# A Nation's Navy
## In Quest of Canadian Naval Identity

Before the navigator can attempt to draw a position line from an observation of
a heavenly body, he requires to know the body's position relative to his own
assumed meridian ... and declination.

– from *Admiralty Manual of Navigation*

Bounded by three great oceans, Canada is a maritime nation with rich
seafaring traditions. Born of both national and British imperial interests
in 1910 and maturing in two world wars, its navy is a vital national institution that continues to evolve in response to new and complex challenges. *A Nation's Navy* explores the decisive formative forces of the
navy's history and illuminates the characteristically Canadian elements
and values that have defined it.

A collection of incisive essays emerging from the second Fleet Historical Conference in Halifax, Nova Scotia, *A Nation's Navy* documents for
the first time the evolution of a distinctive Canadian naval identity. Contributors explore a wealth of pivotal issues: the popular perception of the
Canadian navy, the navy as an instrument of national policy, the impact
of various wars and conflicts, the navy as an expression of Canadian society, the distinctive role of women and the integration of francophone
Canadians, and the future direction of Canadian naval policy.

MICHAEL L. HADLEY is a prize-winning naval historian and professor of
Germanic studies, University of Victoria.

ROB HUEBERT is assistant professor of political studies, University of
Manitoba.

FRED W. CRICKARD, rear-admiral (retired), is a research associate with
the Centre for Foreign Policy Studies, Dalhousie University, and an associate of the Oceans Institute of Canada.

# A Nation's Navy

## In Quest
## of Canadian Naval Identity

EDITED BY
MICHAEL L. HADLEY
ROB HUEBERT
AND
FRED W. CRICKARD

McGILL-QUEEN'S UNIVERSITY PRESS

*Montreal & Kingston* • *London* • *Buffalo*

Legal deposit 4th quarter 1996
Bibliothèque nationale du Québec

Printed in Canada on acid-free paper

This book has been published with the help of a grant
from the Department of National Defence. Funding has
also been received from the Pacific and Maritime
Strategic Studies Group, Department of History, University
of Victoria.

McGill-Queen's University Press is grateful to the Canada
Council for support of its publishing program.

---

**Canadian Cataloguing in Publication Data**

Main entry under title:
  A nation's navy: in quest of Canadian naval identity
  Includes bibliographical references and index.
  A collection of essays emerging from the second Fleet Historical
  Conference in Halifax, Nova Scotia, October 8–9, 1993.
  ISBN 0-7735-1506-2
  1. Canada – History, Naval – Congresses.
  2. Canada. Royal Canadian Navy – History – Congresses.
  I. Hadley, Michael L.  II. Huebert, Robert N. (Robert Neil),
  1960–  III. Crickard, F.W. (Fred W.), 1930–
  IV. Fleet Historical Conference (2nd: 1993: Halifax, N.S.)
  FC231.N37 1996  359'.00971  C96-990014-7
  F1028.5.N37  1996

---

This book was typeset by Typo Litho Composition Inc.
in 10.5/13 Sabon.

# Contents

# Contents

# Contents

# Acknowledgments

This volume represents the work of many: the participants at the Fleet Historical Conference in Halifax, the presenters of papers, and of course the contributors themselves. The editorial board for the volume included not only the editors, but Dr W.A.C. Douglas, at the time director, Directorate of History, National Defence Headquarters; Dr Roger Sarty, senior historian, National Defence Headquarters; and Dr Marc Milner, Department of History, University of New Brunswick. As well, the book owes its origins to the Maritime Commander's Advisory Committee on the conference. Its members included not only those on the editorial board, but Ms Marilyn Gurney, director, Maritime Command Museum, Admiralty House, Halifax; and Chief Petty Officer F.G. McBride, RCN (retired), curatorial assistant, Maritime Museum of the Atlantic, Halifax. The conference itself was convened by Commodore David Cogden, chief of staff personnel and training, and organized by staff of the Maritime Warfare School: its commanding officer, Captain(N) Douglas J. McClean, supported by Major Fred Bigelow, and Lieutenant(N) Katherine Kincaid. Our copy-editor, Judith Turnbull, rendered signal service.

Publication of A Nation's Navy is a joint undertaking between Maritime Command, the Naval Officers Association of Canada, and two academic centres established by the Military and Strategic Studies Programme of the Department of National Defence: the Centre for Foreign Policy Studies of Dalhousie University, Halifax, and the Pacific and Maritime Strategic Studies Group, University of Victoria, Victoria, BC.

## Acknowledgments

The editors and editorial board regard *A Nation's Navy* as the third volume of a Canadian naval trilogy begun with James Boutilier, ed., *The RCN in Retrospect* (1982) and W.A.B. Douglas, ed., *The RCN in Transition* (1988).

# Abbreviations

| | |
|---|---|
| A/S | anti-submarine |
| ADM | Admiralty |
| AIRCOM | Air Command |
| ASUW | anti-surface warfare |
| ASUWC | anti-surface warfare commander |
| ASW | anti-submarine warfare |
| C-in-C | commander-in-chief |
| CANFORME | Canadian Forces Middle East |
| CDS | chief of defence staff |
| CENTAF | United States, Central Command, Air Force Component |
| CFHQ | Canadian Forces Headquarters |
| CID | Committee on Imperial Defence |
| CinCLANT | Commander-in-Chief, Atlantic Fleet |
| CMR | College Militaire Royal de St Jean |
| CNS | chief of naval staff |
| CO | commanding officer |
| COAC | Commanding Officer, Atlantic Coast |
| COMCARGRU | Commander, Carrier Group |
| COMIDEASTFOR | Commander, Middle East Force |
| COMINCH | Commander in Chief of the US Fleet |
| COMUSMIF | United States Commander, Multinational Interception Forces |
| COPC | Commanding Officer, Pacific Coast |
| COSC | Chiefs of Staff Committee |

| | |
|---|---|
| CP | chief of personnel |
| CPD | chief of personnel development |
| CPF | Canadian Patrol Frigate |
| CWAAF | Canadian Women's Auxiliary Air Force |
| CWAC | Canadian Women's Army Corp |
| DCNS | deputy chief of naval staff |
| DCPD | director of career patterns and development |
| DDSD(Y) | Deputy Director of Signals Division (Y) |
| DHist | Directorate of History |
| DND | Department of National Defence |
| DNI | director of naval intelligence |
| DNOPS | director of naval operations |
| DNP | director of naval plans/director of naval personnel |
| DoD | Department of Defence (Australia) |
| DOD | Department of Defense (US) |
| EG | Escort Group |
| FIS | Foreign Intelligence Section |
| FLU | French-language unit |
| FONF | Flag Officer, Newfoundland |
| FRCC | Fisheries Resource Conservation Council |
| HF/DF | high-frequency direction finding |
| HMCS | His (Her) Majesty's Canadian Ship |
| HQ | Headquarters |
| MARCOM | Maritime Command |
| MIF | Multinational Interception Forces |
| MND | minister of national defence |
| MNF | Multinational Forces |
| MOBCOM | Mobile Command |
| NA | National Archives of Canada |
| NAVCENT | United States Central Command, Naval Component |
| NDHQ | National Defence Headquarters |
| NFB | National Film Board |
| NHS | Naval Historical Section (Ministry of Defence, UK) |
| NID | Naval Intelligence Division |
| NPCC | Naval Policy Coordinating Committee |
| NS | Naval Staff |
| NSHQ | Naval Service Headquarters |
| OIC | Operational Intelligence Centre |
| PANL | Public Archives of Newfoundland |
| PCO | Privy Council Office |
| PJBD | Permanent Joint Board on Defence |
| PPCC | Policy Planning Coordinating Committee |
| PRO | Public Record Office (London) |

# Abbreviations

| | |
|---|---|
| RAF | Royal Air Force |
| RAN | Royal Australian Navy |
| RCAF | Royal Canadian Air Force |
| RCN | Royal Canadian Navy |
| RCNVR | Royal Canadian Naval Volunteer Reserve |
| RMC | Royal Military College, Kingston, Ontario |
| RRMC | Royal Roads Military College |
| RN | Royal Navy |
| SACLANT | Supreme Allied Commander, Atlantic |
| SCNDVA | Standing Committee on National Defence and Veterans Affairs |
| sigint | signals intelligence |
| SOSUS | sound-surveillance system |
| TRUMP | Tribal-Class Update and Modernization Programme |
| UNREP | underway replenishment |
| USN | United States Navy |
| VCDS | vice-chief of defence staff |
| VCNS | vice-chief of naval staff |
| VDS | Variable Depth Sonar |
| WD | Women's Division |
| WEU | Western European Union |
| WNRC | Washington National Records Centre |
| WRCNS | Women's Royal Canadian Naval Service |

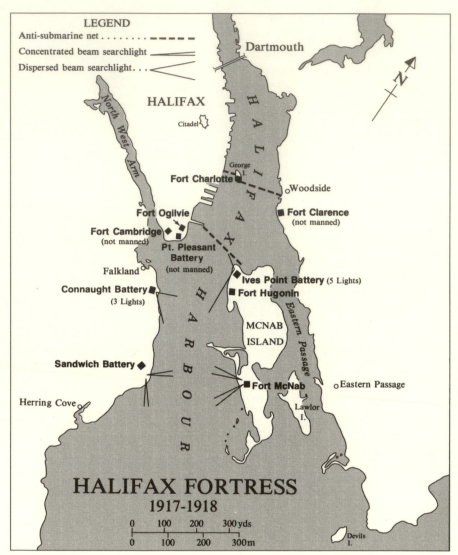

Harbour defences and the Halifax fortress, 1917–1918. [DHist/DND]

# THE ROYAL NAVAL CANADIAN VOLUNTEER RESERVE
### OVERSEAS DIVISION

## TYPE OF MEN NEEDED

**Men of Good Character and Physique are Required in the Above Force for Service Overseas with the Imperial Royal Navy for the Period of the War.**

Candidates must be the Sons of natural born British Subjects.

No previous sea experience necessary.

Applicants must be, for Seamen 18 to 30 years of age, Stokers 18 to 38 years of age.

**THE STANDARD OF HEIGHT AND CHEST MEASUREMENT IS AS FOLLOWS:**

| AGE | MIN. HEIGHT | | CHEST |
|---|---|---|---|
| 18 to 19 years | 5 ft. 3 ins. | 5 ft. 3 ins. and below 5 ft. 5 ins. in height | 33 inches |
| | | 5 ft. 5 ins. and over in height | 33½ inches |
| 19 to 20 years | 5 ft. 3½ ins. | 5 ft. 3½ ins. and below 5 ft. 5 ins. in height | 33½ inches |
| | | 5 ft. 5 ins. and over in height | 34 inches |
| Over 20 years | 5 ft. 4 ins. | 5 ft. 4 ins. and below 5 ft. 7 ins. in height | 34 inches |
| | | 5 ft. 7 ins. and over in height | 34½ inches |

A FREE KIT IS PROVIDED

### Pay and Allowances are as follows:

Ordinary Seamen and Able Seamen (at entry) $1.10 per day. Separation Allowance $20.00 per month.

Men subsequently transferred to Stoker ratings will be paid an additional 10c. per day more.

There are no vacancies for any other ratings than Seamen and Stokers and men can only be accepted as Ordinary Seamen.

**FURTHER PARTICULARS MAY BE OBTAINED FROM ANY CHARTERED BANK IN ONTARIO, OR NAVAL RECRUITING OFFICE, 103 BAY STREET, TORONTO**

A First World War recruiting poster for the Overseas Division of the Royal Naval Canadian Volunteer Reserve. Over a thousand Canadians responded and served in British warships in European waters. [DHist/DND]

Canadian Government Ship (CGS) *Canada* at Shelburne, NS, before the war. Built in 1904 as a fisheries cruiser and a training ship for seamen of the government's marine department, this 200-foot, 14-knot vessel was a mainstay of Atlantic coast defences from 1914 to 1918. [NA]

Officer cadets of the Royal Naval College of Canada at instruction on the bridge of the fisheries-protection cruiser CGS *Canada* in September 1914. [DHist/DND]

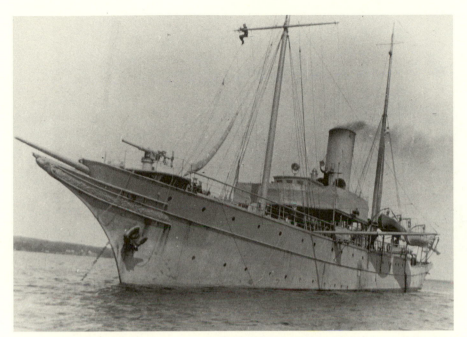

HMCS *Hochelaga*, the 190-foot, 12-knot former US luxury yacht *Waturus*, bought by Canada in contravention of US neutrality laws. She was one of the principal warships of the Canadian Atlantic flotilla from the summer of 1915 to the end of the war. When she faced the much more powerful German submarine cruiser *U-156* in Canadian waters in August 1918, her captain turned away; he was later dismissed from the service. [DHist/DND]

HMCS *Stadacona*, the former US luxury yacht *Columbia*, bought by Canada in contravention of US neutrality laws. With her 4-inch quick-firing gun on the bow and a 4-pounder quick-firing gun on the quarter deck, she was the most heavily armed unit in the flotilla. In 1917 she was equipped with anti-submarine depth charges that were dropped from the stern. [DHist/DND]

The men who kept the Canadian ships running. Maintenance personnel at the patrols depot, Sydney, Nova Scotia, in 1918. [DHist/DND]

Students of the Royal Naval College of Canada at HMC Dockyard, Esquimalt, circa 1920. The college moved to the west coast after its original location at Halifax was severely damaged in the great explosion of 1917. [DHist/DND]

The destroyer HMCS *Skeena* recovering a torpedo with a dummy warhead in 1934. During the 1920s and 1930s, training concentrated on surface warfare, as here, with little thought if any to underwater threats. [DHist/DND]

Commander J.M.B.P. "Jock" de Marbois, RCNR, founder of the Foreign Intelligence Section at Naval Service Headquarters in 1939. He oversaw the growth of the navy's capabilities in signals intelligence and the development of the section into the Operational Intelligence Centre in 1943. [NA]

# Lads, Scoffed at as 'Saturday Night' Sailors In Peace Days Now Defenders of Canada

Article II.
By ERNEST H. BARTLETT

"Being in all respects ready for sea and to engage the enemy . . ."

Our orders had come. Details of these orders were none of my business and, at the risk of being rude, none of yours, either. Our ship, a unit of the Royal Canadian Navy, was going on station, forming yet another link in the chain of ships with which the Empire's navies have girdled the world, and by which they hold the seas. Our movement were being kept a guarded secret.

"And to engage the enemy . . ."

That is the purpose of this ship of war, one of the armed merchant cruisers which Canada has added to her navy so that she may play an increasing part in the conflict at sea. There are thousands of miles of ocean to be patrolled; thousands of merchant ships to be guarded as they carry supplies to beleaguered Britain; there are enemy raiders to be chased and harried and brought to their end.

These armed merchant cruisers are no innovation. They made their name in the last war. They have added to the glory of their name in this.

Remember Rawalpindi?

And Jervis Bay?

They are in goodly company, these erstwhile ships of peace which now bear guns—heavy, hard-hitting guns.

For several days, as the first and only newspaperman yet to be attached to one of these armed merchant cruisers, I have seen this ship at work. Much of what was seen cannot be described, and that is understandable. Details of the ship's armament, for instance, might make interesting reading for you. They would certainly make useful reading for the enemy.

Sufficient to say that the armed merchant cruiser was a crack liner in days of peace. She has speed enough to chase and guns heavy enough to engage an enemy raider. She has depth charges to cope with the undersea skulkers and high-angle guns to blast at hostile aircraft. She is equipped with smoke floats in case she has to lay a covering screen—you will recall that the smoke floats laid by H.M. armed merchant cruiser Jervis Bay brought safety to 34 of the ships in the convoy she was guarding. She has anti-mine devices for her own protection and the protection of those in her keeping.

She is very much a warship.

Structural alterations have been made ruthlessly so that none of her peacetime trappings shall hamper her in her new role. Her brilliant paint has been covered by an over-all coat of battleship grey, the dull, leaden hue which merges her into near-invisibility against the leaden seas and leaden skies where she patrols.

Below decks, seamen's hammocks are slung where once passengers danced. Some of the smaller cabins have been left for officers' accommodation, others have been ripped out to allow space for messes for the different units in the large ship's company.

There is more comfort than would be expected on board a warship, but this comfort in no way softens efficiency.

In many respects the term armed merchant cruiser is somewhat of a misnomer. More current would be the title "converted cruiser" for the changes have made her more closely akin to a cruiser than to an armed merchant ship. With this ship and others of her type, Canada's navy has gone into the "big ship class". Her seamen have proved their worth in the smaller ships—the destroyers and corvettes and escort vessels and minesweepers. Now they are proving their ability in cruisers.

Which brings us to the crew.

Where have they come from, the officers and ratings who man this new ship of war?

We are a mixed crowd. Our captain carries the three rings of criss-crossed braid which denotes him a commander in the Royal Canadian Naval Reserve. In the last war he served in destroyers. In the days of peace he went back to the merchant service. He has commanded his own ships for years, and has proved himself a seaman who has the right to hold his head high in the company of men who know the sea. At the outbreak of this war he held rank of captain, retired, in the R.C.N.R. He dropped one ring of his rank so that he could get back in service again.

Our commander, the second in command of the ship, and her executive officer, also bears three rings on his sleeve as sign that he holds commander's rank. His rings are the wavy type of the Royal Canadian Naval Volunteer Reserve. In the last war he served in Britain's famous "M.L's", as the speedy, deadly motor launches which were the submarines' greatest menace were known. In peacetime, before he "swallowed the anchor", he served in merchant ships—he was a liner officer—and continued his naval service ashore as a volunteer officer in one of the many inland shore stations where long-sighted patriots took their training against the day when their services would again be needed in war.

Canada's navy is questing far afield, doing its share of guarding the Dominion's shores and taking its place in the Empire's ring of ships which girdle the world and hold control of the seas. The photograph above, taken by the writer of these articles in one of Canada's armed merchant cruisers, gives a vivid idea of vastness of the work the navy is doing. The menace of the grim, grey gun whose barrel is seen at the left backs up the vigilance of the guard kept by the men. The lower photographs show how officers have come from two services to reinforce those of the permanent force as Canada's war needs demanded that more and more men give their service. In the centre is shown the "straight lace" badge of rank of an officer in the Royal Canadian Navy. At the left is the "curly lace" of an officer in the Royal Canadian Naval Reserve. To the right is the badge of rank of an officer in the "wavy navy", the Royal Canadian Naval Volunteer Reserve. Permanent, "curly" or "wavy", all are now working so that Canada's ships shall keep the seas.

The First Lieutenant has two broad rings of gold lace with a narrower one between. His rank is lieutenant commander. His rings are of straight gold lace; the lace of the permanent force. In the last war he was a sub-lieutenant in the Royal Navy, with destroyer experience to his credit. The days since have been for him always days with sea connection. He has taken his commands to sea under steam and also under sail. He knows the sea and also its traditions.

There you have three branches of the Service.

The "Curly Navy", as the naval reserves call themselves, thanks to their criss-crossed rings of rank.

The "Wavy Navy", the name similarly gained by the Volunteer Reserves.

And the "P.F." (short for "permanent force") or "Pukka Navy").

The same holds true in the lower deck. Here have been drafted lads from volunteer units the whole Dominion wide. They used to be termed "Saturday Night" sailors by the cheap scoffers of pre-war days. These "Saturday Night" sailors today are proving themselves true seamen, and the scoffers can rest easy in their beds thanks to them.

Reinforcing them are professional seamen from the naval reserve. These men, many of them from the merchant service, maintained their naval training in peacetime so they would not lose touch with the Service. Now they have come with years of experience behind them to fill the roles for which they are so well fitted.

Finally there are the men of the permanent force who well know the navy and its requirements, and whose training and skill are given the backing of the enthusiasm of the newer joined men.

How do they work together? The answer to that has been one of the most inspiring things I have seen during my days with this ship.

Forgetting differences of wavy rings and curly ones, the officers and men have welded themselves into one ship's company. It is almost a mutual admiration society. These fellows certainly know their job", say the volunteers of the permanent force.

"We could not have carried on without them", says the permanent force of the volunteers.

And so it goes on.

On the lower deck a tattooed veteran of the sea slings his hammock beside that of a man whose first ship this is, and there is equality between them. They are a perfect example of a large group of men who have only one aim—to do the job ahead of them.

(Another article in this series will appear tomorrow.)

An early vindication of Canadian naval volunteerism in the the *Ottawa Journal* of 18 February 1941. [DHist/DND]

**MEN** *of* **VALOR**

*They fight for you*

**Two-man boarding party from the Canadian corvette 'Oakville' subdues crew of German sub in Caribbean**

"The Gunslingers." Wartime promotional poster portraying the actual high-seas boarding of *U-94* by two naval reservists from the corvette HMCS *Oakville*, Sub-Lieutenant Hal Lawrence and Petty Officer A. Powell, on 24 August 1942. (For an account see Lawrence's *A Bloody War*.) [DHist/DND]

Wartime publicity poster for the Women's Royal Canadian Naval Service, which played an important role in fields such as signals, operational plotting, and intelligence. [NA]

Posed wartime photo showing an Area Combined Headquarters of the type that existed at Halifax and St John's, Newfoundland, to direct maritime naval and air operations. Note in the left foreground a member of the Royal Canadian Air Force Women's Division. [DHist/DND]

Launching a high-speed patrol craft for the Canadian navy from the Canadian Power Boat Company Ltd, Montreal, circa 1940. [DHist/DND]

Female apprentices in the Power Boat Building Plant of Montreal's Canadian Power Boat Company Ltd, 1940. [DHist/DND]

"Little Britain." This wardroom scene aboard a Canadian destroyer early in the Second World War reflects the strongly British flavour of the RCN at the time. Note as well the five different types of rank and service stripes: (l. to r.) "straight stripe" of the permanent-force RCN; "wavy" stripe of the Royal Canadian Naval Volunteer Reserve; the intertwined braid of the Royal Canadian Naval Reserve; the thin stripe of the commissioned gunner; and the white medium of the Paymaster Branch. [NA]

Life below deck. A typical scene in the messdecks – where sailors ate, slept, and spent their off-duty hours – during the Second World War. [NA]

*A Nation's Navy*

# Introduction

Those who have served in Canada's naval forces share bonds of common identity that are as much underscored by the term "navy" as they are obscured by it. Having experienced a distinctive lifestyle with its institutional and historical values, the sailors' understanding of this identity is more existential than intellectual. One knows who one is and the group to which one belongs because of shared traditions and values; one has undergone the same rites of passage, faced the same challenges, been inspired by similar ideals, and been motivated by similar aspirations. Thus, for many the question of "Canadian naval identity" is not a matter of definition, but of description and celebration. Being in the navy may for some be best described as membership in the Nelsonian "Band of Brothers"; for others it is best described in larger patriotic terms as the seagoing Service, a service in which women have played vital roles beginning with the Wrens of the Second War. Both terms imply community, the cult and culture of seafaring, and ultimately nation-building. Through ceremony, tacit understandings, and the shared experiences of a society within society, sailors celebrate traditions both in current practice and in memory. Thus, by evoking the terms the "navy," the "Service," and the "RCN," one bears witness to the fact that, whether veteran or new recruit, man or woman, regular or reserve, one shares a unique fellowship in a vital national institution whose distinct identity is undoubted, if sometimes changing and unclear.

None of this is self-evident to the layperson, for many of whom the Canadian navy offers no clear legacy of national culture at all. Repeatedly reminded by cultural and political critics that Canada is a nation without identity, Canadians might be forgiven for not knowing their navy. If the nation seems not to have the requisites for identity – neither myth of origin nor overarching civil religion – how could its naval forces have one? Not even the most nationalist of general reference works, *The Canadian Encyclopedia*, (1985), offers easy access. One finds no entry under the generic term "navy" (though one does find "Naval Service Act") and none under "Royal Canadian Navy." (Significantly, the Royal Canadian Legion and Royal Canadian Mounted Police do have entries of their own.) Tucked away under the rubric "Armed Forces," a thumbnail sketch of one and a half columns outlines Canada's naval heritage. The editorial limitations imposed on the entry permit but a lean impression of the navy's importance and meaning for national history.

Formed by the Naval Service Act of 4 May 1910, the Royal Canadian Navy (RCN) ultimately participated in critical action in two world wars. Its formation had been a major political issue of the day that inflamed the passions on all sides of the arguments, making for some uncomfortable accommodations between regional and philosophical interests: for instance, between anglophone Canadian nationalists loyal to Britain but who wanted a separate Canadian force responsible for home defence and francophone Quebec *nationalistes* who endorsed the very same national force but who did so in order not to have to support British imperial interests abroad. These were deeply felt and passionately argued points of view. They established a tradition of debate about naval issues that focused primarily on the national purpose. Yet after the First World War, subsequent Liberal and Conservative governments virtually starved the navy out of existence, triggering Commodore Walter Hose's innovative creation of the Royal Canadian Naval Volunteer Reserve (RCNVR) in 1923 as a means of sustaining a nationwide grass-roots basis for the naval concept. It was largely the infrastructure of the RCNVR that facilitated recruitment and mobilization for the Second World War. In creating a major oceanic fleet, the navy and its reserves expanded from some 13 warships and 3,000 personnel in 1939 to some 365 warships and 100,000 personnel at the end of the war in 1945. During this time Canada's navy served in virtually all the major theatres of war.

The navy's achievements are a matter of record. While struggling for autonomy within the constraints of coalition warfare, the Canadian navy developed its distinctive character. Key among the datum marks in the emergence of a Canadian identity during the war was 1 May 1943. Having resented its subordination to United States forces in the region, Canada negotiated a reorganization of coalition forces, and Rear Admiral L.W. Murray became the Commander-in-Chief, Canadian Northwest Atlantic. This was an appointment unique in Canadian history. Similar struggles for autonomy in coalition warfare have marked the Canadian navy's history up to the present day. Demobilization and new strategic thinking after the Second World War triggered many changes, including government vacillation. Yet, fed by Cold War tensions, the Royal Canadian Navy had by 1964 again grown to a major fleet: an aircraft carrier, twenty-two Canadian-designed and Canadian-built destroyers, seventeen wartime-vintage ocean-going escorts, ten minesweepers, and 21,000 personnel. The Royal Canadian Navy was abolished on 1 February 1968 under the Canadian Forces Reorganization Bill. In the process of unification, it emerged as the Sea Element of the Canadian Armed Forces and later as Maritime Command. What elements of tradition and identity remain? Are there any lessons of history that shed light on the Canadian navy's identity?

Historians, as Alec Douglas reminded us when he gave the opening address at the Fleet Historical Conference of October 1993 on which these papers are based, do not subscribe to "the lessons of history." History teaches no lessons, it explains things. It explains change more than anything else. It is nonetheless noteworthy, he continued, that those who have suffered failure tend to recall the past more vividly than those who have enjoyed success. It is perhaps ironic that the country that once stood against us in two world wars should be the inspiration for the re-examination of our own naval heritage in the context of Maritime Command, for that was the origin of this particular Canadian conference. Concerned that his officers examine and evaluate their past, Germany's first Commander-in-Chief, Fleet, Admiral Rolf Johannesson, had instituted the annual Historical-Tactical Conference of the Fleet in 1960. Here his officers would gather in the naval college in Mürwik to tackle problems of German naval history, and they were given academic freedom to address issues without regard to their rank or station. Provided they exercised intellectual honesty, they could argue against past or present assumptions and against traditions and policies. The conference has become a firm tradition of the German fleet, and the late "Johann Nelson," as the old admiral had been affectionately known since the early years of the war, is among the most revered admirals of the postwar era.

Dr Jürgen Rohwer, Germany's leading naval and military historian, had been an organizer and mentor of Germany's fleet conference from the very beginning, and in 1978 he came to Canada for an international meeting of military historians. Among the first cooperative ventures that emerged from this visit were the graphic reconstructions of Second World War convoy battles on which Douglas and Rohwer collaborated, both in seminars and in print. Those, too, form an important part of Canadian naval scholarship and lore. After two more visits to Canada, as Douglas informed his audience, Rohwer invited Michael Hadley – a German-speaking historian with broad contacts among U-boat veterans – to lecture to the German fleet conference on shallow-water operations of German snorkel-equipped U-boats. On his return to Canada, Hadley submitted a report to the Directorate of History and easily persuaded Douglas that such an exercise would be useful to Canada. Encouraged by Rear Admiral C.M. Thomas, who was soon to become Maritime Commander, Douglas then briefed the Naval Board on the proposal in June 1987. One of Admiral Thomas's last acts as Maritime Commander in 1989 was to decree the holding of a Maritime Command Historical Conference. In 1990, with the enthusiastic support of Vice-Admiral Robert George, we held our first conference. This led to the 1996 appointment of an executive services support officer, with responsibilities for developing a comprehensive heritage policy for Maritime Command. The rest, as they say, is history.

In designing Canada's second Fleet Historical Conference at the Canadian Forces Maritime Warfare School in Halifax, the Maritime Commander and his Advisory Committee aimed at encouraging both serving and retired members of the navy, as well as young scholars of naval affairs, to examine the historical and contemporary record of Canada's naval forces. The theme "In Quest of Canadian Naval Identity" was intended to provoke a wide-range of reflection upon the defining moments of the navy's history and upon the characteristic elements and values that have made the navy a national institution. In response to a general invitation, over thirty-five papers were received: from students, historians, naval and military service people, strategists, scientists, and defence analysts. The papers presented at the naval conference triggered discussions and debate on a number of issues and opened up the inquiry to areas that had not been covered by the program.

Our editorial board appreciated the significance of this lively exchange and decided to invite papers on aspects of Canadian naval identity that had not been addressed formally during the conference. We could not, of course, hope to examine all of the important questions raised, nor could we hope to publish in this collection all the papers that had been prepared for the conference. Though gaps still remain – there is, for example, nothing on heraldry, uniforms, and ceremonies – other themes are explored in detail. Thus, the reader will not be surprised to find various leitmotifs running as unifying structural components throughout the volume: the imperial connection with Britain, the naval arms race, voluntarism and reserves, Canada-US tensions, icebreakers and submarines, fisheries and national sovereignty, the Battle of the Atlantic and air power, to name but a few. Central to each of them is the decision-making process itself.

Despite their diversity, the contributions in this volume on Canadian naval identity share a common approach best characterized in naval terminology as "Sun, Run, Sun"; this is the navigator's technique of taking successive sextant shots of the sun while voyaging across the trackless ocean beyond pilotage waters. Each "sun shot" gives but a single position line, somewhere along which the ship must lie. The point at which a number of position lines intersect serves to "fix" the ship's position. In all this, the wise navigator will bear in mind the largely hypothetical character of that fix and will account for a variety of possibly intrusive factors: errors caused by flaws in the tools of his trade, such as the timepiece and sextant; errors induced by transferring earlier lines and calculations; and errors induced by the natural elements in which he lives, such as set and drift. This technique of "Sun, Run, Sun" provides us with a metaphor for our exercise of establishing Canadian naval identity. Each contributor has raised the sextant to the eye and carefully worked out a position line somewhere along which the Canadian navy's identity may be found to lie. It has been the editors' task to transfer these lines into a navigational fix, in itself a purely historical point in the journey of exploration. The navigational record reveals a rich and varied naval culture that, like the national culture itself, continues in its search for role and meaning.

Entitled "Soundings," the first group of essays attempts to fathom the sea frontier of Canadian naval identity: what we already know, how it has been portrayed, and its intercultural associations. Against the background of the navy's eighty-four years of history, Marc Milner charts the contours and pinnacles of Canadian naval historiography. The navy's story, he argues, is a thread in a much larger tapestry of British imperial and Allied endeavour; it is a thread imbedded in the broader story of Canada. The Canadian navy's identity has therefore been determined by a blend of both national and international military and political themes. Though marked by participation in two world wars, the Korea conflict, and peacekeeping missions, the Canadian navy's story does not offer us the unbroken panorama of great battles and heroic leaders that one popularly associates with the naval history of major powers. Always a coalition partner, Canada has traced a complex record of policies, politics, and plans, though these are punctuated by sometimes remarkable wartime exploits.

Milner reminds us that the principal work of Canadian naval historiography did not appear until 1950, some forty years after the navy had been founded. He highlights the next peak as the navy's seventieth anniversary in 1980, when a conference of sailors and scholars at *Royal Roads* awakened the navy itself to its history. An academic conference in 1985 then launched a new analysis of the naval achievement, drawing increased analytical activity in its wake. Both of these conferences led to the publication of major books, thus buoying the channel and laying on the course for the future. By this time, as Milner explains, a wealth of memoirs and analyses written by veterans, hobby historians, and professionals alike had been contributing to what is now recognized as a substantive published record. Thus, our ability to understand our navy on the basis of a complex and substantial corpus of historical writing is a very recent phenomenon indeed. In examining the context in which Canadian naval history is discussed and taught, and in pointing to the work that remains to be done, Milner ponders whether Canadian naval history has by now grown sufficiently distinct in both substance and identity to be regarded as an independent discipline. Has Canada's naval history, in other words, advanced from being the thread in a composite tapestry to being a tapestry of its own? How distinct, in fact, is Canada's navy?

The popular image of the Canadian navy, as Michael L. Hadley's pilot study shows, is a composite pattern made of public perceptions and media representations. The image derives in large measure from the navy's wartime experience and not, as might be expected, from the periods of peacetime policy-planning. It was primarily the Battle of the Atlantic (1939–45) – the navy's symbolic equivalent to the army's Vimy Ridge (1916) – that has provided its self-defining mythology and lore. This was the battle that in fact turned the "colonial" navy into the Canadian navy. Here the media could find action and tangible achievement, and here the offices of propaganda could find motivational material that would encourage the population to support the war effort. Drawing on a variety of media sources, Hadley traces the development of the navy's image and self-understanding from the earliest days to the present. Destined by international politics to play a minor role in the First World War, the navy received bad press. Overshadowed by the exploits of the Canadian Army in Europe and largely disbanded by the government, the navy – and its image – withered in the 1920s and 1930s. Fighting the Germans and Japanese in the Second World War, of course, easily gained widespread national support, and the navy's positive image flourished. Here the media found (and in many cases invented) valour and the romance of seafaring. Ultimately, it was here that the navy gained its most enduring images – convoy escort, "gun-slinger," and U-boat killer – all of which were then deemed honourable trades. Its media image vacillated in the postwar years: indifference during Korea and ambiguity during the Gulf War. Hadley shows the navy's image to be determined not only by what the navy is designed to do and what it can actually accomplish, but by what the public and the media feel the navy ought to be doing. Thus, today, when combat seems for many the least appropriate role for a peacekeeping nation and when placing one's own people at risk and perhaps having to kill seems least acceptable, having a combat-ready fleet might seem of relatively little importance. Given such perceptions, who needs warships for missions of peace?

The answer lies in Canada's foreign policies and international relations. Here, in "Strategy, the Fleet-in-Being and the Strategic Culture of the Officer Corps," Fred W. Crickard provides the theoretical basis for the international context to which the previous two essays allude, namely naval strategy. Strategy, to his mind, is not so much a science as it is a cognitive development. Rooted in knowledge and shared experience, it is a way of looking at the sea and at a country's national interests. It is the medium in which a nation's oceans policy, its maritime doctrine and development, exists and lives. Basing his study on a comparative assessment of Australian and Canadian naval policy during the Cold War, Crickard argues that operational strategy and to a large extent naval policy are primarily driven by the concept of the fleet-in-being. In Canadian parlance, the term "fleet-in-being" refers to the maintenance of a fleet of active units. The term, therefore, differs from the traditional strategic use of the expression to describe a conflict situation in which a country confronted by superior naval forces constrains the enemy through the deployment of a combined fleet, which has the effect of complicating the enemy's range of choices. For Canadians, the fleet-in-being is a force ready for active deployment. Moreover, what that fleet can actually do once deployed is largely determined by the traditions, values, and behaviour of the officer corps, in other words by their strategic culture. Thus, whereas convoy escort in the Second World War had fallen mainly to the Royal Canadian Naval Volunteer Reserve and its small corvettes, the strategic culture of the career regular-force officer (RCN) had sought offensive action in destroyer gunfights in the European theatre of war. In fact, the Canadian navy had always been predicated on the assumption that it would fight alongside the Royal Navy (RN), just as today it is predicated on alliance or coalition warfare.

Ultimately, of course, the navy is always an instrument of national policy. This is an issue dealt with by the second division of papers ("The Navy as an Instrument of National Policy." In his overarching study "The RCN: Royal Colonial or Royal Canadian Navy," William Glover argues that the problems of national policy and identity are inextricably linked and are as old as the Canadian navy itself. Evoking the mutinies of 1949, Glover seeks answers to why the colonial-imperial relationship between the British and Canadian navies had been perpetuated as late as into the post–Second World War Canadian navy when such sentiments and loyalties had long since been overtaken by demographic and political changes in the country as a whole. Why, in other words, was a colonial-minded navy serving a country whose independence had been assured by the Balfour Declaration (1926) and the Statute of Westminster (1931), and whose independent character had been demonstrated during the Second World War? Part of the answer is deemed to lie in the navy's understandable ignorance of its own history, part in the naval culture (what Crickard would call strategic culture) in which the permanent-force officers worked and were trained, and part in the fact that the navy was completely out of touch with the nation it served.

In exploring "The Roots of the Royal Canadian Navy," Graeme R. Tweedie examines Canada's maritime security concerns in the period prior to the Naval Service Act (1910), highlighting the sovereignty interests of the maritime provinces and the needs for fisheries protection. In doing so, he focuses on the tension inherent in the navy's earliest aspirations both to sovereignty and to an emerging internationalism. Founded amidst conflicting criticism at home to the effect that it was either the instrument of imperial policy intruding in Canadian domestic affairs or the necessary response to the defence needs of the mother country abroad, the Royal Canadian Navy is seen as the child of controversy. Tweedie reminds us that the tug-of-war issues like fisheries protection, coastal sovereignty, free trade, and international power have since the earliest days played crucial roles in determining the character of the navy.

In a contrapuntal piece entitled "The Rise of Proto-nationalism," Siobhan J. McNaught focuses on the political development of the Naval Service Act (1910) from its beginnings in the Colonial Conference of 1902, drawing attention not only to the national vision but to the emotions involved. She argues that the Canadian policy-makers behind the Naval Service Act were actually searching for a Canadian naval identity in part because of their desire for Canadian recognition in the sphere of international politics. Indeed, she found evidence, not the least of which was government propaganda issued as late as 1913, that a distinct naval identity was evolving within the framework of British imperialism. The founding of the Royal Canadian Navy was therefore a major step in the process of nation-building.

In highlighting the crucial position of Halifax and Nova Scotia in Britain's worldwide system of imperial defence, Barry Gough and Roger Sarty explore the complex tensions between naval and military power. Their study "Sailors and Soldiers: The Royal Navy, the Canadian Forces, and the Defence of Atlantic Canada, 1890–1918" puts the case strongly that in the two decades leading up to the First World War, Britain and Canada were forging an alliance of convenience; each country was working out its own destiny in conformity with the other. Central to this consideration is the special role that strategic thinkers were beginning to see for their navies: not so much as a defensive tool of security, but rather as a means of deploying armed force wherever and whenever required. Canada's assumption of responsibility for the fortress town of Halifax on the withdrawal of the British met almost universal approval in Canada, including Quebec. In its role as "Warden of the North," as it has been romantically called, Halifax played crucial roles as naval base, fortress town, and convoy assembly port. Ultimately, Halifax and its bases became a symbol of nationhood, a symbol that derived its meaning not so much from military might as from its free and willing membership in the world's greatest empire.

Among the many crises that the Canadian navy has experienced, perhaps few have been regarded as so bent upon destroying naval identity as Paul Hellyer's policies of armed forces unification. In his chapter entitled "Fleet Replacement and the Crisis of Identity," Michael A. Hennessy argues that those historical accounts that blame Hellyer's "unification crisis" for having marked the demise of Canadian naval identity in 1968 obscure more fundamental issues. They fail to account for the real distinctions between the naval policy of the late Diefenbaker administration and the early policies of the Liberals under Lester B. Pearson. Hennessy argues that where Diefenbaker's Conservatives had been forging ahead with plans for creating and maintaining a large, balanced naval force, the Liberals attacked these initiatives almost immediately after coming into office. Hennessy addresses the difficulties that governments faced in attempting to define the roles and purposes of the Canadian navy in the late 1950s and 1960s. Not the least of these were shifting strategic assumptions, declining defence budgets, and vacillation at the highest levels of the decision-making process. He thus shows that even before Hellyer's process of integration, and well before actual unification of the armed forces in 1968, the Liberals had already shelved the navy's plans. Promoted primarily as a means of fiscal restraint, Hellyer's measures ultimately restricted the fleet to an essentially anti-submarine role, a specialization that only made sense if the Canadian navy operated principally as a component of the NATO alliance. Canadian naval identity, in other words, was now almost entirely predicated upon its integration in NATO.

The core of the Canadian navy's identity as a fighting fleet derives from its achievements in the Second World War. It was known then as the Royal Canadian Navy, and its experience has been communicated to us in a wealth of scholarly and popular accounts. For this reason our third division of essays, "The Navy as a Fighting Service," does not rehearse what is already known. It offers instead new insights into naval intelligence and revisits Canadian tactical doctrines that had first been presented to us from the German submarine perspective; it examines as well the navy's role in the 1991 Gulf War and then investigates postwar fleet and strategic concepts. The unity of the papers in this section derives from their conviction that compromise was always a key to Canadian success – or failure.

Reflecting on the crucial importance of wireless intercepts and codebreaking then headquartered in the Government Code and Cipher School in Britain's Bletchley Park, Catherine E. Allan investigates the personalities and problems involved in the establishment of the Canadian Naval Operational Intelligence Centre during the years 1939–43. Described approvingly by a British admiral as "a minute Bletchley Park," the Canadian centre ultimately made a major contribution to the concept of Canadian identity. At the beginning of the Second World War, the Royal Canadian Navy was engaged in a struggle to exert Canadian control over the resources for Canadian signals intelligence (sigint) in both Canada and Newfoundland. The navy was determined to exert national authority over areas of national concern, but to do so as a fully sovereign, though integrated, country in the Allied war effort. Working in concert with its Allies, the navy thus aimed at assuring itself of the capability to process information about enemy units, and having done so, to promulgate it within its own primary area of operations. Its increasing success coincided with, and ultimately supported, its bid for an independent sea command in the northwest Atlantic in the winter of 1942–43.

Meanwhile, Canadian warships had been escorting convoys across the Atlantic and as far abroad as the Mediterranean, the Arctic, and into Cuban waters. Though the tide of war had turned against the Germans by 1943, their submarines continued to pose a very serious threat. As late as 1944 and 1945 they undertook sorties into Canadian waters, sinking ships within sight of Nova Scotia shores. Although Canadian warships had proven themselves capable of sinking u-boats elsewhere, they never succeeded in Canadian inshore waters. In examining just why this was so, Doug M. McLean, in his "Muddling Through: Canadian Anti-submarine Doctrine and Practice, 1944–1945," focuses on questions of tactical doctrine and efficiency. He discusses the naval training system that the Canadians had been developing, reviews how tactical doctrine was disseminated in the fleet, and contrasts the Canadians with both the Royal Navy and the United States Navy (USN). In finding "muddling through" to have been "typically Canadian," McLean highlights the historical reasons for seeking compromises between the conflicting attitudes and views of Canada's senior alliance partners.

Canada's distinctive contributions as coalition partner continued into the postwar period. Thus, when the Canadian navy went to war during the Korean conflict in 1950, its destroyers rendered distinguished service but never as an identifiable task group. Instead, they were allocated to Commonwealth and American naval task groups wherever and whenever required. Because of this, the Canadians evolved no distinctive combat identity as had been the case in the Second World War with the famous "Maple Leaf" and "Barber Pole" squadrons. Many observers have seen the Korean conflict's absorption of Canadian naval forces into those of larger international groups in a negative light; they point out that such absorption meant that the Canadian navy's impact was actually weaker than it would have been had it operated as a distinct national unit. By contrast, the Canadian navy's operations in the Gulf War coalition of 1991, as Richard H. Gimblett carefully explains, were decidedly different. His paper "MIF or MNF? The Dilemma of the 'Lesser' Navies: in the Gulf War Coalition" illustrates this point by means of a striking current example of deployment in both the UN-sponsored Multinational Interception Forces (MIF) and the US-led Multinational Forces (MNF). Where the MIF enforced the maritime embargo against Iraq by intercepting shipping, the MNF gathered to defend Saudi Arabia from further Iraqi aggression. As Gimblett reveals, the differences between these two acronyms were far greater than one simple letter. The Canadian naval task group underwent a significant change of roles in switching from MIF to MNF during the transition to war in early January 1991. So did other task groups, but arguably none quite as dramatically as the Canadians. The Canadian experience in the Gulf illustrates the tensions at work between the United States and the United Nations, and offers insights into the demands of multinational coalition operations. As it turned out, the lines of demarcation between MIF and MNF became blurred in practice, a feature that posed the coalition navies with serious dilemmas. Within the ground rules established by their respective national governments, each one had to decide if and when it should cross the boundary from MIF to MNF, that is, from being satisfied with intervention in the UN style or escalating into power projection with the USN. In the process of negotiating skilfully between the demands of both types of coalition without injuring relations with either major player, Canadian naval forces made a distinctive contribution. They did so, Gimblett shows, while retaining both their integrity and their national identity.

Seen against the background of postwar policies for developing a war-capable fleet, the Canadians' experience in the Gulf War constitutes the logical outcome of the long and often painful process of "shrinking and expansion" that the navy has been forced to undergo since 1945. It can be argued, in fact, that the navy has been developed less in response to consistent and ongoing strategic threat analysis than in response to tensions between Canada's domestic and foreign policies.

In addressing the question of Canadian naval policy for the years 1945–50, Jan Drent, in his chapter, "A Good Workable Little Fleet: Canadian Naval Policy, 1945–1950," focuses on three critical factors: Canada's defence relationships with the United States, its fear of vulnerability to Soviet attack over the undefended North, and the emerging Cold War. Here as elsewhere he observes conflict between naval authorities and the government of the day over what was best for the nation's maritime needs. Where the wartime Naval Staff had wanted a strong, well-balanced fleet, the peacetime government had sought the minimum nucleus force capable of rapid expansion in any emergency. Locked into the apparent lesson of the Second World War – namely that Canada could fulfil a major international role by maintaining a skeletal force of experts and augmenting them exponentially with reservists at the first sign of crisis – the government at first neglected radical new changes in technology and strategy. While focusing on what Minister of Defence Brooke Claxton called "a good, workable little fleet," Drent explores the difficult choices that confronted policy-makers during the years 1945–50. In the event, the Canadians did manage to have a sufficiently versatile fleet-in-being to undertake UN deployment to Korea and Egypt in the 1950s. In fact, the policies of this period yielded a fleet that is only now being replaced. As senior naval leaders had expressed it in January 1950, the navy had the responsibility of being in all respects ready for sea on the very first day any war was declared and of achieving the largest possible operational fleet within the limited budget the government granted.

As Peter T. Haydon shows in his "Sailors, Admirals, and Politicians: The Search for Identity after the War," this tension caused the severest of "shrinking and growing pains." The Honourable Brooke Claxton had used this expression in describing the root causes of the "incidents" (some call them mutinies) aboard HMC Ships *Magnificent*, *Athabaskan*, and *Crescent* in 1949, but as both Drent and Haydon show, it has wider application. Haydon in particular concentrates on the issue of national identity in describing the shift in our naval role that the new era triggered: from a Second World War convoy scenario in which Canada was subordinated to Britain to a fast-moving nuclear scenario in which Canada was integrated into NATO. In the event, this change of maritime role brought the Canadian navy into ever closer contact with the United States, its armed forces, war matériel, and defence industries. As Haydon explains, the gradual transformation of the Canadian navy into a North American navy was driven by a series of tactical and technical factors, not the least of which was the role of naval air power. Ultimately, however, the uniquely Canadian design for the new St Laurent–class destroyers marked the break with British influence in warship design, and subsequent modifications were based on Canadian rather than British operational requirements. Once again, compromise emerged as a distinctly Canadian trait.

The extent to which the navy is an expression of the national culture whose interests it was deemed to serve is explored in the fourth division of essays, "The Navy and Canadian Society." Diverse in method and focus, the papers shed new light on the navy's social origins. Thus, in his paper "A Nursery of Fighting Seamen?" Bernard Ransom examines the role of the Newfoundland Royal Naval Reserve during the period 1901–20.

Rooted in maritime trades like boat-building and fishing, the Newfoundlanders were natural candidates for the Newfoundland Division of the Royal Naval Reserve. This is the special nautical sense in which Ransom regards Newfoundland as a "nursery." Dependent upon the sea, the island colony offered Britain skilled human resources, a contingency of naval manpower. By exploring the Newfoundland Royal Naval Reserve's organizational history and its involvement in Great War operations, Ransom undertakes the first exploratory steps in providing us with a sociology of reserve participants. As histories of the early years of Canada's naval forces remind us, the Newfoundland experience forms a major component of the national mosaic. Not so well known, if indeed even recognized at all, is just how problematic the Newfoundland experience actually was. Newfoundlanders, it turns out, had a greater preference for joining the army than the navy, a fact, as Ransom points out, that seems to contradict the myth of the island colony as a "nursery of fighting seamen." Cast between the navies of both Britain and Canada, their experience nonetheless helped form the Canadian naval ethos. In breaking new ground, Ransom hints at questions of critical importance for today's defence review: for example, whether the apparent need for naval reserves is a myth perpetuated by a failure to grasp historical and strategic realities.

In like manner, David Zimmerman's chapter, "The Social Background of the Wartime Navy," provides us with an important exploratory description of the Royal Canadian Navy of the Second World War. Zimmerman observes that despite all the anecdotal evidence about the Britishness of the navy of the day, particularly of the officer corps, a quite independent Canadian identity was demonstrably emerging. Drawing on the personnel records of almost 1,200 personnel who served during the war, Zimmerman sketches the profile of a naval force. Recognizing the limitations of the statistical evidence and viewing it with a suitably sceptical eye, he draws the tentative conclusion that the navy had by the end of the war emerged as a distinctly Canadian institution.

One of the most neglected fields of military history has been the role and contribution of women. Given the fact the women have until very recently not been involved in combat roles, their military employment has tended to be regarded more under the rubric of labour or women's studies. Such studies have tended to reach rather negative conclusions about women's experience in the armed forces, despite the fact that servicewomen themselves regarded their service during the Second World War as the most exciting and enriching time of their lives. For many, if not most, it was a period of emancipation. Our understanding of women's experience largely depends upon anecdotal evidence and rather thin and nostalgic memoirs. In explaining the Canadian scene, Barbara Winters, in her "The Wrens of the Second World War: Their Place in the History of Service women," points out that the only academic work on the subject has misrepresented women's experiences by concentrating solely on the army and then extrapolating from it onto the air force and navy. Her exploratory analysis in this volume reveals quite a different story. When formed in July 1942, the Women's Royal Canadian Naval Service was by law just as much an integral component of the Royal Canadian Navy as was the Royal Canadian Naval Volunteer Reserve. Female officers were given the same powers and responsibilities as their male peers, and they enjoyed almost all the same allowances and post-discharge benefits. Differences in remuneration she attributes less to any societal prejudice that woman's work was of less value than a man's than to the intention to distinguish between combat and non-combat forces and to compensate men for the higher risks of combat service. In underscoring the need for in-depth studies of naval and military women, she highlights the evolutionary role the Wrens of the Second World War played in paving the way for women's permanent admission into the Canadian navy a few years later. They were thus a crucial component in the navy's process of nation-building.

Education, as William A. March shows in "A Canadian Departure: The Evolution of HMCS *Royal Roads*, 1942–1948," was also a critical factor in the Canadianization of the navy. Beginning with the Royal Naval College of Canada (RNCC) at Halifax in 1911, the officers' education and training had been based on the Royal Navy model: turning junior officers into competent ship-handlers and sailors just as soon as possible and giving them only as much supportive formal education as did not interfere with the primary training aim. The RNCC closed its doors in 1922 during a period of severe naval attrition, which Commodore Walter Hose had called "the great starvation time." Opening on Vancouver Island in 1942, the Royal Canadian Navy's successor college, HMCS *Royal Roads*, inherited the same principles. Yet unlike its predecessor, the new institution resisted closure for a period of six years by undergoing a series of transformations that matured it from a Royal Navy clone into a distinctive Canadian institution. Chief among the influences brought to bear upon it were not only fiscal pressures to maximize the facilities, but government pressures on the Royal Canadian Navy and other armed services to adopt a university-level education comparable to what was available in Canadian civilian universities. In detailing the changes, March highlights tensions between tradition and reform, and clarifies the stages through which the college was reshaped: from Royal Canadian Naval College (1942–49), to a joint navy–air force college (1947–48), and finally to the tri-service Canadian Services College in 1948. As March is careful to explain, the end of each phase brought about radical changes in the college's curriculum and orientation, and fundamentally attacked the principles on which the naval college had first been based. The college's broader scope, accessibility, and constituencies had thereby established its Canadian identity.

In the civilian sector as well, education proved a key to Canadianizing the navy. In a largely anecdotal survey of the University Naval Training Division (UNTD) that regrettably could not be included in this collection, Robert J. Williamson reminded the conference of the role that this unique, nationwide officer-training corps achieved. Founded in 1943, the UNTD provided a broad spectrum of university students with access to the navy. As Williamson concluded in part, the UNTD not only tempered the influence of the Royal Navy but created a distinct national unit. The program produced some 500 officers for the wartime fleet. Reorganized and expanded in 1947, it arguably pioneered officer education for both the regular force (RCN) and the reserve (RCNR), for where regular-force officers of the day normally undertook only two years of college followed by seatime, the UNTD officer completed four years of university, interspersed with summers of naval training, and received his commission only after having completed his degree. Williamson saw in this a major shift in accent, for like the American system, the UNTD had produced a well-educated officer corps, thereby contrasting with both the RN and RCN, which produced a well-trained naval officer. Based on university campuses and naval reserve units across the country, the UNTD offered in effect the first opportunities for francophone students to enter the navy in large numbers. The UNTD concerned itself with inculcating leadership, and as career patterns have shown, its graduates have assumed leading roles in Canadian society, if not always in the permanent force. In societal terms, the UNTD managed to create a broadly based naval constituency throughout civilian society. When it was disbanded in 1968, its loss deprived the navy not only of a valuable presence on university campuses, but also of the potential for sustaining a constituency of citizens who might support its interests. No subsequent plan ever duplicated what the UNTD had achieved.

The francophone identity of the naval service had meanwhile been seriously neglected, though indeed the commissioning of a francophone warship had been proposed as early as 1910. As Serge Bernier explains in his chapter, "HMCS Ottawa III: The Navy's First French-Language Unit, 1968–1973," despite the social justice issue that clearly backed the idea of a francophone ship, the realization of this dream had to await a constellation of mutually impinging factors. Not the least of these were the Royal Commission on Bilingualism and Biculturalism (1966) and the appointment that year as chief of defence staff of a remarkable francophone officer with wartime experience, General Jean V. Allard. Convinced that the sole means for making francophones feel at home in Canada's armed services was to provide them opportunities for serving in their mother tongue such as the anglophones had always enjoyed, Allard introduced new policies. In the light of experience with the "Van Doos" (le Royal 22$^e$ Régiment) and against the background of major societal changes in Canada, Allard and his staff initiated a major transformation in the navy's self-image and identity. Bernier sets the stage with two images from the ship's scrapbook: the ship's launching in 1956 in Montreal under the inherited White Ensign with crew in British-style uniforms and a monolingual souvenir program for visitors; and in 1992 the ship's decommissioning with Canadian uniforms and ensign and a bilingual program. In this process of Canadianization, the Department of National Defence had shown itself a leader despite the many tensions and ambiguities that the changes implied – not only for educating a navy, but for educating a nation.

HMCS *Ottawa* served as Canada's first francophone warship (bilingual ship, as some might prefer) from 1968 to 1973. Bernier aptly describes her first commanding officer, Commander Pierre Simard, as "a missionary at once inspired and disappointed by many turns of events." He had previously served as Allard's policy adviser. The policy was of course fraught with many difficulties. Internal politics, misperceptions, prejudices, training, and manning were salient among them. But as Bernier explains, while undertaking this experiment in nation-building, HMCS *Ottawa* fulfilled her operational missions and provided a vital training ground for many who have carried their positive cultural and linguistic experience with them through their later promotions to the higher ranks. The *Ottawa* experience therefore bears witness to the navy's openness to the society it serves and to the broader vision of its own identity.

Although the Fleet Conference focused primarily upon historical issues, its participants quite naturally explored the implications of this history for the navy's future roles and operations. Did the navy's "Canadian" identity suggest any especially meaningful routes? In fact, a number of conference papers not included here addressed the theme explicitly. Predicating its thesis on the view that the navy's major strength has always been its people, P.R. Moller's "Leadership through Customer Service" argued that a philosophy based upon customer service could be used to strengthen the navy's ties to Canadian society. David Hill and Hugh Culliton's "In Search of a New Relevance in the Twenty-first Century" argued that the navy had always had difficulty demonstrating its relevance and value to society – except, of course, in wartime. After singling out historical examples of rifts between the navy and the public attitude, they suggested that the navy must become innovative by accepting the concept of "value for money" in the prosecution of naval and military affairs. Only thus, they argued, could the navy ensure public support in the next century. Helena Maria Cerigo discussed the navy's contributions to peacekeeping, one of several operations subsumed under the concept of international conflict resolution. Recognizing not only Canada's limited resources but also the navy's past successes and the necessity to "leverage" our investments by involving the navy even further in international affairs, she argued that greater participation in conflict resolution would enhance the navy's public profile and identity.

The final section of this volume, "Perspectives and Policies for a New Century," ponders the navigator's track covered by the Canadian navy, and having taken a positional fix, it casts an eye towards a future consistent with national character and purpose. Fittingly, the three concluding essays present the comprehensive grasp of an Australian naval officer-historian, the exploratory perspective of a young Canadian scholar, and the operational forecast of the Maritime Commander.

Comparing the Canadian and Australian naval forces reveals some striking similarities and differences that have long fascinated historians and political scientists alike. In "Strangers in Their Own Seas?" James Goldrick focuses on a predominant determining factor in the national characters of the Australian and Canadian navies: the identifying links both have with the British Admiralty and the culture of the Royal Navy. In doing so, he discerns distinctive continuities not only in the individual services themselves, but in the place they came to occupy within their respective nations. Key among the continuities are the cross-cultural strategic and personal relationships in both the Canadian-British and Canadian-American contexts, the junior partners' emulation of the major power as a means for greater efficiency, and the political tensions implicit in the imperial connection.

In formulating his title as a rhetorical question, Goldrick invites reflection on whether we observe in this process – in both the Australian and Canadian cases – a cultural identity that had actually been imposed upon the dominions by this imperial connection. One persuasive answer is seen to lie in a process of acculturation during which the dominions developed both a national and a national-naval identity. Breaking with the purely cultural-political nexus of the identity problem, Goldrick reminds us that, despite whatever else might influence the character of navies, they remain technologically oriented services that tend to draw their culture in large measure from the technological matrix in which they find themselves. In terms strikingly close to Fred Crickard's theory of strategic culture as expressed in his opening chapter of this volume, James Goldrick concludes that what has sometimes been viewed negatively as "blue water navalism" might well characterize the ethos – and, we might add, the identity – of the future navy.

The linchpin of this, as James D. Kiras argues in "Maritime Command, Naval Missions, and Naval Identity," is Canadian sovereignty. By taking the navy's past as a model for its future, he examines the thesis that one might get better value for money by reconfiguring the fleet for national, rather than international, duties: sovereignty patrol, fisheries, and constabulary duties, for example. But in making his case, he recognizes that in the event of any international conflict such a fleet would be reduced at best to a merely passive observer status. Recognizing as well that the navy is a function of Canadian foreign policy and that the Canadian government is committed to supporting its allies and humanitarian causes, Kiras underscores the need for capable and flexible forces with equal utility and endurance on foreign missions. Indeed, he finds that the navy as envisioned for the next century allows Canada to continue its liberal interventionist foreign policy while retaining a nucleus fleet for domestic operations.

A British guest at the conference who confessed to never having pondered the national issues then being discussed, remarked with a quixotic touch: "It is surely a very fine thing to be in quest of Canadian naval identity, but I'm really not quite sure what I'd do if I found it." Secure in the self-evident definition of both his navy and his culture, he had viewed the proceedings at the Maritime Warfare School in Halifax as an engaging intellectual enterprise. Canadians, by contrast, could take no comfort in tacit understandings and axioms about national character as other nationals might do. For Canadians, identity was neither a sojourn nor a description of where one is as immutable fact, but a journey. Canadian naval identity was no different. In this book's concluding chapter, "Points of Departure: Towards the Next Forty Years," Peter W. Cairns, at the time Maritime Commander in Halifax, draws the conclusions of a journey through Canadian naval history. If historians can be accused of not being forward-looking enough, as once actually happened at a conference on military and strategic affairs, then Vice-Admiral Cairns plays a critical role in what he calls "prospective history": he explains where the navy is going and how this new direction is a reflection of its historical character and evolving purpose. By emphasizing such technical matters as the need for a more flexible, general-purpose capability, the need for inter-operability with one's coalition partners, and the Canadian navy's easy integration into joint and combined operations, he suggests that the past has indeed been evolving into the future as it should. Throughout, he strikes that tone of optimism and self-assurance that only comes from knowing who one is.

PART ONE

*Soundings*

· I ·

# The Historiography of the Canadian Navy: The State of the Art

MARC MILNER

Canada scarcely ranks as a naval power in the historical sense.[1] The Canadian navy dates only from 1910, and although it had flexed its nascent "seapower" muscle during convoy duty in the First World War, only in the Second World War and the Cold War did it show strength of any international importance. As a nation, Canada has fought no wars on its own, nor have its armed forces been the object of particular enemy attention. Indeed, one might say that Canada has no independent national naval history at all. Moreover, as a distinct field of scholarship, Canadian naval history is a very recent phenomenon. It is also, at present, a subfield of Canadian military history and as such is poorly integrated into the wider maritime history of the country. Not surprisingly, the brevity and peculiar nature of Canada's naval history have profoundly shaped its historiography, the extent to which Canadian naval history is taught, and our perceptions of naval identity.

For these reasons any discussion of the state of Canadian naval history must be prefaced by a short discourse on the nature of that history. Perhaps more than that of other nations, Canada's naval history is but a thin thread in a much larger tapestry. This situation is somewhat paradoxical, since by the end of the nineteenth century Canada had become a very considerable maritime state. But Canada, like its antecedents, the British North American colonies, rested secure in the bosom of British seapower. With the mother country as the predominant naval power in the world, it would have been absurd for the new self-governing Dominion of Canada to even try to develop its own navy in the nineteenth century. Quite apart from the fact that Britain retained responsibility for Canadian foreign affairs, the metropolitan power, whether French or British, had always been responsible for the maritime security of its North American colonies. It was the colonists' task to defend the land frontier, and so it remained after 1867, when the new dominion's military efforts were devoted to the raising of militias. Paradoxically then, Canada was a "British" nation, dependant upon the sea for its well-being, and many of its people followed the sea; but its military heritage was decidedly continental in flavour.[2]

The founding of the Royal Canadian Navy (RCN) in 1910 did little to alter that situation. The debate over the establishment of a naval service reflected the increasing ambiguity of Canada's constitutional position: should Canada simply give money to Britain to support the mother country's naval armaments race with Germany, or should it establish a Canadian branch of the imperial navy. A Canadian navy might keep problems at arm's length, it was argued, but conversely, it also might draw Canada into confrontations that might otherwise have been avoided. Something also had to be done about policing Canada's fishing grounds. It is a moot point whether German hostility in war or the American threat to the fisheries was more responsible for the establishment of the RCN.[3] Sir Wilfrid Laurier's Liberal government prevailed and the RCN was born on 10 March 1910. The issue of a tiny local navy, too small to fight yet big enough to get into trouble, was so contentious that the 1911 federal election was fought partly around it. The Conservatives, who favoured direct financial aid to Britain, won the election, but Robert Borden's government could not bring itself either to nurture the new navy or to abolish it entirely.

The RCN's tenuous existence in the defence firmament lasted for the next thirty years. The First World War did nothing to salvage it from obscurity. The fleet in 1914 consisted of two aged cruisers acquired for training purposes. One of these, *Rainbow*, was at sea off Vancouver Island when war was declared. Slow, tired, under-gunned, and equipped only with sand-filled training rounds, *Rainbow* was ordered to search for von Spee's powerful East Asia squadron of modern cruisers off the US coast. Admonished by Ottawa to "remember Nelson and the British Navy," she got by all accounts to within fifty miles of at least one German ship (*Leipzig*) but the enemy "escaped."[4] What Edwardian writers would have made of *Rainbow*'s valiant and utterly futile end at the hands of such powerful ships we can only guess. But no gallant tradition of death and glory befell the fledgling service. Instead, Canada poured troops onto the European western front, where the Canadian Corps earned an enviable reputation for its fighting effectiveness. The First World War also produced a number of internationally famous Canadian airmen, with the likes of Bishop, Collishaw, and Barker household names within Canada and throughout the Empire by 1918. Nothing in the RCN's wartime experience compared with this: most of it was a dreary war of patrols. Even the U-boat operations of 1918 off the east coast failed to feed the public imagination with images of Canadian naval heroes. Quite the contrary, newspapers unfairly maligned the RCN for its supposed bungling, and postwar debates in Parliament accused the navy of incompetence, "culpable negligence," and worse.[5]

The navy nearly disappeared in the interwar years despite some attempts to put the RCN on a firmer footing after the war. At the height of the Depression, the General Staff, dominated by the army and the air force, voted to reduce the RCN to care and maintenance status: ships were laid up, recruiting and training halted, and bases all but closed. Although it was ultimately saved, the RCN never forgot its brush with extinction and came to see that its principal enemies were perhaps those closest to home.

As another major war loomed on the horizon in the late 1930s, another Liberal government, this time under William Lyon Mackenzie King, saw the RCN as a marvellous vehicle for contributing to imperial security without having to send thousands of troops overseas again. Although King could not forestall public clamouring for another big Canadian army on the western front once the war got under way, he did develop a very large navy (and a large air force as well). The navy, in particular, suited King's desire to involve Canadian industry in war production, as many of the basic ships needed for the escort fleet could be built in Canada. By 1943 fully half of the Allied escorts in the main theatre of the Atlantic war were RCN, and by the end of the Second World War, Canada, for a brief moment, had the third-largest navy in the world.

The wartime fleet was overwhelmingly small-ship and reservist in flavour. The ships themselves were almost all war-built for basic escort roles and had little long-term value to the postwar navy. Their crews too were "hostilities only" (non-professional sailors recruited to meet the crisis of national emergency). Only 5,000 of the navy's wartime personnel strength of nearly 100,000 belonged to the professional naval service. Not surprisingly, the tiny fraternity of professional RCN officers used the war to secure the basic elements of a balanced postwar navy and kept most of their own personnel in what they regarded as "proper" warships: fleet-class destroyers, cruisers, and the like. This dichotomy of wartime experience – between the reservists in small ships battling U-boats and the RCN waging a struggle for long-term viability – coloured not only the conduct of the war itself, but also much of the naval historical writing that followed.[6]

The expansion of the RCN during the Second World War was a remarkable accomplishment, truly staggering by Canadian standards and a significant event in naval history in general. For the RCN, however, it was a precarious victory, and the navy's fortunes were only salvaged by the advent of the Cold War. Under King's successor, Louis St Laurent, postwar Liberal governments built a large and capable navy in the 1950s. To a considerable extent, this early Cold War fleet was simply an outgrowth of the wartime experience. Moreover, the wave of new construction and modernization of reserve vessels that followed the Korean War was part of a general military expansion. While the navy was large and modern by the early 1960s, in terms of budgets and personnel the RCN remained clearly in third place within the Canadian defence establishment. Little new was added after the early Cold War building boom, and by the 1980s the navy faced block obsolescence. The last deep freeze in the Cold War produced orders for a new fleet in the mid-1980s, which is just now being completed. None of the new ships saw service in the Gulf War, where the navy fought largely without incident and without loss. It is too early to tell just how the navy will fare in the new world order.

Several key points affecting the development of Canadian naval historical writing emerge from this very brief survey. The first, and most obvious, is that the history itself is only some eighty years old. It is difficult, although by no means entirely impossible, to push the antecedents of the RCN much further back than 1900. Secondly, much of that history is uneventful. Apart from the Second World War and the early years of the Cold War, the RCN has lived a low-key, often marginal existence. The third point is that since the navy's founding in 1910 Canada has acted within the confines of much larger international organizations, initially the British Empire and latterly the North Atlantic Treaty Organization (NATO) and the United Nations (UN). This has left little scope for distinctly Canadian naval operations and none whatever for distinctly Canadian wars. Where other nations might well have resorted to gunboat diplomacy abroad to secure their national interests, Canada has been able to rely only on collective action. After all, who was Canada likely to fight, on its own, in the twentieth century? As presently structured, Canadian naval history is therefore drawn from a very narrow base in space and time. Ironically, the only uniquely Canadian naval missions in defence of Canadian sovereignty have been typically directed at our friends in peacetime. The final point is that for the first sixty years of its existence the RCN defined itself within a largely British context. Until 1939 the RCN was simply a flotilla of the Imperial Navy: training, uniforms, equipment, ships, tactics, and doctrine were all British, and Canadian officers appeared on a combined Empire and Commonwealth seniority list. This was much less so after 1945, but the notion of the RCN as a direct descendant of Nelson's "Band of Brothers" survived in the RCN until the full effects of armed forces unification were felt in the early 1970s. Even now Nelson's ghost surfaces on occasion.

It is important to understand, therefore, the very restricted nature of the Canadian naval experience, its very British character, and the importance of Canada's powerful militia tradition when assessing the development of Canadian navy historiography. While many recent works on the origins and early days of the RCN take their accounts back into the latter stages of the nineteenth century, the colonial period and great age of sail have not been embraced as part of Canadian naval heritage. In part this is because the Canadian military establishment has been loath to adopt any of the military or naval traditions of the French era. The work of Guy Fregault on the first distinctly Canadian naval hero, Pierre le Moyne d'Iberville, and that of Jacques Mathieu on French naval building in Quebec in the eighteenth century remain solidly part of Canadian colonial history.[7] D'Iberville, a native son of New France, sailed his lone ship *Pelican* into Hudson Bay in 1697 and in a brilliant action against three English ships sank two and secured command of the area, a feat unremembered in the myths and culture of the Canadian navy.[8] In fairness, though, the British colonial period also stands outside of mainstream Canadian naval history, despite the efforts of W.A.B. Douglas, Faye Kert, Richard Wright, and others.[9] Even the substantial body of work done by Barry M. Gough on naval activity in British North American waters during the nineteenth century, such as his *The Royal Navy and the Northwest Coast of North America, 1810–1914* (1971), fall into imperial, colonial, or maritime history, not naval.[10]

The failure of the often desperate and typically disparate naval efforts of the colonists of New France and British North America to find resonance within Canadian naval history remains enigmatic. Among academics this disconnection is almost certainly due to the fact that the study of history itself is subdivided into fields that often do not talk to one another – military and colonial history, for example. The navy, cleaving first to its Royal Navy lineage and involved in a constant battle to maintain its "blue water" capability, finds little of value in puny colonial antecedents. The result is that Canadian naval history as presently constituted derives none of its traditions from the age of sail, the key formative period for many of the navies of the world.

Moreover, nothing occurred in RCN history prior to 1939 that could be saved from obscurity, particularly when set against the deeply entrenched national militia tradition and the tremendous accomplishments of the Canadian Corps overseas in the First World War. Prior to 1939, legitimacy for the RCN derived from its connection with the Royal Navy (RN); it could hardly have been otherwise. However, set against the RN standard, the only measure suitable among Canadians until a generation ago, there was not much to say of Canada's experiment in naval power before the Second World War.

The first thirty years of RCN history were thus seen as something of a wasteland: little but policy and unfulfilled dreams. By contrast, the scope and scale of the RCN's Second World War accomplishment captured the imagination of the first generation of post-1945 historians, and with good reason. The RCN rose from utter obscurity to a global standing in a few short years. And while the wartime fleet had not been a balanced one in the traditional sense, the acquisition of heavy cruisers and light fleet carriers at the very end of the war gave promise that one day it would be. Further, Canada had demonstrated its naval potential in time of crisis, and the myriad small ships required of modern naval warfare gave it tremendous leverage. Not surprisingly, the RCN's postwar official histories, Gilbert Tucker's *The Naval Service of Canada* (two volumes, 1952) and, more especially, Joseph Schull's *The Far Distant Ships* (1950, reprinted in 1990), were celebrations of Canadian accomplishment. Tucker's first volume covered naval developments up to 1939 and seemed to say all that was needed about that colourless period. His second volume, on naval administration ashore between 1939 and 1945, chronicled the growth of the RCN's institutions as they coped with the rapid expansion of the fleet. Tucker planned a series of three operational volumes on the war, but these were axed by the Naval Staff and a minister of defence, who were not interested in a detailed accounting of the exploits of reservists in small, hastily built escorts.[11] What the navy wanted, and what it commissioned Schull to write, was a popular history that would foster support for postwar naval expansion plans. Schull's delightfully written *The Far Distant Ships* was therefore long on colour and short on analysis or context. To what extent it helped in the building boom of the RCN during the 1950s is an interesting, and unexplored, historical question.

What is clearer is that the combination of Tucker and Schull, both official histories, satisfied the need for information on the wartime RCN for a generation. Two other monographs on RCN history appeared over that period, Thor Thorgrimsson and E.C. Russell's *Canadian Naval Operations in Korean Waters, 1950–1955* (1965), and J.D.F. Kealy and E.C. Russell's *A History of Canadian Naval Aviation* (1965). These too were official histories, and it is possible to see them both as celebrations of Canadian naval maturity and broadsides in the ongoing budgetary battles of the 1960s. Until the 1980s these official histories constituted the total of scholarly monographs on RCN history.

The lack of scholarly monographs on the navy, or even of wider academic interest in the RCN by nongovernment historians in the twenty-five years following the war, is hard to explain. It may be that the RCN's wartime experience failed to capture anyone's imagination. Certainly there was the notion that Canada as a seapower was a new, and perhaps transitory, phenomenon, and few Canadian academics were interested in the subject. Gerald Graham, a Canadian who became a distinguished historian of imperial Britain, had served briefly as an official historian during the war, but he preferred to concentrate on the intellectually more rewarding delights of the British Empire. So, too, did Donald Schurman. A veteran of the Royal Canadian Air Force (RCAF), Schurman was drawn to naval history through an interest in the intellectual roots of twentieth-century British maritime strategy. Both of these men, Graham and, perhaps more so, Schurman (whose career has been spent at the Royal Military College of Canada [RMC] and Queen's University, both in Kingston), profoundly influenced the way in which aspiring Canadian academic naval historians viewed their field.[12] Both forswore the particular in favour of breadth and depth, emphasizing the larger context of naval history. It seems fair to say that the very recent nature of Canada's expression of seapower and Tucker and Schull's emphasis on the uniqueness of the Canadian experience failed to stir them. Moreover, while the army's historical section under C.P. Stacey nurtured a coterie of young historians who went on to academic posts – Reg Roy, George Stanley, Jack Hyatt, and Don Goodspeed to name a few – the collapse of Tucker's project in the late 1940s left Canadian naval history in the hands of a few devoted amateurs in the naval historical section.[13] In the end, however, perhaps the most compelling reason for the dearth of published material on the RCN in the generation after 1945 is that the files were still closed to everyone except the official historians.

It was possible, therefore, until 1970 to count the number of monographs on RCN history on the fingers of one hand, and all of them were government publications. There were a few memoirs of note,[14] a few articles, some passages on the RCN in Don Goodspeed's *The Armed Forces of Canada, 1867–1967* (1967), and some wartime public relations publications, but apart from the official histories, the only thing that passed for serious scholarship on the RCN were the sections in James Eayrs's first two volumes of *In Defence of Canada* (1964 and 1965).

Several things conspired to alter this complacency during the 1970s. Perhaps the most important was that sometime between 1960 and 1980 Canada cast off its colonial mentality and Canadians started measuring the RCN in its own right, as the service of an independent, sovereign state. This was facilitated by armed forces unification, announced in 1964 and put into effect on 1 January 1968. With that the Royal Canadian Navy ceased to exist, becoming "Maritime Command" of the new Canadian Armed Forces and adopting the new standard green uniform of the combined forces. Unification shook the navy to its very core, forcing a process of redefinition and the retirement of many of the last wartime veterans, who either did not or could not accept Canadianization of the navy. The navy, which had seen itself in 1960 as more Royal than Canadian, was by

1980 distinctly Canadian in outlook, right down to its green uniforms and the replacement of Trafalgar Day in favour of Battle of the Atlantic Sunday as the feast day of the Canadian fleet. The navy has since gone back to distinctive naval uniforms, modelled, appropriately enough given its new "imperial" orientation, largely on those of the United States Navy (USN).[15] Concurrent with this altered state within the navy and the nation was the opening of wartime archival material, which allowed non-official historians a more critical look at the navy's most significant experience: the Second World War.

The need to look more closely at the RCN's Second World War experience, and the inadequacies of Tucker and Schull on the subject, had been evident for some time. The only critical assessment of the RCN's contribution to the actual fighting to appear in the generation after 1945 came from the pen of Captain Donald Macintyre, RN. One of the war's best escort commanders and a naval historian of note, Macintyre savagely attacked the RCN's wartime operational efficiency in his memoir *U-Boat Killer* (1956). He charged the RCN with bungling incompetence, described its fleet as "travesties of warships," and accused the Canadian Naval Staff as bent on nothing more than the maximum number of RCN ships on operational plots.

The issue of the fleet's efficiency was addressed briefly in C.P. Stacey's official volume on Canadian defence policy during the war, *Arms, Men and Governments* (1970). However, by the 1970s the conventional wisdom on the wartime RCN was a blend of the Canadian and Macintyre themes: the navy had been big, but probably misguided. The difficulties of such a limited Canadian literature and its concentration on the peculiarly Canadian exploits of the war years were demonstrated in 1979 with the publication of John Swettenham's *Canada's Atlantic War*. Swettenham, one of Canada's best-known military historians, produced a very conventional account of the war at sea in which he attempted, without much luck, to integrate the Canadian story. What he achieved in the end was the standard British interpretation of events, punctuated by Canadian incidents. In that sense, *Canada's Atlantic War* accurately reflects the state-of-the-art, at least with respect to Second World War history, at the end of the 1970s; it was hardly Swettenham's fault.

By the 1970s, however, Canadians were beginning to awaken to their naval history largely, although by no means exclusively, through an examination of the Second World War experience. Several major research projects were under way, and the voices of veterans began to be heard in the first of what has become a fairly steady stream of memoirs and nostalgia. In 1972 the first postwar graduate master's thesis in RCN history was completed, and another followed by the end of the decade.[16] By the end of the 1970s, two doctoral dissertations were under way[17] and the appearance of two new wartime naval memoirs, James Lamb's *The Corvette Navy* (1977) and Hal Lawrence's *A Bloody War* (1979), marked the beginning of a series of books by these two writers and the commencement of a significant memoir phase in the field. The decade also brought the first serious, scholarly questioning of the navy's wartime policy in the form of W.A.B. Douglas's seminal article "Conflict and Innovation" in Arthur Marder's festschrift (1977).

If the 1970s was the decade of gestation, then the birth of modern Canadian naval historical writing – it cannot truly be called a renaissance – dates from a historical conference convened in 1980 at Royal Roads Military College, Victoria, BC. The conference was the work of James Boutilier, a member of the Royal Roads Department of History and Political Economy. Boutilier was spurred by what he saw as the astonishing failure both of historians and naval personnel to analyse RCN history. His solution was to get the navy and a few scholars together to think and write about the subject for a conference convened in March 1980, the first on RCN history. It brought together many, if not most, of the surviving senior officers of the RCN, who dominated the program. Of the nineteen speakers during the three-day conference, eleven were "old salts" speaking largely within their own sphere of expertise. Among the more innovative elements of Boutilier's conference were papers on RCN history prior to 1939, especially on its origins. Significantly, no paper dealt with operations in the First World War.[18]

"The RCN in Retrospect" conference was not an academic tour de force, but it met Boutilier's expectations: the navy awoke to its history.[19] The publication of the conference proceedings in 1982 marked a watershed in RCN historiography. When Alec Douglas produced his review of Canadian naval history for the *Mariner's Mirror* in 1984, he could count among the existing literature the five volumes of official history, the proceedings of Boutilier's conference, a few more memoirs (including the first of a series of collective reminiscences published as *Salty Dips* by the Naval Officers Association of Canada [Ottawa Branch]), "a half dozen theses," a number of scholarly articles, and the first volume of Rear Admiral Jeffry Brock's two-volume memoir, *The Dark Broad Seas* (1981) and *The Thunder and the Sunshine* (1983), the only memoir of any substance, however fanciful, by a senior RCN officer.[20] Douglas tactfully omitted reference to another memoir and to the only biography ever written on a Canadian naval officer. H.N. Lay's *Memoirs of a Mariner* (1982) had the potential to make a major contribution to the field, but spoke more to his family than to those interested in the navy. J.M. Cameron's *Murray: The Martyred Admiral* (1980) was a seriously flawed attempt to vindicate the career of the RCN's most famous operational commander, Rear Admiral L.W. Murray, who moved to England in 1945 after rioting servicemen destroyed much of downtown Halifax. Douglas's 1984 listing also neglected two substantial recent books on RCN history, Fraser McKee's *The Armed Yachts of Canada* and Macpherson and Burgess's *The Ships of Canada's Naval Forces, 1910–1981*.

Alec Douglas gave this burgeoning field a push in 1985 with his own conference commemorating the seventy-fifth anniversary of the founding of the RCN. He filled the program with a largely academic crowd. Among their contributions were the first serious scholarship on the First World War since Tucker's volume one and the first serious academic work on the post-1945 period to emerge since Eayrs's earlier material in the 1960s.

The proceedings of "The RCN in Transition" conference were published in 1988, when the stream of publications on Canadian naval history had, to use Douglas's words, "turned into a torrent."[21] By 1991 Douglas was able to list as many substantial publications in the seven short years since his *Mariner's Mirror* article appeared as had been published in the previous seventy-four years of RCN history.[22] The first scholarly monographs on Canadian naval history by academic historians were published in 1985, both dealing with the Second World War: Michael L. Hadley's *U-boats against Canada* and Marc Milner's *North Atlantic Run* (the latter was one of the two Ph D dissertations completed on RCN history up to that point). David Zimmerman's *The Great Naval Battle of Ottawa* (1989) had also begun as a Ph D dissertation (the third on RCN history) at the University of New Brunswick. Amid this torrent of new publications were more memoirs,[23] David Perkins's monograph on Canadian submariners in the First World War, Alan Snowie's history of the carrier *Bonaventure*, and some popular and privately published histories of individual ships and ship types.[24] Indeed, there was enough scholarship available by the late 1980s to permit the writing and publication of Tony German's *The Sea Is at Our Gates* (1990), the first popularly written, comprehensive, one-volume history of the RCN.[25]

The 1980s, then, mark a major watershed in the historiography of the RCN. Since then the pace has not slackened. There is no space here to list all that has been written, but some key works warrant mention. In 1991 the first scholarly monograph on pre-1939 RCN history appeared: *Tin-Pots and Pirate Ships: Canadian Naval Forces and German Sea Raiders 1880–1918*, by Michael L. Hadley and Roger Sarty. The heavy emphasis on the Second World War has continued apace, and many young scholars are entering the field. In recent years substantial scholarly articles on the RCN have appeared in *The Mariner's Mirror, The Northern Mariner, The Canadian Historical Review, The Canadian Defence Quarterly, Military Affairs, Canadian Military History, The Naval War College Review*, and *The RUSI Journal*. Many of these new historians are working on the Cold War era, for which the documents are becoming available.[26] Others are pushing their research back into the pre-1939 period, and volume 1 of the forthcoming new official history of the RCN will go a long way to filling that crucial gap.[27] Work is under way at the University of Victoria on the social history of the pre-1939 navy, and an official account of the Gulf War is forthcoming from the Department of National Defence. Ships, too, remain a source of interest, especially Second World War escort vessels. Two major books on Canadian corvettes appeared in 1993.[28] If there is a major gap in the current state of Canadian naval historiography, it would be on the role of individuals. At present only one biography, of Engineer Rear Admiral G.L. Stephens, is in the wind, as are a couple of memoirs by retired senior officers.

A complex and comprehensive Canadian naval historiography is, therefore, a very recent phenomenon. Probably for that reason there is little evidence that Canadian naval history is yet widely seen as a viable field of instruction for academic credit in Canada. Military history, of which naval history in Canada is a part, is offered as a bona fide academic subject at only a few Canadian universities and at the Royal Military College. The emphasis in such courses is usually on Canada's military past or on the broader international military experience, approaches strongly biased towards land warfare. Few of those who teach military history in Canada have either the expertise or the interest to separate Canadian naval history from the general pattern of the nation's military history. In that sense, the Canadian navy's experience remains an aberration even in Canadian military history courses, an obligatory reference in an otherwise traditional survey of Canada's long and colourful army heritage.

Those like myself who teach both Canadian military history and courses in the history of seapower also invariably set the Canadian naval story in a much wider context. It forms a piece, sometimes bigger, usually quite small, of a much larger tapestry. Perhaps surprisingly, Canadian naval historians accept such an approach as a given. They do not see an independent existence for the RCN outside of the large context of either the British Empire or the collective security organizations Canada has joined since 1945. In that sense, Canadian naval history is always subordinated to another mainstream military or naval (seapower) field. In only one instance, from what preliminary enquiries could determine, has the focus been reversed and a Canadian naval history course been given for academic credit. In 1991 Michael Hadley, of the Germanic Studies Department at the University of Victoria, gave a one-time term-length honours seminar on naval history, funded by the university's Military and Strategic Studies Program. Hadley was given the liberty by the Department of History to do whatever he wished in a seminar on seapower, and he presented a case study using the RCN as the model. The course, "The Canadian Navy and the Major Powers," has continued to evolve.

Apropos of the comments made earlier here, there is no indication that Canadian naval history is ever taught within the context of Canadian maritime history.

It remains to be seen whether Hadley's course itself is an aberration or a reflection of the maturity of Canadian naval historical writing. In 1980 it was possible to conduct a couple of individual seminars on aspects of Canadian naval history, especially its origins and the controversy over fleet efficiency, as part of a course on naval or Canadian military history. But it would have been difficult to do more. Hadley demonstrated that by 1990 it was possible to mount at least a term-length course for academic credit on Canadian naval history. It is ironic, and indicative of the strong contextual bias evident among naval historians (writ large) within Canada, that many of those historians who were consulted for this paper could still not see the merit in offering a course in Canadian naval history. Maybe they are right, since much remains to be done. Important new scholarship on the early Cold War will emerge within the next few years with Ph D theses from Michael Hennessy and Shawn Cafferky. Hennessy's work, in particular, draws together many of the elements of national naval and maritime policy and will help bridge that gap between naval history proper and the wider fields of which it is a part.[29] There are now a number of substantive articles available on the interwar years, and a new and thorough volume of official history is in the wings. Hadley and Sarty's *Tin-Pots and Pirate Ships* seems to have satisfied interest in the First World War for the time being. However, despite their efforts, a comprehensive monograph on the navy prior to 1914 is still needed. And another is needed to bridge the gap between the events of the twentieth century and all that went before. Perhaps when the navy finds its roots in the age of sail and in the larger context of Canadian history, Canadian naval history will truly have come of age.

## · 2 ·

# The Popular Image of the Canadian Navy

MICHAEL L. HADLEY

Then here's to the lads of the Maple Leaf Squadron,
At hunting the U-Boat it's seldom they fail;
Though they've come from the mine and the farm and the workshop,
The bank and the college and maybe from jail.
– *The Maple Leaf Squadron*

The Canadian navy has had a variety of faces. Perceived in the First World War as a "tin-pot" navy and a "bum-boat fleet," it became a "wavy navy" and "corvette navy" in the Second World War. Other epithets, from "royal" to "sea trappers" and "sheep dog," have defined the sublime and ironic limits of perceived identity; they have revealed the varieties of emotion and affection involved. Of course, image and actual identity may well be two quite different things. Yet the image – how the navy has understood itself and shown itself to the nation – is closely linked to how the public has perceived it to be. The image emerges not only from histories, memoirs, and "salty dips" (tall tales), but also from music, novels, newspaper stories, and film. These media provide a promising and largely untapped source in which this exploratory essay takes the first soundings.

Other navies, notably those of Germany and Britain, have successfully appealed to the classical principles of maritime prestige and seapower whenever national purpose and identity were at risk. The principles have helped such fleets justify themselves even in periods of severe fiscal restraint. This was certainly so in the battleship armaments race of the late 1890s, and no less so in the years leading up to the Second World War. It was arguably also the case when Britain's Royal Navy (RN) re-established its credibility during the Falklands War in 1982. Appeals to such heady "imperial" principles would for obvious reasons have been too fanciful and lofty for the Canadian naval forces of 1910, as indeed for any other period in their life. Quite different principles were involved, and these in turn helped create the matrix in which public perceptions grew.

35

The nascent Royal Canadian Navy (RCN) of the First World War suffered bad press despite the fact that it actually fulfilled the government's policies, as limited as these were. Cast in a rather minor role – as much because of Canada's priority of mobilizing an effective army as because of Britain's overriding control and centralized imperial command – the force remained essentially a fleet of drifters and trawlers. There was little mystique or romance about conducting coastal patrols and protecting convoys, however successfully the job was actually done. Citizens seem to have wanted to see their navy in the kind of "real" action the army had been experiencing, if indeed they wanted a navy at all. As the *Halifax Herald* trumpeted querulously in 1918: "What's the good of a fleet of patrols that can not catch submarines?"[1] The Royal Canadian Navy had never caught any. It had earned itself no battle honours such as the Canadian Expeditionary Force had won at Vimy Ridge. Thus, unlike the army, it was not seen to have participated in any central historical acts that might have helped the whole nation along the road to a distinct identity. Nor is that surprising, for the navy had in fact had no Vimy. Given the national and geopolitical circumstances in which it operated, that would have been asking too much.

Significantly, perhaps, the new battle-class trawlers that entered service towards the end of the First World War were named not after British or Canadian naval lore but after actions fought by the Canadian Corps in France and Belgium: HMCS *Arleux*, *Armentières*, *Givenchy*, *Ypres*, and others. Speeches in the House of Commons at war's end savaged the navy's modest record. Not even the navy minister himself, C.C. Ballantyne, defended it when challenged. Newspapers easily echoed the politicians' rejection of the national fleet. Even when German U-cruisers were operating within sight of Nova Scotia, critics charged, the navy and its leaders had fiddled while Rome burned. The armistice marked the end of the meagre and unflattering public image the navy had garnered. Significantly, Canada's first war at sea gave rise neither to memoirs nor to published yarns. "Unsung, and with little lore to fuel traditions, the 'tin-pot' navy disappeared from the national consciousness."[2] The government soon saw to it that the Canadian navy virtually disappeared from the national scene as well. The government's responses to the Washington agreements of 1921 soon reduced the fleet to "a severely restricted reserve force with two destroyers, HMCS *Patrician* and *Patriot*, and a few trawlers."[3] There was little in the 1920s and 1930s that would inspire any public interest or imagination.

It was the Battle of the Atlantic (1939–45) that provided the self-defining mythology and lore surrounding the Canadian navy; it also provided Canada the opportunity to begin developing the concept and practice of national autonomy.[4] Here the navy came of age in a way that various books have recounted in considerable detail. The intricacies of its growth and development could scarcely have been understood by many serving personnel in those years. Certainly, they were not themes for public discourse. Instead, naval and other government offices concerned themselves with creating images, which then crystallized into what one might call popular tradition. Seen in this light, Canada's naval identity was as much a creation of manipulated information as it was an outcome of national policy. "Manufacturing consent," in the phrase of Walter Lippman, was the job of propaganda, and effective propaganda depended upon communicating at least some element of the truth. As the director of the National Film Board (NFB), which was ultimately responsible for propaganda, exhorted his crews, truth is "a many-headed monster and you may have at times to make people believe what they ought to believe rather than what they want to believe."[5] Both the National Film Board of Canada and the Information Branch of the Royal Canadian Navy actively involved themselves in packaging "facts" for public consumption. This was all the more necessary because, prior to the imposition of strict censorship rules, many journalists were operating like loose cannons.[6]

Newspaper stories of the war years reveal Canada's stalwart fleet of warships as a doughty, down-to-earth band of defenders and their crew as true-blue virtue itself. The relative freedom of the press prior to the period of censorship left the newspapers ample room for the expression of patriotic feelings, as well as for fantasy and speculation. People seemed to want the navy to win its place in the sun. In the words of the *Victoria Daily Times* (18 November 1939), the nation's front-line defence was her "jolly, well-behaved sailor boys ... Canada's splendid young blue jackets [whose] hard-working mothers and fathers have taught [them] to live well and honestly and face the world and its troubles with a grin." Canada's warships of 1939 were touted in the press as the "Watchdogs of the Navy." The *Ottawa Journal* boasted somewhat hastily on Trafalgar Day (21 October 1939) that "Canada's Navy Plays Big Role [in] Convoy System." With breathless flim-flam it continued: "Night and day, in mist, fog, rain and snow, the watchdogs [stand on guard while] the vigilance of Canada's sea fighters [plays] a big role in smoothing the war for Great Britain." Significantly, the war was portrayed as not so much Canada's as it was Britain's, and the mother country needed the colony's help. In this vein, the *Winnipeg Free Press* (18 November 1939) highlighted "Grey Vigil – Canada's Warships Alert for Raiders." Canada's forces were intrepid, undaunted, wakeful, and strong: "... look-outs comb every foot of the heaving green through powerful glasses [while] on the bridge sleepless officers keep watch." Indeed, "weather or no weather, that gate to the world of sea commerce [Halifax] is being guarded against all comers, grimly, efficiently naval guarded." Throughout the war Canada's sailors were a "watchful" lot. Even once war had ended, the press continued to write of an unrepentant foe who might attack again. But Canadians need never fear, for "Canada's sheepdog navy of corvettes, frigates and other small craft," as the *Halifax Herald* expressed it in May 1945, "will still maintain constant vigilance while shepherding the sprawling convoys across the oceans." Such specious rhapsodies enhanced the navy's image and would help encourage public support for a strong postwar navy.

In the meantime, the character of the navy had been rapidly changing from a tiny regular force into a burgeoning force of naval reservists. As early as 1941 the *Ottawa Journal* announced that "Lads Scoffed at as 'Saturday Night' Sailors in Peace Days Now Defenders of Canada."[7] A centrepage photograph showed the three types of officers' stripes – "curly" for Royal Canadian Naval Reserve, straight for Royal Canadian Navy, and "wavy" for the Royal Canadian Naval Volunteer Reserve – and portrayed in overlay a jaunty sailor standing under the "menace of the grim, grey gun" of the armed merchant cruiser aboard which the report was written. The reporter claimed to have been the first to have been taken aboard a Canadian warship, which may well have been true. But since, as he claimed, everything he saw was top secret, the reporter did little more than assure the reader that hard-hitting guns, naval efficiency, and officers and men "that have welded themselves into one ship's company" will take the battle to the enemy. The story's major thrust left no doubt that the largely reserve force aboard this ship symbolized the nation's naval war effort: "Canada's navy is questing far afield, doing its share of guarding the Dominion's shores and taking its place in the Empire's ring of ships which girdle the world and hold control of the seas."

Behind the wartime image-makers was a nascent culture that expressed itself in both graphic art and music, or more properly, in gun-shield graffiti and bawdy ballad. Gun-shield graffiti and ships' crests added unofficial local colour to the navy's iconography and image, for officialdom would not authorize ships' badges until 1946.[8] But in the meantime shipboard artists set about capturing the essence of their vessel. The crews were invariably young; they saw the ship as their home and their fellow crewmen as their extended family. Little wonder that they decorated their gun-shields with graffiti that celebrated a breezy youthfulness, irrepressible energy, artless irreverence, and robust invincibility. The comics inspired figures like Daisy Mae, Donald Duck, Mickey Mouse, and Pluto; Walt Disney films provided fanciful creatures like Jiminy Cricket; there were Indian heads, native lore, and heraldry reflecting the Wild West devil-may-care, learn-as you-go style of naval warfare that seemed to be so Canadian: HMCS *Rimouski* bore a mounted bronco-buster lassoing an escaping u-boat; HMCS *Sorel*, a sorrel horse biting a u-boat in half; HMCS

*Sackville*, a muscular arm holding a bulging "sackful" of u-boats with bows and sterns protruding; and HMCS *Moosejaw*, a startled Hitler on the run from a fierce-eyed, fire-breathing moose that had skewered a u-boat on its horns and was now biting the seat out of Adolf's pants. One can only speculate on the impact such artwork had upon the inhabitants of the ports the ships frequented. The ethos they communicated, in the words of the popular song of the day, was certainly "free and easy, bright and breezy … for you know what sailors are." Newspapers provide some evidence of popular interpretation. The *Toronto Daily Star* (19 December 1942) featured a photograph of HMCS *Moosejaw*'s crest and explained that "most Canadian naval vessels have crests in which humour and grim intent are mingled," and on 19 January 1943 it featured a photograph of HMCS *Chambly*'s graffiti – a snarling bulldog wearing sailor hat and boxing gloves – subtitled "Battling Bulldog Shows What Corvettes Do to Subs." *Chambly* had won a high-seas battle with a German submarine sixteen months earlier.

Offspring of a youthful culture, the navy's songs were "irreverent at best, blasphemous at worst."9 One of the earliest, "Roll Along, Wavy Navy," extolled the voluntarism of the naval reserve, which formed the major component of Canada's rapidly expanding naval forces. With self-congratulatory self-irony, successive verses told of how "we joined for the chance to go to sea," then "for the payment and the fun" and "for the glory of it all." But of course, seen against the reality of war, both the song and the sentiment were sham, though still great fun to sing. The lyrics of "The Maple Leaf Squadron" ("We'll zig and we'll zag all over the ocean, / Ride herd on our convoy by day and by night") pilloried the stark boredom and debilitating discomfort of Atlantic escort, where "from Newfy to Derry's a bloody long way." The song also highlighted the supposedly unprofessional "cowboy" tactics which the British accused the Canadians of having adopted. But its cathartic strains also uttered the unspeakable by invoking fears of not making it home: "So we're off to the wars where there's death in the making, / Survival or sacrifice, fortune or fame; / And our eyes go ahead to the next wave that's breaking, / It's the luck that's before us adds zest to the game." Jaunty, to be sure, but heavy with gallows humour. Corvettes, too, the backbone of Canada's war at sea, were enshrined in song. The most famous was sung to the tune of the First World War favourite echoed in the opening line: "Bless 'em all, bless 'em all, / These bloody corvettes are too small. / In a rough sea they'll heave and they'll pitch, / They'll make you as sick as a son-of-a-bitch. / And it's up to the railing you'll sprawl, / And spew up that good alcohol. / You'll finish the war on this one-funnelled whore, / So, cheer up, my lads, bless 'em all." And in sheer explosive release at having survived one more crossing unscathed, what better bar-room ditty than the raunchy "North Atlantic Squadron," perhaps the most famous of Canadian service songs: "Away, away with fife and drum, / Here we come, full of rum, / Looking for women who peddle their bum, / In the North Atlantic Squadron." It was perhaps scarcely the kind of song that the expatriate reporter of the *Victoria Daily Times* might have expected his "jolly, well-behaved sailor boys" to have indulged in while gallantly fighting Britain's war. But this war at sea was different from the imported British public-school adventure tales of the *Boys Own* and *Chums Annual* variety on which perhaps not a few had once been nourished. War was a rite of passage, a man's business, and such ribald war songs revealed more about the visceral affirmation of male bonding than they did about morals or sexual prowess.

Graphic details of combat in what one senior officer described to the press as "trench warfare of the seas" proved a mainstay of image-making.[10] A case in point was the story of the destruction of *U-501* by HMCS *Moose Jaw* and *Chambly* on the evening of 10 September 1941. Despite what was incorrectly described as the Canadians' inexperience in Escort Group EG9, *Chambly*'s depth-charge attack forced *U-501* to the surface some 400 yards off *Moose Jaw*'s bow. In what rightly became a swashbuckling legend, the U-boat skipper leapt aboard *Moose Jaw* when the corvette ran alongside, leaving his sinking submarine to be boarded in turn and captured by a crew from *Chambly*.[11] This kind of drama needed little massaging for the popular market. Indeed, stories of "death-dealing" rammings, gunnery duels, and boarding contributed to an already developing lore of Canadians as roughriders and cowpunchers: the corvette *Regina* destroyed an Italian submarine with depth charges and heavy gunfire on 8 February 1942 and captured most of its crew; the corvette HMCS *Oakville* outgunned and then twice rammed *U-94* in the Caribbean on 28 August 1942; on 18 January 1943 the corvette *Port Arthur* in the Mediterranean brought the Italian submarine *Tritone* to the surface with depth charges, subjected her to withering gunfire and turned to ram; the frigates *Waskesiu* and *Nene* brought a U-boat to the surface and sank it by gunfire in the North Atlantic on 24 February 1944; and on 5–6 March 1944 HMC Ships *Gatineau*, *St Catharines*, *Chaudière*, *Chilliwack*, and *Fennel* hounded *U-744* to death, bringing her exhausted to the surface to have her hull ripped open by point-blank gunfire from the corvette HMCS *Chilliwack*.

These and other news stories shaped the mythology of Canadian sea-power. As an *Ottawa Journal* editorial (20 November 1941) observed of the achievement of *Chambly* and *Moose Jaw* on 10 September 1941, up to now our naval history had "not been a proud one" because of political neglect, but with the success of these ships "we are now making atonement for the past and living up to the traditions of the British fleet." The attack symbolized nothing less than a turning-point in Canadian naval history that will "not allow us to go back to our naval folly [of neglect], since so much of our future is on the seas." Subsequent stories were made to prove the case.

Press releases from the information branch of Naval Service Headquarters often read like dime-novel narratives. *Chambly*'s adventure of 10 September 1941, for instance, became "the story of the Nazi submarine Commander who abandoned his U-Boat for a haven aboard a Canadian Corvette and left his crew to their fate."[12] In highlighting the life of *Chambly*'s commanding officer, Victoria-born Commander "Chummy" Prentice, the press writer drew out the major theme of gun-slinger action. Prentice had entered the Royal Navy in 1912, had served both in the Battle of Jutland and as first lieutenant of the British battleship HMS *Rodney* in the 1930s, and had then returned to his roots at the family's "Gang Ranch" in the Caribou country of British Columbia. Here he "traded his naval uniform for cowboy regalia, but retained his monocle." A colourful character, he left the ranch with its 6,000 head of cattle to join the Royal Canadian Navy when war began. He was as professional on a warship's bridge as he had been in the saddle, for Prentice "is still on the job, rounding up U-Boats and applying the 'depth charge' brand." The writer struck a similar note with HMCS *Oakville*'s exploit on 28 August 1942, during which two pistol-packing Canadians dressed only in shorts actually jumped aboard U-94 and gunned down Germans. What linked the two stories was not only the events themselves, but the fact that *Oakville*'s Sub-Lieutenant Hal Lawrence had been with *Moosejaw* when she destroyed U-501 earlier.[13] He became a public-relations star. In support of the War Bond Drive, the Wartime Information Board distributed large coloured posters depicting the shooting scene aboard the submarine – "Men of Valor: They fight for you" – and sent Lawrence across Canada on a lecture tour.

The government was not alone in exploiting patriotism as a marketing medium. As a vehicle for promoting products and services in a buoyant wartime economy, the sentiment appealed to many private firms as well, for they could share uplifting values with fellow citizens and potential customers while receiving tax concessions by tagging on to the War Bond advertising campaign. In initiating its promotional series "Famous Signals of the Royal Canadian Navy," the Montreal firm of John A. Labatt Limited published an illustrated anecdote of *Oakville*'s now famous adventure in a quarter-page ad and then made its patriotic pitch: "We Canadians are proud of our Navy. Let us show our pride by giving them more ships, more guns, more shells ... by buying at least one *extra* War Savings Certificate for the Royal Canadian Navy – every week!"[14]

Such advertising was commonplace. The corvette HMCS *Ville de Québec* was another of many ships whose exploits enhanced the lore by serving as means for private-enterprise advertising. While participating in Operation Torch off North Africa on 13 January 1943, she had picked up a promising contact and attacked with depth charges, forcing the damaged u-boat to the surface. After riddling the u-boat with Oerlikon shell, *Ville de Québec* rammed her sharp bow into the u-boat between forward gun and conning tower. It was a lethal blow that sent the submarine into the depths, where it exploded with tremendous force, leaving debris and human remains bubbling to the surface. The whole process, from contact to kill, had taken scarcely ten minutes.

In an enlarged version of the same "Famous Signals" series, John Labatt Limited this time paid for a full-page coloured ad in the *Standard* of Montreal in September 1943. The ship's name alone might have been reason for this rich treatment, for as the *Montreal Star* had headlined its story on 25 January 1943, she was a "Quebec Corvette." In any event, the portrayal was graphic. The upper half of the page depicted a u-boat bursting apart in the depths while writhing in a swirl of flame and debris. Below, writ large, was the daring tale and its political message: "Seamen from all over Canada manned the Ville de Quebec. You can best thank them by increasing your regular purchase of War Savings Stamps and Certificates ... so that Canada may build more and more ships to guard the freedom of the seas."

Of course, the press did not always have such "knock-down and drag-em-out" stories to assure its readers that the navy was doing its job. Unlike the home situation in the First World War, where the press and public were largely indifferent or hostile to the Royal Canadian Navy, the public now could no longer be allowed to see the navy as a "loser." The image of efficient home defender was always invoked in the war years, especially whenever it was necessary to wrest spiritual victory from actual defeat. Thus, when u-boats struck without warning in the Battle of the St Lawrence from May through October 1942, the information branch was faced with having to acknowledge some of the reality as well as having to create counter-truth. Thus, while the *Ottawa Journal* ran two ominous headlines on 7 October 1942 – "u-Boat Sinks Ship below Rimouski" and "Submarine Menace Creeps Stealthily up St Lawrence" – an eye-catching heading then announced the unsubstantiated claim that "Canadian Escorts 'Got u-Boat' at Metis Beach." The "success," which Navy Minister Macdonald neither confirmed nor denied, added one more piece to the fascinating composite drawing that was emerging from the popular press. As tenuous as allusions to such counter-attacks might have seemed to the attentive reader of the day, their cumulative effect would have been persuasive. The myth of Canada's success in the Battle of the St Lawrence, for example, still found adherents into the 1990s, but has doubtless been laid to rest in the popular media by the Brian and Terry McKenna film *War at Sea* aired on the CBC in October 1995.[15]

The loss of the corvette HMCS *Shawinigan* in Cabot Strait on 25 November 1944 documents another case of claiming some sort of victory in defeat. The headline of the *Ottawa Journal* announced on 7 December 1944, "Canadian Corvette Sunk with All Crew," but quickly explained that she had been struck down while "on operational duty in the North Atlantic" and was "the ninth corvette and the tenth warship whose loss has been announced by the R.C.N. in this war." But *Shawinigan* had been "one of the work-horses" of the escort fleet. "Few ships of her class spent more time at sea during the period when Hitler's underseas raiders were most active in the North Atlantic." She had never lost a single ship from a convoy, the report explained. But with little derring-do to describe, the information branch could ultimately do little more than crib from one of her recent work-up reports. Captain(D), Halifax, had commented: "Conditions throughout [the ship] are above average [and] I consider the ship among the most efficient and best organized of its class." Prosaic and understated, the language of quiet self-assurance and reliability was not the stuff of gripping public relations. Still, the navy emerged from such descriptions as workmanlike, reliable, and sound. More importantly, it was a national institution.

Other press stories were manipulated to dramatic effect. When *U-517* sank HMCS *Charlottetown* in the St Lawrence River on 11 September 1942, the action left the press an intensely human story of quiet determination and suffering.[16] This was admirable and important, and became a major part of Canadian naval iconography. It was not, however, aggressive action at a time when such action was politically needed, despite the fact that the press had massaged the account to show that HMCS *Charlottetown* had been "sunk in battle with subs in Atlantic [while] fighting off an enemy submarine attack on a convoy." The *Halifax Herald* had perhaps made matters look worse by linking her loss to the sinking of HMCS *Ottawa*. Yet by splicing disparate stories and drawing inferences from the resultant "truth," the media could produce the desired results. On 19 September 1942, for example, the *Halifax Herald* subordinated the *Charlottetown* story to a banner heading announcing HMCS *Assiniboine*'s "Spectacular Victory over Huns" by ramming and sinking *U-210*. The press did not, or perhaps could not, reveal that *Assiniboine*'s action had actually taken place some six weeks earlier, on 6 August 1942. The clever blending of the stories led one to conclude that the ships had been involved in simultaneous action. The result identified the Canadian navy as that "gun-smoke" style of high-seas force the public doubtless wanted: "That story of the hours-long combat on the surface of the

Atlantic, of guns firing at point-blank range, of destruction of fire controls, of flames sweeping the bridge area – of men cheering as they rained explosives on the enemy – that story is one of the most dramatic in the annals of Canada's young and growing naval establishment."[17] This was precisely the kind of roughrider tactics reported throughout the war and exploited in the propaganda movies. Here as elsewhere, truth and fiction were mutually authenticating.

The official wartime movie-makers attempted to capture navy life for public consumption, following the National Film Board's broad policy of propagandizing the country on military and economic matters. John Grierson, the NFB's director, was the leader of the British documentary movement in the 1930s and 1940s, and in taking over the NFB, he exploited special opportunities for developing a Canadian industry. His films were a means of drawing the public to the government's view of things and, in some cases, to his own special perspectives. To this end, he conceived and produced commercial-quality films for both the national and international market. Three in particular appeared in the series "Canada Carries On." The film *Atlantic Patrol* (1940) spliced prewar British naval footage with shots taken off Halifax aboard a Canadian destroyer. Simulating an attack on a U-boat, it marketed the message: "Today, tomorrow, till the peace comes again, they will be on Atlantic patrol."[18] The "voice of authority" narrative intoned by Canadian actor Lorne Greene became a convention in the genre. *Heroes of the Atlantic* (1941) told the story of freighters and tankers being herded to Britain, while *Fighting Sea Fleas* (1944) not altogether successfully spliced actual and staged sequences of Canadian motor torpedo-boats in high-speed scraps with German E-boats.[19] The year 1943, now recognized as the turning-point in the Battle of the Atlantic, saw three major contributions to the genre: the National Film Board's *Corvette Port Arthur* and *Action Stations*, and Universal Pictures' feature film *Corvette K 225*.[20] HMCS *Port Arthur*'s kill in the Mediterranean on 18 January 1943 had already been celebrated in the press in February as "Canadian Craft Sends Another U-Boat to Bottom."[21] In fact, the prime minister had reportedly sent personal congratulations to both *Port Arthur* and *Ville de Québec* for winning battles within five days of each other. By filming legends, the NFB provided dramatic demonstration of the important role that Canada's corvettes were playing in securing the freedom of the seas against Nazi aggression.

Under advice from Naval Intelligence and Security, the filmmakers showed life aboard ship, an "authentic" convoy conference, and a rather overblown surface action against a supposedly enemy submarine. Casting either a Dutch or British training submarine in the role of marauding Hun, the scriptwriter designed a climactic scenario in which a U-boat burst to the surface under HMCS *Port Arthur*'s blazing guns. An aggressive boarding party launched from the corvettes's sea boats captures the "craven Germans" at gunpoint just before the scuttled U-boat slips beneath the waves. The NFB marketed the film throughout Canada, and it played in cinemas across the land. *Action Stations*, an expanded version of the *Port Arthur* scenarios, developed similar themes: a young, resourceful, and professional navy embodied the grand ideals of an emergent nation.

Universal Pictures' feature film *Corvette K 225* projected essentially the same theme. It was based on an original screenplay by Lieutenant John Rhodes Sturdy, RCNVR, and the Royal Canadian Navy worked closely with Hollywood to produce its story. In this case, to judge by the words that opened the film, it had been produced in order to honour the corvettes, whose sterling service had assured the freedom of the seas: "The name Corvette has become a byword for endurance and sacrifice among the submarine lanes of the North Atlantic." The film tried to impart a mystique about these small ships by showing that the whole nation was marshalled in support of its proud navy in Halifax. As one of the characters points out when touring the Halifax dockyard (the scene was actually shot in Toronto), there were "forty thousand men working on putting out a Corvette every four days."

As might perhaps be expected, the leading roles were played by Americans. The "typically Canadian" commanding officer who returns to Halifax after having lost his ship to a U-boat attack and who now assumes command of the fictitious corvette K 225 (HMCS *Montcalm* in the film) was played by Randolph Scott, best known for his roles in Westerns as heroic lover and lawman. Barry Fitzgerald, a naturalized American Irishman best known for his role opposite singer Bing Crosby, played the "3-badge AB" (the lower deck's "career corporal" and wise old man of the sea). Robert Mitchum, later a major Hollywood star in sultry "tough guy" roles, played a bit part as a Canadian sailor. Judged by the taste of the times, it was not an altogether unsuccessful film, despite the overblown love interest that even contemporary reviewers held to have overshadowed the action.

The film's principal images are nonetheless clear: corvette sailors are the hard-working, unsung heroes of the Allies' war at sea; they persevere in the face of seemingly insurmountable odds to fulfil their duty to country and fellow crew; Canadians, from all over the country and all walks of life, have come to the sea to defend freedom. Portrayed as rough and ready, relaxed and efficient, the gritty and determined young lads quickly grow into a creditable and cohesive ship's company. On the larger scale, the Canadians prove themselves as reliable and highly competent allies. Unlike their ruthless foes, Canadians are a compassionate people, and naval music – "Heart of Oak," "The Maple Leaf Forever" – symbolizes their values and traditions. In fact, the corvette emerged as a much larger than merely national symbol. As the concluding scroll imparts: "She will carry on, and those who come after her, for her name is legion, and the legend of her and of those who fight in her is an inspiration for all men who believe in courage and hope." It was doubtless a morale-builder in its day.[22] Certainly, even in the 1950s, the film *Corvette K 225* was shown to trainees in Cornwallis and Stadacona in order to inculcate a sense of naval history and tradition.

If press reports in the immediate postwar period quickly toned down their euphoria about Canada's proud Senior Service, two personal accounts of the Battle of the Atlantic tried to keep the memory alive in the late 1940s: one a documentary novel written by a naval commander, the other an entirely fictional work by a civilian novelist. Both claimed to capture the distinctive features of Canada's naval experience and to have discerned the identity of the navy. As might be expected, Commander William Sclater's *Haida* (1947) is the more authentic of the two. In the words of its subtitle, the work is "a story of the hard-fighting Tribal-class destroyers of the Royal Canadian Navy on the Murmansk convoy and in the English Channel and the Bay of Biscay." The Tribals were, of course, very different from the largely reservist anti-submarine "Corvette Navy," which the press had lauded. They were the formidable warships the permanent force (RCN) had always wanted, ships that engaged in the dramatic ship-to-ship combat for which the RCN had always yearned. In a special sense, destroyers had been from the beginning the navy's "instruments of security": as virtual "pocket cruisers" they were the best ships of their type and could fight along with the Royal Navy in the principal theatres of war; and no less important, the navy deemed them too expensive to be scrapped out of hand as had happened to Canada's naval forces in the 1920s and 1930s.[23] Having destroyers, it was thought, would not only gain Canada's place in the sun, but serve as an insurance policy against the navy's demise at the hands of uncaring postwar politicians. Doubtless for both political and historical reasons, the author's preface epitomized the "Tribal Class Destroyer of the Royal Canadian Navy [as] a symbol of our times." The author never explained the symbol, for he obviously considered its meaning self-evident. But one of his characters put the matter thus:

The whole bunch of us and the ship are like one. The officers and men are different. I don't mean they're not pusser navy style. They can be plenty pusser when they have to be, but there's a kind of understanding about them where being pusser is concerned. They're a tough lot, the toughest bunch of officers and men, taking them by and large, I ever seen, and there isn't a man aboard who would trade this ship for any other ship in any navy. She's a lucky ship, it's true, but she's got a kind of able viciousness when she's fighting that makes her seem like she's alive. An' she can fight.[24]

In any event, like all symbols, the Tribal-class destroyer in Sclater's book was communicating values as much as anything else. Perhaps this was reason enough for his basically artless narrative to have won the prestigious Governor General's Award.

The fact that the ship has long since rested in restored condition as a museum in Toronto would confirm the Sclater interpretation of the national role his ship played. For the sailors who knew them, both *Haida* in Toronto and the restored corvette HMCS *Sackville* in Halifax are not so much cultural artifacts as cultic relics. They are intimately bound up with rites of passage, with national purpose, and with questions of identity. The places where action took place in Sclater's account were not only the scenes of the navy's coming of age; they marked the Canadian navy's integration into a historical world of great naval enterprise. Place-names that continue to haunt the Royal Navy's centuries-old story – Portsmouth, Plymouth Hoe, Drake's Island, the Lizard, Scilly Isles, Bay of Biscay, the Channel, Roche Douvres, Brest, Gironde – now belonged to Canadian naval lore. The book's linear narrative form and its bugle-and-drum approach lend the tale a largely unreflective, pulp-trade zest. The experiences recounted in *Haida* lent themselves well to clichés: our ships, our men, our flag, and the concepts of duty and patriotism. Sclater's book is memorable literature only to the extent that it succeeds in communicating the experience of a generation who had gone to sea and returned irrevocably changed, matured and moulded – after a job well done. Significantly, perhaps, the tale was authenticated by an official preface from the Admiralty in London, which averred in part: "Canada's emergence as a Maritime power was a significant and striking factor in the fight to maintain liberty and democracy." Equally important, "In the records of many swift offensive forays off the enemy-occupied coast of France, [*Haida*] inscribed a name that will live as long as the White Ensign endures." When HMCS *Sackville*'s story was told in 1960, however, a Canadian admiral would write the preface.

*Storm Below* (1949) was written by landlubber Hugh Garner, who equips his fictional corvette HMCS *Riverford* with portholes, gangplanks, walls, and washrooms (instead of scuttles, brows, bulkheads, and heads), and who summons the watch to work "at 0800 hours in the morning" while setting the corvette's crew cleaning the main gun on the poop. When a crewman begins to sing the bawdy ballad "The North Atlantic Squadron," we are afforded only the bowdlerized fragment – "Away, away with sword and drum, / Here we come, full of rum, / Looking for someone to ..." Yet as the author explained, his corvette is nonetheless "fictitious only to the extent that it is the composite of many" such ships.[25] The sailors themselves "are drawn in the image of hundreds who made up the Royal Canadian Navy." He had, in fact, dished up a stew-pot of a crew: "plough jockeys" from the Prairies, an anti-Semitic Torontonian, a hyphenated West Coaster with British airs, college kids and bank clerks, a Jew with a chip on his shoulder, yachtsmen and ancient mariners, a rough diamond called "Cowboy," and the equally stereotypical character "Frenchy Turgeon," whose atrociously fractured English marks him as an outsider from the very beginning. This, we are led to believe, is the Canadian navy – fashioned in the image of Canada itself. This strange menagerie of reservists actually does become an efficient fighting ship and in her transformation draws her crew into a deeper, compassionate understanding of themselves and their microcosmic world. When all the battling and bonding is done and the last bit of saccharine is wrung from the tale, we are left with a parting image of the corvette navy:

They don't look like a naval crew does in the movies ... [I]f you didn't know them, you'd laugh to see them going out to fight. There's nothing dramatic about them. They have no slogans or war cries, except perhaps an oath or two. If you played "God Save The King" on the P.A. system they'd turn it off. But they're good, and in two or three days' time they'll be showing it again. When it's dark and wet and lonely, and their nerves are jumping with expectation, and the icy wind is blowing through the halyards, they'll be there, and they know what to do.[26]

The fiction and the reality provided the raw material for Joseph Schull's *The Far Distant Ships* (1950), the book that, by marketing the Canadian navy's popular image, exerted – perhaps until the 1980s – the greatest impact on Canadian naval lore. Though touted in the subtitle as "An Official Account of Canadian Naval Operations in the Second World War," it was in many respects cast in the same mould as all that had preceded it. Its genesis is revealing, for this operational history was to have been written by Gilbert Tucker as the third and final volume of his splendid two-volume *The Naval Service of Canada*. However, neither the Naval Staff nor the minister of defence, Brooke Claxton, wanted any scholarly analysis that might uncover unsavoury facts; indeed, Claxton was convinced that after 1948 Canadians would not be interested in examining the war in any detail anyway. Instead, he needed a quick piece of popular history that would support his new fleet plans. Laudatory, largely uncritical, and highlighting deeds of bravado and high adventure, Schull sold the image that the policy planners had wanted since the early

days of the war. In a staff paper of 11 November 1940, for example, senior Canadian officers had defined the Canadian force as an "imperial
navy" with concomitant deep-sea, blue-water responsibilities. Convinced
that Canada must continue this role after the war with a two-ocean policy that would include cruisers and destroyers, the paper had attempted
to forecast the configuration of the postwar Canadian navy.[27] All this
was being formulated while newly built reservist-manned corvettes were
entering the fray with no clearly defined wartime role. As Marc Milner
has argued, the Naval Staff's attitude created the need in the immediate
postwar period for the kind of public image and popular lore that Schull
was commissioned to provide. Now in the increasing frost of the Cold
War, Schull had doubtless found the right idiom. In exploiting it, he carefully dodged questions of wartime inefficiency, a subject the Naval Staff
very much wanted to avoid.

Schull quite properly demonstrates the epic proportions of Canada's
naval battles and evokes the smells of gunpowder and fear. In stressing
the human dimension of the Canadian experience, he portrays the navy's
extraordinary achievements, despite the serious mistakes that a later generation of historians would uncover. Schull had not been commissioned
to question, analyse, and examine, but to recount, extol, and proclaim.
His journalistic style reads sometimes like an adventure novel, at other
times like a taut short story. His brief cameo actions reveal both the flexibility and adaptability of the RCN: Tribal-class destroyers fighting the
more powerful German Narvik-class destroyers off the coast of France;
corvettes combatting surfaced and submerged U-boats in the North Atlantic; MTBS (motor torpedo-boats) in high-speed, rapid-fire shoot-outs
with swift E-boats in the English Channel; destroyers pursuing cruiser
warfare against merchant shipping in Norwegian waters; and, as war
closed, the cruiser HMCS *Uganda* in Pearl Harbor, the cruiser HMCS
*Ontario* in the Red Sea, and the armed merchant cruiser HMCS *Prince
Robert* in Australia.

Schull punctuates his narrative with wartime propaganda images that
starkly contrast the character of the Canadian sailor with that of the
German. Where Germans are wily, cunning, and obsessed, Canadians
are reflective, practical, and committed. Where Germans are sullen and
dangerous, Canadians are stalwart and astute. Thus, where the Germans
struggled fanatically to the end, the Canadians fought tenaciously until
final victory. When, in Schull's account, HMCS *Snowberry*'s depth-charge
and gunnery attack brought "bedraggled supermen" bubbling to the surface, her commanding officer found every reason to observe "no evidence
to make us believe they were members of the Master Race." War against
evil was eminently worth undertaking. How natural, therefore, that
HMCS *Skeena*'s successful hedgehog attack against a U-boat evidenced

what Schull describes as "a soul-satisfying explosion." Here as elsewhere in the account, "raw Canadian youngsters" had mixed it up with the Hun – and won.

Schull's narrative often pivots on the graphic image as it plots the navy's course through world history. Thus, "sailing always with the convoys, herding the slow merchantmen onward through all weather, meeting danger and disaster as it came," the navy reveals itself in 1943 in its true light: "... the thin steel chain which had not snapped in the dark days ... [had now become] the coiled mainspring of the offensive in the year of triumph."[28] He highlights the full range of Canadian ships and operations. With his literary sense of stagecraft, Schull typically evokes the scene of minesweepers clearing paths for the assault ships of the Normandy landing in June 1944: "... the Bangors, which had spent so many years with the coastal convoys along the shores of Canada, began the historic operation upon which the dreams and nightmares of the world were centred."[29] Again, he concludes Operation Neptune with the words of Churchill: "In God's good time, the New World, with all its power and might, had stepped forth to the rescue and liberation of the Old."[30] Of course, Churchill was referring here to the power of the United States, but Schull's deft splicing projects the strong impression of Canada's having played the leading role on the world's stage.

For reasons rooted both in documented fact and propaganda rhetoric, the Battle of the Atlantic was the navy's Vimy Ridge. The navy was deemed to have embodied all that was best about the nation itself: "Our naval effort ... was a revelation of the latent power of the nation."[31] From a naval point of view, the messages were timely, for in the words of Vice-Admiral H.T.W. Grant in 1949, the "Atlantic struggle ... is already fading in public memory" and the navy must do what it can "to keep alive the memory of those most difficult days, and to drive home the many lessons it should have taught."[32] One of the major lessons was that Canada must always have a powerful navy.

The image-makers were well served when, on 5 July 1950, three destroyers – HMCS *Cayuga*, *Athabaskan*, and *Sioux* – sailed to Korea in support of the United Nations' attempts at restoring peace. As we have seen, these were the big ships of the permanent force's early dreams. From a political perspective they heralded the new age of Canadian seapower, for as Minister of Defence Brooke Claxton would announce to the House with some exaggeration almost three years later on 14 April 1953 when introducing a new White Paper, these ships "have engaged in action and in activities on a scale far above anything experienced by similar vessels in the second world war."[33] The reservists' fleet of corvettes had now largely been scrapped, and the new Cold War fleet was emerging under Claxton's guidance with a view to attaining 100 vessels, most of the latest design and with the latest equipment. Where the total personnel strength of the RCN in July 1950 had been just over 9,000, it stood in July 1953 at 15,500.[34] Main items planned between 1951–54, Claxton announced, "include ships, of which we now have some 52 on order, of types varying from the aircraft carrier HMCS *Bonaventure* ... to replace the [aircraft carrier] *Magnificent*, to the arctic patrol vessel *Labrador*, or the escort vessels and minesweepers down to gate vessels."[35]

Yet at the time of the destroyers' deployment to Korea in July 1950, the media seemed strangely indifferent. At least, any news of the Canadian navy was greatly overshadowed by feature stories about the more powerful American armed forces and by reports on Communist aggression and UN peacekeeping operations. Preliminary studies show that "the contemporary media seemed to have forgotten the contribution which Canada had made to the Allied Powers during the Second World War," and to regard the Royal Canadian Navy as now of little use.[36] Indeed, it seems that "by the time of the Korean War, the Canadian Navy had no image" at all.[37] This seemed confirmed one day after the signing of the Korean armistice when the *Ottawa Citizen*'s editorial of 28 July 1953 described "Canada's Laurel Wreath in Korea" by extolling in several paragraphs the achievements of Canada's 25th Army Brigade. Historically legitimized by wearing not only the "red patch ... of the First Canadian Divisions in the First and Second World Wars" but also "the laurel wreath, emblematic of the United Nations," the army was thereby shown to have upheld its grand national traditions and to have heralded "a new concept of Canadian nationhood."[38] The navy, by contrast, got very short shrift, for the editorial tossed off but a single sentence on the RCN's behalf: "And the navy, equally, played a role not to be forgotten." Remembered only peripherally as the "train busters" for its effective coastal bombardment of Korean railroad lines, the navy faded from public view.[39] Ironically, it remained to an editorial from the *Baltimore Sun*, reprinted in the back pages of the *Ottawa Citizen* on 30 March 1955, to praise Canada's naval achievement; considering Canada's small population and its many obligations, the American paper concluded, its " 'token' force in Korea calls for a better name." The Canadian press rarely gave it one.

Against the background of virtual indifference to our naval contribution to the Korean conflict, the Department of Defence tried to tell its own story. Aboard one of the ships, for example, had been Chief Petty Officer Norm Keiziere, the official photographer who would shoot the Department of Defence film *In Line of Duty*. In both tone and style, the story was a carry-over from the Second World War: maritime prestige, high-sounding patriotism, warships on the world's stage, and dedicated fighting men. Now, as then, the script reminds us, we were fighting a festering evil.[40] Showing the aircraft carrier HMCS *Magnificent* (which did not serve in Korea) flanked by destroyers while fighter aircraft took off and landed, the camera panned over sailors manning radar, tactical plotting screens, and guns. Then the narrator's heavily charged voice of authority evoked the apotheosis of Canadian seapower: "They sought no glory. The foe was ill-defined and seldom seen. The actions fought were often inconclusive. The purpose of the war at times forgot [*sic*]. This was a hard thing to do. This was a test of all the months and years of training: that men should stand and fight and bear unceasing watch in distant seas around a distant shore. To halt aggression at its breeding place and thus affirm through *action* that the aggressor *shall not pass*." Then, while the camera zoomed onto and held the White Ensign at HMCS *Athabaskan*'s mast, the unctuous narrator concluded: "These, gathering quiet honour, were *our* men. *Canadian* men. Canadian ships on guard for *freedom* – in the line of duty!"

In point of fact, however, the destroyers' crews would have found little comfort, and perhaps considerable embarrassment, in such overblown rhetoric. As the commanding officer of HMCS *Crusader* reported in an internal document on 6 January 1954, "the inactivity of patrol periods ... and the long periods spent in Japanese ports between patrols tend to destroy the sense of purpose in our being here, consequently there is a tendency to drift into indifference which is difficult to combat."[41] Judging by newspaper coverage of the conflict, the film's sentiments nevertheless remained entirely out of tune with waning public interest in the possibility of Canadian naval power. In an age apparently threatened by intercontinental ballistic missiles, any navy seemed less than useless. Where Korea had failed to create memorable images of Canada's navy, unofficial retrospectives of the Second World War would gradually add to the country's naval culture.

At a time when media interest seemed at an all-time low, it remained for one important book on Canada's fleet to conjure up, as a lone voice, the spirit of a special kind of greatness that once had been. Alan Easton's remarkable memoir, *50 North: An Atlantic Battleground* (1963), projects an unself-conscious image of Canadian wartime naval life in the Second World War by blending both experience and imagination in what he describes as "a factual account." Long underestimated, Easton's book is Canada's *Cruel Sea*, and as such it is a central icon of the Canadian experience. Understated and articulate, reflective and forthright, *50 North* is both sensitive and graphic when describing the sea and poignant moments of the human soul: lonely patrols, fog, fear, anxiety, and the complete interdependence of all the crew. He affords us, moreover, a brief insight into shipbuilding, radar training, and engineering. He communicates the feeling of being on watch during bitterly cold and threatening nights, or in the engine-room when a U-boat attack seems imminent. He sheds light on the conduct of convoys, the hunt for survivors, and "the devastation of attack" when the Canadian warship strikes back. Easton reveals his deep and sympathetic understanding of the merchant marine (in which he had served before 1939) and its experience of war, and imparts sharp images of the Canadian escorts – "like dogs with their noses to the ground" – in pursuit of the German submarine. The narrative pauses briefly for meditations on the pity and misery of war at sea, such as when the convoy came upon an empty lifeboat, an image that always stirred Easton with "a conviction that the shadow of disaster floated close alongside or was hidden beneath."[42]

The image of the Canadian navy with which Easton leaves us transcends the hiatus of Korea and is not easily embodied in the conventional bugle-and-drum graphics or exuberant metaphor that marked so much that had preceded his memoir. Instead, we are left with a cast of mind, an awareness that during the Atlantic battle the Canadian navy had finally come of age on its own terms and with its own distinctive culture. Easton focuses on this very issue in a scene in which the senior officer of the escort group broached the question of naval heritage. The senior officer was in the Royal Navy and, in Easton's words, "was the kind of officer in whom, no matter how fear might assail him, the inbred traditions of the Royal Navy and his loyalty to it would stand fast in any hour of crisis and never allow him to falter."[43] But the tradition that informed the Royal Navy was not Canadian, Easton had pointed out while glancing at the copy of Southey's *Life of Nelson* that his superior was then reading. Canadians, Easton had quietly suggested, had no direct right to such traditions, nor could they properly claim them, for "what made them occurred mainly before we were in existence." Significantly, Captain Herbert Richmond, RN, had raised a similar cautionary note to the Admiralty when discussing the Royal Canadian Navy in November 1918: "It is obviously impossible to transplant an ancient growth to new soil as the basis of an entirely new organisation."[44] The Mainguy Report on Canada's naval mutinies revealed what would befall anyone who might disregard such advice. Easton was deeply in tune with the navy he served. "Our tradition," Easton perceptively suggested, "is probably being made right now," in the Battle of the Atlantic. It was also, he might have added, the primary source of the navy's popular heraldry and image, and one that would outlive the experience of Korea.

The predominant popular mythology about the navy as a distinctly "Canadian" war-fighting maritime force of professional volunteers is marked by two categories of icon: the old defining images derived from British custom and lore, and the Second World War images of "wavy navy" convoy escort and submarine killer. The former – imperial power,

Nelson and Trafalgar, the White Ensign and the crown – still seem more genuine to some Canadian naval veterans of the Second World War than the images that survived both the war and unification. Some of these people seem today not nearly as in tune with the essentially "Canadian" experience of the fleet as Easton had been in 1963, but Canadian images had been emerging throughout the war, and in the postwar period the government created innovative images – uniforms, ships, flag, and ensign – that would reflect the navy's changed character and self-understanding.

A recent exchange of views highlights a major cleavage in perspectives on what the navy once was and what it now seems to have become. The assertion and rebuttal were symptomatic of the division between the "Royal" Canadian naval veterans, who are now fading out of the picture, and their successors, the postwar Canadian naval retirees who, while recognizing the roots of the service, nonetheless foster neither a royal nor a colonial image. Writing in a Victoria newspaper on Trafalgar Day 1993, a commander who had served in the Second World War pilloried the currently fashionable "political correctness" that to his mind had pressured naval authorities into pushing the commemoration of Nelson's great battle (21 October 1805) from Canada's naval tradition, if not even from popular memory.[45] "Informed sources" had revealed to him that in order to appease Quebec and other francophone quarters Canada's navy had been downplaying celebrations of the victory of a British admiral over the French fleet. There were perhaps some grounds for his concern about the dwindling importance of Trafalgar in Canadian naval life, for throughout the history of the Royal Canadian Navy Trafalgar Day had indeed been turned into an occasion for both political and cultural statements: thus, to take but three examples, HMCS *Niobe* had arrived off Halifax on 21 October 1910 in order to symbolize the naval beginnings of "true Canadian national greatness"; the naval college HMCS *Royal Roads* had been commissioned on 21 October 1942; and on 21 October 1947 the navy had invited the press to witness its ceremonial destruction of German U-boat *U-190* off Halifax as a symbol of Canada's final mastery of the German submarine threat.[46] Be that as it may, the Battle of Trafalgar remained a British transplant. The postwar officer who rejected the argument of political correctness pointed out that the modern Canadian navy, now called Maritime Command, had for substantive reasons replaced Trafalgar Day with Battle of Atlantic Sunday (the first Sunday in May). It was in the battle for the security of the seas during the years 1939–45 that the Canadian navy had "established a strong reputation for professionalism and excellence which carries on today."[47] More specifically, "this battle was the RCN's equivalent to Vimy Ridge and deserves prominent recognition as such in the lore of our navy and the military history of Canada." The Battle of the Atlantic, he pointed out, is historically much more relevant than Trafalgar to the men and women of the navy today. It is noteworthy, perhaps, that this ephemeral joust between brother officers from different generations took place in a minor column of a regional newspaper and concerned an issue that triggered little resonance throughout the country. Sadly, the Battle of Trafalgar is still celebrated in some naval quarters as though it were a Canadian event.

The prevalent image of the navy as war-fighter in large measure determines how the Canadian navy is popularly understood today, and thus the degree to which the public is prepared to fund it. So compelling is the American image of naval power projection, and perhaps so strong the residual memory of the halcyon days of the Battle of the Atlantic, that for many citizens there is the impression that today's navy projects itself largely as an aggressive "militaristic" force. This goes a long way in explaining its frequent lack of public support. Convinced that the end of the Cold War means the end of all potential naval conflict, a time when the navy seems no longer needed in its "traditional" role, even professional analysts search for some new kind of authentication. They claim to find it in "non-traditional roles" – fisheries' and sovereignty patrols, constabulary and diplomatic duties – seemingly unaware that these tasks were the distinctly Canadian sources from which Canada's naval force had sprung.

Preliminary studies of the Canadian public's response to the navy's mobilization for the Gulf War reveal just how ambivalent the navy's image is.[48] If a newspaper's political cartoonist could in September 1990 caricature the navy as sending its floating "junk" into a war zone, by January 1991 the same newspaper was marshalling support for a navy that was doing the best it could with the inadequate equipment that successive governments had provided.[49] While the navy continued to be portrayed as a largely antiquated fleet in need of upgrading and refurbishment, the media promoted its mobilization as that heady kind of do-it-yourself zeal that had apparently characterized the 1939–45 Atlantic war. "Ready, Aye Ready" was after all the motto of Maritime Command. In photo stories across the country, newspapers accented last-minute jury-rigging and tearful farewells. Rarely free from sentimentality, such human-interest stories about the navy skewed the arguments away from questions about the need for arms and combat readiness in an unstable world, and blurred distinctions between peacekeeping and peacemaking. The gunslinger image that had prevailed in the Second World War was long since out of vogue and the war-fighter seemed in bad taste; warships taking young sailors to scenes of conflict seemed strangely out of keeping with the so-called traditional role of peacekeeping.

Canada's navy, it can be argued, has been undergoing a crisis of identity. The significance of this crisis will only become apparent once we see how the new class of Canadian Patrol Frigates projects itself in the media: as a belated tool of the Cold War or as a distinctly Canadian innovation in naval technology anticipating the twenty-first century. At the least, the new maritime coastal defence vessels (MCDV), originally designed to train reservists, will seem non-threatening and user-friendly despite their single foredeck gun. A wealth of evidence awaits researchers wishing to investigate the complex and not always happy relationship between the nation and its navy. Here again, symbols and images reveal themselves as the vehicles not only of identity and meaning, but of misunderstanding and calculated ploy.

# · 3 ·

## *Strategy, the Fleet-in-Being, and the Strategic Culture of the Officer Corps*

FRED W. CRICKARD

In the way a nation-state responds to the need to defend itself, there is a connection between national security objectives, defence policy, military strategy, doctrine, and force posture. Strategy, the blueprint by which policy is implemented, also fits into the process. In most Western nations, strategy is arrived at empirically over a long period of time and is largely determined by the type and capability of the military power in hand. Warships take a long time to build and are around for a long time after that, up to thirty or forty years. Moveover, as Admiral Lord Cunningham remarked, "it takes a navy three years to build a ship. It would take 300 years to rebuild a tradition."[1] How, then, does strategy fit into the process of national security, and what influences its nature and quality?

The Royal Canadian Navy (RCN), the United States Navy (USN), the Royal Navy (RN), and the Royal Australian Navy (RAN)[2] share a common strategic culture that has affected fundamentally the values and behaviour of their naval leaders. These navies possess a transnational "operational ethic" transcending national norms. Seafarers generally are a brotherhood, naval men even more so. It is the sailor-scholars' or seaman-tacticians' view of the horizon, all looking at the same point, that has fashioned the naval forces of these countries and will likely continue to do so.

It is the argument of this chapter, based on a comparative assessment of Australian and Canadian naval policy during the Cold War, that operational strategy and to a large extent naval policy are driven primarily by the fleet-in-being. Moreover, the function of that fleet, namely what it

57

can do, is largely determined by the traditions, values, and behaviour of its officers – in other words, by the strategic culture of the officer corps.

There are many ways to analyse behaviour and decision-making. Foreign policy can be viewed through a number of telescopes, each brought to bear on a different horizon: a nation's leaders may act according to rational choice, to the ethic or operational code of the political or military elites, to the bureaucratic accommodation of competing government departments, or to a perception of the country's place in the international system.[3] In reality, all of these factors have a part in the action. With respect to defence policy, the principal relationship is that between the senior military staff and their political leaders, with considerable bureaucratic influence from the civil service and political pressures from legislatures and public-interest groups.[4]

With regard to naval policy, a government can only act with the instruments it has in hand and the fleet with which it finds itself. How that fleet is employed (the strategy) is also largely determined by its capability. This capability, in turn, would have been determined ten or twenty years earlier by the decisions of the government of the day, based largely on the recommendations of the naval leadership that set the features of the fleet they thought was needed to meet "the threat."

This brings up the question of threat assessment. Ken Booth describes threat analysis as best understood at two levels, that of the "statesman" and that of the "colonel." The higher, or statesman's, level is concerned with politics and behaviour, that is, with the intentions of the other players. The lower, or colonel's, level of analysis is concerned with technical analysis or capabilities.[5] In practice, this neat division of viewpoints between political leaders and their military staff is blurred. In theory, it is the responsibility of political leaders to tell the military what they want the armed forces to do. This is unlikely to happen. Since the military leadership often has a better long-term understanding of the military power that is needed than the politician, the result is a two-way process in which the strategic culture of the senior military leadership exerts a strong influence on the policy decision. Under a threat, neither group has that much time. As Booth points out: "Academic strategists, unlike their professional counterparts, have the opportunity to think in the longer term and take hold of problems which policy makers hardly have a chance to think about."[6]

During the Cold War the security dimension of the international system was shaped primarily by East-West ideological and military competition. Now, when a change of the international system is under way, there is a re-evaluation of the relevance of the security policies, strategies, and military-force postures developed by medium powers, like Australia and Canada, to contribute to global and regional security as members of an alliance. This is an important question for powers whose military forces were developed over forty years to fight in an alliance in the worst-case contingency of high-intensity global war.

The Royal Australian Navy and Canada's maritime forces are good examples. Each was shaped to a great degree to fit into or specialize in a broader maritime coalition led by the United States. Although this may be the most efficient way to contribute to an alliance strategy in major conflict, the question that is now being addressed by both countries is, what is the best and most affordable policy, strategy, and maritime capability to meet national interests at lower levels of conflict, particularly in situations where the assistance of the alliance's senior partners may not be forthcoming? Rear Admiral Richard Hill underlines both the priorities and the danger: "If a medium power emphasizes its alliance commitment to the extent of saying its forces are a 'contribution' and that only, it is very likely to get a force structure that is not suited to its national needs."[7]

## Seapower and a Maritime Tradition

The British Empire and the United States entered the twentieth century as maritime powers, one on the decline, the other in ascendancy. Australia and Canada were linked politically to the Empire, and both were protected by the Royal Navy. For the first fifty years, Britain and America maintained ocean-going fleets with worldwide reach to ensure access and influence, and established alliances to maintain the rough balance of naval power. Australia and Canada used their armed forces as political instruments as much to achieve independence from the mother country as to contribute to collective defence.[8]

Because of geography, immense size, and vast ocean approaches, both countries developed ocean-going fleets for the sound political purpose of protecting their coastal and offshore interests and for the equally sensible military one of contributing to collective defence. These were the political justifications for the benefit of their publics and guardians. But the capability of these fleets, whether for offensive operations, the escort of merchant shipping, or coastal defence, originated in the "blue water" tradition and outlook of the naval leadership. The principles of strategy that imbued the naval rearmament and fleet modernization programs in Canada and Australia in the 1950s and 1960s were those of historians, scholars, and sailors of the school of Mahan, Corbett, Richmond, Brodie, Marder, Roskill, and Morison. Australian and Canadian naval officers were trained in the Royal Navy and later in their own countries along the same lines. The primacy of seapower, together with the cultivation of "the fighting spirit," initiative, and offensive action, was the operational ethic that permeated the education of the officers of the USN, the RN, and the "Old Dominions' " navies.[9] In the Second World War, the RAN fought in the Indian Ocean and alongside the USN in offensive operations in the southwest Pacific in the island's campaign. The RCN came of age in the Battle of the Atlantic, but convoy escort fell largely to the "hostilities only" officers and men of the Royal Canadian Naval Volunteer Reserve (RCNVR).[10] The strategic culture of the career RCN officer sought offensive action in destroyer gun-fights in the English Channel and elsewhere.

In a corporate sense, the naval leadership in the dominions took for granted that their navies should be maintained to fight alongside the Royal Navy in a world war. The fall of Singapore in 1942 put the *coup de grâce* on the Australian reliance on the RN for its forward defence, but the USN was there to fill the guardian's shoes. Canada initially shared the burden of the convoy escort in the North Atlantic with the RN, eventually assuming almost the entire mission. The RCN operated as part of the RN in the destroyer sweeps in the English Channel, at Normandy, and with Coastal Forces in the Channel and Mediterranean. As late as the Korean War (1950-53), the RAN and the RCN were comfortably integrated under the operational control of the RN in the Yellow Sea or, in Task Force 77, under the USN in the Sea of Japan.[11]

In short, the doctrine, force posture, and professional focus of the naval leadership of the dominion navies were blue water. Their naval construction, conversion, and modernization programs were designed for fighting in distant waters over a long period of time in high-intensity conflict, integrated with the superior naval forces of the two great powers, especially the USN. This arrangement also meshed with each country's foreign policy goals, at least for the first twenty-five years. At the outset of the Cold War, the foreign policy statesmen and the defence policy colonels were looking through their telescopes at the same point on the horizon.

Three other features of the naval operational ethic are germane to this analysis: conservatism or vested interest in the status quo; the long lead times and lives of naval forces from acquisition to disposal; and the evolution of new strategic concepts into doctrine, usually measured in terms of a generation. This is admirably summed up by Richard Hegmann: "Changes in force structure will not occur quickly, however, for reasons that go beyond the simple one of decades-long ship lives. More permanent perhaps than the steel of ships are their institutional souls, and history shows that organizational beliefs are not easily changed."[12] Little wonder that there is rarely a precise alignment between the current objectives of foreign policy and the capabilities of a fleet-in-being. It is in the nature of naval foreign policy that the statesmen and colonels rarely look at the same point on the horizon. As Denis Stairs has noted in the context of the Canadian 1971 Defence White Paper: "The evidence suggests that alterations in doctrine tended to follow rather than precede the making of specific decisions regarding the deployment of forces and the procurement of hardware."[13] Although the bane of politicians and even soldiers and airmen, there is good reason for the sailor's creed of "a general purpose fleet-in-being."[14]

## Australian and Canadian Security and Defence Policies during the Cold War: The Maritime Dimension

During the Cold War, both countries shared security policy themes in which maritime power was salient. These were collective defence, continental defence, strategic deterrence, regional security, and maritime sovereignty. For the first twenty years of the Cold War, collective defence, manifested in ANZUS (Australia, New Zealand, United States Defence Pact) and NATO (North Atlantic Treaty Organization), was the dominant national security theme in the foreign policies of both Australia and Canada. Australia was also concerned with regional security problems in Malaya, Indonesia, and Vietnam but faced them collectively alongside the United Kingdom or with the United States in the name of containment. Canada was also involved in the air and naval defence of North America in the context of collective defence and central deterrence. Nevertheless, the chief security concern of the four states was Communist expansionism and growing Soviet nuclear power. Collective security and strategic deterrence were the agreed response. From the 1950s to the early 1970s, the respective Australian and Canadian security and defence policies lined up. By and large, their naval force postures were in harmony too.

In the early postwar years, Australia's defence policy was integrated with Empire defence and, subsequently, from 1950, with that of the United States in the ANZUS pact. Australia's aim was to keep the threat of Communist unrest and expansion distant from its shores. During the Korean War the RAN fought alongside the Royal Navy, although Australia's political target was the United States.[15] In 1952 the Cold War in the Far East intensified and Australian defence policy became aligned with that of the United States. In Australia's region, Indochina was held to be the key to the defence of Southeast Asia and Australia's security. This remained the Australian policy for the next twenty years.

The story of Canada's security policy and defence posture in the 1950s and the 1960s is similar to Australia's. At the foreign-policy level, Canada also sought security in an alliance with a major power, through NATO, but its political motives for fighting in Korea remained similar to Australia's. It too adopted the principle that the defence of Canada was best achieved as far away from its shores as possible. The stationing of troops abroad, in Europe, for the first time in Canada's peacetime history not only made an important defence contribution but provided political leverage within the alliance.

During this period the RAN, institutionally, was closer to the RN and the USN than its sister services were to their allied counterparts or, for that matter, even to its own government. The Australian government left the navy to its own devices to the extent that the navy's operational functions could only be deduced.[16] The naval-force posture, however, although fashioned by tradition and custom on that of the RN, happily coincided with Australia's policy of forward defence and collective security. The RAN was designed to work primarily in conjunction with other, larger navies. Its composition was built around a few large ships serving with the RN in an integrated force a long way from Australia. Its main task was the protection of shipping, to be achieved tactically by a carrier anti-submarine warfare (ASW) task group and close escorts. Thus, the RAN's mission was sea control, as part of a larger allied offensive naval strategy in the event of a world war.

At the start of the Cold War, the situation in Canada was similar. In the early 1950s the Canadian government left the decision on the type of navy needed in the hands of senior officers of the Naval Staff. From the diplomatic perspective, some sort of naval contribution to the NATO alliance was needed, but it did not seem to matter what. The RCN chose to specialize in the protection of shipping in the same way as the RAN; tactical ASW in the Atlantic built around a carrier ASW task group and close escorts.[17]

In Australia and Canada during the 1950s and the 1960s, naval policy and strategy were determined by the naval leaderships whose outlooks, assumptions, and judgments were identical to that of their brothers in the RN and the USN. The naval strategy of the dominion navies was allied strategy, primarily the USN's. The political leadership in Australia and Canada seemed to have very little interest in the matter. As often happens in naval affairs, the tactical and the technical determined the policy. The strategy was someone else's.

In the 1970s and 1980s the international system began to change. The Cold War thawed during Detente in the late 1960s, only to see a worsening of relations in the mid-1970s owing to the Soviet military build-up, the invasion of Afghanistan, and assertive Soviet diplomacy in the Middle East, Southwest Asia, and Africa. The process of decolonization was almost complete. A large number of new nation-states in the United Nations sought to make their voices heard, particularly through participation in the Third United Nations Convention on the Law of the Sea from 1971 to 1982.

In the last twenty years of the Cold War, Australian security policy moved towards creating and sustaining a positive security environment in Australia's regions. A rigorous intellectual debate on defence and security policy among Australian academics, serving and retired military officers, and foreign experts took place in universities and service institutes in the 1970s and 1980s. The importance of economic and other non-military strategies to ensure stability in its regions was recognized. What evolved, and is articulated in *Australia's Regional Security*, was a "grand strategy" which takes into account military, economic, social, environmental, and cultural trends affecting Australia in its regional areas of immediate strategic interest in the Pacific and Indian oceans.[18] Regional stability has become the dominant national security theme.

Australia's defence policy changed in step with its security policy. Paul Dibb's *Review of Australia's Defence Capabilities* is the culmination of the debate that resulted in the policy information paper on the *Defence of Australia* in 1987.[19] The concept of "self-reliance" is developed into a set of national military objectives and a related strategy, doctrine, and force posture for the Australian Defence Force. Priority is given to building a balanced defence force, capable of meeting, independently, credible lower-level contingencies in the context of a "defence-in-depth" strategy. The emphasis of the 1987 Australian White Paper is maritime defence: "By its very nature the defence of Australia and its territories emphasizes maritime warfare capabilities."[20] A "two-ocean navy" policy is announced and priority placed on control of the sea-air gap in the north.

In the 1970s the Canadian view of the international system underwent a change as well. Although not as fundamental a change as that of Australia's, Prime Minister Trudeau's "Foreign Policy for Canadians" marked a departure from the internationalism of Pearsonian foreign policy. Trudeau's stamp was distinctly "Canada first." In the 1971 Defence White Paper, the protection of Canadian sovereignty became the first priority of Canadian defence policy, ahead of North American defence, NATO, or international peacekeeping.[21]

In Canada's case, however, the defence-policy priorities in the early 1970s were not transformed into naval doctrine or force posture. NATO's doctrine of flexible response placed a renewed emphasis on the protection of the sea lines of communication in the Atlantic.[22] With the eclipse of Detente in the mid-1970s and the need to encourage European economic links, the 1974 Defence Structure Review culminated in the long-overdue, but slow, naval-ship and maritime-air replacement and modernization programs. Naval-force posture and the new ships and aircraft continued to be shaped to fit NATO's maritime strategy in the traditional Canadian maritime tasks of strategic ASW surveillance and the escort of shipping in the North Atlantic. Collective security returned to centre stage in the beliefs of the Canadian foreign policy establishment.

By the end of the Cold War, Australian and Canadian national security themes had diverged, with each state according a different importance and emphasis on collective defence, continental defence, regional security, and strategic deterrence. Maritime sovereignty and the protection of resources and coastal zones emerged as security concerns for each country, since both are the beneficiaries of enormous wealth.

In Australia today, security and defence policies focus on the direct defence of Australia against low-level threats and on contributing to stable international relations with the states in Southeast Asia and the South Pacific. ANZUS remains important but no longer as a collective-security commitment. Its value is strategic and operational, tying Australia to the alliance as an integral part of the global strategic warning system and a contributor to the regional balance in the South Pacific and the Indian Ocean. Naval policy is given a relatively high priority in Australia's defence and security (and in public acceptance), given the essentially maritime features of its geopolitical setting. Naval strategy is sea control, described as "a complex interdependency of geographical, economic, technical and human factors as well as military capabilities."[23] The RAN's operational missions go beyond maritime surveillance, patrol, and response to include the protection of shipping and offshore territories and strategic strikes.

Canada, on the other hand, remains in the fold of collective and continental defence tied to central deterrence. Its contribution to regional stability, through United Nations peacekeeping, has more to do with foreign-policy objectives than with defence or national security. Canada's defence policy continues to be based directly on "two military alliances: NATO and NORAD."[24] Today its declared defence priorities are defence, sovereignty, and civil responsibilities in Canada, collective defence arrangements through NATO and the continental partnership with the United States, and international peace and security through stability and peacekeeping operations, arms-control verification, and humanitarian assistance.[25] Continental defence is described in terms of collective defence, while regional security could be anywhere in the world where Canada's collective defence or security interests are perceived to be affected.

*Australian and Canadian Maritime Strategies and Naval-Force Postures during the Cold War*

What is revealing about the two navies today is their similar force structures. Although one is based on twenty years of planning and operations for the direct defence of Australia and the other is a response to NATO's requirement to protect allied shipping in the North Atlantic, both will soon comprise balanced air, surface, and sub-surface components capable of ocean and coastal defence operations. Although Canada's maritime forces do not have or need a strike capability or the same shore-support potential as the RAN, the operational missions of each fleet are similar: that is, surveillance, patrol, and response. Both are essentially ocean-going "sea control" navies, with some "power projection" capability in Australia's case. The case to be made here is that the principal reasons for this similarity, in spite of quite different geopolitical circumstances and national security perspectives, lie in their geography and a common institutional belief in seapower held by their naval leaders.

In the first twenty years of the Cold War, the RAN and the RCN were essentially open-ocean navies whose missions were the protection of allied merchant or naval shipping principally against Soviet submarines. Their fleets were based on the aircraft carrier with embarked ASW aircraft or helicopters supported by destroyers, frigates, and supply ships. The RAN acquired its fleet from the RN, and the RCN constructed its own. In the 1960s the RCN specialized further in offensive ASW against ballistic missile-firing submarines. Coastal defence, minesweeping, and Arctic operations virtually disappeared. The RCN became a one-tier, one-ocean fleet specializing in anti-submarine warfare following NATO or CANUS (Canada–United States Defense Agreement) operational doctrine. The RAN, faced with the "wars of diplomacy" in Malaya and Indonesia, expanded its roles in the 1960s to include shore-support and coastal defence operations, as well as to round out its ASW capability. Significantly, aircraft, ships, and equipment were acquired from the United States, and the RAN adopted USN warfare doctrine.

At the mid-point of the Cold War in the early 1970s, Canada's maritime forces were reaching obsolescence but their missions remained the protection of shipping under NATO and area ASW surveillance under CANUS arrangements. The Australian fleet was relatively new. It was becoming an ocean and coastal navy (a two-tier fleet) capable of protecting shipping, shore support, and limited-strike operations. The leadership in both navies continued to see their fleets as part of a greater armada alongside the USN and the RN, preparing for the diminishing eventuality of a global war. Their naval forces were acquired and trained for worst-case contingencies, including major regional conflict with members of the Communist bloc. These expectations were realized by the RAN and the RCN in limited wars and crises such as the Korean War, the Cuban Missile Crisis, and the Vietnam War, alongside the USN and the RN in the first half of the Cold War.

In the late 1960s both navies gave substance to Rear Admiral Hill's cautionary observation about the risk a medium power ran if it considered its forces as a contribution to an alliance and that only. In Canada, national defence meant collective defence in NATO and NORAD (North American Air Defence). In Australia, national defence was beginning to adjust to the changing geopolitics of its region. For Canada the American alliance was the determining basis for defence. In Australia the alliance was becoming less important but remained an enabling factor. Regardless of specialization or diversification of their fleets, both navies shared similar ocean-going force postures highly suited to integrated maritime warfare alongside the major Western naval powers, particularly the USN.

In the 1970s and the early 1980s, the strategic rationales for fleet replacement and modernization in the two navies continued along parallel lines. The Canadian maritime forces remained an open-ocean, specialized force for the protection of shipping and area surveillance. The RAN proceeded along the track, started in the 1960s, of an ocean-going and coastal, general-purpose fleet for the protection of shipping, area surveillance, shore support, and limited-strike missions. Force structure determined the missions and roles, bearing out Denis Stairs's observation that alterations in doctrine tend to follow the deployment of forces and the procurement of hardware.

By the mid-1980s the second postwar naval programs were under way in both countries. In Canada the Canadian Patrol Frigate (CPF) and Tribal-Class Update and Modernization programs (TRUMP) were approved. Plans were made to replace the submarines, and coastal defence and minesweeping forces were approved in principle in a new class of maritime coastal defence vessels. These replacement and modernization programs responded to Supreme Allied Commander Atlantic's (SACLANT) force requirements but also provided a national capability in the western Atlantic, the northeast Pacific, and Canadian Arctic waters. The modernized Tribal-class restored an area air-defence and command-and-control capability that was lost with HMCS *Bonaventure* in 1970. The navy reestablished the Canadian task group concept in 1986 and, with the transfer of HMCS *Huron*, a Tribal-class destroyer, to the west coast in 1987, signalled its return to a two-coast operational force for the first time in thirty years.

The RAN's second postwar fleet-replacement program was also under way at the time of the 1987 *Defence of Australia* policy information paper. The Perth-class guided-missile destroyers (DDG) were undergoing extensive modernization; two additional guided-missile frigates (FFG7) were being built in Australian yards; the ANZAC-class frigates and the COLLINS-class submarines were approved in principle; and the fleet acquired two support ships, HMAS *Success*, an under-way replenishment ship, and HMAS *Westralia*, an oiler, acquired from the United Kingdom's Royal Fleet Auxiliary. In addition, USN Seahawk helicopters were ordered to replace the Sea Kings. A number of options and prototypes were under way to renew the fleet's mine-countermeasures capability. Strategically, the RAN moved towards a two-ocean fleet with the commissioning of HMAS *Stirling* near Fremantle, Western Australia, in 1978.

The combat doctrines and operating procedures of the RAN and the Canadian navy became integrated with the USN's in the last two decades of the Cold War. Both navies passed with distinction the test of interoperability in the Gulf War, which occurred with the invasion of Kuwait by Iraq on 2 August 1990. The Australian navy, a general-purpose force with a capability for power projection and sea control, provided a modern and effective naval instrument in distant operations. The Canadian navy, a surveillance and anti-submarine warfare force, provided older warships, augmented with modern air-defence and communications and control equipment, much of it earmarked for the new Canadian Patrol Frigates. Its contribution was augmented in terms of alliance diplomacy, because it stayed together as a task group under Canadian operational command.

Despite changing government policies and significantly different strategic assessments, both navies have emerged from the Cold War with the same force posture with which they had begun forty years earlier. Moreover, they are similar to each other. At the beginning of the Cold War, the model for their navies was the RN. By the end, the USN had become the model. The RAN and Canada's maritime forces have been built and maintained to fight alongside the principal naval powers in a major war. They are "alliance" navies. This has not been a liability, for the two fleets have served their national interests well in both the diplomatic and policing roles.

## Conclusion

Two deductions may be drawn from this analysis of the naval policies, maritime strategies, and force postures of the two navies during the Cold War. The first is that building and maintaining a balanced ocean-going fleet takes decades, during which time a country's national security priorities may change. The second is that a navy built primarily to meet the needs of an alliance can also meet its country's national needs.

Australia's geopolitical situation during the Cold War was continually changing, quite unlike the Canadian experience, which was locked in the middle of the East-West central balance and at the apex of tension in Western Europe. Australia's defence policy moved from collective defence to self-reliance and continental defence, while Canada's remained collective. Nevertheless, the RAN and Canada's maritime forces were developed to integrate efficiently with the superior navies of the major powers in advanced maritime warfare. At the beginning of the Cold War, the RAN and the RCN operated mostly with the RN in Korea. In the middle of the period, each integrated its operations with the USN in the Cuban Missile Crisis and Vietnam. At its end, each navy fell in with the USN in the Arabian Gulf. Thus, their navies are not so much the product of rational political choice and a subsequent matching strategy and force posture as they are the consequence of institutional beliefs in seapower held by the naval leadership. The type of navy that both Australia and Canada developed and maintained is the outcome of an officer class educated and trained in the Anglo-American maritime tradition of naval mastery, that is, an ocean-going fleet capable of fighting alongside the USN in a major war. Given the fundamental importance of the American alliance to both countries' security during the Cold War, this was a good thing.

Although Australia and Canada have different defence and security policies today, geography has also determined the composition of their fleets, which are remarkably similar. Because of the size and reach of their coastal zones and oceanic approaches, both navies have sought to acquire maritime forces capable of establishing, in Admiral Eberle's words, "control over one's own backyard."[26] Both have also sought the necessary seapower to provide, in those of Sir James Cable's, "a plausible capability to employ force at sea for purposes regarded as nationally important."[27]

Has Australia taken note of Admiral Hill's cautionary dictum about medium powers and the naval contribution to their alliances, and has Canada ignored it? To be sure, Australia's force structure for the 1990s was designed for the defence of Australia, while Canada's was produced primarily to fit NATO's maritime strategy. Nevertheless, Canada's maritime forces also meet the national need to protect its offshore estate while sharing, with the United States, in the seaward defence of the continent. Abroad, both navies are important diplomatic instruments of their country's foreign policy. Yet, ultimately, both have quite deliberately been built, educated, and trained to fight alongside the USN and other naval powers in major conflicts on the world's seas.

In spite of differences in the geopolitical settings and the national security priorities of the two states, their navies are remarkably similar. Both are small, ocean-going, balanced naval fleets, completely interoperable with the USN and built to fight in naval armadas in major wars. By the beginning of the twenty-first century, the RAN and the Canadian navy will be as close to being fleet units of the USN as the Admiralty wished the new dominion navies to be fleet units of the RN at the beginning of the twentieth. Although the international system has changed profoundly in the last one hundred years, and today Canada and Australia are independent medium maritime powers, their navies' lineage and outlook are in the imperial tradition of global seapower. Lord Jellicoe of Scapa, who had written his report on Canada's navy in 1919, would still approve.[28]

# PART TWO

# The Navy as an Instrument of National Policy

# · 4 ·

## The RCN: Royal Colonial or
## Royal Canadian Navy?

WILLIAM GLOVER

Mutiny rocked the Royal Canadian Navy (RCN) in 1949. In three ships, a famed Tribal-class destroyer, a modern fleet destroyer, and an aircraft carrier, in instances isolated in geography and time, a part of each ship's company locked themselves in a mess deck and refused to obey routine pipes.[1] This was a savage assault on the prestige and pride of a navy that had seemingly come of age during the Second World War. The expansion of the Royal Canadian Naval Volunteer Reserve (RCNVR), the number of corvettes and minesweepers commissioned, the importance of the navy's contribution to the Battle of the Atlantic, and the establishment of an operational theatre command based at Halifax, to name only a few, were and remain achievements justly deserving of national pride. By 1945 the naval service had begun to acquire useful experience in the operation of cruisers and aircraft carriers, and plans were being advanced for a peacetime navy ten times the size of the RCN in 1939. At the end of the war it had been decided that a two-year period would be allowed for the transition from the wartime naval service of over 90,000, dominated by the RCNVR, to the permanent peacetime navy of approximately 10,000 men. But even before that transition was completed in September 1947, the problems that would lead to the 1949 mutinies emerged. The attendant publicity clearly revealed to the country that something was wrong in the navy that so recently had done so well in battle.

To investigate and report on the problems, the minister of national defence, Brooke Claxton, himself a veteran of the First World War and of a battalion mutiny in the early days after the Armistice, appointed a commission of inquiry.[2] This became known as the Mainguy Commission, named after its chairman. The evidence presented before it *in camera* put in stark relief a very significant difference of opinion, not merely between the officers and lower deck of the navy, but between the senior officers and the country. Vice-Admiral Harold Grant, RCN, the Chief of Naval Staff, who appeared before the inquiry on 24 June 1949, epitomized the narrow focus of most senior officers:

Of course, I cannot see how any person serving at sea today dare put up the word "Canada" until he is fit or shown himself fit to man a ship and take responsibility ... I certainly would never wear "Canada" myself on my uniform, because it would be allowed on the officers' uniform ... I think it spoils a sailor's uniform too. These young fellows like to go around strutting themselves with "we won the war, we are quite something," but they are not something and until they prove that they are something I don't believe in giving them any advertisement at all ...

I think it looks like hell on any officer. I refused to wear it consistently myself, not because I was not quite pleased to fight under the Canadian flag or any nonsense about trying to wear the RN uniform. I think it ruins the uniform ... The order has already gone out for the other, for the maple leaf, to put it up and we shall see how they like that. If they do not like it and still want to put "Canada" on we will take the maple leaf off and put "Canada" on the seat of their pants ... I think Canada makes enough damn noise in this world without doing anything about it ...

If morale of the troops is suffering as you say, then by pasting this thing on the shoulders you are going to have better men, perhaps we should do it, but I still have to be convinced that they would be better men as a result. What they want is a damn good kick in the seat of the pants in the training period and told that Canadians aren't at the head of the list and not to go around advertising it.[3]

Although Grant's statements may have reflected a strong personal prejudice, they were based in official policy. On 22 February 1946 the Naval Board had decided that "the wearing of 'Canada' Badges [was] to be discontinued." It also refused to permit a maple leaf badge as an alternate form of Canadian identification.[4]

Against that view, Brooke Claxton made the following observation:

During my whole term in office, top officers in the Navy were an extraordinarily homogeneous group. They had all joined about the year [1914/15], had been trained largely with the RN, had served together through every rank and every course, had English accents, and fixed ideas. They really were a fine lot and I came to like most of them very well but they were not overly in tune with Canadian national feeling ...

I had convincing evidence that the senior officers of the Navy, just as the senior members of the Conservative party, were away out of line not only with Canadian sentiment but always with the feelings of the junior officers, petty officers and ratings of our new Navy ...

The out-of-date attitude of some officers in the RCN and conditions of service on the ships helped to build up fairly serious disciplinary troubles. These came to a head on H.M.C.S. Magnificent and I decided to adopt the unusual course of appointing a committee to look into all this ...

The whole tone of the report strengthened my hand regarding modernization of the treatment of Personnel and the further Canadianization of the Navy.[5]

The contrast between these two perspectives begs the question of "RCN: Colonial or Canadian?" Rather, it becomes a question of why had the colonial/imperial relationship between the Canadian and British navies been perpetuated in the postwar permanent navy? To what extent were the senior officers, such as Grant, directly responsible? Or was it a systemic failure that had produced a type of officer of which he was merely representative? What sources of naval policy could have resulted in the crisis of the mutinies? How did national policy influence naval development? To the extent that "Canada" badges and Canadian identity were issues of the mutinies, how had the British identity been able to survive within the navy of the dominion that led the crusade for complete national autonomy within the British Empire?

To answer these questions, it is necessary to trace two separate but parallel paths – the growth of Canadian national identity during the 1920s and 1930s, and the training of RCN officers during that period (these were the officers who would have the responsibility of senior positions in the post–1945 navy). Additionally, the wartime discussions of postwar policy must be reviewed.

In Canada the problems of national policy and identity are inextricably linked and are as old as the Canadian navy. The original recognition of the need for a national maritime capability was quickly lost when the Naval Service Act (1910) was introduced. The partisan political debate hinged on Canada's relationship with Britain. The actual reasons for a Canadian navy were poorly understood even within the navy. A discussion paper about postwar naval policy, written in 1940, said, "Although the question of Canadian Naval defence was first seriously considered in 1902, the real birth of the Royal Canadian Navy occurred as a result of a Joint Resolution by both Parties in the Canadian House of Commons on the 29th March 1909."[6] Recent research has begun to restore the significance of the 1902 discussion.[7] Prime Minister Wilfrid Laurier fashioned the Fisheries Protection Service to advance Canadian interests that were in conflict with those of the United States, a problem Britain chose to ignore in preference to improving Anglo-American relations. Laurier's intention was that the Fisheries Protection Service would evolve into a Canadian navy. That the transition was neither apparent nor easy was largely a consequence of party politics. The imperial emotion that surrounded the dreadnought crisis and subsequent resolutions in the Canadian House of Commons obscured the connection between the existing service and the proposed navy. The conversion, or more properly the return, of the Conservative leader, Robert Borden, from an imperial to a national outlook is noteworthy.[8] As early as 1913, Borden, who had succeeded Laurier as prime minister in 1911, was becoming aware of the importance to defence policies of national sentiment and recognition, albeit within an imperial scheme. In face of Liberal opposition to the Conservative naval policy, Borden wrote to the governor general: "It is highly probable that Canadian Naval Development if initiated some ten years ago along the lines above suggested [essentially Laurier's policy, which was abandoned with his Naval Militia Bill of 1904] would have proceeded smoothly and with little or none of the excitement or criticism which developed under the methods pursued by the late government."[9] The irony of Borden's comment lies in its contrast with his own strident call, during the 1910 naval debate, for a Canadian navy unequivocally under British Admiralty control.[10] At the Imperial War Conference of 1918, an Admiralty proposal for "a single navy at all times under a central authority" was circulated. Borden "reached the unhesitating conclusion that it could not be accepted as it did not sufficiently recognize the status of the Dominions." To help determine naval policies after the war, the various dominion ministers said that they "would welcome visits from a highly qualified representative of the Admiralty who, by reason of his ability and experience, would be thoroughly competent to advise the naval authorities of the Dominions in such matters."[11] Admiral Jellicoe was selected to be the representative.

Jellicoe's report reflected in almost every paragraph the narrow perspective of someone who believed implicitly in the innate superiority of the Royal Navy and its unique suitability for imperial defence. For example, "unity of direction in war being of the first importance it is obvious that during war the control of the whole naval forces of the Empire should be in the hands of the Admiralty. It would be of great advantage if such control were also exercised during periods of strained relations."[12] Virtually all training was to be done both in and by the Royal Navy to ensure complete commonality.[13] To further facilitate this goal, Jellicoe recommended that all officers of all dominion navies be included on the same RN officers' general list: "The promotion of officers on a General List would necessarily be made by the Board of Admiralty on their records of service, recommendations being forwarded from the Dominions in a manner similar to that now done by the respective Commanders-in-Chief on foreign stations."[14] Proposals of this sort cannot be said to have "recognized the status of the Dominions."

The absence of any apparent enemy or of any advantage such an enemy would derive from attacking Canada – "in the case of possible war with Japan, and apart from the difficulties of invasion due to the great distance of Canada from Japan, it is hard to imagine the circumstances in which the Japanese would attempt a landing in Canada"[15] – did not prevent Jellicoe from advocating a considerable naval establishment: "It may perhaps be considered almost inconceivable that war will ever again take place between the British Empire and America, and, if this view is taken, the only influence which such a remote contingency has upon Canadian naval policy is the locality of any future Canadian naval base."[16] Esquimalt was considered satisfactory only as an advanced base for the Pacific coast: "In spite of certain climatic disadvantages and the fact that Prince Rupert is some five hundred miles distant from the main artery of trade – the Straits of Juan de Fuca – it is considered that Prince Rupert Harbour should be ear-marked as the future Pacific coast base of the Canadian Navy."[17] Almost forty years earlier the Carnarvon Commission (for the protection of British overseas trade and possessions) had recommended that Esquimalt be abandoned by the RN because it was too far away from trade routes of any imperial value and defence from an improbable American attack was impossible. For reasons devoid of an understanding of either strategy[18] or finances, at that time the navy had "declined to entertain"[19] the recommendation because it was outside the mandate of the inquiry. Jellicoe's advocacy of Prince Rupert suggests that his understanding of the circumstances was no better.

In Jellicoe's opinion, Canada required, for coastal defences only, a navy of three light cruisers, one flotilla leader with eighteen torpedo craft, eight submarines, and a parent ship. If Canada wished to participate in the broader naval defence of the Empire, he suggested a fleet of one battle-cruiser, two light cruisers, six destroyers, four submarines, two fleet minesweepers, and the necessary auxiliary support vessels.[20] The coastal defence option had an estimated cost of $10 million per year. An absolute minimum fleet of submarines and coastal defence torpedo-boats and minesweepers, with the associated shore establishments, would have cost about $4 million per year. A war-weary Canada lacking a visible or credible naval threat was not prepared to spend even that on a navy. Not surprisingly, the Jellicoe Report was quickly shelved.

After the failure of the Conservative government to win support within its own caucus for Jellicoe's least expensive proposal, naval policy languished. It seemed inappropriate to decide on a definitive Canadian policy before it was known what Britain would provide for the RN, and that was uncertain. The Washington naval limitations talks, which had since the summer of 1921 both anticipated and further delayed any decisions on naval policy, opened on 12 November 1921. The Canadian election of 6 December replaced the Conservative government with a Liberal minority government. Led by Mackenzie King, it was dependent on T.A. Crerar and his western farmer-based Progressive party for parliamentary support. The new minister responsible for the navy, George Graham, wanted to cut naval estimates $1.5 million per year. Captain Walter Hose, who had succeeded Admiral Kingsmill as the director of the naval service, forwarded a proposal to the minister on 28 February. In order to meet the target figure of annual expenditures, in addition to recommending the closing of the Royal Naval College of Canada, reducing the Esquimalt naval base to caretaker status, and effecting some minor economies at Halifax, Hose concluded: "If a further reduction in expenditure is considered necessary, the Naval Committee is of opinion that all Ships should be paid off and the navy reorganized on an entirely new basis, that is to say by the formation of a naval reserve force. The ships with a small permanent force would be used for training purposes exclusively. It is estimated that such a reserve could be maintained for $1,500,000."[21] Graham initialled the memorandum the next day, and it became the basis of naval policy until the late 1930s.

The policy Hose advocated was very much a two-edged sword that did indeed cut both ways. On the one hand it created a naval reserve with a visible presence in the major cities across the country. As such, it was able to ensure at least some naval profile, even in the Prairies, on ceremonial occasions such as the opening of legislatures. Certainly in this manner it attracted the attention of some socially prominent individuals. On the other hand, it meant that all training of the permanent force beyond the basic new entry training for ordinary seamen had to be conducted by the RN, thus ensuring in practical terms the very close imperial naval link that politically had been deemed unacceptable. Because the naval presence within Canada was only barely visible and the focus of the RCN was towards Britain rather than Canada, in the jargon of the 1990s, to a great degree Canadians never "owned" their navy. The beginning of the post-1945 division between the navy and the country can be found in this period. The postwar senior officers were drawn from those who served in the RCN between the world wars.

The most common form of entry into the RCN officer corps was by competitive examination. However, this does not appear to have been entirely exempt from political interference.[22] Candidates had to be between the ages of seventeen and a half and eighteen and a half in the July of the year of application. The teenage boys who were accepted were entered as officer cadets and sent to Britain to be trained by the RN. On successful completion of their exams for the rank of lieutenant, about five years later, they returned to Canada and the RCN. In other words, what is widely recognized as the most important formative period of a person's life was spent in the bosom of the RN, whose general attitudes were so clearly reflected in the tone of Admiral Jellicoe's report. Furthermore, it must be emphasized that the cadets were trained, in a manner equated with an apprenticeship, within the narrow confines of their profession; they were not educated, as university students are, to develop an analytical thought process across a broader spectrum of subjects.[23] The summit of "education" given the junior officers was a two-term academic course at the Royal Naval College in Greenwich on return from time at sea as midshipmen. The course was divided in two parts. Part II, non-science subjects, included history and English. When lecturer in history and English at the Royal Naval College, Greenwich, the famous naval historian W.C.B. Tunstall made the following general comments on the 1934 set of examination papers:

The General history questions, involving issues more intricate and remote from their ordinary experience, were less surely handled, but there is gradually coming a more thoughtful attitude towards political problems and a welcome decline in the past bombastic attitude of five or six years.

The extraordinary ignorance displayed by many of the candidates, during the term, of the elementary facts of world GEOGRAPHY is again reflected in their answers to questions from both parts of the paper.

Unfortunately the candidates ... arrive after being cut off from general and non-service contacts for some considerable time. The result is that many of them find it difficult to establish themselves mentally in an educational course; the change is too sudden; they can memorize facts and they can write down these facts clearly and simply, but they cannot think for themselves and the subject matter of their answers in the English paper is often childish and somewhat stereotyped. Several groups of Essays might each have been written by the same person. They do not betray lack of intelligence or character but rather lack of ability to assimilate the equivalent of a graduate course after spending considerable time at sea.[24]

Trained within the imperial navy environment, for the most part politically unaware, and "unable to think for themselves," as officers in a Canadian navy they got off to a poor start. The narrow focus, of which Vice-Admiral Grant was only representative, was first formed here.

There were two other possible ways of entry into the RCN as an officer: either as candidates who had entered the British merchant navy training ships *Conway* or *Worcester* at their own expense or as cadets who had completed one year at the Royal Military College of Canada (RMC), in

Kingston. The army, which operated RMC, was aware that the academic standards were not high.[25] Officers from both these entry routes joined up with those cadets who went straight into the RCN on the basis of the competitive exam. Together they all followed the normal midshipman's training in the RN leading to lieutenants' exams. It is unreasonable to assume that the few who had entered from *Conway* or RMC were any better educated.

At the very time that officers joining the RCN were being inculcated, in an uncritical manner, in the ways and splendours of the RN and things British, the Canadian political climate was undergoing dramatic change. The popular feeling behind the need, identified by Prime Minister Borden, to "recognize the status of the Dominions," had, at least in Canada, developed steadily during the 1920s and 1930s. At the man-on-the-street level, Canadian nationalism may have been confused with North American isolationism. However, a review of the domestic, defence, and foreign policies of William Lyon Mackenzie King, prime minister from 1922 to 1930 except for a brief interlude in 1926, and again from 1935 until after the Second World War, clearly shows that King was trying to find a distinct place for Canada between the British Empire connection and the consequences of proximity to the United States. His approach, quite different from the "Ready, aye ready" of Meighen's Conservatives, was shared by Crerar's Progressive party. It was also very ably expounded by J.W. Dafoe, initially a Progressive supporter and the editor of the *Winnipeg Free Press*, the most influential paper of the period. Mackenzie King eschewed commitments beyond the limits of Canada's concerns, and policy within those limits was directed by Ottawa. Any issue that challenged, or had the potential to challenge, national unity was avoided if possible, or at least decided in a nationalist manner that did not directly present a unity crisis. The collective security of the League of Nations replaced the British Empire as the guarantor of peace. The League was strongly endorsed, as it provided a safe niche between British imperial policy and continental domination by the United States.

A telling indicator of the demise of imperial sentiment in Canada was the decline in support for the Round Table Movement, an Empire-wide, intellectually-based, imperialist advocacy group. As early as May 1921 it had been decided that no new groups would be created, and eighteen months later the decision was expanded to include the reactivation of old groups. Round Table supporters in Canada "struggled to keep the Canadian organization afloat" throughout the 1920s.[26] On the other hand, the decade did see a considerable growth in nationalist sentiment and a move towards complete independence of policy from Britain.

The independence conferred in the Statute of Westminster (1931) was the formal recognition in law of the statement of independence contained in the Balfour Declaration of 1926. This had been the product of the Imperial Conference of that year. It had described the dominions as

autonomous communities within the British Empire, equal in status, in no way subordinate one to another in any aspect of their domestic or external affairs, although united by a common allegiance to the Crown, and freely associated as members of the British Commonwealth of Nations ... Every self-governing member of the Empire is now the master of its own destiny. In fact, if not always in form, it is subject to no compulsion whatever ...

... the governing consideration underlying all discussions of this problem (of the general conduct of foreign policy) must be that neither Great Britain nor the Dominions could be committed to the acceptance of active obligations except with the definite consent of their own governments.[27]

This had been anticipated by the position that Mackenzie King adopted on the Chanak crisis in September 1922. At that time he had declined to commit Canada to supporting the adventurous intervention policy of British Prime Minister Lloyd George in Turkey. In contrast, Arthur Meighen, the Conservative leader, had made his (in)famous "Ready, aye ready" comment in Toronto. Although his audience of businessmen might have cheered him wildly, his biographer recognized that Meighen's "concept of Empire ... was vulnerable to attack" and not representative of Canadian opinion.[28]

On defence issues, Mackenzie King took great pains at the 1926 conference to ensure that there was no attempt to create an "imperial scheme." Rather, "co-ordination and co-operation has been the note all the way through."[29] On the specific matter of the navy, King was careful to point out that the Canadian navy was meant to meet Canadian concerns, as perceived by the public:

Our naval activities are as yet on a small scale. It is not necessary to detail the circumstances which prevented the growth of the Canadian Navy along the lines anticipated in 1909. The special geographical position of Canada would have made it unnecessary to aspire to very rapid or extensive development, but, had it not been for the circumstances to which I allude, we could doubtless have reasonably expected a more adequate force than as yet exists. I cannot say when that "active and determined support of public opinion" which is so properly stated in the Committee of Imperial Defence memorandum on Empire Naval Policy and Cooperation of 1923 as being essential for the effective maintenance of naval forces will make it possible to advance to a further phase, but the question is receiving consideration.

The policy on which the naval activities of the Dominion are based at present is one of developing the local defence of waters in the vicinity of Canadian coasts and the approaches to our ports. Also it is considered that any naval programme should, as far as possible, be one which will admit of the personnel being for the most part, and as soon as practicable, entirely Canadian. There is also in effect a system of co-operation in staff work and an arrangement of periodical service with the Royal Navy by officers and men of the Royal Canadian Navy in order that they may be trained to carry out their duties in all respects on similar lines.[30]

This policy of Canadian coastal defence to the extent it was supported by the Canadian public had been the Liberal naval policy since Laurier and remained so up to the beginning of the Second World War. When, at the outbreak of war, Rear Admiral Percy Nelles, chief of naval staff, recommended that the navy be placed under British control, Mackenzie King refused, permitting only "close co-operation."[31]

In fact, however, the Canadian navy was more British than Mackenzie King might have wished, despite his policies. The training and "periodical service with the Royal Navy" produced an officer corps that may well have been, as Claxton observed, replete with English accents, fixed ideas, and "not overly in tune with Canadian national feeling." Indeed, there was no reason for the officers to become "Canadian" in outlook or thought. After they completed their five years initial training in Britain, their normal path was to return to Canada to obtain a watch-keeping certificate. This was expected to take no more than six months. They were then eligible for promotion to lieutenant. Thereafter, they were expected to serve at least two years at sea with the RN in each rank, in addition to any courses or shore appointments they might have in Britain. To the extent that any officers were conscious of the growing Canadian national awareness and identity, as enunciated by Mackenzie King's policies and supported by Dafoe's editorials, they would have recognized a conflict with their naval values, instilled in Britain, and probably would have decided in favour of the navy. In Canada there was no apparent need for them to adopt a Canadian perspective. Officers moved within a naval environment that unhesitatingly adopted the British norms. In Halifax and Victoria, where they were most likely to be appointed in Canada, the population readily accepted British values.[32] Trained, not educated, the naval officers probably never recognized the growing gulf between themselves and their country.

War, when it came, seemed at long last to present the chance of creating a "real" navy.[33] It cannot be surprising, though it might be regretted, that in view of their training and background RCN officers defined a real navy in exclusively British terms. One can hardly censure them for this. What is open to serious question is the priority given that goal. At a minimum, the survival of the postwar navy was the second objective of Chief of Naval Staff Vice-Admiral Percy Nelles.[34] Yet sometimes the restructuring of the coastal navy in the image of the RN, an image that was hoped could survive the return of peace, seemed more important than achieving victory.

It is difficult to avoid the conclusion, for example, that the additional accommodation desperately required at Halifax for officers under training was delayed until after a commitment to a naval college had been secured. After all, a shortage of space, satisfied by temporary structures, could not be used to substantiate the need for a college. The former Dunsmuir residence, Hatley Park, had been identified as a possible location for a naval college as early as 18 October 1940. The decision to reopen a naval college was announced by Angus Macdonald, the naval service minister, in his maiden speech on 19 November, and the property transaction was closed on 13 December.[35] By contrast, the shortage of space for RCNVR officer training at Halifax had been identified not later than August of 1940, and the impact of inadequate facilities on training had also been recognized. Yet despite requests for early approval for construction of temporary buildings, it does not appear to have been obtained before November, and the buildings were not ready for occupancy until 15 January 1941.[36]

The emphasis on postwar survival also influenced the attitude of Naval Service Headquarters (NSHQ) towards the conduct of the war at sea. By 1943 it was abundantly clear that the RCN was involved primarily in an anti-submarine conflict. At the Atlantic Convoy Conference in Washington in March 1943, it was "agreed that the R.C.N. should take charge of trade convoys in the Western Atlantic."[37] Yet NSHQ was slow to recognize this in its own organization. The Directorate of Warfare and Training, to be responsible for fighting efficiency, tactical analysis, training, and research and development,[38] was not established until June 1943, and then in response to complaints from commanding officers at sea.[39] At the same time, Lieutenant-Commander D.W. Piers, commanding officer of HMCS *Restigouche*, observed:

A/S Warfare in the Royal Navy is directed and developed by C-in-C. W.A. and D.A/S.W. It is respectfully suggested that the permanent appointment of an R.C.N. Officer both to Derby House and the Admiralty would be greatly beneficial to the necessary close co-operation between the R.N. and the R.C.N. It has recently been learned that a senior R.C.N. Officer has been sent to the U.K. to study the Fleet Air Arm problem. If Officers can be spared for this necessary new development, it might be possible to give greater attention to the outstanding problem of A/S Warfare.[40]

The officer sent to investigate the Fleet Air Arm was Acting Captain H.N. Lay, RCN. When the matter had come before the Naval Staff on

5 April 1943, it was noted that "although it is difficult to foresee the possible size of the Canadian Navy after the war, it is essential to include a Naval Air Service in its organization since no modern Navy is complete without one."[41] Implicit in this was the assumption that after the war Canada would want to have a navy significantly larger than the 1939 force. Thus, Lay, one of the few senior officers with convoy experience, was sent to study Fleet Air Arm problems; yet only a few months later it was necessary for the RCN to borrow an officer from the RN to coordinate escort group training.[42]

Notwithstanding the conspicuous operational success of the United States Navy in naval aviation, the instructions given to Lay for his inquiry laid paramount emphasis on the RN. This British focus was merely a reflection of the bias of the prewar RCN officers and wholly consistent with the earlier naval college decision. The naval college at Hatley Park, considered an essential item of the postwar RCN, was deliberately fashioned on the British model. In September 1940 Captain L.W. Murray, deputy chief of naval staff, had sent a memorandum to Nelles discussing the composition and nature of the proposed naval college.[43] Murray's strong Anglophile leanings were clearly evident. The "interchange-ability of our officers with the Royal Navy ... must be maintained as long as Canada remains a part of the British Commonwealth." Nelles had "concurred" with Murray's recommendation that the cadets on graduation should go to sea with the RN and then remain in England for the sub-lieutenants' courses. He had also agreed with Murray's conclusion that the RCN cadets had to be "in a position to compete on equal terms" with officers joining the RN either from Dartmouth or from the Public School Entry. "From this it is possible to deduce the length of course required and consequently the age of entry into the Royal Naval College of Canada." Unfortunately, secondary education in Canada did not fit the English mould. "As it is not possible therefore to take advantage of the natural breaks in the educational career of Canadian boys, my recommendation, *subject to concurrence by the educational authorities* [emphasis added by Nelles], would be that the Royal Naval College of Canada should take boys between the ages of 15 and 17 and give them a 3-year course, introducing those subjects in which the Canadian educational system is deficient."

A further difficulty was that educational standards, a provincial responsibility, varied among the provinces, and a quota system of candidates from each province would create an uneven entry standard. Murray had recommended entry by competitive exam in preference to quotas. Lack of sufficient numbers to make the college viable could perhaps have been made up by providing the training for boys interested in the merchant service. However, the ultimate goal of interchangeability with the RN could not be challenged:

I am unable to say whether the system I have described as regards educational standards and length of course can be efficiently worked into the educational system of the country for the benefit of those who undertake the Naval College course and do not wish to enter the Navy ... If it is not possible to devote the whole interests of the Naval College to the production of Naval Officers I feel that any changes in curriculum should be as few as possible and that the main object of a Naval College, to provide officers for the Navy, should not be lost sight of. In other words, if it is necessary so to change the system and outlook of the Naval College that it detracts from its value as a Naval College, in order to obtain support of the people towards its establishment in this country, I should strongly advise that we do not embark on such a venture but continue to have our junior officers trained in the British Navy as at present.

Nelles agreed with this assessment, writing, "Common sense. The 1st object must be the RCN."

The lack of importance attached to popular support for the college and the precedence given to achieving the perfect fit with the RN are revealing. The lesson of the failure of support for the navy in the 1922 cutbacks, an event within the service experience of both Nelles and Murray, was at best overlooked. The preoccupation with RN compatibility ignored Mackenzie King's requirement for popular support of the service, which he had outlined in 1926, and ran counter to the professional imperial advice that he cited. It also disregarded the work of Walter Hose, Nelles's predecessor as chief of naval staff. When Hose put forward his scheme for keeping the navy alive in Canada by creating RCNVR units across the country, he was well aware that this naval presence was the first step in creating support for government spending on a larger, better-equipped service. The inability to deviate even in the smallest degree from the British model is evidence not only of the narrowness and enduring nature of the officers' training, but also of the absence both of a broad-based understanding of Canadian conditions and requirements, and of a capacity to recognize the need for modification to meet them.

The slavish pursuit of the English model was not restricted to the question of the college, and the attitude survived the war, at least among some senior RCN officers. By 1944 the navy had grown in size almost to its peak, and its continuance after the war as a sizeable force was also certain. The time had come to put its source of authority on a proper footing. In that year Angus Macdonald, the minister for the naval service, introduced legislation that would consolidate in one place under Canadian control the authorities of the navy. There were "no fewer than eleven different sources. Eight of these [were] Canadian and three from the United Kingdom." The need to replace this "complex body of Canadian and British acts, regulations and orders which can be integrated only with the utmost difficulty even by legal specialists"[44] was accepted without opposition by the House of Commons. When the legislation was implemented, the British King's Regulations and Admiralty Instructions (KR&AI) were replaced by the King's Regulations for the Government of His Majesty's Canadian Naval Service (KRCN). This change was resisted by some. Several years after their introduction, a commodore was described, at about the time of the Mainguy Inquiry, as "an outstanding example of 'the old school.' Intensely 'British Empire' and 'Naval tradition' he deeply resents any change. As a small example he refuses to have anything to do with K.R.C.N. (except when he has to) because he was brought up on KR and AI."[45] Objections such as this at senior rank to parliamentary legislation that did little more than "house clean" represented a real obstacle to changing the colonial outlook of the Canadian navy. Although that officer might have been identified as being extreme, the wartime discussions within the Naval Service Headquarters about postwar policy clearly indicate that none of the senior officers were capable of thinking of the navy in a purely Canadian context.

The achievement of Canadian operational control and direction over Canadian ships has been justly described as a considerable accomplishment during the the Second World War.[46] However, the *form* of the navy over which control was acquired remained British. Indeed, the policy papers advanced by naval officers during the war completely ignored previous Canadian thought and policy. In 1922 Canada had not been interested in the "broader naval defence of the Empire" and of maintaining a navy capable of intervention at that level. There was nothing in the political life of Canada of the 1920s and 1930s to suggest that Canada would be any more willing to embrace such a large-scale defence policy after the conclusion of the Second World War. Yet, at the first opportunity, the Jellicoe plan for a naval establishment was resurrected, advanced, and, as the war continued, expanded upon. In January 1939 Nelles had defined the objective of the naval service as being a fleet of nine destroyers, four anti-submarine vessels, and eight minesweepers on each coast, eight motor torpedo-boats (MTBs) on the east coast only, and parent ships for the destroyers and MTBs. In addition to the naval bases of Halifax and Esquimalt, and without explanation or elaboration, he also called for subsidiary bases at Sydney and Cape Breton, Nova Scotia, and Prince Rupert, British Columbia. Cruisers had not been forgotten; he merely recommended "nil at present." The scale of attack on which a fleet of this size was based included – again without justification – raids by cruisers armed with 8-inch guns and, on the east coast, attack by a battleship.[47] He did not address the problem of what targets on either coast might make attack on this scale profitable. (In 1934 General McNaughton had noted that "it would be a positive advantage to Great

Britain if Japan sent forces to attack our coasts since they would be drawing forces away from the decisive theatre without gaining any comparative advantage.")[48]

By October 1940 the projected size of the RCN had swelled. Captain H.T.W. Grant, director of naval personnel, submitted a complement scheme for the naval services for 1941–42 that called for a significantly increased shore establishment including, by Nelles's amendment, a subsidiary base at Gaspé and a much larger number of corvettes and minesweepers. With this went a submission to increase the RCN component of the naval service. Initially, Macdonald, the naval minister, refused the request. Grant exploded: "In conclusion the whole organisation of the navy with its programme of training, construction and rate of recruiting is entirely dependent on the achievement of a definite numerical strength over a given period. If this strength is not authorized it is quite useless to prepare any programme other than that of the moment. I cannot agree that this is constructive."[49] Grant was overlooking the problem of winning the war – in December 1940 a long way off. He was placing his priority on the postwar navy well in advance of any firm policy decisions on its future size or composition. Macdonald had put his emphasis on winning the war first. Ultimately, the request was approved, but no transfers to the permanent force were to be made until the end of the war.[50]

Also in late 1940 the Naval Staff wrote the memorandum on "Canada's Post-War Navy." It was nothing more than a rehash of Admiralty advice given at the time of the 1910 Naval Service Act, of Jellicoe's report, and of Nelles's January 1939 memorandum. However, four cruisers were added to the eighteen destroyers, and the numbers of A/S (anti-submarine) vessels and minesweepers were increased. The personnel figure was put at 800 officers and 12,000 ratings. The memorandum's insistence that Canada was part of "an Imperial Navy, and the whole Empire shares in its provision and support"[51] and its failure either to address any of the previous political objections to the proposals it was reiterating or to show how Canadian circumstances had materially changed (such that a large postwar navy would be both necessary and supportable) bring to mind Tunstall's comment about the inability of the officers to think for themselves. Commodore G.C. Jones, Commanding Officer, Atlantic Coast, busy fighting a war, remarked, "Let S[taff] O[fficer] O[perations] read this in his spare time and then file it away *safely*."

The next major postwar discussion paper was written in Halifax in 1941 by a special study group. The members were Acting Captain W.B. Creery, RCN; Captain-in-Charge at Halifax, Commander H.G. DeWolf, RCN, Staff Officer Operations to the Commanding Officer Atlantic Coast; and Mr F. Alport, Engineer Works and Buildings. Most of the work on this study, known as the Halifax Paper, was done by the secretary,

Lieutenant Denis Harvey. He was the first of three RCNVR officers to be closely associated with postwar plans. Harvey had been born in England and completed his secondary schooling there. He had earned a bachelor of science degree at McGill University, Montreal, in agricultural economics. He had then gone on to work as a research economist and statistician for an investment banking house. He had joined the RCNVR on the outbreak of war and was sent to Halifax, where he filled shore positions. In November 1941 he became the secretary of the Base Planning Committee and in that capacity was the principal author of the paper about the formulation of Canadian naval policy. This was forwarded to NSHQ by Jones, newly promoted rear admiral, on 22 December.

Harvey's paper represented a significant step forward in the argument for a postwar navy.[52] The basic thrust, not surprisingly, was economic. The Atlantic Charter put Canada in a pivotal position between the United States and the British Commonwealth. "Strategically she is a flanking factor in the United States defence. Economically she is a vital factor to Britain and the Commonwealth. Her position enables her to act in coordinating these otherwise competitive systems. That coordination is essential to her own internal economy and her political union" (8). International trade would overcome sectionalism within Canada, thus promoting unity. It would also help Canadian survival on a continent dominated by the United States. International trade could only be carried by a Canadian-owned merchant marine, which in turned demanded a Canadian navy. A strong Canadian navy would give Canada the requisite voice within the "Empire Naval Policy," thus ensuring the communications link between Britain and the United States. The argument very neatly stood the Statute of Westminster (1931) on its end. Because Canada was autonomous, it was able to participate fully in common imperial policy. That it would want to do so was held to be axiomatic; that Canadian policy might be different was impossible. "Canada's national response in the event of this war was in itself proof of a singleness of purpose on Empire affairs" (1). In the postwar world, "the existence of Canadian naval forces is essential to national prestige and perhaps autonomy" (2). Jones was almost certainly right when he said, "We all feel that we have now got into something which is perhaps too deep for us and not our particular concern." The British imperial sentiment with regard to the Canadian naval lobby had found in Lieutenant Denis Harvey an educated and articulate spokesman. Unfortunately, his own British upbringing meant he was equally divorced from the realities of Canadian political life.

In 1942 Paymaster Sub-Lieutenant J.S. Hodgson, RCNVR, a Rhodes scholar from McGill University, wrote the excellent paper "Post-War Naval Problems."[53] Amidst the many policy discussions and papers of the time, it appears as a breath of common sense, raising many important questions and placing them squarely in a Canadian context. Most telling, he observed: "The present excellent liaison with Great Britain and the United States must not be allowed to lapse. This does not mean the cultivation either of an Imperial or a Pan American Navy. Nor does it mean complete uniformity or imitation, but rather a complete exchange of information. Canada must be kept abreast of new developments in naval affairs abroad." The paper was forwarded by Commander F.L. Houghton, director of plans, who strongly endorsed it, to Commodore H.E. Reid, vice-chief of naval staff. Reid "found it difficult to see how we can plan a post war navy now" when the end of the war was still not in sight.[54] His position was not unreasonable, but it only slowed further discussion temporarily.

The most prolific and certainly one of the most important RCNVR officers to discuss postwar naval plans was George Frederick Todd. He had been born and educated in Glasgow. After obtaining first-class honours in an undergraduate economics degree from the University of Glasgow, he went south to Oxford for further study. He then became a chartered accountant with Imperial Tobacco and took a position with the company in the United States. On the outbreak of war he joined the British consular staff in Wilmington, North Carolina. On 8 June 1942, on the strength of his prewar RNVR commission, he joined the RCNVR as a paymaster lieutenant. He went into the Plans Directorate at NSHQ. When Commander DeWolf left in August 1943 to return to sea, Todd, by then an acting lieutenant-commander (Special Branch), became the acting director of plans.

During his brief tenure as acting director of plans, he wrote several major discussion papers that in course were approved by the Naval Staff. This senior policy forum was normally chaired by the chief of naval staff (Nelles). Todd was a member while acting director of plans. The other members were Rear Admiral Jones, vice-chief of naval staff; Captain W.B. Creery, RCN, assistant chief of naval staff; Captain Eric Brand, RN, director of the Trade Division; Commander G.H. Griffiths, RCN (Temp.), director of operations; and Acting Captain A.R. Pressey, RCN, deputy director of warfare and training. Whenever appropriate, Todd's papers were forwarded to the Naval Board. They were argued with the analysis and skill that would be expected of his academic background. However, like Harvey's work, they too lacked an appreciation of the Canadian political background. Todd's language was frequently jingoistic imperialism and calculated to shame Canada into adopting at least a cruiser-strength navy.[55] With respect to the war against Japan, Todd argued that it was "essential for Canadian prestige that this part of the Canadian Navy should be neither indirect nor meagre ... it is not to be considered that Canada should do proportionately less than the rest of the Empire."[56]

When Captain G.R. Miles (commanding officer of HMCS *Saguenay* early in the war, later chief of staff in Halifax during the VE Day riots, and commanding officer of *Magnificent* when it had the mutiny) arrived in December 1943 to assume the position of director of plans, this argument was seized upon with enthusiasm. At the same time, the role of the RCN in the Battle of the Atlantic was deprecated: "Canadian and allied public opinion has admired the work of the Canadian Navy in the Battle of the Atlantic, yet there is little doubt that this work would have kindled even greater interest had the Naval Service not invariably been thought of in terms of small ships."[57] It was on this premise that Miles built the case for a postwar navy of four cruisers, two light fleet aircraft carriers, three fleet destroyer flotillas, and various escort and minesweeping forces.

In late 1943 the interdepartmental Post Hostilities Problems Committee (PHP) was established. The discussions in that body served only to isolate the strong imperialist sentiment surviving within the navy. The PHP never referred to "empire" but rather to the "British Commonwealth," and it emphasized that each Commonwealth member was completely autonomous, without any obligation to any other, except as arranged by special bilateral agreements.[58] Yet Houghton, by now senior Canadian naval officer (London), writing from London on 11 February 1944, had suggested that after the war there would be a continuing need for complete interchangeability ("when considered necessary or desirable") between the RCN and the RN. Houghton went on to say that "in order to ensure uniformity and homogeneity with the Royal Navy ... the closest possible liaison ... is most essential."[59] His earlier endorsement of Hodgson's paper, which had argued against uniformity, was forgotten. He thought that this liaison could only be achieved by placing inside the Admiralty RCN officers who reported directly to the chief of naval staff (CNS). Although such liaison on technical subjects may have been necessary during the war to improve RCN equipment standards, liaison on the basis of personal contacts outside official channels had been proscribed by Mackenzie King before the war. As an alternative to interchangeability, the option of close cooperation, as was clearly working between RCN and USN ships in escort groups, had not yet been recognized.

The "prestige" accruing to such a navy, a perception used to support many of the postwar suggestions, was defined purely in British terms. When the Canadian government had been manoeuvred into a position of accepting the transfer of two RN cruisers, congratulations were extended by the Admiralty on the "advent" of the RCN "as a 'big ship' navy able to take an even greater part both now and after the war in maintaining the Naval tradition of the British Commonwealth."[60] Like all their predecessors, Todd, in advancing Harvey's prestige argument, and Miles, in using it, had misread Canadian experience when estimating the willingness of a peacetime population to pay for such a large navy – a service capable of global intervention and commitments on a scale unprecedented for Canada. Todd even suggested that if cruisers were acquired for use against Japan, "an opportunity to win battle honours with them [would] greatly enhance the chances of their acceptance by public opinion as part of the post-war Canadian navy."[61]

The importance given to prestige was not entirely misplaced, even if its significance was not clearly understood. To be funded, every organization needs some sort of profile. "Positive PR," or prestige, is an important part of gaining public attention. However, that attention cannot be maintained and turned into support, on the basis of prestige alone. The Canadian Expeditionary Force (CEF) had great prestige in 1918, but this did not ensure a peacetime policy of maintaining an army of several divisions. A naval reserve presence, like militia units, helps to keep defence matters in the public eye in larger towns and cities across the country, but that by itself is not sufficient. The forces must be closely integrated in other aspects of national policy and life. To use current jargon, they must be "relevant." The difficulty of ensuring the relevance of a navy in a country such as Canada, where the capital is 600 miles from an ocean and, in the eyes of many, is yet too far east to be in the "central" part of the country, is a problem utterly unknown in Britain. It adds a complicating dimension to the political questions of policy and funding, one with which the Admiralty could have had no experience. A navy that was a clone of the Royal Navy, one indeed in which the senior officers identified more closely with Britain than with Canada, would not be understood in Canada. The prestige of battle honours alone would never be able to win sufficient support for a "real" navy.

Nor were Todd and his colleagues entirely wrong in describing the use of prestige in the international forum. One of the important accomplishments of the naval service during the Second World War was gaining operational control over its own forces, and over a theatre, rather as the army had won control over the CEF in the first war. Allies would only give that control and authority to an organization with the prestige or credibility of professional competence. To a certain extent, as an organization will be judged by the larger powers, its value must be demonstrated in their terms. What the Canadian naval leadership of the Second World War overlooked, however, was that the RCN had proved its ability with corvettes and destroyers – the small ships disdained by Miles – not cruisers and aircraft carriers. Nonetheless, in the drive to create a real navy, a professional navy, the Canadian officers tried to model the RCN on the RN – to create a clone of it in Canada.

Trained by the RN in a narrow professional manner rather than educated in a broader and more reflective, or analytical, manner, and serving either in the RN or within a British atmosphere in Canada, the RCN senior officers – not surprisingly – either did not recognize or did not understand the environment within which Canadian naval policy had to be made. And so the colonial/imperial relationship was retained within naval thinking long after it had been dropped by the country as a whole. That the navy was out of step with national feeling was made evident by the 1949 mutinies. In the final analysis, mutiny can only be a failure of leadership. The narrow, blinkered perspective of the senior officers was certainly a consequence of their lack of a broad education. Whether Brooke Claxton's efforts at Canadianization of the navy were successful must, in part, be judged by the succeeding senior officers' consciousness of the national political life of the country. The failure to use the nation's own political life as the basis for naval policy is the ultimate hallmark of a colonial navy.

## · 5 ·

# The Roots of the Royal Canadian Navy: Sovereignty versus Nationalism, 1812–1910

GRAEME R. TWEEDIE

In May of 1910, the Royal Canadian Navy (RCN) was born amidst much heated debate. Its formation presented a major controversy in Canada. For Laurier's government, the RCN adequately addressed Canada's obligation to imperial naval defence. However, not everyone was of this opinion. Some felt that the RCN represented too much involvement with imperial defence, while others believed that the "tin-pot" navy was inadequate. To better understand the controversy, one must first review Canada's traditional maritime concerns with regard to sovereignty. This review will examine the history of the Maritime provinces, a region very concerned with its coasts: Nova Scotia, New Brunswick, and Prince Edward Island. The growing obligation to have a naval force, on an international level, will then be discussed.

### The Fisheries and Maritime Sovereignty

Up to 1783, all of eastern North American inshore fisheries – those of Nova Scotia, New Brunswick, Prince Edward Island, Maine, and Massachusetts – were under British control. American fishermen had unrestricted use of the inshore fisheries. After the American Revolutionary War, Americans could still use the Maritime fisheries but Canadians had priority on the use of the shores to dry fish.[1]

During this time, the Nova Scotia government, especially its House of Assembly, which strongly supported Halifax commercial interests, advocated controlling the use of the territorial coastline more to its economic advantage. If the territorial waters were protected, the Americans would be restricted from trading with the local population. It must be noted that, at this time, sovereignty was not enforced to conserve fish, but rather to stop the Americans from trading food and rum for fish. The government considered this US trade as smuggling. In 1788, as Innis has shown, the assembly petitioned Nova Scotia's governor to request that the British government send ships to end American fishing and trading in their waters.[2] This petition was denied, but the issue remained, as the 1783 Treaty of Paris allowed American fishermen to enter local waters to fish where they would trade as well. While this trade represented direct competition to Maritime merchants, resulting in lost revenue and business, it thrived because the local fishermen greatly relied upon Yankee traders for most of their food needs. However, by 1800 the government began commissioning ships such as the *Earle of Moire* to patrol off Cape Breton to protect the fishery and, more specifically, to stop the smuggling.

A chain of world events began to affect the Maritime provinces greatly as well. In 1805 Napoleon attempted to put an end to all European trade with Great Britain when he promulgated his Berlin Decree. In reprisal, the Royal Navy (RN) began to blockade Europe and to board neutral vessels. This led to the boarding of American merchantships and the taking of American seamen suspected of being RN deserters. In 1807 the US government issued the Embargo Act, which stopped all commerce out of American ports. Merchants from the Maritime provinces took advantage of the situation and increased their West Indies trade, which led to a dramatic increase in fishing between 1808 and 1815. By 1812 tension had become so great that the United States declared war on Great Britain and attacked the British North American (BNA) colonies. The British government retaliated by imposing a blockade on the American eastern seaboard. The RN, with eighty-five vessels at its disposal and confronted by only twenty US warships, successfully accomplished this task, and by 1813 all American seagoing trade effectively ceased.[3]

The Maritime provinces, taking the opportunity to capitalize on the anti-US feeling in London, pressed the British government to drive American fishermen out of Canadian territorial waters. In February of 1814, Nova Scotia's House of Assembly began petitioning the Colonial Office to bring this plan into reality. To better their objective, they now added sedition to their list of reasons why the US trade in local waters should be stopped: it was "very injurious to the political morality of the lower classes of people of these provinces whose attachment to the Mother country will be best secured by being barred from such contagious principles."[4]

In 1815 the British government first supported the Maritime provinces by ordering HMS *Jasseur* to seize American fishing ships in Canadian waters. The grounds for such action were that by attacking the BNA colonies, the US government had unilaterally abrogated the 1783 treaty.[5] In 1818 the United States and Great Britain signed a convention ending the War of 1812. The terms of the convention show that the British government finally ceded to the Maritime provinces' particular demands, for the convention completely restricted American fishermen from entering British inshore waters to fish, obtain bait, or trade. They could only enter in emergency situations for repairs, wood, water, and shelter from storms.[6]

The Maritime provinces had thus technically succeeded in barring American fishermen from fishing in local waters. However, until the 1830s, these restrictions were not enforced. Americans freely fished and traded around the coastal waters. The Canadian fishery was also hampered by high costs and taxes, leaving the Maritime provinces unable to compete with the United States. To help improve the fishing industry, the Maritime provinces began pressing for more effective enforcement of the 1818 Convention.

In 1836 Nova Scotia's House of Assembly commenced rigid enforcement of the fisheries by passing the Hovering Act, which allowed revenue officers to board foreign ships within three nautical miles of the coast. In the same year, further enforcement was initiated with the patrolling of the Chaleur Bay, North Shore, and Bay of Fundy by HMS *Champion* and HMS *Wanderer*. This increased enforcement produced results. In 1835 the estimated total tonnage of US ships involved with the fishery was over 61,000 tons, but by 1844 this had been reduced to approximately 12,000 tons. In 1845 American fishermen were not allowed to land on the Magdelan Islands, causing the US government to express its concern to Great Britain. The British government paid heed to the US grievances and, in turn, suggested to the Maritime provinces that enforcement should be slackened. The consequence of this suggestion was that the Maritime provinces started to cooperate among themselves to protect the fishery.

Up to the 1850s the provinces had been ineffectively combining their enforcement efforts. For example, Prince Edward Island did not pass the equivalent of Nova Scotia's Hovering Act until 1843, and New Brunswick not until 1853. However, by 1852 the Fisheries Protection Service (FPS) was formed. Under the agreement, Nova Scotia would supply four ships, New Brunswick two, and Prince Edward Island one. The British would provide a fleet of small steamers. On 28 August 1852 an order was promulgated re-emphasizing the 1818 Convention, which did not allow any foreign fishing boats commercial privileges in Canadian ports.

At this point, fisheries enforcement became a major part of the negotiations for a free trade agreement between the United States and all the BNA colonies. Negotiations for free trade, then better known as reciprocity, began in 1846 and continued inconclusively until 1852, when the fishing dispute was put on the negotiating table by the British government. The rigid enforcement of the 1818 Convention had gained the attention of the US government. In addition, the British had ordered its ships to consider the three-nautical-mile territorial waters to be measured from headland to headland, thus closing a great number of bays where the Americans had traditionally fished. In particular, this interpretation had devastating results for Americans who usually fished in the Bay of Fundy area. The British had reinforced its naval squadron there, and the United States was sending a naval force in reply. By 1853 war was a distinct possibility.

The Maritime provinces withdrew their support of reciprocity when they realized that opening the fisheries to the Americans would be a part of the agreement. However, in the face of Upper and Lower Canada's strong support of the issue and the need for reduced tension between the United States and Britain, the concerns of the Maritime provinces were discounted and the Reciprocity Treaty was signed on 5 June 1854. The treaty permitted US fishermen free access to British territorial waters and Canadian fishermen free access to American waters above the 36th parallel. Duties on the import of such items as grain, flour, fish, livestock, meat, coal, and timber were removed. The treaty was to be in effect for ten years, and each side could rescind it by giving twelve months' notice. This indeed occurred when the victorious northern manufacturing states, which had never supported reciprocity, abrogated the treaty in 1866.

Although the Maritime provinces had initially been unhappy with the treaty, the Maritime economy had flourished under its terms and its cancellation would entail immediate and devastating effects. The Maritime provinces' main export products, fish and lumber, were now not welcome in what had been their largest market. The Maritime provinces decided that to regain reciprocity they would have to restrict American fishermen from the BNA colonies' territorial waters. The fisheries were the only "trump card" the Maritime provinces possessed against the United States.[7] Therefore, they again set about to rigidly enforce the 1818 Convention.

Within two days of the abrogation of the Reciprocity Treaty, Nova Scotia stated that American fishermen were no longer welcome within three nautical miles of the coasts. However, immediate enforcement was not forthcoming, as the British government was very leery of antagonizing the United States.[8] In addition, the governor general of Canada, Lord Monck, strongly suggested that instead of enforcing rigid exclusion, the Maritime provinces should issue licences to the American fishermen and allow them to continue fishing. Therefore, at the insistence of the British government and Canada, Nova Scotia was forced to start issuing licences costing fifty cents for every ton of fish caught; the money would be used to fund a joint maritime police force.[9] Nova Scotia, feeling that this licensing fee was too low, was still dissatisfied. For every ton of capacity, a fishing ship could hold eight to ten barrels of pickled mackerel (a major portion of the American fishery at the time), which could be sold for two to three dollars a barrel. At the same time, Canadians were forced to pay a large duty on fish they exported to the United States. It is estimated that in the first year, 354 licences were sold to the Americans for a total of $13,000. However, Nova Scotians paid over $200,000 to US Customs, while American fishermen caught over $4 million worth of fish.[10] Thus, from the Maritime point of view, licensing was ineffectual. This problem was further compounded by the fact that licensing was not enforced.

However, in December of 1866 the Quebec Resolutions were passed by the British Parliament, setting the stage for Confederation. One of the clauses gave the new federal government control over the seacoast and inland fisheries. By 1868 the new dominion government passed a major maritime law which stated that, henceforth, the governor could issue licences to anyone who fished within three nautical miles of the coast. In addition, specified officers could board foreign ships in harbour and within three nautical miles of the coast and remain on board until the foreign vessels left Canadian territorial waters. If it was deemed necessary, these ships could be ordered to leave harbour or territorial waters within twenty-four hours. If they did not leave, they could be arrested and their ships impounded.[11]

The dominion government tried to enforce this legislation, but at the time the Fisheries Protection Service had all but disappeared and the only remaining maritime force available, the RN, was unable to act, as the Colonial Office did not support rigid enforcement. However, by late 1868, under pressure from the Maritime provinces, the British government ordered the RN to patrol territorial waters but not to arrest any American fishing ships unless they were actually found fishing.[12] Little enforcement resulted, since fishermen could easily see patrol vessels coming and avoid arrest. By 1868 licence fees were increased to two dollars per ton of capacity, but enforcement was so lax that only sixty-one licences were bought that year. As it became obvious that the licensing policy was not working, it was discarded in 1870.[13]

To improve enforcement, the dominion government appointed Peter Mitchel from New Brunswick as the first dominion minister of fisheries and marine. Between 1869 and 1870, he resurrected the Fisheries Protection Service by chartering six small craft, similar in design to American fishing boats, and manned them with ex-RN personnel. These boats were stationed at St John, Digby, Sidney, Port Hood, Georgetown, and

Pictou.[14] This increased force very quickly enraged the US government and alarmed the Gladstone government in London, which primarily wanted to maintain good relations with the Americans.[15]

As Canada was still very interested in reciprocity in 1871, the British government formed a Joint High Commission in Washington. The only Canadian representative on the commission was the Canadian prime minister, Sir John A. Macdonald. Since the British representatives were clearly determined to pacify the Americans, he was in an unfortunate position. Although the Canadians favoured reciprocity, they still wanted the Americans to be restricted from the Maritime provinces' fishery. Nevertheless, representatives from all three countries signed the Washington Treaty, whereby fishermen from both Canada and the United States obtained access to the other's territorial fishing grounds. Since the Canadian fishery was considered the more valuable, compensation would be paid to Canada by the US government. In exchange, fish, fish oil, and lumber were allowed into the United States duty-free. It was not full reciprocity, as the 1854 agreement had been, but the British maintained peace with the Americans and Canadian business received "scaled-down" reciprocity at the expense of Canadian fisheries.[16]

The Washington Treaty remained in effect until 1 July 1885, when again the United States abrogated the treaty. A major reason for this action was that the market for fish had changed. Salted and dry-cured fish were no longer popular, and these were the fish that swam in coastal areas. Therefore, the Canadian fishery was no longer of critical importance to the Americans. However, unrestricted American fishing in Maritime waters continued under the Canadian understanding that a commission would be organized to renegotiate the fisheries agreement, but by 1886 it was apparent that the United States was unwilling to compromise. In response, the Canadian government passed a bill reactivating the 1818 Convention restricting foreign fishermen from Canadian waters and ports. To enforce this bill, the FPS, which by 1885 had diminished to one ship, rapidly expanded to nine ships and conducted 300 boardings in 1886 and over 1,300 the next year.[17]

On 3 March 1887 the US Congress responded by passing a bill authorizing the president to ban all Canadian trade if necessary. This alarmed Canada as well as Britain. Another commission was quickly organized in Washington and an alternative agreement worked out. As Canada's territorial fishery no longer interested the Americans, they agreed to surrender their rights in these waters in exchange for access to Canadian ports. In return, the Maritimes regained the right to export fresh fish to the United States duty-free.[18] Canada ratified the treaty in April 1888, but the US Senate, at the instigation of Massachusetts, voted it down.

However, the agreement remained in effect as a *modus vivendi* by mutual agreement until 1918.[19]

## The Rise of Canada's International Maritime Commitments

By the latter years of the nineteenth century, the question of what Canada's role should be in imperial naval defence was being more seriously considered than it had been up to that time. In 1895 the first Navy League outside of Britain was formed in Toronto. The chief spokesman for the group was Henry Wickham, a former RN officer. Wickham clearly stated that Canada should have a naval reserve of Canadian seamen trained to RN standards but that it should be a distinctly national force under dominion control.[20] Further, a member of the Fisheries Protection Service, Lieutenant Arthur Gordon, promoted the idea of upgrading the patrol ships to include torpedo-boats and gunboats which, in peacetime, would conduct fishing patrols and, in wartime, would protect both coasts.[21]

Previously, this debate took place only between interest groups or nationalist newspaper columnists; the Canadian government generally lacked any interest in the issue. However, this changed in late 1895 when there seemed to be a possibility of war between Britain and the United States over the Venezuelan boundary dispute. This threat necessitated the mobilization of Canada's militia, a mobilization that proved unsuccessful, showing that Canada had many fundamental problems in defending itself against a US threat.

To further investigate Canada's defence requirements, a joint committee from the British Army and the Royal Navy was set up in 1899, under the direction of Major-General Leach. From the army's point of view, a naval force was needed in the Great Lakes to assist the militia in defending Canada against an American invasion. However, the RN had no interest in becoming involved in Great Lakes defence. Hence, the "Leach Report" recommended that a 2,000-man naval militia be formed, under dominion control, to support the army militia on the Great Lakes. It was also recommended that training ships be situated at Montreal and Toronto and that the Fisheries Protection Service be upgraded to a naval force designed to protect the Great Lakes and defend the coasts against European raiders.[22]

Prime Minister Wilfrid Laurier quickly dismissed the idea of naval enforcement on the Great Lakes, since the area had been demilitarized with the Rush-Bagot Treaty in 1817. Nevertheless, the concept of a coastal naval militia built around an upgraded FPS appealed to him. In September 1899 the minister of marine and fisheries, Sir Louis Davies, attended the

Alaska boundary talks in London and was authorized to discuss with the Admiralty the possibility of a naval reserve.[23] However, nothing came of this initiative because the start of the Boer War focused Britain's and Canada's concerns elsewhere.

At the Colonial Conference in 1902, the British representatives reiterated the traditional Admiralty policy of "one ocean and one navy" and voiced the opinion that the best support the colonies could offer would be through subsidies and the assignment of military units to imperial defence. Laurier did not accept this plan but offered that Canada would assume more responsibility for local defence, thereby benefiting British defence by relieving it of some of its duties in Canada. Part of the Canadian effort would be the formation of a naval militia through the conversion of the FPS into a naval force.[24]

When he returned to Canada, Laurier tasked the Marine and Fisheries Department, under the Honourable Raymond Préfontaine (minister of marine and fisheries, 1902–1905), to develop a plan for a naval militia as part of a larger restructuring of the army militia. Laurier proceeded slowly. In April 1903, when Préfontaine publicly announced in a newspaper article that Canada would commission three cruisers for Canadian waters, Laurier was quick to downplay the article.[25]

However, in October 1903, in view of the poor outcome for Canada in the Alaska Boundary Dispute and the fear of more American encroachment in Hudson Bay and the Arctic, Laurier asked Parliament for funds to build two large patrol vessels for the Fisheries Protection Service.[26] This request received no opposition in Parliament, and two ships were commissioned by the Marine and Fisheries Department in 1904. The heavily armed CGS *Canada* went to the east coast and the unarmed CGS *Vigilant* to the Great Lakes. The crews wore naval-style uniforms, and CGS *Canada* commenced naval training for FPS personnel.[27] This is where Canadian naval matters would stagnate for the next five years. The Naval Militia Act, which was to have been enacted in 1904, never materialized into legislation.[28]

In October 1904 Admiral "Jackie" Fisher assumed the position of First Sea Lord at the British Admiralty. He would quickly bring forth a major change in the RN's global stationing. Convinced that the greatest threat now resided in Europe, Admiral Fisher decided to place the bulk of his naval forces in local waters around Great Britain. By December 1904 the Pacific squadron at Esquimalt was disbanded and the North American squadron at Halifax relocated to Britain. The naval dockyards at Esquimalt and Halifax were closed, and the Colonial Office asked Canada to assume some responsibility in defending the harbours of Esquimalt and Halifax, which would still be used for Fisher's roving squadrons.

Laurier quickly offered to take over all responsibility for defence. This was in accordance with his commitment at the 1902 Colonial Conference.[29] The Canadian militia was positively affected by this obligation, and the permanent force tripled in size in order to assume control of the ports and man the coastal guns. In addition, defence expenditures increased from $4.2 million in 1904 to $7 million in 1907. This increased focus on defence was well received by the Canadian people. The withdrawal of the RN fleet from the east coast caused no alarm, since a large RN squadron stationed in England could return to Canada in five days if required.[30] Laurier was therefore under no pressure to proceed with the development of a navy. This was quite apparent when, in November of 1905, he sent Préfontaine to London to discuss the change-over of the bases, but not the formation of a naval militia.[31]

In 1907 another Colonial Conference took place. At this conference, the Admiralty slightly altered its naval policy. It offered the colonies a compromise by allowing them to have a naval force made up of small ships for coastal defence.[32] Laurier was quite pleased with the conference, feeling that by taking control of Halifax and Esquimalt and by upgrading the Fisheries Protection Service for coastal defence, Canada had now properly assumed its responsibilities for imperial defence. In addition, these policies were popular within the country.

However, changes in naval defence would soon be deemed necessary in light of the international naval armament race. In March 1909 it was announced in the British House of Commons that the RN could quite possibly lose supremacy on the high seas. Canadians now strongly favoured supporting the RN. As national leader, Laurier could no longer avoid the issue. In the same month the "Foster" resolution calling for Canada to form a naval force to protect its coasts was unanimously passed in Parliament.[33]

Later that year an emergency Imperial (formerly called "Colonial") Conference took place in London to address the battleship crisis. At this conference the Admiralty completely changed its views on the colonial navies. Now they wanted the colonies to build "fleet units," which for the Admiralty meant a battle-cruiser, three cruisers, six destroyers, and three submarines.[34] Laurier could not accept the Admiralty's proposal, but he countered with a compromise plan to build, in Canada, a fleet of four cruisers and six destroyers for an estimated cost of $11 million.[35]

Two main opinions quickly formed in Canada along political and ethnic lines. One resided predominantly with French Canadians, who wanted no part of imperial defence. Henri Bourassa insisted that the establishment of a "seagoing" navy would alter Canada's historical role with regard to Great Britain and that before the government proceeded, the whole naval issue should be put before the Canadian people in a referendum.[36] According to the second opinion, which resided in English Canada and was mirrored by almost all of the Conservative provincial premiers at the time, Canada should support Britain with a cash donation. The mother country, it was felt, was more in need of dreadnoughts than of Laurier's "tin-pot" navy.[37]

However, although it faced strong opposition, the Liberal parliamentary majority easily passed the Naval Service Act in May 1910. The act enabled the marine and fisheries ministry to form the new Royal Canadian Navy (RCN). The minister became "double hatted," with responsibility for two departments, the Fisheries/Marine and the navy.[38]

If anything, controversy around the new navy increased after its formation. An election was due in 1911. The federal Conservative leader, Sir Robert Borden, and his Quebec lieutenant, F.D. Monk, sensing that Laurier was vulnerable, openly attacked the Naval Service Act and joined forces with the nationalists in Quebec under the leadership of Henri Bourassa in an attempt to defeat the government.

In November 1910 this alliance won a Quebec by-election in a formerly safe Liberal seat on a platform of anti-imperialism and opposition to the navy. Realizing that he was losing his vital Quebec base, Laurier halted all naval development plans.[39] Laurier seized upon a new reciprocal trade agreement that had been negotiated with the Americans, and made it the centrepiece of his platform in the 1911 federal election.[40] This plan failed. Taking a stance against Bourassa and Monk's platform in Quebec, Borden's Conservatives championed the imperial connection in English Canada and stated that reciprocity would weaken that bond.[41] The Conservatives assumed power in September 1911 and, true to their platform, announced that the Naval Service Act was to be rescinded. In the interim it would remain in effect only "for purposes in connection with the Fisheries Protection Service."[42]

Throughout this debate, the Fisheries Protection Service operated without controversy. In 1902 the Department of Fisheries and Marine had been given responsibility for the Arctic. In 1906 Parliament amended the Fisheries Act to proclaim the Hudson Bay area as the territory of Canada. Then, in 1909, a plaque was unveiled on Melville Island by the crew of the FPS ship *Arctic* declaring all of the Arctic as part of Canada.[43] In fact, while Canada's first naval ships, HMCS *Niobe* and *Rainbow*, remained alongside in Halifax and Esquimalt from 1912 to 1914 (disowned and forgotten by the new Conservative government), the thirteen vessels of the Fisheries Protection Service continued to be funded and operated for sovereignty protection.

The Fisheries Protection Service, like its colonial predecessors, had been called into existence and sustained by the pressing need to keep intruders from poaching in territorial waters. Such a police function was so

basic and obvious an element of sovereignty – however that word is defined – that Canadians, like their colonial forebears, could readily agree
on the need. It was Canada's good luck that, because of the country's
increasingly friendly relations with the United States, its distance from
other potential enemies, and the protection afforded by Great Britain's
navy, this was the only obvious need. The idea that the British fleet, the
strongest in the world, should need help from a young, underdeveloped
nation struck many Canadians as fantastic. Those few who were interested in Canada's international naval commitments could not achieve a
national consensus. For some, Laurier's naval plan seemed to promise
only entanglement in remote imperial affairs; for others, it was not
enough. That was the very reverse of nation-building. For these reasons,
the Fisheries Protection Service continued to grow quietly, if modestly,
while the navy was very nearly scuttled by controversy the moment it
was launched.

## · 6 ·

# The Rise of Proto-nationalism:
# Sir Wilfrid Laurier and the Founding of
# the Naval Service of Canada, 1902–1910

SIOBHAN J. McNAUGHT

The term "nationalism" has many definitions. A Canadian political science text states that nationalism is about seeking to formulate a new form of political identity to replace the previous one.[1] The Oxford dictionary, on the other hand, claims that nationalism can mean a patriotic feeling or a policy of national independence. Significantly, such definitions do not describe the attitudes of Canadian politicians during the first decade of the twentieth century. Loyalty towards "the mother country" was still very strong during this period, and there was a proud consciousness of belonging to the British Empire.[2] During this time, however, there was also a growing sense of Canadian distinctiveness, of self-awareness that showed its influence in many areas, including external and defence policies.

This chapter will focus on political developments from the time of the Colonial Conference of 1902, when the Canadian government first formally suggested that it might establish a navy, until the Naval Service Act of 1910, which created the new service amid increasingly bitter controversy. Concern about maritime security, it will be argued, was only one, and possibly a secondary, issue. At least as important were questions about Canada's freedom of action and responsibilities with respect to Great Britain. Conservatives and Liberals agreed that there should be a Canadian navy and that it should be closely connected with the Royal Navy (RN), but disagreed intensely about how these principles should be brought into practice. The new navy survived the political debates, although on a smaller scale than either party had proposed. In the end, the very modesty of the new service reflected distinctly Canadian attitudes more fully than anyone had intended.

Canadian naval development became a prominent question as a result of the strain that the war in South Africa (1899–1902) placed on British resources. The mother country could no longer single-handedly "take on the world." British leaders were particularly worried that the accelerating naval construction by competing nations, including Germany, threatened the supremacy of the Royal Navy, the anchor of British and Empire security.[3] In response to these unfavourable shifts in the balance of power, the British government called on the self-governing colonies to join together in much tighter defence relations, including the permanent commitment of colonial money and troops to strengthen the mother country's armed forces.[4] Admiral Sir John Fisher, a prominent RN officer, was particularly blunt about "colonial laggards," especially Canadians, who "more often than not were willing to let the British do the work and pay the bill."[5] The self-governing colonies, it is true, had provided troops to fight in South Africa, but Canada's prime minister, Sir Wilfrid Laurier, had done so reluctantly.

Joseph Chamberlain, the British secretary of state for the colonies, called a conference of colonial representatives in London for 30 June 1902.[6] Despite Laurier's attitude, the secretary hoped to convert the recent colonial participation in the South African war into long-term defence integration.[7] At the conference Chamberlain made a plea to the colonial leaders: "We do require your assistance in the administration of the vast Empire which is yours as well as ours. The weary Titan staggers under the too vast orb of its fate. We have borne the burden for many years. We think it is time that our children should assist us to support it."[8] Among the measures the secretary urged was that Canada should pay annual subsidies to the Royal Navy, as Australia and New Zealand were already doing. Laurier refused but at the same time "acknowledged the obligation of the Dominion to assume an increasing responsibility for its naval defence."[9] He explained that "his government was contemplating the establishment of a local naval force."[10]

"The secret of the Empire's strength," Laurier asserted, "lay in local diversity and freedom."[11] For this same reason he and his ministers also rejected Chamberlain's proposal for the creation of a permanent imperial council of British and colonial representatives. The Canadians feared that "such a council might demand commitments for imperial policies which Canada was not prepared to make."[12] That was the central issue in all of the schemes for greater imperial defence integration, as the Canadians made clear in a formal memorandum: "The Ministers desire to point out that their objections arise, not so much from the expense involved, as from a belief that the acceptance of the proposal would entail an important departure from the principle of colonial self-government."[13] This attitude was not limited to the governing Liberal party. The Conservative opposition also saw financial contributions to Britain as a long constitutional step backwards. Indeed, Sir Charles Tupper, a former Conservative prime minister, had resigned from the Imperial Federation League of Great Britain "because it expected Canada to furnish money for [Empire] defence."[14]

Britain's reaction to Canada's attitude was not sympathetic. Chamberlain regarded Laurier as unassimilated because of his French blood. Lord Minto, governor general of Canada, agreed: "At heart Sir Wilfrid is not thoroughly British."[15] Admiral Sir John Fisher, not realizing the extent to which Canada had written off the possibility of war with the United States, the traditional enemy, advocated the withdrawal of British naval units from Canadian waters, to "leave Canadians to get along more agreeably with their American neighbours."[16] Fisher, when commander-in-chief of the North America and West Indies Station in 1897–99, had been angered by Canada's unwillingness to assist or support his force. Laurier's talk about the organization of a local Canadian naval action seemed nothing more than a smokescreen for the usual shirking of responsibilities.

This perception was incorrect, however understandable. In his study of the Laurier government's maritime policies, Nigel Brodeur noted that "though there was little attention paid to or money made available for the building of a navy ... it does not mean that there was not a concern or interest in naval matters in certain segments of the Canadian government and the public."[17] Canada's ambitions, and geography, would not permit Canadians to turn their backs on the maritime dimensions of national development, and steps were taken to assert more effective control over territorial waters. Among new vessels ordered for protection of the fisheries in 1903 and 1904 were the Canadian Government Ships (CGS) *Vigilant* and *Canada* – fast, modern, all-steel gunboats suitable for defensive patrols in wartime.[18]

By 1904 moreover, Marine and Fisheries was the largest department in the Canadian government. Fisheries protection was only one part of its responsibilities, which also included the operation and maintenance of hydrographic services, lighthouses, other navigation aids, and port facilities, as well as the regulation of shipping. The department was very active in improvements to navigation, including an ambitious project to deepen the St Lawrence channel.[19] Although Marine and Fisheries was a civilian department, it was nevertheless carrying out many functions that in other nations, including Britain, were the responsibility of the navy. What was more, Fisheries Protection Service (FPS) personnel received some military training in the militia schools and aboard CGS *Canada*, which had been acquired, in part, to serve as a training ship.[20] The most important defence initiative, however, was the Laurier government's willing agreement to the British request of late 1904 that the Canadian militia should relieve the some 2,000 British regular army troops who garrisoned the defences that protected the Royal Navy bases at Halifax and Esquimalt. Significantly, rather than accept the much cheaper British suggestion that Canada should subsidize the British force through a transition period of some years, Laurier insisted that Canadian troops should take over the fortresses. He was determined that his government have real and complete authority over what had been the last British bases in Canada.[21]

The withdrawal of the British garrisons from Canada was part of a larger reorganization of imperial defence that also saw the concentration of much of the Royal Navy in Britain's home waters. The reassignment of ships in 1904–1905 virtually denuded Canada's coasts of warships. On the Pacific, for example, the only vessels that remained in Canadian waters were the sloop HMS *Shearwater* and a hydrographic survey ship.[22] The British government maintained, and Canada accepted, that powerful squadrons of fast warships concentrated in European waters, closest to the most likely sources of danger, afforded the best protection to Canada and the rest of the Empire. Fortified bases like Halifax and Esquimalt were kept up to allow RN warships to hurry back to the scene in the event of an unexpected emergency.

The European threat that worried British planners was changing from the traditional enemies, France and Russia, to Germany, which was aggressively expanding its fleet. In the words of a British Admiralty memorandum: "The new German navy has come into existence; it is a navy of the most efficient type and is so fortunately circumstanced that it is able to concentrate almost the whole of its fleet in its home waters."[23]

At the Colonial Conference held in 1907, Lord Tweedmouth, First Lord (that is, minister) of the Admiralty, stated that the Royal Navy had served Canada well and that Canada "should have faith in the British government and the Admiralty."[24] He also underlined the British policy of "one sea, one Empire, one Navy"[25] in making a renewed bid for financial subsidies from the self-governing colonies. Once again there was a resolute "no" from Canada. In private correspondence Laurier explained that it was imperative "to resist with a firm hand the highly sentimental fads of Imperialism and militarism."[26] During the conference Laurier further insisted that the term "colonies" be "drop[ped]" for Canada, Australia, and New Zealand in recognition of their development, and that they should instead be known as "self-governing dominions." This was a demand for recognition of status that had evolved beyond that of the simple possessions of an imperial mother country.[27]

Louis-Philippe Brodeur, minister of marine and fisheries, also spoke strongly at the 1907 Colonial Conference. He demanded appropriate recognition of Canada's contribution to the British Empire in the areas of fishery protection (for which Canada was fully responsible at a cost of over $3 million per year), wireless stations that provided marine communications on both coasts, the training of Canadian seamen in naval matters, hydrographic work, and maintenance of the dockyard facilities that the Royal Navy had vacated at Halifax.[28] By the thirteenth day of the conference, Lord Tweedmouth altered his attitude, stating that "with regard to Canada, I think I may say there has perhaps been some exaggeration in the idea that Canada does not do anything for the Empire in this manner."[29] Moreover, Tweedmouth conceded that if the dominions so desired, they could construct coastal defence vessels.[30] He acknowledged the value of local squadrons, though it is doubtful that this acknowledgment was sincere.

Less than two years after the 1907 conference, public confidence in the supremacy of the Royal Navy was profoundly shaken. On 16 March 1909 Britain's Liberal government warned that naval expenditure would have to be substantially increased because of evidence that Germany had accelerated battleship construction. Even with the spending increase, the government admitted, Britain's advantage would narrow. The Opposition was more alarmist still, declaring that even with the proposed spending increase, Germany might have twenty-one modern battleships to Britain's twenty by the spring of 1912. These shocking revelations (which later proved to be wildly exaggerated) provoked an emotional response throughout the Empire, not least in Canada.[31]

On 29 March 1909 George Foster, a senior Conservative MP from Toronto, rose in the Canadian House of Commons to present a resolution on naval defence. He had actually placed the resolution on the order paper some months before, merely to tweak the government about its failure to do more, but now the words took on much greater weight: "In view of her great and varied resources, of her geological position and national environment, and of that spirit of self-help and self-respect which alone befits a strong and growing people, Canada should no longer delay in assuming her proper share of the responsibility and financial burden incident to the suitable protection of her exposed coast line and great sea-ports."[32]

Foster believed that two possible policies presented themselves. Canada could either give a contribution of money or ships to the Admiralty, or Canada could assume the defence of its own ports and coastline. He strongly favoured the latter choice because a contribution "looked too much like someone hiring someone else to do what Canadians ought to do."[33] As Foster told the Commons: "I want to see something grafted on the soil of Canada's nationhood, which takes root and grows and develops until it incites the spirit of defence in this country, leads to a participation in the defence, leads to that quick interest in it, its glories, its duties and its accomplished work, which is after all the one great thing that benefits all people for great expenditures, either on land or on sea, in the way of defence and of the maintenance of the rights of the country."[34] Foster argued that if Canada continued to develop its resources without making fuller provisions for defence, aggressive nations would begin to see the country as a tempting target, and they would be right. Without the discipline of proper commitment to defence, the moral fibre of the population would fray.[35]

The leader of the Opposition, Robert Borden, also emphasized national responsibilities in his speech in the Commons that same day: "Canada today is a nation and we are all proud to recognize and hail Canada as one of the greatest nations in the greatest Empire that the earth beholds ... but let us not forget that a national status implies national responsibilities – a primal responsibility is the defence of their territories and the protection of their commerce."[36]

The government, seeking to quiet emotional calls from pro-Empire elements in both parties for an "emergency" cash gift to the Royal Navy, accepted and strengthened Foster's resolution. The revised motion, which passed unanimously the same day, approved expenditure designed to promote "the speedy organization of a Canadian naval service," while recognizing that "the naval supremacy of Britain is essential to the security of commerce, the safety of the Empire, and the peace of the world."[37]

On 30 April 1909 the British government sent an invitation to all of the dominion ministers to visit England for a conference to "discuss afresh the relations of the Dominions and the United Kingdom, in regard to the question of Imperial Defence."[38] The conference was held that summer. Representing Canada were the Honourable Sir Frederick Borden, minister of militia and defence; the Honourable Louis-Philippe Brodeur, minister of marine and fisheries; Major-General Sir Percy Lake, chief of general staff; and Rear Admiral Charles E. Kingsmill, a Canadian who had retired from the Royal Navy in 1908 to take the position of director of marine services.[39]

In London the Canadian delegation was greeted with a complete surprise: an entirely new Admiralty policy. Their lordships now wanted the dominions to raise their own full-fledged navies, each to include a big dreadnought battle-cruiser, three Bristol-class cruisers, six destroyers, and three submarines. What had brought the change was not the German threat, but longer-term worries about the Pacific, where Japan was expanding its fleet while the Royal Navy was withdrawing vessels for redeployment to European waters. In the face of a potentially huge commitment in the Far East, the Admiralty had decided to acknowledge the dominions' desire for greater autonomy and channel this energy into a genuinely useful effort. Australia, which was most concerned about the Royal Navy's declining strength in the Pacific, undertook the full scheme recommended by the Admiralty. Tiny New Zealand preferred to make a cash gift sufficient to build a dreadnought for the Royal Navy. The Canadian delegates, on Laurier's instructions, ruled out the dreadnought battle-cruiser and the Pacific focus of the Admiralty scheme, but did agree to acquire most of the ships – four Bristol-class cruisers and six destroyers – for a Canadian navy that would be divided between the Atlantic and Pacific coasts.

When the Canadian ministers returned home, the government promptly drafted a bill for the creation of a Canadian naval service.[40] The parliamentary session opened on 11 November 1909, and on 12 January 1910 Laurier introduced the legislation. During the second reading, Robert Borden objected that the bill failed to provide immediate aid for the Empire. Claiming that war would break out in Europe before the new Canadian service could become effective, Borden wanted to give Britain a subsidy sufficient to pay for the construction of two dreadnoughts.[41] He also suggested that the government's plan for the two-ocean cruiser and destroyer fleet was too ambitious given Canada's lack of experience in naval organization. Laurier's legislation, he further charged, did not allow for sufficiently close integration with the Royal Navy. "Naval forces" under the Naval Service Act were defined in the bill as "the naval forces organized for the defence and protection of the Canadian coasts and trade, or engaged as the Governor-in-Council may from time to time direct."[42] The meaning of this last clause was that Canadian warships could not be placed under British command except when the Canadian government specifically authorized it and sought the approval of Parliament. Laurier made it clear that such extraordinary action would be taken only if a "severe crisis should develop in which the security of Britain was actually threatened."[43] This emphasis on Canadian control bothered Borden. He believed that there should be provision for Canadian fighting ships automatically to pass under the charge of the Admiralty because of the speed with which conflict could break out at sea.[44]

Laurier and his ministers held firm. They were much more optimistic about the prospects for peace. They also pointed out that Canada's military development had always taken the form of raising forces under Ottawa's control and helping the Empire by relieving British forces that had been committed for the defence of Canada.[45] On its third reading, the Naval Service Bill was passed, 111 to 70, and it received royal assent on 4 May 1910.[46] "The Act Respecting the Naval Service of Canada" created the Department of the Naval Service, under the minister of marine and fisheries, Louis-Philippe Brodeur.[47] In addition to responsibility for the new naval force, the department also took over the four branches of the large marine and fisheries department, which had carried out essentially naval functions: fisheries protection, tidal and current survey, hydrographic survey, and wireless telegraphy. A naval reserve force and a naval volunteer force were authorized, and a naval college would be provided to train officers "in all branches of naval science, tactics, and strategy."[48] The purchase of two obsolescent British cruisers and the secondment of nucleus British crews for them, which provided training ships and instructors for Canadian personnel, was already under way. So too were negotiations with British shipbuilding firms to establish facilities in Canada for construction of the modern cruisers and destroyers.

This promising beginning soon faltered. The Laurier government fell in the election of 1911, in part because of fears in French Canada that the planned navy was so large that it would inevitably lead to participation in Britain's brush-fire wars around the globe. Robert Borden, the new prime minister, attempted to give a $35-million subsidy for battleship construction to Britain in 1912–13, but this failed as well in the face of a bitter Liberal backlash. In fact, prominent Conservatives also had growing doubts about the wisdom of giving away large sums instead of more fully developing Canada's own forces.[49]

Still, Borden did not carry through with his earlier commitment to replace the Laurier Naval Service Act with more Empire-oriented legislation. Although he let the training cruisers languish, he was considering, when the First World War broke out, means of completing the organization of the service with smaller ships that might be acceptable to a broad range of Canadians.[50] During the war, when the Royal Navy was too heavily committed in European waters to provide comprehensive protection to the Canadian coast, the Canadian service used armed civil ships and hastily built anti-submarine vessels to do the job. In all these efforts, Borden stood by Laurier's Naval Service Act, finding that it well served Canadian interests to keep the coastal defence patrol fleet under Canadian command rather than relinquishing it to the British.[51]

The division between the federal parties in 1910–14 over naval policy had in fact been about politics, not fundamentals. Neither party had accepted Britain's traditional policy of a single Empire navy permanently under close central control from London. Whatever the disagreements over particulars, both parties had agreed that Canada's self-governing status dictated that the country must have its own forces. In this light, there was justice in a piece of Liberal propaganda circulated in 1913 that reminded Borden of the reasons he had given for initially supporting the Laurier administration in the establishment of a Canadian navy in 1909:

– because Britain's policy of centralization of her fleets near home exposes the outlying dominions to danger.

- because a local Naval Service affords protection which Great Britain could not
  give in time of need.
- because by a Naval Service, Canada would do her duty to herself and the Empire – we would be rendering a real service in the defence of the Empire and
  we would be doing our duty not only to Canada but to the Empire as a whole.
- because self-respect demands protection of our own shore – I believe that the
  defence of our own commerce is due to the self-respect which should fill the
  heart of every man in the country.
- because contribution implies that Canada has a status of a crown colony, not
  of a self-governing Dominion.[52]

None of this was anti-Empire. Quite the contrary. Laurier insisted that "the true conception of the British empire is the conception of new, growing, strong and wealthy nations, each one developing itself on the line of its own needs and conditions, but all joining in the case of common danger, and from all points of the earth, rushing upon the common enemy."[53] There was, he explained, no contradiction in loyalty to either Canada or the Empire: "I am a Canadian, first, last, and all the time. I am a British subject, by birth, by tradition, by conviction – by the conviction that under British institutions my native land has found a measure of security and freedom which it could not have found under any other regime."[54]

Given the agreement on essentials, why then did the Canadian navy have such a troubled birth? There was something in Borden's charge that Laurier had done too little for too long after the 1902 Colonial Conference and had then suddenly tried to do too much too quickly in 1909–10 for reasons that seemed transparently political.[55] Those sorts of swings could not earn public confidence. Borden was also right in his belief that a major war was looming on the horizon. However, in his unsuccessful bid to make the "emergency" $35-million battleship gift to Britain, he too learned the dangers of pushing beyond consensus in the country, of underestimating the conviction that Canada must look first to its own armed forces.

Perhaps the most salient element was the willingness of Canadians to allow political squabbling to forestall large-scale action. One cannot escape the impression that many Canadians shared a pride in their country, a loyalty to Britain, and an overriding conviction that defence was not a priority because the dominion was secure in its geographical isolation from the world's trouble spots, and because of its friendship with great powers. A private letter from Laurier at the time of the initial naval scare of March 1909 captured these sentiments: "That the superiority of the British navy should be maintained at its present strength over all nations is a proposition to which I am quite prepared to agree, but this policy should not be taken up in a panic ... the whole Canadian people will stand behind England in her troubles if it comes to that, but we are very far from this."[56]

There was, nevertheless, more to Canada's naval identity than much talk and little substance. Although the planned fighting fleet was virtually stillborn, the new navy controlled a substantial proportion of the considerable marine resources the government had built up during the preceding decades, including the coastal radio system, the former British bases on both coasts, and the fisheries protection and hydrographic survey fleets. In 1914–18 the service also had the necessary powers to marshal the whole range of government marine services and port facilities to assist the Royal Navy while also protecting Canadian maritime interests. The loosely formed ideas of 1902 and the Naval Service Act of 1910 proved in the end to be sound and flexible – an effective embodiment of both loyalty to the Empire and aspirations to nationhood.

## · 7 ·

## Sailors and Soldiers:
## The Royal Navy, the Canadian Forces,
## and the Defence of Atlantic Canada, 1890–1918

BARRY GOUGH AND ROGER SARTY

During its earliest years the Royal Canadian Navy found its identity by working hand-in-glove with the Canadian Army in the ports and along the shores of Atlantic Canada. The large scale of the coastal defence mission that these small armed forces inherited from Britain in the first two decades of this century has not been understood, and neither has the co-dependence of the two services in meeting the challenge. Further, their efforts were more essential to the Royal Navy, which retained strategic responsibility for the security of the northwest Atlantic, than has been appreciated. This intimate cooperation with the British service, however, produced tensions in Canada that ultimately strengthened the country's commitment to self-sufficient maritime forces.

In hindsight, the strategic shift that committed Canadian forces to a substantial role on the Atlantic seaboard seems simple enough, even if breathtaking in scope. There was a complete reversal in the flow of support. Canada, instead of being the recipient of British transatlantic military assistance against a threatening United States, came to be a source of support for Britain against dangerous enemies in Europe. Little in the unfolding of these events, which were driven by changes in the international situation, technological innovation, and the vagaries of domestic politics in all of the nations concerned, was straightforward, least of all in Canada, the junior participant.

The pivot on which the shift in Britain's Atlantic strategy turned was the magnificent harbour, naval base, and fortress at Halifax.[1] "War is the business of positions," remarked Napoleon, and in Halifax the British

Empire boasted one of its greatest bulwarks, as well as one of its greatest fulcrums for making war. As with other keys of influence, Halifax's strategic value grew from its position in relation to strategic lines of communication. Thrust into the North Atlantic, 600 miles east of New York and 600 miles from Quebec City, it is the port closest to the great ocean routes between Europe and North America. It is, in fact, a bridge between the Old World and the New, a gateway to deploy European resources in the Americas or, as later became apparent, to project New World power into Europe.

During the nineteenth century, the ultimate strategic role of Halifax, and of the other imperial bases in the Americas, was to contain the United States. Bermuda was given priority by British naval and military planners for the reason that its position was more strategically advantageous for conducting a war against US shipping and mounting raids against the vulnerable American seaboard. Halifax nevertheless grew in importance, first over the period that the British North American (BNA) colonies developed in their trade, populations, and settlements, and then after the Dominion of Canada came into existence as a federal state. Indeed, the British government strongly sponsored Confederation in 1867 in the expectation that, united, the colonies could better defend themselves. The massive scale of American mobilization during the Civil War had raised doubts that Britain's relatively small regular army could hope to hold the Canadian interior against an invasion from the south.[2]

Halifax, more than ever, became the key to Britain's strategic position in North America and to Canadian security. The last imperial army garrisons were withdrawn from the Canadian interior in 1871, but some 2,000 British troops were maintained at Halifax until 1905–1906 and the harbour fortifications, massively rebuilt in the 1860s and 1870s, were modernized repeatedly thereafter. This effort ensured that an American assault would not deprive the Royal Navy of the base it would need to secure the safe arrival of reinforcements from across the Atlantic and organize counter-offensives. With the development of the Canadian transcontinental railway in the 1870s and 1880s, moreover, Halifax became a terminus in a global British Empire transportation route, joining the Atlantic and the Pacific. The Canadian railway provided the final link for this new "all-red" route between the British Isles and Australasia, an alternative to routes via the Suez corridor or the Cape of Good Hope to India and Eastern seas upon which the Empire's existence depended, or so imperial strategists argued.[3] Finally, Halifax, as always, was the base from which British warships maintained a watch over the vast and precious Newfoundland fishery.

The number of vessels assigned to the North America and West Indies Station (the Royal Navy's command post in the western Atlantic) had fluctuated according to the state of Britain's relations with the United States. The number soared to over forty major warships during the American Civil War, but then, with British efforts to avoid further confrontations and the United States' absorption in internal reconstruction and development, it was allowed to fall back to around fifteen generally smaller vessels, sufficient to "show the flag" and carry out what amounted to routine police duties, such as the Grand Banks fishery patrol. Maintenance of Pax Britannica was actually more a convenience than a hindrance to the United States, which was weak at sea. The Royal Navy's work in preserving the status quo in the Americas was the real muscle behind the United States' Monroe Doctrine, a statement expressing opposition to expansion of the territories of non-American powers in the Western Hemisphere.

Even so, Americans, as they began to look outward to the larger world and rebuild their armed forces in the 1880s and 1890s, found the looming British presence off their shores galling. Captain Alfred Thayer Mahan of the United States Navy, one of the leading promoters of naval expansion, marvelled at the chain of maritime possessions that the British could boast – Halifax, Bermuda, St Lucia, and Jamaica – saying that they "strengthen the British hold upon the Atlantic, the Caribbean, and the Isthmus of Panama." The United States could not compete, remarked Mahan: "It is upon our Atlantic seaboard that the mistress of Halifax, of Bermuda, and of Jamaica will now defend Vancouver and the Canadian Pacific. In the present state of our seaboard defense she can do so absolutely."[4]

Mahan was not an Anglophobe. Far from it. His *The Influence of Sea Power upon History* (1890) celebrated the success of British maritime strength in the age of sail as a model his own nation should follow. Yet, as G.S. Graham has remarked, "it is an interesting commentary on human affairs that Mahan's exposition of the influence of sea power on the course of European and American expansion should have occurred at the very time when new instruments of the Industrial Revolution were beginning to erode principles and theories upon which his doctrines were based."[5] From the 1860s, the development of the steam-driven, steel-built warship had undercut the traditional British advantages of a large stock of wooden vessels and a seafaring population experienced in the arts of sailing them. The United States was not the only newly industrialized nation with big navy ambitions in the 1890s: Japan, Russia, and Germany were undertaking fleet expansion as well.[6]

Britain was already hard-pressed to match the steam-and-steel navies of France and Russia, at that time the most dangerous potential enemies. By the late 1890s British naval and political leaders were having doubts about the economy's capacity to sustain an expanded effort to run a three-, four-, or five-way race against all comers. These doubts were confirmed by the course of the South African war of 1899–1902. British armed forces were stretched to the limit to fight this minor regional conflict while maintaining some margin to guard against possible hostility on the part of European powers. This strain gave further impetus to the search for diplomatic settlements with naval competitors, resulting in the Anglo-Japanese alliance of 1902, the beginnings of the entente with France in 1904, and the resolution of outstanding disputes with the United States.[7] Most significant with regard to the latter was Britain's complete abandonment in 1901 of its treaty right to share in the construction and control of a canal across the Panama isthmus, thus freeing the United States to proceed independently with the project. The British fully realized that this would secure American strategic dominance in the Western Hemisphere, as their hitherto divided fleet could now be rapidly deployed between the Atlantic and Pacific, but the Admiralty and the political leaders had already accepted that a war with the United States was unwinnable. Given the burgeoning strength of European fleets, the Royal Navy could no longer afford to despatch sufficient forces to the western Atlantic to counter the US fleet.

When in late 1902 the Admiralty informed the army that in the event of a conflict with the United States early naval reinforcements could not be sent, the soldiers were dumbfounded. The army defences at the western Atlantic and Caribbean dockyards had been organized on the basis of close army-navy mutual support. Because the navy had always agreed that its forces would be adequate to prevent the Americans from laying siege to the bases with a large force, the army had kept its defences at a level that could counter the sort of *coup de main* that might slip by the British squadrons. The army had thus assured the navy that its bases would be sufficiently secure to allow for a rapid and sustained reinforcement of the Caribbean and western Atlantic forces.[8]

As the soldiers came to realize that the Admiralty and the government were writing the United States out of war-planning, they put up a resistance. The Admiralty's policy was tantamount to leaving Canada hostage to American good will, to abandoning one of the Empire's great land frontiers, where the army had a significant role to play – all on the basis of faddish naval theories.

The army did not have a chance. In October 1904 the politically influential Admiral Sir John Fisher became First Sea Lord, the senior professional appointment at the Admiralty. Fisher had promised Canada's financially hard-pressed Unionist government that he could save money and provide more for less. He had received prior approval to reduce overseas squadrons and establishments drastically in order to concentrate the fleet in European waters and thus counter continental threats more effectively. He also proceeded with the construction of a new class of battleship, the large, fast, all-big-gun dreadnought, and the still faster battle-cruiser *Invincible*. The battle-cruisers, he argued, could be rapidly deployed to wherever they were needed, given the increased powers of centralized control afforded by trans-ocean cable telegraphs and the promising development of long-distance wireless telegraphy.[9]

In 1905 a sweeping fleet reorganization came into effect whereby the North America and West Indies, South East Coast of America, and Pacific stations were abolished. The waters of the Americas from Labrador to Tierra del Fuego, from Halifax to Esquimalt, were no longer to see British flagships of size or men-of-war in number. Virtually all of the naval establishments, including those at Halifax and Esquimalt, were closed, and Bermuda, the sole one to survive, was cut to the bone. Routine duties, such as patrolling the Newfoundland fisheries and giving assistance to the isolated island colonies in the Caribbean, were relegated to one or two small cruisers on permanent station and the four to five vessels of the 4th Cruiser Squadron, which, based in England, made annual visits to North American waters.[10]

The wholesale navy cuts enabled the British government to impose similar economies on the army. Significantly, with the exception of a few of the most minor and isolated bases like St Lucia, that did not mean abolition of the western garrisons. The Admiralty was at pains to insist that even the closure of dockyards did not mean that the army defences could be dispensed with. In the event of a crisis, civil port facilities could readily be used by fleet units that rushed to the scene, while additional workmen, supplies, and equipment could quickly be sent without provoking a potential enemy; by contrast, port defences could not easily be improvised, and the despatch of troops and armaments to the vicinity of a diplomatic hotspot could well become a *causus belli*. In short, secure, defended overseas bases for refuelling and repair were no less essential to Fisher's doctrine of flexible response than they had been to the previous system of permanent squadrons. Without safe replenishment havens, the fleet would lack the very mobility Fisher had emphasized.[11]

However, the western garrisons could safely be reduced. With the discounting of the American threat, the only foreseeable attack was a hit-and-run raid by one or two cruisers despatched by European powers on long-range missions to harass shipping. In the case of Halifax that meant that the existing garrison of about 1,800 troops could be cut to less than 400, and several of the harbour batteries, which paradoxically had recently been completely reconstructed and rearmed to counter modern US men-of-war, could be dismantled.

The War Office made a spirited resistance in 1904–1905 against naval dictation of policy by insisting upon maintenance of Halifax's full defences and garrison. With its ability to draw on Canada's continental resources, it argued that the fortress was in a very different position from the isolated and exposed island bases. The geographical position of the city, moreover, was extraordinarily strong: the formidable seafront defences would deter even a capital fleet, while the tangled wilderness on the interior would allow the existing garrison to hold out against the maximum force of 10,000–15,000 men the United States might be able to throw into a land-front assault.

The British government ruled that the Halifax defences could be kept up only if Canada provided troops beyond the cadre of 300–400. This seemed a slim hope. The Canadian government was known not to take the American threat seriously and had long refused to supply substantial assistance at Halifax. Although it was true that the dominion government had been helpful in reinforcing Halifax during the South African War, that seemed to have been a narrowly political manoeuvre designed to avoid the commitment of additional Canadian troops to South Africa and thereby quell domestic controversy over participation in a foreign conflict. The imperial authorities were right about the Canadian government's attitude but had failed to grasp that the chariness of politically divisive imperial entanglements had evolved into a willingness to undertake "national" military expansion, provided there was genuine Canadian control of these forces.

The British were delighted when in December 1904 the prime minister of Canada, Sir Wilfrid Laurier, responded to the suggestion that help would be welcome by offering to take over fully both Halifax and Esquimalt. In the following months he refused the British offer to leave some technical units in place until Canadians could be trained for their work because that would entail continued British command on dominion soil. By inviting British specialist troops to transfer to the Canadian service, borrowing expert British officers, and employing permanent force stations across the country as reinforcement depots, Canada was able to provide a regular garrison of 1,200 troops at Halifax by early 1906 and formally take over both that station and Esquimalt. The effort was largely responsible for tripling the size of the permanent force to nearly 3,000 personnel and increasing the defence budget from $4.2 million in 1904 to nearly $7 million by 1907.[12]

The defences left by the British included nine batteries of the latest concrete and heavy earth-bank construction. These mounted twenty-six modern breech-loading guns: three long-range 9.2-inch Mark X, ten versatile 6-inch Mark VII, and thirteen 4.7-inch and 12-pounder quick-fire. The permanent garrison, although a third smaller than the imperial force, was nevertheless sufficient to man the most important of these works and supporting infantry positions, and despatch a force to erect field defences at Sydney, Cape Breton, a key centre for transatlantic radio and cable telegraph communications. Canada, moreover, assigned additional units of the non-permanent militia to reinforce the Halifax garrison in the event of war and improved training programs in fortress duties for these units. Plans in place by 1912 provided for the mobilization of over 5,000 militiamen from across the Maritimes for service at Halifax.[13]

This large and sustained military effort, unheralded in Canada, was closely watched over by the imperial authorities. Under the terms of transfer of the fortress, the Canadian Maritime Provinces Command updated the Halifax mobilization plan every year to reflect resources actually available and experience gained in exercises. These revisions were forwarded to the Colonial Defence Committee (CDC) in London, a subcommittee of the prime minister's Committee of Imperial Defence (CID), for review in detail. On any substantive question, the CDC and the CID produced special studies and recommendations for Canadian authorities.[14]

The purpose of the strong defences at Halifax, as the CDC and CID regularly confirmed at the insistence of the army, was to resist a major American assault consisting of capital ships and landing forces of up to 15,000 men. Because the British government maintained the pretence of there being a need for a bastion against the United States, scholars working from British documents have concluded that the Canadians were duped.[15] Canadian archives show that this was not the case. The British fleet reorganization of 1904–1905 received instant and detailed coverage in the Canadian press on the basis of cabled reports from the United Kingdom in which Admiralty officials declared that conflict with the United States had been all but ruled out. The reaction in the Canadian press was almost universally calm approval of the progress of Anglo-American friendship.[16]

Leading nationalists, including Québécois, applauded the departure of the last British units on Canadian soil and the clear advance of Canadian military autonomy. Imperialists on both sides of the Atlantic were pleased that the mother country had at long last been relieved of an ancient burden. Laurier, with an eye to forestalling domestic imperialist pressure for the allocation of Canadian funds and troops to the British forces, took care to ensure that the British government recognized his action as an imperial contribution by agreeing to maintain the fortress at the standard prescribed by imperial authorities. He and Sir Frederick Borden, the minister of militia and defence, regularly made reference to that agreement in Parliament, noting that the Canadian government was living up to its commitment.[17] The Laurier administration had no interest in the rationale laid down in secret correspondence for the standard of defence the British government prescribed. The irony is that the dominion government's public circumlocution about the continuing importance of Esquimalt and Halifax to the Royal Navy was in fact exactly appropriate.

Certainly the Canadian government had no intention of preparing for war with the United States. Laurier, like his Conservative predecessor, Sir John A. Macdonald, had anticipated the thinking in Britain that had led to rapprochement, that is, a deep-seated conviction that war with the United States was impossible and unthinkable.[18]

Ultimately, the big garrison at Halifax, like the whole of the militia, which was still organized on the basis of plans for mobilization against American invasion, constituted one symbol of nationhood. It did not mean serious preparation for armed conflict in North America; rather the garrison served as a reminder that Canada was a distinct nation whose distinctiveness derived in no small part from its free and willing membership in the world's greatest empire.

Nicely as the maintenance of the fortress fit Laurier's political needs and those of the British defence bureaucracy, the Canadian militia staff soon found that they faced challenges in sorting out the details. Although the defences were modern, the concept of harbour defence was undergoing fundamental changes, largely as a result of the development of naval technology and tactics. In the 1880s and early 1890s, the navy had eschewed involvement in the direct protection of harbours and coastlines, promoting instead the expansion of a fleet of large, fast warships free to roam the seas to protect trade and strike at the enemy before it could reach imperial territory. Admiral Sir John Fisher's reorganization of the fleet, which had resulted in the disbanding of far-flung smaller-ship squadrons such as the one on the North America and West Indies Station, had been the logical outcome of this "blue water" policy. However, the development by Britain's competitors of fast torpedo armed craft and such other economical weapons of stealth as contact mines provided new means for attack on harbours and coasts that existing fixed defences and major warships were ill-suited to counter. The result had been to bring the navy back into close-in defence with the assignment of its own torpedo craft to screen harbour approaches and coastlines. The progress of these craft, notably the torpedo-firing submarine and the fast, seagoing destroyer, enabled the Admiralty in 1904–1905 to achieve abolition of the Royal Engineers' controlled mining service, a part of the army harbour defences that the navy had never trusted.[19]

Among the first questions the Canadian militia staff posed to the British about development of the Halifax fortress concerned controlled mining. This was in some respects the heart of the defences. On mobilization for war, fields of mines were to be laid between Point Pleasant and Ives Point, the entrance to the inner harbour; six of the nine coast artillery batteries and almost all of the searchlights for night-fighting had been placed so as to provide covering fire over these fields. In January 1906 the Colonial Defence Committee confirmed that Britain was doing away with the mines, and advised Canada to follow suit. The CDC also assured the Canadians that the end of mining did not entail an increase in the artillery defences. To the contrary, current reassessments at British ports were finding that many of the guns that had been associated with the minefields were too far inside harbours to be useful against modern naval attack, and they were therefore being removed. The committee warned, however, that such reductions in the army establishments had been possible largely because Royal Navy torpedo craft were available locally to provide an advanced defence. Using the yardstick of the American scale of attack, the committee advised that Canada should acquire its own torpedo flotilla, particularly large destroyers.[20]

The Canadian militia staff were glad to escape the difficulty and expense of organizing a mine service, but doubted the adequacy of the existing gun armament. Their concern probably derived from the knowledge that there was no prospect that the Laurier government would tackle the contentious question of Canadian naval development. Although the two outermost heavy batteries were advantageously placed for long-range fire seaward, several of the inner forts were not. Fast-moving modern craft, which could evade the outer forts in fog or darkness, would be within torpedo range of port facilities and moored ships before they came under concentrated fire from the inner works. The Canadian staff at Halifax, with benefit of naval advice from the captain of a visiting British cruiser, therefore recommended the construction of at least three new batteries seaward of Point Pleasant to mount armament from the inner forts and some additional guns as well. Because a torpedo attack would probably come at night, rearrangement of the electric searchlights to create a long illuminated "killing" zone over the approaches to Point Pleasant was a particular priority. Early in 1908 the Colonial Defence Committee approved these recommendations but again emphasized the importance of a destroyer flotilla.[21]

While the officers at Halifax and in Ottawa lobbied, none too successfully, for the necessary funds, the naval defence question burst forth in early 1909. A panic in Britain over reports (in fact false) that Germany was outbuilding the Royal Navy brought demands by pro-Empire Canadians that Canada should take dramatic action, such as a special cash gift to Britain for battleship construction. Laurier, in the face of this political crisis, became willing to proceed with development of the existing Fisheries Protection Service (FPS) into a naval defence force. A competent adviser in Canadian employment was now available. In 1908 Rear Admiral Charles Kingsmill, a Canadian with over thirty years' service in the Royal Navy, had accepted command of the Fisheries Protection Service. Kingsmill urged that the first step must be to complete the naval elements of the schemes at Halifax and at Esquimalt on the west coast, including the acquisition of large destroyers.[22]

This plan and the unanimous, if tenuous, support it had achieved in the House of Commons came apart in August 1909, when Sir Frederick Borden and the minister of marine and fisheries, Louis-Philippe Brodeur, attended a special Imperial Defence Conference in London. There, in meetings with the Admiralty, the Canadian delegates ran headlong into disagreement among the British services about Canadian plans and received an analysis of defence requirements markedly different from the one in the careful, consensual documents of the CID and CDC. The Admiralty dismissed any threat from the United States and was not, moreover, as Laurier had rightly suspected, overly concerned about the British/German armaments balance. The worry was about the rapid expansion of the Imperial Japanese Navy and the possibility of Japanese-German cooperation. The Admiralty therefore recommended that each of the dominions should raise a full "fleet unit," including a dreadnought battle-cruiser for service in the western Pacific. The Canadians refused to procure a battle-cruiser but did agree immediately to set up a full-fledged navy with the remaining elements of the fleet unit: four substantial cruisers and six destroyers. When Borden and Brodeur insisted that these ships would have to be divided between the coasts in order to appeal to voters in the eastern part of the country, the Admiralty replied that this was unsound. The RN's concentration in the Atlantic would block any dangerous strike at Canada from that direction. So much for the urgency of improvement of the Halifax defences.

Laurier followed through with the organization of the Canadian naval service in 1910. Canada purchased the obsolescent cruisers *Niobe* and *Rainbow*, manned by some 600 British seamen on secondment, and began recruiting and training programs pending construction of the modern cruisers and destroyers. The programs soon began to fall apart in the political backlash from imperialists who believed Canada should do much more and from Quebec nationalists who were convinced the country should do nothing.

Robert Borden, whose Conservative government came to power in 1911, attempted to satisfy critics at both extremes. Letting the nucleus of Laurier's service languish, he proposed proceeding with a limited, purely coastal defence scheme, while also making a cash grant in aid of Britain's battle fleet. When he went to the UK in the summer of 1912, he discovered that the Admiralty was now deeply concerned about the situations in the Atlantic and the Mediterranean and wanted special cash grants for battleship construction.

As for Prime Minister Borden's coastal defence ideas, the Admiralty suggested they were off the mark. Close-in defence against the vast forces of the United States would require an impossibly large effort, and against the much more likely threat of raids by one or two cruisers of a European enemy, little or nothing need be done. Acknowledging Borden's political interest in acquiring the most modest vessels, the Admiralty obliged with an anti-raider scheme for extended harbour defence by small torpedo-boats and submarines, but warned that it was not necessary. Halifax, the Admiralty noted, was already over-fortified to counter the light attack that might be expected by European raiders. In any event, these attackers were extremely unlikely to risk themselves by pushing in close to coast-lines. They would almost certainly strike some hundreds of miles off-shore at the vast trade from North America that flowed to Great Britain past Nova Scotia and south of Cape Race. The Admiralty admitted that the maintenance of adequate cruiser forces to meet this threat was be-coming a major worry, and therefore urged Borden to carry on with the Laurier scheme, that is, to procure substantial, seagoing cruisers for trade defence in the northwest Atlantic. This was a nearly complete turn-around from the cold reception the officials had given Laurier's politi-cally motivated intention to station some of the cruisers of his 1910 scheme in the Atlantic.[23]

When Borden returned to Canada, his first priority was to push the fi-nancial aid to the Royal Navy through Parliament. That ended in utter failure, for the bill was killed by the Liberal majority in the Senate in May 1913. Borden left the whole naval question on the back burner, while sailors continued to desert the embryo Canadian service and the cruisers lay alongside.

Nevertheless, it still fell to the soldiers and sailors to do what they could with what they had. The very existence of a naval staff was helpful. Despite Laurier's claims that Marine and Fisheries represented an em-bryo navy, the department had completely failed to respond to the mili-tia's pleas for advice on maritime aspects of the Halifax defence scheme. In 1909, however, Rear Admiral Kingsmill, the director of the naval ser-vice, had been authorized to form an interdepartmental committee with the militia. From that time the militia brought every important question about the fortress defence scheme to the committee. Although the new service was soon left to atrophy, its officers were able to accomplish a good deal by arranging for Marine and Fisheries craft to participate in fortress exercises for such wartime roles as intercepting and identifying incoming shipping (the "examination service") and minesweeping.[24]

There was some other progress at Halifax, for the Conservative gov-ernment provided funds to begin the reorganization of the land defences. The leading figure in the execution of the program was Colonel (later Major-General) Willoughby Gwatkin, a British officer on loan to militia headquarters in Ottawa. He had been the founding militia representative on the interdepartmental committee, and he retained his membership when in 1913 he was appointed chief of general staff. With this increased authority, Gwatkin was able to exercise his sometimes ruthless instincts for economy.[25] Since 1907 the proposals for the fortress had become more elaborate still, but with naval support from the interdepartmental committee, Gwatkin slashed the program to only one new battery and reduced to reserve status all five of the innermost batteries, for a total of only five operational forts. At the same time, taking naval advice, he continued to press the priority of expansion of searchlight coverage on the main channel.[26]

Gwatkin knew that full economy ashore and truly effective coastal defence could only be achieved with local naval forces. He therefore joined with the Naval Staff at the end of 1913 in urging the prime minister to act on at least the small-vessel coastal flotilla proposal he had discussed with the Admiralty. By the time Borden had considered this and had in the meantime received the Admiralty's renewed request for trade-defence cruisers rather than coastal craft, war was only weeks away.[27]

In arguing for the coastal defence flotilla, the Canadian Naval Staff had noted that the Royal Navy's increased activity in the western Atlantic was evidence of growing concern about strong transocean raids in the event of a major war. The Canadian officers were right. During 1913 the Admiralty had permanently assigned the 4th Cruiser Squadron (under Rear Admiral Christopher Cradock) to the West Indies to protect British interests in Mexico, then in the throes of civil war. As the Admiralty staff commented, the force would also be useful in light of the greater importance of the region that would result from the opening of the Panama Canal in 1914, and as a ready nucleus for the protection of trade off Canada and Newfoundland, a target in which, intelligence suggested, Germany was interested.[28]

Because of the plans and preparations made by the Admiralty and the Canadian forces, mobilization of defences in the northwest Atlantic on the outbreak of war in August 1914 was quickly and effectively done. The Halifax defence scheme was still geared to war with the United States, and therefore Gwatkin and Colonel (later Major-General) R.W. Rutherford, General Officer Commanding, Maritime Provinces, limited call-outs of non-permanent militia units. At Halifax-Dartmouth a total of 2,600 men provided the infantry detachments in and around the cities and manned six of the nine batteries. (Because the single new seaward quick-fire battery was still far from completion, the Maritime Provinces Command brought into service two of the five inner works slated for abandonment). Some 400 troops, with mobile artillery, established the extemporized defences planned for Sydney in Cape Breton. Local panics had persuaded the Maritime Provinces Command to develop similar defences at Saint John, New Brunswick, a port not included in the mobilization plans.[29]

Reports in the last days of peace and first of war that German raiders were in position off Newfoundland and New York (later proved to be unfounded) undermined the confidence of shippers, particularly at the latter port. Cradock promptly despatched two of his cruisers north, while reinforcements from the United Kingdom sped to the western Atlantic to build up the squadron to about a dozen warships, now designated "Force H." Approximately one-half of this force operated from Halifax because of its closeness to the focal points of transatlantic trade south of Newfoundland and off Nova Scotia. Halifax was also well placed to maintain a patrol off New York. At this, the most important North American Atlantic port, shippers had to be reassured and a guard maintained against break-outs by fast German liners, well suited for service as armed raiders, that had taken refuge in the neutral US port on the eve of the war. The Royal Canadian Navy, with the help of resources from the Department of Marine and Fisheries, provided base services together with shipping intelligence and communications facilities without which the northern part of Force H could not have operated. In addition, the Canadian service, with the help of Newfoundland naval reservists and British personnel, brought the cruiser HMCS *Niobe* into commission, and the warship joined Force H's New York patrol.[30]

The division of labour in the northwest Atlantic, with Canada mainly providing shore services and defences, received the stamp of approval from the highest authorities. Borden, worried about a political backlash against the failure of his naval policy, received assurance from Winston Churchill, First Lord of the Admiralty, that Canada should continue to concentrate on raising land forces for service with the British field armies on the fighting front in France.[31]

Nevertheless, Canadian coastal defence was becoming an issue. In September 1914, when there was no doubt that the Royal Navy had contained the German fleet, Gwatkin began to cut back the Halifax garrison. This was the first of his efforts to ensure that inflated forces at home did not detract from the effort overseas. Protests from Rear Admiral R.S. Phipps Hornby, who had replaced Cradock in command of Force H, resulted in the Admiralty signalling Ottawa that "Halifax is an essential base for British cruisers protecting trade to and from Canada and the reduction ordered the safety of the base considerably."[32] Gwatkin, who consistently respected naval advice about coastal defence, complied. "There is no cause for alarm," he informed Rutherford, "and I hope you will keep the sailors in hand. But I quite agree that the situation will change when German vessels break through the Grand Fleet – as some of them, in the course of time, are not unlikely to succeed in doing."[33]

In the absence of a coastal defence naval flotilla, Phipps Hornby rightly felt utterly dependent upon the Canadian fortifications. He had no formal authority over Canadian forces save for *Niobe*, but his relationship with the RCN was intimate and the Canadian government respected his views. Phipps Hornby was especially worried that the frequent dense fogs off Nova Scotia would mask a raider until it had penetrated deep into the harbour. He thought that the German navy might attempt such a mission, especially as a measure of desperation when the Central Powers were facing defeat. He therefore supported the modernization of the fortress and insisted that it was essential to keep even the innermost forts in action to guard against nasty surprises. The frequently rotten Nova Scotia weather, he warned, made even these substantial defences less than adequate: two torpedo-boats and two submarines should be on station to watch the outer approaches.[34]

In fact, there was often no vessel available at Halifax capable of patrolling in the heavy seas off the port. On mobilization the RCN had assembled about ten craft from the civil marine services and by charter from commercial firms for lookout duty, the examination service, and daily minesweeping runs. The best of these ships, however, were rotated in and out of defence duties while they also continued to fulfil civil functions.[35]

Early in 1915 the east coast naval defence question rose to the highest levels. Amidst a new scare about German transatlantic raids, Borden was shocked to discover that modern submarines were being built in Montreal. Without a word to Canada, the Admiralty had conspired with American firms to evade US neutrality laws by having components for submarines shipped for completion and assembly at Canadian Vickers. Borden was furious, not least because Britain had consistently rejected his proposals for warship construction at Montreal as impractical.[36] Phipps Hornby's calls for submarine patrols off Nova Scotia and the Admiralty's refusal to assign any of the Montreal boats for this duty added to his ire.

As the Admiralty attempted to close the door on the question in the spring of 1915, the German navy launched "sink on sight" submarine warfare against British shipping in the Western Approaches to the British Isles. Intelligence from German circles in the United States had it that efforts were under way to establish secret fuel caches on isolated parts of the Canadian coast to support a transatlantic U-boat assault. The Admiralty advised Canada not to overreact. The submarines would be helpless without refuelling facilities, and these could be countered by a few armed civil steamers.[37]

Vice-Admiral Sir George Patey, who had succeeded Phipps Hornby, knew that the Admiralty's casual approach was unrealistic in view of the

RCN's non-existent resources. Patey, whom the Admiralty had elevated to the old title Commander-in-Chief, North America and West Indies, urged Naval Service Headquarters immediately to expand the little flotilla at Halifax into a force of armed steamers that could keep watch all along the east coast. This was essential, he warned, as his cruisers would be easy targets in the event of a U-boat attack. A worried Canadian government gave the go-ahead to the RCN in late June but, after a few additional ships had been acquired, called a halt. The Admiralty had persuaded Borden, who was then visiting the United Kingdom, that Canada was doing too much. Thus, the expanded RCN coastal defence force was limited to no more than twenty vessels, a dozen for Halifax (only a slight increase in the existing force) and eight at Sydney for the Gulf of St Lawrence, the main summer shipping route. Only half of these craft, including three American yachts that had been secretly purchased in the United States, were commissioned into the navy. As a further precaution, the naval service also installed an anti-submarine net across the harbour at Halifax, on either side of Georges Island.

The Admiralty's soothing assurances to Borden were shattered in October 1916. While Britain continued to advise that U-boats could not cross the Atlantic without vulnerable refuelling arrangements, U-53 did just that and sank five Allied ships off Massachusetts.[38] This was part of a renewed U-boat campaign that in the first half of 1917 would inflict such heavy losses to ocean shipping in Britain's Western Approaches that defeat seemed only months away.

In the wake of U-53's adventure, the Admiralty caused ill feeling in Ottawa by declaring that no assistance could be sent and that the RCN must greatly improve its coastal patrol with its own resources. The blow was somewhat softened when the Admiralty shortly augmented Canada's order for the building of 12 anti-submarine trawlers in domestic yards with orders for 160 additional trawlers and drifters that, although built on British account, would be released to the RCN if needed.[39]

Fortunately, the Germans did not attempt to repeat U-53's feat in 1917. Few of the anti-submarine vessels building in Canadian yards were completed before late in the year, and only a handful of suitable civil craft could be found. In the meantime, both Canadian services did what they could to improve the security of ports in close consultation with Patey's successor in the North America and West Indies command, Vice-Admiral Sir Montague Browning. The RCN installed a second anti-submarine net at Halifax, between Ives Point and Point Pleasant, and placed a net across Sydney Harbour. The militia had in 1916 already completed the new seaward quick-fire battery at Halifax as well as the full system of searchlights, but also maintained the two inner batteries that had been mobilized as an emergency measure in 1914. During 1917 the shore defences at Saint John and Sydney were upgraded with 4.7-inch quick-fire guns on coastal defence mounts that were a great improvement over the field mounts previously at these ports.[40]

The importance of the east coast ports increased enormously in the summer of 1917 with Britain's introduction of transatlantic convoys as a last ditch, and ultimately successful, counter to the U-boat campaign. Sydney and Halifax were two of the principal convoy assembly ports. Their harbours were soon teeming with both merchant vessels and American and British cruisers that served as escorts. (Because the Germans had only a limited number of long-range submarines, the main threat at mid-ocean was of surface raider attack; anti-submarine destroyers, which were in desperately short supply, did not join the escort screen until the convoys neared the Western Approaches.) Although RCN shore staffs and establishments, not to mention Canadian civil transportation facilities, were vital to the convoy system, Canada soon found that the new Anglo-American naval alliance had completely closed the dominion out of the picture. Only by making direct inquiries in Washington did the RCN learn that Browning had arranged for the bulk of US anti-submarine resources to be deployed in European waters, to the exclusion of Canadian needs. It then took the despatch of a Canadian naval officer to London to learn that high-grade intelligence had revealed that long-range U-boat cruisers would probably strike in Canadian waters as early as the spring of 1918. The Admiralty warned that the little anti-submarine drifters and trawlers would have to be supported by a force of destroyers to counter the big submarines, and promised to provide them either from British or US sources. Early in 1918 Vice-Admiral Sir William Grant, Browning's successor as Commander-in-Chief, North America and West Indies, asked the Admiralty and the American navy department about these promises, only to discover through back-door sources that Washington and London had secretly closed ranks against what they denounced as unreasonable Canadian demands.[41]

Meanwhile, in late 1917 and early 1918, growing difficulties with the militia's east coast garrisons came to a head. Despite Major-General Gwatkin's best efforts, during 1915 the Halifax garrison had crept up to 3,500 personnel because of the demands of long-term readiness. With the beginning of shortages of reinforcements for the overseas corps in 1916, the chief of general staff stepped up the pressure for reductions, only to meet with increasingly impolite rejoinders from Major-General Thomas Benson, Rutherford's successor in the Maritime Provinces Command, who pointed out that the garrison was insufficiently manned to provide adequate reliefs of watches on the guns, lights, and infantry outposts. The situation was more complicated still because the home garrisons, as non-permanent militia on call-out, were under lower pay rates and different terms of service than men who had joined the Canadian Expeditionary Force (CEF). Men were less willing to volunteer for boring, underpaid home service than for the CEF. Thus, Benson was facing a major morale problem and insuperable difficulties in finding replacements for garrison members who, in their hundreds, pleaded to be allowed to join the CEF and go overseas.[42]

The headquarters staff saw the solution to the home garrisons question when the government implemented conscription in early 1918. This would allow the disbandment of the many militia units on service and the amalgamation of their personnel into CEF depots that would carry out truly essential garrison duties, with personnel undergoing training before their despatch overseas. Gwatkin sent his trusted colleague, Major-General F.L. Lessard, to take over the Maritime Provinces Command. Lessard and his staff put the case for deep cuts in the Halifax defences to Admiral Grant and the RCN staff at Halifax in February 1918. According to the soldiers, expansion of the Canadian anti-submarine patrol provided sufficient immediate defence. Reinforcements from the mighty American fleet would be available should the RCN need support. The sailors blew these arguments out of the water. The Canadian patrol craft were so light that in the event of any concerted German action they "would have to retire quickly behind [the covering fire from the shore] batteries." American assistance was "potential … rather than actual," and the US Navy already had its plate full.[43]

The militia was obliged to keep the garrison up to strength. Additional artillerymen, moreover, were needed for Sydney, where, as a result of its new importance as a convoy port, additional coast guns were being mounted in concrete positions. The consolidation of the Nova Scotia garrison into CEF depots did allow early despatch overseas of a few hundred urgently needed infantry reinforcements, but the overall effect of the new organization was to bring in draftees from across the country to keep the garrison up to strength until war's end. The garrison was probably at the peak of its wartime efficiency, for the staff implemented intensive training programs for rapid gunfire against fast targets at night, upgraded communications, and made sure full reliefs were available at all of the most important sites. Until the last day of the war the land forces compensated for the inability of the RCN, USN, and RN to provide proper coastal defence vessels.[44]

The naval officers had been speaking from the heart about the weakness of the anti-submarine patrol. During the summer of 1918, deliveries of the new construction trawlers and drifters expanded the flotilla to something over 100 craft, with about 40 at Halifax, mostly for convoy escort in coastal waters, and 60 at Sydney, for both convoy escort and patrol of the Gulf of St Lawrence and the waters around Newfoundland.

A mission to Washington brought a reinforcement of 6 wooden US Navy submarine chasers, which were only somewhat more effective than the trawlers, and the promise of two seaplane squadrons, which did not begin to operate from Halifax and Sydney until September.[45]

The big U-cruisers, armed with torpedoes, mines, and 5.9-inch guns, began to hunt in North American waters in May 1918 but confined themselves to the US coast. Wireless intelligence suggested that *U-156*, which announced her arrival at the end of July by sinking a three-masted schooner in the mouth of the Bay of Fundy, would also head south. However, on 5 August she suddenly appeared within fifty miles of Halifax and destroyed the independently sailed tanker *Luz Blanca*, which had defied naval regulations by leaving port in daylight. A passing steamer quickly radioed word of the action, but all of the best patrol ships were at sea on a convoy escort mission, and it took some hours for a warship to reach the position. With this evidence of the vulnerability of the near Halifax approaches and further wireless intelligence that suggested additional U-cruisers would soon operate in the area, Admiral Grant shifted the assembly port of the main Halifax transatlantic convoy to Quebec City. Although Halifax continued as the main naval base and the centre for the assembly of coastal convoys, the weakness of the RCN and the failure of the Allies to give assistance had forced a retreat from Canada's major strategic port.[46]

*U-156* continued to run amok among the little schooners of the fishing fleets off Nova Scotia. *U-117* then briefly operated offshore between Nova Scotia and Newfoundland. In September *U-155* lay fourteen mines southwest of Halifax, but these did no damage, and there is evidence that the U-cruiser was deterred from more aggressive action by the strengthened patrols the RCN mounted in the Halifax approaches. Aside from the losses the submarines inflicted on the fishing fleets, they sank only one large steamer other than *Luz Blanca*. This was the result of the efficient ocean and coastal convoy system in which the RCN played a major role, both ashore and afloat.

In fact, Canada's slender maritime defences had played a part far more important than could have been anticipated before 1914. Incomprehensible as the maintenance and improvement of the Halifax fortress for conflict with the United States may have seemed, from the moment war broke out with Germany those land defences provided security to both commercial shipping and naval forces, making Halifax one of the foundation stones of North Atlantic trade protection. Truncated by politics as the RCN was, the Naval Staff helped keep the militia's coastal defence policy on the right lines. The RCN also marshalled the largely civil marine resources Canada possessed, and provided a vital link with the British commander-in-chief. The Canadian sailors ensured that the British forces in the northwest Atlantic received necessary support, but at the same time served as a check against the inclinations of the Allies to ignore Canadian interests.

The war administered two shocks in the matter of coastal defence, both of which had an important influence on the government, the armed forces, and especially the navy during the 1920s and 1930s and well into the Second World War. Not only had entirely unexpected threats rapidly developed, but the response to those threats had entangled Canada in tricky questions of sovereignty with respect to both Britain and the United States. As a result, Canadian defence planning now took account of the possibility that the United States might be neutral in a war involving the Empire, or that the Empire might remain neutral in the event the US went to war. For its part, the Naval Staff negotiated with the Admiralty to delineate lines of authority in Canadian waters and ports as between the Royal Navy and the Royal Canadian Navy.

All the services, including the newly organized air force, understood the importance of efficient, comprehensive coastal naval and air patrols and of the fortification of major ports in addition to Halifax and Esquimalt. Most of this, with the deep cuts in defence spending in 1922–23, had to await rearmament in the late 1930s, but at that time the government made these requirements the first priority. From the early 1920s, the navy committed its paltry resources to acquiring destroyers and properly organizing the reserves to provide the warships and the trained manpower that had been desperately lacking in 1914–18. In the late 1930s the service, again drawing on the experience of the First World War, urgently called for production of large numbers of coastal escort craft, and this requirement produced the corvette program of 1939–40.[47] To no small extent, Canada's famed reserve-manned anti-submarine navy of 1939–45 was born out of the German sea-raider menace of the First World War.

# · 8 ·

# *Fleet Replacement and the Crisis of Identity*

## MICHAEL A. HENNESSY

Since the days of Mahan, the size and composition of a navy have defined much more than merely the physical dimensions of the fleet. They have also defined the psychological identity of the navy. In the shape of its fleet, the navy expresses whether it is blue or brown water, coastal patrol or high-seas capability. During the late 1950s and early 1960s, the Royal Canadian Navy (RCN) experienced a crisis in its identity, and in so doing, moved towards recapturing a fleet capable of global blue-water offensive operations. The period from 1955 to 1964 was a tumultuous era for Canadian defence policy, but accounts of these years have tended to concentrate on issues of continental air defence and the indecision marking the Diefenbaker administration's acquisition of nuclear weapons.[1]

These issues largely determined the outcome of the election of 1963. Historical studies have focused on Diefenbaker's electoral defeat and the fundamental reforms and reorganization of Canadian defence forces under the Liberal government of Lester B. Pearson. These events were not without consequence for the RCN. It was, after all, dissolved under the incoming minister of defence, Paul Hellyer. However, it would be wrong to blur the real distinctions between the naval policy of Diefenbaker's government and that later imposed by the Liberals. Before the process of integration and well before unification, the Pearson government shelved the navy's plans for a large, balanced naval force. Promoted primarily as a means of fiscal restraint, but actually prompted by the government's desire to generate public support for its defence policy, this action resulted in

131

fleet specialization in anti-submarine warfare (ASW), which only made sense under the NATO umbrella.

The RCN by 1961 had more than sixty warships in commission, forming a sizeable modern fleet. The vessels included the aircraft carrier HMCS *Bonaventure*, fourteen modern Canadian-built destroyer escorts of the St Laurent and Restigouche classes, and a number of war-built but modernized vessels, including eleven Tribal-class (or related) destroyers and eighteen frigates of the Prestonian class. A submarine loaned by the United States Navy operated on the Pacific coast, as did two submarines on loan from the Royal Navy on the Atlantic. The RCN fleet included ten minesweepers, two escort maintenance ships, and seven smaller craft. In addition, there were over 100 auxiliary vessels. These ranged from research ships to oil scows and yard craft. The RCN provided three first-line air squadrons consisting of CS2F Trackers, Banshee fighters, and anti-submarine helicopters. Four other squadrons engaged in training and evaluation duties. Nearly 51 per cent of the navy's uniformed personnel were at sea. This was a very high sea-to-shore ratio in comparison to other NATO navies. Building in Canadian shipyards were several destroyer escorts and the 22,000-ton tanker-supply ship HMCS *Provider*. As Vice-Admiral Herbert Rayner, DSC, CD, the chief of naval staff, explained at the time: "All efforts are directed towards the support of the fleet – for it is the fleet that is the true expression of the Navy's worth."[2] That, at least, was his view. Fleet composition was therefore directly related to the navy's identity. The internal battles over the shape of the fleet are the subject of this enquiry.

Although the fleet may not in fact have been the true measure of the navy's worth, the changing composition of the fleet is a reflection of its changing purposes and roles. The rate of technical change experienced by the RCN through the late 1950s and early 1960s was perhaps unprecedented, but other navies faced similar problems. Norman Friedman describes this period as the "post war naval revolution." This revolution saw most navies of the Western alliance (NATO) following the lead of Britain and the United States.[3] Throughout the decade of 1945–55, both Britain and the United States developed naval forces in response to the new global military situation created by the perceived threat of the Soviet Union and the atomic bomb. In doing so, they sought to incorporate rapidly changing technologies and develop effective strategies within severely constrained naval defence budgets. Surface fleets underwent major restructuring largely in response to the fast submarine, guided missile, and jet aircraft. Because of the inherent difficulties of intercepting these forces near their intended targets, both the Royal Navy (RN) and the United States Navy adopted strategies and structures that equated sea control with power-projection missions. This marked a shift away from escort strategies to concepts such as attack at source, ocean barrier, and under-sea sound surveillance. The fast modern forces required for these various missions rendered many fleets built during the Second World War obsolete or, at best, in need of extensive modernization.

This naval revolution compelled the Royal Canadian Navy to attempt parallel changes in fleet structures and roles. Naval building programs authorized in the last years of the Diefenbaker government were aimed at bringing the RCN through the naval revolution and restoring the navy to a balanced fleet. The scope and pace of this program, while controlled by budgetary, technical, and strategic concerns, fell into three essential phases.

Prior to these three phases, between 1948 and 1955, the navy's manpower had nearly doubled and the fleet had grown from six vessels (frigates or larger) in active service to twenty-seven. Such rapid growth, which was prompted by the Korean War, could not be sustained, and Canada's entire defence mobilization program reached its pinnacle in 1955. In this year all services were told that no new capital program could be undertaken without a previously accepted program being dropped.[4]

The first, and longest, phase of the navy's response, 1955–60, witnessed increased specialization of the fleet in ASW operations in accordance with allied strategies, sound-surveillance systems, and a rapidly changing submarine menace. The RCN responded by developing a ship-replacement program based on the philosophy of "better ships but fewer ships."

The second period, from late 1960 to early 1963, brought short relief from austerity. In the expectation of increased money, the RCN tried to reconstitute a balanced surface capability. Provisional budget increases encouraged RCN participation in the forward maritime strategy that the larger navies of the alliance had come to substitute for tactical ASW operations, but this role was never fully supported by the government. Rather, tactical ASW in the western Atlantic remained the navy's only accepted *raison d'être*. Nevertheless, efforts by the RCN to re-invent itself by building a new balanced fleet capable of contributing to UN actions or a limited war were part of its effort to create a fleet capable of contributing to forward operations in the eastern Atlantic. The short-lived General Purpose Frigate (GPF) program was the physical expression of this desire.

The third phase coincides with the initial steps taken by Paul Hellyer to integrate the armed forces. Facing retrenchment and financial austerity, the RCN planned for missions confined largely to ASW in the western Atlantic. Subsequent steps taken by the navy to restore its mission flexibility following this period are beyond the scope of this study and will not be addressed.

*Fleet-Replacement Planning*

By 1961 the continued existence of much of the fleet was in doubt. Block obsolescence was approaching for most of the prewar and war-built ships. The carrier required replacement before 1975, and the eighteen frigates and eleven Tribal-class destroyers were due for retirement before 1970. Bilateral agreements under the Canada–United States Regional Planning Group (CUSRPG) for the defence of the Pacific coast and NATO multilateral arrangements for the Supreme Allied Command, Atlantic (SACLANT), committed Canada to providing twenty-nine anti-submarine warfare escorts to SACLANT and fourteen to the Canada-US region. With so many vessels requiring replacement, the RCN would have a net deficiency from agreed force goals of twenty-three ships by 1970. Living up to that commitment required a continuing ship-replacement program.[5]

The scarce resources dedicated to defence spending were controlled through the budgetary process. The navy largely determined what types of vessels it required, but obtaining the funding to build ships entailed gaining authority from several other interested bodies. Individual services were required to generate their demands internally before seeking funding first through the tri-service Chiefs of Staff Committee and then through the Cabinet Defence Committee (CDC). Finally, the decisions of the CDC had to receive approval in the federal Cabinet. The Treasury Board and other bodies, such as the departments of Defence Production, External Affairs, or Finance, could intervene at any of these levels.[6]

The Naval Board had responsibility for establishing naval policy. As one former insider recalled, the power to shape the fleet was in the hands of a very small circle of men.[7] Unlike its namesake (created during the Second World War), which included a civilian deputy minister responsible for financial and administrative overview, beginning in 1957 the Naval Board consisted of some half-dozen senior naval officers: the chief of naval staff, the vice-chief, the navy comptroller, the director of personnel, the assistant chief of naval staff (Plans), and the assistant chief of naval staff (Air & Warfare). These last two members controlled the two functional directorates of the Naval Staff responsible for force planning and reported to the vice-chief of naval staff. The coordination of technical, financial, and operational requirements was facilitated through the Policy and Planning Coordinating Committee (PPCC),[8] which, chaired by the vice-chief, vetted most proposals moving forward for consideration by the Naval Board.

Fleet planning for most of this period involved making repeated compromises with regard to new technology and fulfilling new and maintaining old commitments. The task of maintaining commitments in the period between 1955 and 1960 proved exceedingly difficult. Planners had to keep abreast of the technologies required for a changing NATO maritime strategy within the dire financial strictures placed on the Department of Defence in the late 1950s. Naval appropriations were progressively reduced over 1957–61, declining from $326.3 million to $271.3 million by the end of this period. Despite this decline, RCN personnel strength increased from 13,500 to over 20,000, and the size of the fleet had trebled since 1950. However, in real dollars the naval budget in 1961 was only 19 per cent greater than it had been in 1951. Within that budget, the maintenance and modernization of the fleet presented a set of related problems.

*Origins of the Problem*

In 1948 Cabinet set in motion the first postwar naval building program. An arctic icebreaker, three modern ASW escort frigates, and several small harbour craft were authorized. The ASW frigates were to be ultramodern ships, of Canadian design and manufacture, capable of locating and destroying the advanced type of U-boats that Germany had almost brought into service in the closing months of the Second World War. Technologies incorporated into these vessels that would allow them to operate with near impunity in the North Atlantic were known to have been captured by the Soviet Union.[9] The three Canadian ASW frigates became the lead ships of the St Laurent–class building program. The scale and scope of the building program increased slightly with the addition of four ships after the start of the Korean War in June 1950. Following the Chinese intervention, Canadian Cold War rearmament moved into full swing. A major refit for ASW service of older vessels was undertaken. The Tribal-class destroyers were refitted for escort and ASW duties, and eighteen smaller war-built frigates were saved from the breaker's yard, modernized, and rechristened the Prestonian class. All were needed to fill a glaring gap in Canada's ability to patrol its coastal areas. Furthermore, the government placed orders for an additional seven slightly modified St Laurents, which were renamed the Restigouche class. The St Laurents were reaching completion in 1955, while the Restigouche class joined the fleet over the course of 1958–59.

The construction of these vessels proved a major technological feat for Canadian industry. Because there was no secure access to British and American naval components, such as turbines, turbine gearings, fire-control computers, mortars, guns, and many other subcomponents, construction was undertaken in Canada. Financial planning for the original program proved remarkably inaccurate, as the final costs were misjudged by a magnitude of at least three.[10] The perceived likelihood of general war, however, distracted the government's attention from matters of ultimate cost. As Minister of Defence Production C.D. Howe reportedly explained, if the military asked for a gold-plated piano, then "we buy a gold-plated piano."[11]

These hasty mobilization measures bore financial consequences for the future. Once Canada had committed itself to supplying a set number of vessels to NATO, that number received a degree of inviolability in naval planning. Canada's original contributions to NATO's Supreme Allied Commander, Atlantic, and to the forces under the Canada–United States Regional Planning Group for Pacific defence had not been based on any cold calculation of what forces were essential, but rather on what forces Canada could quickly make available. Canada's army and air force commitments were similarly premised on filling an immediate gap. The costs of sustaining those commitments through the long haul soon threatened to overwhelm the government's financial resources. Shortly before leaving office, Brooke Claxton, the minister of defence during the Korean-era mobilization, discovered that the cost of sustaining only the Canadian air commitment would require three-quarters of the defence department's capital procurement budget.[12] Consequently, from 1955, no new major capital procurement project would be undertaken without a reduction in capital allocations within or between the three separate services.

### Fleet Planning

Fleet planning within the resulting constricted budget was further complicated by four developments: NATO naval strategy was changing; the submarine threat was increasing; many of the vessels brought into service were expected to be obsolescent by the mid-1960s; and there began a prolonged period of dissonance between the Naval Staff and those who controlled financial resources over the perceived threat. This final point warrants greater attention than it can be given here except in a brief digression.

Until the mobilization measures adopted during the Korean War came into play, the Canadian government had formed its own strategic/tactical assessments. Following Korea, the lack of an extensive Canadian external intelligence organization made it impossible for Canada to gather the type of intelligence necessary for force planning. Consequently, Canadian military officials were instructed to accept, without official question, evaluations developed by the US and UK governments. During the first half of the 1950s this caused little problem because of the wide degree of political support for defence preparedness. The advent of thermonuclear weapons and an apparent moderation of Soviet actions following the death of Stalin weakened that consensus. Nevertheless, threat analysis within the Canadian military remained premised primarily on British and American assessments. As the Cold War progressed, getting an agreed reading of the threat was complicated by a growing disjunction between what threat assessments the navy developed and those the Cabinet accepted.

Views within the Western alliance were also changing. The efficacy of escort and tactical ASW operations in the age of the threat of thermonuclear war faced serious reconsideration within NATO. Between 1954 and 1962 two fundamental restatements of NATO's defensive strategy were made that tested the RCN's capacity to respond. The first of these came with NATO's adoption of MC-48 in 1954, which brought the "New Look Strategy" into effect. NATO strategy was to rely on nuclear weapons; hence conventional forces were downgraded in strategic planning. MC-70, the policy of flexible response, followed, and the Canadian government accepted it for planning purposes in 1960. Under MC-70, dependence on more conventional forces came into effect. The debates surrounding the origins of these policy statements are examined elsewhere.[13] What is important for this discussion is the "New Look" and "New New Look" force structures that the RCN framed in response.[14] The escort/ASW missions, which had been an unambiguous strategy at NATO's inception, were considered less important. In the belief that a future war would devastate the mobilization base of the nation, only those ships on hand at the commencement of hostilities were judged likely to contribute. This led to a "come as you are" war scenario that reduced the reliance on reserves and long-term mobilization planning. For the navy, the "fleet-in-being" at the commencement of hostilities was likely to be the only force available to contribute in the event of nuclear war.

Complicating how the RCN would respond to these new strategic assumptions was an extended period of fiscal restraint. The chief of naval technical services, Rear Admiral J.G. Knowlton, framed the first guidelines for fleet planning during this period. Given the anticipated slow or negative growth of the annual naval budget, Knowlton argued that the RCN should adopt a policy of "fewer ships ... but better ships."[15] While the full implications of the MC-48 war concept were under study and the and operational requirements for its support were being developed, the planned fleet-replacement building program was postponed. The plan then put forward for the navy by Knowlton argued that the replacement of vessels retiring from the fleet would require laying down four new ships each fiscal year from 1957 to 1960, followed by two ships a year from 1960 to 1966/67. Further, in keeping with the principle of "fewer but better," the construction of a Vancouver class of second-rate coastal defence vessels was cancelled.[16] Following cancellation of these vessels, the Naval Staff redrew the basic performance requirements for the next set of vessels to be built. The new staff requirements called for greater range, speed, and endurance. These improved characteristics were judged essential for meeting the operational requirements then developing.

The role of ASW forces was no longer clearly one of facilitating passage on the high seas. For the navy, this meant no longer preparing simply to refight the Battle of the Atlantic. Instead two clear missions developed. The continental defence of North America now entailed preventing the approach of Soviet submarines capable of launching nuclear missiles. For this mission an extensive underwater sound-surveillance system (SOSUS) was developed.[17] This entailed the emplacement of a series of chains of underwater listening devices at about 100 fathoms and stretching over several hundred miles. The system was developed jointly by the USN and Bell Laboratories. These listening chains were to be laid on both coasts and were eventually to extend to the ocean transit choke-points along the great circle routes. In theory, this passive listening system could detect low-frequency sound transmissions, those typically made by submarines. Through analysis of these sounds, it was hoped that submarine contacts could be plotted.[18] The New Look Strategy adopted by the RCN embraced the possibilities of this system, recognizing that naval strength no longer remained simply a function of hulls in the water. A fleet capable of exploiting SOSUS contacts required greater endurance and speed and improved weapons systems.

The concept of operations in the North Atlantic, in support of SOSUS, required RCN ASW forces to patrol an area approximately 700 by 300 miles. The patrol area was to be sufficiently far from landfall to negate the range of Soviet missiles.[19] To cover the patrol areas, ships were to operate in pairs, with twenty-four ships required to cover the search area. Given that number of ships, one hour and fifty minutes would be required to respond to a SOSUS contact for vessels capable of twenty-seven knots (that is, St Laurent class) or two hours and fifteen minutes for ships of eighteen knots (Prestonian class). These operational requirements highlighted some of the deficiencies of the current destroyer escort forces. The RCN expected to have fourteen twenty-seven-knot St Laurent/Restigouche destroyer-escorts (DDEs), and four Tribal-class destroyers in service by the end of 1958.[20] There were eleven other escorts in the fleet, four Tribals and seven Prestonians, but they possessed neither the speed nor the ASW gear suitable for these missions. As well, all the Tribals and Prestonians were due for retirement by 1970. To reach the required twenty-four long-range patrol vessels promised to SACLANT, six additional ships were required. Further, to keep ships operating at maximum efficiency within the patrol areas, two tankers were essential for the Atlantic coast and one for the Pacific. Obtaining vessels for these various missions became the priority of the ship-replacement plan.

Moreover, the defence mission in the western Atlantic was growing quite distinct from the operational methods being contemplated for the eastern Atlantic. The maritime strategy shaping the British and American navies required the development of balanced fleets, based on carrier task forces, capable of offensive operations against the major Soviet naval bases. As well, ASW barrier operations were being developed. These entailed securing various choke-points through which Soviet naval forces would have to pass to gain the high seas or North American approaches. The RCN did not restructure itself to participate in the strike operations against the Soviet Union, but it had a long-standing commitment to contribute one aircraft carrier and six escorts for operations under SACLANT control in European waters. In keeping with the changing focus of proposed operations, the carrier's area of operations progressively moved into the eastern Atlantic.[21] Whatever the diplomatic value of having forces committed to eastern Atlantic operations, it was a role that became increasingly more detached from the RCN's specialized mission in the western Atlantic. This growing distinction was greatly accelerated by the acute problem of ASW in the western Atlantic in the period 1958–60.

## Problems in Tactical ASW

The ability to localize and engage modern submarines became increasingly important for two reasons: an unanticipated failure of strategic surveillance systems and the improved capabilities of Soviet submarines. Of immediate concern was the advent of the Soviet Union's missile-carrying submarine program. The Soviets' major conventional submarine building program, commenced in 1951, produced several classes of long-endurance ocean-going boats. From 1956 large numbers of these submarines were modified to carry ballistic or cruise nuclear missiles.[22] These missile technologies drastically changed the nature of the threat at sea. Although the missiles were all of short range, approximately 200 nautical miles, all the cities of the Atlantic and Pacific seaboards were vulnerable to annihilation without warning. Compounding the missile threat was the advent of nuclear propulsion. The success of the USN's nuclear-powered submarine USS *Nautilus*, which travelled under the polar ice-cap in 1957, demonstrated to the Naval Board both the viability of the propulsion plant and the fact that Canada's northern waters were no longer immune to submarine operations. The spectre of nuclear missiles in nuclear submarines was a potent combination that, as the chief of naval staff explained to the Chiefs of Staff Committee, "left anti-submarine warfare far behind."[23]

The increasing scale of Soviet submarine operations in the western Atlantic did not help matters. The exact number of SOSUS contacts remains classified, but contacts by other means demonstrate the increase in scale. Four visual contacts were confirmed in 1958, nineteen in 1959, twenty-one in 1960, and twenty-two in 1961. During the Cuban Missile Crisis, the Soviet Union demonstrated its ability to sortie a large number of long-range boats when, from 23 October to 15 November 1962, some 136 Soviet submarines appeared near the Canadian area of responsibility in the Atlantic.[24]

As it then existed, the deep-water sound-surveillance system did not offer an immediate solution. Although it became operational in 1957, the system did not live up to expectations. In light of the RCN's incapacity to detect Soviet submarines in a timely manner, the vice-chief of naval staff informed the navy's senior officers in November 1961 that the RCN had "virtually no ability" to stop missile-firing submarines.[25]

Finding increasingly sophisticated Soviet submarines demanded improving the effectiveness of the ASW fleet. To do so within the restrained naval budget required that economies be made elsewhere. While studying the ASW problem, the Naval Board authorized reductions in the fleet and declined additional missions for the navy. After long debate, the board voted to dispose of the two cruisers HMCS *Ontario* and *Quebec*. Though they were only being used for training missions, the cruisers had been promised to SACLANT for operations in the eastern Atlantic after mobilization. However, the cost of maintaining that commitment threatened to expend funds that were more urgently required for addressing the submarine threat in the western Atlantic.[26] Further, in the name of economy, though it meant reducing the fleet's general service capability, the navy's only ice-breaker, HMCS *Labrador*, was transferred to the Department of Transport.[27] In focusing on the submarine threat in the western Atlantic, the Naval Board declined participation in an American plan to extend the Distant Early Warning radar system at sea.[28] A Canadian contribution to ASW barrier operations closer to the Soviet Union was reduced to allow concentration of resources in the western Atlantic.[29]

The freeing of financial resources was necessary to allow improvements in the ASW effectiveness of the fleet. The performance of the St Laurent class, once they became operational in 1955, proved disappointing. While the vessels were exceedingly expensive, their effectiveness against modern submarines proved marginal. No sooner had the class become operational than major refits were contemplated to improve performance. The vessels of the Restigouche class, to be completed in the time frame 1957–58, were expected to experience similar problems.[30]

With high speed being judged crucial, the chief of the Naval Technical Services designed a truly new ASW frigate. The notional Mackenzie class were to be fitted with improved machinery, sonars, and guided missiles. These were to be the "fewer but better ships." In planning these vessels, the Naval Staff and technical services realized that the Chiefs of Staff Committee would only support a building program under the current budget ceiling. Replacing on a one-for-one basis the thirty-five escort vessels due to leave the navy between 1958 and 1968 could not be contemplated. The planned replacement program proposed in early 1956 therefore sought to replace only twenty-six escorts. The reduced numbers would be compensated by more capable ships and the early introduction of helicopters into the fleet.[31] However, the proposed Mackenzies promised only a marginal improvement in ASW effectiveness. Not long into the planning phase, the estimated cost of $30 million, as compared to $26 million for the Restigouche (itself seen as too expensive), was judged prohibitive. The original Mackenzie-class program that was proposed to the Chiefs of Staff Committee so threatened to exceed the budget that the chairman of the committee refused to pass it on for higher consideration. When the Naval Board contemplated seeking permission to have the ships built outside the country, it was informed that maintenance of Canada's shipbuilding industry must be taken into account.[32] Consequently, the Naval Board sought a ship either of much improved efficiency or of much less expense.

The decision not to build the more complex Mackenzie vessel greatly complicated the orderly replacement of retiring vessels. After assessing the costs and time involved in bringing forward a new Mackenzie-class design, the Naval Board recommended simply ordering vessels of the previous Restigouche design. Though judged obsolescent, that design already existed. This gained acceptance by the Cabinet Defence Committee on 6 February 1957. Before any construction began, however, the Liberals were turned out of office. The new government requested a review of the proposals before authorizing them on 8 August 1957. Finally, in face of the need to replace retiring vessels and to maintain a basis of skill among the shipyards, four "repeat Restigouche" frigates were ordered. Orders for an additional two were authorized the following year.[33]

For the first four vessels, the infelicitous name "repeat Restigouche" gave way to the designation "Mackenzie class" – even though they were not the Mackenzie class as originally designed. The final two repeat Restigouche vessels also emerged from the shipyards under a new name, the Annapolis class. During construction their design underwent substantial modernization, following that prepared for the St Laurent class. This included incorporation of a helicopter hanger and flight deck and the installation of the Canadian-designed Variable Depth Sonar (VDS).[34] Consisting of a large towed sonar array that could be lowered through the ocean's surface layers, which particularly disrupted sonar effectiveness in the western Atlantic, the VDS had by late 1958 achieved effective active sonar detection beyond 21,000 yards and was exceedingly reliable for ranges up to 11,000 yards at fifteen knots, that is, two to three times the effective range of hull-mounted sonar. Consequently, two ships operating with VDS could search the same area previously demanding six. The potential of the VDS and helicopter was recognized very early on by the RCN. After a period of design development and sea trials, their incorporation into the fleet was delayed only by the rate of production and an orderly shipyard schedule.[35]

The fitting of helicopters and VDS to the original St Laurents was undertaken during their mid-life refits,[36] but the modernization program had been under consideration since August 1957.[37] Authority for an extensive modernization program came with little debate because it was apparent that the delays experienced in ordering the repeat Restigouche vessels threatened to seriously erode fleet effectiveness.[38] Once the minister authorized preparation for a major modernization program, studies commenced in 1958 and focused on improving the ASW effectiveness of the fleet.[39] For the current fleet, improving the on-station time of the ASW vessels was judged critical to meeting the increasing operational requirements of the ASW forces. To this end, construction of the first of three fleet-replenishment tankers was undertaken.[40] Beyond improving the on-station time of the fleet, drastic improvements were sought in the ASW vessels. Present forces required immediate improvement,[41] and thus a short-term modernization program began.

More permanent solutions than the short-term program required a series of further studies. These demonstrated that the effectiveness of the fleet would be greatly improved by the deployment of submarines, helicopters, and fixed-wing aircraft working in combination to support the SOSUS barrier. These considerations complicated identification of the next proposed class of ASW vessels. Submarines, it was argued, could be incorporated into the annual estimates for 1958/59.[42] This raised a serious question about the best type of ASW vessel to follow the Restigouche class. In considering the usefulness of surface escorts, planners also had to consider the fleet anti-aircraft capacity. Maintaining an anti-air capability while improving the ASW effectiveness of the fleet and meeting the replacement schedule evolved into a long-running problem that can be summarized by addressing the origins and fate of the submarine-building program.

*Submarines or Surface Hunters?*

By late 1957 the United States Navy was arguing that the best means of hunting Soviet submarines was with submarines. Submarines could operate with virtual impunity, undetected by aerial or surface observation, and their sonar did not have the same problem with temperature gradients that plagued hull-mounted ship sonars. The RCN kept abreast of the technical advances in submarine building in both Britain and the United States throughout this period,[43] but the possibility of acquiring nuclear-propelled submarines particularly intrigued the chief of Naval Technical Services, Vice-Admiral Brian Spencer.[44] From early 1955, he had encouraged the continuous appraisal of nuclear-drive technology and its incorporation into the fleet. When it became a proven technology and when the value of the anti-submarine submarines developed by the Americans and the British became clear, great attention was given to the issue by the Naval Board.

The success of the USS *Nautilus* nuclear submarine prompted Spencer to argue that there there was a need for Canadian nuclear-propelled submarines. At the 564th meeting of the Naval Board, on 2 April 1958, it was agreed that this need existed and that a detailed feasibility study on Canadian construction facilities should be undertaken. After reaching a "Scope and Means" agreement with both the United States Navy and the Atomic Energy Commission, the Nuclear Submarine Survey Team completed its study by July 1959. After an extensive survey of Canadian shipyards and discussion with manufacturers, the survey team determined that Canadian industry could build nuclear submarines, the only limiting considerations being time and money.[45]

In this regard, the team had established that for the conservative cost estimate of one nuclear submarine, the RCN could gain three to five conventional submarines.[46] The latest conventional boats possessed many of the operational advantages of nuclear-powered submarines, the only real disadvantages being submerged endurance and speed. These considerations prompted the chief of naval staff, Vice-Admiral H.G. DeWolf, to call into question the findings of the survey.

However, the ability of the nuclear-powered submarine to generate electricity was also of great benefit. While Britain and the United States were employing with increasing effect submarine-mounted passive sonar and achieving quite exceptional detection ranges in the order of 125 miles, active sonar was still considered an essential requirement. The power requirements of long-range active sonar could quickly drain a conventional submarine's batteries. At the time, a good range for active sonar was 10 miles, with some demonstrated capacity to achieve ranges of 35 miles in the first convergence zone. The tactics and training for ASW had yet to take account of the speed advantages of nuclear boats. Most tactics and methods had been developed against conventional submarines with submerged speeds of three to five knots. Against such slow targets, ships were given a 5 to 1 speed advantage and aircraft a 40 to 1 advantage, but with nuclear boats capable of high-speed operations in excess of twenty knots, the surface craft often had a speed disadvantage and maritime aircraft were reduced to approximately a 7 to 1 advantage.

These operational conditions were not widely known at the time, and for Defence Minister George Pearkes, VC, speed proved the decisive issue. As he saw it, high speed was not essential for "defensive A/S operations in the Atlantic." Consequently, the chief of naval staff recommended that unless additional funds could be made available to the navy to meet the cost of building nuclear boats, conventional submarines should be undertaken on the basis of equal priority with the surface vessels of the planned replacement program.[47] However, until the submarine program was settled, the surface fleet replacement program was also delayed.

A detailed proposal for Canadian production reached the Chiefs of Staff Committee in November 1959. The chief of naval staff recommended that Canada introduce a submarine service for the purpose of improving its ASW capability and at the same time augment, and eventually replace, the present submarine training squadron on loan from the United Kingdom. The RCN proposal demonstrated a marked preference for nuclear boats but indicated that the RCN would accept conventional boats if no additional funds to offset the additional cost were authorized for the naval appropriation. The Chiefs of Staff Committee endorsed the conventional building program. Ministerial approval for a complete study of such a program came in March 1960. This further survey was completed in conjunction with the Department of External Affairs, Treasury Board, and the Department of Defence Production. The results were presented to the Defence Minister Pearkes on 16 August 1960.

The report proposed introducing submarines into service for training and operational purposes as part of the ship-replacement program. With regard to the operational characteristics, the navy recommended construction of six Barbel-class boats. These were conventional submarines of American design. It further recommended that production be undertaken in Canada at a rate of two ships a year, commencing in 1961. The entire program, including spares, essential stores, and support facilities, bore an estimated cost of $171.35 million. This recommendation was passed to the prime minister, who requested further study. The RCN was asked to assess the conventional building programs of other NATO navies and to ascertain from SACLANT whether conventional submarines could serve as one-for-one replacements of six overage anti-submarine surface escorts. On 9 January 1961 the reply to these questions was presented to the minister: SACLANT agreed to the one-for-one replacement, and the United Kingdom, France, the Netherlands, and West Germany were all committed to conventional efforts. Only the United States stated a clear preference for nuclear submarines.[48]

However, in an interim submission to the minister, on 27 October 1960, the chief of naval staff compared the costs of building the six Barbels in Canada, $164 million, to building six Oberon-class conventional boats in the United Kingdom. Of all available conventional submarine designs, only the Oberons approached the operational profile of the Barbels. For the same money the Oberons would allow the navy to obtain an additional four surface ASW vessels, at the cost of $22 million each. Although the chief of naval staff concluded that the Barbels would make the most effective ASW force, the usefulness of additional ASW ships could not be discounted.[49]

In the absence of ministerial decision, the RCN persisted with the Barbel proposal, taking it to the Chiefs of Staff Committee on 18 May 1961. The program for ship replacement then discussed included not only the six submarines, but an eight-vessel General Purpose Frigate program. Had both programs been adopted, the resulting fleet would have included twenty-six ASW escorts, nine submarines, and eight General Purpose Frigates. Once the submarines and GPFs had been completed, the RCN would commence a six-vessel ASW frigate program. This building program was markedly more ambitious than that proposed to the minister only nine months earlier.

## J.V. Brock's Wish Fleet

The most important event prompting the enlarged building program was the promise of additional money. That money came in accordance with a new NATO strategy articulated under the MC-70 policy. Within NATO strategy the MC-70 concept entailed for maritime forces a policy of forward engagement as developed by the RN and USN. Tactical ASW in the western Atlantic, while troubling for the navy, was neither the true end of NATO strategy, which was to deter aggression, nor the most efficacious means of counteracting Soviet submarine operations. Keeping the bear in its pen was better than dealing with it on the loose, at least acording to SACLANT's naval strategy, whether or not Canada participated.

Requirements for support of MC-70 had influenced NATO fleet planning since 1958, but Canada did not move to increase its participation in forward strike operations. Subtle pressures through SACLANT had been brought to bear on the Cabinet for the deployment of a second Canadian aircraft carrier. Whatever the Cabinet's reluctance to contemplate contributing to strike operations, the financial requirement proved decisive in killing further talk of a second carrier:[50] there were already enough financial, operational, and political difficulties dealing with the submarines in Canada's coastal area of responsibility. Nevertheless, in keeping with MC-70, the federal Cabinet agreed on 22 March 1960 to increase the Canadian defence budget from its present level of approximately $1.5 billion annually to $2 billion by fiscal year 1964/65.[51] Although

Cabinet agreed to implement the requirements of the Medium Term Defence Plan outlined in MC-70, the government did not make any new commitment to participate in strike operations. However, for the first time since the early 1950s, the planning for a balanced fleet could be undertaken by the navy. While real additional funding would only come in 1962,[52] the horizons for naval planning broadened immediately.

Within the navy, the long delays in obtaining approval for any fleet-replacement plan had caused grave concern. Concern also developed over the specialization in the ASW mission. General-purpose forces had been pared away in pursuit of a better ASW force at a time when allied navies were changing their approach to the submarine problem by building strike forces. Once it appeared to the Naval Staff that some form of submarine program would be authorized, attention turned to developing designs for follow-on surface vessels that would preserve the general surface capacity of the fleet.[53] Through 1960, with Cabinet approval of any submarine program uncertain, the Naval Staff still listed a low-cost "austerity" ASW frigate as the top-priority building requirement.[54] But then it was an "either/or" proposition, that is, either submarines or ASW frigates.[55]

However, the replacement program sent forward on 18 May 1961 discarded the austerity frigate and instead sought permission to undertake simultaneously the construction of a submarine and a new surface vessel program. This proposed building program was elaborated on in the *Ad Hoc Report on Naval Objectives* sent to the defence minister in December 1961. The report bore the hallmark of the incoming vice-chief of naval staff, Vice-Admiral Jeffry V. Brock.[56] By his own admission, it was the "first opportunity to put my own hands on the helm after all these years."[57] There is no doubt that Brock's forceful personality influenced the contents of the committee's final report.

The Brock Report clearly identified most of the recent trends in naval technology confronting the Naval Board. Transitions in air, surface, and sub-surface operational requirements were portrayed as calling for many new surface and sub-surface vessels. In sum, the report endorsed a fleet based on the concept of "cheap and many." To forestall serious deficiencies in the fleet's escort forces, Brock called for a replacement and modernization program. The future fleet needed replenishment vessels to allow the fighting units to stay within their patrol areas longer. The fighting fleet required six Barbel-class conventional submarines and eight general-purpose frigates. These frigates were to be capable of shore bombardment, limited air defence, and ASW missions. These ships would replace the Tribals. To replace the old, slow ocean-escort Prestonians and the aircraft carrier, Brock called for construction of a number of "heliporters." These would be frigates only marginally larger than the Prestonians but capable of operating three helicopters in the ASW role. These heliporters could also easily be converted to provide moderate troop-lift capacity, something that would be greatly reduced with the retirement of the *Bonaventure* in 1975. Finally, the RCN was to continue an extensive research program into unconventional ASW craft, such as hydrofoils and hovercraft. This new construction, argued the report, could be funded through a modest increase in naval appropriations. The funding goal was 1 per cent of the gross national product annually for fifteen years.[58] In dollar terms, the fifteen-year program called for naval capital expenditures to increase from $275 million to a peak in 1972 of $525 million.[59]

In a series of eleven meetings held between the last week of September and 12 December 1961, the Naval Board endorsed the Brock Report and approved its submission to the minister of defence and the Chiefs of Staff Committee. From then until early 1964, the report formed the fundamental planning document for fleet development.[60] Although neither the Chiefs of Staff Committee nor the federal Cabinet endorsed the full recommendations of the Brock Report, many of its recommendations were acted upon. In representing the outcomes of several divergent developments, the Brock Report did not mark a major departure for naval planning. Instead, it brought together most of what the Naval Board and government had already authorized or were about to authorize. However much Brock himself set the tone of the Brock Report, it was the developing submarine threat, the limitations of current underwater-surveillance techniques, and the almost prohibitive expense of modern surface ASW vessels that combined to suggest the force requirements and building program that this entailed. Although the Brock Report is given to diverse interpretations, its acceptance by the entire Naval Board demonstrated a shared belief that, unlike most other NATO navies, the RCN should not – or politically could not – restructure around carrier task groups or strike forces.[61] That it included a call for the maintenance of a general-purpose capacity does not contradict that finding.

The genesis of the General Purpose Frigate program illustrates these points. By early 1961, with impending approval of the submarine program, serious doubts were raised within the Naval Board about the advisability of building another specialized ASW ship. The Tribal-class destroyers, it was pointed out, would soon require replacement, and their disposal would greatly diminish the flexibility of the fleet. The vice-chief of naval staff, then Rear Admiral Ernest Tisdall, pointed out that he had a team working on a GPF design. With grave doubts about the replacement of the current carrier task force and the Tribal-class destroyers, the GPF promised only to maintain the RCN's general surface capacity. The GPF would have allowed a contribution to NATO's developing forward defence posture, but the surface flexibility sought by the Naval Board was aimed more towards the support of UN or other limited war operations. As the GPF design moved forward for consideration by the board, further decision on an ASW frigate was deferred.[62]

In developing the design of the GPF, the Naval Staff looked to similar work undertaken by the RN and USN.[63] Both of these navies developed general-purpose vessels both in response to new missile technologies and because, given a new concept of operations, they recognized the precarious place that strictly ASW forces occupied in their strategies. From the late 1950s onwards, the RN and USN increased their reliance on strike operations. For an attack on source missions or the imposition of near-source ASW barrier operations (designed to hold Soviet submarines in the eastern Atlantic), surface fire and anti-aircraft forces were essential.

Unlike the general-purpose vessels of the RN and USN, which were intended for littoral operations and regional wars, the Canadian General Purpose Frigate was earmarked for deployment in the eastern Atlantic. In seeking a Canadian GPF, the Naval Board did not put emphasis on its role in strike missions, but its air-defence capabilities would soon become an essential element in the defence of the Canadian carrier task force. The *Bonaventure*'s Banshee fighters were scheduled for retirement in 1962 and it had been decided that they would not be replaced. Consequently, steps were taken to plan the carrier's conversion into a commando or heliporter carrier.[64] The decision to develop the carrier along these lines marked a loss for the proponents of carrier aviation within the navy. It also marked a step away from operations in the eastern Atlantic and was closely tied to acquisition of the GPF. Maintenance costs of the naval air arm consumed approximately 20 per cent of the annual naval appropriation. It was a large share of the budget for a rather small force. The vice-chief of naval staff, Vice-Admiral Tisdall, certainly questioned the worth of maintaining the entire fixed-wing force, noting in a presentation to the incoming chief of naval staff that Australia planned to eliminate its carrier arm over 1962–63.[65] Funds not used to replace the Banshee fighters would be turned to new ship construction.[66] The limited air-defence capacity planned for the GPF would ensure that the navy retained operational capabilities in the eastern Atlantic.

In seeking authority for the GPF, its proponents marshalled two further arguments. First, they pointed to the GPFs potential contribution to United Nations operations and to brush-fire wars. Although the chairman of the Chiefs of Staff Committee had been wary of recommending construction of the GPF because it threatened to move the RCN towards participation in strike operations in the eastern Atlantic, the UN and small-war argument won him over.[67] The argument was not without merit. Canadian destroyers were among the first Canadian forces to participate in UN operations during the Korean War. In 1956 the RCN had transported a Canadian battalion to Suez for UN deployment. Given the contemporary UN military actions in the Congo, possible participation in brush-fires was not easily discounted. To emphasize the point, a sentence was inserted into the RCN long-term planning guide noting that the "successful deterrent in global war will tend to increase the likelihood of limited war."[68]

The second major argument marshalled in favour of the GPF was that the vessels would have a role in the RCN's newly developed concept of a balanced ASW force. By April 1961 the Naval Board had outlined the constituents of the ideal modern, balanced ASW fleet: one-fifth submarines, three-fifths ASW escorts, and one-fifth general-purpose ships. With Canada committed to provide a forty-three-ship ASW force to SACLANT, the required force mix would yield a fleet of twenty-six ASW escorts, nine ASW submarines, and eight General Purpose Frigates. This was the precise mix later included in the Brock Report.[69] A memorandum from the director of naval operations indicates at least one other primary interest. In light of the possible acquisition by Canada of nuclear weapons[70] and submarines, the guided-missile frigate would be far better for morale "than our obsession with the submarine threat." The present ASW forces could hold "the thin red line" until relieved by the submarines.[71] Through circuitous means, the Naval Staff succeeded in having SACLANT recommend just such a fleet structure to the Chiefs of Staff Committee when it generated new force requirements in support of the MC-70 Medium Term Defence Plan.[72]

All of these diverse strands came together in the building program proposed in early 1961. This proposal was presented to the Chiefs of Staff Committee in early May 1961, and the RCN gained permission to include the GPF in its annual estimates for fiscal year 1962/63. Consideration of the annual estimates came in November 1961, which also saw a detailed ship-replacement building program brought before the Chiefs of Staff Committee. As outlined in the submission prepared for the Cabinet Defence Committee, eighteen frigates and eleven Tribal-class destroyers would exceed their useful lives by 1970. Without their replacement, the RCN would have a net deficiency from agreed SACLANT goals of twenty-three ships by 1970. Given the scale of approaching obsolescence, the Naval Board argued that there was a greater need for submarines in reasonable numbers than for very capable nuclear submarines in small numbers. Two options were presented to the Cabinet Defence Committee. Programme A recommended construction of six Barbel-class submarines and eight General Purpose Frigates. Programme B recommended that if cost was the major concern, three Oberon submarines should be produced in the United Kingdom while detailed proposals for construction of advanced submarines in Canada were being developed. Eight GPFs, to be undertaken in Canadian shipyards, rounded out this proposal. The Cabinet Defence Committee recommended procurement of the Oberons and the GPFs. Cabinet agreed on 19 March 1962.[73] Following the finalization of arrangements regarding British defence purchases in Canada to offset the expenditure for the Oberons in the United Kingdom, the minister of defence announced the new naval construction program in the House on 11 April 1962.[74] After nearly four years of consideration, the ship-replacement program was signed and sealed. Delivery proved another matter.

## Farewell the Wish Fleet

The consequences of not undertaking any new warship construction in Canada since the early 1950s were being felt, and Cabinet agreed that GPFs should be built as a means of preserving the backbone of the nation's shipbuilding capacity. However, the design capacity built up within the industry for the St Laurent and Restigouche programs during the early 1950s had been all but lost by the time the GPF program was begun. None of the vessels undertaken by the navy in the late 1950s, including the Mackenzie- and Annapolis-class vessels still building, demanded the retention of the design staffs essential for this major departure in warship construction.[75] But before the industry's diminished technical capacity made itself apparent, the technical deficiencies of the government agencies responsible for construction became clear with telling effect.

Neither the RCN nor the Department of Defence Production (the former responsible for detailed design work, the latter for contract and program management) demonstrated that they possessed the requisite technical staff or the knowledge needed to control program costs. Time was against their chances of gaining that expertise. The defence minister's announcement to the House had indicated that construction would commence before the end of 1963. Both agencies found themselves short of the skilled engineers and draftsmen necessary to finalize the design. Compounding this shortage were design changes voted by the Naval Board. Delays and costs quickly mounted. By December 1962 the keel-laying was postponed to July 1964, and vessel costs had risen from $33 million per ship to $36.2 million. Then the Department of Defence Production, under pressure from the Treasury Board, insisted on establishing the projected costs for the entire program. It was determined that an additional $150 to $200 million would have to be found. The RCN had chosen the USN's Tartar surface-to-air missile system when it was still under development, and in May 1963 word came that this system was experiencing major delays and that the USN would have to commit $250 million to solving the problem. To keep to the replacement schedule set by the minister's statement, the RCN tried to shorten the design development phase by choosing the component suppliers it preferred. The Department of Defence Production balked at these proposals. Further, in investigating how the RCN devised its original estimates, Defence Production learned that the Naval Technical Services had relied simply on the manufacturers' "ball park" figures, which turned out to be completely insufficient for completing designs or for forming the basis for contracts. By early 1963 the GPF program estimates had risen from $275 million to between $450 and $500 million, and design refinement was still at an early stage.[76] The growing concern of the Department of Finance and Treasury Board was soon shared by a new government, Diefenbaker's Conservatives having lost a vote of confidence in the House on 5 February 1963.

The very public nuclear weapons acquisition controversy had toppled Diefenbaker's administration. This ensured that the incoming Liberal administration of Lester B. Pearson would focus on matters of defence. The "sixty days of decision" that Pearson promised the electorate heralded a commitment to action and reform. The reforms set in train took much longer than sixty days to implement, but the new minister of defence, Paul Hellyer, turned his immediate attention to the GPF program. In May a program review began. In June all government capital programs were suspended, pending a full review of government expenditures. By early October the Cabinet had agreed to cancel the general-purpose frigate. The cancellation cannot be explained as simply a response to the expected cost overruns. Rather, it was directly tied to the more fundamental reforms of defence policy and defence spending sought by the new government.

The nuclear weapons controversy had severely undermined public confidence in Canada's defence policy and defence commitments. In part to alleviate that confusion and in part to rationalize for the public the reforms already drafted in the mind of the defence minister, the new Liberal government formed the Special Committee on Defence. Under the chairmanship of Maurice Sauvé, the committee commenced public hearings in June 1963. By October 1963 the GPF program was being debated before the committee and in the press. Much of the public controversy over the issue had been sparked by retired commodore James Plomer's article "The Gold-Braid Mind Is Destroying Our Navy," which appeared in *Maclean's* in September 1963.[77] Plomer elaborated on his criticisms of the RCN in subsequent statements, especially in his call to the Sauvé committee on 10 October 1963 for more submarines and ASW frigates. In response, Chief of Naval Staff, Admiral Herbert S. Rayner, was sent before the committee to defend the entire building program. He did this several days after the Cabinet had already approved its cancellation![78] The cancellation became public a few days later when the defence minister rose in the House on 25 October. The following explanations were offered: the GPFs too expensive, too specialized, and too inadequate in ASW operations to fulfil Canadian needs.

Given the management problems demonstrated during the early phases of the GPF program, the issue of expense carried the ring of truth. However, despite the cost escalations noted above, neither the navy nor the Department of Defence Production had argued for cancellation of the program. The navy was prepared to meet the costs within its proposed budget even if that entailed reducing orders to only four ships, but even that proved unacceptable to the new government. The entire naval budget was at issue. The minister of finance, Walter Gordon, was insisting that the defence appropriations be reduced from the projected $2 billion required under the MC-70 Medium Term Defence Plan to $1.5 billion, and be maintained at that level for three years. Well before the public debate over the GPF, Hellyer had begun exploring major reductions in the defence appropriation. The RCN was asked to develop a plan to live within a budget of $280 million for three years, with allowance for 3 per cent growth in the last two years. For a navy that had planned on a budget of $300 million for fiscal year 1963/64, $335 million for 1964/65, and $425 for 1965/66, the squeeze placed on procurement was acute. The operations and maintenance expenditures alone for 1962/63 accounted for $218 million.[79]

In its response, the navy recommended postponing the GPF program for one year, borrowing submarines from the United States instead of building the Oberons, and deferring the major refits already planned for the fleet. In outlining these cuts to the full Cabinet, the chief of naval staff pointed out that the RCN would effect savings of $280 million as requested by the minister by taking $197 million from capital programs over the next two and a half years, the balance to be reduced by cutting the uniformed strength from 21,324 to 20,500 and removing four Tribal-class destroyers from service. By 1970 the RCN would be reduced to twenty-seven warships, sixteen of which would be obsolete and overdue for replacement, and eleven of the twenty St Laurent/Restigouche/Mackenzie-class vessels would be lacking the most effective ASW equipment. The ramifications of the proposed cuts were spelt out in detail to the Cabinet, wrote Hellyer, so that the Cabinet could adequately judge the "order of magnitude."[80] Cancellation would yield a fleet "incapable of meeting current NATO commitments." There would be no "satisfactory anti-air defence for the fleet." SACLANT considered that the move would reduce the effectiveness of the Canadian carrier ASW group. The twenty-three surface vessels of Second World War construction would remain in service for years past their effective life.[81]

The Cabinet minutes indicate that the prime minister was moved by the passion of the arguments presented by the service chiefs as they outlined the consequences of reducing the defence appropriation. But the minutes also record Pearson's conclusion: "In order to get public support for the defence programme, there would have to be radical change in its character."[82] The GPF took the first real blow in this long process of radical reform.[83] Although these cuts represented the first of major reforms to come, Finance Minister Gordon noted the excellent job Paul Hellyer was doing in reversing the upward curve in defence expenditures. He observed that this move was all the more difficult in light of it being done "before long-term policy decisions were reached."[84]

Regardless of the steps being taken within the navy to manage its own decline, the minister had determined on a course of action whose ultimate aim remained uncertain. Where or when the reductions would cease was still unknown when, on 1 August 1964, in accordance with the White Paper, the Chiefs of Staff Committee, independent service heads, the Naval Board, and the Naval Staff were struck down as the first step in integrating agencies within the Department of National Defence. The White Paper argued that the new force posture made sense given the total capabilities of the "entire group of NATO nations and ... the Alliance objectives of creating balanced collective forces."[85] For the navy, this meant doing more with less. Operation "Cut-back" as the defunct vice-chief of naval staff called it, continued. How the now headless navy fared after 1964, however, is beyond the scope of this chapter.[86]

The appreciable pressures resulting from the increased Soviet submarine presence and the demand-side pressure imposed by a changing NATO strategy led to the appearance that the navy had achieved real funding increases. That those systems' designs reflected the latest of allied technologies and capabilities must be accepted. That they had been designed to support a forward defence strategy not accepted by the government proved to be only a short-lived problem, solved by the Liberals' reforms.

The search for identity through a large fleet structured to provide direct support for operations well beyond the Canadian coastal area had helped fuel the new government's reordering of defence priorities. The questionable worth of ASW in the western Atlantic underscores the point that, strategically, the new Liberal Cabinet rendered the RCN a sop to Canada's allies, specifically as a contribution to deterrence. This is the charitable interpretation, thus making a virtue of the necessities that sprang from the budget cap imposed by the minister of finance before the long-term policy decisions were made. For the navy, the ASW mission became an imposed identity.

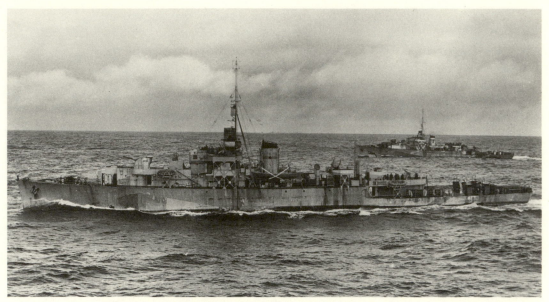

The River-class frigates HMCS *LaSalle* (foreground) and *Coaticook* from the Support Group EG-27 in December 1944. The next month this group was involved in action resulting from *U-1232*'s bold attack on convoy BX-141 in the Halifax approaches. [DHist/DND]

"Killed in Action." Public-relations poster distributed in memory of the crew of HMCS *Saguenay*, 1 December 1940. [DHist/DND]

Newspaper sketch commemorating the sinking of HMCS *Valleyfield* on 7 May 1944. This was one of a series by celebrated Halifax newspaper cartoonist Chambers that marked the loss of each Canadian warship. [DHist/DND]

Four future chiefs of naval staff, at Plymouth (UK), in the summer of 1944: (l. to r.) Lieutenant-Commander H.S. Raynor, Rear-Admiral H.E. Reid, Commander H.G. DeWolf, and Captain H.T.W. Grant. At the time these officers were, respectively, captain of the destroyer HMCS *Huron*, head of the RCN mission in Washington, captain of the destroyer HMCS *Haida*, and captain of the British cruiser HMS *Enterprise*. [NA]

The Bangor minesweeper HMCS *Esquimalt*, sunk by *U-190* on 16 April 1945 off Halifax with heavy loss of life. She was the last Canadian warship sunk in enemy action. [DHist/DND]

The Canadian crew of German submarine *U-190* that had sunk HMCS *Esquimalt*. The U-boat surrendered to the Canadian navy on 11 May 1945, three days after the capitulation of Germany. After brief service in the Canadian navy as HMCS *U-190*, it was ceremonially sunk on 21 October 1947. [Maritime Command Museum, Halifax]

The Tribal-class destroyer HMCS *Micmac*, the first Canadian-built destroyer. Severely damaged in a collision on 16 July 1947, she served as a trials and training ship until paid off on 31 March 1964. Note the experimental mounting of a squid anti-submarine mortar in "A" position, and a quadruple 40 mm Bofors anti-aircraft weapon in "B." [DHist/DND]

HMCS *Labrador*, built in recognition of the growing strategic importance of the Arctic region, breaking ice while westbound through Bellot Strait in 1957. Her records show that "on this passage much four-engine ice was encountered." Paid off 22 November 1957 after only three years in service, and transferred to the Department of Transport. [DHist/DND]

The 6-inch-gun cruiser HMCS *Quebec* (ex-HMS *Uganda*) alongside at HMC Dockyard, Halifax, with the light fleet carrier HMCS *Magnificent* in the background. The incomplete span of the Angus L. Macdonald Bridge dates the photograph circa 1953–54. [DHist/DND]

The new Annapolis-class helicopter destroyer HMCS *Nipigon* entering Halifax in May 1964. Alongside at HMC Dockyard are seen many other vessels, including the aircraft carrier HMCS *Bonaventure*, Tribal-class destroyers, St Laurent-class destroyer escorts, Prestonian-class ocean escorts, and escort maintenance ships. [DHist/DND]

Artist's conception of a proposed design for a General Purpose Frigate, for which the navy had great expectations in the late 1950s and early 1960s. A new Liberal government cancelled the program in 1964. [DND]

The Great Lakes Training Centre in 1964. Here the crew of the "minor war vessel" HMCS *Scatari*, operating out of docks at the Reserve Unit HMCS *Star*, Hamilton, Ontario, with gate vessels HMCS *Porte St Jean*, and *Porte St Louis*, and the occasional frigate. [DHist/DND]

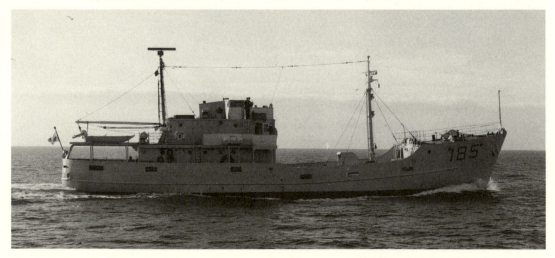

Reserve training on the west coast with gate vessels HMCS *Porte Quebec* (shown here), HMCS *Porte de la Reine*, and (on return from the Department of Transport in 1974) HMCS *Porte Dauphine*. Named after the fortress gates of Quebec City and launched between 1950 and 1952, all ships of this class are being paid off in 1996 to make way for the new Maritime Coastal Defence Vessels. [DHist/DND]

"Mohammad's Junk" (Victoria *Times-Colonist*, 20 September 1990), a public image of Canada's navy when mobilizing for deployment to the Persian Gulf in September 1990. Courtesy of Adrian Raeside.

The Canadian Persian Gulf task force alongside at Dubai, United Arab Emirates. The operational support ships HMCS *Protecteur* (right foreground), with the DDH-280 destroyer HMCS *Athabaskan* and the Improved Restigouche-class destroyer-escort HMCS *Terra Nova*. Note use of radar-absorbent material (RAM) padding on *Protecteur*'s superstructure for anti-missile defence. [DHist/DND]

HMCS *Protecteur*, the only operational support ship in the central Gulf, refuelling the battleship USS *Wisconsin* on 26 November 1990. She proved her worth in the Gulf, among other things by refuelling the ships of many Coalition navies. [DHist/DND]

The CPF (Canadian Patrol Frigate) HMCS *Toronto*, one of Canada's newest Canadian-built class of warship, departs her namesake city in the summer of 1993, during her commissioning cruise. [DHist/DND]

# PART THREE

# The Navy as a Fighting Service

# · 9 ·

## A Minute Bletchley Park: Building a Canadian Naval Operational Intelligence Centre, 1939–1943

CATHERINE E. ALLAN

Military communications systems are designed to facilitate command and control, and technological advances in the 1920s and 1930s steadily improved the ability of naval shore authorities to communicate with units at sea over great distances. Technology also made communications more vulnerable to interception and analysis. Exploiting enemy communications systems to ascertain hostile intentions and force dispositions – signals intelligence (known as sigint) – had proved useful in the First World War.[1] Interwar advances in long-distance communications increased the number of targets for electronic eavesdropping and expanded the suite of activities that produced sigint. Research and development facilities devoted considerable effort to improving protective measures such as manual and mechanical code and cypher systems, and developing countermeasures and counter-countermeasures. Navies in particular recognized the value of operational intelligence (opint), which is collated from a wide range of sources, including interception and analysis of enemy signals ("Y" operations), high-frequency direction finding (HF/DF), and the products of cryptanalysis. They perceived the ability to gather, analyse, and disseminate useful and timely opint to commanders at sea as a powerful force-multiplier. So vital was this resource considered by the Allies that the Royal Canadian Navy's hard-won expertise in operational intelligence provided the basis for its successful bid for an operational command in the northwest Atlantic.

The RCN's operational intelligence capability was the product of pre-war Admiralty planning and wartime guidance, and a long but successful learning curve. As with the rest of the RCN, the new intelligence branch strove to overcome interwar dependence on the Royal Navy. Its realization of full partnership with allied operational intelligence centres parallels the RCN's struggle to earn a credible operational role in the Battle of the Atlantic. Between 1939 and 1943, the Canadian navy assembled most of the elements for an operational intelligence centre capable of locating enemy submarines and diverting Canadian and Allied convoys from danger areas.

### The Foreign Intelligence Section and the East Coast Intercept and Direction-Finding System

The Royal Canadian Navy had had no independent sigint capability prior to 1939. Its First World War and interwar direction-finding resources had been lost in 1922 when stations assigned these duties reverted to the Department of Marine and Fisheries.[2] Then, in 1936, the stations were transferred to the newly created Department of Transport. Prewar Canadian naval intelligence had existed in an imperial context, for the RN had built its wartime sigint plan on centralized analysis and dissemination. As part of its "World Wide Intelligence" organization, the Admiralty had established a limited naval intelligence capability in Canada in the person of the director of naval intelligence (DNI), in Ottawa.[3] Intercept stations operated at Gordon Head near Victoria, BC, and at Rockcliffe in Ottawa; all raw material was sent to the Admiralty in England.[4] Intelligence staff officers assigned to each Canadian coast supervised ship-movement reporting officers.[5]

The principle of centralized Admiralty control continued while the first steps were taken to establish the wartime organization in Canada. The Canadian navy's Commander Eric S. Brand, RN, assumed his duties as the DNI in the summer of 1939, supervising naval intelligence activities in Canada. All planning, tasking, and priority-setting, however, were to remain within the purview of the Admiralty.[6] Brand's mission included establishing a direction-finding and wireless intercept organization that could provide raw material to the Admiralty's Operational Intelligence Centre and disseminate information to RN operational authorities in his geographical portion of the worldwide system.[7] The Department of Transport possessed the only organization that could undertake these activities, and it began naval assignments at the request of the British High Commission in mid-August 1939.[8]

The Admiralty provided Brand with a retired Royal Naval Reserve (RNR) officer to establish and supervise a sigint section: Lieutenant-Commander Jean Maurice Barbé Pougnet de Marbois. This colourful officer was called up from his teaching duties at Upper Canada College in

August 1939, and by 10 September he headed the new Foreign Intelligence Section (FIS).[9] De Marbois had served in the Royal Navy during the First World War on transfer from the British army, and he had been assigned to the Naval Intelligence Division in the Admiralty from 1917 until 1923, when he retired.[10] He faced a considerable challenge in his new post. For guidance, he had the latest Admiralty instructions for high-frequency direction finding and the wireless telegraph (WT) intercept file handed over by the director of plans, Commander Frank L. Houghton. His most important resource, the Department of Transport stations, was less than ideal. Many stations retained their primary responsibility of navigational assistance to transatlantic flights. Sites and equipment were not up to the new taskings. Peacetime operations were a far cry from those required in wartime to monitor and record sporadic, elusive, often breathtakingly brief, distant enemy transmissions on dozens of constantly changing frequencies; nor were they up to taking bearings on ships that did not ask to be found. The Department of Transport did provide one essential ingredient: a communications system capable of passing bearings to Naval Service Headquarters (NSHQ). Naval Service Headquarters had limited communications resources, but Transport had meteorological reporting circuits, and its Radio Branch station was fortuitously located above NSHQ in the Robinson Building in Ottawa.[11] Command and control followed the communications: the RCN agreed that Transport would direct the stations' activities.[12]

De Marbois began by creating a record system in the headquarters, recruiting officers for his staff, retraining civilian operators, and acquiring equipment. He also requested that the British Air Ministry permit Botwood airport in Newfoundland to be assigned naval direction-finding duties.[13] So far, the Admiralty had directed almost every action taken, including the establishment of a joint naval–Department of Transport intercept and DF station near Halifax. The Admiralty further requested that bearings from Canadian stations be passed, not to the Admiralty, but to the headquarters of the Royal Navy's North America and West Indies Station in Bermuda. In the Caribbean, a small plotting centre and an intercept station were to be established near a DF station then being erected. The RCN would neither control HF/DF and intercept resources nor coordinate assignments and the flow of information in the western Atlantic.[14] More significantly, the Bermuda sigint facilities would be co-located with an RN operational headquarters.

Admiralty-directed expansion on the western side of the Atlantic was intended to conform to the concept of centralized control. Construction of the new HF/DF station near Halifax at Hartlen Point, however, became a catalyst for major change in the east coast direction-finding system and ultimately for reporting relationships with the Admiralty. The

Department of Transport conceived the new station as a model for future Canadian-built HF/DF and intercept stations. It rejected the Admiralty's model, which used one intercept station to control a number of HF/DF stations. Instead, Transport co-located both HF/DF and intercept to overcome the limitations imposed by Canadian geography and a poor communications infrastructure, problems not faced in the tightly knit UK system. Brand approved the new station's set-up and directed the staff signal officer (SSO) in Halifax, Lieutenant-Commander George (Sam) Worth, to monitor its construction and arrange suitable communications. Worth was a hard-drinking officer who had left the RCN in the early 1930s in order to avoid court martial, and he harboured no love for the RN. He was qualified in both intelligence and signals, and was one of the few officers in the RCN to have completed the Long Signals course. He understood that Ottawa's ability to task Hartlen Point's intercept station depended on good communications. Worth attempted to use Transport's station arrangement to exploit the proximity of potentially useful information on enemy dispositions for operational purposes. He believed that good communications for Hartlen Point were inseparable from Commanding Officer, Atlantic Coast's (COAC's) requirement for timely information, and he discarded any solution that could cause delay. He accordingly argued that Hartlen Point should be the central and controlling station of a system of direction-finding and intercept stations for the western Atlantic, and that Bermuda be rejected as a viable control station. He shifted the communications priority to the link between Hartlen Point and Naval Service Headquarters rather than between Halifax and Bermuda as the Admiralty desired and Brand had agreed.[15] He intended to provide a communications infrastructure for a Canadian- and Newfoundland-based DF and intercept system under Canadian direction that could support a Canadian operations staff.[16]

Worth's communications plan – particularly that of providing adequate links to Newfoundland – took years to complete, but his vision of a Canadian-controlled HF/DF and intercept system was realized within months, in spite of Brand's vigorous opposition.[17] De Marbois came to endorse Worth's view. He ultimately accepted Worth's assessment that distance and overly complex arrangements precluded efficient control of western Atlantic stations from Bermuda, and that in case Bermuda were cut off, at least a skeleton "Y" organization was required in either Ottawa or Halifax, based on Hartlen Point. Ottawa would pass bearings directly to the Admiralty. De Marbois's January 1940 tour of the east coast stations with Lieutenant W.S.L. Bartram, RN, the officer who would take over the sigint operation at Daniel's Head, Bermuda, proved to be the turning-point. As long as he believed that the RN officer's mission was to assist Naval Service Headquarters in speeding up communication of bearings to the

Admiralty, de Marbois supported Bartram.[18] His cooperation disappeared once it became clear that the Daniel's Head station was to control and therefore limit the Canadian effort. The argument raged for months while de Marbois continued to improve the productivity of the Foreign Intelligence Section: more than a dozen bearings were being passed daily to the Admiralty, a short-wave radio on top of the headquarters building monitored foreign broadcasts, and intercepts were being recorded at the Ottawa station.[19] However, the DF system was still incapable of producing credible fixes, for technical problems continued to plague Transport's stations and communications problems remained unresolved. For example, the station at Strathburn, Ontario, lacked a recorder or a clock, had no spare tubes for its only receiver, and was sending its intercepts by rural mail.[20]

In March 1940 de Marbois reported that the Canadian east coast stations formed a DF unit with Hartlen Point as the controlling station.[21] His statement was misleading, for the question of control remained unresolved. Meanwhile, Vice-Admiral Sir Charles E. Kennedy-Purvis, Commander-in-Chief, America and West Indies Station (C-in-C AWI), continued to make every effort to merge the Bermuda intercept and plotting organization with the DF stations in Canada.[22] His aim was to ensure that operational intelligence arrangements paralleled operations in the western Atlantic, that is, that they were RN-directed.[23] Bartram and de Marbois met and reached a compromise. Daniel's Head would control the whole system, which was to include Caribbean and South American stations, while Hartlen Point would be "sub-control" for the stations in Canada and Newfoundland.[24] Over the next few weeks, communications between Bermuda and Hartlen Point were tested successfully, and Bartram remained convinced that his scheme would work. The Canadian portion of the network continued to have problems, however. Bearings from two stations, St-Hubert and Botwood, were passed to Hartlen Point through Ottawa, while communications between Bermuda and St-Hubert, and between Bermuda and Newfoundland, remained unsatisfactory. Naval Service Headquarters proceeded to implement its own scheme. Captain L.W. Murray, the deputy chief of naval staff (DCNS), informed Kennedy-Purvis in May that a naval liaison officer (NLO) was to take over the Hartlen Point station, after which Naval Service Headquarters would send bearings directly to the Admiralty, repeated to Bermuda, and, "for the defence of Canada," to COAC and the RN commander in Halifax.[25] COAC operations staff would continue to plot their own bearings. This was no less than a bombshell, for it revealed NSHQ's intention to decentralize analysis and to disseminate the products of its own intercept and DF, both to the Admiralty and to operational headquarters in Canada.[26]

Kennedy-Purvis argued for centralization, emphasizing that only the Admiralty, with the breadth of information at its disposal, could gauge an enemy unit's position.[27] He was correct. The facilities in the western Atlantic could not match the Admiralty's Operational Intelligence Centre (OIC), even in calculating accurate fixes based on bearings from a large number of well-placed HF/DF stations. The Foreign Intelligence Section had not earned the right to supply sigint for use by Canadian headquarters. The Canadians did win concessions, however, when Worth's fears about Bermuda's ability to control the Canadian chain were realized.

In late August 1940 the undersea cable between Bermuda and Halifax broke. For six weeks, no bearings could be exchanged except by wireless, and the operators at Daniel's Head could not handle the extra workload.[28] The cable was restored on 9 October, and by then even Brand accepted that Daniel's Head could not exercise control over the northern portion of the network. In a personal letter to Captain Humphrey R. Sandwith, who headed the Admiralty's "Y" and DF section, Brand wrote that Hartlen Point had not only operated well without Bermuda's "interference," but had, in his opinion, operated better. He also acknowledged the value of the Canadian concept of co-located DF and intercept stations and suggested that, given Canadian geography and the brevity of German signals, a network controlled by a single station was not viable.[29] For Brand, there was no question that the Admiralty should continue to collate bearings and determine fixes.

De Marbois continued to pursue the goal of establishing a "Y" centre in Ottawa. The Foreign Intelligence Section still had a small staff of two officers and two civil servants, and its responsibilities were relatively unchanged from September 1939.[30] He used his analysis of Canadian station statistics and those of the RN's Far Eastern Direction Finding Organization (FEDO) to further his aims.[31] Though the FEDO had successfully overcome great distances between stations and from the Admiralty, de Marbois lacked its qualified naval operators. He was making progress, however. The Foreign Intelligence Section regularly received bearings from all western Atlantic stations, and the accuracy of its submarine plotting improved.[32] De Marbois trained and despatched a naval liaison officer to Newfoundland in January 1941 and another to Esquimalt. By the end of 1940, an impressive number of intercepts had been sent to the Admiralty. The east coast stations, including Newfoundland, had passed 1,685 by cable and 10,270 by safe hand; Gordon Head on Vancouver Island, now forwarding traffic to Ottawa as well as to London, had sent even more.[33]

Early in 1941 de Marbois met with Kennedy-Purvis and his staff. All agreed that Naval Service Headquarters would pass HF/DF fixes rather than bearings to the Admiralty,[34] but Kennedy-Purvis proposed that Bermuda direct Ottawa's German assignments and that Ottawa pass bearings to Bermuda. C-in-C AWI's "Y" staff would analyse western Atlantic results and forward its report to the Admiralty. Kennedy-Purvis was proposing no less than that Bermuda become the "Y" intelligence centre for the western Atlantic. De Marbois objected and requested that either arrangements remain unchanged or that all HF/DF analysis and "Y" intelligence be centred in Ottawa.[35]

The implications of C-in-C AWI's proposal were recognized by Rear Admiral Percy Nelles, the Canadian chief of naval staff. He corresponded directly with Kennedy-Purvis and explained that Canadian "Y" efforts had to focus on "anything and everything affecting our enemies and potential enemies which is passed by any form of wireless telegraphy communications." Given the great distances involved and the ensuing delays, he could not accept Bermuda control of such important operational information. He argued that the RCN's partnerships with the Royal Canadian Mounted Police (RCMP) and the Canadian Army, its new western stations, and its effective use of western Atlantic data supported a mandate for an Ottawa regional centre for German "Y."[36] Kennedy-Purvis continued to press in favour of Bermuda setting watches on German frequencies for all western Atlantic stations.[37] He did not accept the FIS's claims of effectiveness and indeed accused Canada's NSHQ of trying to supplant the Admiralty's authority.[38]

Nelles supported his position with impressive statistics and acknowledged Admiralty primacy. But he did add a telling argument: "There may come a time when because of invasion, threat of invasion, interruption of communications or lack of facilities that it will be impossible for the Admiralty to receive or transmit HF DF intelligence ... it would be negligent to remain unprepared."[39] He noted as well that Naval Service Headquarters did not intend that local analysis become the basis for operational action except in special circumstances. By May the affair was all but resolved when the head of Admiralty's "Y" and DF section, Captain Sandwith, granted approval for NSHQ in Ottawa to send its own fixes and analysis to the Admiralty. He had acted on behalf of Rear Admiral J.W. Clayton, the deputy director of the Admiralty's Intelligence Centre. Clayton then visited Kennedy-Purvis in Bermuda, and in June Kennedy-Purvis visited Ottawa and finalized arrangements for the western Atlantic system.[40]

The Foreign Intelligence Section emerged from this with a strong mandate. While the Admiralty would exercise overall coordination by identifying which frequencies were to be watched, Naval Service Headquarters in Ottawa would allocate duties to its stations. C-in-C AWI would not assign DF watches for Canadian or Newfoundland stations.[41] Ottawa was now a regional "Y" centre. The right to promulgate fixes to operational headquarters and units would follow expansion and reorganization.

## The Expansion Phase: June 1941–Fall 1942

With the questions of control and direction apparently settled, de Marbois proceeded with development. He organized the Foreign Intelligence Section into three sub-sections: field officers (that is, the naval liaison officers); research officers, who were concerned with improving equipment and methods; and watchkeepers, who were in charge of plotting and traffic analysis.[42] De Marbois recruited and trained most of his officers. He sought skilled linguists, such as his deputy, C. Herbert Little, recruited from Upper Canada College. Some, such as B.C. MacDonald, also had qualifications in science or mathematics; others, such as Charles W. Skarstedt, had communications experience. De Marbois aimed to establish a centre for "thorough and intelligent study of enemy telecommunications ... and promulgation of intelligence from these studies." He had not lost sight of his goal. He planned to expand from four intercept stations to twelve, in part by despatching naval ratings to augment six Royal Canadian Air Force (RCAF) facilities that were available for naval as well as air force assignments.[43]

The first RCN-built and -operated station, at Harbour Grace, Newfoundland, became operational in July 1941. This station was largely the work of Lieutenant R.J. Williams, the naval liaison officer, Newfoundland, whom de Marbois had recruited from the Department of Transport. Still, the new arrangements with the RCAF and the continued use of Transport stations represented the only way to augment the Foreign Intelligence Section's capability to collect raw material promptly, gather intercepts and bearings that it could analyse, as well as tackle the Admiralty's assignments. De Marbois's selection of some RCAF and Transport intercept stations located in British Columbia may indicate his conviction that Naval Service Headquarters should also be conducting "Y" operations against Japan, even though that power had not yet declared war.[44]

The RCN still lacked the sophisticated techniques and up-to-date equipment needed to refine and broaden the scope of its "Y" operations. Significantly, these resources were not available in Canada. Two related events nonetheless ensured continued growth and improvement. The first was the increasing intensity and close proximity to Canada of U-boat activity. The second was the Admiralty's recognition of the importance of an effective Canadian sigint organization.

Following the resolution of the relationship between Bermuda and Ottawa, Sandwith invited Brand to send one of his officers to visit the RN's "Y" operation in Britain.[45] Recognizing that any expansion would require advice on training as well as on the latest equipment and techniques, Naval Service Headquarters seized the opportunity. The Foreign Intelligence Section believed that the purpose of the Admiralty assistance was to equip the Canadian system so that it could expand to "become the Admiralty's OIC in case the English system [became] inoperable."[46] NSHQ sent Lieutenant J.R. Foster, a Royal Canadian Naval Volunteer Reserve (RCNVR) officer with a background as a telegraphist and radio technician.[47] His return in August 1941 marks the beginning of major FIS expansion under the Admiralty's guidance. The Admiralty permitted Foster to see everything relevant to Canada's increased contribution, although he was not initiated into ULTRA or other higher-level intelligence-gathering techniques. He visited all of Sandwith's departments in the Admiralty's combined signals and intelligence section known as DSD/NID 9; as well as the Signal School at Haslemere, he attended the Scarborough "Y" and DF station and the Flowerdown experimental wireless station.

Foster's report dealt with personnel, equipment, and techniques. He devoted the major portion of the report to new equipment and research and development. He included notes on development and operation of cathode ray direction-finding equipment, radar range and bearing equipment, radio finger-printing (TINA) and range estimation equipment, as well as remote control techniques, multiple receivers, and ionospheric research. Foster also saw the direct benefits of research and development when he visited the plotting rooms and the special section of the Operational Intelligence Centre. At his request, the Admiralty forwarded a copy of its DF classification system to help increase plotting accuracy.[48] It also supplied Naval Service Headquarters with UK stations' bearings on enemy units operating in the northwest Atlantic so that the Foreign Intelligence Section could assess the accuracy of its own stations. At the same time, the FIS began twenty-four-hour operation for plotting and traffic analysis and increased liaison with both the army and the RCAF.[49]

The Admiralty's interest and assistance realized both short- and long-term dividends. Naval Service Headquarters ordered new DF equipment as well as TINA and range estimation equipment during Foster's visit.[50] The Foreign Intelligence Section recognized the potential not only of the new equipment, but of research and development, and acted on Foster's recommendation to enlist the assistance of the National Research Council (NRC) and create a naval research department. Foster had reported on British advances in ionospheric research, and the Admiralty had emphasized the importance of collecting ionospheric data to achieve more accurate plotting.[51] One successful joint effort, the so-called P'f project, produced NRC-designed and -built ionospheric research equipment that was installed at Chelsea, Quebec, providing the FIS with up-to-date information on atmospheric conditions affecting high-frequency propagation.[52] At the behest of the Admiralty and in response to the increasingly tense situation in the Far East, the Foreign Intelligence Section also augmented its Pacific operations. De Marbois formed a Far Eastern

Intelligence (FEI) sub-section in the summer of 1941 and recruited a Japanese linguist, D.R.H. (Ross) MacDonald, to head it.

The new capability was acquired only a few months before war broke out in the Pacific in December. By then, the Foreign Intelligence Section had grown significantly to include six sub-sections: Wireless Telegraphy Intelligence, DF Analysis, Far Eastern Intelligence, Research, Field Officers, and Training. Its school opened in November to prepare special operators for "Y" and DF duties in Canadian stations, and the Foreign Intelligence Section began providing regular bulletins and summaries on enemy procedures and unit identifiers to its operators and sigint analyses to Canadian naval and air staffs.[53] The section also began cooperating with the United States Navy's east and west coast DF stations, while de Marbois finalized arrangements with Washington to exchange fixes from Pacific DF analysis.[54]

In spite of the news from the Far East, the new year began on a high note for the Foreign Intelligence Section: the Admiralty granted the NSHQ authority to promulgate fixes to all western Atlantic units.[55] The Admiralty introduced improvements to ensure security and quick transmission of "Y" material; Typex (or Type X), a security device that scrambled land-telegraph signals, was used in trials between Australia and London, and fielded shortly afterwards.[56] The Admiralty also directed the Canadians to cooperate with the USN's new "Y" effort, and ultimately, the FIS transferred control of its entire west coast operation to the USN.[57] The Far Eastern Direction Finding Organisation, which was in disarray as a result of Japanese successes in Hong Kong and Singapore, relinquished its responsibilities for evaluation, classification, and promulgation of bearings to the USN in February 1942.[58] There is no evidence that either de Marbois or the Naval Staff resisted these steps at the time, possibly because the Far Eastern Direction Finding Organisation had controlled the operation from the beginning and the RCN's ships had a less significant role in the war against Japan than in the struggle with Germany.[59] In any case, the mandate of the Far Eastern Intelligence sub-section was nebulous, and poor communications with the west coast precluded effective NSHQ control of the west coast stations.

Although the Admiralty was interested in furthering sigint cooperation among the three allies, particularly for high-grade cryptography, it had some difficulty dealing with the USN.[60] The United States had not centralized its sigint efforts, nor did operations staffs in the navy department acknowledge the need for a U-boat tracking room in Washington, in spite of the major successes enjoyed by U-boats off the American east coast. In April 1942 the Admiralty despatched Commander Rodger Winn to convert Admiral Ernest J. King, Commander-in-Chief of the US Fleet (COMINCH). He was successful.[61] His visit coincided with the joint

British-American-Canadian sigint conference in Washington that facilitated the full exchange of raw material from Canadian and American sigint operations. Captain Sandwith headed this mission to Washington and Ottawa.[62] He did so with a mandate to bring Canadian and American sigint authorities up to date about British sigint developments, to learn about the American and Canadian organizations, and to arrange for mutual cooperation.[63] The discussions covered wireless telegraphy interception; WT intelligence, equipment, and antenna systems; special types of WT transmissions; shipborne interception; descrambling radio telephony; and radio countermeasures.

The "Y" Conference in Washington,[64] attended by representatives of all Allied sigint organizations, produced a series of agreements that coordinated British, Canadian, and American intercept and DF programs – including exchanges of intercepted raw material and DF bearings.[65] More significantly, the Allies agreed to establish two U-boat tracking rooms on the western side of the Atlantic.[66] They also allocated interception assignments for the western Atlantic and agreed that Canadian and American "Y" organizations would exchange inferences.[67] All would expand their operations: the Foreign Intelligence Section, for example, was to grow from 425 to 700 operators.[68] Naval Service Headquarters in Ottawa was to coordinate all Canadian naval sigint and to promulgate operational intelligence to shore authorities and to ships in Canadian waters. The conference confirmed Canadian responsibility for DF fixes and WT intelligence west of the 35th meridian of longitude.[69] Thanks in part to Admiralty assistance in 1941 and to the fruits of Foster's visit, the Canadians were able to participate fully.

Captain Sandwith then visited Ottawa to provide detailed technical advice. This advice, combined with the general direction he had given in Washington, became the blueprint for sigint expansion and ensured that the Canadian operation remained attuned to Allied imperatives. His formula for success consisted of four elements: separation of the RCN from the Department of Transport; reassignment of some intercept resources to the Canadian Army; a general shift in emphasis from German naval to Japanese traffic; and changes in allocation of resources.[70] He believed that the early benefits from the RCN's "clever" adaption of existing Transport resources were outweighed by limited control over personnel and equipment. In addition, he recognized that the stations shared with the RCAF and Department of Transport could not be fully exploited. He noted that planned new stations in the West (Masset, Grand Prairie, Red Deer, and Lethbridge), which would provide bearings on enemy units in the Pacific, and the new "Y" and DF station at Coverdale in New Brunswick would increase Canadian intercept capacity dramatically. But they would do so only provided that adequate land-line communications could be installed. Moreover, he saw that these new resources would permit NSHQ to hand back the Transport stations for reassignment. As part of his plan to eliminate duplication of effort, he directed that all non-naval assignments, such as monitoring diplomatic traffic, be turned over to the Canadian Army. He reopened the debate about control by one master "Y" station, this time on the grounds of personnel and equipment savings. He also recommended that the number of receivers at each station be increased and that outdated receivers be replaced. Finally, he recommended that Canada's Foreign Intelligence Section shift its emphasis from DF to intercepting Japanese naval traffic so as to support the Allied requirement to devote more resources to the attack on Japanese codes and cyphers. Significantly, however, he ignored any connection between FIS priorities and RCN fleet assignments, and argued in particular that the Canadian emphasis on plotting German U-boats was a duplication of the Admiralty's efforts.

Sandwith's proposals were directed towards supporting a coordinated Allied effort, with the Admiralty tackling German and Italian naval sigint problems and both the Canadians and Americans dealing with the Japanese. Naval Service Headquarters was to be primarily a supplier of raw material to Allied cryptographic centres. It would be dependent on the Admiralty for information about German and Italian fleet dispositions, while the Canadian effort against Japanese traffic would be subordinate to and controlled by the USN. Rodger Winn's visit to Ottawa complemented Sandwith's. His direction created well-defined areas of responsibility in the Atlantic for the U-boat tracking rooms in Ottawa, Washington, and the Admiralty; the FIS broadcast area for its U-boat estimate included only warships north of the 40th parallel north latitude and west of the 40th meridian of longitude.[71]

The Foreign Intelligence Section implemented most of Sandwith's recommendations over the next year and thereby transformed a loosely organized system that produced uneven results into one capable of serving Allied requirements. The creation of a national "Y" Committee in May 1942 ensured national coordination of all "Y" operations and collaboration with Allied sigint policy-making bodies.[72] At Naval Service Headquarters, de Marbois reorganized the FIS to reflect its new scope and alignment with the UK and US organizations, separating "Y" operations from support. Ottawa and Washington started to exchange bearings.[73] In May 1942 the U-Boat Tracking Section of the FIS promulgated its first daily U-boat estimate to COAC, to the Flag Officer, Newfoundland (FONF), and to Washington;[74] and in July the FIS began to send sigint material regularly to Canadian operational authorities on both coasts.[75] The expanded staff began to analyse Canadian station bearings, integrate ionospheric data, and evaluate fixes. By autumn 1942 the Canadian sigint organization was functioning smoothly in an Allied context. It possessed most of the requisite elements for effective operation within the limits of low-level sigint. Admiral John Godfrey, the Admiralty's director of naval intelligence, favourably assessed its progress during his September visit to Ottawa: "A minute 'Bletchley' is doing some excellent work. The Canadian Intelligence Department ... is making a real contribution, and the good work put into its evolution by Captain Brand is now bearing fruit."[76]

The Canadian organization did not generate any intelligence of its own based on decryption of enemy signals. Its mission was to track enemy naval units, promulgate fixes in its area of responsibility, and provide raw material in the form of intercepts and bearings to other intelligence organizations. However, it still suffered from unsatisfactory communications and needed to invest more in training. It also needed to expand to achieve the daunting aim set by the Admiralty prior to the war: to intercept every enemy transmission. Finally, the Foreign Intelligence Section and its successor organization, Deputy Director of Signals Division (Y) [DDSD(Y)], needed to acquire credibility with operations staff and commanders at sea.

De Marbois blamed the operations staff for the Foreign Intelligence Section's failure to have an impact on operations. He saw sigint as the key element in exercising strategic control in the northwest Atlantic. In his view, Naval Service Headquarters could direct its own convoy diversions and anti-U-boat operations with an operational intelligence centre. The marriage of sigint and operations was not consecrated until after the Atlantic Convoy Conference. The Allied command and control crisis in winter 1942–43 forced the Canadian Naval Staff and its subordinate headquarters to refine Canadian anti-submarine operations. In the process, the three nations confirmed DDSD(Y)'s mandate as a separate centre within an Allied sigint system and ensured a high profile for sigint among Canadian operations staffs.

## Crisis in Command and Control, November 1942–March 1943

Communications problems on the east coast precipitated adjustments to command and control of convoy operations and anti-submarine warfare in the northwest Atlantic. The arrangements for passing sigint between the U-Boat Tracking Room in Ottawa and the headquarters in Halifax and St John's were unreliable, inadequate, and complicated. Despite the critical need for direct links between Ottawa and the Commanding Officer, Atlantic Coast, in Halifax and the Flag Officer, Newfoundland, in St John's, all communications between Ottawa and St John's still passed through Halifax; a single overworked RCN teleprinter circuit linked Halifax and

St John's.[77] Leasing additional lines and installing more equipment, however, treated symptoms, not the problem. Operational relationships had to be adjusted: because air and naval operations staffs in Ottawa, Halifax, and St John's were separate, the exchange of sigint was unnecessarily awkward and ineffective. Between November 1942 and March 1943, RCAF and RCN staffs at first resisted and then agreed to establish joint headquarters.[78] Significantly, the staffs recognized "DF Intelligence" as a primary source of information upon which ASW operations should be based.[79] As director of the Signals Division at Naval Service Headquarters, Worth addressed sigint and communications issues on behalf of NSHQ, and with de Marbois he also tackled the serious problem of delays in promulgating fixes, not only within Canada, but between Allied sigint organizations. According to de Marbois, the Admiralty's daily U-boat estimate took an average of seven hours to reach Ottawa. Estimates from Washington, on the other hand, took only two. An additional two hours and twenty minutes passed before these messages reached COAC and FONF from Ottawa.[80] After the war, de Marbois confessed the difficulty: "It was slowly but painfully dawning on all concerned that without speedy communications we could not adequately hope to compete with German U/Boats' wireless control of his fleet."[81] In short, if intelligence could not be delivered to operational staffs and commanders at sea when they required it, Ottawa's increasing the accuracy and completeness of its "Y" operations was of no avail.

Other problems required attention as well. In spite of Winn's efforts to delineate areas of responsibility, western Atlantic convoys were sent fixes by both Canadian and American U-boat tracking centres. Worse, COAC transmitted the very same fixes as Ottawa. Thus, sigint overloaded the airwaves and tied up already busy communications staffs decrypting messages they had already received. Commodore H.E. Reid, the Canadian naval commander in Newfoundland, alerted Naval Service Headquarters to these problems by sending copies of message traffic from Convoy SC 107 as examples.[82] Worth attempted to correct this problem, first by requesting COMINCH to reduce its promulgations in the northwest Atlantic.[83] He resolved the domestic situation by clarifying which headquarters had authority to release messages. COAC thereupon ceased promulgating its own fixes, and the U-Boat Tracking Room in Ottawa became the central authority for U-boat estimates for both the RCN and the RCAF. Resolution of which national authority – Ottawa or Washington – would promulgate fixes in the northwest Atlantic awaited definition of operational control.

In November 1942 the British Admiralty Delegation (BAD) in Washington had asked Canada to accede to COMINCH's demand for control of DF promulgation for the entire western Atlantic.[84] When Nelles pleaded his case to COMINCH in December, he knew that the Canadians stood alone. He specifically addressed the issue of which authority should promulgate U-boat information to Allied ships in the northwest Atlantic.[85] In doing so, he tied Canadian promulgation of fixes to the number of Canadian ships actually operating in that area; he supported his contention that events had overtaken the Anglo-Canadian agreements on operational control of 1941 by detailing the substantial Canadian contribution to the Mid Ocean and Western Local escort forces.[86] Admiral King (COMINCH) told Nelles that the RCN would only be permitted to issue warnings of attacks and U-boat positions once it had acquired general operational control of the North Atlantic.[87] With the aim of amending all agreements governing operational control of North Atlantic convoys in general, Nelles continued to press for a three-nation conference. He believed that the USN should retain "strategic control" and overall responsibility for routing in the western Atlantic, but that Canada should have operational control in the northwest Atlantic, specifically north of the 40 degrees north latitude and as far east as "present strategic limits."[88] In Nelles's and his staff's view, Canada's assumption of major responsibilities for convoy escort compelled the Allies to amend all agreements governing operational control of the North Atlantic.

*The Atlantic Convoy Conference, March 1943*

Repeated pleas by the Canadian chief of naval staff for an inter-Allied conference on Atlantic convoy arrangements were answered, and the RCN finally won recognition of its contribution to the defence of the Atlantic convoys at the Atlantic Convoy Conference in Washington, 1–12 March 1943.[89] This was a singular victory for the RCN and specifically for the officers who had directed the Canadian navy's signals intelligence activities. The conference was held against the background of a crisis in the North Atlantic campaign – soaring successes by German U-boats, the result of recent failures in reading German naval Enigma settings. Vice-Admiral Victor G. Brodeur, chief of the naval mission, Canadian Joint Staff in Washington, was not optimistic. Given that both the RN and the USN sought control of the Atlantic convoys, he believed that Canada would be squeezed between "the two big boys."[90] On the opening day of the conference,[91] he stated the RCN's position clearly, if not succinctly:

I wish to impress this most important fact about Canada which appears to be so little understood, that is, that all Canadian armed forces are under the control of one, only one, higher authority which is the Canadian Government and only by the latter's consent can any armed forces be moved from Canada or from one theatre of war to another and if all sub-committees studying the present agenda will remember that very important factor, a great deal of time will be saved and many misunderstandings avoided.[92]

Brodeur set out the three-point Canadian proposal: that the 40th parallel north latitude mark the southern limit of British and Canadian control of convoys and anti-submarine warfare; that the Commanding Officer, Atlantic Coast, become Commander-in-Chief, Canadian Northwest Atlantic (C-in-C CNA), with general direction of all anti-submarine forces in the northwest Atlantic; and that control of convoys, the dissemination of U-boat information, and convoy diversions in the northwest Atlantic be exercised by Naval Service Headquarters and C-in-C CNA, much as in Britain the Admiralty and Commander-in-Chief, Western Approaches, controlled the northeast.

Admiral King and the senior RN representatives insisted that the RCN could not be given operational control of any area without having an organization that could detect and report the presence of enemy U-boats and surface forces. They were convinced that an operational intelligence centre like the Admiralty's was a cornerstone of success against German naval forces, particularly the U-boats. Brodeur alerted Nelles, who despatched de Marbois and his deputy on 2 March 1943.[93] They successfully argued that they could indeed form an effective operational intelligence centre from the RCN's "Y" and HF/DF system, and Canada was granted its sea command.

The Atlantic Convoy Conference provided for the communications systems that ensured that the new Operational Intelligence Centre in Ottawa could freely exchange information with its sister operational intelligence centres. Each would be co-located with plotting and operations rooms to form "battle organizations," with improved communications connecting them to deployed naval forces.[94] This assured the RCN the means with which to assume a full partnership in the war against the U-boats, and created the organization that gave the members of the Canadian Naval Staff the means with which to plan and direct operations with sigint input. Over the next two years, the Operational Intelligence Centre played a considerably more significant role in the anti-U-boat campaign than that envisioned in 1939. Those who had laboured to ensure the proficiency of the Canadian "Y" and HF/DF system had earned the authority, both within the Allied context and their own service, to support operations against the enemy in Canadian waters.

# Muddling Through:
## Canadian Anti-submarine Doctrine
## and Practice, 1942–1945

DOUG M. McLEAN

The crucible of war rapidly transformed the Royal Canadian Navy (RCN) from a shadow force in 1939 to a fleet of hundreds of warships supported by a large and complex shore establishment. Yet even as the service reached its peak in 1944–45 and achieved notable successes in several theatres, it remained incapable of destroying the handful of U-boats that continued to penetrate deep into Canadian waters.[1] This frustrating result demonstrated the persistence of difficulties that had long plagued the RCN, most particularly since the service had undertaken vastly increased commitments and accelerated expansion in 1942. Poorly defined and implemented tactical doctrine was among the most important failing in the crises of that year. This chapter argues that although there was important progress thereafter, doctrinal weakness goes far to explain the shortcomings of the RCN's anti-submarine operations in home waters during the last months of the war. What is more, the central question of doctrine reveals much about the identity of the RCN in this difficult period: how it absorbed the influences of the predominant American and British navies, and how it addressed the evident need for increased self-sufficiency.

Canada's small prewar navy had been firmly dependent on the Royal Navy (RN), widely regarded as the world's best, for training, technology, and tactical ideas. The Canadian service relied upon access to British training for all of its officers and senior ratings. New developments in naval technology were monitored by observing British trends, and methods of dealing with hypothetical foes were developed by observing British practice. The reason for this situation lay partly in small defence budgets.

The Canadian government, under the rearmament program of the late 1930s, had provided the navy with funds to purchase warships, but it had not provided resources to develop a naval bureaucracy capable of accomplishing these complex and unglamorous support tasks on its own.

Though always a popular recourse in Canada, blaming politicians is perhaps too easy. There is room to doubt that the prewar RCN believed it could develop all the trappings of an independent navy. No doubt most of those concerned assumed that all this would come to pass in due course, but like Admiral P.W. Nelles, chief of naval staff in 1939, they also believed that the RCN would do best in wartime to remain closely integrated with the Royal Navy. Prewar planning by Nelles relied on this intimate connection, and his immediate advice to Cabinet in September 1939 was to fight the war with the RCN essentially as a division of the RN. It was here that Prime Minister William Lyon Mackenzie King caused consternation in the senior elements of the RCN by insisting that Canada retain authority for national control of its fleet and not totally surrender decisions on deployment to the Royal Navy.[2]

Too much can be made of this decision. In practice the RCN did what the Admiralty asked, and continued to rely heavily on the RN for the loan of experienced officers, supplies of equipment, and training and tactical procedures. However, the greatly increased strategic, industrial, and manpower pressures experienced by the RN after the fall of western Europe in 1940 dictated that the Admiralty ask, and expect, the RCN to assume much larger responsibilities for its own training, equipping, and development. The resulting devolution of authority was perhaps more a matter of circumstance than deliberate policy, but the impact on the RCN was severe. The junior service was more on its own than it had ever been, while at the same time it faced the most demanding challenge in its history.

This situation resulted in many problems that might generously be called teething pains, though they have been called far worse by some naval historians.[3] Setting up a shore establishment to support a fleet that had begun to grow at an exponential rate proved terribly difficult. The official historian of the RCN admitted that "operational training in Halifax was not fully organized until May 1942,"[4] and even this is too charitable. Creating a staff capable of identifying and fostering the development of new technology proved still more difficult.[5] The German navy, moreover, complicated the issue by bringing the war to Canada's doorstep.

The naval war that Canada fought did not conform to the one Canadian naval officers had expected. Prewar naval thought, naturally reflecting that of the RN, assumed that the greatest potential threat to Canada would come from surface raiders.[6] Submarines were considered less threatening because of the development of asdic, or sonar, which was believed to render them vulnerable if they chose to attack shipping aggressively. The first year of war seemed to confirm prewar beliefs. This was a result not of Allied strategic prescience but of the poor state of the German navy at the start of the war.[7] The Kriegsmarine had only a small number of submarines, few with the range required for operations out in the Atlantic. The fall of France in the summer of 1940 marked the beginning of a new naval war. The growth of the U-boat fleet in combination with its access to the Biscay ports, which significantly reduced the time U-boats took to reach Allied shipping routes, escalated the struggle between the submarines and escorts into what Churchill dubbed the Battle of the Atlantic. This was the campaign in which the bulk of the RCN fought. A generation of Canadian sailors learned their craft in this grim war of foul weather, sudden attacks, and endless searches for evasive opponents. While a thin leavening of professionals could be found in the Canadian escort fleet, most were volunteer reservists who had never sailed in warships before.[8] The inadequate naval infrastructure and amateur sailors of the wartime RCN created a distinctive style of naval tactics. This was never as effective or efficient as might have been hoped for in a perfect world, but it was a remarkable achievement when assessed in context.

The RCN initially followed RN tactical doctrine reasonably closely. However, this changed when the RN reversed its early emphasis on hunting for U-boats and adopted a new tactical philosophy of "safe and timely" arrival of convoys.[9] This prudent but unglamorous approach emphasized defending merchant ships over killing U-boats. While destruction of U-boats remained a desirable objective, it was not essential so long as the merchant ships got through, regularly and on schedule. The United States Navy (USN) never found the "safe and timely" concept a convincing idea, and throughout the war it saw convoys themselves not so much as the supreme object of concern but as bait to draw U-boats to their destruction.[10] When the USN did develop new tactical procedures, it focused on new offensive methods of finding and killing U-boats.[11] The RCN appears to have remained committed to offensive tactics, stressing the necessity of killing U-boats more than the importance of defending against them. The reasons for this are not entirely clear. It may have been the result of the Canadian navy's exposure to the USN's offensive orientation, or it may have reflected the persistence of prewar concepts. Marc Milner argues that the comparative security of North America from strangulation by U-boat attack allowed the USN and RCN to remain wedded to offensive concepts, while the British, whose very survival depended on the merchant ships, were forced to adopt less exciting but more effective defensive tactics.[12] An alternative explanation is that the RCN simply lacked the capability to analyse effectively either the RN's or the USN's policy. The service stayed with offensive ideas more as a result of human nature than conscious choice. Instinct, after all, is to strike back at a foe, rather than to drive him off and carefully husband your strength to keep ready for the unexpected strikes of other enemies lurking over the horizon.

If the tactical doctrine followed by the RCN in the early stages of the Battle of the Atlantic was poorly defined, the decision to follow RN organization was more evident. The setting-up of a mid-ocean force in Newfoundland in 1941, well described by Marc Milner in his seminal work *North Atlantic Run*, marked Canada's growing commitment to the defence of Atlantic shipping. The new Commodore Commanding, Newfoundland Force, Commodore L.W. Murray, adopted the organization worked out by the British headquarters responsible for Atlantic shipping, Western Approaches. The growing presence of the USN in the northwest Atlantic subjected Canadian sailors to its influence as well. Being sandwiched between two large allies is not a unique experience in Canadian history, but it is never completely comfortable. The RCN would remain in this position through the rest of the war.

Milner has argued that the RCN would have made "quicker and surer advances towards the type of operational efficiency expected of [it] by the RN during 1942" if it had had only one authority to deal with, rather than two – the RN and the USN. Perhaps. The years 1941 and 1942 were without doubt the most difficult years for the RCN. Mushrooming commitments, more aggressive tactics by the expanding U-boat fleet, the commissioning of new ships faster than crews could be properly trained, and the need to keep up with the swift development of essential equipment and tactical methods by Allied fleets stretched the neophyte navy right to, and perhaps a bit beyond, its breaking-point. Yet by 1942 the growing differences between British and Canadian outlooks and needs – and the strains on the RN itself – militated against the RCN slavishly following British models. Nor could the RCN adopt USN practices overnight – not with its senior officers so steeped in British procedures and virtually all of the ships and equipment being of British design. The growing size of the RCN and the growing weight of responsibility upon the service, especially for home defence, encouraged a mild independence, a realization that the perspective in Canada did truly differ from that at the Admiralty and in Washington. Willy nilly, the ordeal of war forced the RCN overnight into adolescence, and the absorption of innovations introduced by allies became a matter of selective choice and subsequent adaptation, an infinitely greater challenge than simple imitation.

The RCN, lacking the shore organization needed to assess, develop, and disseminate tactical ideas, was never fully equal to the challenge. At best, it followed a "muddling through" approach that allowed Canadian ships to use whatever tactics developed by their allies best suited a situation. At worst, the Canadian reaction to German initiatives was confused and disorganized. The result for units operating in Canadian waters was somewhere between these two poles, and the lack of a fully coordinated system of analysis and dissemination gave broad scope to individuals. There were a number of instances where uniquely Canadian innovations were developed. These were often the result of a creative response by individual naval officers in the face of difficult situations and inadequate resources. However, crafting these innovations into a coherent doctrine proved difficult, although the RCN made progress as time passed and better methods of assessing and disseminating tactics were developed.

The situation for ships under the direct operational control of the Royal Navy was more complex. Although Canada gained operational control over what became known as the Canadian Northwest Atlantic in 1943,[13] the number of Canadian ships that operated under the RN remained large and increased in the latter part of the war to support the Allied invasion of Europe and to counter a renewed U-boat offensive in British waters. Those ships that sailed under British operational control were exposed to the British method of developing and disseminating tactics, which remained superior to Canadian practice throughout the war. The result was two significantly different experiences for ships deployed on different sides of the Atlantic.

RCN ships learned early in the war that they would often be expected to operate with inferior equipment, and sometimes numbers, as compared to their British or American counterparts. The inability of the RCN to keep Canadian warships as technologically advanced as RN or USN ships is a complex issue, one that will not be addressed here. It is sufficient to remark that this discrepancy existed. While the degree to which Canadian ships fell behind is debatable, the consequences are not. The RCN often found it impossible to adopt new Allied tactics because the fleet lacked the equipment to carry them out. Somewhat desperate expedients were developed in the Canadian service, one of the more notorious of which was an operation known as "Major Hoople," an attempt to compensate for the lack of radar. Milner has well described this daring ploy, which called for an escort commander to illuminate the area around a convoy before U-boats attacked, basing his decision on little more than his visceral assessment.[14] While a timely illumination could deter a wolf-pack about to attack, a premature decision could light up the convoy for miles, exposing it to the eyes of many U-boats that might not have spotted it otherwise. Not all Canadian tactical innovations were this dependent on gambling, but this one is illustrative of how different the RCN perspective could be.

The issue of Canadian performance and methods came to a head during a series of bitter convoy battles in the fall of 1942. The Admiralty's anti-submarine warfare specialists were sharply critical of the RCN, arguing that the poor level of training of Canadian escort groups contributed significantly to the fact that the heaviest losses were suffered by Canadian-escorted convoys.[15] The RCN's frustration with the RN's criticism, particularly with the apparent inability of British authorities to understand the tactical constraints under which poorly equipped Canadian ships laboured, contributed to a desire to have a Canadian tactical doctrine.[16]

One of the roots of the difficulties between the RN and the RCN in the autumn of 1942 lay in the RCN's dramatic overextension. The RCN entered the war determined to prove itself.[17] For this reason, and out of unselfish patriotism, the service responded over-generously to pleas from Britain, and from the US as well, for help. RCN ships were thrown into the Battle of the Atlantic at a reckless pace and then committed to schedules that left little time for such things as training, especially advanced-group and refresher training, and maintenance. There was never enough time to develop and disseminate tactical ideas and doctrine. The best that could be hoped for was that ships would cope as best they could. The result of keeping too many ships in the fight, despite growing concerns on the part of the Allies about Canadian fighting efficiency, was the near collapse of several RCN groups in the difficult conditions of the fall and winter of 1942–43.[18]

The basic document for British tactical policy in the Battle of the Atlantic was a set of orders first known as Western Approaches Convoy Instructions (WACIs) and later as Atlantic Convoy Instructions (ACIs).[19] This became the primary source to consult when promulgating tactical plans in the convoy war, a matter greatly assisted by the inclusion of a USN section, but a wide variety of other avenues existed for circulating tactical ideas. Senior officers of escort groups often wrote their own orders, which augmented or added instructions to ACIs. Reports of proceedings from convoys or encounters with U-boats occasionally included suggestions for new procedures. As the war progressed, responsibility for developing tactics was assigned to special groups such as the Western Approaches Tactical Unit (WATU), formed by Captain Gilbert Roberts, RN, in January 1942.[20]

A slim set of tactical instructions entitled "Hints on Escort Work" was promulgated in the RCN by one of the more prolific writers on tactical matters, Captain J.D. Prentice, in March 1943 while he was captain(D) at Halifax.[21] These notes were developed to provide a way for local authorities to outline suggestions for escort commanders in their command, and some of these suggestions eventually found their way into ACIs. The "Hints" differed from ACIs primarily in that they strongly emphasized the offensive.[22]

The RCN established its own Tactical Unit at Halifax in 1943, which functioned in a similar manner to WATU.[23] The growing importance of tactical development was acknowledged in Naval Staff Headquarters (NSHQ) by the creation of the Directorate of Warfare and Training (DWT) in early 1943. Its responsibilities included tactical analysis and fighting efficiency.[24] These developments at least theoretically provided the RCN with institutional mechanisms for developing distinctively Canadian tactics. The main problem was finding an effective way of introducing new ideas and procedures into the fleet.

By the summer of 1943 the main U-boat assault on transatlantic shipping had been repulsed. Although driven back from the central ocean, the U-boat fleet remained strong in numbers, strong in morale, and was still able, through continuing technological innovation, to strike offensively at shipping in the face of crushing Allied numerical superiority. Thus, defence of shipping remained the RCN's most important mission right through to the end of the war. In 1944 the defence of transatlantic convoys became primarily an RCN responsibility, as the Royal Navy transferred ships from the mid-Atlantic to other areas. This event is noted with pride in all Canadian histories.[25] A growing number of ships were also sent to European waters to operate with the Royal Navy in what were generically termed "offensive operations," although often these tasks were directly related to the shipping war. The impact of the RCN's increasing commitments in the Battle of the Atlantic was that a steady flow of new warships entered commission, continuing the strain on the Canadian navy's ability to train and maintain warships.

In 1943 the RCN began forming groups of escorts known as Support Groups. These consisted of the best anti-submarine ships in the service and were usually sent to operate in areas where the U-boat threat was greatest. In 1943 this was still the mid-Atlantic, but in 1944 growing numbers of Support and other Canadian groups were deployed to England to assist with the Normandy invasion. The resulting drain of the best ships from Canadian waters continued the difficulties experienced in 1942 in defending Canadian waters from those U-boats that made the hazardous transit to North American waters. It was not until the summer of 1944 that the first Support Group destined for operations in Canadian waters, EG 16, finally came together in Halifax.

In the absence of special groups dedicated to hunting U-boats, searches in Canadian waters were often relegated to ad hoc formations. This policy was known to be less effective than using groups of ships that had trained and operated together. However, the deployment of the best ships overseas, admittedly the most decisive theatre, left no good options. Even the use of Support Groups before they proceeded overseas helped little: the newly formed groups lacked experience operating as a group, and their training in advanced tactics was often rudimentary. The commissioning of HMCS *Somers Isles* in Bermuda 1 August 1944 finally provided the RCN with an east coast sea-training facility that could be used year-round, but the primary aim of this facility remained the work-up of individual ships, either newly commissioned or returning from refit. Once "worked up," Canadian ships had few opportunities for further training, individual or group.

This last factor undoubtedly contributed to the frustration Canadian ships experienced in the last year of the war. In this period U-boats returned in growing numbers (a dozen or more), to operate in shallow coastal waters in the Gulf of St Lawrence and off the coast of Nova Scotia.[26] Fitted with schnorkels for the first time, they proved difficult targets for aircraft, thus reducing the effectiveness of the Royal Canadian Air Force (RCAF) maritime patrol squadrons that had heretofore compensated for the limited strength of the RCN's home commands. The shallow waters off the Canadian coast made sonar detection of these submarines difficult as well, for the poor acoustic conditions found in most areas over the greater part of the year were exacerbated by the rocky and uneven sea bottom. U-boat captains soon learned of these weaknesses and exploited them to good effect.[27] The RCN was also cognizant of these difficulties, but solutions were not easy.[28]

A partial answer was to increase the number of Support Groups, so that at least one could be despatched to an area whenever a U-boat began to operate there. This solution's feasibility rested on the fact that U-boats paid a price for their use of the schnorkel: it substantially reduced their mobility. Since they could no longer move rapidly from one area to another without becoming vulnerable to aircraft, using Support Groups as "fire brigades" to deal with U-boats in specific areas was sensible. The drawback was that since schnorkel-fitted U-boats used their radios quite rarely, little intelligence on even their approximate location was ever available.[29] All too often the first indication of their presence was an attack on shipping. Still, committing organized Support Groups to search in the wake of an attack was better than scrambling to raise ad hoc formations at the moment of crisis.

The RCN created three new Support Groups in the autumn of 1944 as part of the response to the German schnorkel offensive on both sides of the Atlantic, bringing its total number to about seven.[30] In keeping with the priority assigned to overseas waters, only two of these seven groups were retained for operations in Canadian waters, EGs 16 and 27; as usual the RCN had a poverty of resources in home waters. The experience of these two groups compared with those sent overseas illustrates some significant differences between the RCN's approach to tactical proficiency and the RN's. A review of the tactics employed in the two areas reveals more subtle but instructive differences.

The most notable contrast between the two areas was not so much the tactics themselves as the way in which they were disseminated and introduced. Western Approaches, the headquarters that controlled Canadian Support Groups operating overseas, believed strongly in the importance of periodic group refresher training. The purpose of this training was both to hone tactical skills and to provide opportunities for ships to practise newly developed search and attack schemes. For example, before proceeding on patrols in the English Channel or Irish Sea, Western Approaches Support Groups would often spend three to six days at Loch Alsh working with the training commander there. His staff would review the latest tactics with the group officers, and then the ships would practise them at sea, often with a friendly submarine providing a realistic target. The theoretical amount of time spent on this kind of highly focused, practical refresher training was seven days out of every hundred-day cycle.[31] Significantly, however, records of the actual employment of RCN ships overseas reveal that while every effort was made to achieve this percentage, the average time appears to have been closer to five days than seven.[32] Bad weather and breakdowns were part of the problem. The decision to devote this much time to instruction and practice at a time when Support Groups contained the most valuable anti-submarine ships available reflects a very strong commitment indeed to refresher training. (The Germans, we might add, were no less committed to training and upgrading their submarines.) While questions were raised periodically as to whether this amount of training time was justified, Admiral Max Horton, Commander-in-Chief, Western Approaches, always insisted it was.[33]

The contrast of this training with that of Support Groups operating in Canadian waters could hardly be more striking. On formation, the newest Support Group, EG 27, received only one day of what could loosely be described as group training, and EG 16 appears to have fared equally poorly. EG 27 was never again able to train seriously as a group, while EG 16 had to wait until it was transferred overseas before it received the opportunity.[34] Assessing the impact of inadequate training on performance is necessarily subjective, but some generalizations can be hazarded. There is no doubt that the RN practice allowed for the more expeditious transmission of new tactical doctrines and concepts. Since one of the most important elements of success in war is continual adaptation to enemy initiatives, the immense RN effort devoted to refresher training could certainly be justified. Further, group exercises allowed evolutions to be tried that might not be executed otherwise. Most important of all was the chance to hone skills against friendly submarines, as opportunities to detect and attack enemy submarines were all too rare.

The question as to which tactics to employ in Canadian coastal waters provided a lively subject for correspondence both internally in Halifax and between the coast and Naval Service Headquarters in Ottawa. A growing variety of plans were forwarded to the Tactical Unit at Halifax. As might be expected, many were from the Royal Navy, in the form of messages and amendments to tactical publications. These were supplemented by comments from Canadian liaison officers in the United Kingdom. There were also suggestions for new search plans and tactics from ships in the local escort forces. There was no shortage of ideas.

A good example of the difficulties of assessing, adapting, and promulgating new tactics is provided by the response of authorities to the Royal Navy's new search plan known as Operation Scabbard. This scheme provided a pre-planned reaction in the event of definite evidence of a U-boat in an area; in this case the suggested evidence was a torpedoed ship. The plan assumed that the U-boat would bottom immediately after the attack, and prescribed a line-abreast sweep by the escorts through the vicinity of the attack as the first response. The search line was to start at least 5,000 yards from the position of the torpedoed ship, as the assumption was that the attack would be delivered from a range of 2,500–4,000 yards, a reasonable assessment of U-boat attacks based upon periscope capabilities. (In actual fact, however, U-boats off Halifax fired torpedos at a range of 700–1,500 yards from target.) If no detection was made on the initial sweep, ships were to open out and then reverse course to sweep through again, dropping depth charges at frequent intervals. If contact was still not gained, a "box search" was to be organized, with the ships proceeding in line abreast around the perimeter of an imaginary box. The size of the box was based upon a submarine's "probability area," which was presumably calculated using assumptions such as the probable range of the U-boat from its target when it launched its torpedo.[35] The ships proceeded in line abreast at right angles to the perimeter of the box, conducting "EI" turns at the corners.[36] The distance between ships in line abreast depended upon the number of ships available, the interval decreasing as more ships were present. One escort was detailed to assist survivors and gain any information from them about the attack that might assist the search.

This plan was sent out to Canada by message on 25 August 1944. The director of the Tactical Unit at Halifax, Lieutenant-Commander J. Plomer, RCNVR, forwarded his comments on the new proposal to Captain(D), Halifax, Acting Captain W.L. Puxley, RN, on 1 September. Plomer's memorandum provided an assessment and several suggestions for improving the plan. He termed Scabbard "quite straightforward" and felt that "as an area search it was thorough." His improvements were reasonably minor, but it is significant that in one of them he felt obliged to provide ideas on how to improve the search if only a few escorts were available. As many coastal convoys in Canadian waters had small numbers of escorts assigned to them in an essentially random manner, and as organized escort groups were modest in size because of the steady drain of ships overseas, his concern for this detail is hardly surprising. This memorandum was then passed from Captain(D), Halifax, to the office of the Commander-in-Chief, Canadian Northwest Atlantic (C-in-C CNA) on 7 September. The staff spent over a week circulating Scabbard, and reactions ranged from enthusiastic approval to scepticism about its applicability. While an early comment suggested that this plan be sent out to the fleet in an operations order and that it subsequently be included in the Canadian section of ACIs, the final decision appears to have been less formal. The minutes noted that "Operation Scabbard is designed for the shallow water and strong tides experienced in the English Channel" and that "it is unlikely that these conditions would be duplicated in this command." Despite these doubts, it was suggested that the plan be adopted in the tactical school and included for information in "Hints on Escort Work," but "further promulgation [was] not considered to be necessary."[37] In short, after several weeks of staffing, it was decided that while Scabbard was worth paying attention to, there still remained some reservations about whether such a plan really applied to submarine hunting on the Canadian side of the Atlantic.

There were reasons for hesitancy, one of the best being that U-boats were only starting to demonstrate that the Canadian coast was as vulnerable as the English Channel to attack by schnorkel-equipped submarines. Yet the final decision to acknowledge Scabbard and to promulgate it in a general tactical circular instead of including it in the standard tactical instructions of the period meant that doubt remained as to whether it should become a standard procedure at all. The natural result was continued efforts to have some sort of search plan dealing with the situation covered by Scabbard accepted by the naval establishment. Indeed, observing that "there is no [suitable] search plan laid down in A.C.I.s," Lieutenant-Commander Plomer forwarded, on 7 December 1944, yet another search plan to deal with the same sort of situation envisioned by Scabbard.[38] He went on to comment that "in a few instances recently had some form of search been available in various escort groups, that could immediately be carried out, the chances of detection would have been immeasurably increased." The area plan that accompanied Plomer's memorandum was a combination of two plans developed earlier in the war: the first was called "Observant," and the second a square search. This combination called for a group to send two ships to search in the vicinity of a possible U-boat (signalled, again, by a torpedoed ship), while the remaining ships began a square search outside of the two inner ships. The suggested dimensions of the two searches were two miles for Observant and six miles for the square search, although the size of the square search depended on the possible "furthest-on" position of the U-boat, a function of the amount of time that had passed since the submarine attack.

Plomer's memorandum highlights the continued controversy over the best tactics to employ against U-boats in coastal waters. The Secretary of the Naval Board at NSHQ dismissed his "Area Search" proposal on 11 April 1945, noting that "in areas where a U-boat may bottom [essentially, coastal waters] a Group operating independently would achieve better results by the use of the 'Scabbard Search.'"[39] Ironically, despite the fact that NSHQ dismissed area plan and suggested that the Admiralty concept merited adoption, it is clear that the search proposed by Plomer provided inspiration during at least one action off Halifax in the winter of 1944–45. In effect, while there was no real agreement as to whether Scabbard or this new area search should be adopted officially, ships off Halifax could choose to do what they wished. Though this offered flexibility – and doctrine should not be so restrictive as to stifle initiative – it also indicated a lack of clear thinking and made the promotion of effective teamwork much more difficult.

The search for *U-806*, close off Halifax on 24 December 1944, provides a good example of the state of RCN tactical thought. *U-806* had made its presence known a few days before when it damaged a merchant ship in the Halifax approaches.[40] Three warships were sent out of port on the morning of 24 December to sweep the channel in advance of the departure of two convoys. While returning to take station on the first convoy, HMCS *Clayoquot* was torpedoed when she inadvertently closed the U-boat's position. This attack presented the classic situation upon which both Scabbard and the proposed Area Search were predicated: a U-boat was known to be in the area, its presence disclosed by a torpedoed ship. The initial reaction of the escorts was to stream torpedo decoys and search aggressively for the U-boat while shepherding the convoys back into harbour. Given the location of the attack and the experience gained from the Royal Navy concerning U-boat operations, the RCN clearly expected the U-boat to bottom in order to present the most difficult asdic target.[41] In fact, this is precisely what *U-806* did.[42] After the convoys were safely back in Halifax and additional warships arrived on the scene, a more deliberate search began, which closely resembled Plomer's area search. A small group of ships, usually three, were kept in the immediate vicinity of the torpedoing, conducting a slow and careful search. The remaining ships swept a square perimeter outside these ships, patrolling at moderate speeds in order to prevent the U-boat from escaping. This square perimeter grew as time passed, starting at two miles, then five, and finally ten, a procedure consistent with containing the submarine within its furthest-on position, although the rate at which the perimeter grew did not indicate close attention to furthest-on circles.[43]

The ships engaged in this search were an ad hoc assembly of all escorts available at short notice. This naturally presented coordination problems, a point strongly made in later reports.[44] Initially, command of the search lay in the hands of the senior naval officer on the scene, the commanding officer of HMCS *Kirkland Lake*, Commander N.V. Clark, OBE, RCNR. A few hours later, however, the training commander of the port of Halifax, Commander R. Aubrey, RN, arrived to take charge. This event has been characterized by some Canadian historians as "the kind of RN assumption of superiority that really galled."[45] While this might be accurate, there is a another perspective. Given the lack of clear tactical doctrine in Halifax at this time, sending an officer conversant with all the latest anti-submarine concepts could be considered prudent. Whatever the merits of the issue, even Aubrey proved unable to locate *Clayoquot*'s killer. To what degree the improvised nature of the search and ad hoc command arrangements contributed to this outcome cannot be determined with certainty. However, as we now know from the U-boat's log, escorts passed directly over the submarine on at least six occasions.[46] This evidence indicates that the tactics could be considered appropriate and effective, but that detection was extremely difficult in the water conditions off Halifax in winter.[47]

Another disastrous U-boat attack only weeks later tends to confirm that water conditions more than tactics and confusion or lack of skill stymied the RCN. On 14 January 1945 *U-1232* attacked a convoy just before it entered Halifax, torpedoing three ships. This convoy had an escort of two minesweepers of the local escort force and three frigates of Support Group EG 27. The Support Group responded aggressively to the attack, inflicting some damage on the bold U-boat. But the damage resulted from a glancing collision with one of the frigates, not from anti-submarine weapons, and the U-boat was never detected by asdic even at that short range.[48] On this occasion the U-boat decided to leave the area of the attack by travelling slowly and quietly just above the shallow bottom. Again, the search plan organized by EG 27 placed the group in a position where they should have had a chance to detect the U-boat by asdic, and again nothing was heard.[49]

The search plan used by EG 27 did not come from RN concepts but from "the latest tactics as developed by the USN."[50] The three frigates followed a variation on what the USN called a "retiring search plan," in which the ships formed up in line abreast and then followed an expanding spiral course at a moderately high speed towing acoustic-torpedo decoys, searching first in the direction of the U-boat's most likely escape course and sweeping along the submarine's furthest-on position. At the same time as EG 27 set out on this search, other ships were directed by the senior officer (SO) of EG 27 to commence a slow and methodical search in the vicinity of the torpedoed merchantmen in case the U-boat had bottomed. This time the training commander did not arrive to take over the search, possibly as the presence of a Support Group suggested that he was not required. The fruitless retiring search was broken off after about six hours, with EG 27 returning to the vicinity of the attacks to conduct a prolonged search of the Halifax approaches.[51] The US killer group Task Group (TG) 22.9 joined in the search, a testament to the growing USN presence in Canadian waters.

Both the US and RCN ships entered Halifax on 19 January 1945 to discuss procedural issues. This meeting had been in the works for over a month, but now the attack by U-1232 moved it ahead.[52] The tactics decided upon at this meeting reflected a mix of RN, RCN, and USN methods. Elements of Plomer's area search were present, as were some of the ideas developed by Captain J.D. Prentice, RCN, during his period in the English Channel in the summer of 1944.[53] The senior officer of TG 22.9 considered that the final procedure agreed upon at the meeting was close to the USN's Operation SCOUR, itself a variation on Scabbard. In a sense this is not surprising, as all of these plans dealt with the same problem. However, differences did exist. The meeting helped to standardize procedures, thereby promoting quicker responses and better results.

However, two messages in February 1945 again demonstrated the uncertainty surrounding RCN tactical procedures. On the tenth of that month NSHQ promulgated a message directing all ships to use the "retiring search plans" published in the USN's Fleet Tactical Publication 223A.[54] While this might have been taken to indicate a shift to USN procedures, a subsequent message a little over two weeks later showed that much remained to be resolved. The new message hedged the previous direction, stating: "Use of retiring search plans is not intended to replace or conflict with standard operations used in conjunction with protection of convoys or with operational orders which cover specific problems."[55] Clearly, not much was standardized yet and improvisation remained the order of the day.

Results, of course, were the bottom line. Although these could be measured in many ways, the easiest was performance with regard to destruction of the enemy. The failure of the RCN to destroy any U-boats in the wake of the December and January attacks was a sore point. A study by operational research scientists after the war concluded that although conditions in the Canadian Northwest Atlantic were difficult, a comparison with operations in UK waters indicated that the RCN should have been able to destroy at least one U-boat.[56] Like all statistical studies, especially one based on such a small sampling, there is room to doubt the conclusions. Yet the reasons the report offered for this failure sound familiar. The report referred to the requirement for "improved tactical training," "greater experience in inshore A/S operations," and the need for "more hunting forces." One way to provide better escorts for Canadian waters was to bring back groups experienced in inshore operations from UK waters, replacing them there with "newly formed groups … lacking the benefit of such experience and training." The report also suggested that better plotting and communications arrangements in the headquarters at Halifax might have "increased efficiency in coastal A/S hunts."[57] The results achieved by US ships in North American waters in the last year of the war suggest that the scientists might have got it right.

Killer groups such as TG 22.9 were the USN's response to the growing problem of finding and destroying schnorkel-fitted U-boats. These groups first started to form in November 1944, when TGs 22.8, 22.9, and 22.10 were created. Unlike previous USN "hunter-killer" groups, these new TGs focused on surface ASW tactics instead of coordinated air-sea operations in company with escort carriers, a clear indication of the changes schnorkels had wrought in Allied tactics on both sides of the Atlantic. At least some of the ships in these new groups were veterans of the Atlantic battle, and their training emphasized group tactics in contrast to the RCN's concentration on individual ship skills. Prodigious amounts of training and resources were provided to these new killer groups. When first brought together, on average they spent twenty-six days at Casco Bay, Maine, honing their skills as a group. An example of the scale of resources can be found in the exercise time provided with friendly submarines. For TG 22.8 this amounted to "over sixty (60) hours … spent on a manoeuvring submarine perfecting unit tactics and coordinated attacks" during its initial training in November–December 1944.[58] After less than three months of operations, during which this group hunted down and destroyed a weather-reporting U-boat,[59] TG 22.8 returned to Casco Bay for refresher training. Just under thirty hours were spent with friendly submarines this time, twenty on a manoeuvring target and seven and a half with one on the bottom. The contrast with RCN practice is, of course, striking.

The USN had five of these groups by January, and a sixth was formed in April 1945. Together they either sank or contributed to the destruction of at least three U-boats during 1945, two of which were on the fringe of the Canadian coastal zone.[60] While the success of these groups cannot be attributed solely to their better training, there can be little doubt about its importance. The long periods devoted to both group and refresher training ensured that the groups were well coordinated and experienced in the actions required both to detect and to attack u-boats. Canadian ships showed commendable enthusiasm but needed more than this to be successful.

In the Canadian Northwest Atlantic a reasonably effective system for individual and even unit training had been created by the end of 1944.[61] Still, the level of group and refresher training remained far below the standards practised by the RN and the USN. The RCN realized that training of this nature left much to be desired and on 7 April Captain(D), Halifax, wrote that "Western Escort and Support Groups visit H.M.C.S. 'Cornwallis' for Submarine exercises whenever they can be spared"[62] but that, in the press of operational commitments, time for training rarely seemed available. As the war drew to a close, Lieutenant-Commander J.E. Mitchell, senior officer of EG 28, the newest RCN Support Group, protested in April 1945 that his group had had only two days' training since its formation.[63]

While senior officers of Support Groups complained and Captain(D) Halifax, struggled, u-boats claimed another victim in the Halifax approaches, HMCS *Esquimalt*.[64] This sinking, fortunately the last RCN warship sunk by u-boats, occurred on 16 April 1945. The search in the wake of this sinking was soon followed by the end of the war, before any substantial training or tactical improvements could be made. Some measures were taken to increase RCN ship strength just prior to the end of the war, but only tentative ones. A third Support Group sailed for home waters at the end of April, in this case the highly experienced and successful EG 6, the only example of the rotation of experienced groups from UK waters that the operational research scientists would soon recommend as a possible – if roundabout – solution to the RCN's training and experience problem.[65]

As the war ended, the RCN wavered between continuing to adopt RN procedures and embracing new USN concepts. There was also a growing realization that conditions in Canadian areas were different and that therefore new tactics might be required. However, the evident difficulty that the RCN had in determining the best doctrine to adopt can be seen in the prolonged correspondence associated with search plans like Operation Scabbard: after months of discussion on possible alternatives, it was decided that Scabbard was probably best. Naval Service Headquarters' subsequent equivocal direction to adopt USN search plans demonstrates the RCN's ambivalent attitude regarding adoption of another new type of search plan. While the new USN tactics were admired for their scientific basis, concern over conflicts with previous procedures led to a compromise approach where the new could be used so long as it did not interfere with the old. Perhaps it could be said that, in typically Canadian fashion,

NSHQ opted for "muddling through" rather than for taking a strong stand on any one side.

This might be seen as a good general description of the Canadian experience of tactical doctrine throughout the Second World War. Forced to create a naval infrastructure in a rush, the RCN compromised. Many features of the RN were adopted, but even imitation could only be imperfect in the face of the commitments the RCN assumed. By 1945 the service had turned itself into a reasonable facsimile of the larger navies, but it lacked many of their more refined qualities. The RCN had entered the war almost completely dependent on these larger navies, but ended it well on the road to modest self-sufficiency. What is perhaps surprising is not that there was room for improvement, but that so much was accomplished.

## · I I ·

*MIF or MNF?*

## The Dilemma of the "Lesser" Navies
## in the Gulf War Coalition

RICHARD H. GIMBLETT

What are "MIF" and "MNF"? Military organizations are infatuated with acronyms, all too often without great regard for their import. That is unfortunate, for a close examination will invariably expose associations that would otherwise escape the casual user. These two, as used during the Persian Gulf operations of 1990–91, are a case in point. MNF denoted the "Multinational Forces" gathered at the invitation of Saudi Arabia to defend it from further Iraqi aggression. MIF stood for the "Multinational Interception Forces" enforcing the United Nations–sponsored maritime embargo against Iraq. Two means to the same end – arresting Iraq's aggressive behaviour and restoring Kuwait's legitimate government – but the differences between the two terms are crucial, as the very specific meaning of each effectively defined the role that the participating nations, especially those despatching naval forces, saw for themselves within the UN Coalition.

The Canadian naval task group despatched to the region in August 1990 underwent a significant change of roles during the transition to war in early-January 1991.[1] From originally supporting the mandate of the MIF, it came to have a closer affiliation with the position of the MNF. Other Coalition naval forces underwent essentially the same transitional process, but arguably none quite as dramatically as the Canadians. Our national experience illustrates particularly well the forces at play between the MIF and the MNF, and offers insights into the political as well as military considerations to which commanders must be responsive in the course of coalition operations. The whole process provides an enlightening glimpse into the realities of the present-day Canadian naval identity.

When Iraq invaded Kuwait on 2 August 1990, there were eight American warships already in the Gulf, forming the United States Navy Middle East Force (COMIDEASTFOR) that monitored the uneasy ceasefire between Iran and Iraq.[2] They immediately took up defensive positions in the central area northeast of Bahrain. Further amphibious and carrier battle-group reinforcements followed after King Fahd's formal invitation for assistance for Saudi Arabia and, with the army and air force buildup ashore, formed the backbone of the Coalition Multinational Forces under the American auspices of Operation Desert Shield.[3]

In a rare show of unanimity, the United Nations Security Council was quick to criticize Saddam Hussein's invasion, but was somewhat slower at deciding upon the best means to counter it. Beyond the apparent unity of purpose there existed deep divisions as to a solution to the crisis. The United States, supported by Great Britain, held that the independent collective security provisions of the United Nations Charter (Article 51) allowed sufficient scope for the MNF to proceed without further Security Council authorization. France and the Soviet Union, however, were uneasy with the latitude thus bestowed upon the Americans, and wanted the dormant Military Staff Committee (MSC) reactivated to allow direct UN control of operations against Saddam.[4] With China abstaining and most of the non-permanent members on the council as constituents of the non-industrial world,[5] that left Canada to champion the compromise position that the crisis offered a unique opportunity for the world body to manage a solution, but to do so without the potentially inconclusive meddling of the multi-power MSC. American command of the Coalition was inevitable and the incumbent cohesion desirable, but it had to be tempered by the moral authority of the Security Council.

Canada was joined by Australia and the members of the European Community (EC) in the concern to strike a stance supportive yet independent of the Americans. While the Security Council debated the next step, these nations individually came to the conclusion that naval forces offered the best option for representation in the Coalition without fear of establishing an entangling commitment. Besides the Americans, the British and French had long-standing deployments to protect their shipping in the region, and other countries soon announced the despatch of their own warships. In approximate order, they were Australia, Canada, the Netherlands, Italy, Spain, Greece, Denmark, Norway, Argentina, and Belgium.

The title of this chapter alludes to these other naval forces as the "lesser" participants because, on the obvious one-to-one comparison with the USN deployment to the region, even the British and French paled.

Together, however, they constituted a potent assembly. The spontaneous gathering of naval forces encouraged the Security Council to adopt progressively tighter maritime sanctions against Iraq and to arrive at a compromise that would allow a continued Security Council role (under Article 42) but without resort to reactivation of the Military Staff Committee. On 25 August it finally passed Resolution 665 authorizing "maritime forces [deployed] to the area to monitor the sanctions, to use measures commensurate with the circumstances to halt all inward and outward maritime shipping in order to inspect and verify their cargoes" – in essence, to institute a naval embargo, albeit without using the meaning-laden word itself.[6] And there was a further compromise: the United Nations mandate covered only the warships enforcing the sanctions; it did not cover the gathering multinational land and air forces.

By then, the three-ship Canadian task group of HMC Ships *Athabaskan*, *Terra Nova*, and *Protecteur* had already sailed from Halifax, on 24 August. When their despatch had been announced two and a half weeks earlier by Prime Minister Brian Mulroney, on 10 August, the mission statement for the national operation, code-named "Friction," had left ample room for interpretation, broadly given as "to establish [a] military presence in [the] Persian Gulf area in support of Canadian policy."[7] While that "policy" remained undefined, the upgrades to the ships and their embarked helicopters nevertheless got under way, and the media debated the Canadian role, identified by one report as "impotent peacekeeper" or as "toady to the United States."[8] As a constant backdrop, television portrayed the progress of Desert Shield, and the media world was all abuzz over the potential of the Iraqi military. For the most part, the Canadian preparations, too, were for war, for improving the navy's neglected self-defence capability against a modern threat so that it could meet any contingency. The only acknowledgment of its future embargo role was the addition of new high-speed boats – the RIBs (rigid inflatable boats) – radios and flak jackets for the ships' boarding parties, and FLIR (forward-looking infra-red) detectors for the embarked Sea King helicopters.[9] Although the two UN forces had not been defined at this point (in fact, their names had not yet been coined), the expectations on the waterfront were for more MNF than MIF.

Resolution 665 finally clarified the status of the Canadian and the other national task groups, but it would be some time before the allies could attempt to formalize any arrangements. The first meeting of representatives of the Coalition naval forces was in Bahrain on 9–10 September, before many of their forces had even arrived in the Gulf. The Western naval officers who gathered around the table, many of them personal acquaintances, had little difficulty establishing a framework for what they called "Multinational Interception Force" – MIF – operations.

However, the fact that the enterprise fell outside the bounds of any of the traditional alliances (such as NATO) meant that there was no binding structure to the Coalition. The primacy of national command and control was conceded, but some sort of working arrangement was required to avoid both duplication of effort and any mutual interference. Since the formal $c^2$ principal – where "command and control" is delegated to a recognized central authority – was out of the question, an informal $c^2$ was adopted: "coordination and cooperation" became the maxim. Within that definition, no one had any hesitation acknowledging as MIF coordinator the US Navy's Commander Middle East Force. With little acrimony or fanfare, communications nets were promulgated and patrol sectors allocated.

Still, the Americans did not enjoy the same dominant position at sea as they were coming to hold on land and in the skies. Gathered together, the other "lesser" navies discovered they shared common interests and could exert a counter to the dominance of the USN. Collectively, the forty-odd vessels of these others compared favourably with the nearly fifty ships of the USN deployed in the region (compare Tables 11.1 and 11.2).[10] Unlike the forces in the "land" coalition, the forces at sea were more evenly balanced between the USN and the others, allowing even the lesser navies a larger voice in operational discussions, especially where these pertained to interception operations. Given the other members' emphasis on sanction enforcement – that is, MIF operations rather than the broader MNF objective of power projection – they certainly had a different perspective on operations. With MIF, a true naval "coalition" – as opposed to an "alliance"[11] – was emerging. Even with the large variety of forces it had deployed, the USN discovered there were effective limits to the contingencies it could cover, and it capitalized on what it could do best provide the air-defence umbrella under which the embargo could safely be enforced – while implying a secondary priority to sanction enforcement.[12] The lesser navies, as individual services, had insufficient forces available (on average each ranging from two to six vessels deployed) to cover the same variety of contingencies. With each country's deployment geared to reflect a political aim, these navies were left little choice but to concentrate wholly on the embargo enforcement. MIF was quite literally their *raison d'être*.

Nonetheless, the dynamics within the naval coalition complicated relations between the United States and the other navies. The American commander coordinating the MIF effort (COMIDEASTFOR, now double-hatted as "COMUSMIF") also had responsibilities within the MNF. The other members of the naval coalition were bound to the operational restrictions of the embargo effort, and as the crisis dragged on without apparent end, they felt increasing pressure to adopt a more forceful stance.

Table 11.1
USN Deployments to the Gulf Region, 1 October 1990

| Task | Desig | Ship(s) | Side # | Area[1] |
|---|---|---|---|---|
| COMUSNAVCENT | TG 150 | BLUE RIDGE | LCC 19 | CAG |
| COMIDEASTFOR [COMUSMIF] | TG 150.1 | LASALLE | AGF 3 | CAG |
| | | WISCONSIN | BB 64 | |
| | | *ENGLAND | CG 22 | |
| | | *ANTIETAM | CG 54 | |
| | | *O'BRIEN | DD 975 | |
| | | *TAYLOR | FFG 50 | |
| | | *R.G. BRADLEY | FFG 49 | |
| | | *BARBEY | FF 1088 | |
| COMUSNAV LOGSUPFOR | TG 150.3 | COMFORT | T-AH 20 | AG/ |
| | | MERCY | T-AH 19 | GOO |
| | | +3 SUPPORT | | |
| COMCVBGNAS (COMCARGRU ONE) | TG 150.4 | INDEPENDENCE | CV 62 | NAS |
| | | *JOUETT | CG 29 | |
| | | *GOLDSBOROUGH | DDG 20 | |
| | | *REASONER | FF 1063 | |
| | | *BREWTON | FF 1086 | |
| | | +7 AUXILIARY | | |
| COMCVBGNRS (COMCARGRU TWO) | TG 150.5 | J.F. KENNEDY | CV 67 | NRS |
| | | MISSISSIPPI | CGN 40 | |
| | | MOOSBRUGGER | DD 980 | |
| | | *SAN JACINTO | CG 56 | |
| | | *THOMAS.C. GATES | CG 51 | |
| | | *ELM. MONTGOMERY | FF 1082 | |
| | | *THOM.C. HART | FF 1092 | |
| | | *SAM.B. ROBERTS | FFG 58 | |
| | | +3 AUXILIARY | | |
| COMUSAMPHIB TF | TG 150.6 | NASSAU (CTF) +17 | LHA 4 | |
| COMUSCLF | TG 150.8 | SARATOGA | CV 60 | NRS |
| | | PHILIPPINE SEA | CG 58 | |
| | | BIDDLE | CG 34 | |
| | | SAMPSON | DDG 10 | |

\* With ships available for COMUSMIF (as CTG 150.2).
[1] Acronyms for operating areas are as follows:
   CAG  Central Arabian [Persian] Gulf
   SAG  Southern Arabian [Persian] Gulf
   GOO  Gulf of Oman
   NAS  North Arabian Sea
   NRS  North Red Sea
   BEM  [Strait of] Bab el Mandeb

Table 11.2
MIF Deployments to the Gulf Region, 1 October 1990

| Country | Desig | Ship(s) | Side # | Area |
|---------|-------|---------|--------|------|
| CANADA | TG 302.3 | ATHABASKAN (CTG) | DDH 282 | CAG |
| | | TERRA NOVA | DDE 259 | |
| | | PROTECTEUR | AOR 509 | |
| UNITED KINGDOM | TG 321.1 | YORK | D 98 | CAG |
| | | BATTLEAXE | F 89 | /SAG |
| | | JUPITER | F 60 | /GOO |
| | | LONDON (CTG) | F 95 | |
| | | GLOUCESTER | D 96 | |
| | | BRAZEN (8 Oct) | F 91 | |
| | | CARDIFF (25 Oct) | D 108 | |
| | | RFA FORT GRANGE | A 385 | |
| | | RFA OLNA | A 123 | |
| | | RFA DILIGENCE | A 132 | |
| | | +3 MCM | | |
| | | +4 LST | | |
| BELGIUM | TG 418.2 | ZINNIA +2 MCM | A 961 | BEM |
| DENMARK/ NORWAY | TG 420.5 | OLFERT FISCHER (DA /CTG) | F 355 | SAG/GOO |
| | | ANDENNES (NoCG) | W 322 | |
| NETHERLANDS | TG 429.9 | WITTE DE WITH (CTG) | F 813 | SAG/GOO |
| | | PIETER FLORISZ | F 826 | |
| ITALY | TG 620.1 | LIBECCIO (CTG) | F 572 | SAG/GOO |
| | | ZEFFIRO | F 577 | |
| | | ORSA | F 567 | |
| | | STROMBOLI | AOR 5327 | |
| FRANCE | TF 623 | MARNE (ALINDIEN) | A 630 | SAG/GOO |
| | | DUPLEIX | D 641 | /NRS |
| | | MONTCALM | D 642 | /BEM |
| | | COMMANDANT BORY | F 726 | |
| | | DOUD. DE LAGREE | F 728 | |
| | | PROTET | F 748 | |
| | | COMDT DUCUING | F 795 | |
| | | DURANCE | A 629 | |
| AUSTRALIA | TG 627.4 | DARWIN (CTG) | F 04 | GOO |
| | | ADELAIDE | F 01 | |
| | | SUCCESS | A 304 | |
| SPAIN | TG 665.1 | SANTA MARIA | F 81 | NRS/GOO |
| | | DESCUBIERTA | F 31 | |
| | | CAZADORA | F 35 | |
| GREECE | | LIMNOS | F 451 | NRS |

Under those circumstances, it was inevitable that the lines between MIF and MNF would be blurred during the course of operations. The looming dilemma for the Coalition navies was that each in its own way, within the strictures set out by its national government, would eventually have to decide if and when it could, or should, cross the boundary from MIF to MNF – from being satisfied with intervention to escalating into power projection.

The relatively benign operating environment of the southern Gulf, Gulf of Oman, and Red Sea, where the bulk of the MIF operated, allowed their undivided attention to interceptions and boardings. In the tense conditions of the central Persian Gulf, however, where the Canadian task group deployed in concert with the United States and Royal navies, the demands of self-defence tended to blur even more the line between MIF and MNF priorities.[13] Nor did the carefully measured restraint of MIF operations come naturally to the Canadian navy. These boardings were very different from those undertaken in the course of fisheries patrols on the Grand Banks, and unlike the army and air force, both veterans of peacekeeping missions throughout the world, the navy had no long tradition of United Nations operations.

Although a relative newcomer to the game, the navy quickly got into the act. Only six hours into her first patrol, *Athabaskan* was called upon to conduct a boarding of an Indian relief ship that other forces had been unable to effect. Although it was nighttime and a heavy sea was running, the Canadian destroyer accomplished the inspection quickly and professionally.[14] That set the standard, and an unofficial competition was under way among the three Canadian ships, which in turn encouraged a disproportionate Canadian contribution to the overall effort. By the end of November the ships had accounted for 1,041 interceptions – nearly 25 per cent of the MIF total to date, despite their late entry and their having only 10 per cent of the resources.[15] *Protecteur* had added her own solo event as the only Coalition tanker on regular patrol in the central Gulf: during October and November, the Canadian supply ship – nicknamed the "Chuckwagon" – conducted a total of forty-three "replenishments at sea" (RAS), a full half of them with American, British, French, and Dutch warships. Meanwhile, as a whole, the Coalition had swollen to its full membership and, deployed in operating areas ringing the Arabian peninsula, had put a stranglehold on maritime traffic bound for Iraq and occupied Kuwait.

Then, on 29 November, with the adoption of Resolution 678, by which the Security Council authorized the use of "all means necessary" to evict Saddam from Kuwait after 15 January 1991, the MIF rules began to change. The UN mandate was now expanded to cover the actions of all Coalition forces in the region. General Schwartzkopf in Central Command had been working on an "offensive option" for some time and at last had the international moral authority to implement it. At a multinational anti-air-warfare (AAW) coordination meeting on 6 December, COMIDEASTFOR briefed the Coalition partners on the proposed operations and discussed their participation in the event of hostilities. The implication for the Coalition naval partners was clear: the time for decision had arrived – were they to be MIF or MNF?

The response varied considerably. The most immediate and unequivocal replies were from the British and Australians. General Sir Peter de la Billière, commander of the British forces in the Middle East, ordered his task group commander to develop "plans for an offensive campaign by the Navy high up the Gulf."[16] Then, on 5 December, the Australian prime minister announced that Royal Australian Navy (RAN) ships, which previously had been restricted from passing through the Strait of Hormuz, would be deployed from the Gulf of Oman into the Persian Gulf and placed under USN operational command should that be necessary. Within days, the Dutch government similarly committed its task group to the support of USN operations.

At the other extreme was the reaction of the remaining members of the Western European Union (WEU).[17] Coordinating their Gulf policy under the chairmanship of France, this group of nations chose to maintain an independent foreign policy and specifically to refrain from any discussion of offensive operations so as not to jeopardize the possibility of a last-minute compromise.[18] The French, Italian, and Spanish naval forces operating in the southern Gulf, joined by the combined Danish-Norwegian task group, whose governments followed a similar policy, remained effectively assigned to MIF embargo operations.

Falling between these two camps were the Canadians and the Argentineans. The latter had relatively few political restrictions upon their operational employment, this being determined more by the self-defence-only limits of their air defences and incompatibilities of their communications systems with those of the Western allies.[19] The Canadians remained ambivalent for more complex reasons. On the technical side, "connectivity" was certainly not a problem, but anti-air warfare was. Unlike the British, Dutch, and Australians, all of whom were equipped with long-range surface-to-air missiles (Sea Dart for the British, Standard SM-1 for the others), the Canadian ships had no effective area air-defence systems with which to act as long-range "pickets" or "shotgun" close-in escorts of the strike force carriers. Equally important was the domestic political dimension, of which the physical safety of the aging Canadian ships was only one consideration. The Canadian government, second only to the British, was the staunchest Western supporter of American action in the Gulf.[20] Still, Cabinet had been well advised as to the limitations of their hastily upgraded naval task group, and public opinion polls indicated that while Canadians continued to firmly support a tough stance against Saddam, they hesitated to support offensive action before all diplomatic avenues had been explored. Focusing the Canadian deployment on support of the MIF effort remained a popular option. Even with the recent change in the course of events, the mandate of the task group did not change.

The naval coalition was beginning to undergo the transition from a MIF mentality to one more closely resembling that of the MNF, but whereas USN interest in MIF operations was now decidedly secondary,[21] there was little observable change in the scope or tempo of Canadian naval operations. In December 1990 the MIF reached its apex and the Canadians were proud participants in the culmination of the embargo effort. That the Canadians held a different perspective from the American MIF coordinator became apparent over the issue of boarding criteria, the Americans becoming more lenient while the Canadians, supported by their Royal Navy counterparts, continued to put a higher premium on the display of MIF solidarity exhibited through the inspection of *all* Iraq-bound merchant traffic. The commander of the Canadian task group, Captain "Dusty" Miller, felt justified in exercising a degree of independence, primarily because of the loose command and control arrangements in effect (after all, the Americans were only "coordinating" the effort, with each country exercising its right to visit and search in response to national direction) but also because of the conviction that to date the Canadian support for the MIF was arguably at least as great as that of any other Coalition member.

In this light, on 13 December 1990 *Terra Nova* intercepted a small flotilla of tugs and barges returning from a civilian dredging operation at Umm-Qasr, Iraq, to their southern Gulf ports. In the space of six hours, boarding crews from the Canadian destroyer, on the lookout for contraband, inspected eight vessels, a feat quickly claimed as a single-day MIF record. Meanwhile, on 12 December, Commodore Ken Summers, theatre commander of all Canadian forces in the Middle East (CANFORCOMME), headquartered in Bahrain, had hosted a major Coalition conference in the spacious wardroom of HMCS *Protecteur*. Under his chairmanship, for the first time since the earlier Bahrain meeting the military officers of the states of the Gulf Cooperation Council (GCC) were brought into the MIF process, and procedures were formalized for the diversion of vessels to Gulf ports and for information exchange with GCC authorities. Through the end of December 1990, the Canadians continued their unending interception routine. Watching the buildup in the central Gulf of the Coalition naval forces, particularly the American carrier *Midway* with her British, Dutch, and Australian escorts in company, exercising their war stations, Captain Miller was led to remark in his daily report on 27 December that "USN and Allied support of MIF Ops appears to be redirected towards other tasking. Are we the only ones in step?"[22]

Although the Canadian naval commanders were prepared for action in the event of hostilities, they had not formalized plans to join the US-led MNF offensive for a variety of reasons. In large part, this was due to the very success of the MIF operations. The Canadian sailors and airmen had undertaken the tasking with gusto, and the three-ship task group contributed to the interception effort out of all proportion to its numbers. To them it was always a question of how they could best contribute to the Coalition effort. With the task group occupying stations far up in the central Gulf, and with Athabaskan's and Terra Nova's boarding totals (eleven and ten respectively) mounting and Protecteur's RAS services more and more in demand, there seemed little more the Canadian Ships could do. There were already geared to the tense operating conditions on the front line of the interception effort in the central Gulf, where the distinction between MIF and MNF in practice was constantly blurred, and the transition to war seemed like the natural course of events. But the commencement of offensive operations would mean abandonment of the central Gulf by all non-involved forces, and hence the curtailing of MIF operations. Without "area" weapons, there was no vital part for the Canadian ships to move into for the offensive effort. Instead, they would withdraw to the south to take advantage of the protection offered by the MNF. Canada's wartime role was envisioned as the far less glorious escort of the logistics and amphibious ships to be gathered in the southern Gulf, moving northward only behind the strike forces when air superiority was established.[23] Admittedly useful work, this certainly would be a step back from the high profile established in the interception operations. Captain Miller was also facing the prospect of the rotation of the crews of his ships,[24] which meant that for the next three months the effective size of his task group would be reduced by a third, with a consequent drastic diminution in his operating flexibility, compounding further the potential loss of stature of the Canadian task group.[25]

On New Year's day, 1991, all three ships were alongside at once for the first time since the beginning of October, Terra Nova in Manamah and Athabaskan and Protecteur in Dubai. That day, Commodore Summers met with the new American Arabian Gulf battle force commander, Rear Admiral Daniel March, aboard his flagship, the aircraft carrier USS Midway, to discuss Canadian involvement in battle force operations. The Canadian commodore was concerned that his task group have a meaningful role in the forthcoming operations and if at all possible remain as an identifiable group.[26] The American admiral had a problem of his own: the replenishment vessels of his four carrier battle groups were to be consolidated in one large "Combat Logistics Force" (CLF) with the intent that, as requirements arose, designated vessels would be escorted to the appropriate battle group; however, even with all the warships at his disposal, he had insufficient escorts for the task.[27] The two commanders confirmed the Canadian destroyers as escort of the CLF in its holding area in the low-threat environment of the southern Gulf, a tasking well within their capability, freeing USN warships for direct support of the carriers.[28] To help coordinate the planning of the future operations and to maintain this new close liaison with the battle-force commander, Admiral March agreed that two Canadian staff officers – one navy and one air – should be embarked in *Midway* to serve with the flagship staff as of 5 January.[29] The Canadians were back in step with their allies.

It would appear then that once finally embarked upon, the Canadian shift from MIF to MNF was taken in stride. But there was to be yet another twist on the MIF/MNF theme. Though important, the Combat Logistics Force escort duties were still rather inauspicious. Looking for a broadened role, Commodore Summers soon began to anticipate that the Canadian task group, comprising as it did both escorts and a tanker, could form the nucleus of a multinational replenishment task group.[30] The CLF already had a multinational character, as the British, Dutch, and Australians had assigned their tankers to it in the event of hostilities;[31] perhaps others could also be persuaded to join. To reflect the expanded scope, the Canadian commodore proposed replacing the "Combat" in the title of the Combat Logistics Force (which implied American forces only) with the appellation "Combined," and the concept was presented as such to the Coalition forces at their monthly MIF scheduling meeting on 9 January 1991. The other participants perceived the merits of the plan: several of them had already committed forces to the CLF, and for the remainder, joining the CLF either offered greater security to their own replenishment vessels or was easily rationalized in that escort of CLF ships could be seen as a non-offensive "support" function permissable within their national terms of reference. Best of all, it was a genuine alternative to sitting idly by while history was unfolding. When it then came time to decide upon a coordinator, the Canadians had many reasons to commend themselves, not least of which was their excellent communications channels with the Americans, doubly assured by *Athabaskan*'s upgraded radio fit and the presence of the Canadian liaison officer onboard *Midway*.[32]

With only a few days left before the expiry on 15 January of the United Nations ultimatum to Saddam Hussein, there was no longer any ambivalence about the Canadian naval role in the upcoming conflict. As 10 January closed, Captain Miller categorically declared, "Consider TG MIF ops now secondary to concentrating on URG [Underway Replenishment Group] escort ops requirements, with CTG 302.3 as Allied MNF Co-ord."[33] Through a variety of circumstances, therefore, the wartime role of the Canadian task group had been transformed to the extent of Captain Miller ultimately being recognized by the battle force commander as a subordinate warfare commander in his own right – as "UNREP Sierra" he was charged with protection of the Underway Replenishment Group, the only non-USN officer accorded any such "commander" status.[34] This new position brought with it responsibility for much of the southern Gulf and thus put the Canadian commander back into close contact with the Coalition naval forces of the WEU (these, we may recall, had been restricted to MIF operations in that area). Despite the agreement at the planning meeting on 9 January, however, the support of the Europeans remained conditional upon continuation of the MIF mandate. In trying to coordinate operations during hostilities with these other Coalition members, the Canadian task group commander was drawn back into the MIF/MNF dilemma, but this time from the opposite perspective – it was no longer an American officer who had to rationalize the participation of the Coalition partners, but now a Canadian, formerly of the MIF and now of the MNF.

All twelve Coalition naval partners with forces in the Gulf eventually participated in CLF operations (see Table 11.3). By its very nature as an ad hoc organization, the multinational logistics force underwent constant change, as each nation frequently changed the forces it felt disposed to attach to it. In particular, the frigate and destroyer escorts, crucial for the protection of the poorly armed supply ships, came and went seemingly at whim.[35] Captain Miller was now responsible for the protection of up to forty auxiliaries; this he accomplished with usually fewer than a dozen escorts. Through careful negotiation over "permitted" activity, the Canadian commander matched the Americans' CLF protection requirements to the availability of MIF escorts. In the process he helped the often willing Coalition navies find a useful MNF role within the MIF parameters defined by their governments, and he eventually became more of a facilitator than a mere coordinator for the MIF forces.

The strength of the new-found Canadian conviction was put to the test only days after the outbreak of hostilities on 17 January 1991. Sustainment of the Coalition military effort by merchant vessels unloading at the Saudi Gulf ports of Al Jubayl and Ad Damman continued unabated, and demands from the civilian shipmasters for protection against possible Iraqi attack led the USN to plan Operation Desert Turnpike, literally a controlled highway for merchant shipping through the Gulf. The scheme seemed a natural adjunct to the CLF operation and ideally suited to the MIF mandate, so the Americans turned to the commander of the Canadian task group to add this to his coordination responsibilities. Ironically,

Table 11.3

MIF/MNF Units Variously under Canadian Coordination for CLF OPS

| Escorts | | | Amphibs |
|---|---|---|---|
| MNF | MIF | Auxiliaries | (US) |
| HMCS ATHABASKAN* | HDMS OLF. FISCHER* | HMCS PROTECTEUR* | PHIBRON 5: |
| TERRA NOVA* | NoCGV ANDENNES* | HrMs ZUIDERKRUIS* | OKINAWA |
| FNS J. DE VIENNE* | ITS LIBECCIO* | HMAS SUCCESS | FT McHENRY |
| HMS BRAZEN | ZEFFIRO* | RFA ORANGELEAF | DURHAM |
| BRILLIANT | FNS DOU. DE LAGREE | OLNA* | OGDEN |
| EXETER | COMDT BORY | FORT GRANGE | CAYUGA |
| ARA ALM. BROWN* | SPS NUMANCIA | SIR BEDEVERE | |
| SPIRO* | VICTORIA | SIR PERCIVALE | TRIPOLI |
| USS HARRY W. HILL* | BNS WIELINGEN | ITS STROMBOLI* | |
| HORNE* | | VESUVIUS* | |
| FORD | | SAN MARCO* | |
| FRAN. HAMMOND | | USNS KISKA* | |
| FIFE | | SHASTA* | |
| WORDEN | | SPICA* | |
| HALYBURTON | | ACADIA* | |
| HrMsP. VAN ALMONDE | | NITRO* | |
| | | MOUNT HOOD* | |
| | | HASAYAMPA* | |
| | | PASSUMPSIC* | |
| | | KILAUEA* | |
| | | USS KANSAS CITY* | |
| | | PLATTE* | |
| | | SAN DIEGO* | |
| | | NIAGARA FALLS | |
| | | SACRAMENTO | |
| | | MV COURIER* | |
| | | RANGER* | |
| | | ROVER* | |
| | | OREGON STAR | |

* Denotes regular.

Captain Miller had to decline. The situation throughout the Gulf was still unsettled, he was hard-pressed to meet the existing taskings, and he had too few escorts available to take on any new role. The reply to the Americans, made through Commodore Summers, once again underscored the transformation of the Canadian naval contribution to the Coalition effort: "All three Canadian ships are now very involved in [MNF] CLF activities and therefore can no longer be dedicated to MIF Ops."[36] If the Canadians did not have the flexibility to change positions, neither did the Americans, whose warships were all devoted to operations in the northern Gulf. Merchant protection was left to fall under the overall Gulf air-defence umbrella and the Turnpike was held in abeyance until mid-February, by which time the tactical situation had turned decidedly in favour of the Coalition and the Turnpike came under joint American and Canadian administration. Its coordination by any of the other MIF navies was apparently never seriously considered.

In military terms alone, the Canadian task group commander had made a significant accomplishment in the southern Gulf. By bridging the gap between MIF and MNF, he was able to conduct operations on the scale of the Combined Logistics Force without specific command and control over those forces. The unique operational relationship could not easily be explained in terms of familiar command and control concepts. Staff officers at the various levels of the Canadian theatre and national headquarters reflexively rationalized the CLF operations in terms of the comfortable old notion of "tactical control," or "TACON," since in an ideal (NATO) world, that is what Captain Miller would have exercised over the forces assigned to him as a local Anti-Surface Warfare Commander. The battle force commander certainly gave the Canadian officer the authority to coordinate operations in the southern Gulf, but other than over his own Canadian task group, that authority in truth was little more than moral. Even when the WEU forces passed TACON to the USN (most did, but there were exceptions), it was usually with the proviso that it not be re-delegated, and at any rate TACON was somewhat more operationally restrictive than is normally assumed by the term in NATO usage. However, by passing off Miller's efforts as being a result of his exercising TACON, the truth of the existing informal structure lost much of its impact. The Canadian commander had gained the cooperation of his MIF associates not because it was a military alliance requirement, but through persuading them it was for the ultimate benefit of the Coalition, and that he was sensitive to the limitations on their employment.

Perhaps of more import for future multinational operations was the political dimension of the logistics-force coordination. Arguably, Captain Miller was performing a service to the Coalition that few other naval commanders could have with the same degree of success. The Americans, preoccupied with the move to the offensive, were quite happy passing the secondary southern escort role to a proven ally. While recognizing the importance of continuing to project the image of Coalition solidarity, they were less responsive to the sensitivities of the Multinational Interception Force. Most members of that force were doubly handicapped by the political restrictions on their operating areas and their less sophisticated communications suites. The only others who could operate on a close tactical level with the USN – the British, Australians, and Dutch – were already doing just that, involved as they were in the battle force operations to the north. Somehow, through the Combined Logistics Force, Captain Miller was able to square the circle of MIF affiliation with the MNF.

For probably the first time in our nation's military history, the strange juxtaposition of French, British, and American heritages that significantly define Canada proved an advantage in bringing together a diverse group of Coalition nations. Unfortunately, because it strikes at the essence of the Canadian perception of themselves as "helpful fixers," the significance of Captain Miller's undertaking was not fully appreciated by anyone at the time and has reaped scant recognition since.

Ultimately, the MIF/MNF dilemma was not a simple question of tactical control. It was much more a matter of national forces being responsive to the political imperatives of their own governments, and it underlines the political and diplomatic pressures, as well as military, on the forces deployed in the Gulf. Canadian naval commanders were sensitive to their government's desire to define a more active role for the United Nations but to do so without estranging the remaining superpower. They saw they could achieve that end, and preserve their own stature, by marking out an independent yet visible and meaningful contribution. They could afford neither to encourage the continuation of the old way of doing business, as represented by the MNF, nor to squander good relations with the Americans by sticking doggedly to the irrelevant position that to a certain extent the MIF had become. In the process of negotiating a skilful balancing act between the MNF and the MIF, the Canadian forces deployed at sea in the Gulf avoided being relegated to the sidelines, falling neither on the side of obsolescence nor on that of anonymity. By undertaking a leading role in Coalition operations, the navy provided a distinctly Canadian solution to the perennial problem of multinational warfare – measuring the needs of the overall alliance against the aspirations of the individual members – and gave substance to the definition of a Canadian naval identity.

## · 12 ·

# *"A Good, Workable Little Fleet":*
# *Canadian Naval Policy, 1945–1950*

JAN DRENT

Failure by Canada to make a reasonable contribution to her own defence would
inevitably result in loss of national prestige and in undue subordination to other
albeit friendly powers. "Freedom of action" is not a gratuity: it depends upon
the ability to support it. – Naval Staff planning paper, 22 June 1945[1]

A heady awareness of greatly enhanced international status and industrial muscle pervaded Ottawa in the summer of 1945. Canada's military
leaders faced the future with a confidence based on the dominion's prodigious wartime effort. Yet they also had to grapple with a radically
changed international situation and with some all-too-familiar domestic
political constraints. This chapter examines how Canadian naval policy
between 1945 and 1950 was shaped by the emergence of a world dominated by two superpowers and by the onset of the Cold War between
them. By demonstrating singleness of purpose combined with flexibility
and powers of persuasion both at home and abroad, Canada's naval
leadership laid the foundations not only for a substantial peacetime fleet,
but for policies that would endure for forty years.

Uncertain as the future world order seemed in 1945, early that year senior officials and military planners had already identified important basic
elements in postwar planning in documents prepared for the Cabinet
War Committee (CWC). First, while there was optimism about the international situation, it was expected that the victorious powers would
maintain larger armed forces than before the war.[2] Second, the postwar
defence relationship with the United States would be important. The de-
structive potential of long-range bombing had been graphically brought
home. Use of the atomic bomb in August 1945 reinforced earlier perceptions both that warfare had been changed fundamentally and that
long-range air attacks on North America from across the Pole could be

devastating. Canada would be affected in any such attack on the United States. Third, future relationships between the United States and the Soviet Union would be "of special concern."[3] Indeed, as early as April 1944, fully sixteen months before the defeat of Japan, the senior Canadian officer in Washington speculated in a letter widely circulated in Ottawa and seen by the prime minister that the United States might in the future go to war against the USSR.[4]

Canada's greatly enhanced status would become the launching pad for an activist foreign policy of internationalism, but at the same time, the armed forces that had been created in wartime were rapidly reduced in size. In late 1945 the government's priorities were adjusting to a peacetime economy and responding to public expectations for new social policies. The prime minister summarized his approach at the start of 1946: "What we needed now was to get back to the old Liberal principles of economy, reduction of taxation, anti-militarism, etc."[5]

David Bercuson has written, "There had been no real effort ... at the cabinet level to define the overall mission of the armed forces; through the service chiefs proposing, and the government disposing, a policy of sorts emerged almost by accident."[6] The chiefs made proposals about peacetime strengths and structures, and the Cabinet Defence Committee (CDC) set "interim force" levels at the end of September 1945 – only one month after Japan's capitulation. Ultimate peacetime strengths were to be determined later when requirements became clearer. The results of this policy vacuum were later assessed by one of the architects of the new foreign policy, Escott Reid: "At the beginning of 1947, Canada was virtually a disarmed nation."[7] The evolving Cold War was to turn the government's attention back to defence, and a forceful and energetic minister of national defence, Brooke Claxton, would work effectively with his service chiefs to ensure that military requirements received cabinet attention.

## The Policy Process

Brooke Claxton, who became defence minister at the end of 1946, had a major role in shaping defence policy for the next eight years. He faced a daunting task: "My job as the first post-war Minister of National Defence was to bring together and make into a team three mutually resistant and highly competitive services staffed by bands of aggressive young men who had won the war."[8] During his tenure, the Cabinet Defence Committee was the most senior level at which defence policy was developed. Issues were referred to the Cabinet itself when, as Brooke Claxton later wrote, "I thought it desirable."[9]

The committee, the peacetime successor to the Cabinet War Committee, enabled the government to exercise control over defence issues.[10]

Prime Minister Mackenzie King took over as chairman in 1946 to give defence firmer supervision. When he appointed Claxton a few months later, the minister swiftly reconstituted the committee as a smaller and more effective body and became its real leader.[11] By 1948 the CDC included several of the government's most powerful members – the ministers of trade and commerce (C.D. Howe), finance (Douglas Abbott), and external affairs (Louis St Laurent and then Lester Pearson).[12] Its frequent meetings, with their uninhibited exchanges,[13] were attended by the service chiefs of staff and the deputy ministers of the appropriate departments. The chiefs had direct access to the minister, and their scope for making decisions and shaping policy was far greater than in subsequent years, when their department grew larger and more complex. In addition, government departments were more autonomous in the early postwar years, and to effect change, the Department of National Defence (DND) did not have to generate momentum in a structure of overlapping departmental and interdepartmental bodies as was later to be the case.

Reform of defence organization was topical, as governments everywhere were readjusting to peace. Most notably, the United States Congress would pass the act establishing a single secretary of defense in June 1947. Brooke Claxton, who had been the first minister of health and welfare, was chosen to be the first postwar single minister of national defence because the prime minister wanted a firm hand in control of that department and an ally in effecting economies, thus freeing resources for new social programs.[14] The new minister was determined to achieve closer coordination among the services and a measure of unification.[15] Proving to be an energetic, perceptive, and capable administrator, Claxton created a single National Defence Headquarters within three months. He passed on and received policy guidance through a revitalized Chiefs of Staff Committee (CSC), which included strong civilian representation from External Affairs, Finance, the Cabinet Secretariat, and DND itself. The committee produced a yearly joint appreciation and implementation program.[16] Douglas Bland has written that "although harmony was never complete it was in the interests of the Service Chiefs to get along."[17]

In those early postwar years, the afterglow of the wartime importance of the services had practical consequences. Contacts between the service chiefs and senior decision-makers in the government were regular and close.[18] The chiefs and the deputy ministers saw each other at both the Chiefs of Staff and Cabinet Defence committees, and these associations – together with frequent encounters with Cabinet ministers – were part of the formal and informal policy process.

As the Cold war developed, Canada's defence policy came to be decisively influenced by collaborative planning, initially with the United States and after 1948 within the nascent North Atlantic alliance. The service chiefs provided professional advice on the basis of these joint and allied plans, and their recommendations, shaped by spending limits, largely determined how their services evolved. Claxton later described how the chiefs of staff advised him: "Any substantial change or any new addition to the programme on which we had settled, or a proposed major change in organization, would usually be brought about following a discussion of this between the Chief of Staff concerned and myself."[19]

The Naval Board acted as a collegial body of advice for the chief of naval staff (CNS). A staff officer of the time recalls policy being decided "by the Naval Board or by senior officer caucus." He sees this process as having been a throw-back to "how things had been done in the tiny pre-war Navy – by old boy interplay – and a reflection of the desire to get back to the old way of doing things."[20] Within this "caucus" there was an extraordinary degree of policy continuity through the presence of three key officers – Vice-Admiral Harold T.W. Grant, Rear Admiral Frank Houghton, and Captain Horatio N. Lay – all of whom had had considerable experience and influence at naval headquarters during the war.[21]

Vice-Admiral Grant became a member of the Naval Board in 1946 and was appointed chief of naval staff in September 1947 during Claxton's first year as minister. A naval cadet at age fifteen, the admiral had grown up in a tiny service that was a sub-system of the Royal Navy. He had commanded a destroyer and three cruisers during the war, but as chief of naval personnel in 1942, he had also tried in vain to slow the exponential growth of the navy in order, as Milner has written, to consolidate.[22] While there is a lingering impression that Admiral Grant was not as politically nimble as his Royal Canadian Air Force (RCAF) and army opposite numbers, the record shows that he defended the navy doggedly in both Cabinet and Chiefs of Staff committees.[23] The words of Commander Tony German are apt: "Harold Grant was blunt, arbitrary, a firm decision-maker, and a sea-dog to the core."[24]

The second member of the trio, Rear Admiral F. Houghton, came to Ottawa from command of the Royal Canadian Navy's first light fleet carrier, HMCS *Warrior*, to take up the appointment of assistant chief of naval staff in 1947, and he remained when the position was upgraded to vice-chief. Remembered as being restrained in manner,[25] he was the senior member of the Naval Staff and chaired its meetings. Houghton had been director of plans in 1940, when a big-ship navy was first planned.

The acerbic and demanding Captain H.N. Lay became director of plans at the end of 1945. He had commanded the first Canadian-manned escort carrier, HMS *Nabob*, after service in Ottawa, during which he had conducted the study that recommended the creation of a naval aviation branch.[26] As director of plans, Lay was a member of the inter-service Joint Planning Committee on postwar structures and the junior RCN member of the new Canada-US Military Cooperation Committee in 1946. He became assistant chief of naval staff (Plans and Air) in 1948. He then went to Washington in May 1949 as a commodore, just in time to be a member of the North Atlantic Ocean Regional Planning Group as NATO force planning gathered momentum. All three of these members of the naval caucus had key roles in implementing the push towards an anti-submarine warfare (ASW) focus for the fleet and in defending naval aviation from its vociferous critics.

## The Essential Defensive Striking Force

The minimum objective should be to maintain in full commission sufficient ships which when concentrated will form the smallest naval force capable of making an effective contribution to the maintenance of Canadian security.[27]

– Naval Staff planning paper, 22 June 1945

The navy's success in holding to its goal of a fleet structured around a light aircraft carrier task force is a story of perseverance and of difficulties surmounted. Alec Douglas has described how the wartime Naval Staff had pursued its goal of "a strong, well-balanced fleet."[28] It had succeeded in gaining the government's approval for a role in the final Allied effort in the Pacific that would make possible the acquisition of a light fleet carrier and a naval aviation branch. By June 1945 planning for the postwar navy was directed towards a self-contained fleet adequate in the home defence role "to repel all but heavy task force attacks in the adjacent oceans."[29] Other minimum tasks foreseen by the Naval Staff were (a) the protection of sea communications and vital trade routes, (b) cooperation in hemispheric defence, (c) the prevention of "unneutral acts" in national waters, (d) support for a world security organization, and (e) support for national policies and interests.

The Naval Staff argued that the peacetime force should be a minimum nucleus capable of rapid expansion. However, the "essential defensive striking force" – the carrier and cruisers – would have to be kept operational in peacetime, as they could not be rapidly brought out of reserve in a crisis. These arguments reflected painful wartime lessons. Experience had shown that satisfactory operating standards could only be achieved by adequate numbers of trained and experienced personnel. The case for a "fleet-in-being" also rested on the need for sufficient national units to produce a force large enough to matter. The navy had worked hard to gain status in the Allied command structure commensurate with its contributions. In any future joint operations, it was obvious that Canadian influence on how ships were employed would depend on the size and nature of the national contribution.

Under the interim force levels approved by the government in September 1945, the navy's strength was to be reduced to 10,000 by March 1946, sufficient to operate a single light carrier force instead of the two – one for each coast – recommended by the planners.[30] The minister described this in the House in October 1945 as a "good, workable little fleet. It can easily be expanded if need be."[31]

Achieving the goal of a "good, workable little fleet" would not be easy. The support and administrative infrastructure that had been improvised with difficulty during the war to operate a force of relatively small and simple ships would now have to be restructured to handle a new and complex peacetime navy. The most sophisticated ships of the late-war navy, the cruisers and Tribal-class destroyers, had been essentially supported by British infrastructure, and they, along with an aircraft carrier, would now be operating from Canada. The target in the early postwar years was to keep one light fleet carrier, two cruisers (one with a reduced complement), and nine fleet destroyers in commission, with a second carrier and other ships in reserve.[32] Creating a naval aviation branch was one of the earliest and most ambitious goals. The government gave formal approval in December 1945, and the new aircraft carrier HMCS *Warrior* was commissioned one month later. While rapidly discharging personnel (by January 1946, 77,000 officers and ratings had been demobilized) and disposing of ships, the RCN was simultaneously establishing the new air arm and attempting to retain suitably qualified officers and ratings. Personnel shortfalls on the one hand and persistent efforts to man as many ships as possible on the other are consistent themes in the minutes of the Naval Board and other Naval Staff records for the years 1945–50.[33] In 1949 the minister was to tell a conference of senior naval officers that "the Navy, of the three services has had the most difficult job to do in the bringing about of the post war organization. I think that it is a fair summary in four words ... that this situation was brought about by *shrinking and growing pains*."[34]

The war had demonstrated the value of carrier-borne aircraft in anti-submarine operations. Indeed, the RCN had hoped to operate the first Canadian-manned carrier as part of a national support group in 1944, but the ship was used as part of a British force for strike operations instead.[35] In the early postwar period the carrier's operational role was that of the main unit of the "essential defensive striking force." The light fleet carrier, however, had limited political support and became the target of inter-service struggles. Mackenzie King had been uneasy about aircraft carriers when the manning of British escort carriers by the RCN was first officially proposed early in 1944.[36] After the war he continued to see the carriers as overly grandiose for the type of navy he considered appropriate. When he invited Brooke Claxton to become minister of national defence, he buttressed his own opposition with that of his secretary of state for external affairs: "The Navy had no need at all at the present time for aircraft carriers. I had always opposed this from the start. We should have a purely coast defence ... I mentioned specifically that St Laurent was feeling that aircraft carriers should go at once." [37]

Claxton set out his own initial views on defence policy in a memo to the prime minister on 8 January 1947. He considered that the security of Canada should be emphasized as part of the joint defence of North America. A balanced small fleet did not strike a responsive chord: "Our navy's primary purpose is to train personnel rather than to have ready a task force."[38] The new minister circulated his ideas to senior officials. In his reply, Arnold Heeney, clerk of the Privy Council and one of the prime minister's most powerful advisers, suggested that Canada should specialize in selected capabilities in concert with the United Kingdom and the United States. This would probably result in cutting out carriers and other elements.[39]

On 9 January 1947 the Cabinet Defence Committee discussed reducing defence spending and debated eliminating aircraft carriers altogether. By now, however, Mackenzie King had convinced himself that one carrier would be useful in the North in war.[40] Claxton remained sceptical but eventually accepted the carrier. In June 1948 he told a visiting American admiral that naval aviation was financially inappropriate for Canada but that he would try to protect it from public criticism.[41] The second carrier remained a naval planning goal into the 1950s but never received political approval.

During this period the costs of naval aviation and the future utility of aircraft carriers were topics of fierce public controversy between the new US Air Force and the US Navy. It is arguable that these vociferous power struggles could have raised questions in the minds of Canadian politicians and reinforced doubts. Admiral Grant told the Cabinet Defence Committee in 1949 that the naval air arm involved about 9 per cent of the RCN's personnel and 14 per cent of naval expenditures.[42] On more than one occasion he had to argue persuasively to preserve his air arm, and to point out that an autonomous carrier task group was essential to ensure national command of the Canadian contribution in operations with allies.

There were many bureaucratic skirmishes. The chief of air staff, Air Marshal Wilf Curtis, declared at a CDC meeting in September 1948 that "the operation of aircraft carriers by the Royal Canadian Navy was, in principle, undesirable."[43] A year later, during a discussion by the same committee on increased manpower, the minister of finance suggested that the navy should concentrate on a surface escort force.[44] In a committee meeting in October 1949, St Laurent, the acting prime minister, asked pointedly about the role of naval aviation: "It was felt in some quarters that this was an activity somewhat beyond the scope of a navy of the size maintained by Canada."[45]

One of the most direct recorded confrontations occurred in a special Chiefs of Staff Committee meeting in January 1950 concerning the armed forces' Five Year Plan. Air Marshal Curtis "desired to place on record that the Chief of the Air Staff recommended the disbandment of the Naval Air Arm." Earlier in the discussion he had stated that planned expenditures on naval aviation during the next five years "could be put to better use by both the RCAF and the Canadian Army." The chief of air staff and General Foulkes, the chief of general staff and chairman of the committee, suggested that "completely balanced forces" were not required of Canada in NATO. Carrier-borne aircraft could be provided by the United States and the United Kingdom, and the RCN should therefore "concentrate on small ships." Admiral Grant pointed out that "a fleet of surface ships without the Naval Aviation element would of little use." Relying on allied carriers in peacetime would mean that in war "the whole of the Canadian Navy would in fact be under command of either a US or UK Task Force Commander."[46]

## The Impact on Naval Policy of the Defence Relationship with the United States and of the Cold War

When Major-General Pope chaired the Canadian Joint Staff Mission in Washington in 1944, he was looking ahead to the end of hostilities and the need for a continuing close defence relationship with the United States. Writing in April 1944, he observed: "What we have to fear more is a lack of confidence in the United States as to our security, rather than enemy action."[47]

When peace came, the Permanent Joint Board on Defence began working on a new project for North American defence. Although this was to be a contingency plan, joint planning acquired particular significance for Canadian defence policy for two reasons. Since an overall Canadian security policy had not been formulated, the development with the United States of the joint defence plan effectively became the process by which strategic requirements and the types of forces needed by Canada were evaluated. Secondly, and of central importance for the question of national identity, for the first time Canadian defence requirements were being worked out in peacetime in a partnership outside the Commonwealth. Collaborative planning for imperial defence in the 1930s had been hamstrung by misperceptions both in Ottawa and London. Mackenzie King had tended to see all British overtures for increased efforts as attempts to entangle Canada in imperial commitments and had often acted obstructively. The United Kingdom, for its part, had failed to pursue tactics that would respond to the emerging dominion view of a less dependent status. The collaborative planning with the United States that started in 1946 reflected the greatly increased national maturity and status that Canada had gained during the war.

Worsening relations with the Soviet Union gave momentum to Canadian postwar planning in concert with the United States. While Canadian documents used terms like "the potential enemy" or "another great power" in 1946, considerations of possible threats soon concentrated on the USSR. Much of the government's attention became focused on joint planning for defence of the Canadian North. A key concern for ministers and their advisers was to maintain Canadian arctic sovereignty by demonstrating to the United States that there would be a credible national contribution in that region. General Pope had been prescient. A revisionist overemphasis on the dilemmas of security versus sovereignty, however, has subsequently distorted how problems appeared at the time. Both nations were, in fact, responding to what were perceived as real military threats. While the emphasis was on air defence, joint consultation would also directly shape naval planning.

The first stage was a "Joint Canada–United States Basic Security Plan," approved by the newly created Canada–United States Military Cooperation Committee (MCC) in May 1946.[48] The MCC next worked on appendices to specify forces required for implementation. Naval planning concentrated on the "Sea Lines of Communication." The establishment of force requirements developed its own momentum, and by mid-1947 the MCC was producing a yearly implementation program aimed at the two countries' being able to conform to the Basic Security Plan within ten years.[49] Canadian defence planning was soon being dominated by this collaboration. In June 1947 Captain Lay, the director of naval plans and intelligence and a member of the MCC, observed that "the only aspect of defence in which active planning is taking place is the Canada–United States Basic Security Plan. Although no approval has been given to proceed with any part of this beyond the planning stage it already colours defence thinking to the virtual exclusion of all else."[50]

The most far-reaching results for naval policy were, first, an emphasis on anti-submarine warfare to counter the only element of the Soviet navy then capable of offensive operations against North America and, second, equipment standardization on the basis of North American production standards.

Meanwhile, Brooke Claxton outlined the government's postwar defence policy in the House of Commons in July 1947, when he introduced his spending estimates. He listed three defence objectives: the defence of Canada against aggression, aid to the civil power, and undertakings in cooperation with friendly powers or under the United Nations (UN).[51] The Basic Security Plan, Claxton explained, was intended to strengthen and support the UN. As for naval requirements, the minister included higher-speed submarines in a list of devastating new weapons that menaced the Western powers.

The era of "the old Liberal principle of economy and ... anti-militarism" was in fact coming to a close. By the following year, the worsening international situation, marked by the Communist coup in Prague in February 1948 and the Berlin blockade in June, had brought intensive discussions with other Western governments. As an Atlantic alliance began taking shape, Canadian defence planning focused on how Western Europe might be supported in a crisis. The government assigned defence much higher priority, and the DND estimates were increased by almost 40 per cent (although naval expenditures did not start to rise until the following year).[52] Ambitious mobilization and five-year acquisition plans were produced for use in case relations with the Eastern bloc deteriorated further.

A memorandum from the chief of naval staff to the minister in May 1948 typifies how requirements that eventually became government policies were ratchetted upwards.[53] The minister had apparently suggested that the manning restrictions of 75 per cent of authorized service ceilings imposed early in his tenure might be relaxed. Admiral Grant used the opportunity to argue not only for an increase in manpower, but for a shipbuilding program, to start in the following fiscal year, for four fast escorts, four minesweepers/coastal escorts, and, as well, the modernization of existing destroyers to improve their anti-submarine capabilities. The CNS advocated quick action in order to lay the groundwork for further expansion if required. All of these measures were eventually approved – the escorts became the successful St Laurent class[54] – and all were significant in concentrating fleet development on anti-submarine capabilities.

The chief of naval staff based his case on long-term plans for the RCN drawn up in September 1947. These had been built on a worst-case Canadian–US assumption that after 1951 there would be only twelve months' strategic notice of an attack by the USSR and after 1957 one month's notice. Four main Canadian naval commitments were foreseen in the plan: (a) protecting sea lines of communication, mainly in the North Atlantic, (b) defending coastal sea lanes, (c) providing defence for naval bases and ports, and (d) transporting and supporting a mobile air-land striking force designed to deal with incursions in the North. The rationale for Admiral Grant's measures was thus drawn from the ongoing joint planning process with the United States.

The nascent North Atlantic alliance was soon influencing Canadian naval policy. When introducing spending estimates in June 1948, Claxton alluded to the possibility of future roles under "a North Atlantic security understanding." He went on to state the roles outlined in Admiral Grant's paper: "For the short term, however, our roles are clear and evident. At sea our role would largely consist of guarding the lines of communication as the Royal Canadian Navy did so well during the last war."[55]

The signing of the Atlantic Pact in April 1949, which established the North Atlantic Treaty Organization, led to military planning on a regional basis. Admiral Grant headed the Canadian delegation when the North Atlantic Ocean Regional Planning Group (NAORG) met for the first time in October, the same month that the USSR exploded its first atomic bomb. Canada's focus in NATO naval planning was on anti-submarine measures, as concepts about force requirements already worked out in conjunction with the United States Navy (USN) came to be applied in the wider cooperative effort. Nations began pledging specific forces for NATO service in the event of a crisis, and these "force goals" would in time focus effort on living up to national commitments to the alliance. It would not be until 1952 that the NAORG functions were taken over by the Supreme Allied Commander, Atlantic (SACLANT), but the foundations were already in place for a planning system that would, by emphasizing force goals, exert a strong influence on the shape of the RCN over the next four decades.

Meanwhile, alliance preparedness was given a powerful impetus by the Korean War, which broke out nine months later on 25 June 1950. The government instituted an accelerated defence program that included the goal of expanding the naval force from fifty-two to one hundred ships.[56]

Because of the central role that planning with the United States played in the evolution of Canadian naval policy before and after the formation of NATO, it is appropriate here to consider three of the most important aspects of that relationship.

### ASW, Standardization, and the Northern Focus

One of the startling technological developments late in the war had been submarines with greatly improved underwater performance. Alec Douglas, Marc Milner, and Michael L. Hadley have described the difficulties experienced by the Allied maritime forces in coping with the formidable new high-speed, long-endurance German submarines. Indeed, the British official historian Stephen W. Roskill privately considered that they had never been fully and finally mastered.[57] The Soviets had emphasized submarines even before the war,[58] and they were known to have taken over some of the latest German submarines and German production yards.

It was not long before the professional unease born of experience in dealing with the new German submarines led to worry about potential

Russian use of this technology. The Canadian Chiefs of Staff Committee was briefed on the possible problem by Captain Lay in his role as a member of the MCC as early as 7 June 1946.[59] At the same time, the revised Joint Basic Security Plan had assigned the RCN specific tasks in protecting coastal sea communications and in cooperating with the USN in protecting ocean shipping in the North Atlantic and north Pacific.[60]

In late November 1946, the CNS, Vice-Admiral H.E. Reid, explained to the Cabinet Defence Committee that in any future war anti-submarine measures would "constitute the most important and difficult naval task and it was not yet clear as to what means would prove effective in this area."[61] Admiral Reid was not alone in being uncertain about how best to counter modern high-speed submarines. The British and American navies were actively considering a variety of solutions.[62] The joint defence program for the next fiscal year submitted by the Chiefs of Staff Committee in December 1946 assigned priority to anti-submarine measures. It listed "certain types of naval forces that are required to counter the modern high speed submarine" as one of three "immediate deficiencies" and held out the hope of internal economies to free up resources to address the problems.[63] In the event, the Cabinet was determined to effect economies and the defence estimates were cut by one-third.

Anti-submarine capabilities at the time were in fact limited. Organizational energies in the immediate postwar period had been directed to the transition to a peacetime establishment and the creation of a general-purpose fleet. From mid-1947 onwards, the carrier air group consisted of fighters and Firefly Mark IV (and later Mark V) anti-submarine warfare (ASW) aircraft. These were the latest available British type but had poor endurance and day-only capabilities. No Canadian ships were fitted with squid, the stabilized, ahead-throwing, anti-submarine mortar.[64] Naval Staff thinking in 1946 on destroyer requirements for the interim force had stressed the need for good all-round characteristics.[65] The frigates and Algerines commissioned for training periodically on both coasts were far too slow against modern submarines.

Momentum towards improvement took time to develop but eventually produced a mix of versatile ships and aircraft. When a destroyer had to be reconstructed after a collision, the opportunity was used to fit squid. By the time *Micmac* joined the fleet in 1949,[66] there were sufficient funds to fit squid in further destroyers. In 1949 an arrangement was negotiated to procure, on highly favourable terms, Avenger aircraft being discarded by the USN. Refurbished for ASW under an innovative program in Canada, these aircraft greatly enhanced the carrier's capabilities when they entered service early in 1951. Joint force requirements studies had stressed the need for large numbers of escorts in an emergency. When planning took on increasing urgency in 1948, frigates and minesweepers that had been sold for scrap were "frozen" by the government and designated as a "strategic reserve."[67] They were bought back and returned to service under the accelerated defence program after the outbreak of the Korean conflict.[68]

Submarines were needed in the postwar years for anti-submarine training and exercises, but acquisition proved too difficult given the limited size of the RCN.[69] They were borrowed for training each year from Britain and the United States, and eventually were available continuously.[70] By 1948 a role for anti-submarine submarines had been identified. The Naval Staff deliberated their procurement for operational as well as training roles. However, when the vice-chief of naval staff (VCNS) established a committee to investigate submarine requirements, he observed: "Unless circumstances should alter very dramatically, it seems pretty clear that the capital outlay and maintenance costs of a submarine service in the R.C.N. would be regarded as completely prohibitive."[71] It also took time for the Royal Canadian Air Force (RCAF) to reacquire wartime anti-submarine capabilities that had been given up in the peacetime retrenchment. Only in 1950 was the first postwar maritime patrol squadron formed.[72]

As early as October 1948, Admiral Grant told the Cabinet Defence Committee that "the main role of the Royal Canadian Navy was generally considered to be an anti-submarine one."[73] The first definitive political statement was made almost two years later when Brooke Claxton, in explaining NATO roles, told the Commons: "Our role in naval operations is definitely known by all Canadians and certainly recognized by the House of Commons. It is anti-submarine work, largely in the waters across the North Atlantic, and coastal protection on both coasts."[74]

In the early postwar years, former allies, except those under Soviet domination, looked to US technology and methods as models for achieving American-style success. Tendencies in Canada to look south for inspiration rather than across the Atlantic to Britain were reinforced. The advantages of using Canadian sources of matériel and production standards that were closer to American standards than to British had been demonstrated during the war. When postwar joint planning emphasized North American standardization, it thus strengthened views that had long since dominated industry. An agreement on the interchange of information – the encouragement of common designs and standards in "arms, equipment, organization, methods of training, and new developments" – was announced in Ottawa and Washington in February 1947.[75]

The government stressed that this agreement was not a treaty, and it had been carefully worded to preserve sovereignty. Nevertheless, the agreement was important in facilitating cross-border contacts. At the time, there were no regular Canadian-American joint exercises or extensive exchanges of personnel, but the agreement gave impetus to such activities. For the navy the agreement was also significant because it focused attention on the feasibility of procuring new equipment developed for the USN.[76]

The USN's overall influence as a model varied. Aside from the RCN's ingrained familiarity with British methods, there were practical reasons why the USN was not always a suitable example to be copied. Its sheer size and diversity reduced its usefulness as a model, since its complex organization and methods could not readily be applied on a smaller scale. It is true nonetheless that the RCN's organization of ships and aircraft for operations changed to conform to the American task force concept, and this in time facilitated joint operations. The RCN's adoption of tactical signal books based on those used in the USN paralleled similar developments in the RN. Memories of the dominant Anglo-Canadian role in North Atlantic convoy protection during the war were fresh, and it was not clear that USN methods were superior. When, in 1948, the plans for defending Western Europe in a crisis became more specific, it was axiomatic that the Royal Navy would also be a major player. As early as October of that year, the CNS told the Cabinet Defence Committee that "while no definite arrangements had been worked out, protection of the North Atlantic sea lanes in co-operation with the Royal Navy appeared to be a reasonable assignment."[77] The RCN's existing associations with the RN and tendencies to draw heavily on British tactical doctrine were thus reinforced.

In other areas the records show that decisions on using American or British designs and organizations were made pragmatically, with North American sources of supply being used whenever possible. Electrical systems, surface weapons and radars in new construction, and modernization programs were of American design.[78] The St Laurent hull and its propulsion system were derived from UK projects, and the fleet was fitted with British anti-submarine weapons and sonars. The best features of the USN supply system were copied in the overhauling of the RCN's ramshackle naval stores and pay-accounting systems, a decision made in 1948. Naval aviation evolved from its Royal Navy Fleet Air Arm roots; by 1950 it was using a blend of RN and USN operating procedures[79] and, as has been noted, was modifying its first American aircraft for anti-submarine warfare.

Northern defence became a high-profile item for the government, both because there was a perceived developing threat and because of US activities in the Canadian Arctic. A large American military presence in the Canadian North during the war had aroused concern about sovereignty.[80] In the early postwar period, the increased geostrategic importance of the Arctic became one of the most pressing defence issues for the Canadian government. In late 1945 the US Joint Chiefs of Staff had decided on a forward strategy to keep "potential enemies" at a "maximum distance,"[81] and the Americans were soon broaching plans for arctic weather stations, cooperative surveillance, and other research. A paper prepared in the Department of National Defence for the Cabinet in May 1946 noted: "In brief, Canada must now either herself provide essential facilities and services in her Arctic territories or provide them cooperatively, or abandon almost all substantial basis to her claims upon them."[82]

In 1946 the navy's attention was drawn to northern operations by a proposal to freeze a suitable vessel into the ice for a year for the purpose of tri-service research.[83] Although the exercise never occurred, planning began for a northern cruise. In the late summer of 1948, an RCN carrier operated in the eastern Arctic with two destroyers, which then made the first-ever naval visit to Churchill, Manitoba. Officially, it was announced that "the purpose of these cruises is to familiarize personnel in Arctic conditions,"[84] but the navy's ability to operate in anything more than light ice was non-existent.

In fact, a political decision had already been made to change the situation. On 8 January 1948 the Cabinet Defence Committee considered a proposal for a third summer of extensive operations by US naval icebreakers in Canadian waters. The secretary of state for external affairs, Louis St Laurent, focused on a new possibility: "naval participation in arctic activities in relation to North American security, and specifically to ensure a greater measure of Canadian participation in the development of northern projects as might be approved as a result of the Canada–United States Basic Security Plan."[85] Admiral Grant was told to investigate the possibility of procuring one or more icebreakers for the fleet.[86]

Events moved swiftly, and when the committee agreed on 3 March to recommend acquisition of an icebreaker to Cabinet, St Laurent gave the project a further push as one "which should be given a high priority in joint Canada-US defence preparations."[87] The wartime role was foreseen as resupplying friendly forces in the Arctic and breaking ice for amphibious operations against enemy incursions. The project was approved. The icebreaker was the first warship ordered after the war and the first shipbuilding project for the RCN based on American standards.

Soon, however, other priorities emerged as the navy embarked on fashioning the "efficient nucleus anti-submarine force." The Naval Staff started having misgivings about the icebreaker's limited utility in ASW, and long before she was commissioned, there were suggestions that manpower was needed for more warlike tasks. When fleet manning was discussed by the Naval Staff in November 1950, the VCNS acknowledged "the limited strategic requirement for the vessel" but expressed the belief that "public opinion would require that it be commissioned."[88] Just over three years after the icebreaker entered service, the navy turned her over to the Canadian Coast Guard because of economic pressures.[89]

The navy's venture into the Arctic was the result of a political determination to underline Canadian sovereignty. The decision to use a warship for an essentially peacetime role was an echo of the decision early in the century to acquire warships for fisheries protection.

## Conclusion

Peacetime collaborative planning in the five short years between 1945 and 1950 shaped Canadian defence policy for the next forty years. During this period, there was a shift towards using equipment manufactured in North America and major shipbuilding programs began using Canadian designs. Although the RCN for the first time was being significantly influenced by American methodology, the process was selective and techniques were modified to suit Canadian requirements. The government's decision to acquire a special warship – a naval icebreaker – as an instrument of sovereignty was another key development. The Naval Staff guarded its "workable little fleet" from political and inter-service opposition, and worked to ensure that any Canadian contribution to allied operations would be large enough to preserve national control. In response to contingency plans, the small general-purpose navy that existed at the end of the war concentrated on an anti-submarine role while still retaining capabilities in other areas. By 1950 the RCN was busily applying innovative solutions to ASW. The government approved substantial rearmament after the Korean War broke out, and this produced the fleet based on the 1945–50 policies that is only now being replaced.

The 1945–50 period marks a distinct stage in the evolution of the RCN as a national institution and as a navy with unique characteristics. The navy's leaders drew on the experience and confidence gained during the long war years to pilot their service into the new policy areas just described. They were able to make good use of opportunities and to capitalize on their service's strengths. At the time, they appeared to some observers as being too mid-Atlantic in attitude. The record shows clearly that they were no longer functioning as a subset of an imperial navy but were adapting certain of the best features of the Royal and United States navies to Canadian requirements.

The Naval Staff's unrelenting emphasis on a fleet-in-being paid rich dividends in July 1950, when the government was able to respond immediately to the crisis in Korea by despatching three destroyers long before aircraft and troops could be prepared for action. "The Navy must be prepared to put to sea the day war was declared," Admiral Grant had said in January 1950, "and within the limited funds, the plan was to achieve the largest possible operational fleet."[90] These words reflect the ethos of the officers who implemented naval policy in the years between 1945 and 1950.

# · I 3 ·

## Sailors, Admirals, and Politicians: The Search for Identity after the War[1]

PETER T. HAYDON

In the early days after the war, the Royal Canadian Navy (RCN), particularly its search for identity and consensus on force structure, can be studied from several perspectives. An examination of the decision-making process is one of the more interesting approaches. One cannot help but be struck by the similarity between the situation immediately after the Second World War and that of the post–Cold War period. In the late-1940s, for instance, most Canadians believed that military forces were no longer necessary. At first, the politicians were equally convinced that the new peace would hold and were anxious to redirect funds from defence to social programs. The military, however, did not share those views, believing instead that world stability was not yet certain and that a "core" military capability should be retained. The Canadian admirals, naturally reluctant to surrender their recently acquired "blue water" capability, had to embark on a political fight to save their fleet from the politicians' axe.

Canada was forced to rearm a mere five years after the end of the war, but the zeal with which the military was demobilized after 1945 and the scarcity of funds to maintain even a modest fighting capability made rebuilding the navy an enormous challenge, one that continued until 1953–54 when stability returned. The early postwar years have been described as a period of "shrinking and growing pains."[2] Yet that first decade after the war was the formative period for Canada's Cold War navy. They were years of turmoil, often marked more by failure than by success.

Nevertheless, the admirals persevered, and by the mid-1950s the first phase of the RCN's metamorphosis into a highly professional navy, able to maintain modern anti-submarine warfare (ASW) forces in both the Atlantic and Pacific for most of the Cold War, was complete.

During the initial struggle to define the postwar role and structure of their navy, the admirals and their staffs had to deal with two main problems: political scepticism over the need for naval forces and the impact of rapid demobilization. Both were complex issues. The Pacific war was barely over when the senior officers of the RCN had to embark on a campaign to preserve their navy, particularly its infant naval aviation capability. The problem was that the politicians only saw a requirement for a coastal defence navy. The admirals, on the other hand, believed a broader role was needed, and they were determined that the navy would not again be found wanting, as it had been at the outbreak of war in 1939. Planning was also complicated by the changing nature of the Canadian defence relationship with both the United Kingdom and the United States.

Demobilization was essentially complete by mid-1947, but political views of the world situation began to change after the 1948 Czechoslovak coup. Even then, the actual process of rebuilding the navy was far from easy and remained intensely political. By the mid-1950s the navy had essentially completed most of its transition from a wartime navy of over 100,000 people to a much smaller volunteer force prepared to deal with the new threat posed to North America by the Soviet Union, within both the bilateral and the NATO defence-planning structures.

However, in late 1955 NATO's war-fighting strategy, promulgated in MC 48, changed its focus from a concept of operations essentially like that of the Second World War to one involving a fast-moving nuclear scenario in which the first thirty days of conflict were critical.[3] This shift in strategy brought about a major change in the Canadian navy's mission, and it thus marked a turning-point in the evolution of the RCN. Hence, the 1945–55 period forms an interesting window through which to look at the origins of many basic policies that shaped Canada's Cold War navy.

Naval planning in the first postwar decade was dominated by three closely interrelated factors:

- the attempt to define the role and force structure of the navy;
- personnel issues; and
- the changing relationships with the American and the British navies.

In fact, those issues would remain prominent beyond the 1950s in varying intensities. Over the years, however, the last two were generally of secondary importance to the overriding concern for getting political approval of Canadian naval force structures. This should not be surprising, for Canadian admirals have always had trouble selling their concepts for the fleet to the politicians and, unfortunately, to much of the Canadian public. It is, in fact, a consistent theme throughout the recent history of Canada's navy.

This chapter will look at the way the Canadian admirals struggled both to retain the fleet they acquired at the end of the Second World War and to transform it into a professional force able to meet the challenges of the Cold War. To illuminate this struggle, some of the key points within the three dominant factors will be examined. This necessarily brief review will show just how complex and closely intertwined those issues were.

*The Fleet*

The origins of the RCN's Cold War force structure lie in the 1943 Quebec Conference, which saw the Royal Navy (RN) give Canada the opportunity to man and operate capital ships. There is also reason to believe that the origins can be traced even further back in history to the 1919 Jellicoe Report; it was then that the seeds of a Canadian "fleet-in-being" were first planted. However, there were additional changes between 1943 and the onset of the Cold War, as a Naval Staff paper noted in January 1947:

On the 24th December 1943, Naval Staff approved in principle recommendations regarding the tasks which the post-war Navy should be capable of undertaking and for the forces that should be required to fulfil those commitments.

In 1943 the tasks were predicated upon a general state of war without taking into account a particular enemy. It is now possible to give specific consideration in regard to the possible enemy. Moreover, since 1943 developments in weapons have made it possible to foresee with some clarity the nature of the war that will be fought against the probable enemy.[4]

The important point is that when the war ended, the concept of a fleet-in-being was firmly entrenched in the Canadian naval tradition. It was this concept that the admirals had to defend in face of the politicians' plans to reduce the navy to a mere coastal defence force.

Initially, the navy was not quite sure what it wanted the fleet to do beyond the sort of things it had been prepared to do at the end of hostilities. One thing was certain: naval aviation was to be the keystone of any future mission. That concept, however, became the lightning rod for much of the political scepticism concerning and opposition to the post-war navy. Prime Minister Mackenzie King, for one, was firmly convinced that the RCN did not need carriers, noting, "The Navy had no need for aircraft carriers. I had always opposed this from the start as unnecessary. We should have a purely coast defence."[5]

Senior officers of both the army and the air force also challenged the need for a naval aviation capability at every opportunity. Yet the navy was not totally without political support. The interim force model authorized in October 1945 by the minister of the naval service, the Honourable Douglas Abbott, was based on carrier and cruiser task groups. The official statement authorized the establishment of a small postwar navy: "It is now proposed that at the onset Canada's peace-time navy should comprise two cruisers, probably two light fleet carriers, ten to twelve destroyers, and the necessary ancillary craft, all of these of the latest and most modern type, while in reserve and for training purposes we will continue to hold a certain number of frigates. Such an establishment will require a force of about ten thousand officers and men."[6] However, this force structure would not come into being until after the Korean War. The sights were set just too high for the immediate postwar period when the manpower available for the navy fell far short of the ceiling of 10,000.[7] Instead, the navy had to settle for a much smaller fleet, but one that was still formed around a nucleus of an aircraft carrier.

Political opposition to the navy continued in Canada despite growing concern in the United States and Europe that the Soviet military capability, which had not been demobilized after the war, was a growing threat. The United States Navy (USN), for instance, had begun to plan for a future war against the Soviet Union as early as December 1945. Even though the Canadian politicians approved the continuation of the Permanent Joint Board on Defence (PJBD) in 1946 and authorized joint planning for the defence of the continent, they remained sceptical of the need for a blue-water navy. It was not surprising, therefore, that the RCN threw its weight fully behind the joint planning process. It was clear that the survival of the fleet was a function of continental defence.

According to American assessments, the potential Russian threats to North America included attacks on shipping and shore facilities by submarines. Captain H.N. Lay, then director of naval plans, wrote in August 1947:

In view of the vital importance of the defence of the North American war making ability in a future war, R.C.N. planning will in future be largely based on the Naval forces now envisaged in the Basic Security Plan. This will make desirable the complete standardization of the R.C.N. and U.S.N. by the time that the Basic Security Plan must be ready for immediate implementation. The assistance of the R.N. is one of the assumptions in the Sea Lines of Communication Appendix [to the BSP] and therefore tripartite standardization is desirable.

The major threat to sea communications in a war with the U.S.S.R. will, of course, be the submarine. It is known that Russia is placing considerable emphasis on building up her submarine fleet which will be composed of the latest types. The forces required in connection with the protection of sea communications will be primarily anti-submarine and it may be expected that Canadian contribution will be largely confined to this role leaving the provision of heavy cover, support and logistic forces to the U.S.N.[8]

For the protection of the sea lines of communications, Lay and his fellow naval planners on both sides of the border saw the major naval tasks as conducting ocean surveillance to locate and track enemy submarines, controlling and protecting merchant shipping, providing anti-submarine and air-defence ships, and maintaining a centralized command structure. This basis for naval planning stayed relatively constant throughout the postwar period. The way in which the plans were to be implemented, however, remained controversial, as the admirals and their political masters attempted to resolve their differences over how big the navy should be and precisely what it should do.

Maintaining a fleet-in-being was a major problem. In this time of fiscal restraint, the need to spend 25 per cent of the meagre navy budget on naval aviation was often criticized.[9] The fleet also had to be manned under severe personnel constraints, and it had to be modernized to meet changing threats. As the potential threat of the Soviet submarine force became of greater concern to North American and European planners, the need for dedicated anti-submarine forces grew even more pressing. For the beleaguered Canadian admirals, the need to modernize the existing destroyers to give them a better ASW capability became yet another problem. The ideal fleet model adopted in 1946 had to be abandoned. It was impossible to maintain a force of twelve modern, matched destroyers under the prevailing fiscal and manning constraints. As a result, the decision was made to convert the smaller destroyers to ASW escorts and only to man five of the Tribal class; the plan to acquire new Daring-class fleet destroyers was abandoned.[10]

As joint planning progressed, Canadian political opposition to Canadian naval concepts continued to grow. This opposition was largely based on the politicians' scepticism over the interpretation of the threat and the kinds of forces considered necessary as a countermeasure. By 1948 Canadian naval roles had become extensive and can be summed up as follows: (a) defending harbours; (b) convoying shipping; (c) hunting and destroying submarines; and (d) supporting amphibious operations in northern Canada.[11] The related requirement for ships was considerable, ranging from aircraft carriers to harbour patrol craft and submarines. The political opposition, from both sides of the border, to the joint concept of operations is understandable. For instance, in 1946 the joint planning staffs had believed the existing naval forces of Canada and the United States would be sufficient to meet the prevailing threat,[12] but within three years they were calling for widespread increases. Although part of the problem was the planning staff's inability to provide an accurate assessment of Soviet capability, another was their neglect to take economics into consideration in designing a concept of operations.[13]

In Canada the 1947 organization of the Department of National Defence (DND) brought all facets of the department under a single minister, the Honourable Brooke Claxton. His approach to defence planning was far more questioning than that of his predecessors' but he would support, willingly, well-reasoned arguments. He was, as one USN admiral noted in 1948, a consummate politician: "Defence Minister Brooke Claxton, in a private conversation, made it clear that he regarded his position as primarily political. He indicated that any support which he might give to the Naval Board and Staff's analysis of defence needs would be influenced by the political necessity of reconciling those needs with budgets, votes and taxes."[14]

By 1949 – after the Soviet-instigated coup in Czechoslovakia, the formation of the Western European Union (WEU), and the general acknowledgment that Soviet aims were not necessarily compatible with those of the West – the need for an effective Canadian navy was no longer in doubt. Yet despite the changed international situation, economic and political caution still prevailed, as Claxton emphasized: "In Canada, as in every other country, estimates for defence are built up by striking a balance between what is desirable and what is possible. We have programmes set out for every type of defence requirement running into a good many years ahead. We cannot do everything at once and the question we have to answer is which of these do we do first. In Canada, as elsewhere, the Chiefs of Staff never get as much as they want."[15]

The formation of NATO provided a form of collective security not totally dominated by the Americans, allowing Canada the political opportunity to ease out from under the American concept of operations. The Canadian navy, on the other hand, while it had been comfortable with its relationship with the USN, was naturally willing to take on such additional tasks as NATO required.[16] It is probably fair comment that the admirals saw little need to draw clear lines between NATO and North American operations at sea. In practical terms, those operations served a common goal.

The year 1950 became the moment of truth for Canadian naval aviation. There had long been scepticism over the need for Canada to have such a capability, and at various times the Canadian Army and the Royal Canadian Air Force (RCAF) had challenged the concept. The army, mainly through General Charles Foulkes, did not see the need for Canada to spend such a large proportion of the naval budget on what appeared to be a limited capability. Despite an RCN-RCAF agreement on sharing of services, the air force saw the RCN fighter and air-patrol capability as a threat to its own activities. The various issues, which had been debated at a relatively low level before, came to a head in January 1950, when the Chiefs of Staff Committee discussed the new Five Year Plan for the development of the Canadian forces. General Foulkes again challenged the need for Canada to provide carrier aviation to the allied cause when other countries could also do it. Vice-Admiral Grant, the chief of naval staff, steadfastly maintained that the carrier was an essential element in anti-submarine warfare and was necessary not only for wartime use but also to maintain proficiency throughout the fleet. The argument ended in an impasse. Admiral Grant took up the gauntlet again in a March 1950 Chiefs of Staff meeting but ran into a wall of opposition, largely because of the overall cost of maintaining the naval aviation capability. The majority were willing to give up naval aviation altogether. The compromise recommendation to the minister of defence was that "the question of Naval Aviation will have to be reviewed before any major rearming of the carrier is considered."[17] The subject surfaced again in June 1950 without resolution.[18]

The outbreak of the Korean War in June 1950 changed the tempo and scope of Canadian military planning and also solved the naval aviation problem. Once the political decision had been made to join the United Nations (UN) forces in Korea, a rearmament program began.[19] Naval plans included activating ships in reserve, pressing ahead with refits of other ships, improving Halifax harbour defences (the Esquimalt defences were discussed but given lower priority), improving the armament of the Tribal-class destroyers, modernizing anti-submarine and minesweeping equipment, and building a total of seven new ASW escorts (the St Laurent class) and sixteen minesweepers. This program was accompanied by improvements in other fighting equipment and an increase in the overall personnel strength of the navy.[20] However, when the defence minister raised the issue of sending the carrier to Korea, the RCN quickly stated that it was not a good idea because the carrier was committed to NATO.[21] And that was how it would stay!

One thing about the admirals' plans is quite clear: they did not foresee their new fleet taking a purely coastal defence role. Many of the concepts for continental defence that had been agreed upon earlier through the Permanent Joint Board on Defense were incorporated into the new strategic thinking, which saw the Soviet sea-based threat to North America coming mainly from their long-range submarines.

However, by 1950 the RCN had declined to a single carrier, two cruisers, and a destroyer force of eleven, of which four were in reserve and two were not fully operational. The range of regular tasks stretched the limited capability of the fleet to the full. The combined need to train new entries and reservists, meet the requirement for three destroyers in Korea, and modernize the existing destroyers added further pressure. At a time when morale in the fleet was not good (for reasons to be discussed later), the challenge facing the admirals was greater than it had been since the Second World War. But for once, they had adequate funds. Personnel became the limiting factor.

The 30 June 1951 edition of *Canada's Defence Programme* focused on the Korean War and the threat posed by spreading communism. It also included a clear statement of continental maritime defence objectives:

In continental defence the Navy is responsible for the protection of coastal sea lanes and shipping against enemy action, including mines; and for the vital task of keeping our harbours and approaches open. Ships and installations are being constructed to discharge this role. The R.C.A.F is building up maritime squadrons for anti-submarine work.

Naval aviation is playing an increasing part in operations of the Royal Canadian Navy for the immediate defence of Canada. It has been demonstrated in the past that carriers and their aircraft are essential to the successful execution of naval action; especially is this so in the case of anti-submarine warfare which is expected to be a vital commitment of the Royal Canadian Navy in the event of another war.[22]

The NATO role of the RCN was specified as being "anti-submarine and convoy escort work" across the North Atlantic. More importantly, the statement announced an enhanced naval shipbuilding and modernization program. This was to include seven more St Laurent-class destroyer escorts and several new auxiliaries, as well as plans to take thirty-four frigates and minesweepers out of reserve for rearming and modernization. At the same time, navy personnel strength was raised by 27 per cent to 11,709, and the navy budget was increased by 110 per cent. However, the navy's was a relatively smaller increase than that given the other two services. In fact, the navy's share of the overall defence budget dropped from 15.2 per cent in 1950/51 to 13.9 per cent in 1951/52. Some of the rationale for this may have been the perception that the navy could not spend any more than the allotted amount in a given fiscal year because of the long lead time needed for shipbuilding and equipment programs extending over several years.

The new naval program was designed to accomplish four aims within the next three years: (*a*) increase the size of the fleet to about 100 vessels, (*b*) install permanent seaward defences of vital harbours, (*c*) gear up the Canadian shipbuilding industry to produce additional ships more rapidly, and (*d*) improve administrative, training, and logistics systems for all-out mobilization. Before 1952 there had been no real concept of a balanced force or even of a national task group. Instead, planning had been based on a wide range of separate but interdependent tasks for the protection of shipping and ports. The appointment of a NATO Supreme Allied Commander, Atlantic (SACLANT), in January 1952 and the introduction of collective NATO defence planning, which had started at the February 1952 NATO ministerial meeting in Lisbon, provided a multilateral concept of operations to replace the less politically agreeable bilateral planning forum with the Americans.[23]

Naval planning, which became increasingly complex as the Naval Board had to deal with more "big ticket" items, progressed in two main directions: first, the NATO commitment, which included the carrier and most of the naval aviation capability; and second, coastal defence (referred to as "Seaward Defence") for both the Atlantic and the Pacific to meet the universal baseline planning date (Mobilization Day or "M-Day") of 31 December 1955.[24] Planning objectives frequently overlapped, and some ships and aircraft were assigned to meet both national and NATO requirements in the same task. The degree of coordination that was needed can be seen in the 1953 East Coast Defence Plan,[25] which had been worked out with both NATO and US national authorities, including the US Commander, Western Atlantic, who was "double-hatted" as both a national and NATO commander. Within the concept of coordinated operations, Canadian responsibilities were (*a*) to provide anti-submarine patrols adjacent to major ports on the Canadian Atlantic seaboard, (*b*) to protect coastal traffic between Canadian ports, and (*c*) to protect NATO shipping on feeder routes to convoy assembly ports and in other convoy operations under certain joint agreements. The tactical importance of maritime air patrol was also becoming more evident, and in 1953 a formal agreement for the coordination of maritime operations was signed between the RCN and RCAF. From that agreement a lasting tactical relationship developed.[26]

In the mid-1950s the role of the carrier was to provide mobile anti-submarine air patrols to cover areas that could not be reached by land-based aircraft and to provide sea-based air defence. Initially this was to have been in the western Atlantic alone, but NATO also wanted the Canadian carrier task group in the eastern Atlantic.[27] The carrier-borne fighter role was "to eliminate 'snoopers' which act as beacons directing submarines and bombers to the area of a convoy."[28] A concern of the Naval Board was that the NATO carrier commitment could not be maintained by one carrier alone, and as a result, options for acquiring a second were discussed on many occasions.[29] Maintaining the carrier capability was expensive and therefore controversial. This was probably one of the reasons the RCN was continually faced with financial problems in trying to maintain a balanced fleet. The related problem, very much in the RCN's favour, was that NATO had come to depend on the Canadian carrier group. Thus, the grounds for the Canadian fleet-in-being effectively shifted from continental to NATO defence plans.

The escort function, which was being provided by the mixed bag of Second World War destroyers, frigates, and other vessels until the new ships entered service, was another Naval Board concern, and it is the one that forms the focal point of this discussion. Replacing the wartime ships was a high-priority requirement and a constant source of debate between senior members of the RCN and their political masters. By 1954 fourteen St Laurent-class escorts were already under contract, but it would be several years before they all entered service. Moreover, the program was not without its difficulties, as the staff had to balance the availability of new weapons systems with the construction of the hulls. In the meantime, the older ships had to be kept as effective as possible, which in itself was an expensive undertaking.

Because the St Laurents would not replace all the old escorts, another program had to be initiated to replace the smaller Prestonian-class frigates. These new escorts were to have been replacement frigates and had been designated as the Vancouver class, but operational limitations imposed by their smaller size made them impractical and the design was cancelled in favour of additional St Laurents.[30] The Naval Board minutes of the 1 June 1955 meeting explain that the Vancouver class was cancelled because the ships were not suitable for most of the projected roles and, overall, the St Laurents were seen as much better ships. Another factor was that of cost – specifically, that by continuing with the St Laurent class, the RCN could avoid the overhead that a new class of ships would necessarily entail. Another factor was that Canadian shipyards could turn out seven St Laurents every three years. In conjunction with a program of ASW helicopters, these ships would provide an adequate replacement for the Prestonian-class frigates on convoy escort duty as well as fill a great many other roles. Overall, the Naval Staff thought this course of action would provide a significant increase in the effectiveness of Canada's NATO contribution and possibly result in a manpower saving.

By mid-1955 the RCN had re-examined the problems of increased Soviet submarine activity in North American waters and fleet requirements for air defence and had put together a comprehensive force-development plan for surface ships, submarines, and aircraft. Discussions had even been held with the USN in August 1955 on tactical nuclear weapons.[31] A new fleet organization had also been introduced along with various other changes to improve operational coordination and cooperation. These included Rules of Engagement for unidentified submarines detected within

Canadian territorial waters, a direct response to increased Soviet activity in the coastal areas.[32] Fleet strength continued to grow, and at the beginning of 1955 the fleet comprised almost 100 vessels with another 29 under construction.

Overall, the fleet modernization plan was an accomplishment in which the Naval Staff could take some pride. In a relatively short space of time they had recreated a base for mobilization and were making good progress in modernization. By mid-1955 the RCN had commitments in both the Atlantic and the Pacific and had recognized the need to have some Arctic capability. The Canadian fleet seemed to have become accepted as part of the national fabric. But the pleasure was to be short-lived. The political fortunes of the Canadian military were destined to change once more, but that is another story.

*Personnel*

It is not easy to summarize the personnel problems that plagued the Canadian navy in its early postwar years. Although the tendency is to focus on ships as the essential elements of a navy, it is in fact the people that make a navy what it is.

When the war ended, the Canadian navy was made up of more than 95,000 men and over 6,000 women, most of whom had only joined for the duration of the war. Demobilization was a high political priority. The unfortunate experiences of slow demobilization after the First World War and the need to reduce the military payroll as quickly as possible were strong motivators in 1945. But as people now realize, a military establishment cannot be cut back overnight and still be expected to function. There has to be a period of transition. Unfortunately, the period of transition allowed for the Canadian navy to adjust to its peacetime structure was too short. Also, without a strong Canadian naval tradition, there was little incentive for individuals to stay in uniform after the war. Many Canadians, if not the majority, saw the navy as little more than a small, exclusive cadre that was largely British in thought and action. In 1945 this view failed to take account of the changes that had taken place during the war. It was quite clear that the postwar navy would bear little resemblance to its prewar predecessor.

The net result of social and political pressure for quick demobilization was an unbalanced structure of ranks and trades that fell far short of minimum requirements to support the fleet. The situation was not helped by the fact that most of the personnel had to continue to live in temporary quarters and under conditions that were not compatible with postwar standards or expectations. Moreover, the calibre of many individuals who transferred to the new navy was less than ideal.[33]

In 1946 the navy's manpower ceiling was set at 10,000, enough to sustain a modest fleet-in-being. The admirals hoped to be able to maintain that level, but it soon became clear that the numbers could not be met. As the fleet employment plan for 1946–47 acknowledged:

It will be appreciated that the wartime Naval Service was very largely made up of Reserves and their demobilization will leave a very small Royal Canadian Navy. A number of Reserve personnel are being retained for an interim period of two years and recruiting for the Royal Canadian Navy has commenced. The strength of the permanent force is expected to be 6,600 by 1st April, 1946. However, a considerable period will elapse before the service is up to its authorized strength of 10,000 and before all categories of personnel are sufficiently trained to carry out their normal Naval tasks.[34]

The manpower situation was sufficiently grim to impose a major constraint on the number of ships maintained, and by February 1947 fleet strength had been reduced to one aircraft carrier, one cruiser used for training, six destroyers, two ASW frigates for training, and a few auxiliary vessels. The emphasis was placed on ASW training and flying proficiency.[35] In addition, a small reserve fleet of frigates and minesweepers was maintained. In order that reserve training could be conducted during the summer, regular force manning of some ships was reduced. A great deal of importance was placed on maintaining a trained naval reserve. The fleet concept was not greatly different from that of the Second World War: the regular force would operate the "fleet" of capital ships and destroyers, while the reserve would largely be responsible for ASW operations and defending the Canadian coast.

Manning the fleet became a nightmare. Most ships had to operate on reduced manning balanced against requirements for higher levels of new entry training and poor retention. Under favourable circumstances, this process could have worked, but improvements to the conditions of service were not made quickly enough. The result was poor re-enlistment and very low morale. Yet the impact of these problems was masked. Commanding officer after commanding officer routinely sent complaints to the admirals and their staff officers, but little was done. By late 1947 the list of problems had grown to mammoth proportion: inadequate accommodation ashore, lack of medical facilities, rates of pay that were so low that a leading seaman could not maintain a family, poor living conditions aboard ship, poor food, and inferior-quality uniforms. Throughout 1947 and 1948 there were reports of growing dissatisfaction among officers and men, and there was a small incident in HMCS *Ontario* in August 1947 over conditions of service aboard ship. However, it took the incidents on HMCS *Magnificent*, *Athabaskan*, and *Crescent* in February and March 1949 to bring many of those grievances to a head. Even then, progress in making significant improvements was slow. There was not sufficient flexibility in the naval budget to keep the fleet going and deal with all the support requirements for the sailors and their families.

A formal investigation was held into the circumstances of the incidents. The Mainguy Report (named for the inquiry's chairman, Rear Admiral E.R. Mainguy) was blunt both in describing the main causes of dissatisfaction in the fleet and in recommending corrective measures. In the eyes of the three commissioners, much of the problem lay in the need to adapt the Royal Navy system to North American standards and the evident failure to make this happen. Simply put, the fleet was not sufficiently Canadian in its internal structure. There were also serious internal communication problems between officers and men. However, it is easy to overemphasize the significance of the various incidents. Of more importance, as the investigation that followed clearly pointed out, was that the Canadian navy was in desperate need of its own identity.

The Korean War followed quickly on the heels of the 1949 incidents, and the demanding schedules that had to be maintained to keep three destroyers in Korea, meet training requirements, and modernize the destroyers stretched the navy's resources to the limit. But at least now there was reason for hope of relief. The 1950 rearmament and the subsequent budget increases provided some respite and gave the admirals the flexibility to modernize the navy's support infrastructure. However, all this should have happened earlier. As the Mainguy Report so rightly noted, the root causes of the navy's problems were the "shrinking and growing pains" that the RCN endured in the five years immediately after the war. The rush to demobilize in 1945–47 and the premature hope that order would prevail through the world almost precluded the retention in Canada of small naval capability able to respond to the call to arms when it came again in 1950. This is a lesson it would be well to remember today.

## Relationships with Other Navies

In 1945, when the Second World War ended, the RCN had been cast in the RN mould, and it was expected at the time that the relationship would continue. Even though Canadians worked quite closely with the US Navy during the war, a close relationship never evolved. However, the continuation of the PJBD and the recognition that Canadian security was inseparable from that of the United States placed the Canadian military in a new defence relationship with the Americans. Where the RN had provided the entire basis for Canadian naval tradition, equipment, and training, within an essentially "imperial" naval system, the relationship with the USN had a very different foundation. In fact, the relationship was based, to considerable degree, on a concept of mutual benefits. These benefits existed in several areas, not least in the logic of geography, which determined the need for joint defence of the continent: the Canadian admirals, by embracing a continental defence, could protect their new-found naval capability from the sharp knives of their political masters; basic economic advantages would accrue in the creation of a common North American supply system; and a North American perspective could heal the rift between men and officers, for as Canadians slowly realized, whereas sailors tended to see themselves as North Americans rather than displaced Englishmen, the Canadian officer corps had clung to the Royal Navy as a role model.

The new relationship with the Americans did not break the Canadian ties with the "mother" navy. There were changes, many of them gradual, but all of them deliberate. Whereas the links with the Americans were largely forged of geographic and economic necessity, the retention of many British concepts and traditions was voluntary.

The transformation of the RCN into a North American navy was a gradual process driven by a series of tactical and technical factors. For instance, the Canadian naval aviation capability was founded on British concepts, supplied with British equipment, and completely supported, in the beginning, by Britain. But as the RCN became more proficient and was able to integrate naval aviation into collective defence plans, the problems of being tied to British supply and training systems became evident. The need to keep sending the carrier back to Britain as an aircraft ferry started to be counter-productive. Further, having to link Canadian aircraft requirements to British production cycles created several problems. The purchase of American aircraft seemed to be a solution. Eventually, a complete shift was made whereby the RCN operated USN aircraft and all aircrew were trained in the United States. This was not a popular decision with the RN, but under the circumstances, the Canadians had no alternative.

Ship design, on the other hand, remained much more closely allied to British concepts. The carriers, the cruisers, and several of the destroyers were British-built. Initially, many of these vessels were merely on loan to Canada, a situation that presented several maintenance and update problems. Consequently, it became necessary to buy the ships from the RN rather than continue to borrow them. Even though this step decreased the degree of reliance on the RN, there was still a heavy British influence in ship design as a result of links through the Royal Corps of Constructors. By the mid-1950s, however, the fleet began to take on a distinctly Canadian character. The design for the new St Laurent class was uniquely Canadian, and subsequent modifications were based on Canadian rather than British operational requirements.

Even though the RCN still used British equipment to a considerable extent, there was a trend towards American-designed weapons and systems, particularly where they could be made in Canada. Unlike the aviation equipment and procedures, which had shifted to US models, shipboard procedures retained more of a British stamp. Until the 1960s, in fact, most of the highly specialized professional training was done through the RN.

The largest area of change came as a result of continental defence planning. Because of the overriding requirement to defend the North American continent, the RCN had to adopt USN tactical communication and fleet-organization concepts. There was no option. To undertake the joint defence of the continent, common procedures had to exist, and it was logical that the smaller navy adopt the procedures of the larger. When NATO came of age operationally, the RCN also adopted its procedures and thus had to cope with a dual standard. This caused some problems but never to the extent of impeding operations. Through this process, the RCN became a North American navy able to work with ease with its American colleagues and with the other NATO allies. Because it had learned to compromise professionally, the RCN actually developed its own character.

## Conclusion

The problems that faced the Canadian admirals from 1945 to 1955 were much the same as those facing the navy today: the constant quest for political support; public relations, particularly the problem of managing the differing perspectives of the navy's manpower and the rest of society; and relationships with other navies. By 1955 the Royal Canadian Navy had developed a very distinct identity of its own. Largely a continentalist identity, though tempered by strong links with Europe, it was no longer beholden to Britain for its tradition and standards. In this, the RCN was neither British nor American. It was compromisingly Canadian.

PART FOUR

*The Navy and Canadian Society*

## · I4 ·

# A Nursery of Fighting Seamen?
# The Newfoundland Royal Naval Reserve,
# 1901–1920

BERNARD RANSOM

The notion that Newfoundland, or more properly, the Newfoundland trade, was of value as a "nursery" of trained naval manpower originated as a strategic calculation in seventeenth-century British mercantilist thinking. Other commercially expansionist European powers of the period, notably Holland and France, placed equal value on overseas trade and possessions. Pursuing ever greater shares of a global wealth resource then thought to be finite, each nation sought its own vital interest in continuous conflict with its rivals. In addition to this mercantilist imperative, British policy focused upon fears of seaborne invasion by foreign opponents. Memories of the Spanish Armada (1588) and the depredations on the lower Thames during the Second Dutch War (1667) firmly emphasized the importance of the navy as Britain's prime defensive arm.

If the seafaring manpower involved in Newfoundland commerce came to be regarded as an important contributor to the power of that naval arm, then conversely it became axiomatic that the defence of Newfoundland was itself largely a function of the transatlantic effectiveness of the Royal Navy.[1] So vital was the connection that, throughout the eighteenth and the first half of the nineteenth centuries, the civil administration of the colony was linked to the local naval command, and the Newfoundland station and its governorship became a prime Admiralty appointment.

With the recall of Newfoundland's small imperial garrison in 1871, the colony was effectively demilitarized, but it was the Admiralty's strategic reorientation towards the European theatre at the end of the century that proved to be the real turning-point in local defence policy. The variform manner in which RN strategic rethinking in the era of First Sea Lord Admiral Jackie Fisher affected defence capability and policy in the dominions has been well described.[2] When the Admiralty sought colonial participation in financing a unified imperial battle fleet with an organized Royal Naval Reserve (RNR) structure to provide for wartime expansion, it met varied responses. While Australia committed to a reserve and to payment of an imperial subsidy with conditions attached on the deployment of "Australian" vessels, Canada eschewed all imperial arrangements in favour of a minimal, if independent, coastal "fisheries protection" flotilla. For the Newfoundland government, the demands of the new departure in naval policy would conjoin most acutely with long-standing irritation in London about the colony's chronic neglect to provide for its own self-defence. Hence, in the 1898–1902 period, Newfoundland policy would evolve towards covering both obligations through commitment to a local division of the Royal Naval Reserve.

Colonial Office pressure on Newfoundland to attend to its self-defence needs peaked late in 1900, when the colony's signal lack of defence capability was highlighted by its inability to field a single organized unit for the South African War. Contention developed over a proposal by Governor Sir Henry McCallum to raise an 800–man volunteer rifle corps, a scheme flatly rejected by a local Cabinet bent on seeking re-election on a taxation-reduction platform.[3] Cabinet confirmed its decision twice over the course of the year when the question was submitted for reconsideration.[4] This provoked a stinging rebuke from London, deploring the colony's apparent irresponsibility and waywardness: "... the disinclination of the Colony to fulfil its obligation to provide for local defence ... [and the situation where] ... the oldest of Her Majesty's Colonies will continue to be the only unit of the Empire which, although enjoying responsible government, neglects this duty of defence."[5]

Pressed further on the matter and chastened by the secretary of war's observation that such neglect "places the inhabitants of the Colony in a position of far less security than they would enjoy if under the more direct control of His Majesty's government,"[6] Newfoundland Prime Minister Robert Bond indicated a preference for a naval defence force on the grounds that it would enjoy greater success among a seafaring population than a military one.[7]

Bond's rather convenient recourse to a naval option was an explicit attempt to achieve a "total" self-defence policy intended to meet both Admiralty and War Office demands but which minimized the drain on the Newfoundland exchequer. This was the approach he outlined at the 1902 Colonial Conference in London during delegate discussions on imperial naval policy. Bond advocated extensive imperial investment in developing

St John's as both a cruiser base and a defended port from which the North Atlantic cables and grain traffic, so vital for British survival, might be effectively secured in time of war. He regarded a Newfoundland RNR as a pivotal and "direct" contribution to imperial oceanic defence requirements, while cooperative involvement in base construction, he declared, would be "further evidence of ... [Newfoundland's] ... willingness to [contribute] according to its means."[8] On the particular issue of the fitness of Newfoundland's young male population for seagoing duty with the imperial fleet, Bond waxed eloquent in unequivocally traditionalist terms: "They would be of the very best quality of the material upon which the naval greatness of the empire was founded – the sons of fisher-folk cradled on the rocky shore ... and matured in seafaring experience at fifteen or sixteen years of age. It is doubtful if any better naval nursery can be found in all His Majesty's Dominions beyond the seas than on the Newfoundland seaboard."

By 1902 the RNR proposal was seen by the colonial government as a general solution to its embarrassment over lack of defence preparedness, but the actual training scheme for Newfoundland reservists had already commenced and was showing some promise. Fisher himself had first opened discussions about a Newfoundland RNR with the then governor Sir Herbert Murray during the course of 1898, but little had been done in that year to promote the idea among the fishing population.[9] During the summer of 1899, in his first year as governor, the energetic McCallum made a round of the outports of the English Shore in a cruiser of the RN's North American squadron, accompanied by various Newfoundland ministers and by the station commander, Commodore G.A. Giffard, RN. Although worried that his mission had not been well received by the population and that opponents in the press and the competing attraction of the spring seal fishery might undermine the enterprise, McCallum was gratified to learn that he had attracted 300 registrants by early 1900. Premier Bond committed his government to financing the covering-in, heating, and lighting of a training hulk for the reserve corps, a drill facility recommended by the commodore. He further undertook to select fifty men from those who had registered for service and arrange transportation for them to St John's by mid-November for an initial six-month training cruise with Giffard in his flagship HMS *Charybdis*.

While reserving judgment for the moment on the question of provision of a drill ship, the Admiralty enthusiastically took up the commitment for the extended training cruise. Clothing and victualling costs, together with the standard retaining fees, which amounted to £211 sterling gross, would be the Admiralty's responsibility.[10] This inaugural trial cruise, which lasted a full six-month period, from November 1900 to May 1901, was completed to everyone's satisfaction. Giffard had high praise for his Newfoundland reservists, commending their application to big-ship discipline and to acquisition of fighting skills. He noted that "they have made themselves popular to Officers and men alike and ... [are] ... now a useful and efficient body of men who would be a formidable addition to our personnel."[11] He had been able to promote forty of the contingent to the higher grade of qualified seaman and, most revealingly in terms of their nutritional and lifestyle backgrounds, had observed that these young men, all aged between eighteen and twenty-one, had on average put on three pounds of weight and increased their chest measurement by one inch during the cruise. His final analysis was that "the experiment has had a most successful issue," and he expressed the hope that further such training would continue.

The Executive Council of Newfoundland formally expressed its appreciation to Giffard personally, both for his efforts to establish the reserve program and for his considerate treatment of the men. In his reply, the commodore touched upon an issue which perhaps blackened the navy somewhat in the opinion of the colony's fishing population and which would be a chronic obstacle in recruitment for the local RNR: the legal obligation of RN vessels on station to expel any Newfoundlanders encroaching on the fishing grounds of the "French Shore," which were reserved by treaty to French nationals only. Giffard rather sheepishly explained: "The expressions of praise and approval ... are ones I most highly esteem and value and all the more so because they come from those whose efforts – in many instances – for the advantage of the fishing population of Newfoundland were often almost nullified by my necessary actions as the Naval Officer administering the Treaties."[12]

A second contingent – again of fifty reservists, and financed directly by the Admiralty in similar fashion – embarked in HMS *Charybdis* on 11 November 1901.[13] At the conclusion of this second cruise, Giffard was able to promote all but three men to the qualified seaman grade.[14] These two initial training cruises established a pattern for RNR operations in Newfoundland for succeeding years and also a tradition of high levels of performance on the part of the reservists themselves. Newfoundland RNR men proved to be adept at acquiring gunnery and small-arms skills (including cutlass practice) and were noteworthy for their general physical strength and capabilities in small-boat work. In this latter area, they proved to be more than a match for the crack rowing crews of the squadron. Additionally, the 1902–1903 contingent of eighty men saw active service with HMS *Charybdis* in the Anglo-German Venezuelan intervention of that year. Newfoundland reservists performed creditably in action in the bombardment of the Puerto Cabello forts and the landings in Caracas in December 1902 as well as in the subsequent blockade of the Venezuelan coast.[15]

By this time, the full infrastructure required by the RNR program had been completed with the assignment of the refitted obsolescent barque cruiser HMS *Calypso* to St John's for service as a reserve drillship. Arriving in port on 15 October 1902, HMS *Calypso* carried a permanent complement of twenty-eight regular RN instructors and could accommodate up to 300 reservists.[16] Intended to train men as seaman-gunner specialists, the vessel was equipped with modern QF (quick-firing) 5-inch and 6-inch main armament, together with two maxims and two 14-inch torpedo tubes. In command was Commander F.M. Walker, RN, a decorated veteran of twenty-seven years' service whose last appointment had been commanding officer of the drillship HMS *Gleaner* on the lower Thames, the RN's most important reserve training facility.[17]

If HMS *Calypso*'s personnel and equipment indicated the thoroughgoing seriousness of the Admiralty's commitment to the Newfoundland RNR scheme, it has to be said that the Bond government matched it with an unprecedented degree of defence expenditure. Accepting the ten-year term agreed upon at the 1902 Colonial Conference for the Australia–New Zealand RNR scheme, the Newfoundland government committed itself to a contribution of £3,000 sterling per annum for that period – basing the figure on a 600-man force, with proportional reductions for any shortfalls in manning strength.[18] This was additional to a confirmation of its earlier commitment to cover the costs of housing-in, heating, and lighting the vessel for its new role as a training hulk, estimated at £1,800 sterling.

Yet further contingency costs fell to the colonial government following its own insistence that the vessel be moored permanently in St John's harbour, rather than as originally planned at Little Placentia, Placentia Bay. This original location, chosen for its remoteness (in the interests of isolating the men from the distracting temptations of the city) and for its suitability for unhampered live-firing practice, lost favour with the governor, Sir Cavendish Boyle. Ministers agreed with Boyle that the sizeable contingent of regular instructors would tend to discourage indiscipline, that the logistics of government control would be better exercised in the capital, and, perhaps above all, that such a high-profile government investment project would be seen to best advantage at "headquarters" in St John's.[19] Admiralty concurrence with the change was made conditional on the colonial government's willingness to make the eighteenth-century battery sites at the harbour "Narrows" available for RNR gunnery training without charge and to accept costs of emplacing the necessary guns from HMS *Calypso* on site, together with ongoing maintenance charges as required.[20]

The guns – two 5-inch and two 3-pounder QF pieces – were remounted in the Narrows sites after 1904, and with HMS *Calypso* moored in an adjacent berth in the east end of the harbour, a coherent program of shoreside training and deep-water instructional cruises developed. Reservists were required to enlist for a five-year term, during which time they performed a twenty-eight–day drill annually and an extended training cruise of three months on one of the HM ships.[21] By 1905 the RN's North Atlantic squadron was accommodating 120 Newfoundland RNRs annually.[22] In the 1902–14 period the Newfoundland RNR maintained an active cadre of around 150–200 men in any one year and a formal establishment in the 500–600 range.[23] For those who had completed the annual twenty-eight–day drill, seagoing training cruises were offered in two diets: December to February, and February to April. The corps was always regarded as a manpower auxiliary to the regular Royal Navy, members being paid at the imperial rates then current: 66 cents per diem while training, with an annual retainer of $16, for ordinary seamen; and 75 cents, with a $30 retainer, for the higher rank of qualified seaman.[24]

The system of recruitment was an unusual one: under a scheme advanced by Walker in November 1902, reliance was chiefly laid on local magistrates, acting as deputy registrars, to supply men from their localities.[25] The Admiralty hesitated to give full approval to the scheme on account of provision made therein for a $2 "capitation" or "finding" fee to be paid for each recruit the magistrate found.[26] Convinced of the utter necessity of such a measure, Sir Cavendish Boyle authorized it on local Executive Council prerogative, sending what he termed an "urgent whip" on the matter to all magistrates:[27] the prerogative remained the sole authority for the fee. Recruits were drawn chiefly from the settlements of Newfoundland's northeast coast – the old "English Shore." Within the decade, volunteering for RNR service would become so habitual in some communities as almost to constitute a tradition.[28] Young men involved in the inshore fishery, usually aged around twenty, were attracted not only by cash payments for service ("truck" was the norm for fishermen), but by the glamour of the king's uniform, the opportunity to see the wider world, and the chance for some adventure.

Rigorous acceptance standards give some indication of the demographic base of the RNR. Recruits had to be unmarried, be of "good character and good physique," and have basic literacy.[29] It is therefore logical to regard them as something of an elite – as the cream of rural Newfoundland youth – the most venturesome, confident, and articulate young men in their communities. Recruitment remained, however, an arduous and frustrating undertaking, marred by several factors. Perhaps the worst, and least-acknowledged, problem was the navy's association with enforcement of the unpopular French Treaty rights, which seemed to disadvantage the very people whom the RNR most wished to attract. Moreover, the winter training schedule directly clashed with the operation of the seal fishery, itself both a venue for the venturesome and a competitive alternative source of cash earnings. Inevitable *contretemps* of the service also hurt the image of the corps, such as the occasion when HMS *Charybdis* ill-advisedly used headlands south of St John's as target areas for main armament practice. Complaints from local smallholders unimpressed by the fall of shot in home pastures led to something of a public scandal in the winter of 1903–1904.[30] A worrying early sign of low commitment among RNR members themselves was the catastrophically poor level of re-enrolment among those who had finished their first five-year term of engagement in 1905: fewer than 20 per cent indicated interest in re-engagement.[31] Revealingly enough, by 1910 the relative scarcity of individuals offering themselves for service had resulted in some serious dilution of standards. In that year local magistrates were taken to task by the government for a perceived tendency to accept unsuitable individuals and were sharply reminded of the need to maintain the standards originally set.[32]

Despite such difficulties, the high regard for the Newfoundland RNR corps evinced both by UK and colonial officials and by RN officers continued unabated in the prewar period. The consideration shown the men, especially in regard to ensuring their return home in time for the spring fishery, was serious and solicitous. When the 1901 draft ran into delays on the return leg of their training cruise, both Commodore Giffard and the Newfoundland government moved mountains to ensure they made up time lost in transit: all who expressed concern were given special steamer and/or rail warrants to ensure they met the deadlines of their civilian livelihood.[33] The measures taken in relation to the 1906 contingent were even more impressive. Returning from the south Atlantic too late to make Canadian connections, they were routed directly to the United Kingdom, to be landed in Portsmouth on 5 April and embarked on a fast packet from Liverpool two days later. On the intervening day, the entire group were specially received in London by two Cabinet ministers (lords Elgin and Tweedmouth, the colonial secretary and First Lord of the Admiralty respectively), given a sumptuous lunch and dinner, and generally lionized by the London membership of Britain's UK Navy League.[34]

Perhaps the most telling professional comment on the corps was that of Walter Hose. This able officer, later to achieve flag rank and serve as director of the Canadian naval service, was in 1902 a senior lieutenant on HMS *Charybdis*. In this capacity, he was charged with supervision of the shipboard training program of the Newfoundland RNR, a recurrent annual task he performed during his years with the North American squadron, 1902–1905. Hose later recorded his opinion of the Newfoundland RNR men with unequivocal brevity: "They were the best of them all – beat our regulars in boat races all the time."[35]

In these prewar years, the corps became known in the squadron by the curious sobriquet "Quidi Vidi Lancers." Though the origin of this term is obscure, it might refer to the annual St John's Regatta, a day-long event of competitive rowing held each August on Quidi Vidi Lake in St John's. Indeed, it was a crew of the same generation as those who first formed the RNR who, at the 1901 regatta, established an event record that remained unbroken for eighty years.[36] Clearly the training in naval gunnery fitted the men for specialist service in modern warships, but it was evidently their capabilities as small-boat oarsmen that defined their value to the fleet generally. The Newfoundlanders were valued above all for an increasingly rare capability in traditional seamanship within a technologically complex steam-powered armoured fleet.

At the outbreak of war in August 1914, the nominal strength of the Newfoundland RNR stood at 485.[37] The colonial government immediately committed itself to increase the naval reserve to an active strength of 1,000 as well as to raise a land force set initially at 500 men. The then officer commanding the reserve, Lieutenant-Commander Anthony MacDermott, RN, was obliged to take drastic measures with entrance standards in his attempt to reach the new target. The maximum age at entry was raised from twenty-five to thirty-five years, while the physical measurements qualifications were, in his own words, "practically abolished."[38] According to MacDermott, "any well set up young man, likely to be useful on board a man o' war is accepted if physically fit and of generally good physique." Moreover, the stipulation that members should be professional fishermen or seamen also went by the board, many new recruits being city residents with "very little experience of nautical work." Even with these reduced standards, only 660 new volunteers offered themselves in the first six months of hostilities. Of this total, 226 were judged unfit to serve – a rejection rate of 34 per cent.[39]

The contrast with recruiting patterns for the new military force, designated the 1st Newfoundland Regiment, could hardly be more extreme. Under the auspices of a "Newfoundland Patriotic Association," a "Call for Recruits" aged between nineteen and thirty-five years was advertised. Regimental entrance standards were set at a minimal height of five feet four inches, minimal weight of 140 pounds, and a chest expansion of at least thirty-five inches.[40] By mid-September 1914, 750 volunteers had been examined and a total of 520 accepted as fit to serve; this meant a rejection rate of over 30 per cent.[41] By the end of that month, Governor Davidson recommended that recruitment cease, since the numbers far outweighed the association's capacity to process them.[42] In early October the regiment's first contingent, comprising 540 men, embarked for service in the United Kingdom. These were the famous "First Five Hundred" or "Blue Puttees,"[43] who would be the longest-serving members of the regiment and would form its A and B companies. These early volunteers were drawn heavily from the city of St John's, with only 17 per cent from rural areas.[44]

Pay differentials proved to be an additional cause for concern. From the outset, the Newfoundland government intended that both the regiment and the active RNR receive Canadian rates of pay, and it therefore obtained details of current pay scales from Ottawa.[45] Although an improvement on imperial rates then current, these rates clearly discriminated in favour of the army. A private in the Canadian Expeditionary Force (CEF) received $1.10 a day, while ordinary and able-bodied seamen in the Royal Canadian Navy (RCN) were paid daily rates of 50 and 70 cents respectively. The RCN somewhat lamely established a $1 per diem rate for special servicemen enroled for the period of hostilities only,[46] but this did not apply to regulars or reservists enroled before war's outbreak. Imperial daily rates of pay for ordinary and able-bodied seamen, with foreign exchange variables, were then in the equivalency range of 40 to 60 cents Canadian. The genuine wish on the part of the Newfoundland government to ensure equitable remuneration for its RNR servicemen[47] encountered predictable problems for men registered in and mustered for the imperial service. Beyond the basic Canadian differentials, the currency exchange rate proved troublesome. While a standard rate of exchange was quickly arranged for the regiment, this proved impossible for the RN with its widely divergent deployments and manning practices around the globe.[48] Ultimately, the authorities settled for a self-serving rationale: "The inequality is less than it seems – living in the Navy is much cheaper than the Army: they have all sorts of Customs privileges ... They will all come home with a bag full of guineas, as the Prize Money is to be awarded and divided equally."[49] Prize money was an uncertain and, in the event, a marginal recourse: one long-serving reservist had by 1919 amassed the princely bounty of $200.[50] As deterrents to successful RNR recruitment, wartime pay differentials with land forces in effect paralleled the competitive lure of the prewar commercial seal hunt.

Ironically, the Newfoundland RNR's first operational role during hostilities was a Canadian one, providing an extemporized crew component for the cruiser HMCS *Niobe*. Together with Canada's other capital ship, the cruiser *Rainbow*, *Niobe* had been placed at the disposal of the British Admiralty on 5 August 1914.[51] While *Rainbow* put to sea immediately from Esquimalt with a scratch crew to protect British shipping off the American Pacific coast, the Halifax-based *Niobe* lay harbour-bound with only a caretaker establishment.[52] A desperate appeal for volunteers from reservists and the dockyard provided a nucleus for the cruiser's 700-man complement, but extraordinary measures were required to provide trained manpower and regular officers. The Admiralty recalled and laid up at Esquimalt its two sloops then operating in the eastern Pacific, transferring their crews to Halifax for *Niobe*. The intention was to complete the vessel's ad hoc establishment with a draft from the Newfoundland RNR in St John's and to assign it to "special service in patrolling trade routes between the mouth of the St. Lawrence and Newfoundland."[53]

Following a brief work-up, *Niobe* put into St John's and took on board one officer and 106 ratings from the RNR drillship HMS *Calypso*.[54] Security was extremely tight, and the draft departed without fanfare and with little public acknowledgment, something which the governor and his ministers later deplored from the recruiting perspective.[55] For the men themselves, this was likely a marginal concern. Without exception, all were prewar-trained reservists with experience.[56] Indeed, under this new command of Captain Robert Corbett, lately the RN's Senior Officer, American West Coast, and with *Niobe*'s core RN personnel, the Newfoundlanders were on a ship perceived to be "regular" Royal Navy in routine and style. The discipline, treatment, and expectations were familiar to them from the prewar cruises with the old North American squadron. In *Niobe*, they perceived very little that was distinctively "RCN" or Canadian about the vessel.

Joining the thinly stretched RN warships of Rear Admiral Christopher Cradock's 4th Cruiser Squadron, *Niobe* began the tedious duty of blockade patrol of the Atlantic ports of the neutral United States. The patrolling ships were to prevent the escape of enemy merchant vessels caught in port at the declaration of war, especially those suitable for conversion as armed merchant cruisers, and to stop and seize vessels found to be carrying supplies for the Central Powers. Above all, their presence was crucial to sustaining confidence among American shipping interests regarding the hazards of German commerce raiders rumoured to be everywhere. In this early period of the war, before introduction of systematic convoying, such confidence was essential to the maintenance of Britain's Atlantic lifeline.[57] *Niobe* was one of only four cruisers available to carry out this important task. The Newfoundlanders were at a premium, partly because many were trained gunners on heavy naval ordnance, but also because, as might be anticipated on blockade duty, there were heavy requirements for small-boat and boarding work, routines in which they possessed special proficiency.[58] Captain Corbett recorded his "high opinion" of them in a private note to the governor of Newfoundland: "These men ... are almost unknown to me as defaulters. They are most able and willing, which speaks highly for their previous training. The two Sea Boats are manned entirely by them and they have had constant work boarding ships in all weathers, and I am prepared to back them against any boats crew of the Imperial ships on the station."[59]

Recognition of the Newfoundlanders contribution was made early in their stint in *Niobe* by the RCN's insistence that they should be paid at Canadian rates. After some months of correspondence with the Newfoundland government and the Admiralty on the issue, the latter conceded the point: the Newfoundland reservists received the higher rate in December – 70 cents a day (for able-bodied seamen) plus separation allowances for families.[60]

By the summer of 1915, and after almost a year of constant blockade duty, it was clear that *Niobe's* life as a seagoing vessel was nearing its end. Basic structures, including funnels and bulkheads, were in a parlous state, and the boilers were beyond refitting or repair. The vessel's age and the estimated costs of the extensive refit required for further sea service led Ottawa to decide to lay her up in Halifax.[61] Admiralty perceptions of the good service performed by the *Niobe* and her crew led to an immediate offer to replace her with another cruiser seconded from the RN. The RCN's refusal of this capital-ship offer in favour of creating a small-ship fleet of anti-submarine/minesweeping-capable vessels came as a surprise both to Admiralty chiefs and to the Canadian government itself.[62] *Niobe* made her final landfall in Halifax in mid-July, paid off, and was thereafter utilized as a depot hulk. The Admiralty did not countenance any possibility that her Newfoundland RNRs would continue in Canadian service. In company with the 300-odd RN regulars in the cruiser's complement, these valued ratings were summarily transferred at the end of August to depots in Britain for further imperial service.[63]

The ex-RCN Newfoundlanders joined ranks with other newly recruited Newfoundland RNRs on the strength of HMS *Pembroke*; this was the RN's receiving and training establishment at Chatham, Kent.[64] By this time, there were over 1,100 Newfoundland reservists in the United Kingdom. The 1,000-man target had been achieved that May, with an actual figure of 1,003 effectives on *Pembroke's* books. Taken together with 600 additional special reservists, this brought a grand total of 1,102,[65] a figure the colonial government had committed itself to maintain by means of a strengthened recruitment drive in order to make up the shortfall caused by war casualties.[66] Newfoundland RNR men found themselves drafted into three distinct types of service with the RN. Undoubtedly the most fortunate, in terms of conditions and low casualty levels, were those assigned to the Defensive Armed Merchant Ship (DAMS) Program. In the main, these were ex-*Niobe*-trained gunners, who shipped out on fast merchant vessels sailing independently of convoy on the Mediterranean and Indian Ocean trade routes. DAMS personnel operated in very small detached groups, one gun's crew per vessel, and experienced a relatively relaxed mercantile marine regime with commensurate good treatment. Many such reservists spent the remainder of their war service on such duty.[67]

However, by far the majority of imperial Newfoundland reservists served in the armed liners, "armed merchant cruisers" (AMCs) converted for naval use on the northern patrol, or were distributed in small groups throughout the anti-submarine/minesweeping small-boat fleet tasked to secure British coastal waters. This last duty was one of the most hazardous in the navy. Faced from the earliest days of the war with very effective German minelaying in the North Sea, in the English Channel, and along most of the important coastal steamer routes, the Admiralty greatly expanded the prewar RNR Trawler Section to meet the threat. By the fall of 1914, hundreds of former fishing craft were in commission, crewed by reservists and under the coordinated direction of a newly appointed admiral of minesweepers.[68] These small craft carried out myriad tasks: examination of suspicious vessels outside naval anchorages; pilotage for capital ships; reconnaissance and patrol of remote navigable waters; and laying "indicator" anti-submarine barrage nets to impede coastwise movement of enemy submarines. All this was in addition to the conventional minesweeping of coastal shipping lanes. Vessels impressed into this service included not only handy deep-sea fishing craft, trawlers, and drifters, but also tugs, yachts, and paddle-steamers. Casualties on these frail craft when mined or caught in an unequal fight with a U-boat at sea were necessarily high. The Newfoundland RNR suffered around a dozen fatalities each year in the 1915–18 period on this service.[69] Beyond the evident hazards of the duty, conditions were familiar enough to Newfoundland fishermen accustomed to small-boat work and the relative independence involved. Sensitive Admiralty management of the small-boat fleet ensured that discipline was not overbearing, and crews were generally allowed to concentrate on the task at hand rather than service formalities.[70]

Newfoundland RNR's served in drafts of substantial numbers on the AMCs of the RN's 10th Cruiser Squadron on the northern patrol. Tasked to intercept German traffic "Northabout" the British Isles, the patrol area of these ships was principally between the Shetlands and the west coast of Norway. It was a rough weather station second to none and, indeed, had been assigned to AMCs in 1915 after the older cruisers of the original force had shown themselves deficient in the requisite coal capacity and seakeeping qualities. AMC service could combine the worst elements of big-ship discipline with all of the flaws of extemporized equipment, manning, and leadership practices of the expanded reserve fleet. One young Newfoundland RNR volunteer recorded his impressions of shipboard life on the armed merchant cruiser HMS *Clan McNaughton*:

I am one of a gun's crew and have to stand my watch on the fo'c'sle no matter how the water is going over her, with a pair of short lace-up boots on. There were as many as 20 days ... that I never had a dry foot ... I cannot say the treatment is good in this ship – it is far from it ... I would like to be treated as a Man ought to and not like a dumb animal ... we Newfoundlanders are not used to a bugle and the consequence is, if we are a little adrift, we are run in for it and get so many days punishment ... some Newfoundlanders are always adrift and doing punishment ... They don't be adrift intentionally I'm sure, but there is no excuse in the Navy ... [For] a man who has volunteered to fight for his King and Country and then to receive punishment in this way – I say it is far from right. I would fight for my King and Country to the bitter end, but I would not like to be treated as I have seen some treated since I came on board here.[71]

The "bitter end" came all too soon for the *Clan McNaughton* and her crew when, on 3 February 1915, the vessel was torpedoed and lost with all hands: twenty-three Newfoundlanders died with her.[72] This scale of loss was matched in other sinkings of AMCs from the 10th Cruiser Squadron: HMS *Viknor*, mined off Tory Island in the Irish Sea in mid-January 1915, took the lives of twenty-four Newfoundlanders.[73] A dozen Newfoundland RNR men were lost when HMS *Bayano* was torpedoed in the North Channel on 11 March the same year.[74] Nineteen Newfoundlanders died on HMS *Laurentic*, mined off the River Foyle on 25 January 1917.[75] A similar Newfoundland RNR contingent was on board the armed merchant cruiser HMS *Alcantara*, sunk off Norway in a noted single-ship action with a disguised vessel, which proved to be the German raider *Greif*, on 28 February 1916. With both ships foundering, most of *Alcantara*'s crew were picked up by other RN vessels in the vicinity; on this occasion only two Newfoundlanders were lost.[76]

The *Alcantara* action generated prize money for the surviving members of her Newfoundland RNR contingent. With an eye to the fact that the publicity encouraged recruitment, Governor Davidson made the formal share claims on their behalf. He still hoped that the prospect of prize money might stimulate "those men who might join the Navy, but who are afraid to hazard the conditions of soldiering which are new to many of them."[77] The year 1916 had been a desultory period for RNR recruitment, and a summary reduction by the Admiralty in exchange rates for RNR allotments and family allowances had caused serious concern. Davidson made a personal protest against the rate reduction (to $4.76 from the standard $4.86⅔), declaring that it was a gratuitous cause of suspicion and grievance and effected little serious cost saving. He complained that the action "would tend to affect recruiting which is already difficult for the Reserve, most men preferring the higher rate of pay for military [that is, army] service."[78]

On the home front, 1916 also saw the emergence of a serious threat to the Newfoundland and eastern Canadian offshore fishing fleets from

U-boat raiders. Lieutenant-Commander MacDermott of HMS *Calypso* (renamed *Briton* after 15 February that year) organized fisheries–protection patrols of the Grand Banks by using small armed "Q" craft. Foremost of these was the small patrol-steamer–styled HMNS (His Majesty's Newfoundland Ship) *Fogota*, which mounted a 6-pounder quick-firing gun. HMNS *Fogota* was equipped and her commander was paid entirely from colonial funds, while *Briton* provided the crew.[79] Other home-front duties performed by the RNR were minesweeping in the entrance to St John's harbour and adjacent coastal sea lanes, maintenance of the main harbour's (12-pounder QF) defence battery at Fort Waldegrave, and provision of armed guards for the important Admiralty wireless station on Mount Pearl.[80] Whatever their enthusiasm and motivation, the calibre of RNR recruits at this mid-stage of the war was a far cry from pre-war standards. Revealingly, when the Admiralty attempted to provide gunnery courses for the corps in Bermuda, the draft of ninety-three men sent included twenty-three (almost 25 per cent) who failed simply because they were functionally illiterate. However, according to the commanding admiral they were "excellent in every other respect."[81]

In a supreme irony for a corps plagued by persistent recruitment problems, an apparent manpower surplus emerged as a major concern for the Newfoundland RNR in 1917. Conspicuously retained in St John's while attached to HMS *Briton* in the March–October period, some 400 RNRs were without any clear employment. The men were, according to Governor Davidson, "on full pay leave, idling and being a bad example." Worse still, in his view, in the period of catastrophic army losses at Ypres and Passchendaele, these "malingerers" were attracting others to the RNR who should really be enlisting in the Newfoundland Regiment.[82] Davidson and his ministers protested the situation in the strongest terms, even to the point of considering urging London to transfer the entire naval group to the regiment.[83] This undesirable situation was a consequence of the Admiralty's plan to use whatever strength the Newfoundland RNR recruited in 1917 as a manning pool for the 160 new anti-submarine drifters and trawlers that it had ordered from Canadian yards early in the year.[84] The first vessels were not completed until the fall, hence the prolonged wait by their RNR crews. Initially, these vessels were to have been deployed according to RN priorities in European waters, but urgent operational needs would see almost half of them assigned to the RCN over the winter of 1917–18. For the Newfoundland RNR, this would mean a second phase of service with the dominion's navy.

Protection of troop and supply convoys off the North American east coast against the long-range types of U-boat then entering production became an urgent Allied naval concern in late 1917. Convoy assembly and departure zones seaward of Halifax, Sydney, and New York itself were felt to be highly vulnerable to minelaying and torpedo attacks by such stalking "u-cruisers." After much inter-Allied debate, Canada's prime responsibility in the task was recognized and the Admiralty agreed to transfer sixty-six of the new-construction anti-submarine–sweep trawlers and drifters to the RCN's Atlantic patrol to carry it out.[85]

The Admiralty ordered a first draft of Newfoundland RNR ratings to HMCS *Niobe* at Halifax in October and November 1917 to crew the first Canadian-built anti-submarine vessels as they became available for RN service.[86] These seventy or so ratings all sailed with the thirteen RN drifters that departed Halifax before Christmas for service in the Mediterranean.[87] Subsequent drafts from the Newfoundland RNR, which would total 333 men in all,[88] went to HMCS *Niobe* for service in the new drifters and trawlers assigned by the Admiralty to the RCN. The arrangements for such service, which would prove highly troublesome, called for the Newfoundland RNRs assigned to RCN vessels to be paid imperial rates through the paymaster on HMS *Briton* while being subject to RCN administration in other matters through HMCS *Niobe*.[89]

The pay issue was not long in coming to a head. Four Newfoundlanders attached to *Niobe* faced disciplinary action in February 1918 for refusal of duty when ordered to scrape and paint the vessel's hull. Receiving the lowest imperial pay rate of 40 cents a day (when RCN rates were more than double, at $1.10–$1.20 a day) and doing the dirtiest work were obviously beyond endurance.[90] To the credit of the Canadian naval service, the authorities concurred. Within a month the pay differentials were eliminated and no disciplinary action was taken. While serving with the RCN in Canadian waters, Newfoundland RNRs would receive Canadian rates of pay.[91] The incident invites comparison with the "mutiny" of seven Canadian crewmen who refused sea duty on the armed trawler TR 30 in mid-July 1918 and who, after court martial, were sentenced to eighteen months of hard labour.[92] It has been argued that, despite the evident "intolerable living conditions" which caused undue stress and fatigue and which sapped health and morale on these poorly constructed vessels, it was the acute scale of the u-boat threat that summer which brought down such a deferential response to the Canadians. Whatever the reasons, it is entirely consistent with the superior tradition of the Newfoundland RNR that members would accept appalling conditions on active duty without demur, as they did in the RCN's Atlantic patrol in 1917–18. They would "jib," however, at anything that smacked of unfair treatment. Records survive of a very similar protest by Newfoundland RNR men from HMS *Caesar*, assigned – unfairly in their view – to long-term quarry work in the West Indies,[93] and of another by Newfoundlanders held at HMS *Albion*, Devonport, who were experiencing what they considered unreasonable delay in demobilization.[94]

Newfoundland before 1914 had a population of around 230,000, and in the Great War all servicemen from this base were volunteers. The final step of conscription was taken too late for any conscripts actually to see active service. The strong military bias in the preference of those who volunteered is self-evident from the statistics and is noteworthy for a population so wedded to the sea for its livelihood. The total numbers who served in the Newfoundland Royal Naval Reserve were 1,964, with 180 killed in action and 125 invalided home; this meant a fatal casualty rate of 10 per cent.[95] The final accounting of the 1st (Royal) Newfoundland Regiment, in which a total of 6241 served, was strikingly different: 2,314 wounded; 1,305 killed in action, for a fatal casualty rate of 20 per cent.[96] The RNR had a much lower rejection rate than the regiment – 25 per cent as opposed to 50 per cent – and self-evidently fewer applicants.

The reasons for such a heavy bias towards military rather than naval participation on the part of such a population merits special study. Not only does it contradict the mythology of the "naval nursery" idea, but in concrete terms it appears surprising given the actual lifestyle of the people concerned. It can perhaps be suggested that the bias had something to do with the persistence of a local military tradition, which was strongly rooted in service during the Anglo-French wars of the eighteenth century, the War of 1812, and garrison/internal security duties during the nineteenth century. Even after "demilitarization" in 1870, denominational cadet corps kept the martial spirit alive and produced trained men in the prewar period.[97] Undoubtedly, the association of the navy with enforcement of the detested French Shore treaties severely undermined its image both among the fishing population and among Newfoundland's political leaders, who themselves were creators of public opinion.

Psychologically and sociologically, the statistics indicate an overwhelming decision by young Newfoundlanders to abandon seafaring pursuits when offered a choice. This is perhaps to be understood as a psychology of poverty and economic despair associated with the realities of dependency on the fishery resource; the clear importance of the pay factor described above would support this view. Conversely, if this analysis is generally sound, then those who did join the RNR are perhaps confirmed as something of a rural elite, freer than normal from such conditioning. Perhaps in the RNR participants, we are dealing with what might be termed the "kulaks" of the Newfoundland fishery.

To address the question posed at the outset, Newfoundland was indeed a nursery of fighting seamen in the 1901–14 period. But this fact was not something to be taken for granted, and it had to be actively encouraged by government in face of a certain level of popular disdain bordering on resistance. The very real limits of this naval potential not only are surprising to us now, but were actually surprising to political leaders at the time. Such limits raise basic questions about the demography of the fishery and, perhaps more importantly, the appropriateness of the strategic manpower expectations laid upon that population.

Also raised is the very general question in naval and military history regarding the importance and effectiveness of reserves at any time vis-à-vis wartime recruitment and scratch training. Despite considerable official effort and investment, the decade or more of RNR activity in Newfoundland issued in a rather small product of trained, available manpower in 1914. It is hard to avoid the sense of a diminishing-return logic to the entire undertaking, something confirmed by the summary winding-up of the reserve and the sale of the HMS *Briton* for commercial reuse by 1921.

Clearly, the nascent Royal Canadian Navy was a heavy beneficiary of this manpower reserve. But in so being, it compromised its own independent and institutional standing. The necessity to its operations of Newfoundland RNR men confirmed the limits of its own social and political base, emphasized its status as an imperial auxiliary cadre, and displayed its extemporized nature. Newfoundland participation in RCN operations was a good example of inter-dominion cooperation and emphasized a contiguity between the basic security interests of Canada and her smaller neighbour. But it did nothing to strengthen political support for the idea of a continuing RCN, nor indeed for a distinctly Canadian strategic naval role. It was a "dilutee" factor for a service struggling to define and establish itself and for which support at the political level was already too fluid for comfort.

# The Social Background of the Wartime Navy: Some Statistical Data

## DAVID ZIMMERMAN

There are lies, damn lies, and statistics.
— Benjamin Disraeli

It is well known that between 1939 and 1945 the Royal Canadian Navy (RCN) grew exponentially from just 3,843 all ranks to over 95,000, proportionally the most rapid expansion of any navy in this century. At the end of the conflict, the creation of the large wartime navy was rightly viewed as being among the nation's most important accomplishments. Certainly, the industrial, scientific, human, political, and diplomatic resources devoted to the wartime navy were prodigious. Superficial evidence suggests that it is here that we see the emergence of a Canadian naval identity, for it is during this conflict that the Royal Canadian Navy fought its first successful battles, was given command of a major operational area, and emerged as a force seemingly separate and distinct from the imperial navy of Great Britain. But what do we really know about those who served in the greatest Canadian naval effort in history? Was the wartime navy truly "Canadian"? Who were the officers and other ranks who served in it? Was this a navy of all Canadians, or did it represent the achievement of a specific class or social group?

With most available evidence being anecdotal, it has been difficult to provide an accurate assessment of those who served in the navy during the Second World War. The Mainguy Commission, which investigated a series of postwar naval mutinies, concluded that many professional officers had adopted the mannerisms and attitudes of the British officer class, while the other ranks had represented a cross-section of Canadian society. L.C. Audette, one of the members of the commission, later reflected that the artificial distance between officers and men was caused by "the survival of the Senior Service ethic as a result of the training of so many RCN officers with the Royal Navy, their so-called big ship time."[1]

The Mainguy Commission based its findings on the testimony of a large number of naval personnel. The commission undertook no independent investigation into naval recruitment and training practices that might have led to the discovery of other causes of the schism between the officers and the lower deck. The main theme of the Mainguy Report is echoed in William Glover's chapter in this volume, where Glover provides further anecdotal evidence – and substantive arguments – to support the report's conclusions about the cause of the Anglophile tendencies of the officer corps.

As might perhaps be expected, Glover's argument met with some hostile reaction when it was presented at the conference "In Quest of Canadian Naval Identity." Not only had he struck a nerve but there is a great deal of anecdotal data to support quite an opposite conclusion. Even in the tiny prewar navy, there were remarkable instances of the emergence of an independent Canadian identity, even in the presence of the Senior Service. H.N. Lay recalled one such situation in the winter of 1936:

From St. Lucia rendevous'd with the ship of the [North] American West Indies Squadron and did the usual exercise en passage, to Bermuda. Here we anchored in the harbour and although Vice Admiral Sir Matthew Best was still the C-in-C, Captain Brodeur, with his four Canadian ships, flew the Senior Officer's pendant. He called on Sir Matthew and the Admiral returned the call and I well remember his coming up the accommodation ladder looking at the Senior Officer's pendant flying in the [HMCS] *Skeena* and saying to Captain Brodeur, "Brodeur, what are you flying a Senior Officer's pendant for in my Harbour?" Brodeur, who was about the same size as Sir Matthew Best, drew himself up to his full 5'6" and said, "Sir, I am the senior Canadian officer present."

And of course so he was and I don't think Sir Matthew could say very much. They went down to the Captain's cabin and I imagine had a rather unfriendly visit because Sir Matthew appeared on deck within about five minutes.[2]

Joseph Schull's *The Far Distant Ships*, the official operational history, presents the wartime service as representing a cross-section of Canadian society. Like most Canadians, the wartime sailor was unfamiliar with the sea but was willing and eager to learn. Here the myth of the prairie sailor is expounded to its fullest extent. Conflicts between the officers and the lower deck were ascribed to the normal tensions that occured when young men who were "loudly and assertively democratic" came into contact with the rigours of naval discipline. Distinction between the professional navy, the reservists, and the volunteer reservists existed, Schull explained, but were gradually "ironed out" by "continuous association and sharing of hard experience."[3]

Both *The Far Distant Ships* and the Mainguy Report are anecdotal. The former, a thoroughly upbeat account, accentuates the positive. The latter, although it reflects overtones of the wartime navy, describes a situation after four years of debilitating cutbacks and three distressing mutinies. Unquestionably, there were Anglophile officers out of touch with Canadian society, just as there were farm boys from Saskatchewan who joined up without having seen the sea. But the question remains as to whether either Schull or Mainguy truly represent the character of the RCN during the Second World War. For this we must turn to other evidence.

Some four years ago I began a project on the social history of the Royal Canadian Navy from 1939 to 1945. This study has drawn on the records housed in the National Personnel Records Centre in Ottawa to provide a statistical profile of those who had served in the RCN during the war. A total of 1,179 cases were sampled: 251 officers (46 RCN, 53 RCNR [Royal Canadian Naval Reserve], 152 RCNVR [Royal Canadian Naval Volunteer Reserve]), 898 other ranks, and 120 members of the Women's Royal Canadian Naval Service.[4] Data collected came from the short summary cards contained in each personnel file. The front of these cards contains a large amount of basic biographical data: education, pre-enlistment occupation, religion, place and date of birth, place of residence, date of entry into the service, previous military service, height and weight.

This information has some distinct limitations, of which we might note but a few. For instance, anything that might prove to be a variable, such as marital status, was recorded in pencil and was liable to be erased and altered at any time. Because the files were maintained for pension purposes after the war, these changes could take place well after the conclusion of military service. One never knows when the pencilled changes had taken place. As well, it has been impossible to find direct evidence on language background; this entry, it turns out, was completed in less than 5 per cent of the files. Because all manpower studies on the Canadian armed forces in the Second World War have focused on the lack of representation by French Canadians, this latter point is particularly crucial. Nor did an examination of the province of birth and of residence and of religious affiliation help to fill this gap. Information on education is lacking as well for RCNVR officers; less than one-third of all files have information in this area. By contrast, almost all of the files of the other ranks contain data on education.

Separate random samples were taken for each of the three divisions of officers in the navy: the Royal Canadian Navy or professional officer corps; the Royal Canadian Naval Reserve; and the Royal Canadian Naval Volunteer Reserve. This was possible because *The Naval Lists* provided a distinct register of each group from which a random sampling

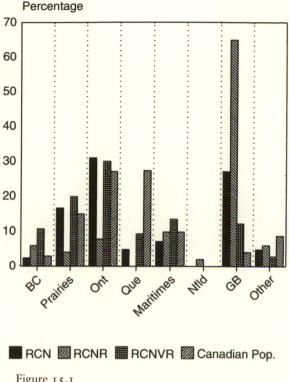

Percentage

RCN  RCNR  RCNVR  Canadian Pop.

Figure 15.1
Place of Birth of Officers

could be undertaken. Unfortunately, the absence of distinct lists pre-cluded a similar sampling method for the other ranks. Sampling for this group could only be undertaken by file number. As a result, comparison between divisions among the other ranks is not possible. The Women's Royal Canadian Naval Service, which Barbara Winters addresses in the next chapter on the basis of seperate data, has been excluded from the study because results are not yet available from this sampling.

*Place of Birth*

The data on the origins of the officers of the Canadian navy in the Sec-ond World War hold not a few surprises (see Figure 15.1). Looking first at the officers of the regular navy, one notes the most apparent variance from the national figures in the large number who were born in the British Isles, over 28 per cent. This contrasts with less than 8 per cent of the total Canadian male population who were British-born.[5] Indeed, it stands in striking contrast to the ratio for officers of the RCNVR, of whom approximately 11 per cent were British-born. Less surprising are the

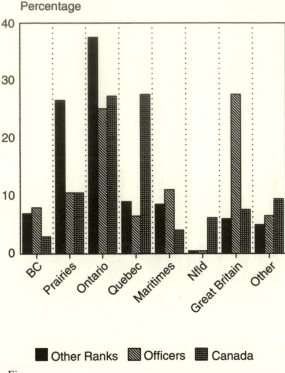

Figure 15.2
RCN Personnel – Birthplace

figures for the RCNR, over 58 per cent having been born in Britain. Many were ex-RNR who had transferred to the Canadian naval service either before the war or at the commencement of hostilities.

Of officers born in Canada, the most noticeable feature is the very small number who were born in the province of Quebec: less than 5 per cent for the RCN and just over 9 per cent for both the RCNVR. These figures deviate greatly from the national statistical norm, which shows that 27 per cent of the male population were born in that province. Once Quebec is factored out, most provinces are represented at about the same ratio as the national census figures. The exceptions to this are the coastal provinces of British Columbia and Nova Scotia. The RCNVR figures in particular show the attractiveness of the navy to people from these two provinces. Less explicable is the large number of RCN personnel from the province of Alberta: nearly 10 per cent, or more than twice the national average. This result may be a consequence of the small number of cases sampled.

The birthplace data on those without commissions reveal a picture much closer to the national profile (see Figure 15.2). Only around 6 per cent were born in Great Britain, slightly lower than the national figures.

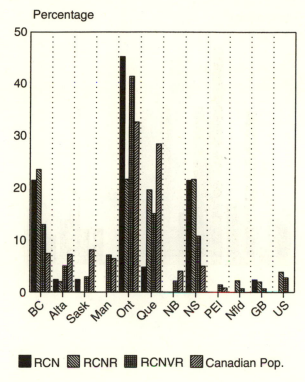

Figure 15.3
Officers' Place of Residence

The major variance from the overall census figure is the very low percentage of those born in Quebec. Just 9 per cent were born in this province, a figure identical to that for the RCNVR officers and less than a third of the national average. Ontario was the place of birth of the largest percentage of the other ranks (37.5 per cent), followed by those from the three prairie provinces (26.5 per cent).

*Place of Residence*

Results concerning the place of residence can be found in two related categories: the province or country, and the size of urban area.

Again the most striking feature is the lack of representation from Quebec (see Figure 15.3). RCN officers were, of course, focused in the three provinces that housed major naval installations: Nova Scotia (21.5 per cent – Halifax), British Columbia (21.5 per cent – Esquimalt), and Ontario (45 per cent – Naval Service Headquarters, Ottawa). Less than 10 per cent listed their place of residence as being outside of these three provinces, and half of these resided in Quebec, mainly in areas close to the

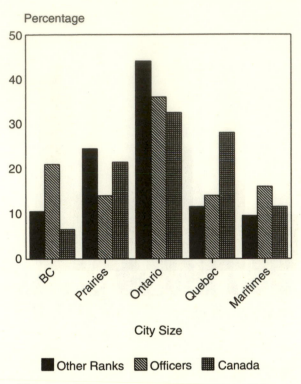

Percentage

City Size

■ Other Ranks ▨ Officers ▦ Canada

Figure 15.4
Other Ranks' Place of Residence

national capital. A few RCN officers (2.4 per cent) listed their place of res-idence as outside of Canada.

Similarly, RCNR officers tended to reside near centres of maritime employment. Since many were merchant marine officers, a large number resided in British Columbia and Nova Scotia (23.5 and 21.6 per cent re-spectively). An almost equal number lived in Ontario and Quebec. Those from Quebec lived mainly in and around Montreal. Very few reservists lived in the other provinces, and slightly less than one in ten were resid-ing outside of Canada, either in Newfoundland, the United States, or England.

The RCNVR officers provide a unique pattern as well. Officers from Quebec are most noticeably under-represented, being only 15 per cent of the total. This figure becomes even more significant when it is consid-ered that 40 per cent of Quebec RCNVR officers were born outside the province. Still, this is a far higher ratio than for the RCN. Once again British Columbia, Nova Scotia, and Ontario are over-represented; this seems further evidence that a large percentage of Canada's sailors came from coastal provinces. As for the Prairie provinces, the myth of the

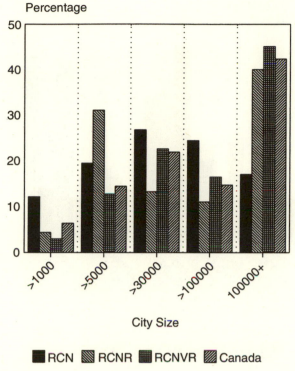

Percentage

Figure 15.5
Size of Place of Residence of Officers

land-locked western sailor does not seem to hold for the officer corps. Both Alberta and Saskatchewan are under-represented, while Manitoba's ratio is just slightly above what might normally be expected. New Brunswick has fewer officers than would be anticipated, but this may be caused by the non-participation of the Acadian minority in that province.

The profile of the place of residence of the other ranks shows a pattern similar to that of RCNVR officers (see Figure 15.4). Once again the small percentage of those enlisting from Quebec (10.5 per cent) is most noticeable. Slightly less than one-quarter (24.5 per cent) of the lower deck lived in the three Prairie provinces prior to enlistment. This is a figure somewhat higher than the overall percentage of the population from this region. We see less indication of large-scale recruitment from the coastal provinces. British Colombians joined at a greater rate than the national figures (11 per cent), but the proportion of Nova Scotians in the navy is approximately equal to their proportion of the Canadian population (5.5 per cent). Ontario is again the place of residence for the largest group in the navy (44.5 per cent).

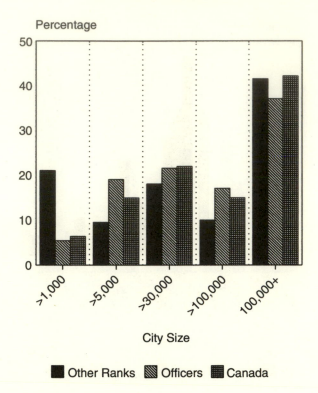

Percentage

Figure 15.6
RCN Personnel – City of Residence

The size of the place of residence of the officers also offers some interesting results (see Figures 15.5 and 15.6). As expected, a greater proportion of RCN officers resided in smaller cities and towns than did
Canadians as a whole. This is primarily a reflection of the sizes of Halifax and Victoria in 1941 (70,488 and 44,068 respectively). RCNR figures
closely follow the Canadian population pattern except for the very large
number (31 per cent) who resided in towns of between 1,000 and 5,000
people. The RCNVR figures closely approximate the urban settlement patterns of Canada as a whole.

One interesting feature is that no officers can be identified as coming
from what the census calls a rural community, although in the 1941 census more than 40 per cent of Canadians lived in these areas. The great
majority of officers, over 75 per cent, came from cities of more than
30,000 people.

The data for those from the lower deck, however, show that a much
larger percentage than the national average are identified as living in
communities of less than a 1,000 people (21 per cent). Cross-referencing
these results with information on occupation reveals that agricultural

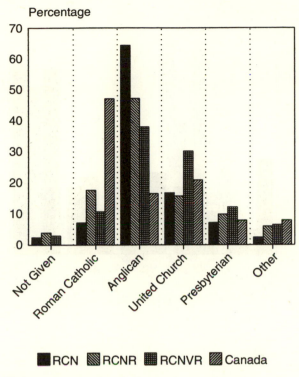

Figure 15.7
Religious Affiliation of RCN Officers

workers, for example, list their obviously rural residence as the nearest urban community. More often than not, the nearest urban centres were the smallest communities recognized by the census, those with a population under 1,000 people. Rural residence still made up a much lower percentage of the lower deck than the 40 per cent national figures. The vast majority of those who served, over 68 per cent, lived in cities with populations of over 30,000 people.

*Religion*

If any one common thread linked the officers of Canada's wartime navy, it was religion (see Figure 15.7). The vast majority of the officers belonged to one of three Protestant faiths: Anglican, United Church, and Presbyterian. Roman Catholics were dramatically small in numbers.

Although Roman Catholics made up close to half of the Canadian population, only slightly more then 7 per cent and slightly more than 10 per cent of the RCN and RCNVR respectively are listed as Roman Catholic. Every single RCN Catholic in the sample turns out to have been born

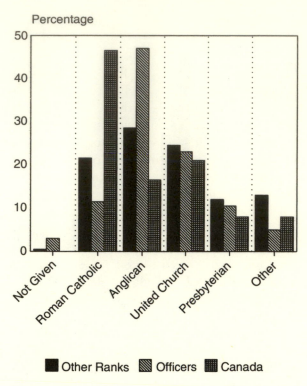

Percentage

Figure 15.8
RCN Religious Profile

in other parts of the Commonwealth. Just under 20 per cent of the RCNR officers were Catholic, but the majority of them were British-born, and not a single one was a Québécois.

The low numbers of Catholics can be in large measure ascribed to the almost complete absence of French Canadian officers. By far the largest number of RCNVR officers born in Quebec were Protestant (61.5 per cent Anglican, 10 per cent other denominations), while only a small minority of around 15 per cent were Catholic. Few of those Catholic officers born in Quebec were unquestionably French Canadian.

The strong Anglo-Saxon Protestant focus of the regular officer corps comes out clearly in examining their religious affiliations. Almost two-thirds of this group were members of the Church of England, as opposed to only 16.5 per cent of the Canadian population who claimed that affiliation. Even if we consider only those RCN officers born in Canada, this would still mean that Anglicans represented 40 per cent of the professional officer corps. There were also large numbers of Anglicans in both the RCNR and RCNVR, although nowhere near as high a percentage as in the regular forces. In the RCNVR almost 40 per cent of all officers were Anglican. Thirty-two per cent of the Canadian-born reservists were Anglican.

There was a far larger proportion of Roman Catholics in the lower deck, slightly more than 20 per cent (see Figure 15.8). Although this figure is still less than half the national average, it does show that ratings and warrant officers more closely followed national patterns. The larger ratio of Catholics is matched with a more modest proportion of Anglicans. Although Anglicans still made up over a quarter of the non-commissioned personnel (28.5 per cent), this figure is significantly smaller than the overall figure for Anglican officers (47 per cent).

The religious profile of residents of Quebec shows that, in comparison to RCNVR officers, the other ranks had a far higher percentage of Roman Catholics (57.5 per cent versus 28.5 per cent) (see Figure 15.9). While this figure is still significantly lower than the provincial average, a large number of francophones served in the lower deck. We still see, however, a disproportionate number of Anglicans in this group (21.5 per cent versus 5 per cent).

The religious affiliations of ratings and warrant officers from other provinces show a close correlation with that of the population at large, with the proviso that Catholics are, generally speaking, slightly under-represented and Anglicans somewhat over-represented (see Figures 15.10, 15.11, and 15.12).

## Occupations

The personnel files also hold a great deal of information on the pre-service occupations of naval personnel (see Figures 15.13 and 15.14). Royal Canadian Naval Reserve officers were, on the whole, those people who had a naval background in either the RN or RCN or who had been involved in sea-related careers; two-thirds were still involved in identifiable maritime-related activities. An examination of this group of reservists shows just how important an influx of skilled personnel it was that came into the navy from this source. Out of fifty-three officers in the sample group, nine were master mariners (17 per cent), three were ship's masters (6 per cent), twelve were merchant marine officers (23 per cent), and four were marine engineers (8 per cent). There was also a weather observer, the chief officer of an RCMP patrol boat, a hydrographic surveyor, and two seamen. Of those in occupations not directly related to nautical activities, the largest groups were professional engineers (6 or 11 per cent) and managers (5 or 9 per cent); there were also several accountants, a salesman, a clergyman, and a teacher.

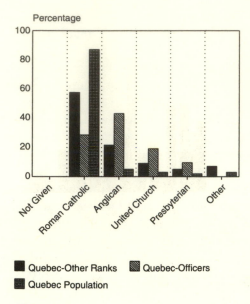

**Figure 15.9**
Religion of RCN Personnel, 1939–45: Quebec

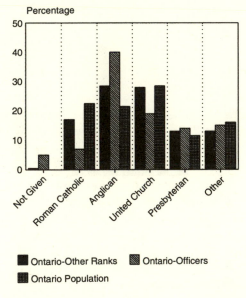

**Figure 15.10**
Religion of RCN Personnel, 1939–45: Ontario

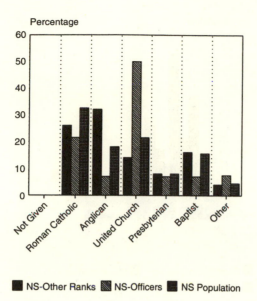

Figure 15.11
Religion of RCN Personnel, 1939–45: Nova Scotia

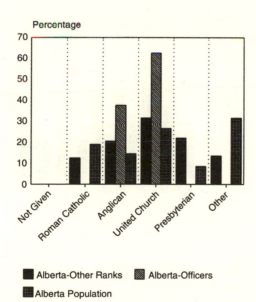

Figure 15.12
Religion of RCN Personnel, 1939–45: Alberta

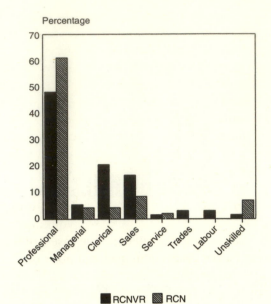

Figure 15.13
Officers' Occupations

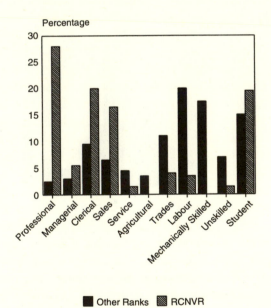

Figure 15.14
Other Ranks' Occupations

While most reservists had skills that could be directly useful to the navy, most volunteer reservists did not. Of the 152 officers in the sample group, only 2, or just over 1 per cent, had a nautical occupation. Twenty-five (16 per cent) of the officers had entered directly as students either from high school or university. Of the remaining 127 cases, the largest single group consisted of professionals: 61, or 40 per cent. The largest number of professionals were engineers, of which there were 10, including electrical, chemical, mining, and mechanical specialists. There was also a large number of accountants (9 or 6 per cent), lawyers (6 or 4 per cent), teachers (6 or 4 per cent), and doctors (5 or 3 per cent).

The second most numerous group consisted of clerical workers (twenty-six or 17 per cent). The only discernable sub-grouping was bank clerks or tellers, the occupation of eight of the volunteer reservists. Sales was the occupation of 14 per cent (twenty-one cases) of the officers, with less than 5 per cent (seven cases) in managerial positions.

The RCNVR officers, therefore, were almost exclusively drawn from white-collar occupations. This conclusion is reinforced by the fact that less than 7 per cent had been in occupations that can be classified as a trade, skilled or unskilled labour (four with trades, four skilled, and two unskilled). But it was not only skills that defined one's ability to become an officer; economics was also a determining factor. Only five of the officers, including one lawyer, are listed as having been unemployed prior to joining the navy, a figure of around 3 per cent. This view of the officer corps as the exclusive preserve of a specific class must be tempered by the fact that large numbers had served time in the non-commissioned ranks prior to being promoted to a commissioned rank (see below).

Not surprisingly, the civilian occupations of the other ranks show that the majority had blue-collar occupations. The largest single group consisted of skilled and mechanically skilled workers, 37.5 per cent of all sailors. Students made up the next largest group: 15 per cent of those who served in the navy entered directly from school. Other labouring groups included tradesmen (11 per cent), unskilled labourers (7 per cent), service-sector workers (4.5 per cent), and agricultural workers (3.5 per cent). The majority of those remaining came from groups whose class/categorization is somewhat ambiguous. Clerical workers made up just under 10 per cent of the total, and sales 6.5 per cent. Professionals and managerial workers accounted for less than 6 per cent of the total. Most of those from the two latter groups were eventually granted a commission.

The ongoing study has as yet made no attempt to relate civilian skills systematically to naval career patterns, and therefore, only the most obvious observations can be made. Engineers served almost exclusively in the engineering branch of the navy, while accountants acted as naval

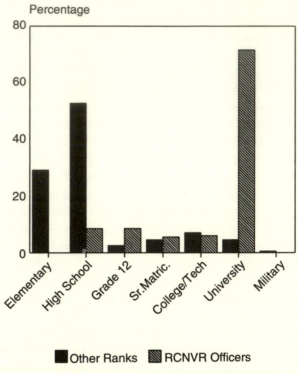

Percentage

Figure 15.15
RCN Education Profile

paymasters, and doctors as naval surgeons. Among the other ranks, those in mechanically skilled occupations tended to serve as stokers and other sub-specialties in the engineering branch. No other clearly defined patterns have yet been ascertained.

*Education*

While officers and the other ranks were separated by social class, it was education, not occupation, that determined who became an officer in the volunteer reserve (see Figure 15.15). Naval regulations stipulated that the normal minimum educational requirement for RCNVR commissions was senior matriculation. This is shown quite clearly in these two groups' educational profile. Fully 71.5 per cent of all RCNVR officers had attended university, while another 11.5 per cent had senior matriculation or some post-secondary college or technical education. High school graduates made up a further 8.5 per cent, and an equal number of officers had no more than some high school education. All of the members of the latter two groups had been promoted from the ranks (see below). No officers had less than some high school education. Among the other ranks, just over half had attended high school but had not graduated. The next largest group had no more than an elementary school education (28 per cent). Only 6.5 per cent possessed a grade 12 or senior matriculation diploma, and just 11 per cent had attended university.

No comparison between the educational backgrounds of the professional and volunteer reserve officers can be attempted here. As William March outlines in his chapter on HMCS *Royal Roads*, it was the standard practice of the professional navy to recruit officer candidates when they were very young and to provide them with a traditional naval training. Thus, from a statistical point of view it is impossible to compare these two very dissimilar groups. It is important to note, however, that in Canadian society education was a crucial factor in determining status. That professional naval officers had a type of education that did not fit into any normal pattern within Canadian society is indicative of their separation from the people they served.

## Promotion from the Ranks

In the second volume of the official history of the navy, Gilbert Tucker relates that for the first two and a half years of the war the majority of officers recruited came directly from civilian life without first experiencing life in the lower deck. This was contrary to the British practice, which required all officers to serve some time as ordinary seamen before being considered for promotion. In August 1940 naval orders were issued that allowed for the promotion from the lower decks of RCNR and RCNVR personnel.[6] The qualifications required for the two divisions were quite different. RCNR ratings needed professional qualifications as well as Board of Trade or Department of Transport Certificates of Competency. On the other hand, RCNVR candidates for commission had to have skills in "Leadership, Character and Education." The normal minimum educational requirement was "Senior Matriculation or its equivalent," a requirement to be waved only "in the face of exceptional practical ability and Officer-like qualities."[7] In May 1941 RCN ratings were given the opportunity for promotion to the regular officer corps. In this case the requirements were more severe. Regular forces ratings had to be unmarried, to be under the age of twenty-three and a half, and to have passed examinations in at least one of mathematics, magnetism and electricity, and navigation.[8]

In February 1943 the navy attempted to adopt the British scheme of requiring officer candidates of all branches, except for medical personnel, to serve at least some time in the ranks. Although Tucker implies that this became the normal procedure for entry, the personnel records suggest otherwise.[9] Of the 152 RCNVR officers surveyed, a total of 25 (under 20 per cent) served for some discernable time as a rating. Of these 25 cases, 1 was promoted in 1940, 5 in 1941, 5 in 1942, 6 in 1943, and 8 in 1944. Although promotion from the ranks was increasingly important after 1940, it never became the dominant form of entry into the commissioned ranks of the RCNVR. Even in 1944 those promoted from the ranks still comprised just half of all new officers. In part, the navy's attempt to emulate the British scheme failed because the Canadian approach still encouraged RCNVR divisional commanders to seek out potential candidates from all new entries and to put them on a fast track for promotion. This is a factor that Tucker failed to consider adequately in the official history.

Although promotion from the ranks accounted for only 20 per cent of all RCNVR officers, a large percentage of those that did not fit the normal occupational or economic background of the officer class benefited from this scheme. Among the twenty-five there was a plumber, a printer, an ice-cream maker, a building superintendent, two unemployed, and at least two others who did not possess the minimum educational qualifications.

Most of those promoted from the ranks went to the executive branch of the navy. Fifteen (60 per cent) had been ordinary seamen, while only one had been an able seaman; three had been writers and were promoted into the paymasters division. Three had been signalmen, all of whom entered the executive branch, although one subsequently qualified as an aircraft pilot. Only one entered the engineering branch, having been a stoker for five months in 1944, but he had also undertaken five and a half years of university and served as an engineer in the army prior to joining the Senior Service. The small number of engineering promotions can be explained by the additional requirement that officer candidates of this branch of the service pass rigorous Admiralty mechanical examinations. Only one person was commissioned into the navy's Special Branch, which looked after radar, this candidate being an electrical artificer. One other had been a supply petty officer and joined the paymasters division.

The average length of service as a rating before promotion increased markedly during the war. In 1941 and 1942 ratings who received commissions had already served an average of around one year; in 1943 and 1944 this period of service as a rating increased to twenty months.

Promotions from the ranks was also a common feature for the RCN and RCNR. There was a marked difference in the type of person selected for promotion. Most of the promotions in these two groups were from warrant ranks. A total of six (12 per cent) reservists were promoted, all from the ranks of mate, skipper, or warrant engineer. There were seven RCN promotions of this type (16 per cent): two gunners, two mates, one acting petty officer, one acting warrant victualling officer, and one warrant telegrapher. At least five of these men had been in the navy prior to the war.

## Previous Military Service

The impression that members of the wartime volunteer reserve had to be gradually trained in everything from basic seamanship and naval discipline to advanced skills such as gunnery, navigation, and, ultimately, operational command is reinforced by data on previous military service (see Figures 15.16 and 15.17). Only 30 per cent of the RCNVR officers and 20 per cent of the other ranks had prior experience in any military service before entry into the wartime navy. Of those with previous military experience, the overwhelming majority of officers (61 per cent) and other ranks (79 per cent) had seen service in non-naval services, the majority with the army or militia. Of these, a few had served with the Canadian Expeditionary Force in the First World War or in the militia prior to the war but the largest number had entered the navy while serving either with the wartime militia or with home defence ("zombie") units. Members of the zombies were conscripted under the authority of the National Resources Mobilization Act of 21 June 1940, and until late 1944 thus could still only serve in home-defence. The phenomenon of conscripts in the home-defence force joining either the navy or air force rather than the overseas army has not been studied to any great extent. It is surprising that this phenomenon should also be observed in the officer corps. The next largest single group of those with previous non-naval service had served in the Canadian Officer Training Corps (COTC) while at university.

All told, eighteen of the wartime RCNVR officers, or just over 10 per cent, had some form of previous naval service. The largest component of this group (6.5 per cent) had been members of the prewar RCNVR; in all likelihood they had received minimal practical training prior to entering active service. There were also five former members of the RCN, one retired Royal Navy officer, and two Royal Navy Volunteer Reserve officer, one retired and one who transferred to the RCNVR during the war.

An even smaller proportion of the other ranks (4.4 per cent) had some form of previous naval experience. Again, the RCNVR provided the largest number of those with some naval background (3.5 per cent). Less than 1 per cent of all other ranks had previously served in some other naval force before entering the RCN.

## Age

Figures can be derived for the average ages of officers and men in service. In 1942, for instance, the average age of an RCN officer was twenty-nine, of an RCNR officer thirty-seven, and of an RCNVR officer twenty-eight. The far greater age of the RCNR officer is of no surprise, for many were

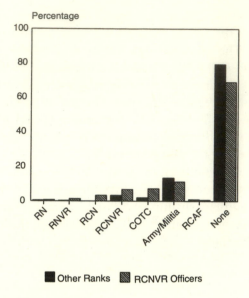

Figure 15.16
Previous Military Service: All Cases

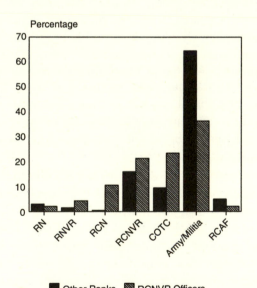

Figure 15.17
Previous Military Service: Valid Cases Only

retired naval officers or long-service merchant marine personnel. However, the closeness in the ages of the RCN and RCNVR officers does require
more explanation. The greatest single factor may be the growth of the
professional officer corps, which had been expanding in the three years
before the war and continued to increase at a faster rate during the conflict. Almost half of all regular officers in the survey group (46 per cent)
were under twenty-five in 1942. The continuing efforts to increase the
size of the professional officer establishment is just one sign of the Naval
Staff's efforts to plan for the peacetime navy.

The average age of those from the lower deck was considerably lower
than that of the officer corps. In 1942 the average age of this group was
twenty-two years. Particularly important in keeping this figure down was
the average age, just eighteen and a half, of those from the lower deck entering directly from school.

## Conclusion

This analysis of the biographical background of Canadian personnel in
the Second World War provides a tremendous amount of information on
who these men were and where they came from. The officer corps
emerges as a homogeneous group of predominantly Protestant men,
many of whom were Anglican, from the middle or upper-middle class.
Statistically speaking, they were much more likely to have been born in
the United Kingdom than the average Canadian, particularly if they were
members of the professional navy. The volunteer reserve officers were
very well educated, the vast majority having had some form of post-
secondary training. They also tended to come from the larger urban
centres. Although promotion from the ranks did go some way towards
breaking these social barriers, it never represented the dominant means
of entry into commissioned ranks.

Those who served in the lower deck represented a better cross-section
of the Anglo-Canadian population. Whereas Protestants, specifically Anglicans, do continue to be somewhat over-represented, the percentage of
Catholics among them is much closer to the national average. There is
also a good representation of those from other ethnic backgrounds.
These men were younger, less educated, and far more likely to have
working-class occupations than the officers. A much larger percentage of
the lower-deck personnel came from small towns and rural areas, although here too the vast majority lived in cities of more than 30,000 inhabitants.

On the whole, the personnel of the RCN were inexperienced in the
ways of the sea, to say nothing of their almost complete lack of the skills
peculiar to fighting naval battles. Many men from the Prairies and

Ontario, in fact, had enlisted without ever having seen the ocean. During the early war years, a massive effort had to be undertaken by the navy to train and mould this group into an effective fighting force. Even among the regular navy, nearly half of the officers consisted of inexperienced wartime entries. Almost no volunteer reserve officers had any maritime-related occupation, although it has proven impossible to trace just how many of these men may have had amateur boating experience. The importance of the RCNR in compensating for this lack of maritime skill in the first three years of the war is clearly illustrated.

Unquestionably, the most noticeable finding of this study for both officers and other ranks is the lack of participation of Québécois. It has always been known that a far smaller percentage of French Canadians than their English-speaking compatriots joined the armed forces during the war. Most of the pertinent studies focus on the army's urgent need for more personnel, which prompted the Mackenzie King government to implement, reluctantly, conscription for overseas service in 1944, but very little research has explored the impact of naval manpower policies on this crisis. Gilbert Tucker's *The Naval Service of Canada* and C.P. Stacey's *Arms, Men and Governments* each devote exactly one paragraph to this topic.[10] Tucker summarizes naval policy on the French language in this way: "In the interest of operational efficiency the RCN had to employ a common language; and since the great majority of its members were English speaking, and its traditions were British, that language was English."[11] English-language courses were established for unilingual francophones in 1941 but were not actually offered until 1943. No mention is made of the fact that Free French, Norwegian, Dutch, and Polish warships – operating in their own languages – all effectively served during the Battle of the Atlantic.

Both the Mainguy Commission and William Glover conclude that by the end of the Second World War, the lower deck was truly Canadian whereas the officers were not. This study tends to confirm these findings, but with one important proviso: the under-representation of francophones. However, the results also caution against resorting to anecdotal evidence alone, for Canadian personnel documentation suggests that it did not take extensive training and operational service in the Royal Navy to create "the artificial distance between officers and men." By their social, cultural, and religious background, the officers, particularly those in the RCN, were already alienated from those they commanded. Service in the RN would only have accentuated these differences.

The extent to which this statistical study addresses the question of Canadian naval identity depends on what one means by identity. Benjamin Disraeli's famous comment on statistics, quoted at the head of this chapter, is apt here because these findings can answer the question both ways.

It can be argued, for example, that the navy was not distinctly Canadian because of the strong British presence among the officers and its failure to accommodate French Canadians. But perhaps in this age of politically correct social engineering we make too much of this, and it is necessary to place things into proper historical perspective. Few Canadian institutions in the 1940s accommodated francophones in ways we would consider acceptable today.[12] The majority of officers and men were born in Canada; they brought with them into the wartime navy peculiarly Canadian ideas about how the service should be organized and run. As the Mainguy Commission surmised, the postwar mutinies were a reflection of this change; they occurred because some officers failed to understand or accept what had happened to the navy since 1939. Although not representing a good cross-section of all Canadians, the Royal Canadian Navy had emerged by the end of the war as a Canadian institution, distinctly different from the Royal Navy.

# · 16 ·

## *The Wrens of the Second World War: Their Place in the History of Canadian Servicewomen*

BARBARA WINTERS

On 31 July 1942 the Women's Royal Canadian Naval Service (WRCNS, in formally known as the Wrens) was established by an order-in-council, marking the first time women were admitted to the Canadian navy in any capacity save that of nurse. A year and a half earlier, in creating the Canadian Women's Auxiliary Air Force,[1] Canada had become the first nation in the Commonwealth to allow women to serve as full rather than auxiliary (notwithstanding the organization's name) members of a service. The decision to allow women to serve in the Canadian military challenged the centuries-old taboo against women in a state's armed forces and forced society to reconsider acceptable roles for women. This being so, the scant attention paid to the phenomenon by historians and other academics is puzzling. Only a handful of women's issues historians have addressed the topic, and within the military history genre, it remains virtually unexplored.

The Second World War remains the most documented conflict in history. Yet a survey of both academic and "official" military writing on the subject leaves one with the impression that the role during the war of the three Canadian women's services was so minimal that it scarcely deserves mention. Gilbert Tucker's *The Naval Service of Canada* (1952) offers the following: "Because the Wrens were doing types of work that had hitherto been a male monopoly, they as women were put on their mettle to an unusual extent, and they earned a reputation for conscientious efficiency which can scarcely be exaggerated."[2] Nowhere in the two volumes of this official history is the name of the senior Wren, Captain Adelaide Sinclair,

280

to be found. By the end of the war, nearly 50,000 women had served in the armed services, but in another official publication, Stacey's *Arms, Men and Governments*, less than one page is devoted to all three of the women's services.[3] Most other histories of the Canadian effort during the Second World War are similar in this respect, and the effect is a near-total eclipse of female service participation.[4] The exclusion of women from Canadian naval history is an oversight that belittles the efforts of thousands of Wrens and obstructs a richer understanding of our true "Canadian naval identity."

Scholarly attention to the military service of women during the Second World War has been, and remains, confined to those interested in women's history.[5] The first historians to write on this subject noted the sense of exhilaration some women felt about their wartime contributions, and described the war as a great watershed in the history of female emancipation.[6] In these early chronicles, wartime reforms were presented as permanent changes to the status of women in society. The women themselves wrote of the Second World War as the most exciting and enriching time of their lives.[7] The novelty of service life, exposure to different women, travel, and, for some, the first taste of independence and responsibility combined to make military service a positive experience.

As the methods and approaches to women's history evolved, scholars altered the way in which they analysed this experience. More recent works by academics such as D'Ann Campbell in the United States, Penny Summerfield in England, and Ruth Pierson in Canada have led to a reconsideration of the subject and to a reversal of opinion. These historians reject the "emancipation" hypothesis. Their studies analyse the era in terms of fundamental, real, and permanent advancements in the status of women. Ruth Pierson asks: "Did this vast mobilization of the female population of Canada lead to a more equal sharing of power and responsibilities between men and women in the public and private spheres of Canadian society? Did war 'liberate' Canadian women from patriarchal divisions of labour and conceptions of proper womanhood?"[8] The conclusions of these revisionist historians are unmistakably negative. Women's position, they argue, was not advanced by the vast mobilization of women during the war; instead, women formed a "reserve pool of labour" to be used at the convenience of a male-dominated society.[9] Equal work was not rewarded with equal pay, and women were segregated into traditional trades and subjected to sexual harassment, including a vicious whisper campaign about their morality.[10] They were accused of spreading sexual diseases and were, in the early stages of the war, dismissed if they had a venereal disease.[11] Any woman found to be pregnant was immediately dismissed.[12] Sexual double standards, occupational segregation, and financial discrimination solidified female subjugation in the face of wartime social upheavals. The Second World War, these historians argue, did little to advance the status of women.

A paradox arises. Why is it that even though many women viewed their service in the military favourably, many historians continue to portray it as oppressive and non-liberating? The answer, it seems, lies in the methods that were used to interpret the experience of these women and its meaning for society.

In Canada the only academic work on the subject of women during the Second World War is Ruth Roach Pierson's *"They're Still Women After All."* In her introduction, Pierson states that the book is intended both as an examination of how women's labour was used by the military in the Second World War and as a consideration of the implications of this non-combatant service "for the place of women in Canadian society in general."[13] The author makes this link between the participation of women in the military and their status as citizens by using the concept of patriarchy.[14] Under patriarchy, Pierson notes, male-female inequality is manifested as a difference in power. This difference is, in part, due to the restriction of women from arms and the military.[15] Arms-bearing duty, she argues, "bestows authority and an aura of power on the officially armed over the officially unarmed."[16] Within a male-dominated society, women are prohibited from assuming combat roles and hence are barred from positions of authority. Since armed might is essential to the power of the state and to powerful positions within it, the pre–Second World War restriction of women's access to the military "must then have contributed to the power of men as a group vis-a-vis women as a group within [Canadian society]."[17]

The large-scale introduction of women into the Canadian military during the Second World War should have represented the dismantling of one the largest barriers to women's full participation in the state's affairs. As Pierson's studies correctly point out, this was hardly the case. Any advances in the status of women made during the war were incomplete and temporary. After the armistice, women were forced out of the military and back into their "proper" sphere – the home.[18]

Pierson's claim that women were excluded from positions of authority in part because they were not allowed to bear arms is less accurate. Canadian society has never been particularly militaristic; indeed, Canada's full participation in both wars would more aptly be labelled "patriotic" rather than militaristic. In Canada the military does not represent the path to power as Pierson claims. More to the point, the issue of women bearing arms remains contentious even in the 1990s. "Women in combat" was not an acceptable idea in the 1940s.

What should be made of Pierson's claims that female service participation was so limited that it precluded any fundamental change in gender relations? To test her hypothesis, Pierson examined the role of women in the Canadian Women's Army Corps (CWAC) in "increasing the power of women as a group in Canada."[19] It appears that she chose the CWAC because it was "the largest of the three women's services."[20] But while the CWAC may have been the largest female service, it was far from being typical. In reality, all three women's services differed from one another in structure, status, and policy. No one service can be taken as indicative of the conditions of women in the military as a whole. Pierson's failure to consider the role of the Women's Royal Canadian Naval Service and the Women's Division of the Royal Canadian Air Force in her analysis calls into question the comprehensiveness of some of her conclusions. Given the emphasis Pierson places on military service as a measure of citizenship, her decision to base an evaluation of the inaugural participation of women in the armed forces on only one service is flawed.[21]

Pierson's incomplete assessment of female participation in the military may be demonstrated by juxtaposing female service conditions in the army with those in the navy. Pierson bases her analysis on the following considerations: trades assigned, pay, benefits, and position within the command structure of the Canadian Army.[22] Using these same considerations – but applying them to the Women's Royal Canadian Naval Service – very different conclusions may be drawn about the nature of Canadian women's service participation during the war. The result distinguishes the WRCNS from its sister services while illustrating the contributions of women in shaping a uniquely Canadian navy.

Pierson's evaluation is based entirely on the Canadian Women's Army Corp, whose status she describes as "at best a stepdaughter of the military."[23] Created on 13 August 1941, the service was established as a separate corps, "supplementary to, rather than an integral part of, the Canadian militia and not subject to military law." She describes CWAC administration as "parallel but unequal," with its own officers, headquarters, and policies, which perpetuated the segregation of women from the regular army. CWAC officer ranks were truncated and of limited authority.[24] Though commissioned, CWAC officers were subordinate even to warrant officers of the army and could administer only minor punishments.

By 1943 the administrative and logistical difficulties arising from the special status attached to the corps were enough to convince the new adjunct general that the CWAC should be incorporated into the Canadian Army proper. The corps' new status did little to increase its power:[25] "All determinants of rank being equal, the CWAC officer or private was junior to her male Army counterpart. And while male Army officers and NCOs [non-commissioned officers] always enjoyed power of command over CWAC personnel junior to them, CWAC officers and NCOs could exercise power of command over junior male Army officers or male other ranks only under exceptional circumstances."[26] The subordinate status of women in society was maintained within the military by segregating the CWAC from the army administration and subjecting its officers to the command of even junior army officers.

In the Women's Royal Canadian Naval Service, the case was quite different. Upon its formation in July 1942, the WRCNS was adjudged by the deputy judge advocate of the fleet to be as much a part of the navy as the Royal Canadian Naval Reserve (RCNVR). "Wren officers received the King's Commission, held the same rank as men and were entitled to salutes and all marks of respect from non-commissioned men and women of the three armed forces."[27] The women serving in the navy held the same responsibilities, were subject to the same chain of command, and followed the same grievance procedures as the men.[28] Further, they took the same oath of allegiance, worked towards the same objectives, and were expected to endure the same inconveniences as men.

This integration, however, was not matched in terms of occupations. At no time were women allowed to assume a combat role, and consequently they were prohibited from enlisting in boating or ship-related trades.[29] Initially, only the following trades were designated Wren trades: stenographer, postal clerk, cook, steward, coder, teletype operator, and motor transport driver.[30] This was later expanded to include librarians, tailors, dieticians, hairdressers, supply clerks, plotters, sick-berth attendants, photographers, dental assistants, messengers, messwomen, switchboard operators, regulators (a form of police), laundry assistants, classifiers, sailmakers, censors, confidential book correctors, and holerwith (punch-card machine) operators. In trades open to women, personnel were trained, employed, and promoted in the same fashion as the men,[31] that is, according to skill, not gender. In her final report, Captain Sinclair advocated that men and women be treated as interchangeable in those categories of employment open to women. Since trades training was identical for men and women, Captain Sinclair advocated that the qualifications and previous training required for entry into a particular position should be identical as well.

As in all female services in Canada, the women in the navy were initially paid only two-thirds the salary of their male counterparts.[32] The rate was later increased to four-fifths the salary of men. This policy was established by the Privy Council and was based on the pay schedules for women serving in Great Britain.[33] The difference was justified by the assumption that it would require three women to replace two men. When statistics proved this to be incorrect and the actual ratio of replacement was determined to be one for one or better, the official explanation offered was grounded on military philosophy, not statistics.[34]

Unlike women serving in the Canadian Women's Army Corp, Wrens received almost all the same allowances and post-discharge benefits as sailors.[35] Wren officers, however, seem to have been the worst off in that the navy alone refused staff pay to women officers "except in a few individual cases where it was conceded only after strong arguments."[36] As Captain Sinclair herself argued, "If women are expected to assume responsibilities for which men require additional pay, the justification for refusing it to them is hard to see."

This brief comparison between the Canadian Women's Army Corp and the Women's Royal Canadian Naval Service highlights some of the fundamental differences between the two services. Clearly, the conditions of service, the degree to which women were integrated, and indeed the jobs they performed and the value it was assigned differed between the two branches of the military. The Wrens were, from the start, fully integrated into the navy. Female officers were given the same power and responsibilities as their male peers. They were entitled to the same marks of respect, and their authority extended over all those for whom they were responsible, male or female. They were granted, furthermore, substantial positions of authority.[37]

No Wren ever served in a combat role, and the discrimination against women in terms of pay continued throughout the entire war. Consequently, it would be too much to conclude that women in the navy enjoyed exactly the same status as their male counterparts, but the Wrens never suffered the same humiliation and frustration in command as the CWACs. Clearly, women's role in the navy was not as limited and circumscribed as that of their CWAC counterparts.

What were the contributions of the Wrens to the Canadian naval identity? The Wrens upheld the established image of the Canadian navy as it existed during the Second World War and as it exists today, that of a professional, well-trained, and highly dedicated service. The Women's Royal Canadian Naval Service, like the Royal Canadian Navy, patterned its organization on the British model. Following the announcement that a women's naval service was to be established, senior Canadian naval officers decided that the service would be set up by three British Wren officers. Sinclair was only appointed once the organization was established. This policy had the advantage of allowing a close link between the British and Canadian navies to be maintained, but it was of little practical assistance to the Canadian Wren officers who assumed command afterwards. In the words of the senior-ranking Wren: "The W.R.N.S. Officers were not familiar enough with Canadian standards to evaluate the capabilities and usefulness of Canadian women ... [and] many Wrens were doomed to serve in categories either beneath or above their intellectual level because of the poor recommendations of the recruiting officer who enroled them."[38]

As shore personnel, the Wrens played a vital role in upholding the image of a professional navy in the eyes of the Canadian public. To that end, the senior Wren, the senior training officer, and all divisional officers established a code of dress and deportment that was strict and effective both on and off base. Wrens were expected to maintain their lady-like demeanour starting at the moment they enlisted. As the senior training officer noted: "The purpose of basic training in the W.R.C.N.S. is different from that of a male training establishment, Wrens were taught to understand sufficient of the organization, traditions and customs to become an integral part of the Navy, yet were encouraged to remain feminine."[39] The Wrens of the Second World War bolstered the image of a smart, professional navy yet remained feminine enough to reassure the public that they were ladies and not sailors.

How do we "identify" the Canadian navy of the Second World War? Do we focus on its organization, its ships, its ceremonies? When we consider the personnel who served, do we consider their religion, their education, or their families? The example of the Wrens of the Second World War makes explicit what is too often overshadowed by other considerations: that Canada was caught in the worst depression of the century when war broke out and that, for many, military service was both an expression of patriotism and a source of employment. Part of the Canadian naval identity, then, is expressed through the women who served and their reasons for doing so.

The Wrens, like all women in the services, were placed in the anomalous position of being at same time part of the navy yet separate from it. Though the single most important factor cited for enlistment was service to the country, the women who served during the Second World War were not combatants. They were "hired" by the Department of National Defence for their labour, not their ability to fight. During the war, economic necessity was cited as one of the most compelling reasons for enlisting. For a young woman in 1942, military service was both a patriotic undertaking and a rewarding means of earning an income that could not likely be matched by civilian employers.

When Canada declared war in 1939, employment stood at record lows.[40] As wartime production began and jobs became available, it was men who were hired, not women.[41] Not only were employers more willing to hire men than women, but the largest increases in employment rates occurred in logging and construction, two industries that rarely hired women.[42]

The level of employment (full and part time) for women in 1941 was still not at its wartime peak. In the two leading industrial provinces, Ontario and Quebec, wage-earning women accounted for only 18 and 19 per cent respectively of the total female population. These low figures are a reflection of the primacy of women's domestic duties and the tendency for men to be hired into the expanding work force before women.

Table 16.1
Women in the Work Force

| | Single Female Wage Earners as a % of Total Female Workers | Single Women (18–25 yrs) as a % of Total Female Workers |
| --- | --- | --- |
| Ontario | 63.7 | 34.7 |
| Quebec | 71.3 | 37.0 |
| British Columbia | 69.7 | 37.0 |
| Manitoba | 76.3 | 42.5 |
| Saskatchewan | 77.6 | 48.5 |
| Alberta | 73.4 | 45.2 |
| Nova Scotia | 70.9 | 40.4 |
| New Brunswick | 72.4 | 41.4 |
| Prince Edward Island | 73.2 | 43.1 |

*Source*: Calculated from *Eighth Census of Canada*, 1941, vol. 6. Tables 1, 2 and 3.

The wartime expansion of industry and manufacturing would not reach its peak in Canada for another one to two years.[43]

The distribution of employment among women varied according to age and marital status. Single women accounted for the vast majority of wage-earners, and within this group no fewer than 63 per cent were aged eighteen to twenty-five (see Table 16.1).

It is also apparent that single women from the ages of eighteen to twenty-five accounted for no less than 34 per cent of the total number of women employed in each province. This is not out of line with the findings of historians concerned with the "life cycle" of female labour. They have found that most women worked for a short while before marrying and exchanging out-of-home waged labour for domestic labour. Thus, it was considered the norm for single young women to work at waged labour.

Despite an expansive economy, a large number of women declared they were seeking employment in the 1941 national census (see Table 16.2). Given the occupational, rather than combatant, nature of female military service during the Second World War, it would be interesting to know how many of the women who had been seeking employment in 1941 (the year in which two of the three women's services were created) chose to enlist in the military. While no figures have yet been complied on this topic, an estimate can be made of what percentage of women who sought employment enlisted. This estimate may be obtained by calculating the number of unemployed women who fell within the age categories for enlistment and then taking the number of women who enlisted as a percentage of this age group. The result, of course, will be only an approximation, since a number

Table 16.2
Number of Women Seeking Employment, 14 Years Old and Up, 1941*

| | |
|---|---|
| Ontario | 20,000 |
| Quebec | 30,283 |
| Saskatchewan | 6,620 |
| Manitoba | 6,470 |
| British Columbia | 6,384 |
| Nova Scotia | 6,003 |
| New Brunswick | 4,572 |
| Alberta | 4,407 |
| Prince Edward Island | 782 |

*Includes all conjugal conditions.
Source: *Eighth Census of Canada*, 1941, vol. 6, Table 3.

of women who enlisted may not have been seeking employment but joined for purely patriotic reasons. The age distribution of women seeking employment is not provided; the data provides only an estimate of the number of unemployed women between the ages of eighteen and thirty.[44] The numbers were calculated as follows:

1 The majority (68.5 per cent) of women earning wages in 1941 fell into the age group of 18–30. The breakdown is as follows: 18–19 years (12.2 per cent), 20–24 years (28.5 per cent), 25–30 years (27.8 per cent), and 30–34 years (12.5 per cent).[45]
2 Taking 68.5 per cent of the figures listed in Table 16.2 (Number of women Seeking Employment), the number of women seeking employment between the ages of 18–30 can be estimated.

| | | | |
|---|---|---|---|
| Ontario | 13,700 | Alberta | 3,018 |
| Quebec | 20,743 | Nova Scotia | 4,112 |
| British Columbia | 4,373 | New Brunswick | 3,132 |
| Manitoba | 4,432 | Prince Edward Island | 536 |
| Saskatchewan | 4,535 | Canada | 58,581 |

The number of women who enlisted in the military during the first year of female enlistment is listed in Table 16.3. The 90 per cent figure is included, since 90.3 per cent of those who enlisted were between the ages of eighteen and thirty. This figure (90.3 per cent) is derived from the age distributions presented in Table 16.4. The vast majority of the women who enlisted were between the ages of eighteen and thirty, as demonstrated by this table.

Table 16.3
Enlistments in All Women's Services as of 31 December 1942

|  | Total Enlistments | 90% of Enlistments |
|---|---|---|
| British Columbia | 795 | 716 |
| Alberta | 1,258 | 1,132 |
| Saskatchewan | 1,433 | 1,290 |
| Manitoba | 513 | 462 |
| Ontario | 3,273 | 2,946 |
| Quebec | 1,101 | 991 |
| New Brunswick | 485 | 437 |
| Nova Scotia | 453 | 402 |
| Prince Edward Island | 70 | 63 |
| Total | 9,485 | 8,537 |

Source: NA, RG 24, vol. 5378, file HQS 45–25–10. Calculated from Interim Tabulation of Occupational History Forms supplied by the Armed Forces, Department of Labour, 16 February 1943.

Table 16.4
Women's Service Enlistments, Age 17–30, as of 31 December 1942
Ages and Corresponding Percentage of Total Enlistments for Province

| Province | 17–19 Years | 20–24 Years | 25–30 Years |
|---|---|---|---|
| British Columbia | 47.7 | 30.4 | 13.1 |
| Alberta | 50.4 | 29.5 | 12.2 |
| Saskatchewan | 55.3 | 28 | 10.1 |
| Manitoba | 48.9 | 27.5 | 16.4 |
| Ontario | 51.8 | 24.2 | 12.0 |
| Quebec | 46.4 | 29.0 | 12.7 |
| New Brunswick | 51.5 | 30.3 | 9.7 |
| Nova Scotia | 53.2 | 24.3 | 14.6 |
| Prince Edward Island | 75.4 | 7.1 | 10.0 |
| Canada | 51.2 | 27.0 | 12.1 |

Source: Directorate of History, DND, Army Headquarters Report D68, 17 June 1954. J.M. Hitsman, " 'Manpower' Problems of the Women's Services during the Second World War," and Directorate of History, DND, 181.003 (D1469), Working Paper used by S/O P. Wetzel in preparing WD History.

Table 16.5
Enlisted Women as a Percentage of Women Seeking Employment

| | |
|---|---|
| British Columbia | 16.4 |
| Alberta | 37.5 |
| Saskatchewan | 28.4 |
| Manitoba | 10.4 |
| Ontario | 21.5 |
| Quebec | 4.7 |
| New Brunswick | 19.9 |
| Nova Scotia | 11.8 |
| Prince Edward Island | 11.8 |
| Canada | 14.6 |

Using the data from Table 16.4, the number of women between the ages of eighteen and thirty who enlisted may be calculated as a percentage of the estimate of women seeking employment who were in the same age group.

As Table 16.5 shows, less than one in seven women, on average, who were seeking work chose to enlist in the military. While these figures are but estimates, they do present a rough indication of the attractiveness of military service for unemployed women. Contributing factors to the low percentage of enlistments are the disapproval of family and friends of military service as appropriate for a woman and a hesitancy to adopt a military way of life.[46]

The above estimates are reaffirmed by the low rate of enlistment of women who had already contacted either the War Service Selection Board or the military. While women would have been discouraged from joining for a number of reasons, a large percentage of them considered the wages too low.[47] In the air force, the highest ratio of female enlistments to applicants was 2:1. While comparable statistics do not exist for the Wrens, their high selection standards would have reduced the ratio even further.[48]

The percentage of women who enlisted who were unemployed (versus the percentage of unemployed women who enlisted, shown in Table 16.5) is listed in Table 16.6. The national average of women who were unemployed previous to enlistment (21 per cent) is slightly higher than the 18.0 per cent average shown in Table 16.5.

Among the women who enlisted, the percentage who had left their jobs to enlist is surprisingly high (71.7 per cent). Since the majority of servicewomen surveyed during the Second World War listed "economic reasons" as their primary motive for enlisting and since unemployment

Table 16.6
Employment Situation at Time of Enlistment as a Percentage of Total Enlistment for Province as of 31 December 1942

| Province | Employed | Self-employed | Unemployed | Never Worked |
|----------|----------|---------------|------------|--------------|
| BC | 73.2 | 2.1 | 17.2 | 7.2 |
| Alta | 65.4 | 1.3 | 26.9 | 5.8 |
| Sask | 60.0 | 1.1 | 28.1 | 10.4 |
| Man | 70.1 | 1.0 | 22.0 | 5.8 |
| Ont | 80.0 | 1.3 | 15.4 | 3.2 |
| Que | 75.7 | 1.3 | 19.4 | 3.5 |
| NB | 64.9 | 1.2 | 26.6 | 6.8 |
| NS | 66.0 | .9 | 26.3 | 6 |
| PEI | 52.9 | 1.4 | 31.4 | 14.3 |
| Canada | 71.7 | 1.3 | 21.0 | 5.6 |

*Source*: NA, RG 24, vol. 5378, file HQS 45–25–10. Calculated from Interim Tabulation of Occupational History Forms supplied by the Armed Forces, Department of Labour, 16 February 1943. Figure quoted for Canada is the national average and is not the average of provincial percentages.

does not seem to have been a motive behind most enlistments, the supposition can be made that for some women employment opportunities in the military were an improvement over what was available in the civilian work force. To investigate this hypothesis, the following factors will be taken into consideration: pay; allowances, including paid leave; sick leave; accommodation; hours worked; training; promotions; and post-employment benefits.

Considering the service of women in the military in terms of labour reveals a great deal about the relative merits of enlistment. Ruth Pierson has pointed out that the pay of servicewomen was at all times disproportionate to that of men, rising to only four-fifths their salary. This ratio, however, was higher than the ratio of women's wages to men's in industry, as women's wages increased to only two-thirds that of men during the war.[49] Though it was far from perfect, the military approached the concept of equal pay more closely than did civilian organizations.

The financial rewards of joining the service were considerable when compared with the employment situation in the general workplace.[50] For some women, military service offered substantially better wages and benefits than they could expect to receive in the civilian work force. This is especially true for women with little education or skills training and for women who had no previous work experience.

Table 16.7
Rates of Pay for Women in the WRCNS, 1942
Substantive Pay of Officers of the Force

|  | ($/Day) |  |  |  |
|---|---|---|---|---|
| Commander | 8.00 |  |  |  |
| Lieutenant-Commander | 6.20 |  |  |  |
| Lieutenant | 5.20 |  |  |  |
| Sub-Lieutenant | 4.00 |  |  |  |
| Probationary Sub-Lieutenant | 3.40 |  |  |  |
| Chief Wren | 3.15 | 2.90 | 2.65 | 2.40 |
| P.O. Wren | 2.50 | 2.25 | 2.00 | 1.75 |
| Leading Wren | 2.10 | 1.85 | 1.60 | 1.35 |
| Wren W/6 Months | 1.95 | 1.70 | 1.45 | 1.10 |
| Wren | 1.85 | 1.60 | 1.35 | 1.10 |
| Probationary Wren |  |  |  | 1.05 |

*Source*: Department of National Defence, *The Regulations for the Organization and Administration of the Women's Royal Canadian Naval Service* (Ottawa: King's Printer, 1942),
article 5.

To begin, consider the salaries that were offered to women in the military. The 1942 salaries of airwomen are listed in Table 16.7. Variations
in the pay schedule for aircraft women and non-commissioned officers
reflects the varying levels of trades pay.

If we take the lowest possible wage that a servicewoman could earn –
$1.05 a day – and compare that wage with the average salaries of civilian
women in the same age category as servicewomen (see Table 16.8), we
obtain a good idea of the earning power of women in the military during
the war. Service personnel were paid for every day they were considered
to be on active service, including days that they were not working as well
as days when they were ill. Theoretically, then, if a woman was enlisted
for a full year, she would have been paid for 365 days of that year. Thus,
the lowest possible salary a women could make in 1941, excluding all
forms of extra allowance, was $383.25.[51] Using the census data of 1941,
we are able to compare these early salaries of servicewomen with the average earnings of women in the civilian labour force during the same year
(see Table 16.9). The figures in boldface represent the average wages that
fell below the minimum military salary.

The absolute minimum salary paid by the military was clearly higher
that the average wage being offered young women between the ages of
fifteen and nineteen. If we consider the highest wage paid to a leading
Wren (the median position in the non-commissioned ranks), $2.10, we

Table 16.8
Female Wages per Year, by Age and Martial Status, 1941

|  |  | Single Women | | | | Married Women | | | |
|---|---|---|---|---|---|---|---|---|---|
|  |  | 15–19 | 20–24 | 25–34 | 35–45 | 15–19 | 20–24 | 25–34 | 35–45 |
| Ont | 574 | 358 | 508 | 703 | 887 | 390 | 489 | 578 | 584 |
| Que | 427 | 274 | 372 | 501 | 634 | 359 | 481 | 554 | 549 |
| BC | 558 | 292 | 473 | 683 | 893 | 264 | 456 | 559 | – |
| Man | 458 | 216 | 360 | 555 | 801 | 149 | 345 | 475 | 523 |
| Sask | 374 | 160 | 322 | 509 | 712 | 120 | 270 | 428 | – |
| Alta | 475 | 221 | 410 | 622 | 852 | 190 | 378 | 500 | 527 |
| NS | 376 | 216 | 324 | 468 | 639 | 271 | 331 | 419 | 456 |
| NB | 365 | 187 | 299 | 463 | 645 | 258 | 322 | 435 | 435 |
| PEI | 292 | 183 | 271 | 372 | 492 | 200 | 373 | 378 | 348 |

Source: Eighth Census of Canada, 1941, vol. 6, Table 5, 70–88.
Note: The provinces are arranged by number of women in the work force. Ontario had the highest number of women in the work force, followed by Quebec and so on.

Table 16.9
Female Wages, by Age and Martial Status, 1941

|  |  | Single Women | | | | Married Women | | | |
|---|---|---|---|---|---|---|---|---|---|
|  |  | 15–19 | 20–24 | 25–34 | 35–45 | 15–19 | 20–24 | 25–34 | 35–45 |
| Ont | 574 | 358 | 508 | 703 | 887 | 390 | 489 | 578 | 584 |
| Que | 427 | 274 | 372 | 501 | 634 | 359 | 481 | 554 | 549 |
| BC | 558 | 292 | 473 | 683 | 893 | 264 | 456 | 559 | – |
| Man | 458 | 216 | 360 | 555 | 801 | 149 | 345 | 475 | 523 |
| Sask | 374 | 160 | 322 | 509 | 712 | 120 | 270 | 428 | – |
| Alta | 475 | 221 | 410 | 622 | 852 | 190 | 378 | 500 | 527 |
| NS | 376 | 216 | 324 | 468 | 639 | 271 | 331 | 419 | 456 |
| NB | 365 | 187 | 299 | 463 | 645 | 258 | 322 | 435 | 435 |
| PEI | 292 | 183 | 271 | 372 | 492 | 200 | 373 | 378 | 348 |

Source: Eighth Census of Canada, 1941, vol. 6, Table 5, 70–88.

obtain a yearly salary of $766.50. Table 16.9 illustrates how this salary compares with the average salary available to the civilian woman. Again, bold figures represent civilian salaries that are less than the leading Wren's salary of $766.50.

The financial advantages of military service for women between the ages of eighteen and forty-five are apparent. The highest average civilian salary listed ($893 in British Columbia for the single woman between the ages of thirty-five and forty-five) is surpassed by the highest salary for a petty officer. It is noteworthy that all women of the rank of chief petty officer and all commissioned officers made more money than civilian women in the highest average income for women category in Canada in 1941. These figures are based on the raised salaries allotted in 1943. No such increase was possible in the civilian work force. In 1939 the government took initial steps to combat the inflationary force that experience had shown to be a natural corollary of uncontrolled economies in wartime. Among other steps taken, a series of orders-in-council were issued to provide for a system of wage and salary controls covering substantially all gainfully employed persons in Canadian industry not above the rank of foreman.[52] These policies would have the greatest effect on women, since they were rarely employed at the skill level of foremen or above.

The financial allure of military service becomes even more obvious when extra allowances are factored into the calculations. Service personnel received the following allowances: transportation and travel allowance, civilian clothing allowance, funeral allowance, the shipment of personal effects at public expense, $15.00 upon enlistment for toilet articles and necessities, and $3.00 every three months after that, and, finally, exemption from income tax and national defence tax. Moreover, service personnel were housed, fed, and clothed for free, and they received discounts on train and bus fares. Military personnel received free health care, estimated by the Department of National Defence at $11.46 for medical treatment and $6.00 for dental work. They were paid on sick leave and on annual leave (vacation leave). A rehabilitation grant of thirty days' pay was issued to officers and Wrens upon discharge (after six months' service).

In practice, women in the military worked roughly the same amount as their civilian counterparts, averaging 8 hours a day, five days a week, and 4 hours on Saturdays.[53] Thus, the normal work schedule was set at 44 hours a week. Military life required service personnel to work more than this, since they had to be available for extra duty.[54] Comparisons with civilian women, however, reveal that in the manufacturing industries, the average female worked 47.3 hours.[55]

Women in the navy were eligible for all the postwar benefits accorded their male peers, including land grants, service credits, service pensions, disability pensions, university and trade school programs, and employment placement services.

As noted above, the majority of women who enlisted had been employed before joining the military. The financial considerations listed illustrate some of the economic advantages of military service. Military service must have been especially attractive to young women who had few skills or little job experience. This is reinforced by the low (average) salaries available to women between the ages of eighteen and twenty-five (see Table 16.9). The appeal of the military to women in this age group is clearly demonstrated by the enlistment statistics provided in Table 16.4.[56]

This brief analysis of the female enlistments has revealed certain indisputable trends. First, only a small percentage of unemployed women (less than 15 per cent) chose to enlist in the military. Conversely, of the women who joined the military, a comparably small number were unemployed at the time of enlistment (21 per cent). Most women were self-employed or worked for some other employer at the time of enlistment. Since most women cited economic reasons as their prime motive for enlisting, we may speculate that the military was a financially more rewarding form of employment than what was available for the average female worker. This is borne out by a comparison of women's average wages in this time period with the salaries offered by the military. Furthermore, most women who enlisted in the military had little education or trades training and were too young to have gained extensive job experience. This is confirmed by the difficulty that recruiting centres experienced in enlisting skilled women, particularly stenographers.[57]

The economic benefits of joining the military for young, unskilled, or underemployed women are clear, and enlistment statistics demonstrate that the young women took advantage of the opportunity. Little information exists on the nature and extent of the post-employment benefits offered women in the civilian work force. Consequently, a direct comparison between servicewomen and their civilian counterparts is impossible. However, the substantial veteran's benefits available to servicewomen is well documented. All servicemembers, male or female, were entitled to obligatory reinstatement in civil employment, preference in the public service, vocational training, resumed education opportunities, and eligibility under the Veterans' Land Act.[58]

## Conclusion

Ironically, military service, with all its regulations, limitations, and restrictions on personal freedom, may have been a liberating experience for women. The temporary inclusion of women into all three services of the Canadian military during the Second World War paved the way for their permanent admission a few years later. Women who served in the military during the war proved what feminists had been arguing all along – women are capable of doing most of the work men do.

The military's highly standardized system of recruiting, selecting, training, and employing personnel ensured that the work of men and women could be evaluated on equal terms. Servicewomen who worked in exactly the same jobs and under exactly the same conditions as men demonstrated, in a way that may not have been possible in civilian occupations, that the only reason women were paid less was because their labour was valued less. In a sense, this was antithetical to military philosophy, which stressed both uniformity and conformity. This may account for the "equal pay for equal work" policy adopted by the military a few years later.

Evaluating female service participation using a labour analysis casts a new light on women in the military and may in part explain the silence of military historians on the issue of women's service. This explanation can only go so far, however, for there is much that we still do not know. In the case of the Wrens, no satisfactory explanation has been found for the Admiralty's quick reversal of opinion on the admission of women into the navy. Nor has the influence of the British Wrens on the formation of its Canadian counterpart been investigated. There is little to tell us how the men in the navy reacted to the Wrens. Indeed, we are uncertain as to whether the creation of the Wrens facilitated or complicated naval activities on shore. Canada was the first nation in the Commonwealth to admit women into its naval service as integral members rather than as part of an auxiliary force, but no comparative studies have been undertaken to determine what effect, if any, this had on the women, the men, and the organization of the navy. The information would be valuable, not only in its own right, but as the historical context to another, bolder, and uniquely Canadian aspect of our navy – the decision to allow women to serve aboard all ships.

## · 17 ·

# A Canadian Departure:
# The Evolution of HMCS Royal Roads,
# 1942–1948

WILLIAM A. MARCH

In just under forty years (1911–48), the Royal Canadian Navy (RCN) saw two naval colleges come and go. The total life span for the two institutions was less than seventeen years. The first, the Royal Naval College of Canada (RNCC), functioned for eleven years, from 1911 until a drastic change in naval policy brought about its closure in 1922. Another twenty years would pass before its successor opened its doors to naval cadets. The RCN's second naval college, the Royal Canadian Naval College, HMCS *Royal Roads*, had an even briefer existence, lasting for a mere six years as a naval college, from 1942 until 1948. Unlike its predecessor, the RCNC did not close down entirely but continued to evolve and adapt, as it had since its inception, as the navy attempted to come to grips both with changing perceptions of how much education an officer required, first in wartime and then afterwards, and with the necessity of rationalizing naval training policy with government directives. During this evolutionary period, 1942–48, HMCS *Royal Roads* went through three distinct transitional phases: first as the Royal Canadian Naval College, from 1942 until 1947; then, briefly, as the Royal Canadian Navy–Royal Canadian Air Force College, from 1947 until 1948; and finally as the Canadian Services College, HMCS *Royal Roads*, in September 1948. These transformations were the result of government pressure on the RCN and the other services to adopt a university-level education for their junior officers. Each phase brought about radical changes in the orientation of HMCS *Royal Roads*, changes that attacked the fundamental principles upon which the naval college had been based. There were three essential principles, all of them inherited from the Royal Navy (RN): acquire officers at as young an age as possible; train and educate them along strictly naval lines; and send them to sea as quickly as possible. By 1948 Naval Service Headquarters (NSHQ) and HMCS *Royal Roads* could only satisfy the last of these criteria.

From its earliest days, the RN had stressed the ability to handle a ship as the supreme quality of a naval officer. This desire for competent ship-handlers led to the development of the naval outlook on education. Education was acceptable, of course, but only to the point where it began to interfere with the naval officer's primary function, the running of his ship. Beyond this point, education was not necessary. To some extent this perception was a corollary of the naval belief that education was no substitute for experience and that the best way to gain experience in manoeuvring a ship was to do it. Such a policy would allow for the acquisition of skills in peacetime that were equally applicable in war.[1] A thorough grounding in basic seamanship skills and experience gained "before the mast" were deemed preferable to long periods of classroom instruction.

Throughout the eighteenth century, the standard practice of enrolling as a "captain's servant" had been the preferred way to commence a naval career and many hopeful officers joined the RN in their early teens or even younger. The ability to "catch 'em young" allowed the RN to recruit raw material that could literally be grown to fit the needs of the service. While serving the captain, these "young gentlemen" acquired some training, and after six or seven years they were appointed to the rank of midshipman. Future promotions depended upon how a sailors ability compared to that of other members of equal rank.[2]

The introduction of "schoolmasters" into the RN early in the nineteenth century combined limited formal education with service training. The schoolmasters provided the minimum amount of education needed to give the young gentlemen the necessary intellectual tools to get the most out of their training. Their classrooms were located on board training ships or active men-of-war, which allowed the students to "learn to read and write as well as splice hawsers and run out on yards."[3] The extent to which schoolmasters, as members of the navy, could ply their trade was determined by the captain's desires and his attitude towards education.

The impact of technology upon the RN brought the need for increased education into the open. Unlike the army, the RN had escaped harsh criticism during the near debacle of the Crimean War. However, the appearance of steam-powered, armour-plated ships called into question the ability of the fleet to defend England. These "new-fangled" inventions called for a technical education then absent in the RN. Once convinced that steam was here to stay, the navy began to lay careful plans for a new engineering branch. Commencing in 1864, engineering officers in the RN received specialist training, which meant that they soon had better educational opportunities than those available to officers of the executive branch.[4] In the late nineteenth century, basic education for both executive and engineering officers was given ashore (although the school teachers, known as "schoolies," remained on board to teach midshipmen), but now the educational opportunities for the two branches diverged. Unlike the executive officer, the engineering officer had no command function and would receive none until the late twentieth century. Therefore, the officers who controlled the navy, perhaps bridling at the superior educational training given the engineers, viewed formal education as but a necessary evil, desirable only in a limited quantity specifically designed to augment an officer's sea training. This attitude towards education was passed on to the emerging RCN.

Part of the Naval Service Act that established the Royal Canadian Navy called for the formation of a naval college along the lines of the Royal Naval College in England. Such an institution would impart "a complete education in all branches of naval science, tactics and strategy."[5] Wilfrid Laurier intended that the naval college should function along the same lines as Canada's other military institution, the Royal Military College (RMC) at Kingston, Ontario, but this was not to be the case.[6] From the outset, the naval college had a completely different purpose from that of RMC. As the minister of militia, Sir Frederick Borden, explained:

The Royal Military College was established at a time when there was no permanent force at all in Canada. The object was very largely to give an opportunity for military training and a course of teaching which would fit young men to enter civil life or the engineering professions, and at the same time give them instructions in military matters which would be of use when they became part of the active militia ... The position now is entirely different. We are starting with a permanent militia, we have no officers at all, and this course is to be limited to the preparation of cadets for the naval service and that only.[7]

Because graduates would serve in a naval force that paralleled the Royal Navy, the college, from entrance requirements to curriculum, followed the practices of the RN and not those of RMC.

Applicants had to be British subjects between the ages of fourteen and sixteen, pass a competitive entrance examination, and meet RN medical standards. Upon successful completion of the program, the graduates would receive commissions in the dominion naval forces. The two-year curriculum, which allowed no personal selection of subjects, provided instruction in navigation, seamanship, pilotage, engineering, applied electricity, physics, chemistry, mechanics, mathematics, English, history, geography, French, and German. Seamanship was the most important course.[8]

Subjects were taught by a mixture of Canadian civilian instructors and ex-RN officers led by Lieutenant Edward A.E. Nixon, who had joined the Royal Navy at the age of fourteen in 1892 and who remained with the RNCC throughout its existence. A former student remembered him as a "strict disciplinarian, a physical fitness fanatic, and a strong believer in naval tradition."[9] Nixon nurtured the college through a rather troubled existence until its closure in 1922. During this period the RNCC trained 148 officers, 60 of whom would still be serving in 1939. These trainees would provide the professional nucleus for a rapidly expanding Canadian navy[10] and would have a fundamental impact on the establishment of the second Canadian naval college.

By August 1940 the RCN had enjoyed rapid growth brought about by wartime demands. With the initial period of expansion complete and a new minister of defence for naval services in office, the chief of naval staff (CNS), Rear Admiral Percy Nelles, felt the time appropriate to broach the subject of a second naval college. Therefore, on 28 August a group of RNCC graduates, led by Nelles, met with the naval minister, Angus L. Macdonald, for the purpose of winning support for the opening of a college. Nelles thought that an institution designed to produce regular officers committed to the RCN would be important for the future of the navy. The CNS had served in a variety of staff positions throughout the dark days of the 1930s when the RCN had almost ceased to exist; he wanted to ensure that the postwar navy would not face the possibility of extinction again.[11] A larger naval establishment, with a suitable complement of ships and permanent shore facilities, would be difficult to do away with. Permanent officers would be required to man these ships and facilities, and Nelles's personal experiences had persuaded him that suitable officers would best be trained at a naval college.

It was obvious from the beginning that the naval officers favoured an institution roughly modelled after the Royal Naval College at Dartmouth and more specifically after the RNCC through which they had passed. Nelles pointed out that, owing to wartime conditions, the current practice of sending Canadian naval officers to England for training was expensive and unreliable. It would be far better, he argued, to train RCN officers at a suitable naval institution in Canada. He recommended that the college accept 100 students, a far greater number than the RNCC had accommodated. He saw this as necessary both because the Canadian fleet that the officers were to support was larger than in RNCC days and because a larger number would decrease the cost per cadet. Nelles informed the minister that not only would a naval college produce naval officers during and after the war, but the training and education provided would be suitable for civilian employment in the merchant marine.[12]

The force of these arguments appeared to influence the naval minister, but the RCN may have been preaching to a convert. A Nova Scotia Liberal and former premier of that province, Macdonald had his own plans for the navy, and these dovetailed with the support that Nelles sought. As he explained to the House of Commons during his maiden speech on 19 November 1940, "it will be a proud day for this country, when our Canadian naval effort will be directed by Canadian men, trained in Canada and operating in ships built in this country."[13] To this end, he informed the graduating class of 1944 that he had arrived in Ottawa with two goals: the creation of a Canadian shipbuilding industry and the re-establishment of a naval college.[14] Both goals were tied to the expansion of the RCN, and although his working relationship with Nelles deteriorated, Macdonald remained true to these aims during his stay in Ottawa.

The growth of the RCN during the first year of the war had strained its training facilities, resulting in a lack of qualified personnel to man the ships.[15] With respect to naval officers, the manning difficulties were exacerbated by the closure in the summer of 1940 of the officer-training establishments of the Royal Canadian Naval Volunteer Reserve (RCNVR), which had barely been managing to cope with the increased demand. The director of naval personnel (DNP), Captain C.R.H. Taylor, advised the CNS on 23 August 1940 that the manning difficulties had reached a critical level. He recommended that a special conference be convened immediately to seek a solution to the problem.[16] This meeting was held one week later, involving Captain Taylor and officers of the various RCN training facilities. At the end of the meeting, the recommendations put forward to the CNS called for the immediate reopening of an RCNVR officer-training establishment, to be in operation no later than January 1941.[17] Faced with an ever-increasing shortage of personnel, Naval Service Headquarters decided to act upon this suggestion, which in turn delayed the opening of the naval college for over a year.

In November 1940 NSHQ directed that the site of the future naval college would initially house the recommended RCNVR training establishment. The location that had been chosen for the college was the Victoria property of the late Lord Dunsmuir, a former lieutenant-governor of British Columbia. The 650-acre estate, complete with several large buildings and a private lagoon suitable for sail training, had been purchased by the RCN for $75,000. Commissioned as HMCS *Royal Roads*, the RCNVR facility received its first cadets in January 1941 and operated until 21 October 1942. Through its gates passed approximately 600 officers to take their place within the Canadian fleet and play a large part in alleviating the officer shortage.

Throughout this period, work on the naval college itself continued apace, directed for the most part by the commanding officer of HMCS *Royal Roads*, Captain J.W. Grant. Grant had had an enormous amount of experience in training officers. Himself a graduate of the RNCC and later an executive officer there, he had more recently served as the executive officer of another RCNVR officer-training establishment, HMCS *Stone Frigate* in Kingston, Ontario. Appointed to command HMCS *Royal Roads* in November 1940, Grant had much to do with the appointment of the various instructors, many of whom had gone through HMCS *Stone Frigate* during his tenure there. For the most part he would be satisfied with their performance at the Canadian naval college.[18] By early 1941, however, his efforts were increasingly focused on establishing the infrastructure for the naval college.

Work quickly commenced on permanent academic and residential buildings, with a target date for completion set for the fall of 1942. A three-man board was appointed in July 1941 to make detailed recommendations to NSHQ with respect to the naval college. The terms of reference provided to the board by Naval Secretary Captain J.O. Cossette, RCN, stated that the college complement would not exceed 100 cadets and that vacancies would exist in the permanent RCN for 30 graduates annually, exclusive of the engineering and paymaster branches. The remaining graduates would be required to serve with the RCNVR for the duration of hostilities. Cossette directed that the "length of the course in War can be accepted as half that required in peace." Age limits for the first war-term were set at seventeen to eighteen years and eight months as of 1 July of the year of entry. Students up to age twenty could be enroled as paymaster cadets for the first term. The college would commence operation in September 1942.

The naval secretary told the board to make recommendations on a college organization that would be suitable in a post-hostilities environment. It was obvious that the intention was to provide a college that would function in peacetime but could be modified to meet wartime requirements.[19] The directions provided by the naval secretary were by no means exhaustive, but they provided the board with a starting-point from which to consider the infrastructure that would be required by the Royal Canadian Naval College. There could be no mistaking the fact that the planning and preparation for the naval college would be guided by the principle that the institution was permanent and that it would continue to exist after hostilities. The speed with which the board's report was returned to Ottawa, on 11 August 1941, suggests the sense of urgency, the effectiveness of preliminary discussions on the structure of the college, and the similar views of the board members, Holms, Grant, and Richardson.

Their recommendations offered no surprises. They agreed that a two-year peacetime course would allow the naval cadets to proceed to sea at a sufficiently young age so as not to place them at a disadvantage with their RN counterparts, and they recommended that after the war the enrolment age should remain sixteen to seventeen years and eight months as of 1 July in the year of entry. After considerable discussion, the board finally agreed that the minimum education standard for entry should be provincial junior matriculation level. However, to provide for a continuous flow of officers, the three members suggested that, for the first entry only, half the candidates be overage students with the equivalent of senior matriculation or one year of university education. These "advanced" students would follow a one-year course.[20]

After the appropriate naval cadets had been selected, it would be necessary to give the cadet in "the two year course ... a complete basic education in Navy Science [which] parallel[ed] roughly the corresponding training in the RN."[21] The board provided a general outline of the types of courses required and the amount of time that should be spent on each. A future RCN officer, it stated, should take mathematics, mechanics, physics, chemistry, English, history, and French. Practical instruction in naval science would be centred around "hands-on" engineering, navigation, pilotage, gunnery, and torpedo classes. Instruction in the practical subjects would combine classes ashore and at sea. The allotment of time between the various courses was comparable to practice in the previous Canadian college and the Royal Naval College at Dartmouth, England; however, it would appear that the board members, all of whom were graduates of the RNCC, favoured a closer approximation to the curriculum of their old college.[22]

With only a few minor changes, these recommendations were accepted by NSHQ and became the blueprint for the Royal Canadian Naval College. Early in the morning of Trafalgar Day, 21 October 1942, the RCNVR training facility HMCS *Royal Roads* was paid off. Two and a half hours later, 137 years after Nelson's naval victory, the Royal Canadian Naval College, HMCS *Royal Roads*, was commissioned by Defence Minister Angus L. Macdonald.

The opening of the college on the anniversary of the famous British naval victory underlined the navy's adoption of RN naval traditions. An American naval officer writing of the RCNC in 1947 stated: "The traditionalism of the Royal Navy is reflected in the designations of the cadet divisions, which are named after heroes of the British Navy. In this connection Nelson, Collingwood, Drake, Rodney, Frobisher, and Hawkins live again as inspirations to give substance and purpose to the cadets in preparing themselves for careers in the fleet."[23]

Discipline, modelled after practices that had been followed at the RNCC and Dartmouth, allowed the practice of caning for serious infractions.[24]

The fact that RN, or British public school, traditions prevailed at the RCNC is not surprising given that the vast majority of the staff had been cadets or instructors at the RNCC or RMC, where RN traditions prevailed, or had had a similar experience at private schools.

In an edition of the RCNC periodical, *The Log*, Admiral Nelles states that it was "important to develop a typically Canadian atmosphere" in the college.[25] In only two areas, however, were significant "Canadian" innovations introduced. The first and most obvious was the college's name, "Royal Canadian Naval College," an indication that this was an institution created to serve the interests of the *Canadian* navy and not those of the Royal Navy. Secondly, the age upon entry of the candidates had been raised. As Nelles pointed out, it was best that the "college ... be operated for the benefit of semi-adults, not school boys in any sense. This is because it fits in better with the Canadian school and college system and will be better supported by the public."[26] Such sentiments did not prevent the RCN from setting the age limitations as low as possible, almost eliminating the possibility of a naval career for French Canadians, who tended to graduate later from the Catholic school system in Quebec. As a result, the college "catered solely to upper middle-class Anglophones, a Canadian version of the public-school boys who found their way to the Quarter Deck in the old RN."[27]

British influence in the Canadian military, especially in the RCN, generated intense discussion within the government as its attention turned to the shape that the postwar military would take. On 25 October 1945 a member of Parliament rose to declare that Canada must "realize that Nelson is dead"; he was responding to complaints that had filtered up through the ranks dealing in part with the low pay and harsh living conditions in the RCN.[28] However, the matter went beyond mere unhappiness with conditions of service to dissatisfaction with the RCN's "slavish conformity to the traditions of the Royal Navy and its outdated code of discipline." Another member of Parliament, Jean Pouliot, informed the minister of defence, Douglas Abbott, that such practices had to cease. The minister promised to inform the naval hierarchy, but the senior officers took little or no action. Eventually, it would take a series of "incidents" aboard three Canadian warships before the prevalence of RN tradition was seriously challenged in the RCN.[29] Although British traditions would remain, the RCN found itself under increasing pressure from the government and the other services to adopt a progressive educational process for its junior officers.

For planning purposes the government had informed the Chiefs of Staff Committee in September 1945 that there would be approximately 10,000 naval, 15,000 air force, and 27,000 army personnel in the postwar Canadian military. These numbers were significantly less than had been requested by the Chiefs of Staff, but they still resulted in the largest peacetime force in Canadian history. A larger force necessitated an increase in the number of junior officers required, and all three services began to consider the question of officer production and training. From the beginning, the Canadian Army hierarchy agreed with the British and Americans that the officer of the future would require increased education and improved technical skills. Discussion centred on whether to support a military or civilian university to provide the required education. Of the three branches of the Canadian military, the RCN was in the best overall position with respect to officer production, for it had a functioning, permanent naval college. The army, by contrast, had closed RMC in 1942 for service reasons and now faced an uphill battle to re-establish it. The air force was in the worst shape with respect to officer-training facilities, as it had never had a college of its own. The notion of tri-service education soon gained favour despite the fact that some members of each branch of the service actively argued for individual service colleges.

One of the first to advocate a tri-service education was the director of naval education (DNE), Dr Percy Lowe. Lowe did not feel that there were sufficient resources, either academic or financial, to support the establishment of several different military colleges. He advocated the creation of a single facility that could serve the needs of all three services.[30] The DNE forwarded a draft of his proposal to the Chiefs of Staff and the defence minister; however, their response was, at best, lukewarm. The chief of naval personnel (CNP) was adamant that there was no need to change and that the RCNC met the navy's needs for educated officers.[31] The chief of air staff (CAS), Air Marshal R. Leckie, favoured the proposal and sought further discussions with his counterparts. Lieutenant-General Charles Foulkes, the chief of general staff (CGS), went one step further: he appointed a committee under Brigadier L.M. Chesley on 8 October 1945 to examine all aspects of the provision of officers for the active army and to assess "the educational requirements of candidates, and how they should be trained."[32] The Chesley committee recommended that a modern army officer obtain a university-level degree.[33] Foulkes agreed and passed the committee's report to the minister of defence, Douglas Abbott.

The call for a university degree as a requirement for an army commission led to a critical examination of the Royal Canadian Naval College. The proposed higher academic standards and increased defence cuts put the future of *Royal Roads* in jeopardy. The CNS expressed his concern to his air force counterpart in late January 1946, and the CAS responded with the suggestion that *Royal Roads* could be preserved by allowing Royal Canadian Air Force (RCAF) candidates to attend.[34] In order to make a joint college possible, the CAS was willing to leave the navy in charge and to place RCAF personnel under naval discipline while they attended the college. Naturally, the CAS wrote, such a plan would depend upon CNS direction with respect to training, cabinet direction on the size of the forces, and detailed examination of the college by both naval and air force staffs.

The CAS proposal had merit. The RCAF and RCN shared many basic beliefs about education and training. Both placed a minimal value on the necessity of post-secondary education except in the case of specialist or technical officers. Believing that an early introduction to the lifestyle and equipment of his service was a necessary requirement for a competent, committed officer, both services wanted their officers to proceed into the air, or to sea, at a young, formative age. In the RCAF, the requirement to "get 'em young" was reinforced by the fact that many of its officers were on short-service commissions. Thus, the RCAF wanted them to get a specific amount of post-secondary education so that by the time they had graduated from the college and had completed flight training, they would be young enough to undertake useful service prior to the end of their engagement. Though it viewed the proposal cautiously, the navy was definitely more enthusiastic about this plan than it was about Foulkes's tri-service suggestion. The acting chief of naval staff sought the opinion of Captain J.M. Grant, now serving at NSHQ, on the RCAF's proposal. Grant considered the plan a sound idea that would appeal not only to the government but to the Canadian people and the navy.[35]

As it turned out, Grant was right in his opinion that a joint college would appeal to the government, for Abbott immediately supported the proposal. He pressed the acting chief of naval staff for "quick" action so that he could announce it to the House of Commons.[36] The air force and navy agreed that the new collage would allow for a common first year of study followed by a second year in which the services would "stream" their candidates. Numbers of air force candidates would be limited so as not to swamp the navy, and the college would continue to be administered by the RCN, with all candidates subject to naval discipline. Nonetheless, the RCAF did wish to do away with the RCN's special selection examinations, preferring a senior matriculation entrance standard. Eventually, the RCAF and the RCN compromised on an entrance examination that not only kept elements of the special examinations, but allowed the testing of mathematics and English at the senior matriculation level.[37]

Abbott continued to support the navy's limited reorganization of their naval college, but a Cabinet shuffle in December 1946 produced a new minister of national defence, Brooke Claxton. Claxton welcomed the opportunity to take on the Defence portfolio, which he viewed as "tough, challenging, and important."[38] Prime Minister Mackenzie King had made it plain to the defence minister that his job was to ensure the greatest possible degree of unification and coordination within the Canadian military. Claxton recalled: "The most urgent problem was the domestic one of organizing the armed forces on a peacetime basis, and of unifying and integrating elements of the Department of National Defence and the armed forces to improve efficiency and to reduce duplications."[39] One of the areas where such duplication could be eliminated was officer training. To this end, Claxton announced to Cabinet on 21 January 1947 his intention to reorient HMCS *Royal Roads* so that it would provide instruction to officers of both the RCN and the RCAF. He explained that he viewed this as the "first step in a combined service college plan for the procurement of officers," which could include the reopening of RMC as a cadet college in 1948.[40]

Having been given firm direction by Claxton, the RCN and RCAF rapidly finalized their plans for the joint college. Major changes to HMCS *Royal Roads* focused on the adoption of a senior matriculation entry standard and on raising the age limits from between sixteen and one-half years to nineteen and one-half years by 1 July of the year of entry. In addition, under pressure from the RCAF, the RCN agreed to offer special consideration to French-speaking applicants. Although the academic requirements remained at the senior matriculation level, such applicants who were up to twenty and one-half years of age could apply.[41] This would allow applicants from Quebec an opportunity to increase their academic suitability by taking one year of university.

The RCN-RCAF College commenced operation in September 1947. However, by establishing a tri-service committee to examine the whole question of officer education and training, Claxton had already laid the groundwork for the next evolutionary change at the college. Unimpressed by previous studies on the subject, he selected retired Air Vice-Marshal E.W. Stedman to head a committee to advise the minister on a wide range of matters pertaining to officer production. Throughout the Stedman committee's meetings, Claxton provided strict guidance and informed Stedman that any points of contention were to be referred to him for settlement. The minister realized that of the three services only the army supported a tri-service plan for officer training, and he himself wished to limit inter-service bickering.[42]

Unfortunately, the inter-service rivalry continued. The Stedman committee quickly became deadlocked, with the navy and air force on one side and the army on the other. Both the RCN and RCAF wanted their officers to enter the service at a young age and with a limited amount of post-secondary education. The army sought a university degree as the basic educational qualification for an officer and believed that an officer trainee could best obtain such a degree by spending time at both a military college and a civilian university.[43] Stedman referred the problem to

Claxton, who took immediate steps to correct the impasse. Firmly convinced that academic credentials were as important as military experience, Claxton told the committee to consider a university degree as the basic goal for technical officers and to examine whether or not education short of a degree would be suitable for non-technical officers.[44]

The Stedman committee continued its discussions throughout the summer of 1947. A subcommittee under Air Vice-Marshal W.A. Curtis recommended that *Royal Roads* and RMC have similar entrance requirements and fees, as well as identical curricula mirroring what was offered at civilian universities.[45] Claxton responded favourably to these recommendations and advised Stedman to accept them "for planning purposes." He could see no reason why the RCAF and RCN cadets who were to commence classes in September 1947 should not follow the same curriculum throughout their two-year program, which, in turn, would be identical to that of RMC as soon as it opened.[46]

Advocates of a tri-service approach to education were heartened when the RCAF representative, Air Commodore Smith, announced on 24 September that the RCAF accepted "the Army plan for Interservice Officer Candidate Training."[47] The reasons for this policy change are difficult to fathom. While the RCAF was not entirely happy with the standard of education provided by *Royal Roads*, it believed that matters had proceeded to a point where backing out of the RCN-RCAF scheme would be detrimental.[48] Moreover, since RMC would soon open again and welcome RCAF cadets, there would be an alternative source of educated officers. Throughout the Stedman committee's discussions, the RCAF had also studied ways of starting graduates on their aircrew training as young as possible. The chief of air staff had finally decided that training could be provided between academic years and that the possibility that cadets could fly with auxiliary squadrons during the academic year would allow the RCAF to graduate relatively well-trained aircrew.[49]

With the air force's change in policy, the RCN quickly capitulated, accepting the recommendations Stedman had sent to Claxton early in 1948. According to the final report, curricula of both colleges would be equivalent to a university combined arts and engineering course, designed to allow cadets, if required, to complete a degree in civil, mechanical, electrical, or chemical engineering. The committee recommended that fees be charged and that cadets wear a "neutral" uniform. A candidate had to be between the ages of sixteen and twenty upon entry – except for those entering the RCN, in which case the normal limits were sixteen to nineteen years of age. Candidates from French classical colleges were accepted up to age twenty. The committee suggested that a certain number of scholarships be awarded and that they be distributed among the provinces according to population. The staffs of the two colleges would include both military and civilian personnel, with the overriding criterion being to get the best man for the position. Army and air force cadets would undergo four years of instruction, while cadets of the naval technical branches would either complete their four years of education at one of the military colleges or continue on to RN facilities in Britain to complete their training. Naval cadets of the executive branch would only be required to undergo two years of instruction at HMCS *Royal Roads*. Finally, the Stedman committee recommended that the collective name for the colleges be the "Joint Services Cadet Colleges."[50] Satisfied for the most part with the report, Claxton set about ensuring that its recommendations were implemented.

The Combined Services College, HMCS *Royal Roads*, which commenced operation in September 1948, differed from the Royal Canadian Naval College. The RCNC had been based on the tried and true principles of RN naval tradition, which called for early entry into the service, an education geared towards naval requirements, and sea duty as soon as possible. By 1948 HMCS *Royal Roads* offered a naval cadet entry at a significantly higher age and a liberal education comparable to that found in a civilian university. Only cadets opting for the executive branch proceeded to sea in two years. These changes had been brought about by postwar pressure to adopt a university-level education for young officers. Supported by the army and Brooke Claxton, the minister of national defence, there was never any doubt as to the final outcome.

The RCN, however, proved reluctant to accept these changes wholeheartedly and, in fighting a successful rearguard action, maintained the ability to get a portion of its officers to sea at a young age. Still, the carefully created incubator that the RCN had fashioned to produce its future officers had been cracked and the naval cadets were now exposed to outside influences. These influences would eventually remove the last vestiges of the old-fashioned British training practices and allow the college to serve all three military services, albeit with a naval flare.

As a sad final note, in May 1995 Royal Roads ceased to exist as a military college. The victim of budgetary considerations, it has now sailed into history as a distinctly Canadian educational facility. However, as part of our naval heritage, it will always be valued for having helped shape Canada's naval identity.

# · 18 ·

## HMCS Ottawa III:
## The Navy's First French-Language Unit,
## 1968–1973

SERGE BERNIER

*Introduction*

Anyone leafing through the photo album of *Ottawa* III, which was commissioned in 1956 and decommissioned in 1992, would be struck by a number of things. The White Ensign and the British-style uniforms of 1956 gave way, in the 1960s, to a Canadian flag and distinctively Canadian uniforms. The curious would also come across some very revealing artifacts. When the ship was commissioned in 1956, the ceremony was conducted at the shipyards of Canadian Vickers Limited in Montreal, but the brochure given to the guests on that occasion contained not a single word of French. In 1992, however, the handout given to her visitors was printed in both official languages. It should also be noted that *Ottawa* III, a St Laurent–class ship, embodied a number of Canadian technical achievements and innovations. For those who sailed in her, she was much more than just another vessel. Ships eventually develop a soul, and *Ottawa* III's was in part moulded by the fact that she was, between 1968 and 1973, the first French-language unit of the navy.

One thing that the ship's photo album cannot give the observer is an idea of what life was like for the men and women who sailed in her over the years. This chapter is not intended to provide a precise description of the crew, whose composition constantly changed over the Ottawa's thirty-six-year life span, or of their day-to-day existence. We would, however, like to offer a few snippets covering the "French" period of

*Ottawa* III,* the heir to the outstanding battle honours won by her predecessors, *Ottawa* I and *Ottawa* II, during the Second World War.[1]

In hindsight, 1968 was a difficult year in many respects for large segments of the Western elites of the day, and the Royal Canadian Navy
(RCN) was no exception. In that year, the admirals had scarcely come to
terms with certain elements of an awakening Canadian nationalism and
had not yet accepted unification – far from it – when the establishment of
a French-language naval unit was announced. Retired Vice-Admiral
Jeffry V. Brock, on learning the news, remarked that it was "sheer, un-
adulterated lunacy."[2] The admirals and other senior officers still in the
service carefully refrained from commenting on the announcement in
such a frank manner (in public, at any rate). How many of them privately shared Brock's view is another matter! One thing is certain: the
men who headed the Royal Canadian Navy in 1968 were not entirely
surprised, although many others certainly were, when this project, which
they had been hearing about for nearly a year, was finally launched.

## Background of a Revolution

There were probably few naval officers who knew General Jean V. Allard
well enough when he became chief of defence staff in the summer of
1966 to foresee that within forty months he would profoundly change
the Canadian Armed Forces. Now that his memoirs have been published,
we have learned that as a result of having experienced certain disappoint-
ments during the war while serving in the armoured corps, Allard believed that francophones would only feel at home in the Canadian Army
if non-infantry units were created that had a francophone identity and
operated somewhat like the Royal 22$^e$ Regiment (R22$^e$R).[3] During the
1950s and up to 1966, he endeavoured, with other francophones, to im-
plant that idea in the army. When he reached the top of an integrated and
soon-to-be unified hierarchy, Allard ensured that his successive ministers
(Paul Hellyer and Léo Cadieux) would support him in implementing his
plan – this time within the three services.

We know a little about the major steps that would ultimately result in
*Ottawa*'s designation as a French-language unit (FLU – ULF in French). In
the fall of 1966, Allard established the Study Group on the Recruitment
and Retention of French Speaking Personnel in the Armed Forces, under

---

* For the sake of bevity, I will, from this point on, dispense with the "III" and refer to the ship
simply as "*Ottawa.*"

the chairmanship of Colonel Armand Ross. One of the naval members of this group was Commander Pierre Simard. The Ross Report released in March 1967, recommended among other things that predominantly French-language units and bases be created in the three services; this would provide an opportunity for francophones to work in their own language, as anglophones had always been able to do.[4] Francophone service personnel would gain their initial operational experience in their own language at these locations, and they would return to them at various stages in their careers. These units would also contain an appropriate proportion of anglophones. Thus, anglophones would come into contact with the French Canadian culture and language, and their francophone counterparts would be exposed to English very early on in their careers. In an environment such as this, French Canadians would not have to prove themselves professionally and socially in their second language.[5]

After considering these recommendations, Allard wrote a memorandum to his subordinates at Canadian Forces Headquarters (CFHQ) stating that the time had come to discuss the possibility of concentrating navy francophones on the east coast with a view to forming two "predominantly French-speaking" crews and making one of the flying squadrons at Greenwood, including its ground crew, a "predominantly French-speaking" unit.[6] We shall not concern ourselves with the matter of the long-range patrol squadron, which, in 1994, is still in the planning stage. Instead, we shall look at what happened in the navy between 1968 and 1973.

## The Decision

It is a matter of fact that Allard wanted to create non-infantry units patterned on the Royal 22e Regiment, but exactly how he visualized a French-language unit would operate outside Quebec in less clear. It is unlikely that he had a precise idea of what the actual result would be in a naval milieu that was traditionally resistant to the French language and culture. The chief of defence staff (CDS) was aware that the problems to be addressed in that environment were much greater than in the army, where the "French fact" already existed, and even in the air force, which had bases in Quebec. The navy, steeped in British tradition and established on both English-speaking coasts of Canada, had no French-language "critical mass." It therefore posed a very special problem, one which the CDS tasked naval personnel to solve.

Basically, was it possible to have a French-language unit in the navy at all? Commander Simard had expressed doubts on the subject in a memorandum to Allard on 12 October 1967. He believed that the viability of a French-language unit in the navy was ultimately contingent upon having an entirely French-speaking crew.[7] His reasoning was as follows: anglo-phones should not be subjected to the very injustices that the navy was now attempting to eradicate from the lives of French-speaking sailors; the situation should be avoided whereby the commanding officer (CO) would have to exercise two kinds of leadership, one for anglophones and another for francophones, as the two groups were so different; and it would be impossible to use French aboard ship with anglophones present – indeed, Simard added, anglophones would probably ask to be trans-ferred elsewhere.

It is difficult to discount arguments voiced by an experienced officer who had previously commanded a ship. It should be noted, however, that as a member of the Ross team, Simard had supported the idea of units composed mainly, but not exclusively, of francophones. Be that as it may, politics will always have the last word. The news release of 2 April 1968 was very clear: 20 per cent of the strength of the French-language units would be anglophones, and that percentage would be reduced to 10 in the 1972 fifteen-year plan.[8] The political acumen of either the chief of defence staff or Simard had made it possible to examine the alternative of an French-language unit comprising 80 per cent francophones. After he wrote his October 1967 memorandum to Allard,[9] Simard rethought the potential advantages of a ship crewed by a mixture of anglophones and francophones. In fact, in the spring of 1968, he suggested that this ap-proach would make it easier to obtain the required number of men, that it would not be necessary to award special promotions to a number of francophones to fill certain positions, that national aims and the conclu-sions of the Ross Report would be observed, that the "separatist" idea that some were already associating with the ship would be instantly dis-pelled, and, finally, that the sailors would find it more acceptable to serve in a bilingual ship than in a unilingual French one.[10]

Essential to the creation of the naval French-language unit would be the availability of a sufficient number of linguistically qualified seamen. According to a detailed analysis taken from the Ross Report and con-tained in Simard's memorandum of October 1967, there were 132 offic-ers and 1,585 non-commissioned officers (NCOs) and seamen who were French-speaking. This highly perfunctory survey, however, which had been conducted less than a year earlier, failed to indicate whether the required skills were available at each level and in all of the specialties. The task of thoroughly investigating the data was delegated to the chief of personnel (CP), who, between November 1967 and January 1968 and in cooperation with Maritime Command (MARCOM), was to determine whether a French-language ship (eventually a second one and perhaps a third) could operate on an ongoing basis. In early February 1968, about two months before the creation of the naval French-language unit was publicly announced, the conclusion resulting from that investigation was extremely pessimistic: in the final analysis, there were purportedly fewer than 1,000 francophones and bilingual anglophones in the navy. This meant that, in the long term, the naval French-language unit could survive only if part of the linguistically qualified crew were kept at sea on an almost permanent basis – an alternative that would certainly not be very popular with the seamen.[11]

Faced with this alarming new situation, Admiral J.C. O'Brien, Commander, MARCOM, who actively supported the concept of a naval French-language unit, suggested to the CDS that he send his naval assistant, Pierre Simard, to Halifax so that he could review *in situ* the facts and figures contained in the report of the chief of personnel and prepare his own recommendations. After three weeks' work, Simard was able to present a more optimistic picture of the situation, although the figures were still lower than those contained in the Ross Report. He claimed that there were 1,157 francophones and bilingual anglophones, a sufficient number to enable the ship to operate as a French-language unit between 1968 and 1971. However, the fact that 20 per cent of the crew would have to be anglophones – not all of them bilingual – would require special measures, including accelerated French courses.[12]

Seventeen days later, the minister's press release included one naval French-language unit in the list of those designated for the three services. It was to be HMCS *Ottawa*, which, besides having a highly symbolic name, was in the first of her three operational cycles at the time. Simard was appointed to command her. In April he began to select his officers, translate standing orders, order publications and typewriters with French keyboards, see to the essential postings both to and from the ship, and attend to a variety of other related tasks. Although the venture was immense, considerable progress had been made by the time he officially assumed command on 15 July 1968.

## The Difficulties

In the letter accompanying his final report as first commanding officer of the first naval French-language unit, sent to Chief of Personnel Vice-Admiral R.L. Hennessy on 25 June 1970, Commander Simard spoke of beginning the process of creating a second French-language unit in the navy, "as I am convinced that if we wait until we have all the bilingual personnel required we will never get underway."[13] MARCOM sent a message to CFHQ on 20 August, requesting that a "feasibility study be conducted to ascertain when a second bilingual ship can be manned with an assessment of what percentage bilingual/unilingual personnel might be held in both ships."[14] The message even added that it was hoped that this second ship could begin to become a French-language unit in July 1971. The message was sent to the director general of postings and careers (DGPC) on 26 August, together with this handwritten minute: "The sooner we can have a second ship the better."[15] On 28 August the DGPC, Commodore R.H. Falls, asked his specialists to look into the matter.[16]

We know now that this second French-language unit would not appear until 1982. This urgent request by MARCOM was probably dropped in the process of producing the "15-year Program to increase Bilingualism and Biculturalism in the Armed Forces" (B&B plan), which was already under way in the summer of 1970. In the event, manning *Ottawa* with a crew of francophones and bilingual anglophones was to prove a generally insoluble problem throughout the entire period from 1968 to 1973. There was to be a high proportion of unilingual anglophones aboard throughout that five-year period. We shall return to this topic.

*Ottawa* encountered other difficulties, probably in part because of the personality of the first officer to command her as a French-language unit. Commander Simard, a down-to-earth pragmatist, consistently described his ship as a bilingual unit rather than a French-language unit. While this was an accurate reflection of the actual situation, it raised a serious question in the mind of every young francophone who had been told when he enroled in Chicoutimi or Drummondville that a sailor lived in French on the *Ottawa*.[17] Granted, the ship operated in both languages, but it seems that Simard had abandoned the term "French-language unit" as soon as anglophones were included in the project. This approach on Simard's part did not sit well with everyone.[18]

In his report of June 1970, as may be imagined, Commander Simard, having been involved with the Ross Report and having served as General Allard's "naval right-hand man," did not just confine himself to describing the situation on his ship. He turned his attention to everything dealing with French in general. His outlook was far-ranging. He dealt with dependants' education, French-language courses for anglophones, the procurement of French-language magazines, films, and technical manuals for his crew or for the purpose of training young francophone sailors in French. Simard referred to meetings he had had with officials of the French Embassy in Ottawa and with representatives of the French navy when his ship had visited France. These discussions must not have pleased everyone, because Simard added: "It is high time that the military establishment ceases to equate negotiations with France with disloyalty to Country."[19]

To all of this, Simard even added a dash of history: "To have a naval vessel manned by a predominantly/entirely French speaking crew has been advocated ever since the R.C.N. was founded some 60 years ago." Anyone reading his report is immediately struck by Simard's caution about the

315

status accorded the French language in his ship. The use of French was introduced only gradually, beginning in the fall of 1968. "This low key approach with respect to languages served us well throughout the cycle and we did not have a single request to leave the ship." Speaking of the three-week French immersion course in December 1968, he added: "I can now confess that I was truly worried prior to sending these people to this course, about the attitude they might have towards it all." One of his recommendations (which would not be accepted) was that a French instructor be kept on board so that the students could continue to progress even during the operational phases.

On the surface, this report is remarkably cautious, even ambivalent. It must be remembered, however, that it reflected the circumstances of the time. Halifax newspaper editorials of the day were sometimes hostile. As well, many of Commander Simard's friends and colleagues, retired or otherwise, generally saw nothing positive in an experiment that senior authorities had launched and were controlling from Ottawa. Perhaps Simard was overly sensitive to criticism that was, in the final analysis, superficial.

The fact remains that, in his own way, Simard was a missionary who was both inspired and disappointed by the turn of certain events. Certainly, he devoted a great deal of his time to his mission and had no qualms about going beyond the normal prerogatives of a ship's captain to advance a cause that he had embraced for over three years (if his involvement with the Ross group is included). This dedication probably played a role in the fact that he subsequently served – initially as a naval officer and, later, as a civilian – as Maritime Command Coordinator of Official Languages; he would establish a record for the length of time that such a position was occupied in the Canadian Armed Forces. When Commander M.H. Tremblay assumed command of *Ottawa*, the problems of this French-language unit were far from solved. They would continue to recur and would be transplanted to *Skeena* when she replaced *Ottawa* in the role.

## Linguistically Unqualified Personnel

In general, the deficiencies that *Ottawa* encountered as a French-language unit were not unique to the navy, but existed in all such units outside the R22eR, although they were less acute in the latter cases. When the fifteen-year B&B plan was being formulated, particularly during the summer and fall of 1971, the documentation was clear with respect to the obstacles that existed everywhere in the forces: a shortage of bilingual anglophones, a lack of coordination between language courses and postings to French-language units, and a shortage of francophones in many trades and ranks. In other words, the planners recognized that a situation that had been allowed to deteriorate for decades could not be rectified within twelve or twenty-four months, or even in sixty. Once the fifteen-year plan was accepted and on the verge of being implemented, many questions remained unsettled, including that concerning the shortage of linguistically qualified personnel, which is central to the operation of a French-language unit.

The "FLU control" group formed at the Treasury Board in 1971 sent three questionnaires to the French-language units in all departments, one part of which dealt with the linguistic qualifications of the staff. Accordingly, for the period from 31 July to 22 November 1971, the commanding officer of HMCS *Ottawa* reported fifty-four unilingual anglophones (23 per cent) among his crew. Approximately one year later (between 24 May and 22 November 1972), this number had decreased to forty-four (16.2 per cent). By 1 April 1973, it had fallen to thirty (16.1 per cent).[20] On that date *Ottawa* ceased to be a French-language unit, and the percentage of unilingual anglophones henceforth accepted in such units was reduced from 20 to 10 percent as a result of the 1972 B&B plan. In *Ottawa*'s case, if the unilingual anglophones (16.1 per cent) are added to the bilingual anglophones, the number of English speakers aboard easily exceeded by a factor of two the number permitted in a French-language unit. In other words, from this standpoint alone, after a period of five years, 1968–73 *Ottawa* could still not be considered a French-language unit. The optimism shown by Simard in the fall of 1967 and the spring of 1968 was shattered by harsh reality.

Until the commanding officer – who was probably in the best position to know – provided these figures, Canadian Forces Headquarters had thought the language situation aboard had been much better. This state of affairs caused such concern in Ottawa that a meeting was arranged on 13 June 1972, chaired by the director general of postings and careers, Brigadier-General Duncan A. McAlpine, and attended by representatives of the director general of bilingualism and biculturalism (DGBB) and the director of manpower distribution control (DMDC), as well as by several career managers. The purpose of the meeting was "to redress some of the existing imbalances on the *Ottawa* by December 1972, at which time a 10% changeover should be possible."[21] The participants acknowledged that the department's central computer did not distinguish between personnel whose bilingualism had been tested and those who declared themselves to be bilingual (and who may not have been as fluent in the other language as they thought). Further, the question of whether a francophone had retained enough of his French to be able to use it in his day-to-day life was systematically ignored. These deficiencies would gradually be rectified. As an immediate measure, however, and after examining the situation, McAlpine "directed that DMDC and the career managers proceed, in consultation with the CO of the *Ottawa* to achieve an improvement in francophone and bilingual manning by December" 1972. The chairman of the meeting also wanted longer-term planning carried out in order to rectify the situation to a large extent before the ship's current twenty-month cycle ended in August 1973. However, as we have seen from the figures cited above with respect to the situation on 1 April 1973, this desire, as sincere as it was, would have very little impact on the actual situation.

In fact, where would things stand in December 1972 as a result of the renewed effort stemming from the meeting of June 1972? With respect to the representation of unilingual anglophones, the situation would be virtually identical to that which obtained in 1968 and 1969 when the proportion stood at 20 per cent. In most cases, however, these individuals were filling the more senior positions, a fact that gave rise to rather awkward psychological and physical situations. In the former case, young francophones readily concluded that, in order to rise in rank, one had to speak English and perhaps even be an anglophone. In the latter, the reality was at variance with the desired image. The following is an excerpt from a memorandum: "The Chief Boatswain's Mate conducts 'hands fall in' on the upper deck in the English language. This is embarrassing when the ship is alongside a predominantly French locale."[22] The author of that document added that although the master warrant officer in question had a French-sounding name, he was a native of Newfoundland and could not even pronounce his own name "à la française." Further, there were no francophones at his level, and the only bilingual individual had just completed his tour in *Ottawa*. *Ottawa* had many other socio-linguistic problems as well: there were a few unilingual anglophone NCOs "who are not suitable employment in French-language units because of their attitude ... [in fact they] could ... best be described as bigoted." Finally, the shipborne helicopter detachment consisted mainly of unilingual anglophones.

In essence, all of this is just a reflection of the general attitude towards the entire B&B question that still existed in MARCOM in 1973. A memorandum dated 14 February 1973 from the director of career patterns and development (DCPD), Lieutenant-Colonel Guy J. Ruston, following a visit to Halifax between 30 January and 6 February 1973, is clear on this point: people on the east coast were very resistant to the B&B policy, seeing only disadvantages in it. Thus, the program called FRANCOTRAIN was regarded as a system for training francophones with a very limited knowledge of English in various trades, and not as a vehicle for providing francophones with the same opportunities as anglophones. After taking all their training in French, these francophones very often found themselves in English-language units because, on the one hand, excessive recruiting was being carried out in an effort to compensate quickly for the virtual absence of francophones and, on the other hand, there was only one naval French-language unit and it obviously could not accommodate all of them. Some of the statements quoted in Ruston's memorandum were shocking. Speaking of francophones in a meeting, one master warrant officer said that they were not really so bad as individuals: "But when they get together the bastards speak French." An anglophone corporal shouted directly to a francophone corporal: "You sons of whores get all the breaks." Later the anglophone confessed that following the discussion, "the Francophone corporal asked me in private just what breaks he was getting."[23] In other words, the general atmosphere in which *Ottawa* found herself was hardly favourable and some of Simard's initial apprehensions, which we mentioned earlier, were confirmed.

In preparation for the end of *Ottawa's* operational French-language unit cycle, scheduled for the fall of 1973, *Skeena* had officially been selected the previous spring to be the next French-language unit. The ship's company in *Skeena* would initially be 77 per cent francophone and 23 per cent anglophone; all things considered, it was felt that 88 per cent of the crew had a satisfactory level of ability in French. Seven of the eleven officers – including Commander Neil Boivin – were anglophones, only one of whom was not bilingual.[24] However, the six-month refit period in Montreal was to be used to provide French courses for everyone who needed them.[25]

## The Status of the French Language in Ottawa

A letter from J.P. Boys, the head of the French-language units group within the Treasury Board, is a document of central importance. In this letter, dated 11 February 1974 and addressed to the deputy DGBB (Lieutenant-Colonel Derek McLaws), Boys draws conclusions concerning *Ottawa's* operation in French based on the three questionnaires completed by the commanding officer (discussed earlier with regards to the linguistic composition of *Ottawa's* crew). However, other questions dealt with the use of French. Boys wrote that, judging by the data gathered in *Ottawa*, one had "to wonder about the chances of French being preferred to English as the language of work in a predominantly bilingual environment in which unilingual Francophones constituted the smallest minority."[26] The use of French, according to the answers provided by the CO of *Ottawa* himself, appeared to have remained "more or less unchanged throughout its existence as a French-language unit." Boys dwelt on all the problems associated with this facet of the question: written communications were very seldom in French internally, never externally; the captain's superior had always been a unilingual anglophone since 1968;

and the ability of the support services to operate in French was on the wane between 1971 and 1973. Boys added: "In sum, the comparative study of the three questionnaires concerning *Ottawa* indicates that *Skeena*'s situation at the outset may be rather problematical ... [Indeed] if no improvement occurs within about a year, serious consideration will have to be given to replacing this French-language unit with another more viable one." This implied, of course, that the replacement FLU might not be a naval unit.

We now know that *Skeena* was to survive as a French-language unit, and in reading the exchanges of correspondence that took place within DND in the spring of 1973, we will see that the experience of *Ottawa*'s acknowledged deficiencies was drawn upon in large measure to rectify to some extent a situation that, as mentioned earlier, was not ascribable solely to *Ottawa*'s commanding officer. Here, then, are two brief, but rather significant, examples of what happened regarding the use of French in *Ottawa*'s time.

On 19 May 1972 a guide for internal and external communications for French-language units, based on the guide issued by the Treasury Board for all such units of the various departments, was forwarded to the commands. In theory, the model proposed therein was to be followed to the letter.[27] However, the commander of MARCOM despatched it to his units with a note indicating that his command would be the exception: "It is not considered possible at this time to comply with the channels of communication prescribed."[28] He added, however, that when through a combination of circumstances it became possible for *Ottawa* to communicate in French either with MARCOM Headquarters or with other naval units, she would have to provide an English translation of the material in order "to facilitate handling of correspondence." One can imagine the effect that such an interpretation of the headquarters' directive would have had in an environment where English had always predominated.

The second example is a further case of administrative obfuscation. When, in August 1972, the time had come for Ottawa to send out a list of French-language units, the director of organization (DO) took the liberty of translating the designation "Her Majesty's Canadian Ship (HMCS)" as "Navire canadien de Sa Majesté (NCSM)." Lieutenant-Colonel C. Tousignant, director of bilingual plans and research (DBPR), and Armand Letellier, one of the DGBB's assistants, suggested to the director of organization that the French abbreviation be done away with because "we risk to enshrine this translation as the official name thereby pre-empting the researchers' decision and confusing those awaiting notification of the official name of Ottawa."[29] So it was that the French term "NCSM" – instead of the traditional "HMCS" – did not come into use until the 1980s. If it had been adopted immediately, in 1972, or if, at least, immediate follow-up action had been taken with respect to the sensible translation proposed by the director of organization, it would be more firmly entrenched today than it is.

## Conclusion

*Ottawa* was adversely affected from 1968 on, throughout her entire period as a French-language unit, by a host of factors. It has only been possible to deal with a few of them here. Not the least among the obstacles encountered was the lack of psychological preparedness within the Halifax military and naval community. Although some problems were resolved much more easily than expected by Simard (for example, the problem of education for francophone dependants, another area only touched upon here), it was not possible to put aside completely, within a period of five years, a Canadian naval tradition built upon a solid footing of British tradition in which the very recent Canadianization process of the 1960s had scarcely made a dent.

Nonetheless, as a French observer noted, "the 'Ottawa' experience is an important test which indicates the desire of the Armed Forces to accommodate its French-speaking personnel."[30] Notwithstanding all the snags encountered, the concept of the French-language unit has survived in the navy and, indeed, has made headway in recent years. In this respect, then, the experiment was a success.

There were other positive aspects as well. *Ottawa* had an operational role and performed it very well. From 16 September 1968 to 21 February 1970, during her first real cycle as an French-language unit (which took place amid rather widespread scepticism), *Ottawa* sailed 379,888 miles, spent 151 days at sea, and did very well in the various competitions within her squadron: "first in flag hoisting, first in the regatta, second in the ASW [anti-submarine warfare] proficiency shield and third in the Murray Trophy competitions."[31] In February 1972 "once again *Ottawa* proved up to the test decisively winning the regatta and the coveted 'Cock of the Walk.'"[32]

Moreover, a perusal of the list of officers who were members of the original ship's company reveals that several of Simard's subordinates went on to pursue rewarding careers. For example, J.G. Comeau, P. Yans, I.S. Foldesi, and D.E. Pollard attained the rank of naval captain. Others, such as sub-lieutenants B. Power and J. Dickson, are commanders today. Among their successors in the early 1970s, we find one commodore (D. Cogdon), several captains (B. Derible among them), and many commanders (including A. Perusse, G.E. Girard, and D. Baltes). In other words, serving in *Ottawa* when she was a French-language unit did not adversely affect the subsequent careers of these men.

These missionaries of French have since scattered throughout various levels and appointments where they can now help to resolve the many unsettled questions regarding the presence of francophones in the Canadian navy. *Ottawa* served for five years as the prototype in this field. It was understandable that she would encounter problems, solve some of them, indicate potential solutions to others, but leave many unresolved. From this standpoint, those who served in her from 1968 to 1973 can proudly say, "Mission accomplished!"

PART FIVE

*Perspectives and Policies for a New Century*

# · 19 ·

## Strangers in Their Own Seas?
## A Comparison of the Australian and Canadian
## Naval Experience, 1910–1982

The Canadian and Australian navies are not mirror images. Differences of nationality and geography make that degree of similarity impossible. Indeed, a superficial comparison might emphasize the distinctions. Despite the fact that the Royal Canadian Navy was created in 1910 and the Royal Australian Navy (RAN) only one year later, the two services have prospered, struggled, or stagnated in curiously converse circumstances. While Australia could field a fleet unit centred on a battle-cruiser in August 1914, Canada mustered only two old cruisers. In 1939 Australia contributed six cruisers to the defence of the British Empire; Canada's largest ships were destroyers. In 1945, however, the RCN was both bigger and better equipped than the RAN and would remain so for more than twenty years. When the RAN began to recover ground in the early 1960s, the Canadian force was suffering the cancellations and reductions that marked the beginning of the era of "rust-out." In 1994, as the Canadian Armed Forces seek to define legitimate roles within a post–Cold War security policy, the large-scale shipbuilding programs of Australia indicate the degree to which the RAN has become an integral part of an increasingly maritime conception of defence and security.

Despite this, the parallels between the two services remain such that any thoughtful Australian naval historian contemplating either the record or the present state of the Canadian navy does so with the same feelings of uncertainty and dislocation that accompany an episode of *déjà vu*. The Royal Australian Navy may not have proceeded along the same paths as the Royal Canadian Navy, but it could have done so. The two were established to meet the same threats, and they were founded on exactly the same principles and in the same way. The only major conflicts in which they have not both been involved were the Vietnam War and confrontation with Indonesia. They have experienced very much the same external social, political, and economic influences and have dealt with them in remarkably similar ways.

Given the nature of their establishment, in defining the identity of both the Australian and the Canadian navy, a key question is whether either has emerged as a truly national entity or whether either one exists simply as a construct of an alien culture.

This is not easy to answer. If we accept that the critical requirement for any navy is a capability to conduct war at sea, we must draw some distinction between elements that are alien to the national culture because they impose unnecessarily different values and elements that are unique because they are integral to the efficient functioning of naval affairs. In other words, we may have to recognize not only that navies can be different from any other organization, military or civil, within a nation state, but that a specific degree of difference is required for them to work well.

That navies operate according to consistent global strategic principles has been generally understood and enunciated for a century or more. That there may be cultural congruencies that transcend nationalities has been the subject of less study, except as part of more general examinations of military behaviour. It is, however, something that navies themselves have always comprehended, if only dimly. The most explicit acknowledgment has been manifest since 1969 in the United States Navy's series of "International Seapower Symposia" at Newport, Rhode Island. One senior Canadian officer has noted that he emerged from one conference "with an increased realisation of the brotherhood of the sea and [the] comforting knowledge that most naval officers share the same problems, the same aspirations, and the same feelings about the importance of sea power on countries and mankind as a whole."[1]

The focus of this chapter is therefore upon a theme that has been a consistent factor in the development of the identity of both the RAN and the RCN. It concerns the connections of the two organizations with the British Admiralty and the Royal Navy. In examining such relationships, it is possible to discern continuities, not only in the development of individual identities by the two nascent services, but in the place each came to occupy within the respective nation. Furthermore, it can be argued that the British naval connection, however distant it may have become in recent years, has left the legacy of an outlook within the two navies that is, despite the limited resources of both, essentially "blue water" and transoceanic.

## The British Connection – Strategic Relationships

Both services were founded by and deliberately modelled upon the Royal Navy. The intent of the Admiralty and the local authorities, in taking this approach, clearly differed. The British focus was upon strategic unity. If imperial forces were not trained and operated to the same standards as the Royal Navy, then they could not be reliably employed in wartime. If the Admiralty did not ensure that it played a key role in defining force structure, resources might be dissipated on forces that were not capable of making efficient contribution. If Whitehall could not be guaranteed operational control in wartime, then the local navies would be liabilities rather than assets in any attempt to provide for the defence of the Empire as a whole. In retrospect, there was a tendency, understandable in the atmosphere of naval arms competition within Europe between 1898 and 1914, to assume that if the security needs of the United Kingdom itself were met, those of the dominions were not an issue. This resulted on at least one occasion in the redistribution of forces intended for the Pacific into British home waters with no prior consultation.[2]

The dominions' perceptions were inevitably different. The guidance and support of the Royal Navy were required in order to produce capable forces as rapidly as possible and, in the long term, to avoid the inefficiencies believed to be inherent within small navies operating in isolation. Operational compatibility was axiomatic, but its existence did not imply the automatic right of Admiralty control. The dominions believed that they could be relied upon to assist the United Kingdom in emergency, but the nature and timing of such assistance had to be their own decision. That the Admiralty continued to look towards Europe at the expense of the rest of the world could only reinforce the dominions' determination to control their own ships.

The contradictions inherent in these attitudes created a dichotomy in naval planning that was to manifest itself at intervals over the following thirty years. The British were slow to accept the concept of independent but compatible dominion forces and, despite the obvious success of the RAN in the First World War, keen to revive a Whitehall-controlled "Empire Navy."[3] This was rejected out of hand by both Canada and Australia in 1918 and again in 1923.[4] Even after these sharp reminders of the dominion position, the United Kingdom's record of consultation was mixed. The failure of the "Main Fleet to Singapore" strategy is a notorious example of strategic coordination by Whitehall with Australia that was at best ambiguous and at worst culpably misleading; the British were themselves confused by their own policies.[5] As late as 1940–41 the Admiralty still showed an occasionally incomplete appreciation either of Australia's concerns or of its rights over the deployment of warships.[6]

This was a time when more timely and complete explanations on the Admiralty's part might well have resulted in more rapid and unstinted cooperation than did in fact occur. There was considerable merit in Canada's refusal to submit its ships to the degree of Admiralty control that Australia permitted.

That insistence on national control, however, never extended to a refusal to allocate ships to operations well removed from either Canada or Australia if there was a reasonable justification on the basis of national interest. Both navies have proved themselves wholly at ease with what are now termed "out of area" operations, and the facility with which they can conduct them has proved convenient to governments seeking to make public, but restricted, commitments to alliances. This was true for Korea in 1950–53 and it remained so for the Gulf War in 1990–91. If the RAN seemed to be more prone to such activity than the RCN during the era of the Cold War, it also did not have the extensive commitments of the latter to anti-submarine operations in the Atlantic theatre.

## Personal Relationships

The suspicion that the Admiralty and its servants sustained an agenda that did not meet the dominions' interests underlay many politicians' attitudes to the naval case in both Australia and Canada. It certainly governed personal relationships between ministers and British officers on loan and was partly responsible for the Canadian government's insistence that senior RCN positions be filled by Canadian personnel.[7] Elements within the other services were also convinced that their naval equivalents on secondment from the Royal Navy were simply mouthpieces of the Admiralty.[8]

It is, however, undeniable that both the RCN and the RAN owe a considerable debt to the loan personnel who provided the substitute for the experience that did not yet exist in each navy and could not be created overnight. While some officers were not suitable for local conditions and it is equally true, short of a personal motivation such as native birth, that the Admiralty did not often deprive the Royal Navy of its most capable officers to serve the dominions,[9] the quality could be excellent and it became more often so as the loan system was replaced by one of outright exchange. As the posts to be filled became more senior, the problem was not so much selecting for quality but finding officers willing to go to expensive, poorly supported, and politically difficult jobs. In the aftermath of the First World War, the Australian government's delay in increasing the salary of the First Naval Member to £3,000 resulted in at least two RN officers turning down the appointment.[10] By the late 1930s refusal was the norm.[11] Furthermore, more junior officers often found their isolation from the Royal Navy could disadvantage them in the selections for promotion.[12]

It was true that some RN personnel did not help their case by maintaining personal contacts with the Admiralty in such a way as to make it obvious that policy was being decided independently of either government.[13] It was also true that the seconded officers could and generally did develop naval policies which, even if intellectually derived from the Admiralty and sometimes inappropriate to Australian conditions, reflected genuine attempts to meet national and not specifically British interests. Ray Jones's study *Seagulls, Cruisers and Catapults* makes clear the extent to which the structure of the RAN, while operating within the increasingly dubious context of the Singapore strategy, mutated to meet local defence priorities.[14] Even the celebrated scuttling of the battle-cruiser *Australia* in 1924 had its origin in the judgment that the ship did not meet contemporary defence needs at a time of economic stress, rather than in Australia's unsought but inevitable inclusion within the Royal Navy for the purposes of the Washington Treaty limitations.[15]

Perhaps the clearest example of disinterest was the bitter denunciation by Vice-Admiral Sir Guy Royle, Australia's First Naval Member and chief of naval staff (CNS) from 1941 to 1945, of Britain's performance in the Far East in 1941–42 during his deliberations as a member of the Australian Chiefs of Staff Committee.[16] This was notable not only for the fact that Royle pulled no punches in his comments but that he had less than a year before he stepped down from the Board of Admiralty as Fifth Sea Lord and chief of naval air services.

The traffic was also not wholly one way. In April 1949, at a meeting in Greenwich with the British Naval Staff, Vice-Admiral Sir John Collins, the first RAN College graduate to serve as CNS, deliberately asked that the Admiralty not inform either the British or the Australian government of the inability of the new light fleet carriers to operate jet aircraft without expensive refits. Collins's justification was that the Australian government might become "disinclined to purchase the second carrier."[17] While Collins's acknowledgment of his personal responsibility for finding a solution to the problem is laudable in one sense, there are obvious ethical and constitutional implications in a national chief of naval staff acting in such a way. The Admiralty, it should be noted, reacted by removing the passage from every set of minutes but that retained in the First Sea Lord's office. Even in the late 1950s the Australian Naval Staff deliberately sought a visit to Australia by Lord Mountbatten, the British First Sea Lord, to assist in making the Royal Australian Navy's case with both the government and the public.[18]

The Admiralty's offers in 1944 to provide cruisers and carriers for the Royal Canadian Navy (and for the RAN) were at least partially motivated by requests from local authorities, conveyed on a navy-to-navy basis without the prior sanction of government.[19] This was also the case with Australia, and it is fair to say that the ground for proposals was often prepared by unadvertised contacts between the naval staffs.

On the other hand, there is evidence, albeit circumstantial, than the overtly "independent" approach of the Canadian government and RCN after 1939 resulted in the Admiralty adopting an attitude that was at best benign neglect and that certainly delayed the identification and rectification of the equipment and training problems that bedeviled Canadian forces in the early years of the Battle of the Atlantic.[20]

## The Politicians and the Imperial Connection

The political arm could play the Admiralty connection for its own purposes, frequently to check and sometimes even to undermine local naval authorities. Admiral Sir Francis Hyde, CNS in Australia from 1931 to 1937, found that any visit to Whitehall by Australia's minister of defence had to be preceded by careful coordination between the Admiralty and the Australian Naval Board because any differences between the two authorities, particularly with regard to force-structure requirements and financial estimates, would be used to the Admiralty's advantage.[21] The same caution is evident in the director of the Canadian naval service's preparations for any visit to Canada by the Royal Naval Commander-in-chief (C-in-C) of the America and West Indies Station in the 1920s. In 1937 Hyde found himself ignored by the Admiralty in its discussions with his minister over the appointment of his successor as chief of naval staff, to the point where he was not even sure of the timing, let alone the identity of his relief.[22]

If there is a judgment to be made, it is that the Australian and Canadian governments proved little more adept than their navies at developing a "home-grown" strategic outlook. This must largely be subscribed to their failure to develop the machinery to allow reasoned assessments that could be matched against the views of Whitehall.

## Emulation Means Efficiency

A more complex question is the extent to which the immersion of young personnel into the ways of the Royal Navy, through wholesale adoption of British customs and traditions and training and repeated service in British ships, warped the form of the young navies. If one is studying the matter from the standpoint of efficiency, it is difficult to see that there was any alternative. Vice-Admiral H.G. DeWolf summarized the feelings of many in both the RCN and RAN when he said, "I don't think I made any mistakes because of anything I had been taught by the RN."[23] The "cloning" system produced forces that were capable of operating as fully efficient units within a few years of the decision to create the new naval services, and the close links sustained the small navies through the inter-war years when their size was such that isolation from the Royal Navy would have rendered them moribund.

When the RCN and the RAN came to acquire fixed-wing aircraft carriers, the British provided infusions of equipment and personnel. Such assistance obviously derived from the Admiralty's judgment that the existence of capable Australian and Canadian naval forces was in Britain's best strategic interests, but it was invaluable to the receiving countries nonetheless. If evidence is needed of the importance of such support, one has only to compare the performance of HMC Ships *Magnificent* and *Bonaventure* and HMA Ships *Sydney*, *Vengeance*, and *Melbourne* and their air groups with that of the aircraft carriers and aircraft that Argentina and Brazil put into service in the late 1950s. The system again operated successfully a decade later when both Australia and Canada acquired submarines. Britain, of course, benefited by the work its shipbuilding industry received. The Royal Navy, however, had to provide not only training billets but key personnel, sometimes from critical shortage categories.

However much may be said about the drawbacks of uncritical acceptance of British doctrine, the two navies derived great benefit from their free access to British infrastructure, to British creative activity, and to the Royal Navy's intellectual property. Both services utilized RN training schools for many years. Even if the payments exacted steadily rose to reflect the real costs of such support to the British, the system meant that the smaller services were not required to divert scarce personnel and funds to do the job themselves. In 1994 the principal factor behind the drive for a joint RAN-RCN "Perisher" (Submarine Commanding Officers' Qualifying Course) is the prospective demise of the RN's diesel-electric submarine force, not a desire for operational self-reliance in its own right. The commitment required to conduct such training is not one that either submarine service must view with great enthusiasm.

In most circumstances, the burden of the expensive and lengthy work required to bring new systems into service was borne by the Royal Navy, not the navies of the Commonwealth. While there were some attempts to pass on costs, these were fitful in the extreme. Notably, the RAN did not always react kindly to the experience of operating with prototype weapons when its ship purchases already represented the leading edge of British technology. While the Australian County-class cruisers made significant contributions to "debugging" the complicated 8-inch turret in 1928–29,[24] there was much surprise and irritation at the trouble caused the destroyers *Tobruk* and *Anzac* in the Korean War by the new 4.5-inch Mark VI turret, which they were the first to take operationally to sea.[25] The RCN was too small before 1939 to be involved in such issues, but any study of the very successful Canadian building programs of 1948–56 shows the considerable extent to which Admiralty products and concepts were melded into the RCN effort.[26]

In the absence of fully manned naval staffs – and it was axiomatic that these could not be brought into being on a national basis until some foundation of practical expertise had been established among seagoing personnel – the Admiralty could and did provide relatively disinterested advice. The Royal Navy sometimes dispensed more than it intended, as officers on exchange service were in ideal positions to report, albeit informally, on the real performance levels of British methods and equipment. It is highly likely, although there is little written evidence to support this, that the Australian Naval Board had become aware through its own sources of the limitations of the British Sea Slug missile when the choice had to be made between that system and the American Tartar.[27]

Another way in which the RCN and RAN short-circuited the normal infrastructure requirements of independent navies was their use of British *Books of Reference* and *Confidential Books*. These had their faults and they were sometimes imperfectly adapted to local conditions. Canada took a long time to produce coherent national legislation for the government of the RCN, relying for more than thirty years on a "complex body of Canadian and British acts."[28] However, neither Australia nor Canada had to engage in the expensive and manpower-intensive processes of "book writing" for technical and operational matters from scratch. What tended to happen instead was that the British texts were modified as much or as little as each service desired.

The warping, if any, of the two navies must therefore be judged as largely favourable in its effects. The necessary infrastructure for independent activity was allowed to grow naturally while the two services developed an adequate corpus of seagoing and administrative experience. Both services were permitted to maintain fighting elements of greater size and manifestly greater efficiency than would otherwise have been possible. The fact that this result met the United Kingdom's strategic requirements as much as it did those of Canada or Australia was not, in the contemporary political and strategic context, either unnatural or undesirable.

### An Imposed Cultural Identity?

The fundamental criticism of the British connection that has legitimacy is a subtle one. The imposition of a wholly British model on the new navies and the long service of so many officers with the RN is said to have prevented the proper identification of the two services with their own national cultures. Nicholas Rodger in his review of *The RCN in Retrospect* in the *Mariner's Mirror* suggested that the link was too close in the case of the RCN and that "in consequence the Service was always isolated and misunderstood, and thus undefended against the assault of the forces of nationalism."[29]

Within the services, the Royal Navy ethos is alleged to have created barriers between officers and sailors. The most notorious manifestation of this in the Canadian context is the now celebrated examination of Vice-Admiral H.T. Grant, RCN chief of naval staff, by the Mainguy Commission in the wake of the 1949 mutinies. He expressed himself as bitterly opposed to any "Canadianization" of the navy and totally out of sympathy with lower-deck and junior officer desires to define a new Canadian naval identity. Louis Audette suggests that too many in the RCN's officer corps had adapted "a type of life and a style of leadership alien" to Canada.[30]

Australian examples of such attitudes are less clear-cut, although Tom Frame in his books *Where Fate Calls*[31] and *Pacific Partners*[32] argues strongly that the RAN sustained a pro-British approach in the fifteen years after the Second World War that was increasingly out of step with Australia as a whole. Certainly, external observers were commenting less than favourably on the apparent Anglophilia of the RAN in the early 1960s.[33] Even in 1993 the British-based customs and traditions of the Australian Defence Force as a whole were the subject of criticism.[34]

The limited direct evidence that exists for the RAN suggests, however, that its personnel quickly developed a very strong idea of their national and their individual naval identity. This was strengthened throughout the 1920s and 1930s as the number of British loan personnel decreased. The process was more marked in the RAN than in the RCN, most probably aided by the greater size of the RAN and the fact that its national training effort, particularly in the form of the Royal Australian Naval College, sustained a continuity not experienced in Canada. It also must have been much helped by the policy of exchanging cruisers between the RN and the RAN. This began with the despatch of the *Adelaide* to join the Special Service Squadron on its round-the-world cruise in 1924 and continued until 1926. Economic factors forced suspension of the program until the end of 1934, when HMAS *Australia* departed for the Mediterranean.

Although Australian ships were regarded as operationally interchangeable with those of the RN for all purposes (but only with the consent of the Australian government as the C-in-C, China Station, discovered with HMAS *Brisbane* in 1925),[35] they were never seen by their British counterparts as anything other than distinctly Australian. It is arguable that the coincidence of so many procedures made the cultural differences all the more obvious. Certainly, unlike the experience in the Canadian navy, whose destroyers were limited to concentrations at Bermuda, the world-wide RN professional experience of the lower deck approximated that of the wardroom. The cheerful recognition by RAN ships of their uniqueness was a feature of the excellent performance of the Australian cruisers *Australia* and *Sydney* in the Mediterranean in 1935–36 and the exploits of the Australian ships on the same station in 1940–41. The response by HMA Ships in Alexandria Harbour to the return of the second *Sydney* from the destruction of the Italian cruiser *Bartolomeo Colleoni* is significant: "The Australian destroyers – each flying seven Australian flags for the occasion – gave her a tremendous welcome, and Waller, leading the cheering in *Stuart*, gave an Australian flavour to his greeting with the signal, 'Whacko, Sydney.'"[36]

That Canadian efforts were made in the same direction is evident in the celebrated case of Captain Brodeur's insistence on flying a senior officer's pendant in Bermuda, despite the presence of the British Commander-in-Chief, America and West Indies.[37] It is also clear that by the end of the Second World War RCN ships were evolving a specifically Canadian identity, with the Maple Leaf on each ship's forward funnel being but one element of the process. All this suggests that the scale on which a navy operates is as important as the distinctness of its national culture in forging a coherent service identity.

Just as it has taken a long time to understand the consequences of the French Revolution, it is probable that it is too early, and that we are too close as historians, to make a final judgment. As Frame implicitly suggests, the disconnection between navies and national cultures might only have been confined to a few years. Any reader of the novels of the Australian Martin Boyd or the earlier works of the Canadian Robertson Davies would be justified in thinking that the navies did not travel alone with the British. Closer to the naval environment, Robert MacNeil's memoir *Wordstruck* conveys very clearly the extent of cultural intermingling between Great Britain and at least one part of Canada in the era of the Second World War.[38]

### Was the Problem Elsewhere?

There is more than one way of looking at the sources of the two navies' problems. It must be significant that both the RCN and the RAN underwent their most severe problems of leadership and morale in the wake of the world wars and after rapid expansion. The RCN suffered them after the Second World War in the form of the disturbances that culminated in the 1949 mutinies, while the RAN experienced similar agonies after the First World War, somewhat better handled than the Canadian controversies but suggesting a degree of insensitivity in the ships that could not wholly be due to the presence of a Royal Navy fleet commander or a largely RN Naval Board.[39] In his 1919 report on the future of the RAN, Admiral Lord Jellicoe was scathing in his criticism of many of the RAN's officers, largely the "turnovers" from the RNR and old colonial services, of whose efficiency and capacity to maintain discipline he was dubious.[40] Yet, some seventeen years after Jellicoe's strictures on the RAN, the martinet Max Horton was unambiguous in his praise for the Australian cruisers he had commanded.[41] It is arguable that the considerable reductions made in the RAN between 1921 and 1933, the intense competition for promotion, and the steady progress of RAN College–trained (but also RN-indoctrinated) officers all had their good effects.

William Glover attacks the question of collective competence in the senior command of the RCN elsewhere in this book. He has not only the dubious record of the Canadian navy's administrative achievements between 1940 and 1950 to back him up,[42] but also the arguments of an actuary: "Only five lieutenants (including two who had served in the RN lower deck in World War I and were commissioned in 1936), and one lieutenant commander in the 1939 navy list who remained in the RCN after 1948 failed to attain at least commodore's rank."[43]

Promotion on this scale made nonsense of any attempts at quality control. Until the early 1950s, Australian willingness to use RN loan officers allowed much more selectivity. Between Hyde (promoted rear admiral in 1928) and Farncomb and Collins (1948), no RAN officer was promoted to the active flag list. This system caused some ill feeling among those whose career aspirations were disappointed, such as H.J. Feakes and C. Farquhar-Smith, and it could be carried to ridiculous lengths. G.D. Moore was never confirmed as a rear admiral, despite serving six years (1944–50) as Flag Officer in Charge, East Australia. Yet the logic was unassailable. During their exchange posting in the rank of captain, such Australian officers had to be recommended for flag rank according to Royal Navy standards, judged by their performance in the RN. As such, the policy was simply a continuation of the selection process applied to more junior officers.

The RAN system broke down (and in this it mirrors the Canadian situation in the 1940s) when political insistence on senior posts being filled by Australians combined with the knock-on effect of small entries to the RAN College and a high casualty rate in the Second World War to reduce the pool for selection to almost nothing.[44] The mixed political record of the RAN between 1955 (when the highly capable Sir John Collins retired) and 1983 (the year of the Labor Government's decision to abolish the fixed-wing Fleet Air Arm) must suggest that there was inadequate human capital to provide for the senior ranks and the staff and administrative machinery necessary for an "independent" navy to operate efficiently.

Given that the Canadian situation was so similar, we may conclude that the identity problems of the two navies may have worsened the difficulties the two faced, but they cannot fairly be said to have been the root cause.

## Going It Alone

It is easier to identify the RCN's and RAN's intellectual points of departure from the RN than it is to identify the cultural separations. Notably, the motivations for separation were not wholly strategic in origin, although the increasing divergence of national interests was always a key element in the process. Navies are and remain technologically oriented services, whose fighting efficiency derives directly from the access they enjoy to the latest methods and equipment. Once it became clear that there were products superior to those of the British on offer, neither RAN nor RCN could be expected to remain at the apron strings forever.

The break with Canada is particularly difficult to pin down but could be put first at 1939, the decisive factor being the Canadian government's determination to organize the expansion of its navy using only Canadian officers. There were, of course, exceptions, but the RCN policy of promoting Canadians to fill appointments without consideration of the "relativities" with respect to the Royal Navy helped create a gap of understanding between the RCN and the RN. This forced the former to rely more upon Canadian resources than it would otherwise have done, clearly with effects both good and bad. A researcher cannot find within the Admiralty 205 series gossipy personal letters between Admiral Nelles and the First Sea Lord. Such correspondence does exist between the latter and the Australian First Naval Member, and it also exists for the years 1931–37 (when the Australian Francis Hyde was CNS) and from 1948 onwards (when the first graduate of the Royal Australian Naval College took up the appointment).

The second break came with the establishment of an independent Canadian command area during the Battle of the Atlantic,[45] and it was finally confirmed in 1947 by the RCN's decision to implement the Canada–United States Basic Security Plan. Under this arrangement, the RCN's responsibilities for sea-lane defence would require "full adaptation by the RCN of USN [United States Navy] methods and doctrine."[46]

The fall of Singapore did not shatter the British-Australian naval nexus, but it and the events of the next few years sowed the seeds. The RAN operated increasingly closely with the USN, appreciating not only its operational techniques, but its technology. Although no formal research has yet been conducted on the effects of exposure to American methods and equipment, there is evidence in the Australian official history of the

Second World War of dissatisfaction with the limitations of British-designed ships in comparison with their contemporaries of the USN, notably in habitability.[47] It is likely that Australian marine engineers experienced the same professional crises as did the officers of the British Pacific Fleet in 1944–45 when they came to realize the inadequacies of their ships.[48]

In an operational sense, Australia gave a quiet reminder to the RN of its independence in 1945, when the cruisers and destroyers of the Australian Squadron were not made available to assist with the reoccupation of Hong Kong but went to the Japanese surrender in Tokyo Bay. Six minesweepers were despatched instead.[49] Australian units were, however, soon afterwards integrated into the Far East Fleet, with which the RAN would maintain a close relationship until the British withdrawal from "East of Suez" twenty-five years later. Nevertheless, the USN connection was not ended, and by the early 1950s, the first in a series of naval agreements between Australia and the United States was set in train, bringing with it slowly but constantly expanding operational interaction.

The significant public break in the RAN-RN relationship did not really come until the 1961 decision to procure the US-built Charles F. Adams–class guided-missile destroyers. The resulting differences in weapons and systems made separation inevitable, perhaps most clearly manifested by the patriation of the Principal Warfare Officer Course to Australia in 1985. As noted above, such separation is not yet complete. Self-interest on the part not only of the RCN and RAN but of an ever smaller and more resource-limited Royal Navy will probably ensure that it never happens.

## A Unity of Outlook?

Despite the ways in which both the RAN and RCN have developed as services wholly independent of the Royal Navy, the organization of their force structures and the operational employment of their front-line units suggest very strongly that there remains a fundamental congruency of outlook, if not of enunciated doctrine. Furthermore, their organization and employment continue to mirror, albeit in miniature, those of the larger Western navies. Neither service is wholly comfortable with the "fortress state" concepts of defence sometimes proposed as appropriate for either Canada or Australia, preferring to focus on the requirement to protect communications and contributions to international alliances as the basis for national security.[50] At least for Australia, the increasing recognition of the importance of regional engagement within current defence policy must owe much to the RAN's activities of the last decade.

The extent to which such attitudes were promoted and sustained in recent years by the United States and the Western alliance is undeniable.

Rear Admiral Crickard's thesis is the most recent in a series of works on the subject.[51] It is also clear that the tyranny of distance in the maritime environments of both Canada and Australia has had the result that a force structure that can span the needs of national defence alone also has the capability to permit operations at great distances from the homeland. This consequent capability was specifically described in the *Defence of Australia* White Paper (1987)as providing Australia's means of contributing to the Western alliance,[52] and its reality was proved by the deployment of a small task group to the Gulf War. It can be no coincidence that Canada's contribution to Allied naval forces both in the Second World War and during the Cold War was on exactly the same scale as that of Australia and that Canadian ships found integration with the USN and alliance forces just as easy.

It therefore seems reasonable to suggest that the two navies have continued to sustain a concept of existence so clearly derived from the Royal Navy because of these two factors. The need to sustain alliances with the United States in the Cold War kept both the RCN and the RAN in close contact with one another, thus requiring cooperation with a navy that, while possessing a very different culture from that of the Royal Navy, maintained much the same worldwide outlook. The vast size of both countries, becoming even more vast as a result of the development of the Law of the Sea, has forced acquisition of ships large enough to do more than assert geographical sovereignty. If they are given such tools in an increasingly complicated and interconnected world, it is hardly surprising that governments will use them.

All this suggests an answer to the question as to whether navies have to be unique to do their work properly. The solution for the future might well be a converse relationship. The ability to operate on a super-national level, the tendency to view national interests as being more wide-ranging than territorial imperatives alone, and the facility with which navies can work far afield all equate to desirable characteristics in emerging defence strategies. It might then be that what has been viewed, often unfavourably as "blue-water navalism" is in fact the ethos of the armed forces of the future.

# · 20 ·

# *Maritime Command, National Missions, and Naval Identity*

JAMES D. KIRAS

A significant part of the Canadian naval identity has been forged by the navy's domestic contribution in "national missions" such as preservation of sovereignty and fisheries patrols, although few Canadians are aware of what these duties entail. National missions have assumed greater importance in Canadian strategic planning over the past quarter century in part because of sweeping changes in the rights of individual nations to manage living and non-living resources within their sovereign territory. Disagreements over the definition of sovereign territory and maritime boundaries often translate into the demonstrative use of naval force between nations. Recently, the veiled threats of unilateral naval intervention in outlying areas of the Grand Banks by Fisheries Minister Tobin and Prime Minister Chrétien are evidence that national "gunboat diplomacy" continues to remain a tool in Canada's post–Cold War diplomatic policy.

This chapter explores three issues on the use and utility of Canadian naval forces for operations in home waters: (1) questions of the preservation of sovereignty and maritime boundary disputes; (2) the suitability and utility of naval platforms for national missions; and (3) the role of national missions in sustaining the Canadian naval identity.

## Sovereignty and Boundary Disputes

One of the cornerstones of national security for any nation is the assurance of its sovereignty. Sovereignty is best defined as "the prevention of trespass, the provision of services and the enforcement of national and international law within (Canadian) territory, waters and airspace."[1] The preservation of sovereignty over some four million square kilometres of maritime territory falls on several branches of the federal government, including the Department of National Defence.[2] By intermittent patrolling, the ships of Maritime Command (MARCOM) and the aircraft of the Maritime Air Group assert Canadian sovereignty or presence in Canadian waters.[3]

The size of Canada's maritime area has grown to its present dimensions owing to Canadian diplomatic efforts at the third United Nations Conference on the Law of the Sea (UNCLOS III) from 1973 to 1982. Prior to this conference, the countries of the United Nations (UN) struggled to agree on a 12-nautical-mile territorial sea.[4] The Canadian delegation at UNCLOS III eventually became the most vocal proponents of the concept of the Exclusive Economic Zone (EEZ), which would give coastal nations the sole right to harvest and manage the marine resources out to a distance of 200 nautical miles from shore.[5]

The UNCLOS III guidelines have yet to be ratified into binding international law, but the Canadian government unilaterally declared a 200-nautical-mile fishing zone in 1977. While not completely the same as an EEZ, the Canadian fishing zone included all of the rights and responsibilities that a coastal state had with regard to living resources in its EEZ. This declaration immediately created problems, as several nations had historic access to Canada's fishing grounds. In exchange for recognition of Canada's fishing-zone claim and compliance with Canadian fisheries laws, Canadian diplomats negotiated surplus stocks or phase-outs.[6] Some boundary disagreements remain to be resolved, most notably with the United States. Binding arbitration can sometimes create more problems than it solves.

No case exemplifies the complexity of the diplomatic and legal process better than Canada's negotiations with France over the islands of St Pierre and Miquelon. The islands are located in the Gulf of St Lawrence, some twelve nautical miles off the southwest coast of Newfoundland. They changed between British and French hands a number of times until 1814 and thereafter remained in French possession.[7] During the Second World War, St Pierre and Miquelon were the focus of an acrimonious Allied debate when they were unilaterally liberated by Free French forces in late 1941.[8] The islands have been newsworthy recently because of French attempts to apply an EEZ claim for increased access to Canadian sections of the Grand Banks.

Attempts to find a bilateral solution to the disagreement between the Canadian and French governments over the division of the Grand Banks continually bogged down over access rights and quotas.[9] After several unsuccessful attempts at reconciliation, most notably in 1972 and 1986, both nations agreed to take their dispute to the International Court of Justice.[10] On 10 June 1992 the court rendered a decision that was "extremely favourable for Canada."[11] Canada received custody over the areas that are richest in groundfish, while France gained a contiguous zone around the islands and an exclusive 12-nautical-mile corridor that extends due south from the islands for 200 nautical miles.[12]

Although many commentators closed the chapter on this disagreement after the court's decision, St Pierre and Miquelon remain newsworthy, as their boundary continues to be a source of diplomatic tension. In late August 1992, shortly after the boundary ruling was handed down, a French warship herded Canadian scallop boats out of the southern corridor. This action contravened prior access agreements between the two nations.[13]

The French utilization of nominal naval force to expel Canadian fishermen demonstrates how naval forces can be used to assert a nation's sovereignty claim. Equally indicative of that commitment is the continued presence of a symbolic garrison on the island of St Pierre.[14] In another resource-based dispute, the French government also relied on naval forces in 1963 off the coast of Brazil, but that event involved the incarceration of French nationals.[15] The 1987 "cod war" between Canada and France and recent heated exchanges over quotas and rights of access demonstrate an emotional intensity over fisheries issues, expressed by both nations, that may lead to future incidents involving coercive naval power.[16]

### The Utility of Naval Forces in National Missions

The Canadian navy works together with various federal departments to carry out national missions that represent the enforcement end of sovereignty protection. These missions include the enforcement of Canadian laws regarding the right to harvest living and non-living oceanic resources; assisting in containing and collecting evidence of environmental disasters, such as oil spills; and drug and immigration deterrence and enforcement.[17]

Each federal department or agency acts as lead agency in its specialized area of national interest. In addition to its indigenous resources, each department receives supplemental resources or time from other departments to ensure that their missions are fulfilled. For example, the Royal Canadian Mounted Police (RCMP) requests the assistance of the Department of National Defence (DND) for law enforcement missions at sea. Maritime Command provides the platforms for RCMP officers in operational missions like narcotics and arms interdiction and deterrence patrols.[18] Both parties benefit from this cooperative effort: the MARCOM crew have an authorized federal peace officer at hand should a situation arise in the course of sovereignty patrol, and the RCMP now has a means of asserting its authority beyond the inshore areas.

Similar arrangements exist between Martime Command and the Canadian Coast Guard (Transport Canada) and the Department of Fisheries and Oceans. These two civilian departments operate their own fleets, but they work in conjunction with MARCOM on national missions. The reason for this close cooperation stems from the fact that the resources of the two civilian fleets are inadequate to carry out their mandated tasks unassisted. Several departmental inquiries and committees, including the 1963 Glassco Commission, the 1970 Audette Report, and the 1987 Nielsen Task Force, have tried to rationalize the consolidation of these fleets.[19] In the end, each committee opted against militarization of the civilian fleets or total integration of fleet resources, favouring the preservation of separate, specialized fleets.

Unlike their American counterparts, Canadian Coast Guard vessels are unarmed and their primary responsibilities are navigational safety, icebreaking, environmental disaster management, and search and rescue. To fulfil these missions, the Coast Guard has its own specialized fleet of 112 ships to manage a vast area that encompasses the three oceans, the Great Lakes, all inland waterways, and the St Lawrence River.[20]

Should a major environmental disaster or several sequential emergencies occur, the resources of the Coast Guard would be quickly overburdened. MARCOM and the Maritime Air Group provide assistance in the form of personnel, vessels, and aircraft for search and rescue and environmental disaster management.[21] Although Maritime Command personnel are well equipped to assist in search and rescue missions, in the event of a chemical spill they would be under the control and direction of the on-scene Coast Guard officials, as the Coast Guard has the suitable equipment and training for such crises.

The lead civilian agency in fisheries research, quota verification, and fisheries enforcement is the Department of Fisheries and Oceans. On paper, it would seem that with 700 available vessels, Fisheries and Oceans has the numerical strength to adequately patrol the Canadian fishing zone.[22] A closer inspection of the fleet figures reveals only 6 offshore patrol vessels and 4 near-shore patrol vessels.[23]

Securing available personnel for all of Fisheries and Oceans' various labour-intensive duties imposes restraints on the capital available for new ship construction. In order to maximize sea time, all of the offshore vessels are double-crewed, and additional personnel are required to verify catch quotas on the foreign vessels that are allowed to fish in Canadian waters.[24] As with the navy, Fisheries and Oceans has had a difficult time recruiting personnel for arduous sea duties. Payroll, ship maintenance, and operational costs represent the most significant portion of Fisheries and Oceans' yearly budget.

The greatest strain on Fisheries and Oceans' resources for the foreseeable future will be the enforcement of the federal ban on groundfish harvesting in the eastern and southeastern fishing zones on the Atlantic coast. The first survey by the Fisheries Resource Conservation Council concluded: "The remaining stocks should be given as much protection as is possible in order to take advantage of better survival conditions when they occur."[25] The council's second study was even more pessimistic in its assessment of the remaining stocks, and on their recommendations, further fishing areas were closed by the federal government. Diligent enforcement within the fishing zone may allow the regeneration of many groundfish species, but threats not subject to Canadian regulations may undermine that process.

Although the Department of Fisheries and Oceans upholds Canadian fishing laws within the fishing zone, compliance to binding quotas outside of it rests entirely in regulations created by the members of collective organizations like the Northwest Atlantic Fisheries Organization (NAFO). Organizations such as NAFO contribute to solving problems like overfishing, but they have their limitations. In the case of the Atlantic cod fisheries, several NAFO-member nations have either refused to abide by the quotas or have reflagged their fishing vessels to avoid them altogether. Gathering evidence of fisheries violations is a time-consuming and expensive process, and a specific amount of evidence must be obtained before any form of punitive action can be taken. An additional frustration for NAFO nations resides in the provision that punishment of quota violations rests entirely with the violator's state of registration, whose authorities may or may not take action.[26]

Those nations that do not belong to organizations like NAFO are not bound by its regulations or quotas. This leads to unrestricted fishing, often just beyond the jurisdictional limit of a nation's EEZ. Diplomatic efforts such as the recently negotiated one-year NAFO moratorium on cod fishing in the Grand Banks will relieve some of the stress on recovering stocks.[27] However, greater diplomatic initiatives, in the form of coercive diplomacy and the deterrent use of naval force, may be required to elicit the compliance of non-NAFO nations. These efforts alone cannot rejuvenate living resources, but they are necessary until the enforceable regulations of the United Nations Conference on Straddling Fish Stocks and Highly Migratory Fish Stocks are defined and codified.

Naval forces throughout the world assist in fisheries-protection duties, and MARCOM is no exception. The navy has a well-established heritage in this domestic mission; patrol vessels and personnel of the Department of Marine and Fisheries were the genesis of the Royal Canadian Navy (RCN) in 1910.[28] Currently, MARCOM assists Fisheries and Oceans in its enforcement duties by patrolling the periphery of the fishing zone. MARCOM vessels act as a visible deterrent and provide support to Fisheries and Oceans for a defined number of ship-days without charge.[29] The Maritime Air Group provides a set number of aerial tracking and surveillance hours with its long-range maritime patrol aircraft, CP-140 Auroras.[30] The time allocated for this by MARCOM is usually in excess of its own training and independent sovereignty patrolling requirements, although national mission patrols are often multi-tasked to take advantage of regular sailings, such as transits to training exercises or as part of routine sovereignty patrols.[31] For example, the submarine HMCS *Oberon* conducted a fisheries patrol during the first week of March 1993. Immediately after completing this patrol, the *Oberon* sailed to scheduled naval exercises.[32]

Several national benefits have accrued through naval participation in national missions. For example, such participation can act as a stimulus for increased cooperation between neighbouring or allied countries. In the *Concordia* incident of 11 December 1989, aerial surveillance detected an American commercial boat fishing illegally in Canadian waters. The St Laurent–class destroyer HMCS *Saguenay* responded and gave chase, but the *Concordia* failed to heave to, even after warnings were issued and shots were fired across her bow. Eventually the *Concordia* fled to American waters where she was seized and interned by the US Coast Guard.[33] This incident resulted in the creation of the Canada–United States Reciprocal Enforcement Agreement. The agreement has streamlined the information-sharing and legal processes between the countries while establishing prohibitive fines for transgressors.[34]

Participation in national missions can also highlight tactical shortcomings that would be hard and costly lessons to learn in a hostile environment. Once deficiencies are identified, naval planners can create solutions that can be tested during training exercises and other deployments. These practical exercises keep naval personnel prepared for incidents that may arise during overseas deployments.[35] This problem-solving process is exemplified in the *Concordia* incident. During the course of the pursuit, the *Saguenay*'s officers discussed the option of boarding the American ship but considered this option to be too dangerous in view of sea conditions and their men's inexperience.[36] Boarding tactics were later examined by naval planners and employed by the Canadian task group deployed to the Persian Gulf.[37] Additional shortfalls in the decision-making processes that staff recognized during the *Concordia* incident were addressed and rectified by the appropriate military and civilian departments.[38]

*Suitability of Naval Force Structure for National Missions*

Some commentators and analysts on defence issues have argued that using warships for national missions has been an attempt by the navy to find relevancy after the end of the Cold War.[39] Although these arguments ignore the historical contributions that the Canadian navy has made in fisheries and sovereignty patrols, no analyst would suggest building destroyers and cruisers strictly for sovereignty protection and national missions. The projected Canadian fleet structure of destroyers, frigates, minesweepers, and supply vessels allows the continuity of a liberal interventionist foreign policy, while retaining a base fleet for domestic operations.[40]

Although Canada's current foreign and defence policies are under review and subject to changes, Canadian security has in the past been inextricably linked with the security of its major trading partners through cooperative organizations like the Conference on Security and Cooperation in Europe (CSCE), the North American Air Defence Agreement (NORAD), and the North Atlantic Treaty Organization (NATO).[41] Canadian naval leaders in turn have opted for platforms that are equipped with the most recent technology and sufficiently adaptable to fulfil various missions overseas. Recently, naval vessels have participated in UN missions off the coasts of Somalia, the former Yugoslavia, and Haiti. If Canada continues with its historically interventionist foreign policy, then the equipment of the Canadian Armed Forces will continue to be built or procured for the worst-case scenario: for example, active participation in a coalition-based regional conflict like the Korean War. For MARCOM, this translates into a few balanced task groups of frigates, destroyers, and supply vessels.

Coinciding with the navy's growing participation in international humanitarian missions is a greater emphasis on domestic operations. National missions offer Canadian policy-makers a greater degree of latitude for unilateral action than they find in cooperative security associations.[42] The federal departments involved in maritime issues have had to deal with unilateral policy declarations, such as the Arctic Waters Pollution Prevention Act and the declaration of the fishing zone, without a commensurate increase in resources. Unilateral domestic actions backed by credible force strengthen the external perceptions of a state's resolve and enhance its prestige. Due to their symbolic value, the utilization of naval forces can have a catalytic influence on issues that might have remained unknown.[43]

Inevitably, the defence analyst must weigh the capabilities and suitability of naval vessels for national missions, including the options that are available. Canadian maritime area surveillance is conducted by CP-140

Auroras and Arcturuses and will be improved by ground-based sensors currently in development.[44] Area surveillance by ground-based sensors only provides range and bearing information, while aerial surveillance is limited by the number of available aircraft and by fuel endurance. The frigates and destroyers of the Canadian navy, which can detect vessels at ranges of twenty-five nautical miles with their organic surface search radar, are equipped with modern command, control, and information-collection facilities and are manned by highly capable, motivated, and professional crews.[45] The communication systems used by major MAR-COM platforms are secure, and after the review of the *Concordia* incident, they are interoperable with those used by other government agencies.[46]

Warships have an advantage over their airborne counterparts in their ability to remain on-station for extended periods of time. Their presence serves both as a persistent reminder of Canadian sovereignty and as a deterrent to those who, for example, might consider fishing within Canadian waters illegally. Teams, under the guidance of a Fisheries and Oceans officer, can investigate suspicious vessels within the fishing zone.[47] Recent advances in the shipborne Global Positioning System translates into the ability to accurately determine whether a fishing vessel is within Canadian waters. Warships can also shadow NAFO-member vessels fishing outside of the fishing zone, for the purpose of collecting photographic evidence of illegal fishing activity.

Most of the larger ships of the Canadian navy have at least one helicopter on board, which drastically increases the ship's surveillance range.[48] Shipborne helicopters, with on-board Fisheries officers, can perform the same surveillance and evidence-gathering missions as their surface and fixed-wing counterparts. High-resolution night-vision cameras currently used by US Coast Guard helicopter crews and available commercially, allow evidence-gathering in conditions that have normally been perennially used for illegal activity.[49]

All of the navy's surface platforms are outfitted with a surface gun that can fire warning shots or be used for self-defence. Historically, in disputes like the Anglo-Icelandic cod wars and the Beira blockade, warning shots have been largely ineffectual in halting determined ship's captains.[50] The use of disabling fire may become lethal, and given the legal issues involved, only the most sanguine nations would consider using potentially lethal force in a dispute over fisheries.[51] In light of the *Concordia* incident, MARCOM's policy-makers identified the need for a level of force to bridge the gap between warning and disabling fire.[52] This led to the review of boarding tactics, including heliborne insertion, which were successfully applied by the Maritime Interception Force in the Persian Gulf.[53]

While the use of naval vessels to actively enforce the maritime laws of a nation may be the cornerstone of maintaining a credible maritime sovereignty policy, their usage also entails the risk of escalating a conflict.[54] The Canadian government could have responded to the French use of naval force described earlier by sending elements of the Canadian navy to escort the expelled scallop boats. This might have led to increased force deployments by both sides and to the escalating use of non-lethal or lethal force, should neither side have been willing to open negotiations or retire.

As fiscal restraint has been the hallmark of Canadian defence policy since the end of the Cold War, a key element of the recent defence policy review was the fiscal accountability of each branch of the Canadian Armed Forces. Even before the review was completed, a group known as the Canada 21 Council advocated further downsizing and restructuring.[55]

While few analysts would deny that using naval vessels to catch illegal immigrants and fishermen is expensive, the costs are relative to the tasks at hand. No one would question the costs of naval involvement in emergencies like oil-spill or rescue operations. For fisheries duties, the costs are equivalent for vessels provided by the Coast Guard and MARCOM, according to the 1990 Treasury Board investigation into federal fleet utilization (the Osbaldeston Report). Unfortunately, these figures are incomplete, and the operating costs for specific vessels are not set out in detail. Other costs that may not be included in the Treasury Board's figures are personnel costs and the operational costs for use of the ship's helicopter(s).

Not only are linear cost comparisons in such matters questionable, but their relevance is arguable given Fisheries and Oceans' paucity of capable offshore vessels. In the course of the Osbaldeston inquiry, for instance, Fisheries and Oceans stated that they could meet only half of their required number of patrol ship-days. The Treasury Board also discovered that the number of days available from National Defence and the Coast Guard for multi-tasked fisheries patrols, in excess of their own requirements, almost equalled the Fisheries and Oceans shortfall.[56]

Each federal fleet, however, remains relatively expensive to staff and get to sea. If the bottom line for the Canadian government is only lower operating costs, several options are available. These include using commercial contractors for fisheries patrols and search and rescue; employing east coast fishermen, with their private vessels, for fisheries patrols; and downsizing MARCOM to the level of a coastal navy.

Fisheries and Oceans is currently experimenting with hiring commercial contractors to carry out aerial fisheries patrols. It has a five-year contract with a St John's chartering company to fill the significant surveillance gap left when the Maritime Air Group's medium-range patrol aircraft, the Trackers, were retired.[57] With no replacement aircraft available, Fisheries and Oceans faced the loss of almost 1,500 hours of flight time provided by National Defence.[58] As these hours had been provided cost-free to Fisheries and Oceans, the contract has added additional pressure to its besieged budget. In its report *Maritime Sovereignty*, the Standing Committee on National Defence and Veterans' Affairs (SCNDVA) expressed reservations about the use of private-sector companies for duties that might have national security implications.[59] Since National Defence has plans for a new coastal patrol aircraft (CPA), the experiment of privately contracting services may end in the near future.[60]

Another idea that has surfaced recently to make the patrolling of Canada's offshore areas more economical involves employing east coast fishermen and their vessels as temporary Fisheries officers.[61] Although potentially attractive as a way to bridge the gap between lower costs and more patrol vessels, this plan raises some obvious concerns. First and foremost, adequate training would have to be provided to familiarize the fishermen with the appropriate laws and evidence-gathering procedures. Government training courses would have to be established, and this process alone would take a significant amount of time. Finally, there is the question of the source of funding for such a plan. Given the Canadian government's current financial situation and deficit-reduction programs, it seems unlikely that it has the resources available to create and sustain a new employment program of this magnitude.

A third option for cutting costs would be to decommission the current naval fleet, with the goal of creating a coastal fleet of large numbers of corvettes and auxiliaries.[62] The benefits of a navy based on the Swedish model include more platforms at sea to assist in national missions, the opportunity for more officers to have ship commands, the liberation of capital for other programs, and reduced fleet operating costs. A coastal navy, however, would ensure that Canada would be a passive observer in any international naval efforts undertaken by its trading and security partners. Even if Canadian politicians decided to send support ships for peacekeeping missions, their protection would rest entirely with our coalition allies, as corvettes have limited defensive capabilities. With a coastal navy, Canadian national sovereignty would be preserved at the expense of our international reputation with our trading partners and allies.

*National Missions and Naval Identity*

MARCOM's domestic contribution in national missions preserves Canadian sovereignty and is a strong linchpin of the navy's relevance. Sovereignty, as we have seen, has a fairly straightforward definition: national assertion and the right to regulate territory unilaterally without external interference, whether on sea, air, or land. MARCOM's efforts to preserve sovereignty is important to Canadians, as its constant assertion is one of the parts of the sum total that helps to define a sense of autonomy. Canadians may not have a clearly defined national identity, but knowing and deciding who uses their territory fosters a sense of independence and self-determination. The inability to assert control over claimed maritime areas or resources leads to conditions like those observed off the coast of Somalia, where the lack of any centralized authority has allowed several nations the opportunity to fish at will, often within sight of the coast.[63]

Any institutional identity, naval identity included, is the product of many interrelated factors. These factors include recognized competence demonstrated by the skill of its personnel and in professional innovations, regular contact with other professionals in order to demonstrate ability and to share ideas, a clearly defined outline for the future as well as pride in past accomplishments, and meaningful contributions in worthwhile domestic and international causes. Canadian naval participation in national missions fulfils many of these criteria, yet is undermined by the navy's inability to extend its presence ashore and further inland.

This inland presence is not associated with power-projection or amphibious operations, but relates to MARCOM's ability to share its naval identity with a larger segment of the Canadian population. Most Canadians live and work a considerable distance away from the oceans and have little if any contact with the officers and vessels of the Canadian navy. This lack of contact, in combination with the continentalist outlook of many Canadians, has worked against their developing an appreciation of naval issues.

Canadian politicians and the taxpaying public have a notoriously short collective defence memory, a fact that strengthens MARCOM's need to inform them clearly and consistently of the importance of issues like the protection of sovereignty and collective security. The recent defence policy review allowed all branches of the Canadian Armed Forces to have the opportunity to articulate their importance to a national audience.

The potential solutions to the problem of sustaining interest in and awareness of naval issues in Canada include such alternatives as expanding the naval reserve and situating them in smaller communities throughout Canada, encouraging and sustaining a relationship with the various national media, and becoming involved in the political process. Each alternative entails sacrifices and risks, from charges of lobbying and influence-peddling to dilution of combat strength. Budgetary support for the Canadian Armed Forces is immutably linked to political support, which itself is pursuant to an understanding and appreciation of the related issues. This acquisition of political support through the spreading of the domestic naval presence, as well as through increased public awareness of the importance of sustained naval participation in national and international missions, is necessary for continued growth of the Canadian naval identity. How this can be achieved will be one of the most vexing and important concerns facing Canadian naval planners and policy-makers into the twenty-first century.

# Points of Departure:
# Towards the Next Forty Years

PETER W. CAIRNS

This book's subtitle, "In Quest of Canadian Naval Identity," illustrates a familiar national propensity. Yet we are sometimes so wrapped up in the "who" of things that we often miss the subsequent insights of "what, where, when, how, and why?" The contributors to this volume have gone a long way in clarifying these issues, and in doing so, they have delineated the complex issues that have determined the historical track along which the navy has developed its evolving nature. The journey continues.

While our final destination may always remain just out of sight over the horizon, however, the navy is not moving forward without a sense of direction. We do have a future vision. We have an achievable plan to guide us along our course, and we know many, if not all, of the obstacles in our path. I want to focus my remarks, not on where the navy has been nor on "who" it has been, but on where it is going.

In the spring of 1994, the United States Naval Institute (USNI) asked the commanders of world navies what they believed the most important naval developments of the coming decade would be. Nineteen of my contemporaries responded, as did I. In reviewing their replies in the *Proceedings* of the USNI, I was struck by the degree of commonality in their outlooks. Albeit from differing perspectives and with different emphasis, most of the commanders touched on five recurring themes:

1 the need for balanced, general-purpose forces;
2 the importance of technology and of command, control, communications, and intelligence ($c^3i$);

3 the evolving importance of joint and combined operations;
4 the growing importance of national roles in the coastal zones; and
5 the need to act within a fiscally restrained regime.

That so many naval commanders from such different backgrounds would share these concerns points towards a general convergence of thinking about the utility and employment of maritime forces. Certainly, each one of these concerns is germane to an understanding not only of the character of the Canadian navy, but of where it is and where it is headed.

Many factors are contributing to the current emphasis on the maintenance of balanced and versatile, general-purpose forces in most navies, including our own. These factors include the disappearance of a single overriding military threat, as well as fiscal pressures that militate against large fleets of highly specialized craft. Nations are building navies that can meet an unknown variety of missions, and they are seeking to employ the synergisms that a balanced force provides. This not only reinforces versatility, but can result in real economies as well.

Thanks to the foresight on the part of naval planners over the past decade, we are well on the way to successfully making the shift from a fleet focused on anti-submarine-warfare (ASW) to a more flexible, general-purpose capability. If, and it is a significant "if," the government is able to deliver the rest of the equipment it is committed to acquiring, we will then have a highly versatile, capable, general-purpose fleet. While it will not be large, the capabilities it will incorporate should allow our navy to address maritime defence requirements across the entire spectrum of likely operations.

When the layers of meaning that have been assigned to the concept of balanced forces have been pared away, the core requirement for credible operational capabilities in all three dimensions of ocean space remains: air, surface, and sub-surface. It is really the geometry of ocean operations that dictates the fundamental requirement for balanced forces.

The principal components of Canada's future maritime force have already begun to arrive with the delivery of five of the proposed twelve general-purpose Canadian Patrol Frigates (CPF), two of the up-dated "TRUMPed" anti-air command-and-control destroyers, and three Arcturus arctic and maritime surveillance aircraft. By the end of the century, our fleet transition should be largely complete, providing my successors with a force consisting of four TRUMP destroyers, twelve patrol frigates, two replenishment vessels, up to six conventionally powered patrol submarines, twelve coastal defence vessels, a number of shipborne helicopters, a variety of maritime patrol aircraft, and a small number of auxiliaries and tenders. The department is also considering a requirement for a multi-role support vessel, which would provide the sea-lift capability to move a land-force battle group and its equipment to an area of crisis on short notice.

The Canadian Patrol Frigates are superb general-purpose warships, laden with capabilities. Like the first generation of Canadian-built warships, the St Laurent–class destroyers, which were called the "cadillacs" of their day, and the Tribals, which were called "sisters of the space age" when they commenced service in the 1970s, the Canadian Patrol Frigates are among the very finest of their class in the world. Their integrated-machinery control systems, the distributed architecture of their command-and-control systems, and their threat-evaluation and weapons-assignment systems are all thoroughly state-of-the-art and designed to meet the demanding requirements of the modern maritime battlefield. They are the right ship for the age, and Canadians will be getting excellent value from them.

Judging from the performance of the first two ships to complete conversion, the TRUMP destroyers should prove an excellent complement to the patrol frigates. One is just completing an initial tour of duty as the flagship of NATO's Standing Naval Force Atlantic (STANVFORLANT), and the second is about to relieve her in the Adriatic. Their weapons systems and command-and-control architecture have been proven in real time on both the test ranges and in the rigorous operational setting of a UN-sponsored NATO–Western European Union (WEU) task group off the former Yugoslavia. Canada is, therefore, well on the way towards possession of a small but well-balanced maritime force. While the resulting force won't be large, it will be the best that Canadian technology can affordably offer. Thus, the navy will be a highly effective one.

*Technology and Command, Control, Communications, and Intelligence (C³I)*

The second theme emphasized by many of my contemporaries was the role to be played by technological developments and particularly the burgeoning information technology.

Perhaps more than in any other environment, technology has changed the way maritime forces conduct their business. Thus, the face of our navy will continue to reflect a reliance upon new technologies; this will continue to be an area of great importance to our future development. We have excellent defence scientists at work in this field, and we are also well placed to take advantage of Canada's status as a world leader in emergent fields of advanced technology. Levering additional capabilities out of new technologies is something of a tradition in the Canadian navy. For example, the "beartrap" helicopter hauldown system and

Variable Depth Sonars rank among the many other innovations to debut in our navy before being adopted by other navies. There is a long pedigree behind the ground-breaking systems on our new classes of ships as well.

We are in the process of substantially upgrading our c³i capabilities in the fleet and in our shore-based operations as well. The effects of this work will be most particularly felt in the Canadian ability to interact effectively with other government departments in the context of national roles and to coordinate operations with other nations in contingency operations and peacekeeping scenarios. When it comes to interoperability, Canada is well out in front of many navies, and recent efforts are reinforcing that lead.

Another area where the Canadian navy takes the lead is in the introduction of electronic chart display navigational systems. These will be fitted in the maritime coastal defence vessels when they are built. This technology has been successfully developed in Canada. It replaces paper charts with digitized versions, which are stored on computer disks and displayed on colour monitors. The system also pinpoints the ship's real-time location on the charts twice every second. A read-out from the ship's radar can be painted over the monitor to show the position of other vessels, and the system includes audible alarms that can be set to warn of approaching shallow water. Canadians are leading the world in the development and employment of this technology, which is described as the most significant development in seafaring since the invention of radar. Canadian naval reservists will be among the first to be using it.

Canada has sweeping northern possessions and responsibilities. Maritime Command has a mandate to be there advancing Canada's security interests, but it has a rather limited capability to do so at present. Breaking through in the Arctic is one of the navy's toughest challenges. Only through new technologies will it be possible to make real progress in the North. The Canadian navy is currently developing an arctic surveillance system that will provide a sonar-based surface and sub-surface monitoring capability near the three most important arctic choke-points. That will go some way towards meeting its requirement, but in the end it will still be necessary to be able to get beneath the ice and respond to what goes on there. That will take submarines with good under-ice endurance. In 1992 the government approved a three-year air-independent propulsion research program. Sufficient advances in this promising field could produce a system for eventual retro-fitting on our submarines, thus making them capable of under-ice operations. These are among the more notable fields in which technology will not only expand the scope of our operations, but contribute to the cost-effectiveness of our efforts and enhance our ability to meet defence policy objectives.

*Joint and Combined Operations*

Virtually all navies are adapting to the increasing prevalence of joint (with the army and air force) and combined (with allied or friendly naval powers) operations. Given a proliferation of regional conflicts, a more active United Nations, and a new openness to multilateral military cooperation, we can expect to see even greater emphasis placed on joint and combined operations in the future. Significantly, improved preparedness for joint and combined operations was one of the considerations driving our command reorganization in 1992. Both of the coastal headquarters – in Halifax and Esquimalt – have been structured to facilitate joint operations, either from their own facilities or while deployed with a Canadian force. Elsewhere, similar concerns are prompting other nations to reorganize their forces. For instance, the United States Navy's Atlantic command has been transformed into a new USA command that will act as a joint force generator for most military forces based in the continental United States. Since Maritime Command (MARCOM) has operated a joint headquarters with the air force for decades and regularly integrates our ship and submarine operations with those of the air force, that aspect of joint operations is not new to us. For the most part, working with the army is still relatively new to us, although operations in the Gulf, in Somalia, and in some of the more traditional peacekeeping operations in which our sailors have recently participated are beginning to build up a store of experience there as well.

Many of our higher-profile overseas deployments since 1990 have also been combined operations: the Gulf War; participation in the maritime interdiction force in the Red Sea and in humanitarian operations in Somalia; and our ongoing presence in the Adriatic. In each case, the navy has profited immensely from years of inter-allied cooperation within NATO and from good working relations with many Commonwealth navies. This is one area where NATO is proving its continuing worth and relevance.

Our new force disposition, which more equitably balances assets between the east and west coasts, will allow the commander on either coast to assemble versatile force-packages to meet most contingencies, whether they are only naval, joint, or combined responses. Thus, each coast commander will be able to deploy an independent, self-supporting task group tailored to the requirements of any contingency. Such a force could include a TRUMP command-and-air defence destroyer, several Canadian Patrol Frigates, a supply ship, and embarked air support provided by its helicopters. Where appropriate, the package could also include either a submarine or an Aurora aircraft. We will also have planning in place for the deployment of a single ship or other smaller tailored contributions to joint and combined forces where that allows us to achieve the best effect.

Of course, the bits and pieces are of limited value in themselves if it is impossible to integrate them into the forces of one's partners. Hence, we continue to place a good deal of emphasis on the development of interoperable command-and-control systems. We are also building on our expertise in joint and combined operations by participating in national and allied exercises. These actions, coupled with our growing level of real-time experience not only with joint and combined operations in home waters, but in support of NATO and the United Nations abroad, should ensure that we can effectively meet the challenge of closer inter-service and multilateral defence partnerships.

*National Roles and the Coastal Zone*

Development of the Law of the Sea regime, increased economic pressures upon coastal areas, and wider public concerns about non-traditional threats to ocean space have combined to develop a new focus of naval activity in the coastal zones. The Canadian navy has been involved in search and rescue, sovereignty and fisheries patrols, and related support to other government departments in coastal waters for many years, and throughout it has been assisted in these tasks by Maritime Air Group. Most of these national tasks are not new to the navy. What has changed, however, is the priority now being placed on national roles and the kind of interdepartmental cooperation going into their achievement. Since 1991, the Interdepartmental Program Coordination and Review Committee and its subordinate committees, located in Ottawa, have been working towards the establishment of sound procedures to facilitate cooperation among those federal departments with maritime responsibilities. Numerous improvements to interoperability within the federal fleet have been identified and implemented. As a result, the navy, Coast Guard, RCMP, Fisheries and Oceans, Revenue Canada, and Environment Canada have been much more effective in fulfilling their maritime mandates. On both coasts, new ground is being broken in regard to the management of the navy's response to national roles. Recently it began using submarines to conduct fisheries patrols and support the RCMP's counternarcotics operations. It will soon install Global Positioning Systems (GPS) on the submarines to further facilitate their effectiveness in such roles. Greater involvement in supporting the mandates of other government departments (known as OGD support) has also provided a tailor-made vehicle for the naval reserve to test and refine its new coastal defence roles. This is finally bringing some reality and genuine utility to the work of reservists. The navy takes advantage of every special resource in discharging its national roles. For example, HMCS *Cormorant* represents the best diving-operations resource in the federal government. She recently recovered drugs from a sunken mothership off Newfoundland and stopped pollution escaping from a sunken oil barge off the Cavendish coast of Prince Edward Island.

Maritime Air Group, as well, continues to play its part in addressing national roles. Its aircrew conduct northern patrols, fly surveillance missions, and provide airlift for fisheries observers. More recently, they have become more involved in the war on drugs. Auroras have been used to good effect identifying ocean polluters and have refined the collection of legally compelling evidence. These kinds of operation in the three dimensions of ocean space are important. They can be very fulfilling, and they can provide our sailors and members of Maritime Air Group with excellent training opportunities that also deliver real value to Canadian taxpayers.

My concern is that we maintain an appropriate balance between the resources and time devoted to national roles and that which we spend on maintaining readiness for combat-related tasks. I am charged with maintaining combat-capable forces, and I can only do that if my sailors are schooled in the requisite skills. Some tasks, like boardings, can be practised during the course of "other government department" operations. Others simply cannot. Given the pressures at work in society at large, maintaining the required equilibrium will not be easy.

*Fiscal Restraint*

The last, but by no means the least, of the common concerns expressed by my contemporaries is that associated with the widespread reduction of defence expenditures. Concerns about the so-called bottom line are by no means unique to Canada, for virtually all NATO allies have made major cuts to their defence budgets and force levels. While members of the military, no less than their civilian neighbours, have welcomed the global adjustments in international relations that may allow a reversal of the arms race that had driven Cold War relations, we must remain concerned that core Canadian defensive capabilities be maintained. We still live in an uncertain, unstable world, and Canadians still have a worthwhile contribution to make to international peace and security.

And yet cuts have been sustained – and they have hurt. Over the past few years, incremental funding cuts have resulted in a 25 per cent reduction in our operations budget. In late 1992 I was forced to reduce fleet operations by one-third. We in the navy still need to do a good bit of work to bring our "tooth-to-tail ratio" into line – that is, the ratio of infrastructure to operations – but the relatively ad hoc nature of many year-end budget cuts makes it hard to do that. Although command operations and maintenance funding have declined 11 per cent over the past five years (1989–93), the amount in the navy's fuel budget has plummeted 26 per cent. As the naval commander, I need to preserve a number of core capabilities. I cannot afford to have a continuing string of relatively ad hoc, short-term budget decisions erode my ability to maintain them. Just about the only way that I can see our delivering a credible and meaningful defence capability, while at the same time coping with fiscal pressures, is to improve how we manage the resources we have. This is under way in a process entitled Defence 2000, which combines a more businesslike, results-oriented way of doing things with a wider delegation of fiscal responsibility to hands-on managers. While this makes managers at all levels more accountable for spending, it also provides them with an incentive. When they find more cost-effective ways of meeting our mandate, they are allowed to keep some of the savings accrued to spend on unit priorities. The rest of what is saved returns to our headquarters where it can be applied to navy-wide priorities. We have only just begun this process, and indications are that there are many areas where significant savings can be made. One of the first things to be done with Maritime Command's share of those savings is to apply them to the fuel budget, so that Canadian ships can be operational for as many days of the year as possible.

## Conclusion

We are getting our own fiscal house in order, and I am sure that we will continue to do our part in meeting the government's wider financial objectives as well. While we could measure that bottom line in terms of production units in a capital plan or the pluses and minuses on a balance sheet, I think that for us the real bottom line is to continue our well-established tradition of contributing to Canadian interests and well-being. And we are doing that. We are making a solid contribution to the achievement of Canadian defence policy objectives. As a partner in Canada's foreign affairs team, the navy continues to bring credit to our flag throughout the world. At home we have been instrumental in advancing national objectives off our coasts. As a national institution we are showing ourselves to be responsive to social change and responsible stewards of public resources.

In short, the Canadian naval identity, which was first embodied in the Naval Services Act of 1910 and which evolved in the course of a colourful history, forms a sound foundation on which to build our future. With this point of departure, our navy will grow as a national institution in which Canadians can take pride. We are ready to embark upon the future with the confidence that we will live up to the proud traditions of our past.

# *Notes*

1 Reproduced with permission from Hattendorf and Schulman, eds, *Ubi Sumus: The State of Naval and Maritime History.* I am especially grateful to J.A. Boutilier, W.A.B. Douglas, M.L. Hadley, R. Sarty, and D. Zimmerman for their comments on the draft of this chapter. The final conclusions, errors, or omissions remain entirely my own.

2 For a discussion of this issue, see Sarty, "Canadian Maritime Defence."

3 The debate over German naval armaments and the need to assist the mother country is the traditional context for the Canadian naval debate of 1909–10; see, for example, Tucker's *Naval Service*, vol. 1. The problem of fisheries protection – although not to the exclusion of the German problem – has been the focus of much recent debate, as in Gimblett's " 'Tin Pots' or Dreadnoughts?" And then there is the "Sarty Thesis": the little-known but sophisticated and sound view that the development of a small Canadian navy in the early twentieth century was crucial to the perfection of Canada's existing system of coastal defence based on long-range gunnery – what might be called "the Navy as an outgrowth of coast artillery theory" of the origins of the RCN. See Sarty, " 'Trouble in the North Pacific.' "

4 Tucker, *Naval Service*, 1:261–79.

5 See Hadley and Sarty, *Tin-Pots and Pirate Ships*, 301.

6 See, for example, Douglas's seminal piece, "Conflict and Innovation," for a discussion of the tension between fighting the war against the Germans and the battle for long-term viability at home.

7 Fregault, *Pierre le Moyne d'Iberville*, and Mathieu, *La Construction Navale Royale à Québec*.

8 A replica of *Pelican* was launched in Montreal in 1993.

9 Douglas, "The Anatomy of Naval Incompetence," and "Nova Scotia and the Royal Navy"; Kert, "The Fortunes of War"; and Wright, "Green Flags and Red-Coated Gunboats."

10 Barry Gough, *The Royal Navy and the Northwest Coast of North America* and *Gunboat Frontier*.

11 See Stacey, "Life and Hard Times."

12 Schurman's influence has been unquestionable. Among his former pupils was the late Barry Hunt, who taught naval history at RMC for twenty years. Schurman's friend and former colleague at RMC, W.A.B. Douglas, has for the last twenty years been writing *the* official history of the Canadian Armed Forces. Gerald Graham's influence has been perhaps less direct but no less profound. Much of recent academic activity on the RCN has been at the University of New Brunswick (UNB), where one of Graham's former students, Dominck S. Graham, ran the military history program until 1986. Milner and Zimmerman were products of that program, which Milner now runs. The latest UNB naval historian, Michael Hennessey, has taken the late Barry Hunt's position in the History Department at RMC.

13 J.M.S. Careless left the naval historical section to pursue a career in Canadian history at Toronto.

14 See Easton's superb wartime memoir *50 North*; Sclater's excellent *Haida*; and Pugsley's two volumes on the lower deck, *Saints Devils and Ordinary Seaman* and *Sailor Remember*.

15 Much of the old RN tradition still survives, however, as evidenced by the practices outlined in Arbuckle's *Customs and Traditions*. Indeed, one is hard-pressed to find anything distinctly Canadian in the customs and traditions Arbuckle describes.

16 Lund, "Command Relationships in the North West Atlantic"; and Milner, "Canadian Escorts and the Mid Atlantic." See Douglas, "Canadian Naval Historiography," for a list of other theses and dissertations in related fields, such as imperial maritime history.

17 Milner, "No Higher Purpose"; and Melville, "Canada and Sea Power."

18 The conference proceedings were published in Boutilier, *The RCN in Retrospect*. The table of contents is unaltered from the list of speakers.

19 The model was used later by Cmdr James Goldrick, RAN, to spur interest in Australian naval history. The proceedings were published in Frame, Goldrick, and Jones, *Reflections on the Royal Australian Navy*.

20 As discussed in Douglas, "The Prospects for Naval History," 19.

21 Douglas, *The RCN in Transition*.

22 See Douglas, "The Prospects for Naval History."

23 Stead, *A Leaf upon the Sea*; Lamb, *On the Triangle Run*; Lawrence, *Tales of the North Atlantic* and *Victory at Sea*; Lynch, *Salty Dips*, vols. 1 and 2; and Law, *White Plumes Astern*.

24 Perkins, *Canada's Submariners, 1914–1923*; Snowie, *The "Bonnie"*; and, for example, Blakely's privately published *Corvette Cobourg* and Macpherson's *River Class Destroyers* and *Frigates of the Royal Canadian Navy*.

25 German's book was accompanied by a video tape as part of the attempt to popularize the navy's history among a younger generation. See also Macbeth, *Ready, Aye Ready*.

26 See, for example, Haydon, *The 1962 Cuban Missile Crisis*, which contains new information on the RCN's role, specifically the chapter "The RCN and the Cuban Missile Crisis," 349–67.

27 See McKercher, "Between Two Giants"; Whitby, "In Defence of Home Waters"; and a series of works by Sarty, including "The Naval Side of Canadian Sovereignty," and " 'Entirely in the hands of the friendly neighbour.' " Sarty is also the principal author of the pre-1939 volume of the new official history of the RCN.

28 Harland and Mackay, *The Flower Class Corvette Agassiz*; and Macpherson and Milner, *Corvettes of the Royal Canadian Navy*.

29 See, for example, Hancox, "Canada, the Navy and the Shipbuilding Industry: Plus ça change?," "The State as Innovator," and "Post-War Ocean Shipping."

### CHAPTER TWO

1 *Halifax Herald*, 12 August 1918, 2.

2 Hadley and Sarty, *Tin-Pots and Pirate Ships*, 303.

3 Hunt, "The Road to Washington," 46. See also Pullen, "The Royal Canadian Navy between the Wars," 62–72.

4 See, for example, Lund, "The Royal Canadian Navy's Quest," 138–57.

5 Cited in Evans, *John Grierson*, 111.

6 While a Censorship Coordinating Committee had existed since 1939, its work was confused and inconsistent. The minister of defence assumed ultimate responsibility for censorship in May 1942.

7 Ernest H. Bartlett, "Lads Scoffed at ...," *Ottawa Journal*, 18 February 1941.

8 See Lynch and Lamb, *Gunshield Graffiti*.

9 Godfrey, "Forward." Squadron-Leader Godfrey's thoughtful foreword discusses the phenomenon of straight-laced, largely middle-class, Protestant young people fostering the raunchy, iconoclastic ballad.

10 LCDR William Strange, RCNVR, Plans and Operations Division, in an address to the Ottawa Canadian Club and the press, 5 March 1942. This was picked up, for example, in the *Daily Star* (Montreal), 5 March 1942, 23, and *Halifax Herald*, 6 March 1942, 2.

11 See accounts in Schull, *The Far Distant Ships*, 83–6; and German, *The Sea Is at Our Gates*, 105.

12 DHist, Chambly 8000. See also the then secret report dated 23 August 1942.

13 See two undated draft press releases and official reports, DHist, Oakville 8000.

14 "Their Lordships Congratulate H.M.C.S. Oakville on destruction of U-boat," DHist, Oakville 8000.

15 A well-intentioned veteran's book on the subject had argued against all evidence that this Canadian defeat was actually a victory and that the government had kept events quiet. See Essex, *Victory in the St. Lawrence*.

16 For a full account of the action, see Hadley, *U-Boats against Canada*, 121–5.

17 *Halifax Herald*, 19 September 1942, 6.

18 Evans, *John Grierson*, 121. For marketing purposes, the film was ultimately edited to about ten minutes.

19 Ibid., 141–2. *Fighting Sea Fleas* ran for eleven minutes, *Heroes* for fifteen.

20 For an account of the NFB productions, see Evans, *John Grierson*, 185–6.

21 For example, in *Ottawa Evening Citizen*, 1 February 1943.

22 A younger generation has endorsed these perceptions. I acknowledge the reflections of students Steve Ball, Simon Cairns, Shawn Hutchings, and David Yuill in my seminar on the history of the Canadian navy, September–December 1993, University of Victoria.

23 See Whitby, "Instruments of Security," 1–15.

24 Sclater, *Haida*, 191.

25 Garner, *Storm Below*. Garner seems to have spliced words from the song "West Atlantic Squadron": "Away, away, with sword and drum, / Hear the corvettes' engines hum ..."

26 Ibid., 207–8.

27 DHist, staff memorandum on "Canada's Post-War Navy," 11 November 1940, Naval Policy 1650-1, vol. 2, NSHQ, Ottawa.

28 Schull, *The Far Distant Ships*, 182.

29 Ibid., 271.

30 Ibid., 359.

31 Ibid., 425.

32 Vice-Admiral H.T.W. Grant, "A Message from the Chief of the Naval Staff," *Souvenir Program*, Canadian Naval Officers Reunion, 28 June to 1 July [1949], Halifax, NS, 5. David Zimmerman Collection.

33 House of Commons, *Debates*, 14 April 1953, 1–8.

34 DHist, "Notes on RCN Operations in the Korean Theatre," 1650-239/187.

35 House of Commons, *Debates*, 14 April 1953, 8.

36 Yuill, " 'Operation Korea.' "

37 Ibid., 11.

38 Editorial, "Canada's Laurel Wreath in Korea," *Ottawa Citizen*, 28 July 1953.

39 See, for example, " 'Train-Busting' Crews in Korea War Honoured," *Ottawa Citizen*, 5 February 1954.

40 This rare footage was subsequently spliced into the CBC Halifax film "Ready, Aye Ready: A Celebration of 75 Years of the Canadian Navy," Halifax: CBC, 1986, minute 27–30.

41 DHist, CO, HMCS *Crusader*, to Commander, Canadian Destroyers Far East, HMCS *Huron*, 6 January 1954, in "Korea," DHist, 1650–239/187.

42 Easton, *50 North*, 85.

43 Ibid., 213.

44 Great Britain, PRO, Captain [later Admiral Sir] Herbert Richmond, minute, 22 November 1918, ADM 137/1619. Cited in Hadley and Sarty, *Tin-Pots and Pirate Ships*, 296–7.

45 A. Tassie, letter to the editor, *Times-Colonist* (Victoria), 21 October 1993.

46 For the arrival of HMCS *Niobe*, see Hadley and Sarty, *Tin-Pots and Pirate Ships*, 53–5. The quotation is from a speech by the minister of marine, the Hon. L.P. Brodeur. For "Operation Scuttled," the sinking of *U-190*, see Hadley, *U-Boats against Canada*, 300–1.

47 Captain(N) Wilfred Lund, OMM, CD, letter to the editor, *Times-Colonist* (Victoria), 29 October 1993.

48 Hutchings, "The Victorian Reaction."

49 Raeside, "Mohammad's Junk" shop cartoon, *Times-Colonist* (Victoria), 23 September 1990; see stories "Kootenay could be off to gulf," "Peace-talk pressures grow," and "Sailpast will help bid goodbye to Huron," *Times-Colonist* (Victoria), 3 January 1991.

### CHAPTER THREE

1 Booth, *Navies and Foreign Policy*, 59.

2 Bill C-243, the Canadian Forces Reorganization Act, established a unified military service incorporating the former single services, the Royal Canadian Navy (RCN), the Canadian Army, and the Royal Canadian Air Force (RCAF). The naval forces of the RCN became Maritime Command (MARCOM), the army became Mobile Command (MOBCOM), and the air forces became Air Command (AIRCOM).

3 Stairs, *The Diplomacy of Constraint*, 297 and chap. 9.

4 Middlemiss and Sokolsky, *Canadian Defence, Decisions and Determinants*.

5 Booth, *Strategy and Ethnocentrism*, 128.

6 Ibid., 181.

7 Hill, *Maritime Strategy for Medium Powers*, 198–9.

8 See Mansergh, *The Commonwealth Experience*, 148; Preston, *Canada and Imperial Defence*, 430–1; Macandie, *Genesis of the Royal Australian Navy*, 272; and Sarty, "The Origin of the Royal Canadian Navy," 98–9.

9 The phrase is borrowed from Dr Thomas-Durrell Young, "The Old 'Dominions' and Their Policies of Defense Independence: Implications for Allied and United States Security" (paper presented at the Annual Conference of the International Studies Association, Strategic Studies Institute, United States Army War College, Carlisle Barracks, PA, 11–12 November 1988).

10 Lamb, *The Corvette Navy*, 18.

11 Thorgrimsson and Russell, *Canadian Naval Operations in Korean Waters*, 145.

12 Hegmann, "Reconsidering the Evolution of the U.S. Maritime Strategy," 324.

13 Stairs, "The Military as an Instrument of Canadian Foreign Policy," 111.

14 Geoffrey Till, "… constant failure to get current long-term political direction encourages the military planner to produce unspecified and general purpose forces … [T]he sailor's … almost mystical faith in the capacity of a first-rate balanced fleet to cope with virtually anything, can be distinctly irritating to the unsympathetic." Goldrick and Hattendorf, *Mahan Is Not Enough*.

15 O'Neill, *Australia in the Korean War 1950–53*, 1:405–6.

16 Millar, "The Australian Naval Situation," 210.

17 Dillon, *Canadian Naval Policy Since World War II*, 53.

18 Australia, Department of Foreign Affairs and Trade, Ministerial Statement, (Hon.) Gareth Evans (QC), *Australia's Regional Security*, December 1989.

19 Australia, DOD, *Defence of Australia*.

20 Bateman, "Towards an Australian Maritime Defence Strategy," 9.

21 Sokolsky, *A Question of Balance*, 36.

22 Joel J. Sokolsky, *Seapower in the Nuclear Age: The United States Navy and NATO* (Annapolis, Ma.: Naval Institute Press, 1941), 72–4.

23 Bateman and Sherwood, *Principles of Australian Maritime Operations*, 2.

24 Cairns, "Foreword," in *The Naval Vision* (Ottawa: DND, 1994), ii.

25 DND, *Statement on Defence Policy*, 1991, 3.

26 Cable, *Britain's Naval Future*, 43.

27 Cable, *Diplomacy at Sea*, 39.

28 *Report of Admiral of the Fleet Viscount Jellicoe of Scapa on Naval Mission to the Dominion of Canada*, 3 vols (November–December 1919), 1:11–13 (hereafter referred as the Jellicoe Report). In his report Admiral Jellicoe suggested two naval options for Canada: one for "Canada's own requirement and Canada's own safety" and the second, a more powerful "fleet-unit," should Canada decide "to cooperate in the general naval needs of the empire."

CHAPTER FOUR

1 To escape the legal ramifications of "mutiny," the actions were officially described as "incidents." However, even at the time it was acknowledged that technically they were mutinies. See Rear Admiral E.R. Mainguy et al., *Report on Certain "Incidents"* (hereafter referred as Mainguy Report), 56.

2 The inquiry was formally charged to investigate the "incidents" on *Crescent*, *Athabaskan*, and *Magnificent*. In the process of its deliberations, the inquiry also reviewed the problem on *Ontario*, which had not attracted similar public attention.

3 NA, Evidence before the Mainguy Inquiry, 3497; NA 3499–3500, Audette Papers, MG 31 E 18, vol. 4.

4 DHist, minutes of the 167th meeting of the Naval Board held on Friday, 22 February 1946, item 167–3, "Canada Badges," decisions 1 and 2. The members of the board present were Deputy Minister W. Gordon Mills; Assistant Chief of Naval Staff Commodore H.G. De Wolf; Chief of Naval Administration and Supply Rear Admiral Harold T.W. Grant; and Chief of Naval Personnel Captain Paul W. Earl, RCNVR. I am indebted to Commodore J. Drent for drawing this to my attention.

5 NA, Claxton Papers, MG 32, B 5, vol. 221, 867–8, 870.

6 NA, "Staff Memorandum on Canada's Post-War Navy," November 1940, NSHQ, Ottawa (attributed to Cmdr F.L. Houghton, director of plans), RG 24, Acc 83–84/167, vol. 11209, file 1017–10–34, p. 10.

7 Gimblett, " 'Tin-Pots' "; Hadley and Sarty, *Tin-Pots and Pirate Ships*; Sarty, "Canadian Maritime Defence"; and Sarty and Schurman, "An Historical Perspective."

8 Gimblett, " 'Tin-Pots,' " 53–4. In 1901 Borden had favoured a Canadian naval militia, a position very close to Laurier's.

9 "Borden to Governor General, 24 March 1913," in *Documents on Canadian External Relations*, 1:281; and Sarty and Schurman, "An Historical Perspective," 61.

10 House of Commons, *Debates*, 12 January 1910, 1739. "Suppose that a Canadian unit of the British navy is organized – and I prefer to speak of it that way rather than as of a Canadian navy pure and simple"; and his concluding remarks (1761–2), "We have no Dreadnought ready; we have no fleet unit at hand. But we have the resources and I trust the patriotism to provide a fleet unit or at least a Dreadnought without one moment's unnecessary delay. Or, and in my opinion this would be the better course, we can place the equivalent in cash at the disposal of the admiralty to be used for naval defence under such conditions as we may prescribe. In taking this course we shall fulfil not only the letter, but in the spirit as well the resolution of March last, and what is infinitely more important we shall discharge a great patriotic duty to our country and to the whole empire." This strong imperialist position may, in fact, over a longer time scale be shown as an aberration, political opportunism of the moment of the dreadnought crisis."

11 Borden, *Robert Laird Borden*, 2:841–3.

12 Jellicoe Report, 3:3, para. 5.

13 "It is of great importance that the Royal Canadian Navy and the Royal Navy should hold themselves in the very closest relationship. The ships should be of

similar types, the personnel actuated by the same motives, trained on the same lines, imbued with the same traditions, governed by a practically common discipline and aiming at the same high standard of efficiency." Jellicoe Report, 2:28.

14 Ibid., 1:30, para 11.

15 Ibid., 3:4, para 9.

16 Ibid., para 8.

17 Ibid., 3:5, para 15.

18 See Ranft, "The Protection of British seaborne trade," 3–10, for a discussion of "the intellectual limitations of the naval high command of [the] day."

19 NA, memorandum (no. 2) of the Colonial Defence Committee, printed with "Confidential. Vancouver: Defence of Esquimalt"; memorandum (no. 3) by CDC; no. 29 printed for the use of the Colonial Office, 23 August 1887, 6, MG 29, E 61, vol. 12.

20 Jellicoe Report, 1:11, 13.

21 DHist, Hose to minister, 28 February 1922, 81/520/1440–5, vol. 8.

22 John Crispo Leckie Annesley failed the chemistry exam, requested a re-mark, and had the failure confirmed. Nonetheless, he was given a place as a cadet in the RCN. NA, Personnel Record Centre, personnel file of Annesley (died 1964), 0-2440.

23 Mainguy Report, 53, specifically commented on the lack of humanities instruction for junior officers. "We therefore recommend that some additional instruction be given in literature and history in order that a wider experience of men may be joined to a deeper knowledge of human affairs from the recorded pages of history and literature. We have already observed that, in our opinion, the young Canadian Naval officer is not as well educated as his British and American contemporary. This condition should not be allowed to continue any longer."

24 DHist, confidential source.

25 Granatstein, The Generals, 13. See also the discussion of Maj.-Gen. Bruce Matthews, 181; having failed French, Latin, English literature, ancient history, algebra, physics, and chemistry in his last year at Upper Canada College, he only "narrowly failed his entrance examinations for admission to the Royal Military College."

26 Kendle, The Round Table Movement, 278.

27 Cited in NA, Claxton Papers, MG 32 B5, vol. 220, 367.

28 Graham, Arthur Meighen, 2:220–1.

29 "Extracts from the minutes of the Imperial Conference, 1926, November 15, 1926," 4:162.

30 "Extracts from the minutes of the Imperial Conference, 1926, November 15, 1926," 159–60.

31 Stacey, Arms, Men and Governments, 308–9.

32 That Victoria might have been "British" in the 1920s and 1930s, when even today it promotes the tourist image of being "a bit of old England," requires no elaboration. MacNeil, in his memoir *Wordstruck*, describes the "psychic colonialism" (18) of growing up in Halifax. Of Halifax and Nova Scotia he says, "Psychologically, the province I grew up in was still in large measure a British colony. Halifax society was conditioned by the presence of generations of well-born, sometimes aristocratic, British officers and showed it. The higher up the social pecking order in that small but cosmopolitan seaport town, the more people identified with England" (15). Either city can be contrasted with, for example, the Winnipeg of James Grey's account of growing up in that city, *The Boy from Winnipeg*.

33 Rear Admiral R.H. Leir had wanted to join the real navy, the RN, but was unable to do so and therefore joined the second-best RCN as a possible backdoor route to the RN. Leir, "Big Ship Time," 76.

34 In January 1940 Commodore Sir Frederick Dreyer reported Nelles as saying that his second object was to establish "a permanent peacetime navy on a much larger scale than before 1939." Cited in Douglas, "Conflict and Innovation," 215.

35 NA, naval superintendent, HMC Dockyard, Esquimalt, to naval secretary, 18 October 1940, AE 33–206–1, RG 24, vol. 11, 908. "During his recent visit here the Minister of National Defence (Naval Service) requested that a site plan of Hatley park be forwarded to him." House of Commons, *Debates* 19 November 1940, 207.

36 DHist, "Monthly Report Officers Training," 2 August 1940, NS 10005–13, vol. 2; NA, summary of the Manning Conference held at NSHQ on 30 and 31 August 1940, 4 September 1940, NS 1078–3–5, vol. 1, RG 24, vol. 4045; NA, message, COAC to NSHQ, (R) C. Stadacona, 1121/5/11/40, message C. Stadacona to NSHQ for DNP, (R) COAC, 1155/5/11/40, NS 1–24–1, vol. 3, RG 24, vol. 5586.

37 DHist, "Review of the Development of Canadian Naval Policy," NSHQ Plans Division, April 1943, p. 6, Naval Policy 1650–1, vol. 1.

38 NA, NS C1070–1–23, 2 September 1943, RG 24, vol. 8162, file NSC 1700 DT 50, vol. 1.

39 DHist, Rear Admiral K.F. Adams interview with H.A.L. Lawrence, no date, 39.

40 NA, "Comments on the Operation and Performance of H.M.C. Ships, Establishments and Personnel in the Battle of the Atlantic," HMCS *Restigouche*, 1 June 1943, RG 24, vol. 3997, file NSS 1057–3–24, vol. 1.

41 NS Meeting, minutes of the 168th meeting held Thursday, 8 April 1943, Decision 168–5, and Appendix B, "Memorandum to VCNS for Naval Staff, Policy re Canadian Naval Air Service," 6 April 1943, para. 15.

42 "Commander J.V. Waterhouse, D.S.O., R.N., has been appointed to H.M.S. 'Canada' additional as Escort Group Training Commander at Halifax," *Royal Canadian Monthly Review* 22 (October 1943): 35.

43 NA, Memorandum to CNS, 30 September 1940, RG 24, Acc 83–84/167, vol. 529, file NSC 1700–121/2, vol. 1. The memorandum is quoted extensively in this and the following paragraphs.

44 House of Commons, *Debates*, 8 June 1944, 4:3655.

45 NA, PRC, personnel file of Commodore Adrian Mitchell Hope (died 15 February 1963). Hope retired in October 1951. During his climb to a commodore's broad pennant, Hope was passed over by Bidwell (who was himself passed over by Mainguy and Roy), Mainguy (who also passed over commodores Godfrey and Edwards and Rear Admiral Houghton), Miles (also passed over by Roy), Roy (who passed over eleven officers when he was promoted to commander and was later lost in HMCS *Margaree*), and DeWolf (who by January 1948 had passed over ten current or future commodores and flag officers). That someone such as Hope, of limited ability and so resistant to change, could reach high rank is indicative of the problem of senior leadership in the expanded postwar navy. Only five lieutenants (including two who had served in the RN lower deck in the First World War and were commissioned in 1936) and one lieutenant-commander in the 1939 navy list who remained in the RCN after 1948 failed to attain at least commodore's rank. Rupert Wainman Wood was the only commander on the 1939 navy list who stayed in the navy after 1945 but was not promoted to commodore. Despite being the brightest cadet of his entry term and being recommended for "the higher ranks of the service," he was passed over for promotion to commander by others who had not been so noted, and sidelined into ordnance before the war, perhaps as a consequence of showing interest in his family. He retired in 1946 as a captain. The need to fill senior positions required all the available officers. There was no selection for promotion on the basis of ability or merit. To some, it appeared to be promotion by nepotism and the old boy net.

46 Douglas, "Conflict and Innovation"; and Lund, "The Royal Canadian Navy's Quest."

47 DHist, "Objective of the Naval Service," 17 January 1939, Naval Policy 1650–1, vol. 1.

48 Great Britain, PRO, "Impression of Canadian Defence Policy – December 1934," by Sir Maurice Hankey, Hankey Papers, London, CAB 63/81.

49 NA, DNP to naval secretary, 23 December 1940 (draft), RG 24, vol. 5586, file NS 1–24–1, vol. 1.

50 NA, memorandum, 27 January 1941, RG 24, vol. 5586, file NS 1–24–1, vol. 4.

51 "Staff Memorandum on Canada's Post-War Navy," 2, para 4.

52 The paper and Jones's covering letter are at NA, RG 24, D 10 vol. 11129, file "Naval Policy."

53 NA, RG 24, D1, vol. 3844, file NS 1017–10–34.

54 Minute by VCNS, 12 May 1942, ibid.

55 From "Summary of Canadian Naval Policy," 1 September 1943, approved
200th Naval Staff meeting, 13 September 1943: "The present Canadian
Navy is not capable of maintaining command of the oceans adjacent to Canada in the face of a substantial challenge by hostile fleets"; from "Post-War
Navy," 4 September 1943, approved 199th meeting, 8 September 1943
para. 5, "The question actually at issue is thus whether Canada seeks the status of an independent power ... or ... intends to depend wholly upon the
United States ... Naval defence is an essential element in national self-preser-
vation"; from "R.C.N. Ship Requirements for the War Against Japan,"
9 September 1943, approved 199th meeting: para. 3, "In fact, by limiting its
participation in the war against Japan to such duties [convoy escort not in
'conflict with the enemy's main naval effort'], the R.C.N. would inevitably
lose much of the prestige it has acquired during the Battle of the Atlantic";
para. 14, "This is not a position which the Canadian Navy can be expected to
accept with equanimity, and it is certainly not fitting that the second Navy of
the Empire should be a mere spectator on such a vital occasion;" para. 19,
"... submarines do not play such a direct part in the fight for general command of the seas as do surface craft, since they merely exploit deficiencies in
the enemy's close protection forces, and it is in the main fight for command
that the R.C.N. should directly participate"; from "The Post-War Canadian
Navy," 17 November 1943, approved 216th meeting, 24 December 1943:
tasks included maintenance of "Imperial sea communications." The "imperial" qualification was added by Todd, since DeWolf's memorandum on a
similar topic was forwarded 14 April 1943. Todd also said (para 8), "To obtain the prestige and recognition of status which it thus seeks, it is essential
that Canada should have as strong a Navy as possible. The Latin American
countries are particularly susceptible to demonstrations of armed strength ...
At present even the Argentine Navy, with two battleships, two cruisers,
16 destroyers and 3 submarines, has more powerful ships than the Canadian
Navy." Additionally, in his papar "Immediate War Plan for the War Against
Japan" (23 October 1943, approved 208th meeting, 1 November 1943), the
imperial connection was kept alive in the recommendation that RCN cruisers,
fleet destroyers, and aircraft carriers be placed under RN operational control,
while escort vessels "be offered to the U.S. Navy for employment under
U.S.N. operational control." DHist, file Naval Policy 1650–1, vols. 1 and 2,
NS Minutes.

56 "R.C.N. Ship Requirements," 1.

57 DHist, "R.C.N. Manning Programme," Captain G.R. Miles, director of
plans, 15 December 1943, Naval Policy 1650–1, vol. 2.

58 See, for example, NA, minutes of the PHP, 28 July 1944, RG 24 D1, vol. 6170,
file HQ 15–48–1, vol. 1.

59 NA, "Post War Navy – Representation in UK," RG 24, D1, vol. 3844, file NS
1017–10–34.

60 Cited in Douglas, "Conflict and Innovation," 211. This article also includes a discussion of the way Mackenzie King was presented with the offer of cruisers in circumstances calculated to make him accept.

61 Todd, "The Post-War Navy," para. 52.

CHAPTER FIVE

1 Waite, *Canada 1874–1896: Arduous Destiny*, 202.
2 Innis, *Cod Fisheries*, 232, 235, 149.
3 Tucker, *Naval Service*, 1:52.
4 Innis, *Cod Fisheries*, 247.
5 Ibid.
6 For this and the following, see Easterbrook and Aitken, *Canadian Economic History*.
7 Morton, *The Critical Years*, 251.
8 Longley, "The Fisheries in Nova Scotia Politics," 83.
9 Innis, *Cod Fisheries*, 353.
10 Longley, "The Fisheries in Nova Scotia Politics," 83.
11 Innis, *Cod Fisheries*, 364.
12 Longley, "The Fisheries in Nova Scotia Politics," 87.
13 Innis, *Cod Fisheries*, 366.
14 Longley, "The Fisheries in Nova Scotia Politics," 89.
15 Morton, *The Critical Years*, 250.
16 Innis, *Cod Fisheries*, 369.
17 Joseph Gough, "Fisheries Management in Canada," 19, 20.
18 Waite, *Canada 1874–1896: Arduous Destiny*, 204.
19 Innis, *Cod Fisheries*, 422.
20 Sarty, "Canadian Maritime Defence," 468.
21 Sarty, "The Australian Connection," 81.
22 Ibid., 86.
23 Gimblett, "Reassessing the Dreadnought Crisis of 1909," 37.
24 Sarty, "The Australian Connection," 87.
25 Gimblett, "Reassessing the Dreadnought Crisis of 1909," 38.
26 Ibid., 39.
27 Brodeur, "Brodeur and the Origins of the Canadian Navy," 16.
28 Gimblett, "Reassessing the Dreadnought Crisis of 1909," 40, 41.
29 Sarty, "The Australian Connection," 89.
30 Ibid., 90.
31 Gimblett, "Reassessing the Dreadnought Crisis of 1909," 42.
32 Sarty, "Canadian Maritime Defence," 477–8.
33 Clippingdale, *Laurier, His Life and World*, 155.
34 Gimblett, "Reassessing the Dreadnought Crisis of 1909," 49.
35 Ibid., 158.

36 Tucker, *Naval Service*, 1:137.

37 Clippingdale, *Laurier, His Life and World*, 188.

38 Tucker, *Naval Service*, 1:141.

39 Sarty, "Canadian Maritime Defence, 1892–1914," 484.

40 Bothwell, Drummond, and English, *Canada 1900–1945*, 46; and Dyer and Viljoen, *The Defence of Canada 1760–1939*, 190.

41 Bothwell, Drummond, and English, *Canada 1900–1945*, 47.

42 Tucker, *Naval Service* 1:174.

43 Joseph Gough, "Fisheries Management in Canada," 24.

## CHAPTER SIX

1 Dickerson and Flanagan, *An Introduction to Government and Politics*, 77.

2 Neatby, "Laurier and Imperialism," 1. It has been argued that there were three reasons for imperialism: the assumption of racial superiority, family ties, and the belief that England symbolized liberty, justice, and civilization in the world.

3 German, *The Sea Is at Our Gates*, 23; and Barry Gough, "The End of Pax Britannica," 93.

4 Skelton, *Life and Letters of Sir Wilfrid Laurier*, 288. This policy of centralization concentrated on political, economic, and military aspects of Great Britain.

5 Barry Gough, "The End of Pax Britannica," 95.

6 McMinn, "Laurier versus Chamberlain," 163–4.

7 Winterbotham, *George E. Foster*, 49; Ollivier, *The Colonial and Imperial Conferences*, 1:151–9; and Stevens, "Laurier and the Liberal Party," 332.

8 McMinn, "Laurier versus Chamberlain," 165.

9 Stevens, "Laurier and the Liberal Party," 332.

10 Neatby, "Laurier and Imperialism," 7; and Robertson, *Sir Wilfrid Laurier*, 114.

11 Skelton, *Life and Letters of Sir Wilfrid Laurier*, 298.

12 McMinn, "Laurier versus Chamberlain," 167. This attitude existed among the other colonial premiers at the conference as well, although Canada was the only self-governing colony that declined to assist in the cost of imperial defence.

13 Ibid., 173.

14 Ibid., 175.

15 Ibid., 192.

16 Barry Gough, "The End of Pax Britannica," 95.

17 Brodeur, "Brodeur and the Origins of the Canadian Navy," 17.

18 Ibid., 16; and German, *The Sea Is at Our Gates*, 23.

19 Brodeur, "Brodeur and the Origins of the Canadian Navy," 18.

20 Gimblett, " 'Tin-Pots,' " 69–70, 98–100.

21 Hadley and Sarty, *Tin-Pots and Pirate Ships*, 16.

22 German, *The Sea Is at Our Gates*, 24.

23 Ibid., 24; and Tucker, *Naval Service*, 1:88. For the impact on Canada in the prewar years, see Hadley and Sarty, *Tin-Pots and Pirate Ships*.

24 Brodeur, "Brodeur and the Origins of the Canadian Navy," 20.

25 German, *The Sea Is at Our Gates*, 24.

26 Stevens, "Laurier and the Liberal Party," 332.

27 Ollivier, *The Colonial and Imperial Conferences*, 237.

28 Brodeur, "Brodeur and the Origins of the Canadian Navy," 20.

29 Ibid., 21.

30 Gordon, *The Dominion Partnership in Imperial Defence*, 217.

31 Rhodri Williams, *Defending the Empire*, 161–70.

32 Winterbotham, *George E. Foster*, 145; Liberal Party, *Canada and the Navy: Reasons*, 2; and German, *The Sea Is at Our Gates*, 25.

33 Tucker, *Naval Service*, 1:123.

34 Liberal Party, *Views of George E. Foster*, 4.

35 Winterbotham, *George E. Foster*, 145.

36 Liberal Party, *Canada and the Navy: Reasons*, 2.

37 Tucker, *Naval Service*, 1:127–8.

38 Liberal Party, *Canada and the Navy: The Real Emergency*, 3.

39 German, *The Sea Is at Our Gates*, 25.

40 Liberal Party, *Canada and the Navy: The Real Emergency*, 4.

41 Allen, "Borden, Britain, and the Navy," 22.

42 Barry Gough, "The End of Pax Britannica," 93.

43 Allen, "Borden, Britain, and the Navy," 21.

44 Sarty, "The Naval Side of Canadian Sovereignty," 90.

45 Preston, *Canadian Defence Policy*, 18. Laurier's refusal can be seen as further evidence of a sense of Canadian identity and the wish for Canadian control.

46 Tucker, *Naval Service*, 1:138.

47 Liberal Party, *Canada and the Navy: The Real Emergency*, 4.

48 Tucker, *Naval Service*, 1:140.

49 Hadley and Sarty, *Tin-Pots and Pirate Ships*, 60–4.

50 Ibid., 70–5.

51 Sarty, "The Naval Side of Canadian Sovereignty," 95–100.

52 Liberal Party, *Canada and the Navy: Reasons*, 4–5.

53 Wilson, "The Canadianism of Sir Wilfrid Laurier," 269.

54 Ibid., 268.

55 Borden to governor general, 24 March 1913, *Documents on Canadian External Relations*, 1:279–81.

56 Allen, "Borden, Britain, and the Navy," 12.

CHAPTER SEVEN

1 Stacey, "Halifax as an International Strategic Factor," 46–56.

2 On British strategy in North America, see Stacey, *Canada and the British Army*; and Hitsman, *Safeguarding Canada*.

3 Dilke and Wilkinson, *Imperial Defence*, chaps 3 and 4.

4 These views, from 1903 and 1890 respectively, are reprinted in Mahan, *The Interest of America in Sea Power*, 37–8, 24.

5 G.S. Graham, *The Politics of Naval Supremacy*, 124.

6 The classic account is Marder, *The Anatomy of Sea Power*; for recent research, see Friedberg, *The Weary Titan*.

7 For an excellent overview of Britain's strategic position and policy, see Williamson, *The Politics of Grand Strategy*, chap. 1.

8 On the army-navy struggle over the defence of Canada, see Bourne, *Britain and the Balance of Power*, chaps 8–9; Wells, "British Strategic Withdrawal," 335–56; and Gooch, "Great Britain and the Defence of Canada," 369–85.

9 See Marder, *From the Dreadnought to Scapa Flow*, vol. 1, chap. 3; Mackay, *Fisher of Kilverstone*, esp. 263–5, 286–321; and Rhodri Williams, *Defending the Empire*, chap. 5.

10 Great Britain, Parliament, "Distribution and Mobilization of the Fleet," December 1904 (Cmd 2335); and Willock, "Gunboat Diplomacy," 102–5.

11 Great Britain, PRO, CID Memorandum 46C, "Memorandum by the Admiralty on the Garrisons of Defended Stations Abroad," 2 February 1907, CAB 5/2.

12 Barry Gough, *Royal Navy and the Northwest Coast of North America*, 220–42, and "The End of Pax Britannica," 19–30; and Sarty, "Silent Sentry," chap. 2.

13 Sarty, "Silent Sentry," chap. 3.

14 Copies of the defence scheme are in DHist, 340.003 (D1); copies of the Colonial/Overseas Defence Committee printed comments and other memoranda are in NA, file 343, pts 7–8, RG 7, G 21, vol. 234.

15 Bourne, *Britain and the Balance of Power*, 364, 389; Wells, "British Strategic Withdrawal," 344–7; Gordon, *The Dominion Partnership in Imperial Defense*, 183–4; and Gooch, "Great Britain and the Defence of Canada," esp. 382–3.

16 Sarty, "Silent Sentry," 123–6.

17 See House of Commons, *Debates*, 10 July 1905, cols 9116–7; 27 March 1908, cols 5734–5; 19 March 1909, col. 2265; 5 May 1911, cols 8515–6.

18 Sarty, "Canadian Maritime Defence," 462–90.

19 See, for example, Mackay, *Fisher of Kilverstone*, 297–303, 376–7.

20 DHist, Clauson, CDC Memorandum 359M: "Submarine Mining Defence at Halifax," 22 January 1906, 340.003 (D20).

21 NA, director engineer services to master-general of ordnance, 19 February 1906, HQS 351, RG 24, vol. 2405; NA, Officer Commanding Maritime Provinces to secretary of the Militia Council, 27 November 1906, enclosing district officer in charge of defence lights, Halifax, 10 November 1906, HQC 544, pt 1, RG 24, vol. 2436; NA, chancellor, Colonial Defence Memorandum 399 M, "Defence of Halifax against Torpedo Attack," 27 February 1908, file 343(8), RG 7, G 21, vol. 234; and Great Britain, PRO, chancellor, CDC 400

M/CID 54C, "Liability of Defended Ports abroad to Attack by Torpedo Craft," 27 February 1908, CAB 8/4.

22 NA, Kingsmill to minister of marine and fisheries, 19 April 1909, NS 1017–1–1, RG 24, vol. 3830.

23 NA, Admiralty memoranda, October 1912, MG 26H, vol. 124, files 66917–21; and DHist, Admiralty, "Supplementary Note to Memorandum on Best Method of Harbour and Coast Defence," 12 October 1912, 81/744.

24 Sarty, "Silent Sentry," 191–2, 219–21. The "Local Naval Arrangements" chapter for the Halifax defence scheme, revised to June 1914, is in NA, NS 1001–1–7, pt 1, RG 24, vol. 6196.

25 Armstrong, "Canadian Home Defence."

26 NA, Stephens to director of the naval service, 6 May 1914, NS 1014–3–2, RG 24, vol. 3824; NA, CGS to officer commanding 6th Division, 16 March 1914, extract from proceedings of 15th meeting of militia-navy interdepartmental committee, 8 May 1914, HQS 66, pt 8, RG 24, vol. 2322; and NDHQ Library, Halifax Defence Scheme revised to April 1914, Table A(ii).

27 Sarty, "Silent Sentry," 220–2.

28 Great Britain, PRO, [illegible signature] to chief of staff, "After CID Inquiry is over," n.d. [early 1913], Jackson to First Sea Lord, "Proposed Redistribution of Cruisers to Be Employed Abroad," 6 May 1913, ADM 116/3088.

29 Sarty, "Silent Sentry," 262–7, 277–80.

30 Tucker, *Naval Service*, 1:212–5, 1:237–44; see also Hadley and Sarty, *Tin-Pots and Pirate Ships*, chap. 4.

31 Tucker, *Naval Service*, 1:218–9.

32 NA, Harcourt to governor general of Canada, telegram, 17 September 1914, MG 26 H, reel C-4440, file 160909.

33 NA, Gwatkin to Rutherford, 1 October 1914, Gwatkin Papers.

34 NA, Phipps Hornby to director of the naval service, telegram, 23 September 1914, NSC 1001–5–3, RG 24, vol. 6194.

35 DHist, Naval Historical Section, "Ships and Vessels of the RCN on the Atlantic Coast in the Great War 1914–1918," 17 July 1963.

36 Gaddis Smith, *Britain's Clandestine Submarines*.

37 Hadley and Sarty, *Tin-Pots and Pirate Ships*, chap. 5; and McKee, *Armed Yachts*, chaps 2–3.

38 Hadley and Sarty, *Tin-Pots and Pirate Ships*, chap. 7.

39 Harris, "Canadian Warship Construction 1917–1919," 149–58.

40 Great Britain, PRO, Admiral Browning's monthly "General Letters," ADM 137/504.

41 Great Britain, PRO, Admiral Grant's monthly "General Letters," ADM 137/504. These are especially useful on all aspects of Canadian and British naval activities in 1918; and Hadley and Sarty, *Tin-Pots and Pirate Ships*, chaps 8–9.

42 For example, see NA, General Officer Commanding Military District 6 to secretary of the Militia Council, 19 September 1916, HQ 54–21–11–102,

RG 24, vol. 850; NA, Mewburn, "Minutes of Meeting of COs of Active Militia Regiments MD 6 ... 14 April 1917," HQC 2042, pt 1, RG 24, vol. 2542; and NA, Mewburn, "Particulars of Guards in Military District No. 6," 18 April 1917, HQ 54–21–11–124, pt 1, RG 24, vol. 853.

43 Quote from Admiral Superintendent, Halifax Dockyards, to General Officer Commanding Military District 6, 22 February 1918, in NA, file 501–1–1, pt 1, RG 24, vol. 11122; for the military's position, see NA, Lessard, "Memorandum and Recommendations from G.O.C.M.D. No. 6, Regarding the Reorganization of the Defences of Halifax, N.S.," 27 February 1918, and appendices, HQS 66, pt 10, RG 24, vol. 2323.

44 NA, Lang, "Memorandum on the Reorganization and Efficiency of the Defences of Halifax and Nova Scotia, 11th February to 11th November, 1918," 12 December 1918, HQS 66, pt 10, RG 24, vol. 2323; see also Sarty, "Silent Sentry," 328–36.

45 Kealy and Russell, *History of Canadian Naval Aviation*, 2–4.

46 Hadley and Sarty, *Tin-Pots and Pirate Ships*, chaps 10–11; and Sarty, "Hard Luck Flotilla," 110–25.

47 For example, see Nelles to minister, "Review of the Naval Requirements of Canada and the Existing Situation, 29th September 1939," NHS 1650–1 (Policy), pt 1, a useful paper that digests the recommendations the Naval Staff had made since 1935.

### CHAPTER EIGHT

1 Representative of these themes are Jockel, *No Boundaries Upstairs*; Granatstein, *Canada 1957–1967*, esp. chaps 5 and 9; and Bothwell, *Canada and the United States*, 70–98.

2 *Crowsnest* 14, no. 1 (November 1961): 7.

3 Friedman, *The Postwar Naval Revolution*, esp. 9–10, 29.

4 On fleet composition, see Hobson, *The Composition of Canada's Naval Fleet*, 58, 71. On the budget restriction, see, DHist, Col. R.L. Raymont, "Report on the Organization and Procedures Designed to Develop Canadian Defence Policy ... ," ref. no. 79/17, vol. 1, February 1978, 187–8.

5 NA, PCO, "Memorandum to the Cabinet. National Defence Equipment Programmes, 1965–1966 to 1969–70," Cab. doc. 497/64, 16 November 1964; and NA, PCO, Cabinet Minutes, 8 December 1964.

6 The Panel on the Economic Aspects of Defence Questions represented these three interests on a continual basis at the COSC level. See NA, "Privy Council Panel of the Economic Aspects of Defence Questions," RG 49 (Defence Production), vols 707 and 708, file 247–5.

7 This according to the former director general of ships, Davis, "The St. Laurent Decision," 194.

8 The Policy Planning Coordinating Committee (PPCC) was renamed the Naval Policy Coordinating Committee (NPCC) in 1960.

9 NA, "Oral Presentation to the Chiefs of Staff Committee, Russia's Naval Capabilities," Captain H.N. Lay, 7 June 1946, RG 24 (National Defence), vol. 8067, file NSM 1270–15–7, v. 1.

10 On this program, see Davis, "The St. Laurent Decision," 187–208.

11 Bothwell and Kilbourn, *C.D. Howe: A Biography*, 257.

12 NA, Brooke Claxton Papers, MG 32-B5, vol. 222, memoirs.

13 Three recent studies prepared by Perras are very illuminating on these strategic policy statements: *The Birth of Forward Defence*; *Massive Retaliation*; and *Nato and the Defence of Europe*.

14 On the consequences of MC-48 for naval plans, see DHist, (Naval) Policy Planning Coordinating Committee, minutes, "Ad Hoc Committee on the Reappraisal of Current War Plans," 17 September 1956, ACC 79/249; and COSC Minutes, "Minutes of Special Meeting," 26 October 1955, 73/1223, file 1303.

15 NA, memorandum from J.G. Knowlton, rear admiral (E), to VCNS, 31 May 1955, "RCN Estimates," RG 24, 83–84/167, box 3549, file 8000–35, pt. 1.

16 DHist, NS minute 32/55–30, October 1955.

17 Canada joined the project shortly after inception and participated as well in an abortive British inshore system, which SOSUS eventually replaced. Most details of this system remain classified, although it appears that the Soviet Union was kept abreast of the technical aspects of these developments through an operative placed in charge of the Admiralty's underwater research establishment. See, DHist, Naval Board Minutes , "Special Meeting," 16 November 1953; and "Special Meeting," 5 October 1954. On the agent Alister Watson, see Peter Wright, *Spy Catcher*, 251–60, 267, 291, 332; and Costelo, *Mask of Treachery*, 145, 156–7, 474, 561, 598, 605, 614.

18 The science of data-sound processing largely had to be invented to produce timely plotting of submarine contacts. Into the mid-1960s computer technologies did not provide for the timely production of these plots.

19 In 1956 that was only 200 nautical miles, but by 1960 it was judged to be between 1,000 and 1,500 nautical miles. See NA, "Some Factors Pertinent to the MC 48 War Concept," esp. "Annex I – Force Requirements for the Support of Sound Surveillance Systems," memo from director of naval plans to ACNS (Plans), 14 February 1956, RG 24 83–84/167, vol. 457, file 1650–26, vol. 15.

20 If there was one helicopter per two ships, then not more than forty minutes was required to reach the DATUM point. As for maritime patrol aircraft, maintaining three on continuous patrol would give a time on DATUM of forty minutes. With those performance requirements, a fleet of forty Neptune patrol aircraft was required to provide twenty-four-hour patrol. DHist, "Some Factors Pertinent to the MC 48 War Concept."

21 These forces were to be stationed at Brest and Milford-Haven in the event of hostilities and would operate at the discretion of SACLANT.

22 For the development of Soviet submarines and missile technologies, see Breemer, *Soviet Submarines*; and Jordan, *Soviet Submarines, 1945 to Present*.

23 At one point the Americans sought Canadian adoption of new rules of engagement that would have authorized ship's captains to force an unidentified vessel, operating within or in proximity to territorial waters, to the surface, by fire if necessary. Although the Canadians prevailed in stating such a response was unacceptable to the Canadian government, this illustrates the level of concern. DHist, Naval Board Minutes, 592–6, 8 April 1959; and DHist, memorandum from CNS to chairman, Chief of Staff, "RCN Submarine Programme," 18 November 1959, 73/1223, series 1, file 379.

24 See NA, "Prediction of Operational Exposure Periods in ASW," in ASW Operational Research Team, Closed Circulation Report, RG 24 83–84/167, cited in German, *The Sea Is at Our Gate*, 272.

25 DHist, "Notes on NSS 1279–118," Brock to 12th Senior Officers' Meeting, 20 November 1961, Naval Policy 1650–1, vol. 3.

26 DHist, Naval Board Minutes, 564–3, 570–4, 1958.

27 DHist, Naval Board Minutes, 540–2, 28 August 1957.

28 NA, PCO, Cabinet Minutes, 19 December 1956, RG 2, vol. 5775.

29 NA, "RCN Position Regarding G-I-UK Study Group Recommendations," Appendix A, 26 September 1960, RG 24 83–84/167, box 89, NSS 1270–78–1, vol. 6.

30 DHist, Naval Board Minutes, 576–4, 24 September 1958.

31 DHist, COSC Minutes, 588, 9 February 1956; DHist, PPCC Minutes, 56–8, 19 March 1956; and DHist, Naval Board Minutes, 482–2, 10 April 1956.

32 DHist, Naval Board Minutes, 482–3, 21 March 1956.

33 DHist, COSC Minutes, 588–9, 9 February 1956; DHist, PPCC Minutes, 56–8, 19 March 1956; DHist, Naval Board Minutes, 482–2, 10 April 1956; DHist, COSC Minutes, 592–4, 12 April 1956; NA, record of CDC 111th meeting, 13 August 1956, and 113th meeting, 6–7 February 1957, RG 24, 83–84/167, vol. 3549, file 8000–35, pt. 2; DHist, Naval Board Minutes, 517, 19 January 1957; NA, letter from George Pearkes, minister of national defence, to CNS, 8 August 1957, RG 24 83–84/167, file, 3549, pt. 2; and 114th CDC Minutes, 19 August 1957.

34 For this analysis, see NA, message from Maritime Commander, Atlantic, to naval secretary, "Analysis of Operations 7–8 September 1958, Analysis of Contact P-86," 15 September 1958, RG 24 83–84/167, vol. 455.

35 DHist, "A/S Detection Equipment – Variable Depth Sonar – AN/SQS 504," 79/246 PPCC files, project EE-5. See also *Maritime Warfare Bulletin: Commemorative Edition 1985* (Maritime Warfare School Halifax/Department of National Defence, 1985), 45–53, 66–74.

36 "The Conversion Program," *Crowsnest* 115, no. 4 (April 1963): 9.

37 See DHist, PPCC Minutes, 103–3, 17 March 1958, 79/246; DHist, Naval Board Minutes, 564–4, 2 April 1958. See "ASW Weapons Effectiveness Study, 1957–1967," Director of Undersea Warfare, 18 September 1957, discussed in 120th PPCC meeting, 15 November 1957, and NS, 24–1957, 29 October 1957, Naval Board Minutes 552, 20 November 1957.

38 The CNS gained authority to plan the modernization program after a private meeting with the ministers of defence, external affairs, and finance. See marginal note by CNS on Cabinet memorandum 4–57, 14 August 1957, in NA, RG 24 83–84/167, box 3549, file 8000–35, vol. 2.

39 DHist, Naval Board Minutes, 575, 10 September 1958; 79/246 PPCC files, project D-4, see memorandum VCNS to CNS, "Policy on Bringing Fleet to Maximum A/S Capability," 23 September 1958. On the recommendation to hurriedly fit the VDS, see NA, "Message from Maritime Commander Atlantic to Naval Secretary," 15 September 1958, RG 24 83–84/167, vol. 455.

40 These vessels were essential for enabling the fleet to operate for prolonged periods approximately 1,000 nautical miles from Canada's shores. DHist, Naval Board Minutes, 573–4, 583–5, 1958, in which the draft characteristics were approved.

41 On helicopter effectiveness and need for VDS, see DHist, Naval Board Minutes, 576–4, 24 September 1958. Before committing to these new systems, Naval Board recommended further study using two vessels converted to test the concept. The vessels converted were HMCS *Sioux* and HMCS *Crusader*. As well, an examination was to be made of the feasibility of converting the five frigates with the longest remaining operational service so that they could carry up to three helicopters.

42 DHist, Naval Board Minutes, 564–4, 2 April 1958; 79/246 PPCC Minutes, 103–3, 17 March 1958. See "ASW Weapons Effectiveness Study, 1957–1967," Director of Undersea Warfare, 18 September 1957, discussed in 120th PPCC meeting, 15 November 1957, and NS, 24–1957, 29 October 1957, Naval Board Minutes, 552, 20 November 1957.

43 DHist, Naval Board Minutes, "Special Meeting," 16 November 1953, provides an early example of the British response to American ASW submarines.

44 Davis lends many particular insights on Spencer's views in "It Has All Happened Before," 34–41.

45 DHist, "Progress Report on the RCN Nuclear Submarine Study," 79/246 PPCC files, project L-2 NSS 8000-SSN.

46 The Canadian Nuclear Submarine Survey Team concluded that an atomic boat could be built in Canada according to an American design for approximately $65 million. A British-designed conventional boat of the Porpoise (progenitor of the Oberon) class could be constructed for $15 to $18 million in Canada or $9 million in the UK. See "RCN Submarine Programme," memorandum from CNS to COSC, 18 November 1959, 2. For the entire Nuclear Submarine Survey, see DHist, 79/246 PPCC files, projects L-1 and L-2.

47 See NA, (Staff) minister's memo to CDC, 9 January 1961, cited, R.J. Pickford, director of naval plans, to VCNS, 12 November 1961, RG 24 83–84/167, vol. 3549, file 8000–35, pt. 4, NSS 8000–35. On the operational advantages and disadvantages, see DHist, J.C. Arnell, science adviser to CNS, comments on "A Nuclear Powered Submarine Program" by Dr. R.J. Sutherland, memorandum to CNS, 16 March 1964, 79/246 PPCC files, project AA-4; and DHist, Directorate of Naval Operational Requirements, "Operational Requirements for RCN Submarines," 17 June 1963, 79/246 PPCC files, project M-4.

48 DHist, "RCN Submarine Programme," 18 November 1959, 73/1223 series 1, file 379, and draft submission to CDC, "RCN Submarine Programme," 10 November 1960; DHist, "The Report of the 1962 Submarine Committee," July 1962, 79/246 PPCC files, project F-3, all provide detailed historical survey and comparative statistics on the operational performance of the Barbel-and Oberon-class boats.

49 DHist, "The Report of the 1962 Submarine Committee," July 1962, 79/246 PPCC files, project F-3.

50 NA, "NATO Annual Review. Draft Comments for Guidance of Canadian Delegation on Prepared List of Questions," 23 October 1958, RG 49, vol. 708, file 247–5, vol. 4.

51 NA, PCO Cabinet Minutes, "MC 70, The Minimum Essential Force Requirements 1958–1963," 22 March 1960.

52 DHist, Naval Board Minutes, 630, "An Examination of the Implications of Implementing the 1961/62 Defence Programme within the 1960/61 Budget Limitations," 6 September 1960.

53 DHist, 79/249 PPCC files, project D-4. See especially "Minutes of Special Meeting of the Ship Characteristics Panel," NSS 8885–1, 12 November 1958.

54 DHist, PPCC Minutes, 192–2, 3 May 1960, memorandum to CDC, "Ship Replacement Programme," 21 January 1960, RG 24 83–84/167, vol. 3549, file 8000–35, pt. 3, which called for a six ship program, with the vessels expected to cost $20 million each.

55 DHist, COSC Minutes, 649, 19 November 1959.

56 DHist, *The Report of the Ad Hoc Committee on Naval Objectives* (Ottawa, 1961) (hereafter Brock Report).

57 Brock, *The Thunder and the Sunshine*, 80.

58 During the Korean War, naval expenditures represented 1.24 per cent of GNP; over the decade of the 1950s they declined to a low of 0.7 per cent. The ten-year average was 0.98 per cent. See Brock Report.

59 Jeffrey V. Brock, *The Thunder and the Sunshine*, 95–8.

60 DHist, Naval Board Minutes, 659, September–December 1961.

61 Compare Haydon, "When Military Plans and Policies Conflict," 2:59, with Cuthbertson, *Canadian Military Independence*, 129–30.

62 DHist, Naval Board Minutes, 642–3, 17 January 1961.

63 The RN recently produced a new Tribal class, the Type 81 frigate, and the USN the guided-missile Charles F. Adams–class frigate.

64 DHist, Naval Board Minutes "Special Meeting," 22 July 1960; NA, memorandum from VCNS to CNTS, 8 August 1960, RG 24 83–84/167, vol. 3549, file 8000–35, pt. 4.

65 DHist, Naval Board Minutes, "Special Meeting," 22 July 1960; 12th Senior Officers' Meeting, 20–21 November 1961.

66 DHist, COSC Minutes, 686, 16 March 1961.

67 Ibid., 692, 18 May 1961.

68 DHist, PPCC/NPCC Minutes, 255–2, 18 December 1962.

69 DHist, Naval Board Minutes, 648, 21 April 1961.

70 The possible acquisition of nuclear weapons was under constant study through the late 1950s. However, no major steps were taken to actually retain nuclear depth bombs in Canada or on its warships until 1964. See DHist, COSC Minutes, 667-VI, 11 August 1960; PPCC Minutes, 293–1, 4 March 1964.

71 NA, memorandum from DNOPS Captain J.C. Littler to ANCS(P) Commodore D.W. Piers, 11 August 1960, RG 24 83–84/167, vol. 3549, file 8000–35, pt. 4. See also Piers's reply attached.

72 DHist, COSC Minutes 680, 9 January 1961.

73 See NA, RG 24 83–84/167, vol. 3549, file 8000–35, pts 3 and 4; DHist, NPCC files, "The Report of the 1962 Submarine Survey"; and NA, PCO, Cab. doc. 54/62, 7 February 1962, and Cabinet Minutes, 19 March 1962.

74 House of Commons, *Debates*, 11 April 1962, 2835.

75 NA, "Naval Shipbuilding Economic Considerations General Purpose Frigate Programme," 27 May 1963, RG 49, vol. 1, file 39-N-1521–2.

76 For these developments, see NA, report of A.W. Allan, J. Longhurst and G. Hughes-Adams to J.C. Rutledge, director of shipbuilding, DDP, 28 June 1962, RG 49, vol. 1, file 39–N–1521–2; NA, letter from director general of ships to A.J.C. Pomeroy, Defence Supply Naval Shipbuilding Panel, 14 December 1962, RG 49, vol. 1, file 39–N–1521–2; and NA, letter from G.W. Hunter, deputy minister of defence production, to secretary of Treasury Board, 29 January 1963, RG 49, vol. 1, file 39–N–1521–2.

77 Plomer, in *Maclean's*, 7 September 1963, 22–3, 44–5, 50. The program had been attacked in the press when first announced; see Charles Lynch, "A Wasteful Make-Work Navy Project," *Ottawa Citizen*, 14 April 1962. Lynch's criticism was unceasing.

78 See Rayner's testimony in Sauvé Committee proceedings, 15 October 1963.

79 NA, J.C. Rutledge to W.H. Huck, assistant deputy minister, Defence Production, 15 July 1963, RG 49, vol. 1, file 39–N–1521–2.

80 NA, PCO, Cab. doc. 195–63, 1 August 1963; and NA, Cabinet Minutes, 2 August 1963.

81 NA, PCO, CDC doc. D9–63, 27 September 1963, attached to Cab. doc. 293–63, "Naval Ship Procurement," 4 October 1963, and Cabinet Minutes, 10 October 1963.

82 NA, PCO, Cabinet Minutes, 2 August 1963.

83 Ibid., 10 October 1963.

84 Ibid., 4 December 1963.

85 DND, *White Paper on Defence* (1964), 9.

86 DHist, VCNS files, "Naval Programmes"; vols 1 and 2 are devoted exclusively to the reduction of forces under Hellyer. See also DHist, NS Minutes, 1/64, 7 January 1964, and NPCC files, project AA-3, "Ad Hoc Working Group, and project AA-4, "Studies on the Future Composition of the Fleet." See also Cameron, "The Royal Canadian Navy and the Unification Crisis," 334–44.

## CHAPTER NINE

1 Deacon, *The Silent War.* Chapter 5 gives a general account of German and Allied naval sigint in the First World War.

2 Great Britain, PRO, "Report of Committee regarding Government Wireless, Telegraphs, Cables and Other Means of Communications" (n.d., c. 1922), 1880–13, RG 11, vol. 2851.

3 Great Britain, PRO, "N.I.D. History 1893–1923," NID 10388/21, ADM 116/1842 (n.d., c. 1923), copy held at DHist.

4 Hinsley et al., *British Intelligence*, 1:40.

5 DHist, Cmdr E.S. Brand, RN, "Annual Report of DNI, Ottawa Year 1939," 31 December 1939, 81/145, 29.

6 DHist, Captain E.S. Brand, RCN, to DNI Admiralty, 19 April 1944, 81/145, vol. 1, 1; and DHist, "History and Activities of Operational Intelligence Centre, N.H.Q. – 1939 to 1945" (n.d., c. October 1945), 1440–18, Introduction, 1 (hereafter OIC History).

7 Brand to DNI Admiralty, 19 April 1944, 1.

8 NA, Radio Division, Department of Transport, "Report on Wartime Interception Service," in Department of Transport War Activities 1939–45, 11–19–20, Ottawa, 12 October 1948, RG 12, box 2157 (hereafter DOT Radio Div. Report).

9 NA, "Extract from 'Y' Log, 11 February 43, NSS 1008–75–44, RG 24, vol. 3807; and Brand, DNI Annual Report 1939, 12.

10 Much of what we know about de Marbois, unfortunately, comes from his own hand: see DHist, de Marbois biographical file (hereafter DHist Biog deM).

11 DHist, C.H. Little, "My Early Days in Naval Intelligence 1939–41" (hereafter DHist Biog L), 1.

12 NA, naval secretary to COAC, 22 November 1939, 501–2–6, RG 24, D 10, vol. 11123.

13 NA, NSHQ to Admiralty, 1246, 5 September 1939, 501–2–6, RG 24, D 10, vol. 11123.

14 NA, Admiralty to NSHQ, 2159, 15 September 1939, 501–2–6, RG 24, D 10, vol. 11123. The Admiralty message said it would be "desirable" that bearings be passed to Bermuda.

15 NA, Brand to Worth, 23 October 1939, 501–2–6, RG 24, D 10, vol. 11123.

16 For Transport's assessment, see NA, Deptartment of Transport district superintendent (Halifax) to COAC, 15 November 1939 and 30 November 1939, 501–2–6, RG 24, D 10, vol. 11123. See also NA, SSO to COAC, 17 November 1939, 501–2–6, RG 24, D 10, vol. 11123.

17 Brand's reaction to Worth's initial proposals was swift and negative. He informed Worth that there would be no direct connection between Hartlen Point and NSHQ – or any other Canadian naval facility. See NA, naval secretary to COAC, 30 November 1939 and 5 December 1939, NS 1008–75–1, RG 24, D10, vol. 11123.

18 NA, de Marbois to DNI, 7 February 1940, NSS 1008–75–44, RG 24, vol. 3807.

19 DHist, "Naval Weekly Reports," nos 16, 17, 18 for 4, 11, and 18 January 1940, NSS 1000–5–7; and DNI Annual Report 1939, 12–13.

20 NA, de Marbois to DNI, "Report on Strathburn w/t Station," 14 February 1940, NSS 1008–75–44, RG 24, vol. 3807. Strathburn monitored German commercial traffic, which was sometimes interspersed with naval messages.

21 DHist, "Summary of Naval War Effort 1 January–31 March 40," NS 1000–5–8, Naval Historian's Files.

22 NA, Bartram to C-in-C AWI, 9 February 1940, NSS 1008–75–44, RG 24, vol. 3807.

23 Admiralty had also stationed a senior British sea commander, Rear Admiral Commanding 3rd Battle Squadron (RA3), at Halifax.

24 NA, de Marbois to DNI, "H/F D/F Unit in Eastern Canada, Report of FIS's visit to Halifax 20 March to 30th," 1 April 1940, NSS 1008–75–44, RG 24, vol. 3807; and DHist, "Naval Weekly Reports," no. 27, 21 March 1940, NSS 1000–5–7, 2.

25 NA, DCNS to C-in-C AWI, "DF Communications," 6 May 1940, NSS 1008–75–32, RG 24, vol. 3807.

26 NA, de Marbois to COAC, 11 May 1940, 501–2–6, RG 24, D 10, vol. 11123.

27 NA, C-in-C AWI to NSHQ, 8 June 1940, NSS 1008–75–32, RG 24, vol. 3807.

28 NA, Lt-Cmdr D.E. Cox to de Marbois, 4 October 1940, NSS 1008–75–32, section 1, RG 24, vol. 3807.

29 NA, DNI to Captain H.R. Sandwith, RN, Signal Department Section 9, Admiralty, 15 October 1940, NSS 1008–75–44, RG 24, vol. 3807.

30 NA, FIS to DNI, "Foreign Section Naval Int," 31 December 1940, NSS 1008–75–44, RG 24, vol. 3807.

31 NA, SO FIS to Lt-Cmdr D.E. Cox, RN, HMS *Malabar*, 28 October 1940, NSS 1008–75–32, RG 24, vol. 3807. Far Eastern Combined Bureau and Far Eastern Direction Finding Organization reports arrived at NSHQ starting in July 1940.

32 NA, FIS to DNI, "WT I and HF DF period October–14 December 40," 16 December 1940, NSS 1008–75–44, RG 24, vol. 3807.

33 Ibid.

34 NA, NLOs Hartlen Point and Newfoundland and de Marbois, "Observations made by W/T Int Officers for NSHQ during visit to Bermuda 'Y' and D/F Organisation," 12 February 1941, NSS 1008–75–32, RG 24, vol. 3807; and NA, C-in-C AWI to NSHQ 377, 3 June 1941, NSS 1008–75–44, RG 24, vol. 3807.

35 NA, de Marbois to Cox, 11 February 41, NSS 1008–75–32, sec. 1, RG 24, vol. 3807.

36 NA, CNS to C-in-C AWI, 13 February 1941, NSS 1008–75–10, RG 24, vol. 3805.

37 NA, C-in-C AWI to CNS, AWI 377, 7 March 1941, NSS 1008–75–10, RG 24, vol. 3805.

38 NA, C-in-C AWI to NSHQ, "Analysis of D/F Bearings," 21 April 1941, NSS 1008–75–10, RG 24, vol. 3805.

39 NA, CNS to C-in-C AWI, 6 May 1941, NSS 1008–75–10, sec. 1, RG 24, vol. 3805. A copy remains of Brand's revisions to de Marbois's draft of this letter: FIS to DNI, n.d., NSS 1008–75–10, sec. 1, RG 24, vol. 3805.

40 Great Britain, PRO, "America and West Indies Station – War Diaries February 41–January 42," War Diary No. 19, pt 1 (May 1941); and War Diary No. 20, pt 1 (June 1941), ADM 199/402 (copy held at DHist).

41 NA, C-in-C AWI to CNS, "D/F and 'Y' Organisation on America and West Indies Station," AWI 0511, 28 June 1941, NSS 1008–75–10, RG 24, vol. 3805.

42 DHist, DND, "Summary of Naval War Effort 1 April–31 June 41," item 7, Intelligence.

43 Ibid.; and NA, Brand to Sandwith, 7 July 1941, NSS 1008–75–10, pt 1, RG 24, vol. 3805. Only the station at Gordon Head had been exclusively manned by naval personnel.

44 DHist, DND, "Summary of Naval War Effort 1 April–31 June 41," item 7, Intelligence.

45 NA, Sandwith to Brand, 4 June 1941, NSS 1008–75–10, sec. 1, RG 24, vol. 3805.

46 NA, Lt J.R. Foster, RCNVR, to Cmdr J.M. de Marbois, "Report on Visit to Admiralty" (n.d., c. 30 August 1941), NSS 1008–75–44, RG 24, vol. 3805.

47 John Ralph Foster's background is difficult to confirm. He claimed service in the RN and RNCVR as a warrant officer telegraphist and, from 1922 to 1926, in the Canadian Corps of Signals. See Canada, DND, DHist Biog F.

48 NA, "Admiralty Classification of Bearings Reference Sheet," 19 September 1941, NSS 1008–75–10, RG 24, vol. 3805. Bearings were classified according to their quality.

49 "Summary of Naval War Effort, 1 July to 30 September 1941," item 6.

50 NA, NSHQ to Admiralty DSD 9 for Lt Foster, 5 August 1941, NSS 1008–75–10, RG 24, vol. 3805. The TINA and range estimation equipment had to be released by the Admiralty before the RCN could purchase it; see NA, Admiralty DSD to NSHQ for DNI from Lt Foster, 2 August 1941, NSS 1008–75–10, RG 24, vol. 3805.

51 NA, Admiralty to NSHQ, 10 September 1941, NSS 1008–75–10, RG 24, vol. 3805.

52 The National Research Council of Canada, Radio Branch, Report No. ERA 141, "The War History of the Radio Branch" (Ottawa: August 1948), 37. A few years later, an ionospheric research station was established at Churchill, Manitoba.

53 NA, FIS memorandum, 4 December 1941, NSS 1008–75–10, RG 24, vol. 3805.

54 "Summary of Naval War Effort, 1 October to 31 December 41," item 6.

55 NA, Admiralty to NSHQ, 1716A, 7 January 1942, NSS 1008–7–44, RG 24, vol. 3807.

56 NA, untitled, 19 February 1942, MG 42, DO 35/548D B-4963; the title and author of the document were omitted during photocopying.

57 NA, Sandwith to de Marbois, 3 February 1942, NSS 1008–75–10, RG 24, vol. 3805.

58 NA, NSHQ to COPC, 0100Z, 21 January 1942, NS 1008–4–7, sec. 1, RG 24, vol. 3803; and OIC History, OIC 3 1942, 1.

59 De Marbois did resist later when it became obvious that there was no role for Canadian west coast resources, except as suppliers of raw material to the USN's far larger system.

60 NA, Sandwith to Brand, 19 February 42, NSS 1008–75–10, RG 24, vol. 3805.

61 Beesly, *Very Special Intelligence*, 106–10; Hinsley, *British Intelligence*, 2:48; and Great Britain, PRO, Rodger Winn, OIC 8s, "Submitted herewith the following account of my recent visit to Washington made with the object of establishing an effective U/B Tracking Room," 3 June 1942, NID 002956/42, ADM 223/107, Godfrey Archive, vol. 39; copy held at DHist (hereafter Winn Report).

62 NA, Sandwith to Brand, 19 February 42, NS 1008–75–10, RG 24, vol. 3805.

63 NA, RN, Signal Department Section 9, "Composition and TORs of Y Mission to US and Canada," 9 February 1942, NSS 1008–75–20, RG 24, vol. 3806 (hereafter TORs, Y Mission). This copy has marginal notes that assign NSHQ officers to the various areas to be covered by the Y Mission.

64 The Americans referred to "Y" as Radio Intelligence (RadInt) and named the meetings accordingly. De Marbois and Sandwith both refer to the conference as the "Y" Conference.

65 Hinsley, *British Intelligence*, 2:56; and NA, "Canadian Report on United States–British Radio Intelligence Conference, April 6–16, 1942 in Washington, D.C. at the Navy Department," n.d., NSS 1008–75–20, RG 24, vol. 3806 (hereafter "Canadian Report").

66 Hinsley, *British Intelligence*, 2:48, 551; and NA, DDSD(Y) to DOD, 30 November 1942, NSS 1008–75–44, RG 24, vol. 3807.

67 "Canadian Report," Sub-committee A1, "W/T Interception."

68 NA, FIS to DNI and DSD, "'Y' Organisation at NSHQ," 4 May 1942, NSS 1008–75–44, RG 24, vol. 3807.

69 "Canadian Report," Sub-committee A2, "W/T Interception," note; and FIS to DSD and DNI, "'Y' Organisation at NSHQ," 4 May 1942.

70 NA, Captain H.R. Sandwith, RN, "Report on RCN 'Y' Organisation," 19 May 42, NSS 1008–75–20, RG 24, vol. 3806. This document is an excellent overview of the Canadian system in April/May 1942.

71 Winn Report, June 1942, 5–6.

72 DHist, COSC miscellaneous memoranda, 193.009 (D8).

73 NA, OpNav to NSHQ, DN 006 1934/27/4/92, NSS 1008–75–44, RG 24, vol. 3807.

74 OIC History, 1942, 6. Eastern Air Command and the Admiralty were added later.

75 DHist, NS Minutes, 108, 30 July 1942, item 108–2, "Teletype Installation Ottawa Vancouver; Ottawa Esquimalt."

76 Great Britain, PRO, DNI Admiralty, "Notes on D.N.I.'s Visit to Washington September-October 1942," 1 November 1942, NID 005790/42, ADM 223/107, Godfrey Archive, vol. 39; copy held at DHist.

77 NA, FONF to NSHQ and COAC, 1659Z/11/12/1942; and NA, NSHQ to FONF, 2147Z/22/1/43, both in NA, NS 1300–1, sec. 1, RG 24, vol. 11927; and NA, FONF to NSHQ, 27 February 1943, NSS 1008–75–29, RG 24, vol. 3806.

78 For a full discussion of Canadian prosecution of ASW, see Douglas, *The Creation of a National Air Force*, vol. 2, chap. 14, esp. 523–5.

79 Great Britain, PRO, "Minutes of a Meeting Held on 1st and 3rd November, 1942, to Consider the Present Methods Employed in Anti-Submarine Warfare in the Northwest Atlantic and to Make Recommendations for Improvement Thereof," 3 November 1942, NSS 1001–1–16, ADM 1/11750; copy held at DHist.

80 NA, DDSD(Y) to DSD, 7 December 1942, NSS 1008–75–10, RG 24, vol. 3805.

81 OIC History, 1942, 5.

82 NA, FONF to NSHQ, 9 November 1942, NSS 1008–75–29, RG 24, vol. 3806. Using different codes to protect the same text was also poor security.

83 NA, DDSD(Y) to DOD, 30 November 1942, NSS 1008–75–24, sec. 1, RG 24, vol. 3806. Minutes on FONF's 9 November 1942 letter indicate that DSD was building up evidence of COMINCH's and COAC's duplication.

84 NA, DDSD(Y) to DOD, "Promulgation of D/F bearings obtained at NSHQ," 30 November 1942, NSS 1008–75–44, RG 24, vol. 3807.

85 NA, Nelles to King, 1 December 1942, NS 8740–102/1, sec. 1, RG 24, vol. 11928. Much of the credit for Nelles's supporting arguments goes to Horatio Nelson Lay, then director of Operations Division: Tucker, *Naval Service*, 2:406–7. De Marbois drafted those sections concerned with Canadian contribution to sigint and U-boat locating.

86 For a full discussion of ABC (American-British Conversations) 1 and ABC 22, see Stacey, *Arms, Men and Governments*, 159–60; 349–54 for ABC 1; and 349, 354, 356–7, 360, 362–4, 366, 389 for ABC 22.

87 NA, King to Nelles, "Operational control of northwest convoy lanes west of 35 degrees West," 17 December 1942, NS 8740–102/1, sec. 1, RG 24, vol. 11928.

88 NA, Nelles to COAC, FONF, and NMCJS, 19 January 1943; and NA, NS 8740–102/1, sec. 1, RG 24, vol. 11928.

89 For a full account of the Atlantic Convoy Conference and its significance, see Douglas, *The Creation of a National Air Force*, 2:546–9.

90 NA, Brodeur to Murray, 5 February 1943, NS 8740–102/1, pt 1, RG 24, vol. 11928.

91 DHist, "Atlantic Convoy Conference Washington, D.C. March 1 to March 12, 1943, Report of Conference," Copy No. 38, NDHQ, Directorate of History 181.009 (D268) (hereafter ACC March 1943), 5–6; and Stacey, *Arms, Men and Governments*.

92 ACC March 1943, 6.

93 NA, DDSD(Y) to DSD, director of Operations Division, VCNS and CNS, NS 1008–75–41, 23 February 1943, RG 24, vol. 11928; and "History and Activities of Operational Intelligence Centre, N.H.Q. – 1939 to 1945" (unpublished MS, c. October 1945 – copy held at DHist), 1–2.

94 Recommendations of the Sub-committee on Communications and Operational Intelligence (A.C.C. 5), 5 March 1943, in ACC March 1943.

CHAPTER TEN

1 The operation of German submarines in Canadian waters was first thoroughly documented by Hadley, *U-Boats against Canada*. As it turned out, the RCN failed to sink any U-boats near the Canadian coast throughout the entire war. Milner sums it up by stating that "no U-boat was sunk by a Canadian warship west of 50W and north of the Caribbean." Milner, "Inshore ASW," 158. See also Hadley, "Inshore ASW: the U-Boat Experience."

2 Stacey, *Arms, Men and Governments*, 308–9.

3 Zimmerman, *The Great Naval Battle of Ottawa*, 5, 24–5. Zimmerman describes the failure to equip the RCN with modern equipment in a timely manner a "national failure."

4 Tucker, *Naval Service*, 2:261.

5 Zimmerman, *The Great Naval Battle of Ottawa*, 4.

6 Whitby, "In Defence of Home Waters," 169, 171.

7 Milner, *North Atlantic Run*, 10–11.

8 Schull, *The Far Distant Ships*, 428–9.

9 Roskill, *The War at Sea*, 1:134–5, 352–3.

10 Meigs, *Slide Rules and Submarines*, 49.

11 Ibid., 111–12, 146–9.

12 For this and the following, see Milner, *North Atlantic Run*, 102–3, 49–51, 59–60.

13 Lund, "The Royal Canadian Navy's Quest for Autonomy," 138–57.

14 Milner, "The Technological Implications of Technological Backwardness," 46–53.

15 Milner, *North Atlantic Run*, 139.

16 Ibid., 181.

17 Douglas, "Conflict and Innovation," 223–8.

18 The negative impression created by the RCN circa 1942 is best illustrated by the description in Macintyre, *U-Boat Killer*, 88–92.

19 Milner, *North Atlantic Run*, 60.

20 M. Williams, *Captain Gilbert Roberts*.

21 Milner, *North Atlantic Run*, 246.

22 NA, RG 24, vol. 11938, file NS 8440–2, vol. 1. See especially the comments with respect to "Persistence" on page 3.

23 I have been unable to determine the exact date of establishment. Monthly reports for the Halifax Tactical Unit dating from October 1943 are in Canada, DND, DHist, NS 1000–5–13, vol. 20.

24 Tucker, *Naval Service*, 2:427.

25 Schull, *The Far Distant Ships*, 216.

26 Hadley, *U-Boats against Canada*, chaps 8–10. The first schnorkel U-boats to arrive were *U-107* and *U-1222* in the early summer of 1944. They were followed by *U-802*, *U-541*, and *U-1221*. *U-1229* left Norway for the coast of North America on 26 July 1944 but was sunk on 20 August 1944 by aircraft from USS *Bogue* before reaching her destination. These submarines were followed by *U-1223*, *U-1228*, *U-1230*, *U-1231*, and *U-806* by the end of 1944. *U-1232* arrived right at the end of 1944 and scored several successes in the first part of January. *U-190* sank the last Canadian ship of the war off Halifax in April 1945, while *U-805* and *U-889* were also operating in Canadian waters when the war ended. *U-858* surrendered to the USN just on the edge of the Canadian zone, some 300 miles southeast of Newfoundland. *U-889* and *U-190* surrendered to Canadian forces.

27 Hessler, *The U-Boat War in the Atlantic*, sec. 472.

28 NA, memorandum from Acting/Commander D.L. Raymond, RN, DWT, to ACNS, dated 19 October 1944, "Asdic Conditions in the Gulf and off the Nova

Scotia Coast in the Winter," RG 24, 83–84/167, vol. 2616, 16128–1, vol. 1. This memorandum was produced in anticipation of U-boat activity off Halifax during the winter of 1944–45. It stated bluntly in its preamble that "in the light of previous experience it is extremely probable that A/S conditions in the Gulf and off the Coast will be very poor during the winter months due to a severe positive temperature gradient." See also NA, "Minutes of BT Conference Held at NSHQ," 18 to 21 December 1944, RG 24, vol. 11026, file CNA 7–16.

29 McLean, "Confronting Technological and Tactical Change," 92.

30 This generalization is imprecise because numbers kept changing in light of ship availability. There were four Support Groups at Normandy, EGs 6, 9, 11, and 12. By the fall the ships of EGs 11 and 12 were on their last legs mechanically and were combined into one group. In the meantime, EGs 16, 25, 26, and then 27 were formed. Macpherson and Burgess, *The Ships of Canada's Naval Forces*, Appendix 8.

31 Chalmers, *Max Horton*, 207.

32 This assessment is based on a detailed review of the reports of proceedings of EGs 9, 26, and 27 during the winter of 1944–45. A subsequent general re-view of the Reports of Proceedings of EGs 6, 16, 25, and 28 during the same period generally confirms the research done to date. Reports of proceedings can be found at DHist, EG (6,9,16,25,26,27,28), NHS 8440.

33 Chalmers, *Max Horton*, 206.

34 DHist, reports of proceedings for EG 16 and EG 27, NHS 8440.

35 DHist, Admiralty monthly anti-submarine report for August 1944, DHist Library, D 780 M66 1944, July-December.

36 "EI" turns were where ships in line abreast turn in succession commencing with the ship furthest away from centre. The second ship turns as the first passes approximately astern of it. When all ships have turned, the order of ships in line abreast will have been reversed. All ships will then be proceeding in the new direction at the same interval as before. Most importantly, all of the area in the vicinity of the change of direction will be swept equally, which would not be the case if the ships performed an extended wheel in line-abreast formation to alter direction. The diagram accompanying the discussion of the attack on convoy HX 332, found in the January 1945 issue of the Admiralty Monthly Anti-Submarine Report, DHist Library, well illustrates the manoeuvre.

37 NA, memorandum from director of the Tactical Unit, Dockyard, Halifax to Captain(D), Halifax, 1 September 1944, and memorandum from Captain(D), Halifax, to CINCCNA, 7 September 1944, and covering minutes, RG 24, vol. 11022, file CNA 7–6–1.

38 NA, Memorandum entitled "Area Search" from director of the Tactical Unit, Dockyard, Halifax, to Captain(D), Halifax, dated 7 November 1944, but should read 7 December 1944 (enclosure is dated 29 November 1944), RG 24, vol. 11022, file DO23–2–1.

39 NA, NSS 16121–5 FD 894 (Staff), memorandum from secretary of the Naval Board to CINCLANT, 11 April 1945, RG 24, vol. 11022.

40 Douglas, *The Creation of a National Air Force*, 2:604.

41 NA, HMCS *Kirkland Lake* to Ships in Company, 242040Z December 1944, RG 24, vol. 11111, file 55–2–1/542.

42 DHist, log of *U-806*, entry for 1506 on 24 December 1944: "Touched bottom with keel. Decided to remain on bottom at this location," SGR II 257.

43 Time and size of box derived from the following messages:

    a *Kirkland Lake* to Group, 241754Z December, 1944;

    b Literate to All Literates, 241822Z December, 1944;

    c *Kirkland Lake* to Ships in Company, "Appreciation of Situation," 242040Z December, 1944; and

    d *Kirkland Lake* to *Fennel*, 242251Z December, 1944.

All messages in NA, RG 24, vol. 11111, file 55–2–1/542. The order to expand the box to ten miles came approximately nine and a half hours after the torpedoing of *Clayoquot*. In the event the U-boat had not bottomed, the size of the box should have been expanded more rapidly, as a U-boat could travel at about three knots for prolonged periods submerged. Ten miles should have been ordered some three and a half hours after the torpedoing if containment was to be assured.

    *U-806* considered the rate at which the search expanded quite accurate. Her log recorded: "Since the sub had not been detected by nightfall, the search was resumed in circles around the site of the attack. These circles were then extended commensurate with a fairly well calculated submerged running speed." DHist, SGR II 257.

44 Hadley, *U-Boats against Canada*, 267.

45 German, *The Sea Is at Our Gates*, 178–9; and Hadley, *U-Boats against Canada*, 265.

46 DHist, *U-806* log entry for 0200 25 December 1944, SGR II 257.

47 McLean, "The Last Cruel Winter," 59–60.

48 Doug McLean, "The Battle of Convoy BX-141," 23; and Hadley, *U-Boats against Canada*, 278–84.

49 McLean, "The Battle of Convoy BX-141," 28–9.

50 The fact that SO EG 27 followed "the latest tactics as developed by the USN" was revealed to the author by St Clair Balfour through personal correspondence (2 August 1991).

51 The reason that the search was broken off is not entirely clear from the records. Balfour remembers that he was ordered back to the scene of the attack by "a signal from Operations." Correspondence with the author, 7 October 1991.

52 Three letters between CINCLANT and CINCCNA led up to this meeting. The first was sent from the chief of staff to CINCLANT to CINCCNA 13 December

1944 (file A4–3[00895]). CINCCNA replied on 3 January 1945, suggesting the end of the month as the most suitable period. CINCLANT responded on 16 January indicating that TG 22.10 would arrive at Halifax 29 January 1945. Evidently, events overtook these plans and TG 22.9 was despatched shortly after the attack. All correspondence in NA, RG 24, vol. 11022, file CNA 7–6.

53 NA, report entitled "Submarine Warfare in the Channel," from SO EG 11 (HMCS *Ottawa*), Commander J.D. Prentice, RCN, to Commodore(D), Western Approaches, dated 17 July 1944, RG 24, vol. 11575, file D-01-18-0.

54 NA, message from NSHQ to large number of addressees, 101630Z February 1945, RG 24, 83–84/167, vol. 2616, file 16121–5, vol. 3.

55 NA, message from NSHQ to AIG 161, 251557Z, February 1945, RG 24, vol. 11022, file CNA 7–6.

56 NA, RCN Operational Research Report No. 35, dated 28 August 1945, "A Comparison of A/S Hunts in Canadian and British Coastal Areas," RG 24, vol. 11464.

57 The question of communications efficiency has been avoided in this chapter, but it is another area that deserves further attention.

58 "Achievement of Killer Groups Trained at Casco Bay," letter from Commander Destroyers, US Atlantic Fleet, to Commander in Chief, US Atlantic Fleet, 28 August 1945, NARA, WNRC, RG 313, Red Series, box 137 (TS-585), Secret, 1945, folder A16–3(1), "ASW Warfare Misc," #2 Jacket.

59 D. Syrett, "Weather-Reporting U-boats in the Atlantic: The Hunt for U-248," *Mariner's Mirror* 52, no. 1 (Winter 1992): 16–24.

60 U-866 was destroyed on 18 March 1945, by TG 22.14, in position 43 18N, 061 08W. U-548 was destroyed 19 April 1945, by TG 22.10, in position 42 19N, 061 45W. Both locations are southwest of Sable Island, approximately 200 miles southeast of Halifax. TG 22.10 was originally assessed as having destroyed U-879 on 19 April, but recent historical reassessment has resulted in the credit of that U-boat being given to USS *Natchez*, USS *Bostwick*, USS *Coffman*, and USS *Thomas* on 30 April. The reassessment was based on identification of debris resulting from the attack on U-548 by TG 22.10, which allowed a positive correlation with U-548 to be made. This reassessment was brought to the author's attention by Axel Niestle in personal correspondence, 18 November 1993.

61 Milner, "Somers Isle," 41–7.

62 DHist, A/Captain W.L. Puxley, RN, Captain(D), Halifax, to CINCLANT, Minute II on the training commander's Monthly Report of Proceedings for March, dated 7 April 1945, NSC 1445–102/4.

63 Milner, "Inshore ASW," 157.

64 For details, see Hadley, *U-Boats against Canada*, 289–92.

65 EG 6 left Northern Ireland 18 April 1945 and arrived in Halifax 3 May 1945.

The group did not leave harbour again before the end of the war. DHist, "Report of Proceedings 6th Escort Group for Period 18th April to 4th May 1945," dated 4 May 1945, NHS 8440, "EG 6."

CHAPTER ELEVEN

1 Task Group (TG) 302.3, consisting of HMCS *Athabaskan* (DDH 282, destroyer-flagship), *Terra Nova* (DDE 259, frigate), and *Protecteur* (AOR 509, operational support ship). The task group was under the command of Commodore Kenneth J. ("Ken") Summers until mid-October 1990, when he was appointed commander of the Canadian Forces Middle East Headquarters (HQ CANFORME) established in Manamah, Bahrain. Captain(Naval) Duncan ("Dusty") Miller then became commander of TG 302.3.

2 A cruiser, a destroyer, and five frigates under the command of Rear Admiral William M. Fogarty, Commander, Middle East Force (COMIDEASTFOR), permanently based from Bahrain. Marolda, "A Host of Nations," 3; and Palmer, *Guardians of the Gulf*, 98–9.

3 The official report to Congress affirms that "during the first two weeks of the crisis, the focus was on defending Saudi Arabia from a possible Iraqi invasion and building a coalition in support of Kuwait." United States, *Conduct of the Persian Gulf War* [hereafter CPGW], 62.

4 Dannreuther, "The Gulf Conflict," 29.

5 The five permanent members (with veto status) of the Security Council are the United States, the then Soviet Union, China, Great Britain, and France. The council also includes ten non-permanent members elected by the General Assembly for a two-year term, half that number changing each year to allow some continuity. In August 1990 they comprised Canada, Colombia, Ethiopia, Finland, Malaysia, Cuba, Ivory Coast, Romania, Yemen, and Zaire. The first five were due to retire their seats at the end of 1990, to be replaced by Austria, Belgium, Ecuador, India, and Zimbabwe.

6 For the complete text of the UN Security Council resolutions, see Safry and Cerf, *The Gulf War Reader*, 137–56.

7 NDHQ DMOC, "Deployment to Persian Gulf Area – OP FRICTION," 11 August 90.

8 "O Canada, must thee be on guard?," *Globe and Mail* (Toronto), 18 August 90.

9 The 40 mm Boffin guns in all three ships were fitted primarily for the interdiction role, as they were far better suited to the firing of warning shots than the bigger-calibre main armament, but they were more the object of ridicule as museum pieces given the attention focused on their original purpose of manufacture during the Second World War as anti-aircraft armament. See CP story filed by Paul Mooney, *Ottawa Citizen*, *17–18 October 1990*.

10 For descriptions of the forces, see Friedman, *Desert Victory*, 88ff. and Appendix C, "Naval Forces in the Embargo and the War," 319–23; and Gilchrist, *Sea Power*. The inherent mobility of naval forces and fluctuating force levels due to reinforcements and replacements make the comparison of national deployments problematic. A representative date is 1 October 1990, which coincides with the first day of operations for the Canadian task group.

11 Silkett, "Alliance and Coalition Warfare," 74–85, discusses the differences between alliances and coalitions, with occasional reference to the Gulf War.

12 See Table 11.1. Of the fifty-odd USN warships deployed to the region, CO-MUSMIF (COMIDEASTFOR) had fifteen available to him for embargo operations, spread among the Persian Gulf and the Red and Arabian seas. Of these fifteen, five were cruisers whose primary function was anti-air warfare.

13 In early October, shortly after the Canadian task group joined the interception effort in the central Gulf, a squadron of Canadian CF-18 Hornet fighters began operations from Doha, Qatar. Their mandate was to provide air defence for the ships enforcing the embargo below, and they were not directly attached to the Central Command Air Forces (CENTAF) in Riyadh. Ostensibly this further defined Canadian support of the MIF. However, every other coalition air component came under the MNF. Unlike their naval brethren, who at least had ample company in the MIF, the Canadian pilots could not help but feel a closer affiliation to the MNF.

14 Burrowes, "Patrolling the Gulf," 18.

15 CTG 302.3, "ASSESSREP/001/DEC," 1 December 1990; and CTG 150.2 [CO-MUSMIF], "Multinational Maritime Interception Operations/SITREP," 1 December 1990. Note the distinction between interceptions and boardings. An interception is the act of coming upon a merchant vessel and demanding from it (usually over radio) information to determine if further action – a boarding – is required to verify its cargo. In their time in the Gulf, the ships of TG 302.3 found it necessary to board only twenty-two ships bound to and from Iraq.

16 De la Billière, *Storm Command*, 137. He took advantage of a coincidentally planned 3 December rotation of senior naval staffs to define the order. He does not state it in so many words, but de la Billière clearly implies that Commodore Paul Haddacks, the outgoing Senior Naval Officer, Middle East, had been slow to develop plans for offensive action (compare pp. 61 and 137). The general, who only arrived in Riyadh on 7 October, was definitely pro-MNF in his outlook and had little time for the niceties of the MIF. One of his first actions upon arrival in-theatre was to advise Haddacks, until then autonomously conducting the embargo with his Armilla Patrol, that "I now wanted a fundamental change: I wished the Navy to make plans for war at the northern end of the Gulf – a far cry from their role in the area so far" (61). Perhaps Haddacks, who had been in charge of the Armilla Patrol since before the invasion, better appreciated the subtleties of the MIF operations.

His replacement, Commodore Christopher Craig (the veteran commander of HMS *Alacrity* in the Falklands War), who did not carry the MIF "baggage," favoured the more emphatic British response in early December.

17 The role of the WEU in the crisis has been at once both underappreciated and overstated, and in itself could be the profitable subject of investigation. More than just a sub-set of the larger European Community, the WEU, a military and economic association with roots predating the birth of NATO, provided a mechanism allowing its member states (Belgium, France [then occupying the rotating position of chair], West Germany, Italy, Luxembourg, the Netherlands, and the United Kingdom) to project the semblance of united foreign and defence policies beyond the territorial restrictions of NATO. Based upon its apparent success in the Gulf crisis (five of the seven nations despatched naval forces – the only exceptions being Luxembourg, which has no navy, and Germany, which has overriding constitutional limitations on its military forces), it has been proclaimed as the model for future European military cooperation and even a replacement for NATO after American withdrawal from the European continent. Indeed, the WEU is seen as the core of the common security and defence policy embodied, in highly vague terms, in the Maastricht Treaty. The national policies of the several members covered the spectrum of opinion on the subject; attempting to rationalize them was problematic, and inevitably the WEU could agree upon only the lowest common denominator – the enforcement of the UN-authorized sanctions. Individual members that felt constrained by this took the pragmatic step of splitting their task groups between the MIF operations sanctioned by the WEU and the less-restrictive (i.e., more aggressive) national taskings. The British had done this from the start, but they were eventually joined by the Dutch and even the French, who as we shall see later dedicated a warship for non-WEU Gulf operations. For a well-balanced and insightful discussion of Europe's collective role, see Cromwell, "Europe, the United States, and the pre-war Gulf crisis," 124–50. A more explicit critical analysis of the military role of the WEU in the Gulf crisis is Young, "Preparing the Western Alliance," 32–6.

18 Cromwell, "Europe, the United States, and the pre-war Gulf crisis"; and Hiro, *DESERT SHIELD to DESERT STORM*, chap. 8. Both chronicle the doomed diplomatic efforts of President Mitterand and the EC to avert hostilities.

19 Edward R. Rosenthal, "La Armada Argentina en el Golfo Pérsico," *Boletin del Centro Naval* (Argentina) 109, no. 763 (Winter 1991): 259.

20 This intuitive statement is made on examination of the Canadian diplomatic role (both from Ottawa and at the United Nations) and military support for the MIF to mid-December 1990. At the time of writing, the only full-length treatment of the Canadian role in the Gulf crisis is Jocelyn Coulon, *La dernière croisade* (1992).

21 CTG 150.2, "December Multinational Sked Conference," 4 December 1990 (to CTG 429.9).

22 CTG 302.3, "ASSESSREP/027/DEC," 27 December 1990.

23 CTG 302.3, "Transition to War," 9 December 1990. Captain(N) Miller had already given the matter some preliminary thought. In a message to his task group giving his "assessment of where we stand and where we are going" in the wake of UNSCR 678, he offered that, "realistically, I expect that our task will be to provide close escort to High Value Units in the Central Gulf, enforce a naval blockade, contribute to maintaining an accurate surface plot and perform Search and Rescue operations" CTG 302.3, "CTG's Evaluation," 30 November 1990.

24 The rotations were planned to start, in sequence, on 1 January with *Protecteur*, followed by *Athabaskan* and his own task group staff in February, culminating finally with *Terra Nova* in March. Coupled with necessary maintenance and work-up periods, the plan called for each of the ships in turn to be out of operations for a full month.

25 The reluctance to consider operations other than MIF was a reflection, therefore, not only of government policy, but also of the state of the Canadian fleet, which had neither the modern anti-air equipment to accord it a frontline escort role nor the depth in numbers to allow a complete, one-time task group rotation. The TRUMP (Tribal-class Update and Modernization Programme) and CPF (Canadian Patrol Frigate) programs then in progress would go a long way to solve both these structural problems, but the force reductions incurred on the rest of the fleet in 1990–91 for their introduction were in the short run as much a curse as a blessing.

26 When the Canadian navy was last at war, off Korea, its destroyers had done great service, but never as an identifiable Canadian task group. Instead they were allocated to Commonwealth and USN task groups as required. This was subsequently seen as having diluted the impact that the navy could have made.

27 The USN logistics plan was laid out in CTF 154, "Battle Force Zulu (AGBF) Jan Logistics Plan," 3 January 1991.

28 CTF 154, "AGBF Stationing Intentions," 4 January 1991. The Canadian supply ship, *Protecteur*, was scheduled to be included in the CLF upon resumption of operations in late January.

29 The naval officer, LCDR G. Romanow, joined the staff of Commander Destroyer Squadron 15 (AGBF ASUWC-designate), while the air officer, Maj. J.L.J Cloutier (CF-18 pilot), joined the staff of COMCARGRU 5. The idea of placing Canadian officers as liaison on US theatre staffs was not new: three pilots were working quite effectively as liaison officers to CENTAF in Riyadh, coordinating the employment of the Canadian CF-18s from Doha so as to meet the various intentions of CANFORME, NAVCENT, and CENTAF. The extension of the idea to encompass air and naval coordination with Battle Force Zulu seemed to lend itself to the present situation.

30 NDHQ DMOC, "OP FRICTION Brief to Ad Hoc Committee on the Persian Gulf Crisis," 8 January 1991.

31 This was to ensure the resupply of their warships attached to the American battle groups. Logistics sharing within the coalition was quite extensive, especially with regards fuel, for which exchange agreements existed, but on the whole logistics remained a national responsibility.

32 Whatever the shortfalls of the Canadian task group in other than self-defence main armament, the command-and-control facilities of the ships had been given special attention. Even before the present crisis arose, interoperability with the USN was at a high level, as required for NATO operations and the joint defence of North America. Those facilities were upgraded for the Gulf deployment such that the Canadian "connectivity" with the USN was arguably the best in the Coalition – possibly even better than between the USN's own Atlantic and Pacific forces.

33 CTG 302.3, "ASSESSREP/010/JAN," 10 January 1991. Highlighting the MIF/MNF reversal further, reports from the Canadian headquarters in Manamah were already beginning to elaborate upon "post-MIF operations with the Multi-National Force (MNF)" (for example, see CANFORCOMME, "Post MIF Operations," 10 January 1991).

34 CPGW, 260. "UNREP" is an acronym for "underway replenishment"; "Sierra" is a codeword indicating that the tasking falls within the "anti-surface warfare" (ASUW) principle warfare discipline. Besides "UNREP Sierra," there were three other subordinate surface-warfare positions: "NAG Sierra" (covering operations in the northern Gulf), "Strike Sierra" (coordinating cruise-missile and air-bombing missions), and "Eagle Sierra" (screening for the carriers), all held by USN officers. No other principle warfare duties were delegated from American control. A discussion of the USN's "Composite Warfare Commander" (CWC) concept as exercised in the Persian Gulf can be found in Schneller, "Persian Gulf Turkey Shoot," 11–13.

35 CTG 302.3, "War – The Way Ahead," 1 February 1991, and "ASSESSREP/009/FEB," 9 February 1991, in which he noted, "Have gone from feast to famine with availability of escorts for CLF duties."

36 CANFORCOMME, "Multinational MIF Ops," 22 January 1991, in reply to CTF 152 (COMUSMIF) message of 21 January 1991.

CHAPTER TWELVE

1 NA, "The Continuing Royal Canadian Navy," RG 24, vol. 8186, NS 1818–9. This paper was forwarded under a covering memorandum by Captain H.S. Rayner, director of plans, on 2 June 1945.

2 NA, Cabinet War Committee document 917, 4 January 1945, "Post-War Defence Relationship with the United States: General Considerations," RG 24, RCN vol. 8125, file 1818–2.

3 Ibid., para. 3.c.

4 Maj.-Gen. Pope to Col. Jenkins, 4 April 1944, quoted in Eayrs, *Peacekeeping and Deterrence*, 321.

5 Mackenzie King was reflecting in his diary on a Cabinet meeting on 3 January 1946. Pickersgill and Foster, *The Mackenzie King Record*, 4:6.

6 Bercuson, *True Patriot*, 159.

7 Reid, *Radical Mandarin*, 244.

8 "Autobiography," Claxton Papers, quoted in Eayrs, *Peacekeeping and Deterrence*, 117.

9 Eayrs, *Peacekeeping and Deterrence*, 116

10 The committee's lineage can be traced back to 1937, when Mackenzie King established the "Defence Committee of the Cabinet," which apparently met only sporadically and was not very effective. It was succeeded by the powerful Cabinet War Committee in late 1939. Stacey, *Arms, Men and Governments*, 119.

11 Bland, *The Administration of Defence Policy*, 13–16; and Bercuson, *True Patriot* 160, 162.

12 DND, *Report of the Department of National Defence for the Fiscal Year Ending March 31, 1949*, 8.

13 Eayrs, *Peacekeeping and Deterrence*, 109.

14 Pickersgill and Foster, *The Mackenzie King Record*, 3:394.

15 By 1948 DND noted that "Canada has proceeded further in military unification than any other country," *Report for the Fiscal Year 1949*, 8.

16 *Report for the Fiscal Year 1949*, 8.

17 Bland, *The Administration of Defence Policy*, 150. This book describes the Claxton system in some detail.

18 Earlier associations were also useful. Vice-Admiral H.E. Reid for example, as CNS in 1946–47, made use of a relationship with Lester Pearson formed when they had served together in Washington. Interview with Vice-Admiral D.A. Collins, who was Admiral Reid's secretary, 14 September 1993.

19 Claxton Papers, quoted in Eayrs, *Peacekeeping and Deterrence*, 116.

20 DHist, letter from Admiral A.H.G. Storrs to Admiral Davis, 1983, Admiral Storrs file. These remarks are particularly interesting as A.H.G. Storrs had several appointments with increasing responsibility on the Naval Staff between 1946 and 1958.

21 Douglas, "Conflict and Innovation," 215.

22 Milner, *North Atlantic Run*, 124.

23 Discussion with Rear Admiral R. Murdoch, 24 September 1993. Brooke Claxton came, however, to recognize the difficulties Grant faced in grappling with expansion while simultaneously raising standards of efficiency. His working relationship with Grant appears to have been productive. When Grant retired in 1951, Claxton's public tribute was fulsome.

24 German, *The Sea Is at Our Gates*, 206.

25 Discussion with Rear Admiral Dillon, secretary to the Naval Board in 1947 and 1948, 15 September 1993.

26 Technology developed so rapidly that H.N. Lay's thinking about naval Canadian aviation in fact was able to span developments over several decades. He prepared a paper for a 1951 Senior Officers' Meeting advocating the employment by the RCN of helicopters equipped with dunking sonar from ships. Soward, *Hands to Flying Stations*, 215.

27 NA, "The Continuing Royal Canadian Navy," RG 24, vol. 8186, NS 1818–9, para. 2(a).

28 Douglas, *The Administration of Defence Policy*, 213.

29 NA, "The Continuing Royal Canadian Navy," RG 24, vol. 8186, NS 1818–9, para. 2(c).

30 NA, "Royal Canadian Future Planning – to 1956," RG 24, Acc 83–84/167, vol. 610, file TS 11818–1, vol. 1 of 4 November 1946.

31 House of Commons, *Debates*, 1945, vol. 2, 1368, quoted in Eayrs, *Peacekeeping and Deterrence*, 87.

32 NA, "Royal Canadian Navy Future Planning – to 1956," note 30 above.

33 For example, DHist, NSS 1650–26 file, vols. 1, 2, and 3, chronicle successive fleet composition, employment, and manning plans.

34 NA, Claxton Papers, RG 24, Acc 83–4/167, vol. 2, 141, ACS 1279–6.

35 Douglas, "The Prospects for Naval History," 22.

36 Manning escort carriers were part of a package that came about because the RCN was able to scale back its escort manning requirements and thus would have surplus manpower. At the same time, the RN was facing manpower shortages. The Naval Staff made sure that carriers were included because they almost certainly planned manning as a first step to procurement. Douglas, "Conflict and Innovation," 211–12.

37 Mackenzie King Diary, December 1946, quoted in Pickersgill and Foster, *The Mackenzie King Record*, 3:394.

38 NA, Claxton Papers, RG 32, B 5 vol. 122.

39 Ibid., memorandum from A.D.P. Heeney, 3 March 1947.

40 Pickersgill and Foster, *Mackenzie King Record*, 4:9. The prime minister's visceral unease about carriers never left him. More than a year later, in April 1948, after recording in his diary the danger posed by recent Soviet submarine developments, Mackenzie King noted how "I cannot but shudder each time I think of the enormous aircraft carrier which we are having brought out ... it would be about the first of the large vessels to disappear" Ibid., 183.

41 US National Archives, Joint Chief of Staff, CCS 092 (9–1–45), PO 32-FIII of 8 June 1948. Report of conversation with Claxton by Admiral T. Inglis, chief of naval intelligence.

42 NA, minutes of CDC meeting of 22 December 1949, RG 2. Yearly figures that show that naval aviation's share was an overall average of 10 per cent of naval

expenditures for the period 1946 to 1952–53 are given in Soward, *Hands to Flying Stations*, 233.

43 NA, minutes of CDC meeting of 21 September 1948, RG 2, vol. 2748, vol. 3/46. Transfer of the air station in Dartmouth from the RCAF to the RCN was on the agenda and was approved.

44 NA, minutes of CDC meeting of 20 September 1949, RG 2, vol. 2748, vol. 4, 156.

45 NA, minutes of CDC meeting of 26 October 1949, RG 2, vol. 2748, vol. 3/49.

46 NA, minutes of special meeting of the COS Committee, 31 January 1950, RG 24, Acc 83/84/167, vol. 223. Both other services were already allocated substantially more than the RCN: over the five years the navy was to receive $400 million, the army $670 million, and the air force $835 million. It must have been a heated discussion.

47 Maj.-Gen. Pope to Col. J.H. Jenkins, 4 April 1944, DEA files, quoted in Eayrs, *Peacekeeping and Deterrence*, 321.

48 Jockel, *No Boundaries Upstairs*, 17.

49 NA, memorandum on Implementation Programme 1948–49, 24 June 1947, RG 24, RCN vol. 8084, TS 11272–11–14.

50 NA, memorandum on the "Relative Size and Roles Canadian Armed Services," 30 June 1947, RG 24, Acc 83–84/167, vol. 1, TS 11400–25.

51 Eayrs, *Peacekeeping and Deterrence*, 95. Dr Roger Sarty has drawn attention to the fact that these objectives echoed those of 1909: defence against invasion, aid to civil power, cooperation in imperial defence.

52 Middlemiss, "Economic Considerations and the Canadian Navy," 259.

53 NA, RG 24, Acc 83/84/167, vol. 223, DC (Gen) 51, 31 May 1948.

54 The Naval Staff wanted to repeat the river names of the first destroyers built for the RCN in the 1930s. Interestingly, the director of naval information (Public Relations) pointed out the public-relations value of using the names of cities and towns. In hindsight he may have been right. DHist, NS Meetings file, minutes of 5012st meeting, 31 October-6 November 1950, item 501–5.

55 House of Commons, *Debates*, 24 June 1948, 5785.

56 NA, "Accelerated Defence Programme Recommendations for the increase in strength of the R.C.N.", 31 July 1950, MG 32, vol. B 5, vol. 94, NSS 1650–26, vol. 3. The commitment to NATO was already quite heavy, as it included both the cruisers and six destroyers. Joel Sokolsky gives detail on the early evolution of NAORG and on how NATO commitments were used as a lever for increased naval expenditures. On the other hand, External Affairs reacted to the modest increases to defence programs proposed by the service chiefs with a hawkish prod that Canada would have to do much more to be a credible ally. Eayrs, *Growing Up Allied*, 200–1.

57 Milner, "The Dawn of Modern Anti-Submarine Warfare," 61–9. See also Douglas, *The Creation of a National Air Force*, vol. 2, chaps 16 and 17. A

postwar American assessment of the German submarine technology is described in Palmer, *Origins of the Maritime Strategy*, 33.

58 By 1937 the Russian submarine force was the world's largest. Moore et al., "Developments in Submarine Systems," 151.

59 NA, RG 24, vol. 8087, NSTS 11270–15–7, vol. 2. I am grateful to Cmdr Peter Haydon for drawing my attention to this reference.

60 NA, "Royal Canadian Navy Future Planning – to 1956," note 30 above.

61 NA, minutes of CDC meeting of 26 November 1946, RG 2, vol. 2748.

62 Friedman, *The Postwar Naval Revolution*, 157–8.

63 NA, "Memorandum to the Cabinet: Joint Defence Programme for the Fiscal Year 1947–48," 11 December 1946, RG 2, vol. 3730, 2750.

64 Zimmerman has described the wartime reluctance of the Naval Staff to adopt squid in *The Great Naval Battle of Ottawa*, 127–9. The postwar gap in squid-fitted ships was a result, and this equipment did not reach the postwar fleet until 1949 in HMCS *Micmac*. Canadian wartime squid-fitted frigates and corvettes had been built in the UK and were returned to the RN in 1945.

65 DHist, minutes of Naval Board meeting of 29 March 1946, NS 1279–65.

66 *Micmac* had been heavily damaged in 1947.

67 NA, Naval Programme 1949–50, 29 September 1948, RG 2, vol. 2720. These ships were also seen as a valuable resource because of the leverage gained in NATO through sheer numbers. At a Naval Staff meeting the director of plans, Captain J. Brock, said, "If these Frigates are not available in an emergency, it may well be that the R.C.N. is relegated to a vastly inferior status, relative to the USN and the R.N. in the Command Organization which will be established in the North Atlantic Ocean." DHist, minutes of 480th meeting of Naval Staff, 7 March 1950.

68 Twenty-one frigates were modernized as ocean escorts, the first commissioned in 1953. While the Naval Staff acknowledged their slow speed and lack of air warning radar, it argued that they "would be useful for A/S Escort work, at least during the next three or four years." DHist, Naval Staff Meetings file, meeting of 18–30 October 1950, item 500–41. In the event, the rebuilt frigates served an average of eleven years. With their imaginative modernization and excellent endurance, they proved valuable peacetime training ships. They are an interesting example of how a decision to accept a less-than-optimal operational solution meant that useful ships were on hand when naval expenditures began shrinking in the mid-1950s.

69 The Naval Board attempted to acquire a British submarine in 1946, but the minister did not give approval because such a vessel had not been included in the austere naval program already authorized. DHist, minutes of Naval Board meeting of 15 May 1946, item 177–4.

70 Hobson, *The Composition of Canada's Naval Fleet*, 17.

71 NA, minutes of the 420th meeting of the NS, 20 July 1948, RG 24, Acc 83–84/167; and memorandum to Captain Peers, 22 July 1948, and minutes of the

first meeting of the RCN Submarine Committee in same file. In recommending such a group, Captain H.N. Lay wrote, "As you know, I have for some time been of the opinion that the R.C.N. should get with S/M's (and possibly out of air). No doubt the R.C.A.F. would co-operate in such a proposal" (same file, handwritten memorandum). What makes this glimpse of private views fascinating is Lay's key involvement in establishing and furthering naval air.

72 Goodspeed, *The Armed Forces of Canada*, 219.

73 NA, minutes of CDC meeting of 26 October 1948, RG 2, vol. 2748, vol. 3/49.

74 House of Commons, *Debates*, 9 June 1950, 3427.

75 NA, "PJBD Progress Report – R.C.N. USN Standardization," 14 February 1948, RG 25, Acc 92/109, vol. 78, file 50218.40.

76 Ibid. This report in early 1948 was already enumerating common electrical standards and listing for "probable" acquisition the USN gunnery and fire-control equipment fitted three years later in the Tribal surface armament modernizations and in the St Laurents.

77 NA, minutes of CDC meeting of 28 October 1948, RG 2, vol. 2748, vol. 3/49. At the time, the USN was focused on "hunter-killer" ASW concepts. The precise roles foreseen for RCN and RN carrier groups in defence of trade had not been checked.

78 When gunnery rearmament was discussed by the Naval Staff, the sponsoring director observed that his proposals, albeit involving USN systems, were very close to those proposed by the Admiralty for HM ships; see DHist, minutes of 434rd NS meeting, 7 December 1948, item 435–5. American radars were chosen partly because they were available. The USN was actively modernizing their systems, while the RN program was five to seven years in the future; see minutes of 459th NS meeting, 12 July 1949, item 459–1. The RN obtained some of the same air warning radars under US military assistance and fitted them in carriers.

79 Soward, *Hands to Flying Stations*, 179.

80 Grant, *Sovereignty or Security?*, 103–9. A more balanced view of postwar US military intentions is in Jockel, *No Boundaries Upstairs*.

81 Jockel, *No Boundaries Upstairs*, 6; and Palmer, *Origins of the Maritime Strategy*, 20.

82 NA, "Sovereignty in the Canadian Arctic in Relation to Joint Defence Undertakings," RG 2, vol. 2750, file D-65.

83 DHist, minutes of Naval Board meeting of 6 November 1946, item 199–3.

84 *Report for the Fiscal Year 1949*, 35.

85 NA, "Memorandum to Cabinet Defence Committee Provision of Ice-Breaking," 20 February 1948, RG 2, 2750 D 166.

86 The CNS appears to have been forewarned about St Laurent's intentions, as he went to the meeting armed with a memo containing background information on icebreakers. NA, memorandum from secretary to CNS, 7 January 1948, RG 24 83/84/167 int 205, vol. 3493, file 8000 AW 50. DEA records on

icebreakers have not been checked. There had been much informal discussion in headquarters about sovereignty in the North in 1946–47. DHist, Admiral Storrs file, letter to Dr Douglas, 21 October 1991. At the annual Senior Officers' Meeting in May 1947, *Micmac*'s CO, Cmdr Littler, had advocated a naval icebreaker "for control of our own navigable waters." NA, RG 24, Acc 83-4/167, vol. 11, 141 Senior Officers' Meetings file, DMCS 1480–135/14 of 19 April 1947. The official Naval Staff reaction was frosty and in the oracular prose of the time: "The R.C.N. does not propose to enter into this type of operation to any great extent ... procurement ... would only lead to commercial commitments ... personnel could not be made available. Planning in this field was considered to be in the same category as fire boats, fleet trains, etc." Ibid., memorandum NSC 8000–408 of 23 June 1947.

87 NA, CDC minutes extracted 18 March 1947, RG 24, Acc 83/84/167 vol. 3493, file 8000, TS 11400–ABC–22.

88 DHist, minutes of NS 502nd meeting, 7 November 1950, item 502–1.

89 The Naval Staff had originally proposed the name *Hudson Bay*. Minutes of NS 480th meeting, 7 March 1950, item 480–1. The bilingual name *Labrador* was an inspired decision apparently made at a higher level. Major Canadian icebreaker projects are interesting case studies in government decision-making. The Mackenzie King government's success in ordering a naval icebreaker contrasts with the failure of the Mulroney government to follow through with its 1985 announcement in Parliament about acquiring a Polar 8 icebreaker. In the late 1940s, government was simpler. A unified Cabinet instructed officials to implement a political decision and made funds available. Almost forty years later, major projects were far more difficult to implement. The initial problem may have been a lack of collective resolve by ministers. The Polar 8 was pushed by External Affairs and Transport, but neither had sufficient funds in their "envelopes." Officials in other departments naturally protected their own envelopes. The government appeared unable to concentrate sufficient political energy on the issue, which deteriorated into several years of contracted feasibility studies and eventual abandonment.

90 NA, RG 24, Acc 83/84/167, vol. 223, file 1400–25, pt 2.

CHAPTER THIRTEEN

1 The research for this paper was made possible under a grant from the former Canadian Institute for International Peace and Security given to Joel Sokolsky, J.T. Jockel, and myself for a larger project on Canada-US naval relationships. I would also like to thank the archivists at both the DND's Directorate of History and the National Archives (Government Records) for their patient help in making the various files available to me.

2 The concept of "shrinking and growing pains" was used by the minister of national defence, the Hon. Brooke Claxton, in an address to the sixth meeting

of RCN senior officers on 3 November 1949, to describe the root causes of the incidents aboard HMCS *Magnificent*, HMCS *Athabaskan*, and HMCS *Crescent*. NA, RG 24, vol. 11141, file ACS 1275–6.

3 This document has not yet been declassified. A good description of the implications on Canadian defence planning can be found in the minutes of the COSC for 26 October 1955.

4 NA, A/D.N.P.I. Memorandum NS 1650–26 F.D. 5183 to ACNS: "R.C.N. – Future Planning," dated 17 January 1947, RG 24, Acc 83–4/167, vol. 455, file 1650–26, pt 1.

5 Pickersgill and Foster, *The Mackenzie King Record*, vol. 3, quoted in Eayrs, *Peacemaking and Deterrence*, 22–3.

6 House of Commons, *Debates*, 22 October 1945, 1364.

7 According to the Fleet Employment Plan for fiscal year 1946/47, the estimated strength of the RCN for 1 April 1946 was 6,600. NA, NS memorandum NSS 1650–26 (Staff), 17 January 1946, RG 24, Acc 83–4/167, vol. 455, file 1650–26, pt 1.

8 Naval Member PJBD files, "Implementation of Canada-U.S. Basic Security Plan," file TS 11272–11, 26 August 1947.

9 See NA, minutes of the 4th meeting of RCN senior officers, 26–27 November 1947, I, RG 24, vol. 11141, file ACS 1279–1.

10 See Naval Board Minutes, item 171–1, 29 March 1949; item 178–3, 15 May 1946; and item 229–2, 23 October 1946.

11 NA, minutes of the 420th NS meeting, item 420–1, RG 24, Acc 83–4/167, vol. 455, file 1650–26.

12 US National Archives, "Appreciation and Outline: Joint United States–Canadian Security Plan," document JPS 788/6 of 18 May 1946, JCS Records, RG 218, file 092(9–10–45), ser. 4.

13 For instance, see NA, "Basic R.C.N. Plan – 1947–1957 (Plan A)," file TS 11272–11 of 26 September 1947, RG 24, Acc 83–4/167, vol. 8067, file NSTS 11270–15–1 (vol. 1).

14 Chief of naval operations internal staff memorandum no. op–32–FIII dated 8 June 1948 (from the Records of the Chief of Naval Operations.)

15 DND, *Canada's Defence Programme 1949–50*, 18.

16 Ibid. The rebuilding of Canada's naval capability was not formally authorized until the autumn of 1949, when a new defence statement, with a heavy NATO emphasis, was published. The naval role was specified (14) as defence of shipping, and plans were made for new capabilities to meet this task; requirements would include "minesweepers, an icebreaker and, especially, fast escort vessels." This concept of defence planning was based on partial mobilization, but it would have only provided resources that fell far short of Naval Staff requirements.

17 Minutes of the COSC, 6 March 1950, 5.

18 Ibid., 21 June 1950.

19 Direction to the department was issued by the deputy minister in a paper entitled "Acceleration of Defence Program," dated 20 July 1950.

20 See Naval Board Minutes, 21 July 1950.

21 Minutes of the COSC, 17 July 1950.

22 DND, *Canada's Defence Programme 1951–52* (with revisions to 30 June 1951), 7.

23 This was discussed in detail by the defence minister at the 9th meeting of RCN senior officers on 17 and 21 March 1952. NA, RG 24, vol. 11141, file ACS 1279–9.

24 See DHist, NS letter "Naval Mobilization Plan Based on an M-day of 31 December 1953 [sic]," file NSTS 11650–35 of 30 March 1953. This actually discusses 31 December 1955 national mobilization plans: Flag Officer, Atlantic Coast, "Emergency Plan for the Protection of Coastal Sea Lines of Communication – East Coast" (undated), file ACTS 11420–13–7. NA, RG 24, Acc 83–4/167, vol. 11.133.

25 Ibid., 1. Plans for the Pacific Command have not yet been found, but it can be presumed that they were based on a similar command relationship. The full scope of integrated NATO and bilateral planning was described in a brief by VCNS to the 11th Senior Officers' Meeting, 12–14 May 1954. NA, RG 24, Acc 83–4/167, vol. 11129, file ACTS 11279–11.

26 Minutes of the 11th Senior Officers' Meeting, A(ii).

27 NA, minutes of the 10th Senior Officers' Conference, 6–8 May 1953, Appendix A, RG 24, Acc 83–4/167, vol. 11129, file ACTS 11279–10.

28 Naval Board Minutes, item 360–2, 24 June 1952.

29 See Naval Board Minutes, items 405–2, July 1954; 422–6, 29 October 1954; and 423–2 9 November 1954.

30 Naval Board Minutes, items 446–1, 1 June 1954; and 448–6, 15 June 1955.

31 Naval Board Minutes, item 457–3(a), 7 September 1955.

32 Naval Board Minutes, items 448–1, 15 June 1955; and 456–3, 31 August 1955.

33 The problems of morale and conditions of service were raised frequently at a series of RCN Senior Officers' Meetings held after the war, but the concerns that were expressed by commanding and staff officers on the coasts seemed to fall on deaf ears until the 1949 "mutinies."

34 NA, NS memorandum, "Employment of Canadian Naval Forces During the Fiscal Year 1946–47 – Annex 'A' Estimated Ship Manning Programme," file NSS 1650–26 (Staff) of 17 January 1946, RG 24, Acc 83–4/167, vol. 455, file 1650–26, pt 1.

35 NA, NS memorandum, "Employment of the Canadian Fleet," file NSS 1650–26 of 24 February 1947, RG 24, Acc 83–4/167, vol. 455, file 1659026, pt 1.

CHAPTER FOURTEEN

1 For a statement of the argument in the most general thematic treatment of British imperial expansion, see Woodcock, *Who Killed the British Empire?*, 24.

2 Gordon, *The Dominion Partnership in Imperial Defense*; Hadley and Sarty, *Tin-Pots and Pirate Ships*, 3–75; and Sarty, "Canadian Maritime Defence."

3 PANL, governor to colonial secretary, 14 November 1899, GN 2/38 #2.

4 PANL, colonial secretary to governor, 28 November 1899, GN 2/38 #2; PANL, administrator to secretary of state (Colonies), 18 June 1900, GN 1/1/7 1900; and PANL, governor to secretary of state (Colonies), 14 August 1900, GN 1/1/7 1900.

5 PANL, secretary of state (Colonies) to governor, 6 December 1900, GN 1/2/0 1899–1900.

6 PANL, R.H. Knox (War Office) to under-secretary of state (Colonies), 27 March 1901, GN 1/2/0 1901.

7 PANL, R. Bond to Sir H. McCallum, 18 April 1901, GN 1/2/0 1901.

8 For this and the following quotation, see PANL, "Statement" by Sir Robert Bond on the question of imperial defence, 5 July 1902, GN 1/2/0.

9 For this and the following, see PANL, Sir Henry McCallum, governor of Nfld, to Joseph Chamberlain, colonial secretary, despatch #64, 9 September 1900, GN1/1/7 – 1900.

10 PANL, C.J. Thomas, Admiralty, to under-secretary of state, Colonial Office, Confidential Minute M-01045, 15 October 1900, GN1/2/0, 1899–1900; PANL, Sir C. Boyle, governor of Nfld, to colonial secretary, 29 October 1901, GN 2/38 #2.

11 PANL, Commodore G.R. Giffard, HMS *Charybdis*, to the Administrator, Nfld, 13 May 1901, GN 2/38 #3.

12 PANL, Commodore G.A. Giffard, HMS *Charybdis*, to Sir C. Boyle, governor of Nfld, 15 November 1901, GN 2/38 #2.

13 PANL, Admiralty to C-in-C, North America and West Indies (Vice-Admiral F.G.D. Bedford), Telegram #94, 25 October 1901, GN 2/38 #2; PANL, Vice-Admiral F.G.D. Bedford, HMS *Crescent*, St John's, to Sir C. Boyle, governor and C-in-C, Nfld, 25 October 1901, GN 2/38 #2.

14 McGrath, "Colonial Naval Reserves," 535.

15 Ibid.; and Saunders, "The First Naval Incident," 14–17.

16 *St. John's Daily News*, 16 October 1902.

17 *Evening Telegram* (St John's), 15 September 1902.

18 PANL, Robert Bond to Lord Selbourne, Admiralty, 5 August 1902, GN 2/38 #2.

19 PANL, Boyle to Acting Premier E. Morris, 22 September 1902, GN 2/38 #2.

20 PANL, E. MacGregor, Admiralty, to under-secretary of state, Colonial Office, M – 15041, 27 November 1902, GN 1/2/0 (1902).

21 McGrath, "Colonial Naval Reserves," 534.

22 PANL, Vice-Admiral Day Bosanquet to governor of Nfld, 8 July 1905, GN 2/6/B (1905).

23 PANL, *Vide*, monthly returns, NF RNR, OC *Calypso* (registrar-general) to governor of Nfld, GN 2/38 #4.

24 McGrath, "Colonial Naval Reserves," 534.

25 PANL, copy of scheme attached to correspondence from Sir C. Boyle, governor of Nfld, to Rt Hon. J. Chamberlain, MP, secretary of state for colonies, 20 January 1903, GN 1/1/7.

26 PANL, Message N. 174426/02 – 121, under-secretary, Admiralty, to C-in-C, HM Ships and Vessels, North America, 26 March 1903, GN 1/2/0 (1903).

27 Boyle to Chamberlain, 20 January 1903.

28 Personal testimony of Sidney Randell of Fogo (Nfld RNR no. 1084X).

29 PANL, notice of call for volunteers, Magistrate J.G. Conroy, Central District Court, St John's, Nfld, 28 September 1900, GN 1/1/7 (1900).

30 PANL, C. Boyle to colonial secretary, 28 March 1904; and Captain R.A.J. Montgomerie, RN, to Boyle, 20 February 1904, GN 2/38 #3.

31 PANL, OC *Calypso* to governor, 1 December 1905, GN 2/38 RNR #1.

32 PANL, colonial secretary to governor, 16 May 1910; and governor to colonial secretary, 4 May 1910, GN 2/38 #4.

33 PANL, Giffard to administrator, Nfld, 1 May 1901; and administrator, Nfld, to Giffard, 2 May 1901, GN 2/38 #3.

34 For this and the following, see Elgin, secretary of state, Colonial Office, to governor of Nfld, 12 April 1906.

35 Note, "Walter Hose & the Naval Reserve in Nfld," in *The RNR in Nfld*, report by Captain O.C.S. Robertson, RCN, HMCS *Cabot*, St John's, 1950, Duff Papers, Nfld Museum.

36 Local tradition has it that this celebrated crew – fishermen from a small community some five to six miles from St John's – actually carried their boat that distance to the regatta venue and, following a day of competitive rowing, including the record-setting pull, carried it home again. In 1910 the noted naval reformer and enthusiast, Lord Brassey, supported the regatta with a generous donation that was used to strike a set of medals to be awarded to the crew who would surpass the 1901 achievement. The "Lord Warden's medals" (thus named because Brassey held the honorary office of Warden of the Cinque Ports at the time) were won and duly awarded to a record-breaking crew only in 1981.

37 PANL, Sir W. Davidson, governor of Nfld, to L. Harcourt, dominions secretary, 23 November 1914, GN 1/10/1 (RNR 1914–17).

38 For this and the following, see PANL, LCDR A. MacDermott to Governor W. Davidson, 28 November 1914, GN 1/10/1 (RNR 1914–17).

39 PANL, LCDR A. MacDermott, OC, NF RNR, to Sir W. Davidson, governor of Nfld, 29 January 1915, GN 1/10/1 (RNR 1914–17).

40 PANL, Nfld, Patriotic Association proceedings, 3rd meeting, 20 August 1914, MG 632, 1 (1914).

41 Ibid., 5th meeting, 11 September 1914, MG 632, 1 (1914).

42 Ibid. 6th meeting, 28 September 1914, MG 632, 1 (1914).

43 So called because these men were initially kitted out in St John's with locally fabricated uniforms that included puttees fashioned with navy-blue cloth. Tradition has it that insufficient khaki-coloured material was available: like the aspersion "old contemptible" in the UK, the makeshift "blue puttee" accoutrement became a mark of special pride of service in Newfoundland. Once landed in the UK, the men were wholly re-kitted to standard British army specifications.

44 PANL, Nfld Patriotic Association, 5th meeting, 11 September 1914, MG 632, 1 (1914).

45 PANL, secretary, Naval Service (Ottawa), to governor of Nfld (HQ #47–1–1), 1 October 1914, MG 632 #28; and PANL, report, Finance Committee, Nfld Patriotic Association, 28 September 1914, MG 632–7–17.

46 PANL, secretary, Naval Service (Ottawa), to governor of Nfld (coded telegram #216), 30 November 1914, GN 1/10/1 (RNR 1914–17).

47 PANL, Governor Davidson to prime minister of Nfld, (Despatch no. 139), 19 December 1914, GN 1/10/1 (RNR 1914–17).

48 PANL, report, Finance Committee, Nfld Patriotic Association, 3 October 1914, MG 632–7–17. The rate arranged was $5 to the pound sterling.

49 PANL, Governor Davidson to Rev. A.G. Bayly of Bonavista, 12 March 1915, GN 1/10/1 (RNR 1914–17).

50 Personal testimony of Sidney Randell, NF RNR #1084 X.

51 DHist, telegram, governor general of Canada to secretary of state for the colonies, London, 5 August 1914, NHS 1700–100/78-CS 43–2–1.

52 Hadley and Sarty, *Tin-Pots and Pirate Ships*, 88–9.

53 DHist, L. Harcourt, secretary of state for the colonies, to governor general of Canada and governor of Nfld, cypher telegram, 6 August 1914, NHS 1700–100/78-CS 43–2–1, and Duff Papers, Nfld Museum.

54 DHist, NHS, "Brief History of HMCS Niobe," 26 October 1961, 47; DHist, Governor Davidson (Nfld) to colonial secretary (St John's), 13 October 1914, Duff Papers, Nfld Museum.

55 PANL, Governor Davidson (Nfld) to Rt Hon. L. Harcourt, secretary of state for the colonies, London, 23 November 1914 (not sent – filed for record only), GN 1/10/1 (RNR 1914–17).

56 Personal testimony of Sidney Randell, NF RNR #1084 X.

57 Hadley and Sarty, *Tin-Pots and Pirate Ships*, 84–5.

58 Personal testimony of Sidney Randell, NF RNR #1084 X. Randell, trained at the Fort Amherst battery prewar, was assigned in company with many other NF RNRs to main ordnance duty on HMCS *Niobe*. His particular station was on the #3 (Port) 6-inch gun.

59 PANL, Captain Robert Corbett, RN, HMCS *Niobe* at sea, to the governor of Nfld, 27 March 1915, GN 1/10/1 (RNR 1914–17).

60 PANL, secretary, Department of the Naval Service, to Hon. Sec., Nfld Patriotic Association, 28 December 1914, RG 24, 5592, 18–6–1.

61 DHist, "Short History of *Niobe*," 58.

62 Hadley and Sarty, *Tin-Pots and Pirate Ships*, 125–6.

63 NA, Dept of Naval Service, Ottawa, to OC HMS *Calypso*, St John's (signal no. 102), 27 August 1915, RG 24, 5592, 18–6–1.

64 PANL, governor (Nfld) to prime minister (Nfld), despatch #139, 19 December 1914, GN 1/10/1 (RNR 1914–17).

65 PANL, Governor Davidson to colonial secretary, 31 May 1915, GN 1/10/1 (RNR 1914–17).

66 PANL, Harcourt to Governor Davidson (despatch #98), 2 March 1915, GN 1/10/1 (RNR 1914–17).

67 Record and testimony of Sidney Randell, NF RNR #1084 X.

68 Bowen, *History of the Royal Naval Reserve*, 129–30.

69 Nominal Roll, Nfld RNR Fatalities, 1914–18, Duff Papers, Nfld Museum.

70 Bowen, *History of the RNR*, 136–7.

71 PANL, letter home from Stephen Dicker of Flat Island, Bonavista Bay, Nfld, serving on HMS *Clan McNaughton*, 19 January 1915, quoted in letter from Elias Bishop, school principal in Flat Island, to Sir W.E. Davidson, governor of Nfld, 20 February 1915, GN 1/10/1 (RNR 1914–17).

72 Nominal Roll, Nfld RNR Fatalities, 1914–18, Duff Papers, Nfld Museum.

73 Corbett, *Naval Operations*, 2:135, Nominal Roll, Nfld RNR Fatalities, Duff Papers, Nfld Museum.

74 Ibid.

75 Ibid.

76 Bowen, *History of the RNR*, 119–20.

77 PANL, Governor Davidson to ministers, 24 November 1916, GN 1/10/1 (RNR 1914–17).

78 PANL, Governor Davidson (Nfld) to secretary of state for the colonies (code telegram no. 89) 20 April 1916, GN 1/10/1 (RNR 1914–17).

79 PANL, colonial secretary (Nfld) to Governor Davidson (Nfld), 4 October 1916, GN 1/10/1 (RNR 1914–17).

80 PANL, Ft Waldegrave Records, 1914–17, MG 562.

81 PANL, Vice-Admiral M.E. Browning, C-in-C, N. America & W. Indies, to governor of Nfld, Despatch P 27, 7 May 1917, GN 1/10/1 (RNR 1914–17).

82 PANL, Governor Davidson (Nfld), note to file, 20 October 1917, GN 1/10/1 (RNR 1917–20).

83 PANL, Cmdr A. MacDermott, OC *Briton*, to governor of Nfld, 20 October 1917, GN 1/10/1 (RNR 1917–20).

84 For this and the following, see Hadley and Sarty, *Tin-Pots and Pirate Ships*, 187–8.

85 Ibid., 211. No responsible naval authority at the time believed that numbers of such small vessels – severely outgunned by the 6-inch main armament mounted by the large U-boats – were an adequate response to the threat. However, since neither the RN nor the USN was prepared to allocate scarce destroyer types to the theatre, the small-ship RCN escorts had to assume the burden. This permitted the decimation of the eastern Canadian and Newfoundland offshore fishing fleets by U-boat raiders in 1918.

86 NA, CO, HMCS *Niobe*, to chief accountant, Dept of the Naval Service, 3 August 1918, RG 24, 5662, 58–53–30.

87 Ibid.; and Hadley and Sarty, *Tin-Pots and Pirate Ships*, 211.

88 NA, chief accountant, Dept of the Naval Service, to paymaster, Dept of Militia, St John's, Nfld, 9 December 1919, RG 24, 5662, 58–53–30V2.

89 NA, Cmdr H.E. Holme, OC *Niobe*, to admiral superintendent, Halifax, n.d. [February 1918], RG 24, 5662, 58–53–30V1.

90 NA, A/AG Canadian Militia Circular, 19 April 1917, RG 24, 5662, 58–53–6V2.

91 NA, admiral superintendent, Halifax, to secretary, Dept of the Naval Service, 25 February 1918; and command memorandum, Naval Service, to admiral superintendent, Halifax, 25 March 1918, RG 24, 5662 58–53–30V1.

92 For this and the following, see Hadley and Sarty, *Tin-Pots and Pirate Ships*, 223.

93 PANL, Samuel Petten, RNR, attached HMS *Caesar*, Bermuda, to Hon. W. Coaker, MHA, St John's, n.d. [August 1917]: attached correspondence, governor of Nfld to General Staff officer, Dept of Militia and Defence, St John's, 2 August 1917, GN 1/10/1 (RNR 1917–20).

94 C. Cobb, Nfld RNR, HMS *Albion*, Devonport, to Hon. W. Halfyard, colonial secretary, St John's n.d.: attached correspondence, Cmdr A. MacDermott, OC HMS *Briton*, to Hon. W. Halfyard, 3 March 1919, Duff Papers, Nfld Museum.

95 PANL, Return of Number of Recruits, HMS *Briton*, 22 February 1920, GN 1/10/1 (RNR 1917–20).

96 Nicholson, *The Fighting Newfoundlander*, 509.

97 See ibid., 1–106.

CHAPTER FIFTEEN

1 Audette, "The Lower Deck," 247.

2 Lay, *Memoirs of a Mariner*, 88–9.

3 Schull, *The Far Distant Ships*, 127–8.

4 This represents a 4 per cent sampling of RCN and RCNR officers; a 2 per cent sampling of RCNVR and WRCN officers; and a 1 per cent sampling of the other ranks.

5 All figures for the Canadian population are from the 1941 census.

6 Tucker, *Naval Service*, 2:245.

7 DHist, Naval Order 1296, 12 April 1941.

8 DHist, Naval Order 1322, 6 May 1941.

9 Tucker, *Naval Service*, 2:245–7.

10 Ibid., 2:277; and Stacey, *Arms, Men and Governments*, 420.

11 Tucker, *Naval Service*, 2:277.

12 For instance, the Department of External Affairs had few francophone foreign service officers. English, *Shadow of Heaven*, 1:149.

### CHAPTER SIXTEEN

1 The Canadian Women's Auxiliary Air Force was later redesignated (in February 1942) the Royal Canadian Air Force (Women's Division). From Roach Pierson, *"They're Still Women After All,"* 95.

2 Tucker, *Naval Service*, 2:320. It is difficult to understand the context of Tucker's comments. The roles assigned to the Wrens were support roles – that of secretary, clerk, cook, and messwoman – work that was hardly a male monopoly.

3 Stacey, *Arms, Men and Governments*. Though not an official publication, this volume was published "by the Authority of the Minister of National Defence." These services were: the RCAF (Women's Division), the Canadian Women's Army Corp (CWACs), and the Women's Royal Canadian Naval Service (WRCNS).

4 The official history of the RCAF states only that "groundcrew recruiting never proved a real problem during the war, particularly after women were enroled in the Canadian Women's Auxiliary Air Force – later called the RCAF (Women's Division) – starting in 1941." (Douglas, *The Creation of a National Air Force*, 220.) This brief treatment is startling given that this work was written in 1986, a full two decades after the establishment of women's history as a legitimate and worthwhile field of enquiry.

5 Interestingly, this is not the case in the United States, where an entire volume of the official history of the US Army during the Second World War was devoted to women. See Treadwell, *The Women's Army Corp*.

6 See J. Cassin-Scott, *Women at War*; Kevin Sim, *Women at War*; Eric Taylor, *Women Who Went to War*; Martin Binkin, *Women and the Military*; Hugh Conrod, *Athene, Goddess of War: The Canadian Women's Army Corp, Their Story*; Beryl Escott, *Women in Air Force Blue: The Story of Women in the Royal Air Force from 1918 to the Present Day*; Elizabeth Ewing, *Women in Uniform*; Arthur Marwick, *Women at War 1914–1918*; Ursula Mason, *The Wrens 1917–1977 – A History of the Women's Royal Naval Service*; J. Piggot, *Queen Alexandra's Royal Nursing Service*; and Roy Terry, *Women in Khaki*.

7 Based on the responses of 150 women to the questionnaire I distributed at the 50th anniversary reunion of the formation of the Wrens, held in Halifax,

August 1992. The same pleasure is expressed in written works as well, where a sense of liberation appears to be common. One British woman described her experiences as "being let out of a cage." See the introduction in Gail Braybon and Penny Summerfield, *Out of the Cage*; Hugh Conrod, *Athene, Goddess of War*; Rosamond Greer, *The Girls of the King's Navy*; and Adelaide Sinclair, "Women's Royal Canadian Naval Service."

8 Pierson, *"They're Still Women After All,"* 9.

9 Only the Canadian and British military dismissed women at armistice; in the United States women were permitted to remain as part of the permanent peacetime force.

10 See Milkman, "Redefining 'Women's Work,'" 336–72.

11 This, at least, was the policy in the Canadian military. In the American Women's Army Corps, service women who had contracted a venereal disease during her service or whose disease had not been detected before enlistment because of a faulty medical exam were treated. Women who were found to be suffering from a venereal disease during an enlistment medical were not permitted to join. See Treadwell, *The Women's Army Corps*, 615–18.

12 This is true of both the American and Canadian services. Ibid., 622.

13 Pierson, *"They're Still Women After All,"* 13.

14 "The term 'patriarchal' refers to power relations in which women's interests are subordinated to the interests of men … [these power relations] rest on the social meanings given to biological sexual difference." Weedon, *Feminist Practice*, 2.

15 Ibid. It should be noted that Ruth Pierson offers no explanation of what she means by the term "power."

16 Ibid., 127.

17 Ibid., 13–14. As some historians have noted, women were not barred entirely in their dealings with the military. Women served as laundresses, cooks, and "camp followers" in pre–Second World War conflicts, but always as civilians. In a similar fashion, nurses were first incorporated into the British, American, and Canadian military as a separate corps and not as part of the regular army. During the First World War, nearly 13,000 women were recruited into the US Navy and Marine Corps as clerks and telephone operators. The ruling that had permitted their admission was later questioned, and the enlistment of women subsequently ceased. Large-scale, government-sanctioned admission of women into the military, then, did not occur in Britain, Canada, and the United States until the Second World War.

18 See Pierson's conclusion, "When Fluffy Clothes Replace the Uniform," in *"They're Still Women After All,"* 215–20.

19 Pierson, *"They're Still Women After All,"* 96.

20 No explanation is offered for why the CWAC was the only service to be considered or why it was chosen over the Women's Division of the RCAF or the WRCNS. See Pierson, *"They're Still Women After All,"* 96.

21 Pierson states that "a link existed in Canada between the military, power and prestige." Furthermore, as Patricia E. Roy has pointed out with respect to Canada's reluctance to recruit Canadian-born Japanese and Chinese for military service during the Second World War, "Military Service is the ultimate test of citizenship. By allowing Chinese and Japanese Canadians to serve in the armed forces, Canada would concede them a claim for equality." Roy, "The Soldiers Canada Didn't Want," 341, quoted in Pierson, *They're Still Women After All,*" 96.

22 Pierson, *"They're Still Women After All,"* 96.

23 For this and the following, see ibid., 117.

24 The highest rank was initially equivalent to a colonel. Pierson, *"They're Still Women After All,"* 118.

25 The revised army regulations of 1943 stipulated that rank was to be assigned according to the following guide:

5. Officers, Warrant Officers and Non-Commissioned Officers in other branches of the Army according to the dates of their appointments in their respective ranks, but where such appointments bear the same dates, Officers and other Ranks of the Canadian Women's Army Corps shall rank junior.

6. Officers, Warrant Officers and Non-commissioned Offers of the Army, of corps other than the Canadian Army Corps, shall have power of command over personnel of the Canadian Women's Army Corps who are junior to them by rank, appointment or seniority.

7. Officers, Warrant Officers and Non-Commissioned Officers of the Canadian Women's Army Corp shall have power of command only over Officers and Other ranks of other Branches of the Army as may from time to time be placed under their command. Pierson, *"They're Still Women After All,"* 121.

26 Pierson, *"They're Still Women After All,"* 122.

27 Greer, *The Girls of the King's Navy,* 32.

28 While the procedures were the same, women unit officers were the commanding officer's adviser on female matters, and did possess a right of direct access to him. Hitsman, *Report No. 68,* 18.

29 Tucker, *Naval Service,* 2:322.

30 Hitsman, *Report No. 68,* 7.

31 Ibid., 18. On the matter of promotions, see DND, *Organization and Administration of the Women's Royal Canadian Naval Service,* article 5. To be clear, the women were trained in classes separate from the men, but the content and structure of their training were the same as for men.

32 The exceptions to this were female doctors and nurses. Female doctors were paid at the same rates of pay as male doctors. NA, Treasury Board Minutes, 1 October 1941, RG 24, vol. 3371, file 428–1–2.

33 During a discussion of the War Appropriations Bill in the House of Commons on 3 June 1943, Mr. Power stated, "The original rate of pay for women in the

Armed Forces was laid down in Britain, early in the war, when surveys showed that three women would be required to replace every two men in uniform. The RAF accordingly paid its airwomen two-thirds as much as airmen received, and the RCAF fell into line with this when establishing the CWAAF in 1941. Recently, however, Britain has found that women in the service have increased in efficiency to the point where five women effectively replace four men. Accordingly, the RAF raised its rates of pay for women to four-fifths its rates of pay for men." DHist, 181.009 (D876), Press Release, 27 July 1943. The army and the navy soon followed suit and raised their rates of pay for women.

34 An accurate figure on the replacement ratio of women to men has never been determined. During one War Cabinet Committee meeting, the minister of national defence for air stated that "experience in the RCAF (WD) had shown that the employment of women did not result in an equivalent reduction in the number of men needed. Substitution would, of course, take place but it was not safe to count upon 100 percent replacement of male personnel." War Cabinet Committee Minutes, 4 September 1942. On the other hand, reports from other sources indicated that three women could often replace four men.

35 NA, RG 24, vol. 8105, file NSS 1280–125.2. Captain Sinclair notes in her final 1946 report and recommendations for future service that it was only due to the "concerted effort" of all three women's services that inequalities in income tax exemption, pension rates and out-of-work benefits were obtained. Adelaide Sinclair, "Report on W.R.C.N.S.," 1946, NS file 1700–190, vol. 1, sec. 9.

36 For this and the following, see Adelaide Sinclair, "Report on W.R.C.N.S.," 1946, NS file 1700–190, vol. 1, sec. 9.

37 Adelaide Sinclair, for example, noted that "WRCNS controlled traffic coming in and out of Newfoundland." In Janice Middleton, "Canada's Forgotten Veterans," Ottawa Citizen, 10 November 1981, sec. B, p. 1.

38 Sinclair, "Report on W.R.C.N.S.," 1946, NS file 1700–190, vol. 1, sec. 5.

39 Isabelle MacNeil, quoted in ibid., sec. 6.

40 Employment in Canada increased only 26.3 per cent in the decade between 1931 and 1941; almost all of this increase occurred in the last year and a half of the period. Government of Canada, Monthly Employment Statistics (Ottawa: Dominion Bureau of Statistics), 11 SC 71-d-52.

41 Little work has been done on the changes in Canadian industrial employment from the Depression era to peak wartime production using a gender-based system of analysis. Gail Braybon and Penny Summerfield have described the shifts in England as less than "smooth." They point out: "It was assumed that if 'non-essential' industries were concentrated in a few firms, factory space and resources would become available and workers would be freed for employment in more important industries like

munitions ... Because so many women worked in consumer industries such as textiles, clothing, pottery and books and shoes, which as in 1914, cut their workforces in the face of the threat war posed to their markets, there were more women out of work during 1940 than there had been in 1939 whereas the number of unemployed men fell ... For example some 20,000 women were 'freed' from the cotton industry during 1940–1941 but only half of them found new jobs, in spite of the war situation." Braybon and Summerfield, *Out of the Cage*, 155–6.

42 The increase in employment figures for the logging industry was a remarkable 84 per cent while employment in construction increased 68.1 per cent. Government of Canada, *Monthly Employment Statistics* (194?), 2.

43 For example, the index number of employment for the nation as a whole climbed 18 points from 1 January 1940 to 1 January 1941, while the next year's increase (1941–42) was 31.6, slightly less than double the rate of growth. Government of Canada, Table 1, "Index Numbers of Employment by Provinces and Economic Areas," in *The Employment Situation at the Beginning of October, 1942*, 24.

44 The ages eighteen to thirty were selected because eighteen was the minimum age required for enlistment and women over thirty were initially discouraged from enlisting unless they held special qualifications. Over 90 per cent of the women who did enlist during 1941 were between the ages of eighteen and thirty (see Table 16.7).

45 Calculated from *Eighth Census of Canada, 1941*, vol. 7, Table 5, "Wage Earners... ," 70.

46 NA, RG 24, vol. 5378 file HQS 45–25–10, calculated from Interim Tabulation of Occupational History Forms supplied by the Armed Forces, Department of Labour, 16 February 1943.

47 The Directorate of Manning's survey of 1941 revealed that 43 per cent of those interviewed stated that the primary reason their friends had decided not to enlist was low pay. Other reasons included the lack of privacy, dress regulations, and unlady-like companions. DHist, DND, 181.003 (D1469), working paper used by SO P. Wetzel in preparing WD history; and Dhist, DND, 181.009 (D891), 15.

48 Air force enlistments as a percentage of approaches:

| British Columbia | 55.4 | Nova Scotia | 40.8 |
|---|---|---|---|
| Alberta | 49.9 | PEI | 39.4 |
| Manitoba | 49.9 | Ontario | 37.6 |
| New Brunswick | 45.5 | Quebec | 27.5 |
| Saskatchewan | 45.3 | | |

Calculated from RCAF (Women's Division) statistics, DHist, DND, vols 74–7, 427–9.

49 Pierson, "*They're Still Women After All*," 117.

50 The largest exception to this were the war-based industries. A fair-wages policy established by the government in 1942 established "the minimum rates to
be paid in the case of contracts for manufacture of government supplies and
equipment to 35 cents an hour for males and 25 cents per hour for females,
18 years of age and over." Thus the minimum wage for women in such industries was double that of minimum wage for a servicewoman. The servicewoman's wage, however, was supplemented by allowances, discounts,
benefits, and regular pay promotions. Few of these industries existed in the
West, where the rate of enlistment into the service was highest.

51 In 1943 the pay rate of women was raised to four-fifths that of men. It should
be noted that while servicewomen received this increase, the salaries of civilian women working were frozen in agreement with the ruling of the Privy
Council in 1942.

52 Department of Labour, *Report of the Department of Labour* (1945), 11.

53 Conversation with Dr Roger Sarty, DHist, DND, January 1991.

54 Only an estimate is possible, since the overtime worked by service personnel
varied greatly according to trade, rank, location, and operational demands.

55 Canada, *Weekly Earnings of Employees Engaged in the Manufacturing
Industries of Canada* (1946), Table 1, p. 2.

56 The figures are calculated from the birth rates of all 9,485 women who had
enlisted by the time the survey was conducted.

57 Stenographers, for example, were trained under the War Time Emergency
Plan. DHist, DND, file 74-7, 299–311.

58 Memorandum from deputy minister to Robert England, executive secretary,
General Advisory Committee on Demobilization and Rehabilitation,
13 November 1942, DHist, DND, file 74-7, 299–311.

CHAPTER SEVENTEEN

1 Masland and Radway, *Soldiers and Scholars*, 95.

2 Gardiner, *The British Admiralty*, 102.

3 Ibid., 250.

4 Ibid., 266.

5 P.W. Brock, "Nixon and The Royal Naval College of Canada, 1910–1922,"
33.

6 Hines, "The Royal Naval College of Canada," 165.

7 Ibid., 165–6.

8 Ibid., 166–9.

9 Ibid., 167.

10 Ibid., 186.

11 Eayrs, *From the Great War to the Great Depression*, 274–5. In 1933 the
newly created position of chief of defence staff was filled by Maj.-Gen.
A.G.L. McNaughton, who felt that the growing importance of air power had

rendered the navy obsolete. When the government decided to reduce defence expenditures that year, McNaughton recommended that the majority of the cuts come from the naval budget, which would have left the RCN an insufficient amount to function with. The CNS, Admiral Hose, managed to convince the Treasury Board not to make the proposed cuts, but it was close.

12 NA, minutes of meeting held in the minister's office, 28 August 1940, 11 a.m., RG 24, file 83–84/167, vol. 529, NSC 1700–121/2(1).

13 House of Commons, *Debates*, 19 November 1940, 202–6.

14 *The Log*, Graduation 1944, speech by the Hon. Angus L. Macdonald to the graduating class. *The Log* was the unofficial publication of the cadets at the college.

15 Milner, *North Atlantic Run*, 15–19.

16 NA, memorandum from DNP to CNS, 23 August 1940, RG 24, vol. 5586, file NS 1–24–1, vol. 3.

17 NA, memorandum of Conference on Manning and Training held at NSHQ, 30 August 1940, RG 24, vol. 4045, file NS 1078–3, vol. 1.

18 DHist, Biog G., interview with Captain J.W. Grant, 37–8.

19 NA, memorandum from naval secretary to COPC, 22 July 1941, RG 24, vol. 11848, NE 15–13, NS 100–7–1. The naval secretary, Paymaster-Captain J.O. Cossette, informed the COPC on 22 July of the formation of a board consisting of Acting-Captain W.B.L. Holms, J.M. Grant, and Professor L. Richardson, who had recently been appointed as the director of naval education.

20 NA, report by the Naval College Board to COPC, 11 August 1941, 1, RG 24, vol. 11848, NE 15–13, vol. 1.

21 Ibid., 2.

22 Ibid., Appendix 1.

23 Mahoney, "The Royal Canadian Naval College," 436.

24 Preston, "MARCOM Education," 68–69.

25 *The Log* 5, no. 2 (1945): 12–15.

26 Ibid., 13.

27 Preston, "MARCOM Education," 68.

28 House of Commons, *Debates*, 25 October 1945, 1509.

29 Eayrs, *Peacemaking and Deterrence*, 124–5. The incidents took place on board HMC Ships *Magnificent*, *Athabaskan*, and *Crescent* in early 1949. All three cases involved a number of Canadian sailors refusing to obey orders. An investigation of the incidents by a committee, chaired by Rear Admiral R. Mainguy, called into question certain RCN practices and stressed the need to "Canadianize" the navy.

30 NA, memorandum from DNE to CNP/CGS/MND, 26 September 1945, RG 24, vol. 83–84/167, file 529, NSC 1700–121/2(3).

31 NA, memorandum from CNP to CNS, 15 October 1945, RG 24, vol. 83–84/167, file 529, NSC 1700–121/2(3).

32 Preston, *Canada's* RMC, 310.

33 DHist, "Report to the Chief of the General Staff on the Provision of Officers – Post-War Active Force," 12, 113.3m3.009(D7).

34 For this and the following, see NA, letter from CAS to CNS, 31 January 1946, RG 24, 83–84/167, file 529 1700–121/2(3).

35 NA, letter from CAS to CNS, 31 January 1946, attached note from Grant to A/CNS, undated, RG 24, 83–84/167, file 529 1700–121/2(3).

36 NA, note from A/CNS to CNP, 9 March 1946, RG 24.

37 Preston, *Canada's* RMC, 325.

38 NA, unpublished memoirs of Brooke Claxton, MG 32, B5, vol. 221, 828.

39 Ibid., 827.

40 NA, message from AFHQ to COPC, 4 April 1947, RG 24, D 11, vol. 11819, 1700–121/2.

41 NA, memorandum from naval secretary to CO, HMCS *Royal Roads*, 3 April 1947, RG 24, D11, vol. 11819, 1700–121/2.

42 NA, unpublished memoirs of Brooke Claxton, MG 32, B5, vol. 221, 827–8.

43 DHist, HQS 403–0–1, "Report of the Inter-Service Committee on Officer Training," Appendix M, minutes of the 1st meeting, 18 June 1947, 4.

44 Ibid., Appendix C, telegram from Claxton to Stedman committee, 22 June 1947.

45 Stanley, *Canada's Soldiers*, 328.

46 DHist, "Report of the Inter-Service Committee on Officer Training," Appendix F, letter from MND to CAS/CGS/CNS, 21 July 1947.

47 Ibid., Appendix M, minutes of 7th meeting, 24 September 1947.

48 Preston, *Canada's* RMC, 325.

49 Ibid., 328–9.

50 DHist, HQS 403–0–1, "Report of the Inter-Service Committee on Officer Training," 6–13.

CHAPTER EIGHTEEN

1 The third *Ottawa* displayed the following battle honours: Atlantic, 1939–45 (convoy escort); Normandy, 1944 (Operation Neptune); English Channel, 1944 (sinking of the German submarine U-678); and Bay of Biscay, 1944 (sinking of the German submarines U-621 and U-984).

2 *Ottawa Journal*, 3 April 1968, in National Defence Records Management System (NDRMS) 1211–14–3, vol. 1.

3 Allard and Bernier, *Jean V. Allard*, 366.

4 NDRMS, 1211–0, vol. 3; 1211–17, vol. 1; and Pariseau and Bernier, *French Canadians and Bilingualism*, 1:210, and Annex PP, recommendation no. 33.

5 NDRMS, 1211–0, vol. 3, 14–15.

6 DHist, Memorandum P1210–2 from CDS to VCDS/CP/CTS/CG, 2 May 1967, 84/126, file 9.

7 For this and the following, see NDRMS, 1211–14–3, vol. 1, Simard to Allard, 12 October 1967.

8 DHist, Program to increase Bilingualism and Biculturalism in the Canadian Armed Forces, 84/331, vol. 18.

9 Simard to Allard, 12 October 1967.

10 DHist, Reports and Returns – General, vol. 1, Simard to Allard, 15 March 1968, 90/444, file 15.

11 NDRMS P1211–14–3, vol. 1. *Progress Report – Bilingual Ship – HMCS Ottawa*, sent to CP, 25 June 1970.

12 Simard to Allard, 15 March 1968.

13 NDRMS P1211–14–3, vol. 1, Simard to Hennessy, 25 June 1970.

14 NDRMS P1211–14–3, vol. 1, message 201300Z August 70, CANMARCOM to CANFORCEHED.

15 NDRMS P1211–14–3, vol. 1, minute from Maj.-Gen. J.A. Dextraze to DGPC.

16 NDRMS P1211–14–3, vol. 1, DGPC to DMOC, 27 August 1970.

17 NDRMS P1211–14–3, vol. 1, Simard's report, 25 June 1970 (Simard to Hennessy, 25 June 1970).

18 NDRMS P1211–14–3, vol. 1, Simard's report, 25 June 1970. See the comment of Maj.-Gen. J.A. Dextraze, then chief of personnel development (CPD), of 24 July 1970 on the Simard report of 25 June 1970. "The *Ottawa* should be referred to by its name and not be called the bilingual ship. This ship's working language is French; hence it is a French speaking unit." Dextraze reiterated the point further on in the same memorandum. "The purpose of having the *Ottawa* as a French speaking ship is to allow the Francophones of this country to identify themselves as a French speaking component of the Canadian Naval Forces. It is therefore, important that we do not call these ships bilingual ships."

19 For this and the following, see NDRMS P1211–14–3, vol. 1, Simard's report, 25 June 1970; covering letter in Simard's report from Simard to Hennessy, 25 June 1970. Another similar reference can be found in the body of the report.

20 See Pariseau and Bernier, *French Canadians and Bilingualism*, 189, Table 13.

21 For this and the following, see DHist, Col. Hanna to DBPR and DLT, 16 June 1972, 90/444, file 37.

22 For this and the following, see NDRMS P1211–14–3, vol. 3, DGBB to DGPC, 16 August 1972.

23 NDRMS, 1211–14–3, vol. 4, DCPD to ADM(Per) through DGCD.

24 NDRMS, 1211–14–3, vol. 4, D/DGBB to DGBB.

25 NDRMS, 1211–14–3, vol. 4, VCDS to Commander, MARCOM, 17 June 1973.

26 For this and the following, see NDRMS, 1211–14–3, vol. 5, Boys to McLaws, 11 February 1974.

27 Very briefly, according to this model, FLUs were to send and receive all correspondence with superior formations in French; they would receive correspondence in English from English-language units and reply to it in French.

28 For this and the following, see NDRMS PI211–14–3, vol. 3, Rear Admiral Timbrell, Commander, MARCOM, to his units, 11 July 1972.

29 NDRMS PI211–14–3, vol. 3, DBPR to DO, 29 August 1972. Armand Letellier was the DGBB. Tousignant, as DBPR, was one of Letellier's assistants.

30 Breheret, "La francophonie dans les Forces armées canadiennes," 435.

31 DHist, Ottawa Historical Report, 6 May 1970, file 1326–1295.

32 DHist, Ottawa Historical Report, 1 June 1973, file 1326–1295.

## CHAPTER NINETEEN

1 Rear Admiral H.A. Porter, RCN, to Vice-Admiral Richard G. Colbert, USN letter dated 27 November 1969, cited in Hattendorf, "International Naval Co-operation," 248.

2 See Lambert, "Admiral Sir Francis Bridgeman-Bridgeman." Lambert notes that Winston Churchill, as First Lord, determined not to send out the battle-cruisers *Indomitable* and *New Zealand* to the Pacific (China Station) despite Britain's promise to do so at the 1909 Imperial Conference.

3 See, for example, Barry Gough, "The End of Pax Britannica," esp. 98–100.

4 Roskill, *Naval Policy between the Wars*, 1:271–5 (1918) and 1:401–2 (1923).

5 See Coulthard-Clark, "Richmond's Australian Connection," 265–75. This gives a fascinating insight into Richmond's intellectual schizophrenia resulting from his deep concerns about the inadequacies of a poorly thought through and insufficiently resourced policy and his need to support the Admiralty's case for a unified maritime strategy in the 1930s.

6 Gill, *Royal Australian Navy 1939–1942*, 73–77.

7 Zimmerman, "The RAN and the RCN," 212.

8 Coulthard-Clark, *The Third Brother*, 59–63.

9 Rear Admiral J.S. Dumaresq (commanding the Australian Squadron 1919–22) and Rear Admiral (later Admiral Sir John) Crace (commanding the Australian Squadron 1939–42) are two outstanding examples of highly competent Australian-born officers in the RN who served on loan to the RAN. As a lieutenant-commander, Crace also commissioned the battle-cruiser *Australia* in 1913.

10 Hyslop, *Australian Naval Administration*, 93.

11 Admiral Sir Max Horton refused the appointment before the Second World War, despite his "happy experience" of Australian cruisers under his command in the Mediterranean. See Chalmers, *Max Horton*, 55–56. At least one officer refused the job in 1941 before Sir Guy Royle consented to accept, and the same happened in 1944–45. The officer eventually selected, Admiral Sir Harold Burrough, then had to be diverted to replace Admiral Sir Bertram Ramsay as C-in-C, Allied Naval Expeditionary Forces in Europe after the latter's death in a plane crash. Vice-Admiral Sir Louis Hamilton was finally persuaded to go, although he assumed the post reluctantly and with very mixed feelings.

12 Rotherham, *It's Really Quite Safe!*, 296–7.

13 See Goldrick, "Carriers for the Commonwealth," 225.

14 Ray Jones, *Seagulls, Cruisers and Catapults*.

15 See Ray Jones, "A Fall from Favour," 53–61, for an interesting discussion of the factors behind the ship's decommissioning and eventual destruction.

16 Horner, *High Command*, 161.

17 Great Britain, PRO, secretary to First Sea Lord, minute 1912/89c of 27 April 1949, ADM 205/72.

18 See Admiral Sir Charles Lambe (C-in-C, Far East Fleet) to Admiral the Earl Mountbatten (First Sea Lord), letter dated 24 November 1955, Mountbatten Papers (Hartley Library, University of Southampton).

19 Tucker, *Naval Service*, 2: 88–94.

20 Zimmerman, *The Great Naval Battle of Ottawa*, 166.

21 Goldrick, "Captain James Bernard Foley," 515–16.

22 Hyslop, "Admiral Sir George Francis Hyde," 420–2.

23 DeWolf cited from a 1985 interview in the *Maritime Warfare Bulletin Commemorative Edition 1985*, 24. See also note 4 in Barry Gough, "The End of Pax Britannica," 364.

24 Pound, *Evans of the Broke*, 207–8.

25 Conversation between the author and Rear Admiral G.R. Griffiths, AO, DSO, DSC, RAN (Ret.), 2 July 1989. Only HMS *Saintes* had carried an experimental Mark VI mounting before *Tobruk* commissioned. See Cooper, "At the Crossroads." This gives a useful summary of many of the problems facing the Australian Naval Staff in the period.

26 Knox, "An Engineer's Outline of RCN History," 319–24.

27 See P.D. Jones, "Buying the DDGs," 316–29.

28 Glover "The RCN: Royal Colonial Navy or Royal Canadian Navy?," in this volume, cited from original paper prepared for the Second Naval Historical Conference, "In Quest of a Canadian Naval Identity," 19.

29 Rodger, "Review," 99.

30 Audette, "The Lower Deck," 247.

31 Frame, *Where Fate Calls*.

32 Frame, *Pacific Partners*.

33 Millar, *Australia's Defence*, 168.

34 See Smith, "Minority Representation in the ADF," 33–5.

35 See Gill, *Royal Australian Navy*, 22–3.

36 Ibid., 195.

37 Zimmerman, "A Question of Identity: The Statistical Analysis of the Social Background of the Wartime Navy," in this volume, citing Lay, *Memoirs of a Mariner*, 88–9. It is worth noting that Brodeur was not only one of the relatively few French Canadian officers in the RCN, but also politically well connected. W.G.D. Lund elsewhere cites Admiral Lay as suggesting that Brodeur's treatment at the hands of the RN as a junior officer helped instil an

anti-British approach that was to manifest itself during the war. See Lund "The Royal Canadian Navy's Search for Autonomy," 354–5, nos 48 and 49.

38 MacNeil, *Wordstruck*.

39 See Holden, "The Learning Curve," 125–9.

40 See Patterson, *The Jellicoe Papers*, 2:312–15, 332–8.

41 See Horton to the naval secretary, letter cited in Chalmers, *Max Horton*, 55–6. See also Collins, *As Luck Would Have It*. Collins was the executive officer of HMAS *Sydney* in her first commission, much of which was spent in the Mediterranean.

42 See also Milner, *North Atlantic Run*, and Zimmerman, *The Great Naval Battle of Ottawa*, for descriptions of the consequences of the too rapid expansion of the RCN.

43 Glover, "The RCN: Royal Colonial Navy or Royal Canadian Navy?," in this volume.

44 Four captains were killed between 1941 and 1944: Burnett (lost in HMAS *Sydney*), Waller (lost in HMAS *Perth*; he was probably the finest seagoing commander the RAN ever produced, and would likely have become CNS in the mid-1950s instead of Dowling), Getting (HMAS *Canberra*), and Dechaineux (killed in a kamikaze attack on HMAS *Australia*). Two more, Howden and Armstrong, became medically unfit for sea service (and thus promotion), while the highly competent Farncomb was forced to leave the service in 1951 because of alcoholism, just at the time he might have expected to relieve Collins as CNS. Farncomb's condition had been brought on by the strain of spending all but six months of the Second World War in seagoing command. The promotion rates between 1935 and 1938 explain the problem:

|  | Seagoing Forces (Executive Branch) | |
|---|---|---|
|  | To Captain | To Commander |
| 1935 | 1 | 2 |
| 1936 | 0 | 3 |
| 1937 | 3 | 3 |
| 1938 | 2 | 3 |

The rates during the Second World War were little better, the Naval Board being determined not to allow expansion that would require postwar reductions as traumatic as the "Axe" of the early 1920s. This policy was reflected in the entries to the RAN College. In 1919 there were thirty-two cadet midshipmen entered. By 1921 the annual intake had dropped to twelve. By 1940, even with the addition of a Special Entry, the total number for permanent career service was only thirty-seven. There was no entry for 1931. See Cunningham, *Work Hard Play Hard*, 121–46.

In consequence of this limited-entry policy, the promotion rates for certain years were quite extraordinary. The 1932 entry had twelve cadet midshipmen. One became a vice-admiral, three rear admirals, and one a substantive commodore. This was exceptional, but it does indicate just how small the "pool" was.

45 See Lund, "The Royal Canadian Navy's Quest for Autonomy," 138–57.

46 Cited in Crickard, "A Tale of Two Navies," 86.

47 Gill, *Royal Australian Navy*, 102–3.

48 See Le Bailly, *The Man around the Engine*, for a scathing account of the tribulations of the British Pacific Fleet in 1944–45.

49 Gill, *Royal Australian Navy*, 676–7.

50 See, for example, Dibb, *Review of Australia's Defence Capabilities*.

51 See Young, "ANZUS Naval Relations 1951–1985"; Sokolsky, *A Question of Balance*; and Frame, *Pacific Partners*.

52 Australia, DOD, *Defence of Australia 1987*, 8.

## CHAPTER TWENTY

1 SCNDVA, *Maritime Sovereignty*, 5.

2 Haydon, "The Future of the Canadian Navy," 8.

3 DND, *The Maritime Command Vision*, 1–5, 2–3, 2–4.

4 Gray, *Canadian Defence Priorities*, 138–9; and Hunt, "Strategy and Maritime Law," 44.

5 Johnson and Middlemiss, "Canada's 200-Mile Fishing Zone," 67–8.

6 Ibid., 93, 99–100; and VanderZwaag, *The Fish Feud*, 68–9.

7 Day, *The Saint-Pierre and Miquelon Maritime Boundary*, 1–2; and Anglin, *The St. Pierre and Miquelon Affaire of 1941*, 4–9.

8 Anglin, *The St. Pierre and Miquelon Affaire of 1941*, 135–8.

9 Touchette, *Canada-France Maritime Relations*, 1–3.

10 Department of Fisheries and Oceans (DFO), "Canada-France Fishing Relations."

11 DFO, "Canada-France Boundary Decision Is in Canada's Favour."

12 Marston, "St. Pierre-Miquelon arbitration," 160–2; and Joseph Gough, "Fisheries and Sovereignty in Canada," 16.

13 "Fishermen consider blockade," *Globe and Mail*, 3 September 1992.

14 "France to bring home 3500 personnel," *Jane's Defence Weekly* 20, no. 16 (16 October 1993): 23.

15 Cable, *Gunboat Diplomacy*, 101, 221.

16 McRae, "Canada and the Delimitation of Maritime Boundaries," 161; "Crosbie stands firm as France retaliates with new fish quotas," *Globe and Mail*, 13 October 1992; and Tracy, *The Diplomatic Utility of Canada's Naval Forces*, 21.

17 Thomas, *The Canadian Navy*, 16; and DND, *The Maritime Command Vision*, 1–1 to 1–6.
18 Treasury Board, *All the Ships That Sail*, 38 (hereafter referred as the Osbaldeston Report); SCNDVA, *Maritime Sovereignty*, 39, 46–7; and Murray, "Optimal Fleet Utilization."
19 Osbaldeston Report, 1–2, 54.
20 Sharpe, *Jane's Fighting Ships: 1993–1994*, 93.
21 Murray, "Optimal Fleet Utilization," 16; and SCNDVA, *Maritime Sovereignty*, 35, 46, 65.
22 Sharpe, *Jane's Fighting Ships: 1993–1994*, 100.
23 Ibid., 100–2; and Joseph Gough, "Fisheries and Sovereignty in Canada," 116.
24 Middlemiss, "Canada's Maritime Enforcement Policies," 318; and SCNDVA, *Maritime Sovereignty*, 49.
25 FRCC, *Report on the Status of Groundfish Stocks*, 6.
26 Copes, "Canadian Fisheries Management Policy," 5, 13; and SCNDVA, *Maritime Sovereignty*, 10–11.
27 "Hook pulled on cod fishing," *Toronto Sun*, 18 February 1994.
28 German, *The Sea Is at Our Gates*, 24–6; and Joseph Gough, "Fisheries and Sovereignty in Canada," 111.
29 Griffiths, "The Maritime Command Concept of Operations," 46; and Murray, "Optimal Fleet Utilization," 16.
30 Murray, "Optimal Fleet Utilization," 16.
31 Osbaldeston Report, 35; and SCNDVA, *Maritime Sovereignty*, 34.
32 Murray, "Optimal Fleet Utilization," 16–17; and Silverstone, "Naval Intelligence," 181.
33 SCNDVA, *Maritime Sovereignty*, 53–4; and Murray, "Optimal Fleet Utilization," 17.
34 Joseph Gough, "Fisheries and Sovereignty in Canada," 116.
35 Murray, "The Maritime Warfare Bulletin Interview," 26, 28.
36 Murray, "Optimal Fleet Utilization," 17; Murray, "The Maritime Warfare Bulletin Interview," 33; and SCNDVA, *Maritime Sovereignty*, 54.
37 Murray, "The Maritime Warfare Bulletin Interview," 33–4; and Murray, "Optimal Fleet Utilization," 17.
38 SCNDVA, *Maritime Sovereignty*, 55–6, 58.
39 "Canadian navy unfurls sales pitch," *Globe and Mail*, 26 July 1993; and "High tech on the high seas," *Globe and Mail*, 27 July 1993.
40 DND, *The Maritime Command Vision*, 2–1, 2–3, 2–5.
41 Honderich, *Arctic Imperative*, 104; and Baird, "Canadian Naval Considerations," 13, 17.
42 Tracy, *The Enforcement of Canada's Continental Maritime Jurisdiction*, 63.
43 Cable, *Gunboat Diplomacy*, 49.
44 Hobson, "Advance for Ground Wave Radar," 10.

45 Sharpe, *Jane's Fighting Ships: 1993–1994*, 85; and Byrne, "Notes on Canadian Defence Policy," 38.
46 Gunn, "Early Navy Initiatives," 52; and Murray, "The Maritime Warfare Bulletin Interview," 32.
47 Griffiths, "The Maritime Command Concept of Operations," 46.
48 Haydon, "The EH-101 Helicopter," 26.
49 Dewhirst, "Comment and Discussion," 21.
50 Tracy, *Enforcement of Canada's Continental Maritime Jurisdiction*, 21, 26, 44.
51 Ibid., 20–1; and SCNDVA, *Maritime Sovereignty*, 54.
52 Griffiths, "The Maritime Command Concept of Operations," 46.
53 Delery, "Away the Boarding Party!," 71; and Tracy, *Enforcement of Canada's Continental Maritime Jurisdiction*, 24.
54 "Update urged for foreign policy," *Globe and Mail*, 17 March 1994.
55 Tracy, *Enforcement of Canada's Continental Maritime Jurisdiction*, 56; Osbaldeston Report, 106.
56 Tracy, *Enforcement of Canada's Continental Maritime Jurisdiction*, 24–6, 106; and "Canadian navy unfurls sales pitch."
57 SCNDVA, *Maritime Sovereignty*, 50–1; and "They're Canada's fish police," *Toronto Star*, 15 November 1993.
58 SCNDVA, *Maritime Sovereignty*, 30.
59 Ibid., 50–1.
60 DND, *The Maritime Command Vision*, 2–4.
61 "Retrain fishermen to police our waters," *Toronto Star*, 25 September 1993.
62 Jessen, "Surface Vessels for the 1980s," 29–30; and Tracy, "Matching Canada's navy," 461.
63 "Somali clans threaten foreign fishing boats," *Globe and Mail*, 3 February 1994.

# Bibliography

Allard, Jean V., and Serge Bernier. *The Memoirs of General Jean V. Allard.* Vancouver: University of British Columbia Press, 1988.

Allen, Ronald Michael. "Borden, Britain, and the Navy 1909–1914." MA thesis, University of Calgary, 1971.

Anglin, Douglas. *The St. Pierre and Miquelon Affaire of 1941: A Study in Diplomacy in the North Atlantic Quadrangle.* Toronto: University of Toronto Press, 1961.

Arbuckle, Graeme. *Customs and Traditions of the Canadian Navy.* Halifax: Nimbus Publishing 1984.

Audette, L.C. "The Lower Deck and the Mainguy Report of 1949." In *The RCN in Retrospect,* edited by Boutilier, 235–49.

Australia, Department of Defence. *Defence of Australia.* Canberra: Australian Government Publishing Service, March 1987.

Baird, Katherine. "Canadian Naval Considerations within the Context of United States and NATO Maritime Strategies: Policies, Problems and Perspectives." *Canadian Defence Quarterly* 22, no. 3 (December 1992): 13–18.

Baskerville, Peter A., ed. *Canadian Papers in Business History.* Vol. 2. Victoria, BC: Public History Group, University of Victoria, 1993.

Bateman, W.S.G. "Towards an Australian Maritime Defence Strategy." In *Australia's Navy, 1990–91,* 8–9. Canberra, Department of Defence, Australian Government Publishing Service, 1990.

Bateman, W.S.G., and R.J. Sherwood. *Principles of Australian Maritime Operations.* Strategic and Defence Studies Centre, Working Paper No. 265, Canberra: Australian National University, November 1992.

Beesly, Patrick. *Very Special Intelligence: The Story of the Admiralty's Operational Intelligence Centre 1939–1945.* London: Hamish Hamilton, 1977.

Bercuson, David. *True Patriot: The Life of Brooke Claxton.* Toronto: University of Toronto Press, 1993.

Binkin, Martin, and Shirley Back. *Women and the Military.* Washington, DC: Brookings Institution, 1977.

Blakely, Tom. *Corvette Cobourg: The Role of a Canadian Warship in the Longest Sea Battle in History.* Cobourg, Ont.: Royal Canadian Legion Branch No. 133, n.d.

Bland, Douglas. *The Administration of Defence Policy in Canada 1947 to 1985.* Kingston: Ronald P. Frye, 1987.

Booth, Ken. *Navies and Foreign Policy.* London: Croom Helm, 1977.

–. *Strategy and Ethnocentrism.* London: Croom Helm, 1979.

Borden, Robert Laird. *Robert Laird Borden: His Memoirs.* 2 vols. Toronto, Macmillan, 1938.

Bothwell, Robert. *Canada and the United States.* Toronto: University of Toronto Press, 1992.

Bothwell, Robert, I. Drummond, and J. English. *Canada 1900–1945.* Toronto: University of Toronto Press, 1987.

Bothwell, Robert, and William Kilbourn. *C.D. Howe: A Biography.* Toronto: McClelland and Stewart, 1979.

Boutilier, James A., ed. *The RCN in Retrospect.* Vancouver: University of British Columbia Press, 1982.

Braybon, Gail, and Penny Summerfield. *Out of the Cage: Women's Experiences in the Two World Wars.* London: Pandora Press, 1987.

Breemer, Jan. *Soviet Submarines: Design, Development and Tactics.* London: Jane's Publishing, 1989.

Breheret, J. "La francophonie dans les Forces armées canadiennes." *Revue maritime*, no. 286 (April 1971).

Brock, Jeffry V. *The Dark Broad Seas.* Toronto: McClelland and Stewart, 1981.

–. *The Thunder and the Sunshine.* Toronto: McClelland and Stewart, 1983.

Brock, P.W. "Commander E.A.E. Nixon and The Royal Naval College of Canada, 1910–1922." In *The RCN in Retrospect*, edited by Boutilier, 33–43.

Brodeur, Nigel D. "L.P. Brodeur and the Origins of the Canadian Navy." In *The RCN in Retrospect*, edited by Boutilier, 13–32.

Burrowes, James. "Patrolling the Gulf." *Sentinel* 26, no. 6 (1990/6): 18.

Byrne, L.J. "Notes on Canadian Defence Policy." *Canadian Defence Quarterly* 21, no. 3 (December 1991): 38–40.

Cable, James. *Britain's Naval Future.* London: Macmillan Press, 1983.

–. *Diplomacy at Sea.* Annapolis: Naval Institute Press, 1985.

–. *Gunboat Diplomacy: Political Application of Limited Naval Forces.* New York: St Martin's Press, 1981.

Cameron, A. Keith. "The Royal Canadian Navy and the Unification Crisis." In *The RCN in Retrospect*, edited by Boutilier, 334–44.

Cameron, James M. *Murray: The Martyred Admiral*. Hantsport, NS: Lancelot Press, 1980.

Canada. "Extracts from the minutes of the Imperial Conference, 1926, November 15, 1926." *Documents on Canadian External Relations, 1926–1930*. Ottawa: 1971.

–. *Monthly Employment Statistics*. Ottawa: Dominion Bureau of Statistics, 194?.

–. *The Employment Situation at the Beginning of October, 1942*. Ottawa: Ministry of Trade and Commerce, 1942.

–. *Weekly Earnings of Employees Engaged in the Manufacturing Industries of Canada*. Ottawa: Dominion Bureau of Statistics, 1946.

Canada, Department of Fisheries and Oceans. "Canada-France Boundary Decision Is in Canada's Favour." *News Release*. NR–HQ–92–51E. Ottawa: Fisheries and Oceans, 11 June 1992.

–. "Canada-France Fishing Relations: The History." *Backgrounder*. B–HQ–92–021. Ottawa: Fisheries and Oceans, June 1992.

Canada, Department of Labour. *Report of the Department of Labour*. Ottawa: King's Printer, 1945.

Canada, Department of National Defence. *Canada's Defence Programme 1949–50*. Ottawa: King's Printer, 1949.

–. *Canada's Defence Programme 1951–52* (with revisions to 30 June 1951). Ottawa: King's Printer, 1951.

–. *Report of the Department of National Defence for the Fiscal Year Ending March 31, 1949*. Ottawa: King's Printer, 1949.

–. *The Regulations for the Organization and Administration of the Women's Royal Canadian Naval Service*. Ottawa: King's Printer, 1942.

–. *White Paper on Defence*. Ottawa: Queen's Printer, 1964.

Canada, House of Commons, Standing Committee on National Defence and Veterans Affairs. *Maritime Sovereignty*. Ottawa: Supply and Services, November 1990.

Canada, Treasury Board. *All the Ships That Sail: A Study of Canada's Fleets*. Ottawa: Treasury Board, 1990.

Cassin-Scott, Jack. *Women at War, 1939–45*. London: Osprey Publishing, 1980.

Chalmers, W.S. *Max Horton and the Western Approaches*. London: Hodder & Stoughton, 1954.

Clippingdale, Richard. *Laurier: His Life and World*. Toronto: McGraw-Hill Ryerson, 1977.

Collins, John. *As Luck Would Have It*. Sydney: Angus & Robertson, 1965.

Conrad, Hugh. *Athene, Goddess of War: The Canadian Women's Army Corps, Their Story*. Dartmouth, NS: Writing and Editorial Service, 1983.

Cooper, A.J.W. "At the Crossroads: Anglo-Australian Naval Relations 1945–1960." BA (honours) thesis, University College, University of New South Wales, Australian Defence Force Academy, 1991.

Copes, Parzival. "Canadian Fisheries Management Policy: International Dimensions." In *Canada's Oceans Policy: National Strategies and the New Law of the Sea*, edited by Donald McRae and Gordon Munro, 3–16. Vancouver: University of British Columbia Press, 1989.

Corbett, J.S. *Naval Operations*. Vol. 2: *History of the Great War*. London: Longmans, Green & Co., 1921.

Costelo, John. *Mask of Treachery*. London: Collins, 1988.

Coulthard-Clark, C.D. "Richmond's Australian Connection." In *Mahan Is Not Enough*, edited by Goldrick and Hattendorf. Newport: US Naval War College, 1993.

–. *The Third Brother: The Royal Australian Air Force 1921–1939*. Sydney: Allen & Unwin, 1991.

Crickard, Fred W. "A Tale of Two Navies: United States Security and Canadian and Australian Naval Policy during the Cold War." MA thesis, Dalhousie University, 1993.

Cromwell, William C. "Europe, the United States, and the pre-war Gulf crisis." *International Journal* 48, no. 1 (Winter 1992–93): 124–50.

Cunningham, I.J. *Work Hard Play Hard: The Royal Australian Naval College 1913–1988*. Canberra: Australian Government Publishing Service, 1988.

Cuthbertson, Brian. *Canadian Military Independence in the Age of the Superpowers*. Toronto: Fitzhenry & Whiteside, 1977.

Dannreuther, Roland. "The Gulf Conflict: A Political and Strategic Analysis." *Adelphi Papers*, no. 264 (Winter 1991–92): 1–88.

Davis, S.M. "It Has All Happened Before: The RCN, Nuclear Propulsion and Submarines – 1958–68." *Canadian Defence Quarterly* 17, no. 2 (Autumn 1987): 34–41.

–. "The St. Laurent Decision: Genesis of a Canadian Fleet." In *The RCN in Transition*, edited by Douglas, 187–208.

Day, Douglas. *The Saint-Pierre and Miquelon Maritime Boundary*. Boundary Briefing #5. Durham, UK: Boundaries Research Press, 1990.

Deacon, Richard. *The Silent War: A History of Western Naval Intelligence*. London: Grafton Books, 1978.

de la Billière, Peter. *Storm Command: A Personal Account of the Gulf War*. London: HarperCollins, 1992.

Delery, Tom. "Away the Boarding Party!" *Naval Review 1991* 117, no. 5 (May 1991): 65–73.

Dewhirst, Chris. "Comment and Discussion." *Proceedings (USNI)* 119, no. 8 (August 1993): 21.

Dibb, Paul. *Review of Australia's Defence Capabilities*. Canberra: Australian Government Publishing Service, March 1986.

Dickerson, Mark O., and Thomas Flanagan. *An Introduction to Governmental Politics: A Conceptual Approach*. 3d ed. Toronto: Nelson, 1990.

Dillon, G.M. *Canadian Naval Policy Since World War II: A Decision-Making Analysis*. Occasional Paper No. 2, Halifax, NS Centre for Foreign Policy Studies, Dalhousie University, October 1972.

Douglas, W.A.B. "The Anatomy of Naval Incompetence: The Provincial Marine of Upper Canada before 1813." *Ontario History* 81 (1979): 3–26.

–. "Canadian Naval Historiography." *Mariner's Mirror* 70, no. 4 (November 1984): 349–62.

–. "Conflict and Innovation in the Royal Canadian Navy 1919–1945." In *Naval Warfare in the Twentieth Century*, edited by G. Jordan, 210–34. New York: Crane Russack, 1977.

–. *The Creation of a National Air Force: The Official History of the Royal Canadian Air Force*. Vol. 2. Toronto: University of Toronto Press, 1986.

–. "Nova Scotia and the Royal Navy, 1715–1766." PhD dissertation, Queen's University, 1973.

–. "The Prospects for Naval History." *Northern Mariner* 1, no. 4 (October 1991): 19.

–, ed. *The RCN in Transition*. Vancouver: University of British Columbia Press, 1988.

Dyer, Gwynn, and Tina Viljoen. *The Defence of Canada 1760–1939*. Toronto: McClelland and Stewart, 1990.

Easterbrook, William, and G.J. Aitken. *Canadian Economic History*. Rev. ed. Toronto: Macmillan, 1963.

Easton, Alan. *50 North: An Atlantic Battleground*. Toronto: Ryerson Press, 1963.

Eayrs, James. *In Defence of Canada: Appeasement and Rearmament*. Toronto: University of Toronto Press, 1965.

–. *In Defence of Canada: Preacekeeping and Deterrence*. Toronto: University of Toronto Press, 1972.

–. *In Defence of Canada: From the Great War to the Great Depression*. Toronto: University of Toronto Press, 1964.

–. *In Defence of Canada: Growing Up Allied*. Toronto: University of Toronto Press, 1980.

English, John. *Shadow of Heaven: The Life of Lester Pearson*. Toronto: Lester & Orpen Dennys, 1989.

Escott, Beryl E. *Women in Air Force Blue: The Story of Women in the Royal Air Force from 1918 to the Present Day*. Wellingborough, England: P. Stephens, 1989.

Essex, James W. *Victory in the St. Lawrence: Canada's Unknown War*. Erin, Ont.: Boston Mills Press, 1984.

Evans, Gary. *John Grierson and the National Film Board: The Politics of Wartime Propaganda*. Toronto: University of Toronto Press, 1984.

Ewing, Elizabeth. *Women in Uniform: Through the Centuries*. Totawa, NS: Rowman and Littlefield, 1975.

Ferguson, Julie H. *Through a Canadian Periscope: The Story of the Canadian Submarine Service*. Toronto: Dundurn Press, 1995.

Fisheries Resource Conservation Council. *Report on the Status of Groundfish Stocks in the Canadian Northwest Atlantic*. Ottawa: Fisheries Resource Conservation Council, 1993.

Frame, Tom. *Pacific Partners: A History of Australian-American Naval Relations*. Sydney: Hodder & Stoughton, 1992.

–. *Where Fate Calls: The HMAS Voyager Tragedy*. Sydney: Allen & Unwin, 1991.

Frame, Tom, J.V.P. Goldrick, and P.D. Jones, eds. *Reflections on the Royal Australian Navy*. Kenthurst, NSW: Kangeroo Press, 1990.

Fregault, Guy. *Pierre le Moyne d'Iberville*. Montreal/Paris: Fides, 1968.

Friedberg, Aaron L. *The Weary Titan: Britain and the Experience of Relative Decline, 1895–1905*. Princeton: Princeton University Press, 1988.

Friedman, Norman. *Desert Victory: The War for Kuwait*. Annapolis, Md: Naval Institute Press, 1991.

–. *The Postwar Naval Revolution*. London: Conway, 1986.

Gardiner, Leslie. *The British Admiralty*. London: William Blackwood and Sons, 102.

Garner, Hugh. *Storm Below*. Toronto: Ryerson Press, 1949, 1968.

German, Tony. *The Sea Is at Our Gates: The History of the Canadian Navy*. Toronto: McClelland and Stewart, 1990.

Gilchrist, Peter. *Sea Power: Desert Storm Special 3, The Coalition and Iraqi Navies*. London: Osprey, 1991.

Gill, G. Hermon. *Royal Australian Navy 1939–1942*. Canberra: Australian War Memorial, 1957.

Gimblett, Richard. "Reassessing the Dreadnought Crisis of 1909." *Northern Mariner* 4, no. 1 (1994): 35–55.

–. " 'Tin Pots' or Dreadnoughts? The Evolution of the Naval Policy of the Laurier Administration, 1896–1910." MA thesis, Trent University, 1981.

Godfrey, Bob. Foreword to *Songs from the Front and Rear: Canadian Servicemen's Songs of the Second World War*, edited by Anthony Hopkins. Edmonton: Hurtig Publishers, 1979.

Goldrick, J.V.P. "Carriers for the Commonwealth." In *Reflections on the Royal Australian Navy*, edited by Frame, Goldrick, and Jones, 220–44.

–. "Selections from the Memoirs and Correspondence of Captain James Bernard Foley CBE, RAN (1896–1974)." In *The Naval Miscellany*, vol. 5, edited by N.A.M. Rodger, 499–531. London: Navy Records Society, 1984.

Goldrick, James, and John B. Hattendorf, eds. *Mahan Is Not Enough: The Proceedings of a Conference on the Works of Sir Julian Corbett and Admiral Sir Herbert Richmond*. Newport: US Naval War College, 1993.

Gooch, John. "Great Britain and the Defence of Canada, 1896–1914." *Journal of Imperial and Commonwealth History* 3 (May 1975).

Goodspeed, D.J. *The Armed Forces of Canada, 1867–1967*. Ottawa: Canadian Forces Headquarters 1967.

Gordon, Donald C. *The Dominion Partnership in Imperial Defense, 1870–1914*. Baltimore: Johns Hopkins Press, 1965.

Gough, Barry. "The End of Pax Britannica and the Origin of the Royal Canadian Navy: Shifting Strategic Demands of an Empire at Sea." In *The RCN in Transition*, edited by Douglas, 90–102.

–. *Gunboat Frontier: British Maritime Authority and Northwest Coast Indians, 1846–90*. Vancouver: University of British Columbia Press, 1984.

–. *The Royal Navy and the Northwest Coast of North America, 1810–1914*. Vancouver: University of British Columbia Press, 1971.

Gough, Joseph. "Fisheries and Sovereignty in Canada: Some Historical Highlights." *Maritime Warfare Bulletin*, no. 2 (1992): 107–17.

–. "Fisheries Management in Canada, 1880–1910." Halifax: Canadian Manuscript Report of Fisheries and Aquatic Sciences No. 2105, 1991.

Graham, G.S. *The Politics of Naval Supremacy*. Cambridge: Cambridge University Press, 1965.

Graham, Roger. *Arthur Meighen*. Toronto: Clarke, Irwin, 1963.

Granatstein, J.L. *Canada 1957–1967: The Years of Uncertainty and Innovation*. Toronto: McClelland and Stewart, 1986.

–. *The Generals: The Canadian Army's Senior Commanders in the Second World War*. Toronto: Stoddart, 1993.

Grant, Shelagh. *Sovereignty or Security?* Vancouver: University of British Columbia Press, 1988.

Gray, Colin S. *Canadian Defence Priorities: A Question of Relevance*. Toronto: Clarke, Irwin, 1972.

Gray, James. *The Boy from Winnipeg*. Toronto: Macmillan, 1970.

Greer, Rosamond. *The Girls of the King's Navy*. Victoria: Sono Nis Press, 1983.

Griffiths, D.N. "The Maritime Command Concept of Operations." *Maritime Warfare Bulletin*, no. 2 (1992): 35–47.

Gunn, C. "Early Navy Initiatives in Support of Other Government Department Missions and Taskings." *Maritime Warfare Bulletin*, no. 2 (1992): 51–4.

Hadley, Michael L. "Inshore ASW in the Second World War: The U-Boat Experience." In *RCN in Transition*, edited by Douglas, 233–54.

–. *U-Boats against Canada: German Submarines in Canadian Waters*. Montreal/Kingston: McGill-Queen's University Press [1985] 1990.

Hadley, Michael L., and Roger Sarty. *Tin-Pots and Pirate Ships: Canadian Naval Forces and German Sea Raiders 1880–1918*. Montreal/Kingston: McGill-Queen's University Press, 1991.

Harland, John, and John Mackay. *The Flower Class Corvette Agassiz*. Anatomy of the Ships series. London: Conway, 1993.

Harris, Daniel G. "Canadian Warship Construction 1917–1919: The Great Lakes and Upper St Lawrence River Areas." *Mariner's Mirror* 75 (May 1989): 149–58.

Hattendorf, John B. "International Naval Co-operation and Admiral Richard G. Colbert: The Intertwining of a Career with an Idea." In *The RCN in Transition*, edited by Douglas, 233–54.

–, ed. *Ubi Sumus: The State of Naval and Maritime History.* Newport, RI: US Naval War College, 1994.

Haydon, Peter. "The EH-101 Helicopter: Myths and Realities." *Forum (CDAI)* 8, no. 2 (April 1993): 23–6.

–. "The Future of the Canadian Navy." *Canadian Defence Quarterly* 20, no. 3 (December 1990): 7–10.

–. *The 1962 Cuban Missile Crisis: Canadian Involvement Reconsidered.* Toronto: Canadian Institute of Strategic Studies, 1993.

–. "When Military Plans and Policies Conflict: The Case of Canada's General Purpose Frigate Problems." In *The McNaughton Papers*, 37–56. Toronto: Canadian Institute of Strategic Studies, 1991.

Hegmann, Richard. "Reconsidering the Evolution of the U.S. Maritime Strategy, 1955–1965." *Journal of Strategic Studies* 14, no. 3 (September 1991): 299–336.

Hennessy, Michael A., and Kenrick G. Hancox, eds. *Canada, the Navy and Industry.* Toronto: Canadian Institute of Strategic Studies, 1992.

Hessler, Günther. *The U-Boat War in the Atlantic*, edited by Andrew J. Withers. London: Her Majesty's Stationery Office, 1989.

Hill, J.R. *Maritime Strategy for Medium Powers.* London: Croom Helm, 1986.

Hines, G.W. "The Royal Naval College of Canada, 1911–1922." In *Swords and Covenants*, edited by Adrian Preston and Peter Dennis, 164–89. London: Croom Helm, 1976.

Hinsley, F.H., et al. *British Intelligence in the Second World War.* 3 vols. New York: Cambridge University Press, 1979–85.

Hiro, Dilip. DESERT SHIELD to DESERT STORM: *The Second Gulf War.* New York: Routledge, 1992.

Hitsman, J.S. *Report No. 68 Historical Section (G.S.).* Ottawa: Directorate of History, 1954.

–. *Safeguarding Canada, 1763–1871.* Toronto: University of Toronto Press, 1968.

Hobson, Sharon. "Advance for Ground Wave Radar." *Jane's Defence Weekly* 21, no. 5 (5 February 1994).

–. *The Composition of Canada's Naval Fleet.* Halifax: Centre for Foreign Policy Studies, Dalhousie University, 1986.

Holden, Tom. "The Learning Curve: Some Early Courts-Martial." In *Reflections on the Royal Australian Navy*, edited by Frame, Goldrick, and Jones, 125–34.

Honderich, John. *Arctic Imperative: Is Canada Losing the North?* Toronto: University of Toronto Press, 1987.

Horner, D.M. *High Command: Australia and Allied Strategy 1939–1945*. Sydney: Allen & Unwin, 1982.

Hunt, Barry. "The Road to Washington: Canada and Empire Naval Defence." In *The RCN in Retrospect*, edited by Boutilier, 44–61.

–. "Strategy and Maritime Law." In *The RCN in Transition*, edited by Douglas, 34–48.

Hutchings, Shawn. "The Victorian Reaction to the Canadian Forces in the Persian Gulf." Paper presented in the seminar "The Canadian Navy and Major Powers," Department of History, University of Victoria, 6 December 1993.

Hyslop, Robert. "Admiral Sir George Francis Hyde (1877–1937). In *Australian Dictionary of Biography*, 9:420–2. Melbourne: Melbourne University Press, 1983.

–. *Australian Naval Administration 1900–1939*. Melbourne: Hawthorn Press, 1973.

Innis, H.A. *The Cod Fisheries*. Rev. ed. Toronto: University of Toronto Press, 1954.

Jellicoe, Admiral. *Report of Admiral of the Fleet Viscount Jellicoe of Scapa on Naval Mission to the Dominion of Canada*. 3 vols. November-December 1919.

Jessen, S.T. "Surface Vessels for the 1980s: Smaller, Cheaper, All-Purpose." *Canadian Defence Quarterly* 5, no. 3 (Winter 1975/76): 24–30.

Jockel, Joseph. *No Boundaries Upstairs*. Vancouver: University of British Columbia Press, 1978.

Johnson, Barbara, and Danford W. Middlemiss. "Canada's 200-Mile Fishing Zone: The Problem of Compliance." *Ocean Development and International Law Journal* 4, no. 1 (Spring 1977).

Jones, P.D. "Buying the DDGs." In *Reflections on the Royal Australian Navy*, edited by Frame, Goldrick, and Jones, 316–29.

Jones, Ray. "A Fall from Favour: HMAS *Australia* 1913 to 1924," *Journal of the Australian Naval Institute* 19, no. 4 (November 1993): 33–42.

–. *Seagulls, Cruisers and Catapults: Australian Naval Aviation 1913–1944*. Tasmania: Pelorus Publications, 1989.

Jordan, John. *Soviet Submarines, 1945 to Present*. London: Arms and Armour Press, 1989.

Kealy, J.D.F., and E.C. Russell. *A History of Canadian Naval Aviation 1918–1962*. Ottawa: Department of National Defence, 1965.

Kert, Faye. "The Fortunes of War: Privateering in Atlantic Canada in the War of 1812." MA thesis, Carleton University, 1986.

Knox, J.H.W. "An Engineer's Outline of RCN History: Part II." In *The RCN in Retrospect*, edited by Boutilier, 96–116.

Lamb, James B. *The Corvette Navy: True Stories from Canada's Atlantic War*. Toronto: Macmillan [1977].

–. *On the Triangle Run*. Toronto: Macmillan, 1989.

Lambert, N.A. "Admiral Sir Francis Bridgeman-Bridgeman: 1911–1912." In *The First Sea Lords: From Fisher to Mountbatten*, edited by Malcom Murfett. New York: Praeger Press, 1995.

Law, C. Anthony. *White Plumes Astern: The Short, Daring life of Canada's MTB Flotilla*. Halifax: Nimbus, 1989.

Lawrence, Hal. *A Bloody War: One Man's Memories of the Canadian Navy 1939–45*. Toronto: Macmillan, 1979.

–. *Tales of the North Atlantic*. Toronto: McClelland and Stewart, 1989.

–. *Victory at Sea: Tales of His Majesty's Coastal Forces*. Toronto: McClelland and Stewart, 1989.

Lay, H. Nelson. *Memoirs of a Mariner*. Stittsville, Ont.: Canada's Wings, 1982.

Le Bailly, Louis. *The Man around the Engine*. London: Kenneth Mason, 1990.

Leir, R.H. "Big Ship Time." In *The RCN in Retrospect*, edited by Boutilier.

Liberal Party of Canada. *Canada and the Navy: Reasons by the Rt. Hon. R.L. Borden M.P., in Favour of a Canadian Naval Service and against a Contribution*. Ottawa: Central Information Office, 1913.

–. *Canada and the Navy: The Real Emergency – The Nationalist–Conservative Alliance and Some of Its Consequences*. Ottawa: Central Information Office, 1913.

–. *Views of George E. Foster: On What Grounds Should Parliament Decide on Canadian Naval Service*. Ottawa: Central Information Office, 1913.

Longley, R.S. "The Fisheries in Nova Scotia Politics 1865–71." In *Nova Scotia Historical Society (NSHS)*. Vol. 25. Halifax: Imperial Publishing Co., 1942.

Lund, W.G. "Command Relationships in the North West Atlantic, 1939–1943." MA thesis, Queen's University, 1972.

– "The Royal Canadian Navy's Quest for Autonomy in the North West Atlantic." In *The RCN in Retrospect*, edited by Boutilier.

Lynch, Mack, ed. *Salty Dips*. Vol. 1: "... When We Were Young and in Our Prime." Vol. 2: "... and All Our Joints Were Limber." Ottawa: Naval Officers Association of Canada, 1985.

Lynch, Thomas G., and James B. Lamb. *Gunshield Graffiti: Unofficial Badges of Canada's Wartime Navy*. Halifax: Nimbus Publishing, 1984.

Macandie, G.L. *Genesis of the Royal Australian Navy*. Sydney: A.E. Pettifer, Government Printer, 1949.

Macbeth, Jack. *Ready, Aye Ready: An Illustrated History of the Royal Canadian Navy*. Toronto: Key Porter Books, n.d.

McGrath, P.T. "Colonial Naval Reserves." *Canadian Magazine* 20, (1903).

Macintyre, Donald. *U-Boat Killer*. London: Weidenfeld and Nicholson, 1956.

Mackay, Ruddock. *Fisher of Kilverstone*. Oxford: Clarendon Press, 1973.

McKee, Fraser. *The Armed Yachts of Canada*. Erin, Ont.: Boston Mills Press, 1983.

McKercher, B.J.C. "Between Two Giants: Canada, the Coolidge Conference and Anglo-American Relations, 1927." In *Anglo-American Relations in the 1920s,* edited by B.J.C. 81–124. McKercher. Edmonton: University of Alberta Press, 1990.

McLean, Doug. "The Battle of Convoy BX-141." *Northern Mariner* 3, no. 4 (October 1993): 319–35.

–. "Confronting Technological and Tactical Change: Allied Antisubmarine Warfare in the Last Year of the Battle of the Atlantic." *Naval War College Review* 47, no. 1, Sequence 345 (Winter 1994): 87–104.

MacNeil, Robert. *Wordstruck*. Penguin Books, 1989.

Macpherson, Ken. *River Class Destroyers of the Royal Canadian Navy*. Toronto: Charles Musson, 1985.

–. *Frigates of the Royal Canadian Navy*. St Catharines, Ont.: Vanwell, 1989.

Macpherson, Ken, and John Burgess. *The Ships of Canada's Naval Forces, 1910–1981*. Toronto: Collins, 1981.

Macpherson, Ken, and Marc Milner. *Corvettes of the Royal Canadian Navy*. St Catharines, Ont.: Vanwell, 1993.

McRae, Donald. "Canada and the Delimitation of Maritime Boundaries." In *Canada's Oceans Policy: National Strategies and the New Law of the Sea*, edited by Donald McRae and Gordon Munro. Vancouver: University of British Columbia Press, 1989.

Mahan, A.T. *The Interest of America in Sea Power, Present and Future*. Boston: Little, Brown, 1918.

Mahoney, E.J. "The Royal Canadian Naval College." *United States Naval Institute, Proceedings* 73, no. 1 (January 1947).

Mainguy, Rear Admiral E.R., et al. *Report on certain "Incidents" that occurred on board HMC Ships Athabaskan, Crescent, and Magnificent and on other matters concerning the Royal Canadian Navy*. Ottawa, October 1949.

Mansergh, Nicholas. *The Commonwealth Experience*. New York: Praeger, 1969.

Marder, Arthur J. *The Anatomy of Sea Power: A History of British Naval Policy in the Pre-Dreadnought Era 1885–1905*. New York: Knopf, 1940.

–. *From the Dreadnought to Scapa Flow: The Royal Navy in the Fisher Era, 1904–1919*. Vol. 1: *The Road to War, 1904–1914*. London: Oxford University Press, 1961.

Marolda, Edward J. "A Host of Nations: Coalition Naval Operations in the Persian Gulf." Paper presented to the Conference of the Society for Military History, Fredericksbrug, Va., 12 April 1992.

Marston, Geoffrey. "St. Pierre-Miquelon arbitration: Canada–France maritime delimitation award." *Marine Policy* 17, no. 3 (May 1993).

Marwick, Arthur. *Women at War, 1914–1918*. London: Croom Helm, 1977.

Masland, John W., and Laurence I. Radway. *Soldiers and Scholars*. Princeton, NJ: Princeton University Press, 1957.

Mason, Ursula, *Wrens 1917–1977: Women in the Royal Naval Service*. Education Explorers, 1977.

Mathieu, Jacques. *La Construction Navale Royale à Québec, 1739– 1759*. Quebec: n.p., 1971.

Meigs, Montgomery. *Slide Rules and Submarines: American Scientists and Subsurface Warfare in World War II*. Washington, DC: United States Government Publishing Office, 1990.

Melville, Thomas Richard. "Canada and Sea Power: Canadian Naval Thought and Policy, 1860–1910." PhD dissertation, Duke University, 1981.

Middlemiss, Danford. "Canada's Maritime Enforcement Policies." In *Canadian Foreign Policy and the Law of the Sea*, edited by Barbara Johnson and Mark Zacher. Vancouver: University of British Columbia Press, 1977.

–. "Economic Considerations and the Canadian Navy." In *The RCN in Transition*, edited by Douglas, 254–79.

Middlemiss, Danford, and J.J. Sokolsky. *Canadian Defence, Decisions and Determinants*. Toronto: Harcourt Brace Jovanovich, 1989.

Milkman, Ruth. "Redefining 'Women's Work': The Sexual Division of Labour in the Auto Industry during World War II." *Feminist Studies* 8, no. 2 (Summer 1982): 336–72.

Millar, T.B. "The Australian Naval Situation." *Proceedings*, vol. 98, no. 6. Annapolis: USN Institute Press, June 1972, 10–11.

–. *Australia's Defence*. Melbourne: Melbourne University Press, 1965.

Milner, Marc. "Canadian Escorts and the Mid Atlantic, 1942–1943." MA thesis, University of New Brunswick, 1979.

–. "The Dawn of Modern Anti-Submarine Warfare: Allied Responses to the U-Boats 1944–45." *Journal of the Royal United Services Institute* 134, no. 1 (Spring 1989): 61–9.

–. "Inshore ASW: The Canadian Experience." In *The RCN in Transition*, edited by Douglas, 143–58.

–. "No Higher Purpose: The Royal Canadian Navy's Mid-Atlantic War, 1939–1943." PhD dissertation, University of New Brunswick, 1983.

–. *North Atlantic Run: The Royal Canadian Navy and the Battle for the Convoys*. Toronto: University of Toronto Press, 1985.

–. "The Technological Implications of Technological Backwardness." *Canadian Defence Quarterly* 19, no. 3 (Winter 1989): 46–53.

–. ed. *Canadian Military History*. Copp Clark Pitman, 1993.

Moore, K.J., Mark Flanagan, and Robert Heisel. "Developments in Submarine Systems 1956–76." In *Soviet Naval Influences: Domestic and Foreign Dimensions*, edited by Michael McGwire and John McDonnell, 151–81. New York: Praeger, 1977.

Murray, L.E. "Optimal Fleet Utilization." *Forum (CDAI)* 8, no. 2 (April 1993): 21–3.

–. "The Maritime Warfare Bulletin Interview." *Maritime Warfare Bulletin*, no. 2 (1992): 10–34.

Neatby, Blair H. "Laurier and Imperialism." In *Imperial Relations in the Age of Laurier*, edited by Ramsey Cook, Craig Brown, and Carl Berger, 1–9. Toronto, Ont.: University of Toronto Press, 1969.

Nolan, Brian, and Brian Jeffery Street. *Champagne Navy: Canada's Small Boat Raiders of the Second World War.* Toronto: Random House, 1989.

Ollivier, Maurice, ed. *The Colonial and Imperial Conferences from 1887–1937.* Ottawa: E. Cloutier, Queen's Printer, 1954.

O'Neill, Robert. *Australia in the Korean War 1950–53.* Vol. 1: *Strategy and Diplomacy.* Canberra: Australian Government Publishing Service, 1981.

Palmer, Michael. *Guardians of the Gulf: A History of America's Expanding Role in the Persian Gulf.* New York: The Free Press, 1992.

–. *Origins of the Maritime Strategy.* Annapolis: US Naval Institute Press, 1990.

Pariseau, Jean, and Serge Bernier. *French Canadians and Bilingualism in the Canadian Armed Forces.* Vol. 1: *1763–1969: The Fear of a Parallel Army.* Ottawa: Department of National Defence, 1988.

Patterson, A. Temple, ed. *The Jellicoe Papers: Selections from the Private and Official Correspondence of Admiral of the Fleet Earl Jellicoe.* Vol. 2: *1916–1935.* London: Navy Records Society, 1968.

Perkins, David. *Canada's Submariners, 1914–1923.* Erin, Ont.: Boston Mills Press, 1989.

Perras, Galen Roger. *The Birth of Forward Defence: Nato and the Defence of Europe, 1945–1955.* PR502. Ottawa: Department of National Defence/Operations Research and Analysis Establishment (DND/OREA), 1989.

–. *Massive Retaliation, New Look and Nato Strategy, Nuclear Weapons and the Defence of Europe 1954–1960.* PR503. Ottawa: DND/OREA, 1989.

–. *Nato and the Defence of Europe, 1961–1967: Flexible Response Is Adopted.* PR504. Ottawa: DND/OREA, 1989.

Pickersgill, J.W., and D.F. Foster. *The Mackenzie King Record.* Toronto: University of Toronto Press, 1970.

Pierson, Ruth Roach. *"They're Still Women After All."* Toronto: McClelland and Stewart, 1986.

Piggot, Juliet. *Queen Alexandra's Royal Army Nursing Corps.* London: Leo Cooper, 1975.

Pound, Reginald. *Evans of the Broke: A Biography of Admiral Lord Mountevans.* London: Oxford University Press, 1963.

Preston, Richard A. *Canada and Imperial Defence.* Durham, NC: Duke University Press, 1967.

–. *Canada's RMC.* Toronto: University of Toronto Press, 1969.

–. *Canadian Defence Policy and the Development of the Canadian Nation 1867–1917*, Canadian Historical Association Booklet #25. Ottawa: Love Printing Service, 1970.

–. "MARCOM Education: Is It a Break with Tradition." In *The RCN in Transition*, edited by Douglas, 61–89.

Pugsley, W.H. *Sailor Remember*. Toronto: Collins, 1948.

Pullen, Hugh Francis. "The Royal Canadian Navy between the Wars, 1922–39." In *The RCN in Retrospect*, edited by Boutilier, 62–3.

–. *Saints Devils and Ordinary Seaman*. Toronto: Collins, 1945.

Ranft, Bryan. "The Protection of British seaborne trade and the development of systematic planning for war, 1860–1906." In *Technical Change and British Naval Policy 1860–1939*, edited by Bryan Ranft, 1–22. London: Hodder & Stoughton, 1977.

Reid, Escott. *Radical Mandarin: The Memoirs of Escott Reid*. Toronto: University of Toronto Press, 1989.

Robertson, Barbara. *Sir Wilfrid Laurier: The Great Conciliator*. Toronto: Oxford University Press, 1971.

Rodger, N.A.M. "Review of *The RCN in Retrospect 1910–1968*." *Mariner's Mirror* 69, no. 1 (February 1983): 99.

Roskill, Stephen. *Naval Policy between the Wars*. Vol. 1: *The Period of Anglo-American Antagonism 1919–1929*. London: Collins, 1968.

–. *The War at Sea 1939–1945*. 3 vols. London: Her Majesty's Stationery Office, 1954.

Rotherham, G.A. *It's Really Quite Safe!* Belleville: Hangar Books, 1979.

Roy, Patricia E. "The Soldiers Canada Didn't Want: Her Chinese and Japanese Citizens." *Canadian Historical Review* 59, no. 3 (September 1978): 341–58.

Safry, Micah L., and Christopher Cerf, eds. *The Gulf War Reader: History, Documents, Opinions*. Toronto: Random House, 1991.

Sarty, Roger. "Canadian Maritime Defence, 1892–1914." *Canadian Historical Review* 71 (December 1990): 48–73.

–. " 'Entirely in the hands of the friendly neighbour': The Canadian Armed Forces and the Defence of the Pacific Coast 1909–1937." In *Redirection: Defending Canada, the Pacific Perspective*, edited by D. Zimmerman. Forthcoming.

–. "Hard Luck Flotilla: The RCN's Atlantic Coast Patrol, 1914–18." In *The RCN in Transition*, edited by Douglas, 103–25.

–. "The Naval Side of Canadian Sovereignty, 1909–1923." In *The Niobe Papers*. Vol. 4: *Oceans Policy in the 1990s: An Atlantic Perspective*, edited by Fred Crickard and Katie Orr, 87–104. Halifax: Nautica Publishing, 1992.

–. "The Origin of the Royal Canadian Navy: The Australian Connection." In *Reflections on the Royal Australian Navy*, edited by Frame, Goldrick, and Jones, 74–105.

–. "Silent Sentry: A Military and Political History of Canadian Coast Defence 1860–1945." PhD thesis, University of Toronto, 1982.

–. " 'There will be trouble in the North Pacific': The Defence of British Columbia in the Early Twentieth Century." *B.C. Studies* 61 (Spring 1984): 3–29.

Sarty, Roger, and Donald Schurman, "An Historical Perspective on Canadian Naval Policy." *Argonauta* 4, no. 1 (March 1987).

Saunders, Robert. "The First Naval Incident in the Honourable Career of the Newfoundland Royal Naval Reserve." *The Newfoundland Quarterly*, Winter 1963/64.

Schneller, Robert J. "Persian Gulf Turkey Shoot: The Destruction of Iraqi Naval Forces during Operation Desert Storm." Paper presented at the Conference of the Society for Military History, Kingston, Ont., 11–13 May 1993.

Schull, Joseph. *The Far Distant Ships: An Official Account of Canadian Naval Operations in the Second world War.* Ottawa: King's Printer, 1950. Reprint. Toronto: Stoddart, 1990.

Sclater, William. *Haida.* Toronto: Oxford University Press, 1946.

Sharpe, Richard, ed. *Jane's Fighting Ships: 1993–1994.* London: Jane's Publishing, 1993.

Silkett, Wayne A. "Alliance and Coalition Warfare." *Parameters: US Army War College Quarterly* 23, no. 2 (Summer 1993): 74–85.

Silverstone, Paul H., ed. "Naval Intelligence." *Warship International* 30, no. 2 (Spring 1993): 180–1.

Sim, Kevin. *Women at War 1914–1918.* New York: William Morrow, 1982.

Sinclair, Adelaide. "Women's Royal Canadian Naval Service." *Canadian Geographical Journal* 27, no. 6 (December 1943): 286–93.

Skelton, Oscar: *Life and Letters of Sir Wilfrid Laurier.* London: Oxford University Press, 1922.

Smith, Gaddis. *Britain's Clandestine Submarines 1914–1915.* New Haven: Yale University Press, 1964.

Smith, Hugh. "Minority Representation in the ADF: Does It Matter?" *Asia-Pacific Defence Reporter* 20, no. 2/3 (August-September 1993).

Snowie, Alan. *The "Bonnie."* Erin, Ont.: Boston Mills Press, 1987.

Sokolsky, Joel. *A Question of Balance: Canada and the Cold War at Sea, 1945–1968.* Centre for International Relations Occasional Paper No. 21. Kingston: Queen's University, 1987.

–. "A Question of Balance: Canada and the Cold War at Sea: 1945–1968." In *The RCN in Transition,* edited by Douglas, 209–32.

Soward, Stuart. *Hands to Flying Stations.* Victoria: Stuart Soward, 1993.

Stacey, C.P. *Arms, Men and Governments: The War Policies of Canada, 1939–1945.* Ottawa: Department of National Defence, 1970.

–. *Canada and the British Army, 184–1871: A Study in the Practice of Responsible Government.* Rev. ed. Toronto: University of Toronto Press, 1963.

–. "Halifax as an International Strategic Factor." *Canadian Historical Association Annual Report,* 1949.

–. "The Life and Hard Times of an Official Historian." *Canadian Historical Review* 51, no. 1 (March 1970): 21–47.

Stairs, Denis. *The Diplomacy of Constraint*. Toronto: University of Toronto Press, 1974.

–. "The Military as an Instrument of Canadian Foreign Policy." In *The Canadian Military: A Profile*, edited by Hector Massey, 209–32. Toronto: Copp Clark, 1972.

Stanley, George F.G. *Canada's Soldiers*. Toronto: Macmillan, 1974.

Stead, Gordon W. *A Leaf upon the Sea: A Small Ship in the Mediterranean, 1941–43*. Vancouver: University of British Columbia Press, 1988.

Syrett, D. "Weather-Reporting U-boats in the Atlantic: The Hunt for U-248." *Mariner's Mirror* 52, no. 1 (Winter 1992).

Taylor, Eric. *Women Who Went to War*. London: Robert Hale, 1988.

Terry, Roy. *Women in Khaki: The Story of the British Woman Soldier*. London: Columbus Books, 1988.

Thomas, Robert H. *The Canadian Navy: Options for the Future*. Working Paper #41. Ottawa: Canadian International Institute of Peace and Security Studies, 1992.

Thorgrimsson, Thor, and E.C. Russell. *Canadian Naval Operations in Korean Waters, 1950–1955*. Ottawa: Queen's Printer, 1965.

Touchette, Pierre. *Canada-France Maritime Relations*. Backgrounder BP-167E. Ottawa: Library of Parliament, 1987.

Tracy, Nicholas. *The Diplomatic Utility of Canada's Naval Forces*. ORAE Report #R60. Ottawa: Department of National Defence, 1976.

–. *The Enforcement of Canada's Continental Maritime Jurisdiction*. Ottawa: Department of National Defence, 1975.

–. "Matching Canada's navy to its foreign policy and domestic requirements." *International Journal* 38, no. 3 (Summer 1983): 459–75.

Treadwell, Mattie E. *The Women's Army Corp*. Washington, DC: Centre of Military History, 1991.

Tucker, Gilbert. *The Naval Service of Canada: Its Official History*. Vol. 1: *Origins and Early Years*. Ottawa: King's Printer, 1952.

–. *The Naval Service of Canada: Its Official History*. Vol. 2: *Activities on Shore during the Second World War*. Ottawa: King's Printer, 1952.

United States, Department of Defense. *Conduct of the Persian Gulf War: Final Report to Congress*. Washington, DC, April 1992.

VanderZwaag, David L. *The Fish Feud*. Lexington, Mass.: D.C. Heath and Co., 1983.

Waite, P.B. *Canada 1874–1896: Arduous Destiny*. Toronto: McClelland and Stewart, 1971.

Weedon, Chris. *Feminist Practice and Poststructuralist Theory*. Oxford: Basil Blackwell, 1987.

Wells, Samuel F. "British Strategic Withdrawal from the Western Hemisphere, 1904–1906." *Canadian Historical Review* 49 (December 1968): 333–50.

Whitby, Michael J. "In Defence of Home Waters: Doctrine and Training in the Canadian Navy during the 1930's." *Mariner's Mirror* 77, no. 2 (May 1991): 1–15.

–. "Instruments of Security: The Royal Canadian Navy's Procurement of the Tribal-Class Destroyers, 1938–1943." *Northern Mariner* 2, no. 3 (July 1992): 1–15.

Williams, M. *Captain Gilbert Roberts and the Anti-U-Boat School*. London: Cassel, 1979.

Williams, Rhodri. *Defending the Empire: The Conservative Party and British Defence Policy 1899–1915*. New Haven: Yale University Press, 1991.

Williamson, Jr., Samuel R. *The Politics of Grand Strategy: Britain and France Prepare for War, 1904–1914*. Rev. ed. London and Atlantic Highlands: Ashfield Press, 1990.

Willock, Roger. "Gunboat Diplomacy: Operations of the North America and West Indies Squadron 1875–1915. Part II: Fuel Oil and Wireless, 1895–1915." *American Neptune* 28 (April 1968): 5–30.

Wilson, Eugene Strand. "The Canadianism of Sir Wilfrid Laurier: A Study of His Liberalism and Nationalism from 1871–1911" PhD dissertation, Columbia University, 1967.

Winterbotham, Arnold, ed. *George E. Foster: Canadian Addresses*. Toronto: Bell & Cockburn, 1914.

Woodcock, G. *Who Killed the British Empire?* London: Jonathan Cape, 1974.

Wright, Peter. *Spy Catcher*. New York: Viking, 1987.

Wright, Richard J. "Green Flags and Red-Coated Gunboats: Naval Activities on the Great Lakes during the Fenian Scares, 1866–1870." *Inland Seas* 22, no. 2 (Summer 1966): 91–110.

Young, Thomas-Durrell. "ANZUS Naval Relations 1951–1985." In *Reflections on the Royal Australian Navy*, edited by Frame, Goldrick, and Jones, 296–315.

–. "Preparing the Western Alliance for the Next Out-of-Area Campaign." *Naval War College Review* 45, no. 3 (Summer 1992): 32–6.

Yuill, David. " 'Operation Korea': Public Opinion and the Image of the RCN." Paper presented in seminar "The Canadian Navy and Major Powers," Department of History, University of Victoria, 6 December 1993.

Zimmerman, David. *The Great Naval Battle of Ottawa*. Toronto: University of Toronto Press, 1989.

–. "The RAN and the RCN and High Technology in the Second World War." In *Reflections on the Royal Australian Navy*, edited by Frame, Goldrick, and Jones, 206–19.

# Notes on Contributors

CATHERINE E. ALLAN (BA, Queen's; MA, London), a colonel in the Canadian Forces, commanded 723 (Halifax) Communication Squadron prior to accepting an assignment to the Directorate of History, National Defence Headquarters, in 1987. She was subsequently appointed to the staff of the Director-General, Reserves and Cadets, at National Defence Headquarters. Since 1990, she has been employed as a civilian at the Communications Security Establishment in Ottawa.

SERGE BERNIER (BA, honours, Royal Military College; MA, PhD, Strasbourg) is now acting director of history and senior historian (civilian) at the Directorate of History in Ottawa. Included in his numerous publications are *The Memoirs of General Jean V. Allard*, volumes 1 and 2; *French Canadians and Bilingualism in the Canadian Armed Forces*; and *Relations politiques franco-britanniques, 1947–1958*. He has been the president of the Canadian Commission of Military History since 1988.

PETER W. CAIRNS, CMM, CD, enroled in the Royal Canadian Navy in 1956 under the Venture Officers' Training Plan. During his career he has held various staff positions, studied at the United States Naval College, and commanded a submarine, two destroyers, a submarine squadron, and a destroyer squadron. His senior appointments have been as Director General, Officers' Careers; Deputy Chief of Staff, Operations, to the Supreme Allied Commander, Atlantic; Commander, Maritime Forces Pacific; and Commander, Maritime Command. He retired from active duty in the rank of vice-admiral in July 1994.

FRED W. CRICKARD, RCN (retired) (MA, Dalhousie), was educated in Vancouver before attending Royal Roads Military College from 1948 to 1950. He served in the Royal Canadian Navy and the Canadian Forces for thirty-five years, retiring as a rear admiral in 1985. Since 1988, he has been a full-time research associate with the Centre for Foreign Policy Studies, Dalhousie University, and serves as the editor-in-chief of the *Niobe Papers*. He is currently the president of the Naval Officers' Association of Canada.

JAN DRENT, CD, was a career officer in the Royal Canadian Navy for thirty-six years. He served at sea on both coasts and commanded three ships: HMCS *Annapolis*, *Qu'Appelle*, and *Provider*. His shore appointments included an exchange tour with the Royal Navy and two postings as the naval attaché in Moscow. He served in National Defence Headquarters as a senior naval policy analyst and in the NATO Headquarters in Brussels as the Deputy Supreme Allied Commander, Atlantic, and Commander-in-Chief, Channel, representative. Since retiring in 1990, he has qualified as a convoy commodore. He is currently a freelance translator and researches maritime history.

RICHARD H. GIMBLETT (MA, Trent) graduated from the Royal Military College of Canada (RMC), Kingston, in 1979. After serving in various west coast destroyers and on the military staff of RMC, he was appointed combat officer of HMCS *Protecteur* in the Persian Gulf, January–February 1991. He was subsequently engaged as a historian at the Directorate of History to collaborate on an official account of the Canadian participation in the Gulf War, which will be published in 1996. He has also published "Multinational Naval Operations: The Canadian Navy in the Persian Gulf, 1990–91," in the *Canadian Defence Quarterly*, August 1992. He is currently working on his PhD at Laval University.

WILLIAM GLOVER earned degrees in history at Queen's University and war studies at King's College, University of London. Since transferring from the naval reserve to the regular force in 1977, he has served in a variety of ships and appointments on both coasts. He "came ashore" after being combat officer on the HMCS *Yukon*. Before joining the Directorate of History, he taught history, political science, and naval history for five years at Royal Roads Military College. His most recent article, "The Politics of Nation Building and the Defence of British Columbia 1971–1939," appears in *The Journal of the West*.

JAMES GOLDRICK (BA, New South Wales; MLitt, UNE) joined the Royal Australian Navy (RAN) in 1974. An anti-submarine warfare specialist, he has had sea postings with the RAN and the Royal Navy. He commanded HMAS *Cessnock* before serving as a visiting research fellow at the US Naval War College. He later spent two years in charge of the RAN's principal officer training and tactical development unit. Currently executive officer of HMAS *Perth*, he will take command of HMAS *Sydney* at the end of 1996. He has lectured and published extensively on both contemporary and historical subjects; his writings include *The King's Ships Were at Sea: The War in the North Sea August 1914–February 1915* (1984).

BARRY GOUGH (BA, UBC; MA, Montana; PhD, London) is a prize-winning author of many books, including *Northwest Coast* (1992) and *The Falkland Islands/Malvinas* (1992). He has served as the president of the Canadian Nautical Research Society and the North American Society for Oceanic History and is now the editor-in-chief of the journal *The American Neptune: Maritime History and Art*. He is professor of history and coordinator of Canadian Studies at Wilfrid Laurier University in Waterloo, Ontario, and is an archives fellow of Churchill College Cambridge.

MICHAEL L. HADLEY (BA, UBC; MA, Manitoba; PhD, Queen's) is a professor at the University of Victoria, where he teaches German literature in the Department of Germanic Studies and naval history in the Department of History. He is the author of books and articles on German literature and naval history and contributed to both *The RCN in Retrospect* (1982) and *The RCN in Transition* (1989). His books *U-Boats against Canada: German Submarines in Canadian Waters* (1985, 1990) and *Tin-Pots and Pirate Ships: Canadian Naval Forces and German Sea Raiders 1880–1918* (1991, with Roger Sarty) have both won awards from the Canadian Nautical Research Society and the North American Society for Oceanic History. Most recently he has published *Count Not the Dead: The Popular Image of the German Submarine* (1995) and *God's Little Ships: A History of the Columbia Coast Mission* (1995). He began his naval service in the University Naval Training Division (UNTD) in 1954 and attained the rank of captain(N). He served for ten years on the Defence Minister's Academic Advisory Board to the Canadian Military Colleges.

PETER T. HAYDON (MA, Dalhousie), a former career officer in the Royal Canadian Navy, retiring in the rank of commander, is now a defence analyst and research fellow with the Centre for Foreign Policy Studies at Dalhousie University, specializing in naval and maritime security issues. His main interests include the role of naval forces in the post–Cold War period and their function in diplomacy and international crisis management; post-1945 Canadian defence and naval policy; and civil-military relations in Canada. His most recent book is *The 1962 Cuban Missile Crisis: Canadian Involvement Reconsidered* (1993). He is also a senior research fellow with the Canadian Institute of Strategic Studies.

MICHAEL A. HENNESSY (BA, honours, UBC; MA, PhD, New Brunswick) is an assistant professor of naval and military history at the Royal Military College of Canada. Specializing in the history of technology and international relations, he has published on Canadian naval, shipbuilding, and defence policy. He has recently completed a key background narrative on the development of Canadian anti-submarine forces during the Second World War for the official history program of the Department of National Defence.

ROB HUEBERT (BA, honours, Manitoba; MA, Carleton; PhD, Dalhousie) is an assistant professor at the Department of Political Studies at the University of Manitoba. His area of interests include the Law of the Sea, maritime affairs, decision-making theory, Canadian foreign and defence policy, and northern studies. His most recent publication, "Polar Vision or Tunnel Vision: The Making of Canadian Arctic Waters Policy," is in *Marine Policy*. He is a research fellow with the Centre for Foreign Policy Studies, Dalhousie University.

JAMES D. KIRAS (BA, Massachusetts; MA, Toronto) specializes in low-intensity conflict and the organization and operations of the Viet Cong, as well as the coastal and riverine operations of the United States Navy in the Vietnam War. In addition to historical naval research, he is also interested in current naval issues.

DOUG M. McLEAN (BSc, honours; MA, Royal Military College) serves at the National Defence Headquarters as a staff officer in the Directorate of Maritime Force Development. He lectured on history and strategy at RMC from 1992 to 1995. He sailed in various ships on both coasts as a watchkeeper and weapons officer. His shore tours, first in Argentia and then in National Defence Headquarters, were both focused on anti-submarine warfare.

SIOBHAN J. McNAUGHT is a graduate student at the University of Calgary and a sub-lieutenant in the naval reserve. Winner of the James H. Grey Gold Medal for Western Canadian History, she completed her BA with a double major in history and religious studies. Currently she is writing her MA thesis on the American as compared to the British impact on grassland ranching within Palliser's Triangle during the period 1870 to 1930. She intends to continue her studies at the doctoral level.

WILLIAM A. MARCH (BA, first-class honours, Royal Military College; MA, Victoria) joined the Canadian Forces in 1977. In 1983 he received his Air Navigator wings at Winnipeg. After two flying tours on maritime patrol squadrons, he was transferred to Royal Roads Military College as a squadron commander. Promoted to major in 1991, he assumed the duties of the Staff Officer, Cadets and Military Training, at the college. He is currently Senior Staff Officer, History, at Air Command Headquarters in Winnipeg.

MARC MILNER (PhD, New Brunswick) is a professor of war and naval history at the University of New Brunswick (UNB). He is the author of *North Atlantic Run:*

*The Royal Canadian Navy and the Battle for the Convoys* (1985) and *The U-Boat Hunters: The Royal Canadian Navy and the Offensive against the U-Boats* (1994); the editor of *Canadian Military History: Selected Readings* (1993); co-editor of *Military History and the Military Profession* (1992); and co-author of the popular work *Corvettes of the Royal Canadian Navy 1939–1945* (1993). He contributed to *The RCN in Retrospect* (1982) and *The RCN in Transition* (1989). His articles have appeared in numerous journals, from *Military Affairs* to *Canadian Defence Quarterly*. Now director of UNB's Military and Strategic Studies Programme, he was formerly employed with the Directorate of History at the Department of National Defence, Ottawa, where he wrote portions of volume 2 of the RCAF's official history. He was a member of the Canadian Military Colleges Advisory Board.

BERNARD RANSOM (MA, PhD, Edinburgh) is chief curator of the Newfoundland Museum and an adjunct member of the Directorate of History, Department of National Defence, Ottawa. Originally an Irish history specialist, he now conducts research in the area of Newfoundland military/naval history. His publications include books and articles on the Royal Canadian Navy in St John's, armed conflict, and political theory. Among them are *James Connolly – Selected Political Writings* (1974), *Connolly's Marxism* (1980), "For King and Country – The Permanent Military Exhibit of the NF Museum" (1986), and "Canada's 'Newfyjohn' Tenancy: The Royal Canadian Navy in St. John's, 1941–45" (1994).

ROGER SARTY (MA, Duke; PhD, Toronto) is senior historian at the Directorate of General History, National Defence Headquarters. After joining the directorate in 1981, he became a specialist in maritime air operations and was the principal researcher for that part of W.A.B. Douglas's *The Creation of a National Air Force: The Official History of the Royal Canadian Air Force*, volume 2. He then helped to establish the directorate's naval team. He is now working on the new three-volume official history of the Royal Canadian Navy. Dr Sarty is co-author with Michael Hadley of *Tin-Pots and Pirate Ships: Canadian Naval Forces and German Sea Raiders 1880–1918* and has published widely on all aspects of Canadian maritime defence.

GRAEME R. TWEEDIE (BA, Brandon) joined the Regular Officer Training Plan in 1971. After completing his bridge watchkeeping training in 1976, he served in HMCS *Assiniboine* and *Iroquois*. In 1982 he qualified as a combat control officer and served as the weapons and operations officer in HMCS *Nipigon* and *Fraser*. From 1984 to 1988 he served in Maritime Command Headquarters as Staff Officer–Above Water Readiness and Staff Officer–Officer Training. In 1989 he graduated from the Canadian Forces Command and Staff College in Toronto. Upon returning to Halifax, he was employed as executive officer for CSE Division in Canadian Forces Fleet School *Halifax*. In 1990 he was posted to HMCS

*Cormorant* as executive officer. Having attended the continuous French course at CFB Shearwater in 1993–94, he is now executive officer of HMCS *Athabaskan*.

BARBARA WINTERS (BA, Queen's; MA, Victoria) has worked as a heritage building researcher in Halifax for the Department of National Defence, where she produced booklets on the Dockyard Residences, Wellington Barracks, and the admiral's residence, among others. In 1991 she received her MA in history on the subject of women in the Royal Canadian Air Force during the Second World War. Currently studying law at the University of Victoria, she continues to work on her PhD on the subject of women in the Canadian military during the Second World War. She is an active member of the naval reserve in Victoria and was commissioned from the ranks in 1992. She is a lieutenant currently completing her Maritime Surface (MARS) officer training.

DAVID ZIMMERMAN (BA, Toronto; MA, PhD, New Brunswick) is associate professor of military history at the Department of History, University of Victoria. His publications include *Coastal Fort: A History of Fort Sullivan, Eastport, Maine*; *The Great Naval Battle of Ottawa*; and *Top Secret Exchange: The Tizard Mission and the Scientific War*.

# Index

449